Reynolds

1

DESCUBRE

Lengua y cultura del mundo hispánico

VISTA
HIGHER LEARNING

Boston, Massachusetts

Publisher: José A. Blanco
Editorial Director: Beth Kramer
Project Managers: Armando Brito, Daniel Finkbeiner

Director of Art and Design: Linda Jurras
Director of Production and Manufacturing: Lisa Perrier
Design Manager: Polo Barrera
Photo Researcher and Art Buyer: Rachel Distler
Production and ManufacturingTeam: Jeff Perron, Oscar Díez, Mauricio Henao, María Eugenia Castaño

President: Janet L. Dracksdorf
Sr. Vice President of Operations: Tom Delano
Vice President of Sales and Marketing: Scott Burns
National Sales Consultant: Norah Jones
Executive Marketing Manager: Benjamin Rivera

DESCUBRE Level 1 Student Edition ISBN-13: 978-1-60007-252-9
DESCUBRE Level 1 Student Edition ISBN-10: 1-60007-252-6
DESCUBRE Level 1 Teacher's Annotated Edition (TAE) ISBN-13: 978-1-60007-253-6
DESCUBRE Level 1 Teacher's Annotated Edition (TAE) ISBN-10: 1-60007-253-4

Library of Congress Control Number: 2006939624

1 2 3 4 5 6 7 8 9 VH 12 11 10 09 08 07

Table of Contents

Lesson Openers
offer a preview of the content and features to come.

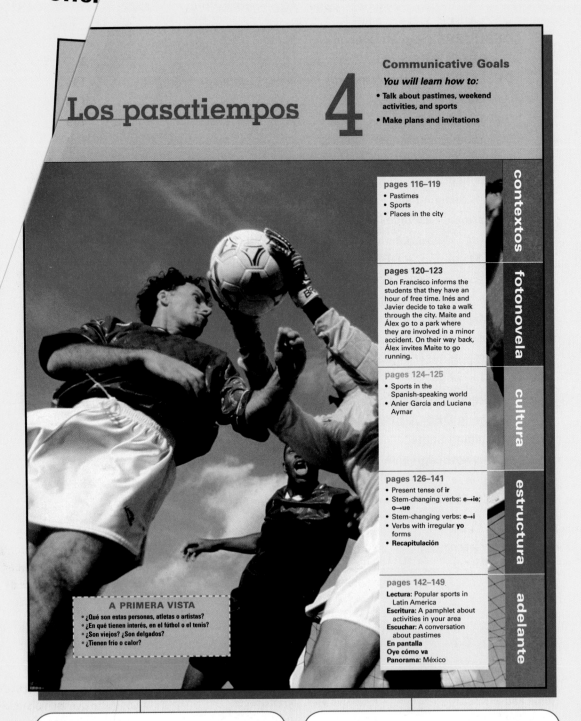

Los pasatiempos 4

Communicative Goals

You will learn how to:
- Talk about pastimes, weekend activities, and sports
- Make plans and invitations

pages 116–119
- Pastimes
- Sports
- Places in the city

contextos

pages 120–123
Don Francisco informs the students that they have an hour of free time. Inés and Javier decide to take a walk through the city. Maite and Álex go to a park where they are involved in a minor accident. On their way back, Álex invites Maite to go running.

fotonovela

pages 124–125
- Sports in the Spanish-speaking world
- Anier García and Luciana Aymar

cultura

pages 126–141
- Present tense of **ir**
- Stem-changing verbs: e→ie; o→ue
- Stem-changing verbs: e→i
- Verbs with irregular **yo** forms
- **Recapitulación**

estructura

pages 142–149
Lectura: Popular sports in Latin America
Escritura: A pamphlet about activities in your area
Escuchar: A conversation about pastimes
En pantalla
Oye cómo va
Panorama: México

adelante

A PRIMERA VISTA
- ¿Qué son estas personas, atletas o artistas?
- ¿En qué tienen interés, en el fútbol o el tenis?
- ¿Son viejos? ¿Son delgados?
- ¿Tienen frío o calor?

The photo-based **A primera vista** helps students anticipate the lesson theme and contexts.

The highly visual layout and design serve as a pedagogical aid. Major sections are color-coded for easy, competent use.

Contextos
presents and practices vocabulary and structures in meaningful contexts.

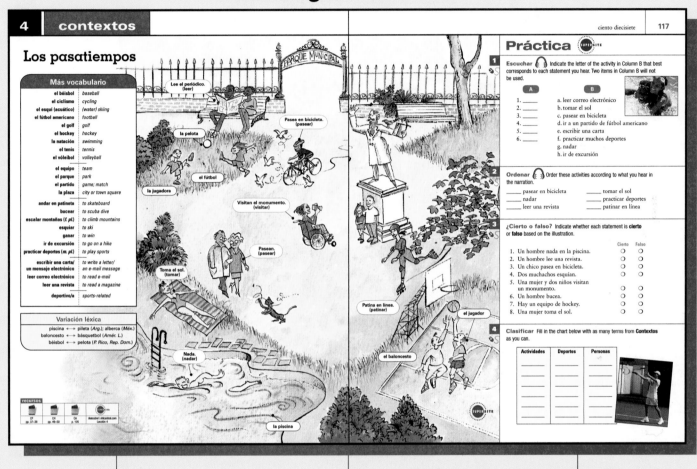

Más vocabulario boxes clearly organize vocabulary in a manner that helps build student confidence.

High-frequency vocabulary is introduced in expansive, clear **illustrations** for a strong language foundation.

The **Práctica** section begins with two listening exercises and continues with activities that practice the new vocabulary in meaningful contexts.

Variación léxica presents alternate words and expressions used throughout the Spanish-speaking world.

Frequent **Recursos** boxes refer to extensive print and multimedia components that support different learning styles.

Comunicación activities allow students to use the vocabulary creatively in interactions with a partner, a small group, or the entire class.

DESCUBRE 1 at-a-glance

The Fotonovela for DESCUBRE, niveles 1 y 2, presents the story of four students traveling in Ecuador.

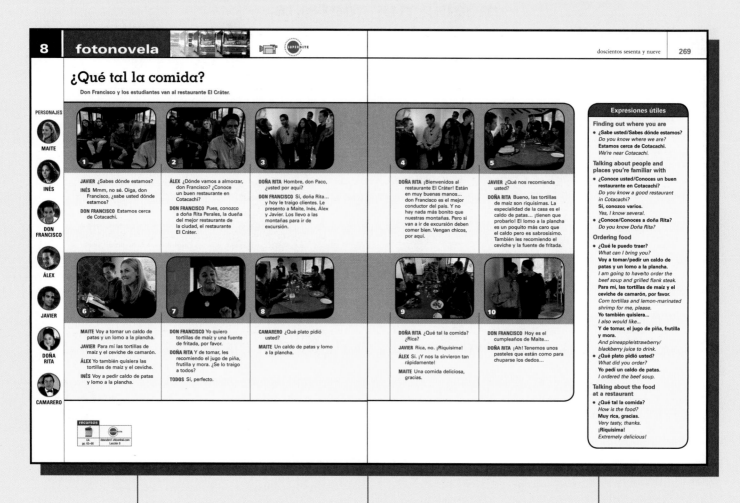

Fotonovela characters and contexts present grammar and vocabulary throughout the lesson.

Fotonovela Video is one of the three video programs on the **DESCUBRE** DVDs. For information about the others, see pages T7 and T14.

Expresiones útiles are the **Fotonovela** conversation "bridge" that re-enters **Contextos** vocabulary and previews grammar concepts of the **Estructura** section.

The **video story board** builds student confidence for learning before, during, and after viewing.

Cultura
explores cultural themes introduced in *Contextos* and *Fotonovela*.

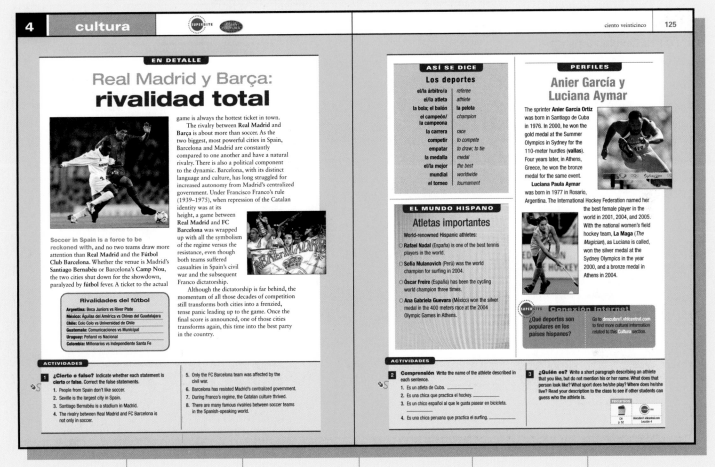

En detalle gives students an opportunity to read in-depth about the lesson's cultural theme, using comprehension-supporting photos.

An icon lets you know this would be an appropriate point to use **Flash cultura,** the second video program on the **DESCUBRE** DVDs.

Perfiles, Así se dice & El mundo hispano spotlight contemporary language, people, perspectives, and practices to show diversity and unity.

Activities with purpose always have the communication-culture connection that keeps learning integrated and relevant.

Conexión Internet leads students to the **DESCUBRE** Supersite—and to the Spanish-speaking world.

DESCUBRE 1 at-a-glance

Estructura
presents grammar in clear, concise, and visually effective formats.

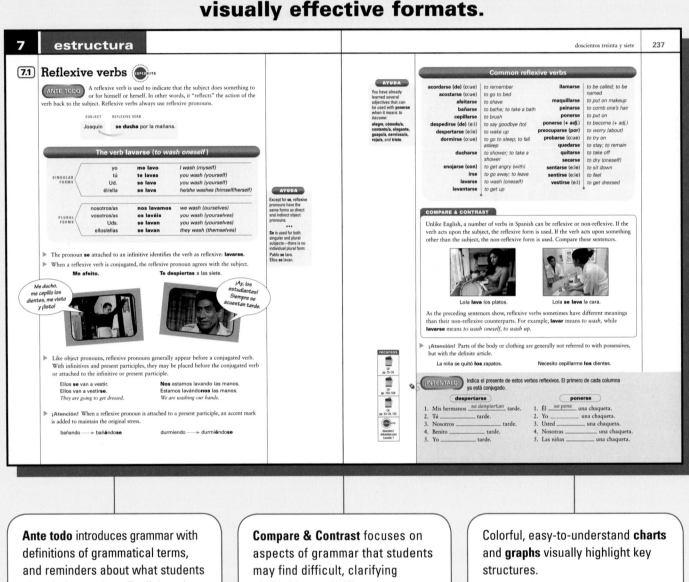

Ante todo introduces grammar with definitions of grammatical terms, and reminders about what students already know about English and Spanish that will help them.

Compare & Contrast focuses on aspects of grammar that students may find difficult, clarifying similarities and differences between Spanish and English.

Colorful, easy-to-understand **charts** and **graphs** visually highlight key structures.

Fotonovela contexts are used to present and practice language structures.

Sidebars provide consistent support for student confidence and success.

¡Inténtalo! eases students into the practice of new grammar points.

Estructura
provides directed and communicative practice.

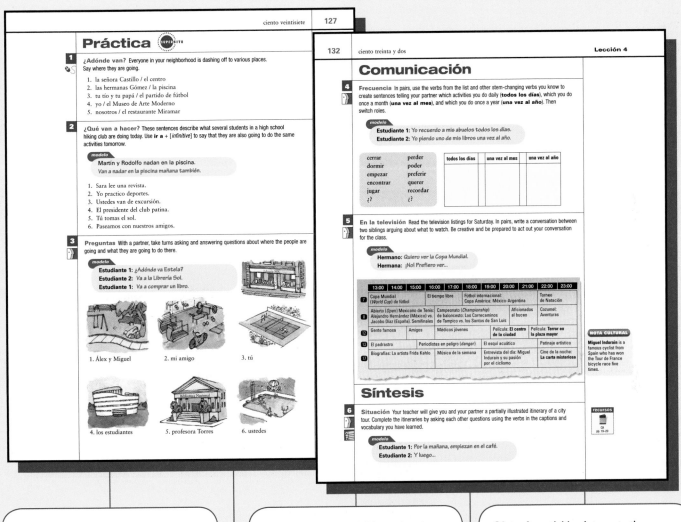

Práctica · SUPERSITE

1 ¿Adónde van? Everyone in your neighborhood is dashing off to various places. Say where they are going.

1. la señora Castillo / el centro
2. las hermanas Gómez / la piscina
3. tu tío y tu papá / el partido de fútbol
4. yo / el Museo de Arte Moderno
5. nosotros / el restaurante Miramar

2 ¿Qué van a hacer? These sentences describe what several students in a high school hiking club are doing today. Use **ir a** + [*infinitive*] to say that they are also going to do the same activities tomorrow.

modelo
Martín y Rodolfo nadan en la piscina.
Van a nadar en la piscina mañana también.

1. Sara lee una revista.
2. Yo practico deportes.
3. Ustedes van de excursión.
4. El presidente del club patina.
5. Tú tomas el sol.
6. Paseamos con nuestros amigos.

3 Preguntas With a partner, take turns asking and answering questions about where the people are going and what they are going to do there.

modelo
Estudiante 1: ¿Adónde va Estela?
Estudiante 2: Va a la Librería Sol.
Estudiante 1: Va a comprar un libro.

1. Álex y Miguel
2. mi amigo
3. tú
4. los estudiantes
5. profesora Torres
6. ustedes

Comunicación

4 Frecuencia In pairs, use the verbs from the list and other stem-changing verbs you know to create sentences telling your partner which activities you do daily (**todos los días**), which you do once a month (**una vez al mes**), and which you do once a year (**una vez al año**). Then switch roles.

modelo
Estudiante 1: Yo recuerdo a mis abuelos todos los días.
Estudiante 2: Yo pierdo uno de mis libros una vez al año.

cerrar	perder
dormir	poder
empezar	preferir
encontrar	querer
jugar	recordar
¿?	¿?

todos los días	una vez al mes	una vez al año

5 En la televisión Read the television listings for Saturday. In pairs, write a conversation between two siblings arguing about what to watch. Be creative and be prepared to act out your conversation for the class.

modelo
Hermano: Quiero ver la Copa Mundial.
Hermana: ¡No! Prefiero ver...

	13:00	14:00	15:00	16:00	17:00	18:00	19:00	20:00	21:00	22:00	23:00
7	Copa Mundial (*World Cup*) de fútbol			El tiempo libre		Fútbol internacional: Copa América: México-Argentina				Torneo de Natación	
8	Abierto (*Open*) Mexicano de Tenis: Alejandro Hernández (México) vs. Jacobo Díaz (España). Semifinales			Campeonato (*Championship*) de baloncesto: Los Correcaminos de Tampico vs. los Santos de San Luis				Aficionados al buceo		Cozumel: Aventuras	
12	Gente famosa		Amigos		Médicos jóvenes			Película: **El centro de la ciudad**		Película: **Terror en la plaza mayor**	
13	El padrastro		Periodistas en peligro (*danger*)		El esquí acuático				Patinaje artístico		
17	Biografías: La artista Frida Kahlo		Música de la semana		Entrevista del día: Miguel Indurain y su pasión por el ciclismo			Cine de la noche: **La carta misteriosa**			

NOTA CULTURAL
Miguel Indurain is a famous cyclist from Spain who has won the Tour de France bicycle race five times.

Síntesis

6 Situación Your teacher will give you and your partner a partially illustrated itinerary of a city tour. Complete the itineraries by asking each other questions using the verbs in the captions and vocabulary you have learned.

modelo
Estudiante 1: Por la mañana, empiezan en el café.
Estudiante 2: Y luego...

recursos
CA
pp. 19–20

Práctica weaves vocabulary and grammar into a wide range of guided yet meaningful exercises.

Comunicación activities take place with a partner, in small groups, or with the whole class.

Síntesis activities integrate the current grammar point with previously learned points, providing built-in, consistent review and recycling.

The **Supersite** icon at the top of the page indicates that content is available on the **DESCUBRE** Supersite (**descubre1.vhlcentral.com**); mouse icons next to individual activities signal that these are available with auto-grading on the Supersite.

The **Notas culturales** sidebars expand coverage of the cultures of Spanish-speaking peoples and countries, while **Ayuda** sidebars provide on-the-spot language support.

Estructura

Recapitulación provides in-text and online diagnostic activities to encourage and support reflective learning.

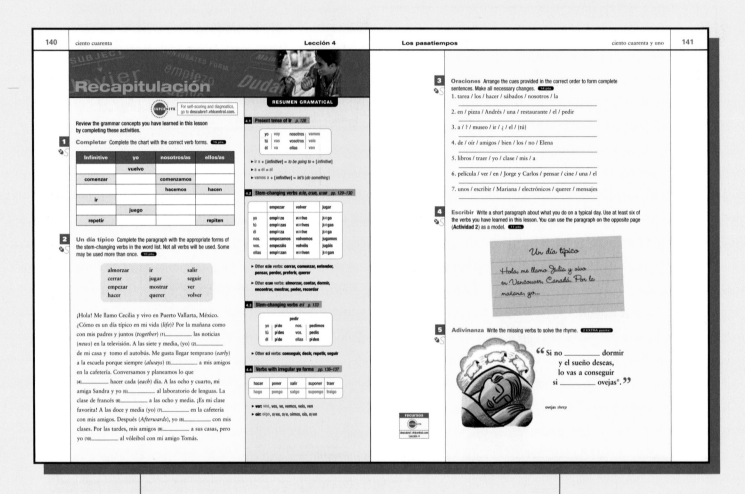

Resumen gramatical This review panel provides a condensed, study-friendly overview of the basic concepts of the lesson's grammar, complete with page references to the full explanation.

Points A point value following each activity serves to help track student progress. All **Recapitulación** sections add up to fifty points, with an additional extra-credit possibility for successfully completing the **Adivinanza**.

Activities A series of activities, moving from directed to open-ended, systematically tests the lesson's grammar. The section ends with an **Adivinanza,** a riddle or puzzle using the lesson's grammar.

Supersite Icon An icon leading to the Supersite lets students know that the **Recapitulación** activities can be completed online with automatic scoring and diagnostics to help identify areas where they need the most review.

Adelante
Lectura develops reading skills in the context of the lesson theme.

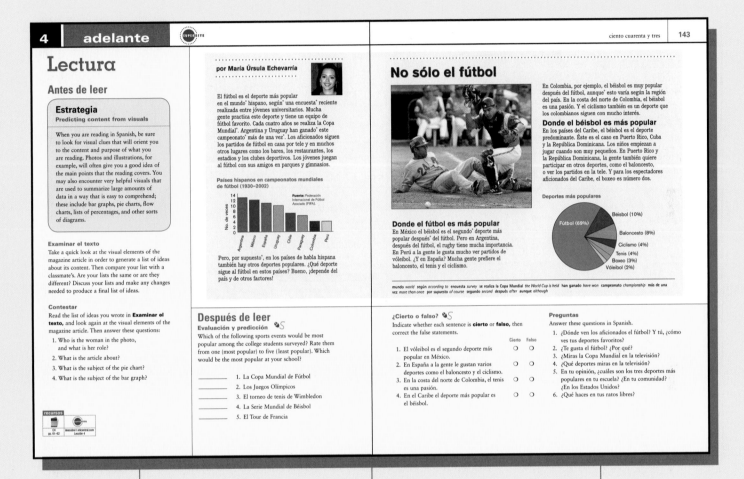

4 | adelante | SUPERSITE | ciento cuarenta y tres | **143**

Lectura

Antes de leer

Estrategia
Predicting content from visuals

When you are reading in Spanish, be sure to look for visual clues that will orient you to the content and purpose of what you are reading. Photos and illustrations, for example, will often give you a good idea of the main points that the reading covers. You may also encounter very helpful visuals that are used to summarize large amounts of data in a way that is easy to comprehend; these include bar graphs, pie charts, flow charts, lists of percentages, and other sorts of diagrams.

Examinar el texto
Take a quick look at the visual elements of the magazine article in order to generate a list of ideas about its content. Then compare your list with a classmate's. Are your lists the same or are they different? Discuss your lists and make any changes needed to produce a final list of ideas.

Contestar
Read the list of ideas you wrote in **Examinar el texto**, and look again at the visual elements of the magazine article. Then answer these questions:
1. Who is the woman in the photo, and what is her role?
2. What is the article about?
3. What is the subject of the pie chart?
4. What is the subject of the bar graph?

recursos

---

por María Úrsula Echevarría

El fútbol es el deporte más popular en el mundo° hispano, según° una encuesta° reciente realizada entre jóvenes universitarios. Mucha gente practica este deporte y tiene un equipo de fútbol favorito. Cada cuatro años se realiza la Copa Mundial°. Argentina y Uruguay han ganado° este campeonato° más de una vez°. Los aficionados siguen los partidos de fútbol en casa por tele y en muchos otros lugares como los bares, los restaurantes, los estadios y los clubes deportivos. Los jóvenes juegan al fútbol con sus amigos en parques y gimnasios.

Países hispanos en campeonatos mundiales de fútbol (1930–2002)

[bar graph: No. de veces — Argentina, México, España, Uruguay, Chile, Paraguay, Colombia, Perú]

Fuente: Federación Internacional de Fútbol Asociado (FIFA).

Pero, por supuesto°, en los países de habla hispana también hay otros deportes populares. ¿Qué deporte sigue al fútbol en estos países? Bueno, ¡depende del país y de otros factores!

Después de leer

Evaluación y predicción
Which of the following sports events would be most popular among the college students surveyed? Rate them from one (most popular) to five (least popular). Which would be the most popular at your school?

_____ 1. La Copa Mundial de Fútbol
_____ 2. Los Juegos Olímpicos
_____ 3. El torneo de tenis de Wimbledon
_____ 4. La Serie Mundial de Béisbol
_____ 5. El Tour de Francia

No sólo el fútbol

[photo of baseball players]

Donde el fútbol es más popular
En México el béisbol es el segundo° deporte más popular después° del fútbol. Pero en Argentina, después del fútbol, el rugby tiene mucha importancia. En Perú a la gente le gusta mucho ver partidos de vóleibol. ¿Y en España? Mucha gente prefiere el baloncesto, el tenis y el ciclismo.

En Colombia, por ejemplo, el béisbol es muy popular después del fútbol, aunque° esto varía según la región del país. En la costa del norte de Colombia, el béisbol es una pasión. Y el ciclismo también es un deporte que los colombianos siguen con mucho interés.

Donde el béisbol es más popular
En los países del Caribe, el béisbol es el deporte predominante. Éste es el caso en Puerto Rico, Cuba y la República Dominicana. Los niños empiezan a jugar cuando son muy pequeños. En Puerto Rico y la República Dominicana, la gente también quiere participar en otros deportes, como el baloncesto, o ver los partidos en la tele. Y para los espectadores aficionados del Caribe, el boxeo es número dos.

Deportes más populares

[pie chart:
Fútbol (69%)
Béisbol (10%)
Baloncesto (8%)
Ciclismo (4%)
Tenis (4%)
Boxeo (3%)
Vóleibol (2%)]

---

mundo *world* según *according to* encuesta *survey* se realiza la Copa Mundial *the World Cup is held* han ganado *have won* campeonato *championship* más de una vez *more than once* por supuesto *of course* segundo *second* después *after* aunque *although*

¿Cierto o falso?
Indicate whether each sentence is **cierto** or **falso,** then correct the false statements.

	Cierto	Falso
1. El vóleibol es el segundo deporte más popular en México.	○	○
2. En España a la gente le gustan varios deportes como el baloncesto y el ciclismo.	○	○
3. En la costa del norte de Colombia, el tenis es una pasión.	○	○
4. En el Caribe el deporte más popular es el béisbol.	○	○

Preguntas
Answer these questions in Spanish.
1. ¿Dónde ven los aficionados el fútbol? Y tú, ¿cómo ves tus deportes favoritos?
2. ¿Te gusta el fútbol? ¿Por qué?
3. ¿Miras la Copa Mundial en la televisión?
4. ¿Qué deportes miras en la televisión?
5. En tu opinión, ¿cuáles son los tres deportes más populares en tu escuela? ¿En tu comunidad? ¿En los Estados Unidos?
6. ¿Qué haces en tus ratos libres?

Antes de leer Valuable reading strategies and pre-reading activities build student skills and confidence.

Readings Selections are specifically related to the lesson theme and recycle vocabulary and grammar students have learned.

Después de leer Students grow in confidence and competence in foundational and higher-order thinking skills.

Charts, graphs, photos, and text provide interpretive skill tools relevant for achievement in and beyond school.

Adelante

Escritura develops writing while *Escuchar* practices listening skills in the context of the lesson theme.

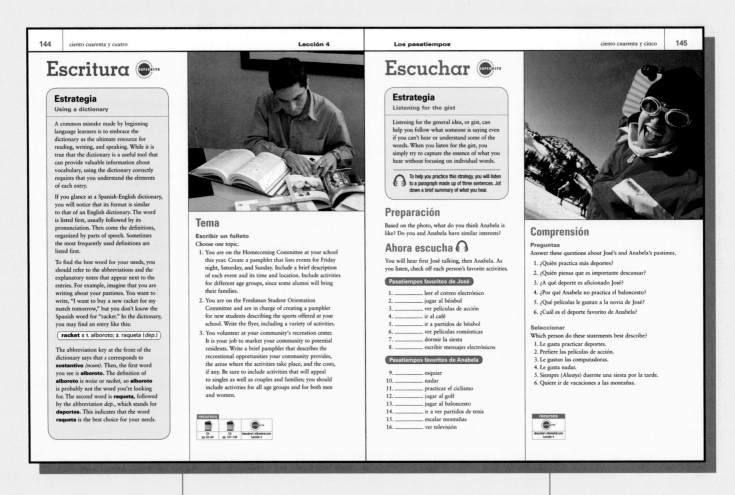

Estrategia Strategies to build a skill repertoire for life.

Escritura The **tema** describes the writing topic and includes suggestions for approaching it.

Escuchar A recorded conversation or narration develops listening skills in Spanish. **Preparación** prepares students for listening to the recorded passage.

Ahora escucha walks students through the passage, and **Comprensión** checks their understanding of what they heard.

Adelante

En pantalla and *Oye cómo va* present an authentic television clip and a song tied to the lesson theme.

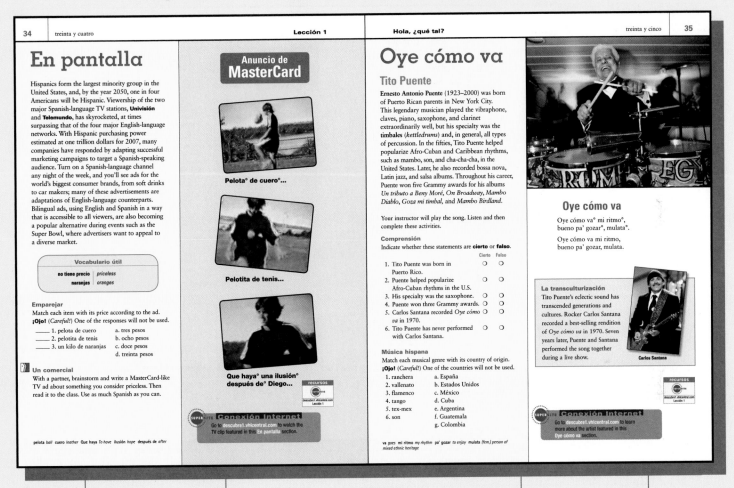

En pantalla **Perspectives and practices are evident in authentic, short video clips that will make students laugh—and think and respond.**

Supersite icons **and** Recursos **boxes lead students to the Supersite (descubre1.vhlcentral.com), where they can view the TV clip and get further practice.**

Activities **A series of activities checks students' comprehension of the material and expands on the ideas presented.**

Oye cómo va **A biography of an artist or group from the featured country introduces students to the music of the Spanish-speaking world. Excerpts from the song lyrics, photos, and explanations of the genre accompany the biography.**

Panorama
presents the nations of the Spanish-speaking world.

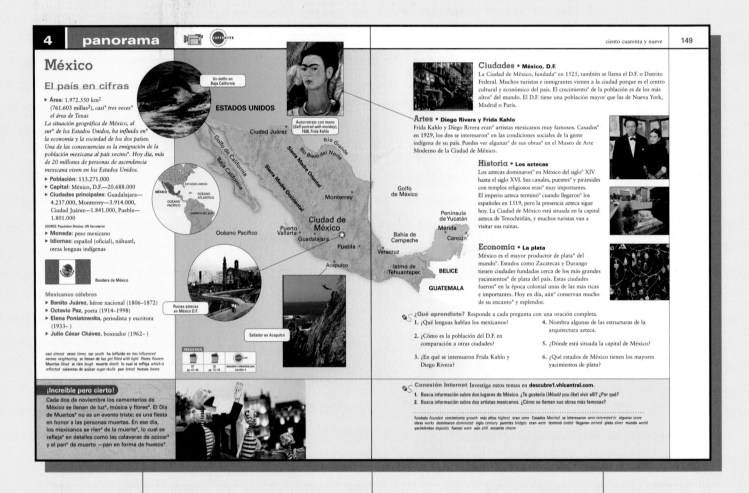

El país en cifras highlights key facts about the featured country.

Maps and **photos** illustrate significant places, people, and products.

Readings explore culture through language-rich highlights on the arts, history, and daily life.

¡Increíble pero cierto! spotlights an intriguing fact about the country or its people.

Conexión Internet offers Internet activities on the **DESCUBRE** Supersite for additional paths to discovery.

Panorama cultural, the third video program on the **DESCUBRE** DVDs, has authentic footage of the featured Spanish-speaking country so students can experience the sights and sounds of its culture.

DESCUBRE provides everything you need to make sure your students succeed.

Teacher Materials

- **Teacher's Annotated Edition**
  The Teacher's Annotated Edition contains a wealth of teaching information designed to support teaching in the classroom and to save teachers time in preparation and class management.

- **Textbook Audio Program**
  This audio program, recorded by native Spanish speakers, integrates directly with the **Contextos** and **Vocabulario** sections of the textbook. It is available in a variety of formats to suit your classroom needs.

- **Video Program on DVD**
  Three separate video programs provide linguistic and cultural input. The **Fotonovela** program features a storyline closely integrated with the lesson's content. The thematically based **Flash cultura** program expands on the content presented in the **Cultura** section of the textbook. The **Panorama cultural** program contains authentic footage and narrations about the Spanish-speaking countries featured in **Panorama** in the textbook.

- **Audio Program**
  The Audio Program provides the recordings to be used in conjunction with the audio activities in the **DESCUBRE Cuaderno de actividades**. It is available in a variety of formats to suit your classroom needs.

- **Supersite powered by MAESTRO™**
  The **DESCUBRE** Supersite utilizes the power of **MAESTRO™** to provide tracking, grading, and monitoring of student performance and to facilitate communication with the class. Teachers have access to the student site, as well as the entire Teacher Package.

- **Audio and Video Scripts ***
  The Audio and Video Scripts contain the Textbook Audio Program and the Audio Program scripts; the video scripts; and English translations of the video scripts.

- **Answer Keys ***
  This contains answers to all activities with discrete answers in the **Cuaderno de práctica** and the **Cuaderno de actividades**.

- **Overhead Transparencies ***
  The Overhead Transparencies include maps of the Spanish-speaking world, drawings to reinforce vocabulary presented in the textbook's **Contextos** sections, and other useful illustrations for presenting or practicing concepts such as telling time. They are available as PDFs as well.

- **Testing Program ***
  The Testing Program consists of four versions of tests for each textbook lesson, a final exam, listening scripts, answer keys, and suggestions for oral tests. It is provided in ready-to-print PDFs, in RTF word-processing files, and in a Test Generator. Testing audio files are also available.

- **Teacher's Resource CD-ROM**
  The Teacher's Resource CD-ROM delivers the teacher materials marked with an * in the following descriptions, all on one convenient CD-ROM.

Student Materials

- **Cuaderno de práctica**
  The **Cuaderno de práctica** provides additional practice and comprehension of the vocabulary, grammar, and cultural information presented in **Panorama** in each textbook lesson. The **Cuaderno de práctica** is a practical homework option for your students.

- **Cuaderno para hispanohablantes**
  For classrooms that require differentiated instruction, this workbook focuses on the development of reading and writing skills for students who have grown up in a Spanish-speaking family environment but have had little or no formal Spanish language training.

- **Cuaderno de actividades**
  The **Cuaderno de actividades** offers audio activities that build listening comprehension, speaking, and pronunciation skills, as well as video activities for pre-, while-, and post-viewing of the video programs. It also provides worksheets for paired communication activities, making it an invaluable supplement for your classroom.

- **e-Cuaderno powered by MAESTRO™**
  The **e-Cuaderno** contains the **Cuaderno de práctica** and the audio and video activities from the **Cuaderno de actividades** in an online environment powered by the **MAESTRO™** engine.

- **Supersite powered by MAESTRO™**
  The **DESCUBRE** Supersite includes, in an auto-graded format, activities found in the textbook; additional, auto-graded activities with feedback for practice, expansion, and research; the complete audio and video programs; and much more!

- **Pocket Dictionary & Language Guide**
  The VHL Intro Spanish Pocket Dictionary & Language Guide is a portable reference for Spanish words, expressions, idioms, and more, created expressly to complement and expand the vocabulary in the student text.

The DESCUBRE Story

DESCUBRE is the deliberately different three-year Spanish program designed to take students to a higher level of learning and success. Since 2000, language textbooks and materials published by Vista Higher Learning have achieved exciting and effective learning outcomes in secondary schools throughout the country. **DESCUBRE** is a bold and appealing student-centered, teacher-friendly program that guides learners of all abilities in today's classrooms through the different stages of learning in order to become proficient and competent users of Spanish.

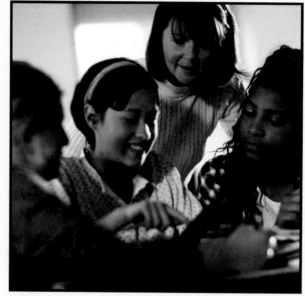

DESCUBRE will help you accomplish your instructional objectives, ensuring high levels of student skill and motivation through:

- Carefully structured lesson organization, built around easy-to-navigate, color-coded sections
- Instructional design that emphasizes language as a tool, not a topic
- Progressive communicative activities incorporated in every section of every lesson
- Unprecedented cultural coverage of the entire Spanish-speaking world
- Culturally accurate contexts that encourage communication and skill-building
- Compelling, visually striking photo and illustration programs that support and enhance students' understanding of the text
- Engaging video selections and storylines, integrated throughout all three levels of the program

DESCUBRE and the *Standards for Foreign Language Learning*

DESCUBRE promotes and enhances student learning and motivation through its instructional design, based on and informed by the best practices of the *Standards for Foreign Language Learning in the 21st Century* (American Council on the Teaching of Foreign Languages).

DESCUBRE blends the underlying principles of the five Cs (Communication, Cultures, Connections, Comparisons, Communities) with features and strategies tailored specifically to build students' speaking, listening, reading, and writing skills. As a result, right from the start students are given the tools to express themselves articulately, interact meaningfully with others, and become highly competent communicators in Spanish.

The Five Cs of Foreign Language Learning

Communication
Students:

1. Engage in conversation, provide and obtain information, express feelings and emotions, and exchange opinions. (Interpersonal mode)
2. Understand and interpret written and spoken language. (Interpretive mode)
3. Present information, concepts, and ideas to an audience of listeners or readers. (Presentational mode)

Cultures
Students demonstrate an understanding of the relationship between:

1. The practices and perspectives of the culture studied.
2. The products and perspectives of the culture studied.

Connections
Students:

1. Reinforce and further their knowledge of other disciplines through Spanish.
2. Acquire information and recognize distinctive viewpoints only available through Spanish language and cultures.

Comparisons
Students demonstrate understanding of:

1. The nature of language through comparisons of the Spanish language and their own.
2. The concept of culture through comparisons of the cultures studied and their own.

Communities
Students:

1. Use Spanish both within and beyond the school setting.
2. Show evidence of becoming life-long learners by using Spanish for personal enjoyment and enrichment.

Adapted from ACTFL's *Standards for Foreign Language Learning in the 21st Century*

Good Teaching Practices

The design and format of the presentations and activities in the **DESCUBRE** program incorporate research-based instructional principles to address your instructional needs and goals.

Contextualized Vocabulary

Vocabulary concepts are explicitly presented, carefully organized, and frequently reviewed—always in context—to reinforce student understanding. Each lesson provides ample opportunities for students to practice and work with all the vocabulary they have learned up to that point. The **Contextos** section presents vocabulary in meaningful contexts and reinforces new words, phrases, and expressions through varied and engaging practice activities.

Ongoing Comprehensible Input

The *Fotonovela* Video Program features conversations that reinforce vocabulary from **Contextos**. The video storyboard—the companion script with accompanying visuals in the textbook—provides students with instructional reinforcement and preparation that ensure successful and confident use of Spanish.

Contextualized Grammar

Grammatical terms are clearly and concisely defined in the **Estructura** section. Grammatical structures are carefully called out and modeled with sample context sentences. Students are encouraged to apply their knowledge of English grammar to make comparisons with grammatical concepts in Spanish.

Communication

The language practice activities provided in the **Contextos** and **Estructura** sections are carefully designed to progress from directed to open-ended to fully communicative, all within context-based, personalized activities. The varied **Comunicación** and **Síntesis** activity formats include pair and small-group work, class interaction, and task-based, to name a few. The **DESCUBRE** program offers ample opportunities for all types of learners to demonstrate what they can do with the vocabulary and grammar they have learned.

Cultural Context for Learning

Language learning, like any academic subject, requires a context. Without it, the vocabulary and grammar students learn lack real meaning. Culture is the framework that provides the necessary context to students. It adds depth and color to their linguistic landscape, and over time it becomes a powerful incentive for continued study.

Culture is a prominent feature of the **DESCUBRE** program. Students are continually prompted to use Spanish in different cultural contexts and to use critical thinking skills to make connections and comparisons. In particular, the **Cultura** and **Panorama** textbook sections, with their respective emphases on culture from thematic and geographical perspectives, provide opportunities for teaching Spanish in a cultural context. In addition to the cultural material in the textbook, you can enrich your students' learning experience with the *Flash cultura* and *Panorama cultural* videos and by bringing to the classroom authentic items from different Hispanic cultures, such as restaurant menus, songs, poetry, podcasts, documentaries, or films.

Universal Access

You can build a unique classroom community by engaging all students and encouraging them to participate regularly in class. Knowing how to appeal to learners of different abilities and learning styles will allow you to foster a positive teaching environment and motivate all your students.

Here are some strategies for creating inclusive learning environments for students who are cognitively, emotionally, or physically challenged as well as for heritage language and advanced learners.

Learners with Special Needs

Learners with special needs include students with attention priority disorders, students with learning disabilities, slower-paced learners, at-risk learners, gifted students, and English-language learners. Some inclusion strategies that work well with the special needs of such students are:

Clear Structure By teaching concepts related to language in a predictable or understandable order, you can help students classify language in logical groups. For example, encourage students to keep outlines of materials they read, classify words under categories such as colors, shapes, etc., or follow prewriting steps.

Frequent Review and Repetition Preview material to be taught and review material covered at the end of each lesson. Pair proficient learners with less proficient ones to practice and reinforce concepts. Help students retain concepts through continuous practice and review.

Multi-sensory Input and Output Use visual, auditory, and kinesthetic tasks and activities to add interest and motivation and achieve long-term retention. For example, vary input with the use of audio recordings, video, guided visualization, rhymes, and mnemonics. Or use specially prepared displays for emphasizing key vocabulary and concepts. Encourage students to repeat words or mime responses to questions.

Sentence Completion Provide sentence starters for students who struggle to remember vocabulary or grammar. Emphasize different sentence structures. Write and encourage students to copy cloze sentences before filling in blanks.

Additional Time Consider how physical limitations may affect participation in special projects or daily routines. Allow extra time for completing a task or moving around the classroom. Provide additional time and recommended accommodations for hearing-impaired or visually-impaired students.

Advanced Learners

Advanced learners have the potential to learn language concepts and complete assignments at an accelerated pace. They may be enrolled in school programs such as Advanced Placement or International Baccalaureate that require them to sharpen writing and problem-solving skills, study subjects in greater detail, and develop the study skills needed for tackling rigorous coursework.

As a result, advanced learners may benefit from assignments that are more challenging than the ones given to their peers. Examples include reading a variety of texts and sharing their perspectives with the class, retelling detailed stories, preparing analyses of texts, or adding to discussions. The key to differentiating for advanced learners is adapting or enriching existing activities by adding a degree of challenge to a given task. Here are some strategies for engaging advanced learners:

Timed Answers Have students answer questions within a specified time limit.

Persuading Adapt activities so students have to write or present their points of view in order to persuade an audience. Pair or group advanced learners to form debating teams and have them present their opinions on a lesson topic to the rest of the class.

Circumlocution Prompt students to discover various ways of expressing ideas and of overcoming potential blocks to communication through the use of circumlocution and paraphrasing.

Identifying Cause and Effect After reading passages in the text or other types of writing, prompt students to explain why something happened and what followed as a result. Encourage them to vary vocabulary and use precise words and appropriate conjunctions to indicate sequence and the relation between events.

Heritage Language Learners

Heritage language learners are students who come from homes where a language other than English is spoken. Spanish heritage learners are likely to have adequate comprehension and conversation skills (although oral proficiency levels may vary widely), but they could require as much explicit instruction of reading and writing skills as their non-heritage peers. Because of their background, heritage language learners can attain, with instruction adapted to their needs, a high level of proficiency and literacy in Spanish. In addition to the suggestions provided in the Heritage Learner notes in the Teacher's Annotated Edition, you may want to incorporate some of the following strategies for harnessing bilingualism and biculturalism among this student population:

Support and Validate Experiences Acknowledge students' experiences with Spanish and their heritage culture and encourage them to share what they know with the class.

Focus on Accuracy Alert students to common spelling and grammatical errors made by native speakers, such as distinguishing between **c, s,** and **z** or **b** and **v** and appropriate use of irregular verb forms such as **hubo** instead of **hubieron**.

Develop Literacy and Writing Skills Help students focus on reading as well as grammar, punctuation, and syntax skills, but be careful not to assign a workload significantly greater than what is assigned to non-heritage learners.

For each level of the **DESCUBRE** program, the **Cuaderno para hispanohablantes** supports the two latter strategies with materials developed specifically for heritage learners. Each lesson of the **Cuaderno** focuses on the development of reading and writing skills, while also providing vocabulary, grammar, and spelling practice appropriate for heritage language learners.

All Learners

Use Technology to Reach All Learners No matter what their ability level or learning style, students are surrounded by technology. Many are adept at using it to understand their world. They use it enthusiastically, but they need your guidance in how to use it for learning Spanish. You can use technology to customize your students' learning experience by providing materials for visual, auditory, and kinesthetic learners, as well as for learners who need more time to accomplish certain tasks.

The **DESCUBRE** program provides a wide range of technology that is designed to make sure that all your students, no matter what their home or school environment, have equal access to all instructional materials—and to success.

Level of Computer Access			
	None	**Moderate**	**High**
Practice activities	Textbook	Textbook and Supersite	Textbook and Supersite
Audio	Audio CDs	Supersite	Supersite and **e-Cuaderno**
Audio activities	Textbook and **Cuaderno de actividades**	Supersite	Supersite and **e-Cuaderno**
Video	Video DVD	Supersite	Supersite and **e-Cuaderno**
Video activities	Textbook and **Cuaderno de actividades**	Supersite	Supersite and **e-Cuaderno**
Homework	**Cuaderno de práctica**	**Cuaderno de práctica**	**e-Cuaderno**

If your students have no access to computers, you can bring audio and video into your classroom with the Textbook and Audio Program CDs and the Video DVDs. Accompanying activities are found in both the textbook and the **Cuaderno de actividades**. If you wish, you can use the **Cuaderno de práctica** for homework to reinforce concepts learned in class.

If students have access to computers through your classroom or a school language lab, they can complete activities on the **DESCUBRE** Supersite. Activities are motivating, as well as instructional, and include interactive flashcards, games, short self-quizzes, and more. Selected activities are connected to an online gradebook, so you can monitor student performance.

If all students have access to computers at home as well as at school, consider having them use the **e-Cuaderno**, which incorporates the **Cuaderno de práctica** with the audio and video activities from the **Cuaderno de actividades** in an online, auto-graded format, connected to a gradebook.

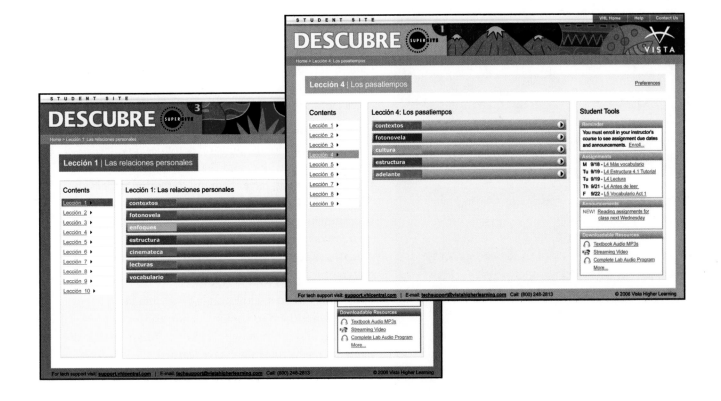

Classroom Environment

The creators of **DESCUBRE** understand that there are many different approaches to successful language teaching and that no one method works perfectly for all teachers or all learners. The strategies and tips provided in this Teacher's Annotated Edition take into account the many widely accepted language-teaching methods applied by successful teachers today.

Strategies for Creating a Communicative Learning Community

The aim of communicative learning is to develop oral and listening proficiency, literacy skills, and cultural knowledge in order to have meaningful exchanges with others through conversation, writing, listening, and viewing. Think of communicative interaction as being an instructional method as well as the ultimate reason for learning Spanish.

Apply the following strategies to address challenges commonly faced by Spanish-language learners. Good strategies will help your students gain confidence to communicate clearly, fully, accurately, personally, and confidently. Always focus on ways to engage students and increase meaningful interaction.

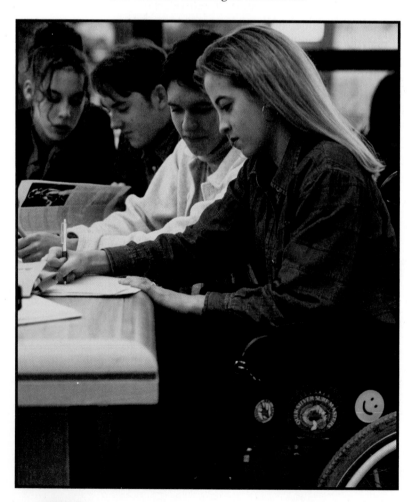

Maintain the Target Language

As much as possible, create an immersion environment by using Spanish to *teach* Spanish. Encourage the exclusive use of the target language in your classroom, employing visual aids, circumlocution, or gestures to complement what you say. Encourage students to perceive meaning directly through careful listening and observation, and by using cognates and familiar structures and patterns to deduce meaning. Employ mnemonics, and encourage students to develop strategies to expand and retain their knowledge of Spanish.

Accommodate Different Learning Styles

Visual Learners learn best by seeing, so engage them in activities and projects that are visually creative. Encourage them to write down information and think in pictures as a long-term retention strategy; reinforce their learning through visual displays such as diagrams, videos, and handouts.

Auditory Learners best retain information by listening. Engage them in discussions, debates, and role-playing. Reinforce their learning by playing audio versions of texts or reading aloud passages and stories. Encourage them to pay attention to voice, tone, and pitch to infer meaning.

Kinesthetic Learners learn best through moving, touching, and doing hands-on activities. Involve such students in skits and dramatizations; to infer or convey meaning, have them observe or model gestures such as those used for greeting someone or getting someone's attention.

Cultivate Critical Thinking

Prompt students to reflect, observe, reason, and form judgments in Spanish. Engaging students in activities that require them to compare, contrast, predict, criticize, and estimate will help them to internalize the language structures they have learned.

Encourage Cooperative Learning

There are many reasons for encouraging cooperative learning among your students, particularly in the context of Spanish-language learning. Pair or group students of differing abilities and levels of proficiency to encourage peer coaching, promote student self-confidence, help enhance individual and group social skills and promote positive relations in your classroom.

Pair and group work can promote learning and achievement among students, create positive learning experiences, and improve students' abilities to retain information for longer periods of time.

Monitor group interactions and presentations regularly. Allow for flexible grouping and encourage movement within and among groups, so that group leaders and facilitators as well as group members are constantly changing. If possible, match students with common interests to encourage them to engage in conversation and share knowledge. You may want to allow for equal special needs or heritage learner representation among groups where possible to allow for different perspectives.

Consider the Affective Dimension

While many factors contribute to the quality and success rate of learning experiences, two factors are particularly important to language learning. One is students' beliefs about how language is learned; the other is language-learning anxiety.

As studies show, students often come to language classes either with a lack of knowledge about how to approach language learning or with mistaken notions about how to do so. Mistaken and unrealistic beliefs can cause frustration, significantly undermining students' ability to achieve a successful language-learning experience.

Similarly, language learning anxiety can have a negative impact on students. The late Dr. Philip Redwine Donley, **DESCUBRE** co-author and author of articles on language-learning anxiety, spoke with many students who reported feeling nervous or apprehensive in their classes. They mentioned "freezing" when called on by their teachers or going inexplicably blank when taking tests. Some so dreaded their classes that they skipped them or dropped the course.

DESCUBRE contains several features designed to reduce students' language anxiety. Its structured, visually dramatic interior design was conceived as a learning tool to make students feel comfortable with the content and confident about navigating the lessons. The Teacher's Annotated Edition includes recurring Affective Dimension annotations with suggestions for managing and reducing language-learning anxieties. The student text provides a wealth of helpful sidebars that assist students by making immediately relevant connections with new information or reminding them of previously learned concepts.

Student Sidebars

¡Atención! Provides active, testable information about the vocabulary or grammar point

Ayuda Offers specific grammar and vocabulary reminders related to a particular activity or suggests pertinent language-learning strategies

Consulta References related material introduced in previous or upcoming lessons

¡Lengua viva! Presents immediately relevant information on everyday language use

Nota cultural Provides a wide range of cultural information relevant to the topic of an activity or section

The Four Skills and Grammar

Effective second-language teaching equips students with the ability to recognize, understand, and produce the target language. Think of listening and reading as forms of input, and focus on speaking and writing as student output.

Listening/Speaking Skills

As students begin to study Spanish, it is likely that they will expect to need to recognize every word they hear in order to understand. The audio and video materials in the **DESCUBRE** program build on what students have already learned but also introduce words, phrases, and structures to which they will be exposed later. It will be important for you to train students to listen for tone, the gist of the message, and cues that will help them situate meaning, such as **ayer** or **mañana** to distinguish between past and future.

The **DESCUBRE** audio program is adaptable to the method for developing listening skills that works best for you and your students. Remind students to look for the headset icons that appear throughout the lessons, but particularly those in **Contextos** and **Escuchar**. Remind students also to approach listening passages in stages in order to understand them and to become proficient listeners.

Three Stages of Listening In the first stage, students should read any pre-listening strategies and post-listening activity items before listening to a passage. This will help them anticipate the main ideas as they listen to the passage the first time. Encourage them to listen to it in its entirety while jotting down words and ideas and while keeping in mind what the comprehension items ask. Remind students that they should not expect to understand every word. As students listen to the passage a second time, they should attempt to answer as many of the activity items as they can, leaving the more challenging ones for the final time they listen to the passage. If you choose to do these activities as a class, modeling the various listening stages for students will establish constructive precedents for future listening situations, both in and out of the classroom.

Sequence of Speaking Activities DESCUBRE activities progress from guided to open-ended, with speaking opportunities becoming more numerous from one section to the next. In the **Contextos** and **Estructura** sections, the activities found in the **Comunicación** panel were specifically designed to elicit abundant oral production. Often, the **Síntesis** activity in this panel is a Communication Activities worksheet that requires students to work in pairs to perform a common task. Some of these activities require students to fill in information on a worksheet. In both cases, students communicate orally with classmates in a fully open-ended context in order to complete the task.

Before starting open-ended speaking activities in any section, make sure students have practiced and understood any relevant lexical or grammatical forms by completing guided activities that precede the communicative ones. Practice circumlocution with your students on a regular basis as part of your curriculum so that it is always clear to them that talking their way around an unknown word or expression is a normal communication strategy in Spanish just as in their first language. This way, when students carry out the open-ended speaking activities in **DESCUBRE**, they should already feel comfortable expressing themselves. After any type of speaking activity, remember to review what students have said in their groups and share the information with the entire class.

Reading/Writing Skills

As students develop reading comprehension skills in Spanish, encourage them to access texts by applying the reading strategies they learn both within and beyond your classroom. Remind them to predict or infer content by observing supporting information such as pictures and captions. Have them focus on text organization (main idea and details, order of events, and so on).

Every lesson of **DESCUBRE** contains ample reading opportunities, not only in sections with longer reading passages such as **Cultura, Lectura,** and **Panorama,** but also in the video still captions of **Fotonovela** and in reading passages for practicing grammar points in **Estructura** activities. As with listening practice, students should approach reading in stages.

Three Stages of Reading Remind students to look over pre-reading activities or strategies to familiarize themselves with the topic of the reading passage. They should also look at post-reading activities in order to anticipate the reading's theme. They should keep this information in mind as they read the selection through the first time. At this point, they should only stop to jot down notes, but they should strive to reach the end of the selection without looking up English translations since their focus should be on understanding the gist of the passage. Remind them that it is fine if they do not understand every word.

As students read the passage a second time, they should consult the glosses of unfamiliar words or phrases, and when finished, revisit post-reading activities in order to answer as many items as possible, leaving the more difficult ones for the time being, before beginning a third or subsequent reading of the passage. Most importantly, any reading assignment should be integrated into a broader framework of tasks consisting of all the language skills, giving students the opportunity to speak, listen, and write about the reading selection's topic. To this end, consider using the reading as a springboard for pair or group discussions or a short essay soliciting students' reactions to the reading's theme.

Writing Activities Writing skill development should focus on meaning and comprehensibility. As needed, remind students to take into account spelling, mechanics, and a logical structure to their paragraphs.

Differentiate assignments to allow for more accurate evaluation of individual students' abilities. For example, assign specific questions to different individuals or groups. Have each student or group answer the same number of questions, but vary the complexity of questions from group to group.

DESCUBRE offers many opportunities for writing practice. Most prominent of course is the **Escritura** section of **Adelante** and the writing activities in the **Cuaderno de actividades**, where students learn and practice strategies for becoming more proficient writers in Spanish. However, other activities in strands such as **Cultura** and **Estructura** provide writing practice via shorter tasks.

Grammar in a Communicative Environment

Help students understand that learning Spanish is about communication, that is, about understanding and expressing oneself. While vocabulary and grammar are the basic elements of language, rules and patterns in themselves are not the goal of Spanish study. Help students experience grammar—that is, effective form and usage—as a tool that permits them to engage in varied, meaningful, and broader written and spoken interactions in Spanish.

The **Estructura** section in **DESCUBRE** begins with clear, brief, and meaningful introductions to a limited number of concepts on which students are asked to focus. Examples (including photos) from the lesson **Fotonovela** episode reinforce the communicative context for the grammar point. After introducing the grammar point, the **Práctica, Comunicación,** and **Síntesis** activity sequences provide a fully-integrated, carefully-sequenced progression of practice activities, moving from directed to open-ended to fully communicative, all having a context-based, personalized focus.

Use a variety of methods to help students focus on meaning conveyed by different forms. For example, the Communication Activities allow students to use Spanish in a communicative way. An implicit focus on grammar, especially when integrated into communicative activities, should increase motivation and allow students to express themselves relevantly, use an acceptable level of accuracy, and, most importantly, make themselves understood.

Assessment

As you use the **DESCUBRE** program, you can employ a variety of assessments to check for student comprehension and evaluate progress. You can also use assessment as a way to identify student needs and modify your instruction accordingly. The program provides both traditional assessments that are comprehensive in scope and elicit discrete answers, as well less traditional ones that offer a more communicative approach by eliciting open-ended, personalized responses.

Diagnostic Testing

The **Recapitulación** section that follows the **Estructuras** sections in each lesson of Levels 1 and 2 provides you with an informal opportunity to assess students' readiness for the listening, reading, and writing activities in the **Adelante** section. If some students need additional practice or instruction in a particular area, you can identify this before students move on.

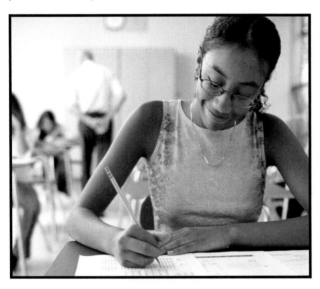

If students have moderate or high access to computers, they could complete the **Recapitulación** auto-graded quiz, also available for Level 3, on the **DESCUBRE** Supersite. After finishing the quiz, each student receives an evaluation of his or her progress, indicating areas where he or she needs to focus. The student is then presented with several options—viewing a summary chart, accessing an online tutorial, or completing some practice items—to reach an appropriate level before beginning the activities in the **Adelante** section. You will be able to monitor how well students have done through the **MAESTRO™** gradebook and be able to recommend appropriate study paths until they develop as reflective learners and can decide on their own what works best for them.

Writing Assessment

In each lesson of Levels 1 and 2, the **Adelante** section includes an **Escritura** page that introduces a writing strategy, which students apply as they complete the writing activity. The Teacher's Annotated Edition contains suggested rubrics for evaluating students' written work.

You can also apply these rubrics to the process writing activities in the **Cuaderno de actividades** and the **Cuaderno para hispanohablantes** for all three levels of **DESCUBRE**. These activities also include suggestions for peer- and self-editing that will help students focus their attention on what is most important for attaining clarity in written communication, while at the same time helping them develop into reflective language learners.

Testing Program

The **DESCUBRE** Testing Program provides four tests for each lesson. All of the tests include listening, reading, and writing sections. There are additional sections about culture that you may choose to use, as well as oral test suggestions. **Pruebas A** and **B** are discrete-item tests that are effective measures of progress in contexts where you may want to stress a balance between form and usage as well as communication. **Pruebas C** and **D** use open-ended formats and can be effective in contexts where the focus is solidly on communication. The Testing Program also provides cumulative tests that allow you to assess students' spiraling knowledge of vocabulary and grammar and evaluate listening, speaking, reading, and writing abilities.

You can use the tests just as they appear in the printed Testing Program. They are also available on the Teacher's Resource CD-ROM and the Supersite so you can customize the tests as you wish, adding, eliminating, or moving items according to your classroom and student needs.

Portfolio Assessment

Portfolios can provide further valuable evidence of your students' learning. They are useful tools for evaluating students' progress in Spanish and also suggest to students how they are likely to be assessed in the real world. Since portfolio activities often comprise classroom tasks that you would assign as part of a lesson or as homework, you should think of the planning, selecting, recording, and interpreting of information about individual performance as a way of blending assessment with instruction.

You may find it helpful to refer to portfolio contents, such as drafts, essays, and samples of presentations when writing student reports and conveying the status of a student's progress to his or her parents.

At the beginning of the school year, ask students to consider which pieces of their own work they would like to share with family and friends, and help them develop criteria for selecting representative samples of essays, stories, poems, recordings of plays or interviews, mock documentaries, and so on. Prompt students to choose a variety of media in their activities wherever possible to demonstrate development in all four language skills. Encourage them to seek peer and parental input as they generate and refine criteria to help them organize and reflect on their own work.

Strategies for Differentiating Assessment

Here are some strategies for modifying tests and other forms of assessment according to your students' needs and your own purposes for administering the assessment.

Adjust Questions Direct complex or higher-level questions to students who are equipped to answer them adequately and modify questions for students with greater needs. Always ask questions that elicit thinking, but keep in mind the students' proficiency and readiness.

Provide Tiered Assignments Assign tasks of varying complexity depending on individual student needs. Refer to the Universal Access section on page T19 for tips on making activities simpler or more challenging.

Promote Flexible Grouping Encourage movement among groups of students so that all learners are appropriately challenged. Group students according to interest, oral proficiency levels, or learning styles.

Adjust Pacing Pace the sequence and speed of assessments to suit your students' learning needs. Time advanced learners to challenge them and allow slower-paced learners more time to complete tasks or answer questions.

Block Scheduling and Pacing

Planning is essential to block scheduling, as it allows you to establish routines, pace instruction, integrate concepts thoroughly, and modify activities to respond to individual and group learning needs. Refer to the sample pacing guides on pages T28 and T29 for suggestions for sequencing and timing instruction. The guides have been generated to help you establish engaging routines (such as warm-ups and quick reviews) as well as use either 50- or 90-minute periods to cover lesson objectives effectively and keep students on task with receptive and productive oral and written communicative activities.

The sequence of instruction in each **DESCUBRE** lesson and accompanying activities (noted in teacher tips as well as student practice workbooks) provide you with an effective instructional progression that integrates all four language skills (listening, speaking, reading, and writing) within a single class period, whatever its length.

50-Minute / 18-Day Suggested Lesson Pacing Guide

Day 1	Present Communicative Goals. Go over the contents of each section presented on the lesson opener page. **15 min**	Discuss the **A primera vista** question. Preview **Contextos** section. Present **Contextos** vocabulary. **25 min**	Begin **Práctica** activities. **10 min**
Day 2	Review **Contextos** vocabulary. **10 min**	Complete **Práctica** activities. **20 min**	Begin **Comunicación** activities. **20 min**
Day 3	Review **Contextos** vocabulary. **10 min** Complete **Comunicación** activities. **15 min**	Present **Fotonovela** and **Expresiones útiles**. **15 min**	Begin reading the **Fotonovela** as a class. **10 min**
Day 4	Review the **Expresiones útiles**. **10 min**	Finish reading the **Fotonovela** as a class. **20 min**	Show the **Fotonovela** video episode. **25 min**
Day 5	Review the **Fotonovela** and **Expresiones** útiles. **20 min**	Complete the **¿Qué pasó?** activities. **20 min** Preview **Pronunciación** section. **10 min**	
Day 6	Present **Pronunciación** section. **10 min** Have students complete the **¿Cierto o falso?** activities. **15 min**	Present and work through the **En detalle** reading in the **Cultura** section. **25 min**	
Day 7	Present the **Así se dice** vocabulary. Present and work through the **Perfiles** reading in the **Cultura** section. **20 min**	Have students complete the **Actividades** questions. **10 min** Show the **Flash cultura** video. **20 min**	
Day 8	Present and work through the first **Estructura** grammar explanation. **25 min**	Have students complete the **Inténtalo** and **Práctica** activities. **25 min**	
Day 9	Review the first **Estructura** grammar explanation. **5 min**	Have students complete the **Comunicación** and **Síntesis** activities. **25 min**	Present and work through the second **Estructura** grammar explanation. **20 min**
Day 10	Review the second **Estructura** grammar explanation. **5 min**	Have students complete the **Inténtalo** and **Práctica** activities. **20 min**	Have students complete the **Comunicación** and **Síntesis** activities. **25 min**
Day 11	Present and work through the third **Estructura** grammar explanation. **20 min**	Have students complete the **Inténtalo** and **Práctica** activities. **20 min**	Have students begin the **Comunicación** and **Síntesis** activities. **10 min**

Day 12	Review the third **Estructura** grammar explanation. **5 min**	Have students complete the **Comunicación** and **Síntesis** activities. **15 min**	Present and work through the fourth **Estructura** grammar explanation. **20 min**	Have students begin the **Inténtalo** and **Práctica** activities. **10 min**
Day 13	Review the fourth **Estructura** grammar explanation. **5 min**	Have students complete the **Inténtalo** and **Práctica** activities. **10 min**	Have students complete the **Comunicación** and **Síntesis** activities. **20 min**	Recycle lesson vocabulary. **15 min**

Day 14	Present and work through the activities in the **Recapitulación** section. **25 min**	Present and work through the **Lectura** section in **Adelante**. **25 min**	
Day 15	Present and work through the **Escritura** section in **Adelante**. **35 min**	Present and work through the **Escuchar** section in **Adelante**. **15 min**	
Day 16	Present and work through the **En pantalla** section in **Adelante**. **5 min**	Present and work through the **Oye cómo va** section in **Adelante**. **15 min**	Present and work through the **Panorama** section. **20 min**
Day 17	Show the **Panorama cultural** video. **20 min**	Review and recycle lesson vocabulary and grammar points. **30 min**	
Day 18	Administer the lesson **Prueba**. **30 min**	Preview the next lesson theme. **20 min**	

90-Minute (Block Schedule) / 10-Day Suggested Lesson Pacing Guide

Day 1	Present Communicative Goals. Go over the contents of each section presented on the lesson opener page. 10 min	Discuss the **A primera vista** question. Present **Contextos** vocabulary. 20 min	Complete **Práctica** activities. 40 min	Go over **Comunicación** activities in preparation for Day 2. 20 min	
Day 2	Review **Contextos** vocabulary. 10 min	Complete **Comunicación** activities. 35 min	Present **Fotonovela** and **Expresiones útiles.** 10 min	Read the **Fotonovela** as a class. 25 min	Wrap up and review the topics and vocabulary covered in class. 10 min
Day 3	Review **Expresiones útiles.** 10 min	Show the **Fotonovela** video episode. 25 min	Complete the **¿Qué pasó?** activities. 25 min	Present **Pronunciación.** 15 min	Wrap up lesson. 15 min
Day 4	Review **Pronunciación** section. 10 min	Present and work through the **En detalle** reading in the **Cultura** section. 35 min	Have students complete the **¿Cierto o falso?** activities. 15 min	Present the **Así se dice** vocabulary. 10 min	Work through the **Perfiles** section as a class. 20 min
Day 5	Review the **Perfiles** reading. 5 min	Have students complete the **Actividades.** 10 min	Show the **Flash cultura** video. 25 min	Present and work through the first **Estructura** grammar explanation. 25 min	Have students complete the **Inténtalo** and **Práctica** activities. 25 min
Day 6	Review the first **Estructura** grammar explanation. 5 min	Have students complete **Comunicación** and **Síntesis** activities. 25 min	Present and work through the second **Estructura** grammar explanation. 20 min	Have students complete the **Inténtalo** and **Práctica** activities. 15 min	Have students complete **Comunicación** and **Síntesis** activities. 25 min
Day 7	Review the second **Estructura** grammar explanation. 5 min	Present and work through the third **Estructura** grammar explanation. 20 min	Have students complete the **Inténtalo** and **Práctica** activities. 25 min	Have students complete **Comunicación** and **Síntesis** activities. 25 min	Present and work through the fourth **Estructura** grammar explanation. 15 min
Day 8	Review the third and fourth **Estructura** grammar explanations. 10 min	Have students complete the **Inténtalo** and **Práctica** activities. 20 min	Have students complete **Comunicación** and **Síntesis** activities. 25 min	Recycle lesson vocabulary. 10 min	Present and work through the activities in the **Recapitulación** section. 25 min
Day 9	Present and work through the **Lectura** and **Escritura** sections in **Adelante.** 45 min			Present and work through the **Escuchar, En pantalla,** and **Oye cómo va** sections in **Adelante.** 45 min	
Day 10	Present and work through the **Panorama** section. 20 min	Show the **Panorama cultural** video. 20 min	Review lesson vocabulary and grammar points. 20 min	Administer the lesson **Prueba.** 30 min	

Professional Resources

Printed Resources

- American Council on the Teaching of Foreign Languages (2006). *Standards for Foreign Language Learning in the 21st Century*. Third Edition. Yonkers, NY: ACTFL.

- Brown, H Douglas (2000). *Principles of Language Learning and Teaching*. Fourth Edition. White Plains, NY: Pearson Education.

- Crawford, L. W. (1993). *Language and Literacy Learning in Multicultural Classrooms*. Boston, MA: Allyn & Bacon.

- Hughes, Arthur (2002). *Testing for Language Teachers*. Second Edition. Cambridge, UK: Cambridge University Press.

- Kramasch, Claire (2004). *Context and Culture in Language Teaching*. Oxford, UK: Oxford University Press.

- Krashen, S.D., & Terrell, T.D. (1996). *The Natural Approach: Language Acquisition in the Classroom*. Highgreen, UK: Bloodaxe Books Ltd.

- Larsen-Freeman, D. (2000). *Techniques and Principles in Language Teaching*. Second Edition. Oxford, UK: Oxford University Press.

- Nunan, D. (1999). *Second Language Teaching and Learning*. Boston: Heinle & Heinle.

- O'Malley, J. Michael and Anna Uhl Chamot (1990). *Learning Strategies in Language Acquisition*. Cambridge, UK: Cambridge University Press.

- Ommagio Hadley, Alice (2000). *Teaching Language in Context*. Third Edition. Boston, MA: Heinle & Heinle.

- Richards, Jack C. and Rodgers, Theodore S (2001). *Approaches and Methods in Language Teaching*. Cambridge, UK: Cambridge University Press.

- Shrum, Judith L. and Glisan, Eileen W. (2005). *Teacher's Handbook: Contextualized Language Instruction*. Third Edition. Boston: Heinle & Heinle.

- Tomlinson, C. A. (1999). *The Differentiated Classroom: Responding to the Needs of Learners*. Alexandria, VA: Association for Curriculum and Supervision Development.

- Tomlinson, C.A. (2001). *How to Differentiate Instruction in Mixed-Ability Classrooms*. Alexandria, VA: Association for Curriculum and Supervision Development.

Online resources

American Council on the Teaching of Foreign Languages (ACTFL)
www.actfl.org

American Association of Teachers of Spanish and Portuguese (AATSP)
www.aatsp.org

Modern Language Association (MLA)
www.mla.org

Center for Applied Linguistics (CAL)
www.cal.org

Computer Assisted Language Instruction Consortium (CALICO)
www.calico.org

The Center for Advanced Research on Language Acquisition (CARLA)
www.carla.acad.umn.edu

The Joint National Committee for Languages and National Council for Languages (JNCL/NCLIS)
www.languagepolicy.org

International Association for Language Learning Technology (IALLT)
http://iallt.org/

Linguistic Society of America Learning Technology (LSA)
www.lsadc.org/

National K-12 Foreign Language Resource Center (NFLRC K-12)
http://nflrc.iastate.edu/homepage.html

National Foreign Language Resource Center (NFLRC)
http://nflrc.hawaii.edu

National Capital Language Resource Center (NCLRC)
http://www.nclrc.org

Center for Advanced Language Proficiency Education and Research (CALPER)
http://calper.la.psu.edu/

Center for Applied Second Language Studies (CASLS)
http://casls.uoregon.edu/

Index of Cultural References

DESCUBRE

Lengua y cultura del mundo hispánico

VISTA
HIGHER LEARNING

Boston, Massachusetts

1

Publisher: José A. Blanco
Editorial Director: Beth Kramer
Project Managers: Armando Brito, Daniel Finkbeiner

Director of Art and Design: Linda Jurras
Director of Production and Manufacturing: Lisa Perrier
Design Manager: Polo Barrera
Photo Researcher and Art Buyer: Rachel Distler
Production and Manufacturing Team: Jeff Perron, Oscar Díez, Mauricio Henao, María Eugenia Castaño

President: Janet L. Dracksdorf
Sr. Vice President of Operations: Tom Delano
Vice President of Sales and Marketing: Scott Burns
National Sales Consultant: Norah Jones
Executive Marketing Manager: Benjamin Rivera

Printed in the United States of America.

DESCUBRE Level 1 Student Edition Text ISBN-13: 978-1-60007-252-9
DESCUBRE Level 1 Student Edition Text ISBN-10: 1-60007-252-6

Library of Congress Control Number: 2006939626

1 2 3 4 5 6 7 8 9-C-12 11 10 09 08 07

DESCUBRE

Lengua y cultura del mundo hispánico

Table of Contents

	contextos	fotonovela

cultura	estructura	adelante

Table of Contents

	contexts	fotonovela

cultura	estructura	adelante

Table of Contents

	contextos	fotonovela

cultura	estructura	adelante

The Spanish-speaking World

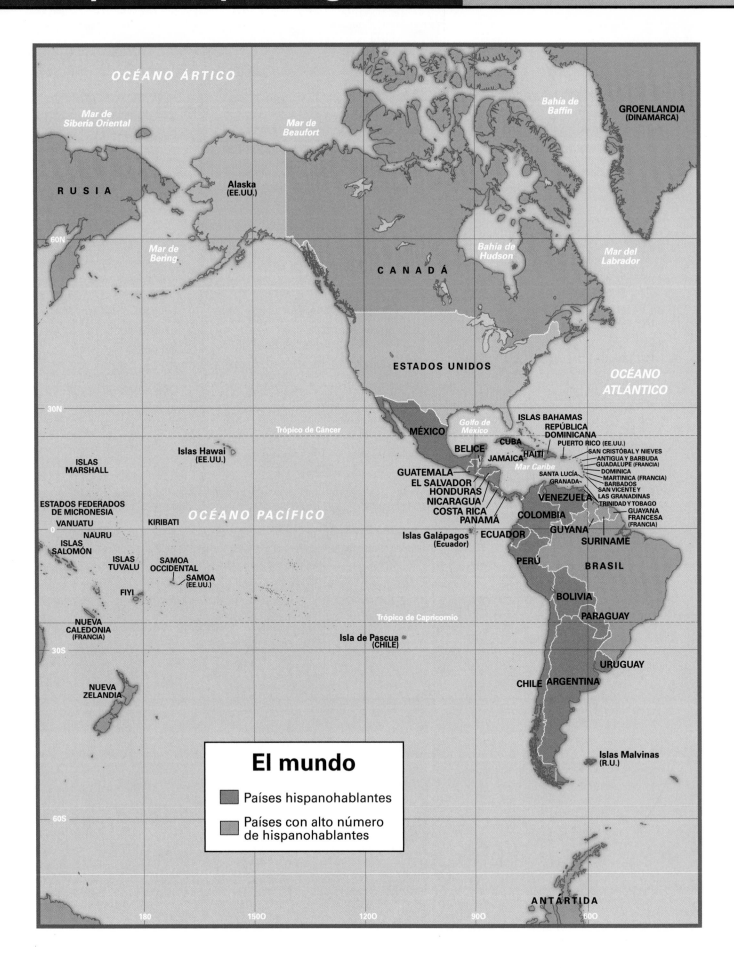

OCÉANO ÁRTICO

Mar de Siberia Oriental

Mar de Beaufort

Bahía de Baffin

GROENLANDIA (DINAMARCA)

RUSIA

Alaska (EE.UU.)

Mar de Bering

60N

Bahía de Hudson

Mar del Labrador

CANADÁ

ESTADOS UNIDOS

OCÉANO ATLÁNTICO

30N

Trópico de Cáncer

Golfo de México

ISLAS BAHAMAS

REPÚBLICA DOMINICANA

MÉXICO

CUBA

PUERTO RICO (EE.UU.)

Islas Hawai (EE.UU.)

BELICE

HAITÍ

SAN CRISTÓBAL Y NIEVES

ISLAS MARSHALL

JAMAICA

ANTIGUA Y BARBUDA

GUADALUPE (FRANCIA)

Mar Caribe

DOMINICA

GUATEMALA

SANTA LUCÍA

MARTINICA (FRANCIA)

EL SALVADOR

GRANADA

BARBADOS

HONDURAS

SAN VICENTE Y LAS GRANADINAS

ESTADOS FEDERADOS DE MICRONESIA

NICARAGUA

VENEZUELA

TRINIDAD Y TOBAGO

COSTA RICA

VANUATU

OCÉANO PACÍFICO

KIRIBATI

PANAMÁ

COLOMBIA

GUYANA FRANCESA (FRANCIA)

0

GUYANA

Islas Galápagos (Ecuador)

ECUADOR

SURINAME

NAURU

ISLAS SALOMÓN

PERÚ

BRASIL

ISLAS TUVALU

SAMOA OCCIDENTAL

SAMOA (EE.UU.)

BOLIVIA

FIYI

PARAGUAY

Trópico de Capricornio

NUEVA CALEDONIA (FRANCIA)

Isla de Pascua (CHILE)

30S

URUGUAY

NUEVA ZELANDIA

CHILE ARGENTINA

Islas Malvinas (R.U.)

El mundo

Países hispanohablantes

Países con alto número de hispanohablantes

60S

180   150O   120O   90O   60O

ANTÁRTIDA

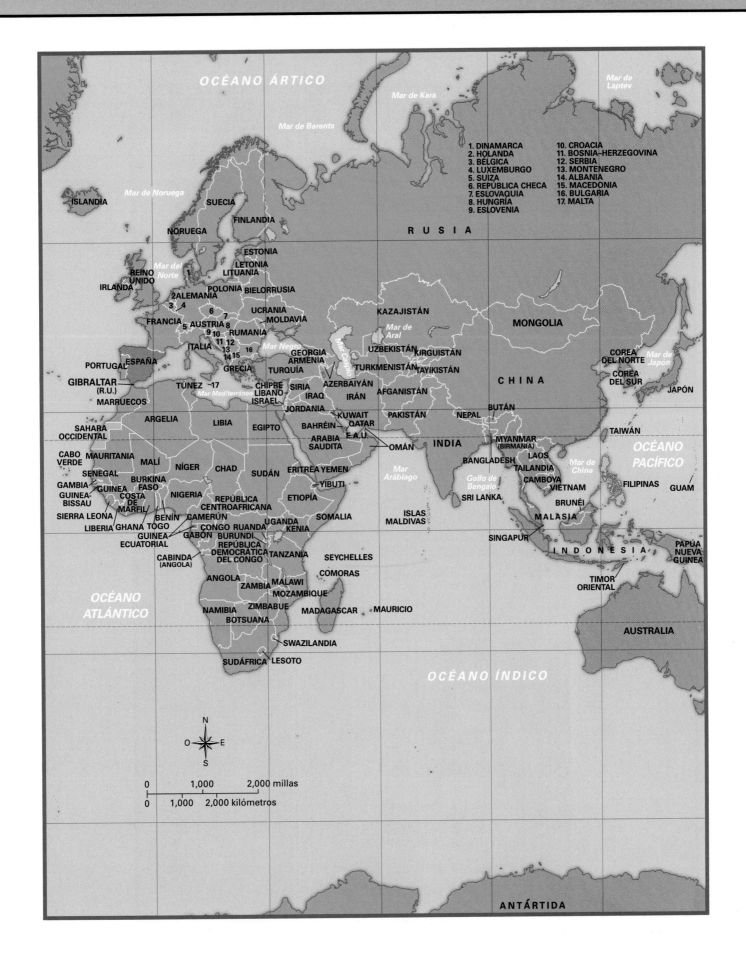

OCÉANO ÁRTICO

Mar de Kara

Mar de Laptev

Mar de Barents

1. DINAMARCA   10. CROACIA
2. HOLANDA   11. BOSNIA-HERZEGOVINA
3. BÉLGICA   12. SERBIA
4. LUXEMBURGO   13. MONTENEGRO
5. SUIZA   14. ALBANIA
6. REPÚBLICA CHECA 15. MACEDONIA
7. ESLOVAQUIA   16. BULGARIA
8. HUNGRÍA   17. MALTA
9. ESLOVENIA

ISLANDIA

Mar de Noruega

SUECIA

FINLANDIA

NORUEGA

RUSIA

ESTONIA

LETONIA
Mar del   LITUANIA
Norte   1
REINO
UNIDO   POLONIA   BIELORRUSIA
IRLANDA
2 ALEMANIA
3 4   6 7   UCRANIA
FRANCIA 5 AUSTRIA 8   MOLDAVIA
9 10   RUMANIA
11 12
ITALIA 13 14 15 16   Mar Negro
GRECIA   GEORGIA
PORTUGAL ESPAÑA   ARMENIA
TURQUÍA
GIBRALTAR   CHIPRE   SIRIA
(R.U.) TÚNEZ 17 Mar Mediterráneo LÍBANO
ISRAEL   IRAQ
MARRUECOS   JORDANIA

KAZAJISTÁN

Mar de
Aral

MONGOLIA

UZBEKISTÁN   KIRGUISTÁN
TURKMENISTÁN TAYIKISTÁN

Mar Caspio

AZERBAIYÁN
IRÁN
AFGANISTÁN

CHINA

COREA
DEL NORTE   Mar de
Japón
COREA
DEL SUR

JAPÓN

ARGELIA   LIBIA   EGIPTO
SAHARA
OCCIDENTAL

BAHRÉIN QATAR
KUWAIT
E.A.U.
ARABIA
SAUDITA   OMÁN

PAKISTÁN
NEPAL   BUTÁN

INDIA

TAIWÁN

OCÉANO
PACÍFICO

CABO   MAURITANIA
VERDE   MALÍ   NÍGER   CHAD   SUDÁN
SENEGAL
GAMBIA   BURKINA
GUINEA FASO
GUINEA- COSTA
BISSAU   DE   NIGERIA
MARFIL
SIERRA LEONA
LIBERIA GHANA TOGO   REPÚBLICA
GUINEA   CENTROAFRICANA
ECUATORIAL GABÓN

ERITREA YEMEN
YIBUTI

ETIOPÍA

SOMALIA

Mar
Arábiago

ISLAS
MALDIVAS

MYANMAR
(BIRMANIA)   LAOS
BANGLADESH   TAILANDIA
CAMBOYA
SRI LANKA   VIETNAM

Golfo de
Bengalo   Mar de
China

BRUNÉI

MALASIA

FILIPINAS   GUAM

BENÍN CAMERÚN
CONGO RUANDA   UGANDA
BURUNDI   KENIA
REPÚBLICA
CABINDA   DEMOCRÁTICA
(ANGOLA) DEL CONGO   TANZANIA

SEYCHELLES

SINGAPUR

INDONESIA

PAPÚA
NUEVA
GUINEA

ANGOLA   MALAWI
ZAMBIA   MOZAMBIQUE
ZIMBABUE
NAMIBIA   MADAGASCAR   MAURICIO
BOTSUANA

COMORAS

TIMOR
ORIENTAL

OCÉANO
ATLÁNTICO

SWAZILANDIA
SUDÁFRICA LESOTO

OCÉANO ÍNDICO

AUSTRALIA

N
O   E
S

0   1,000   2,000 millas
0   1,000   2,000 kilómetros

ANTÁRTIDA

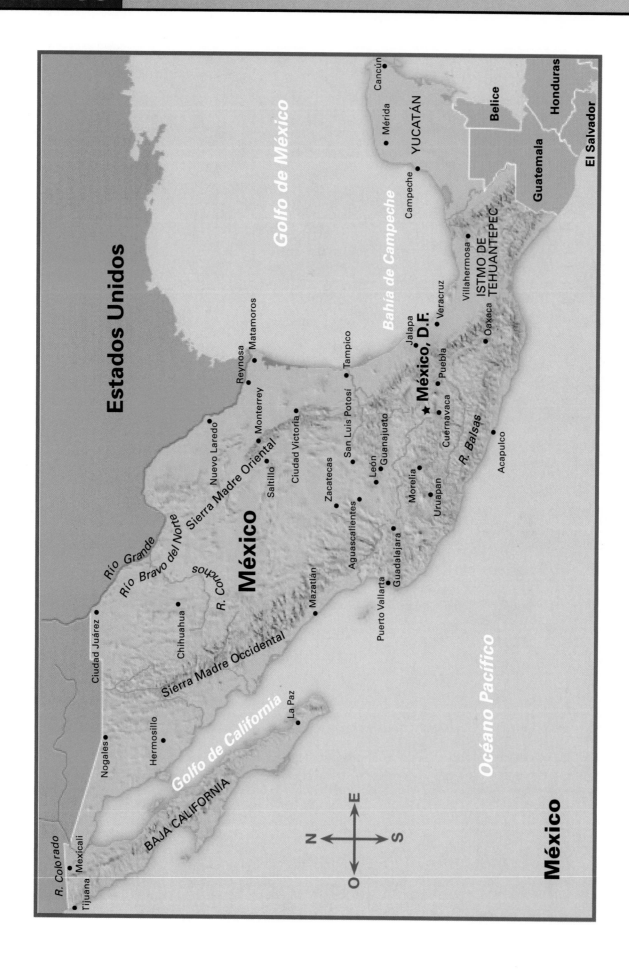

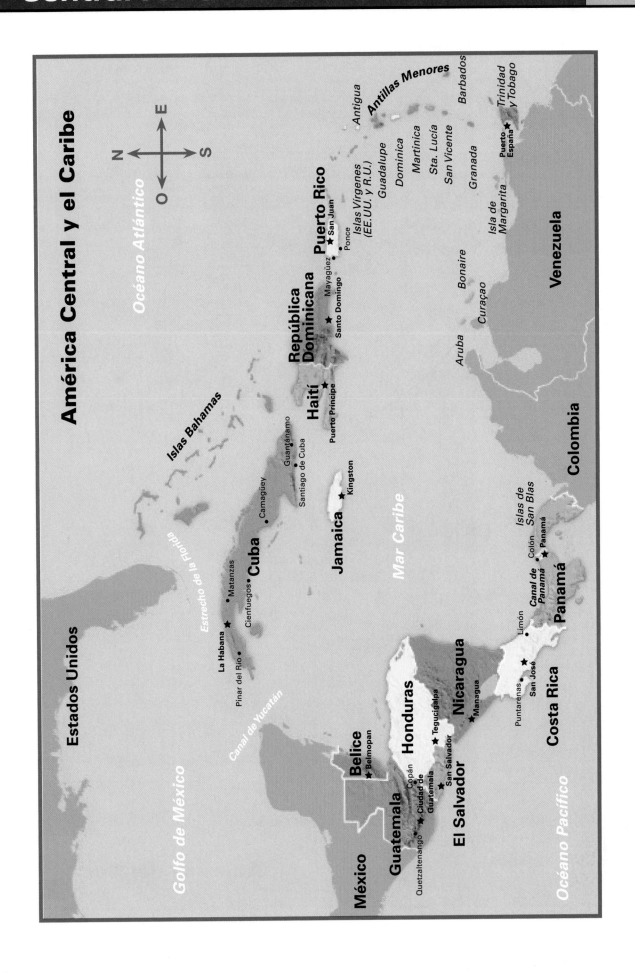

América Central y el Caribe

Océano Atlántico

N — E — S — O

Estados Unidos

Golfo de México

Islas Bahamas

Estrecho de la Florida

La Habana ★
Pinar del Río ●
Matanzas ●
Cienfuegos ● Matanzas
Cuba
Camagüey ●
Santiago de Cuba ●
Guantánamo ●

Canal de Yucatán

México

Belice
★ Belmopan
Copán ●
Quetzaltenango ● ★ Ciudad de Guatemala
Guatemala
San Salvador ★
El Salvador

Honduras
Tegucigalpa ★

Nicaragua
Managua ★

Puntarenas ●
San José ★
Costa Rica
Limón ●

Colón ● Panamá ★
Canal de Panamá
Islas de San Blas
Panamá

Jamaica
Kingston ★

Mar Caribe

Haití
Puerto Príncipe ★

República Dominicana
Santo Domingo ★
Mayagüez ● San Juan ★
Ponce ●
Puerto Rico

Islas Vírgenes (EE.UU. y R.U.)

Antillas Menores

Antigua
Guadalupe
Dominica
Martinica
Sta. Lucía
San Vicente
Granada
Barbados

Aruba
Bonaire
Curaçao
Isla de Margarita

Trinidad y Tobago
Puerto España ★

Venezuela

Colombia

Océano Pacífico

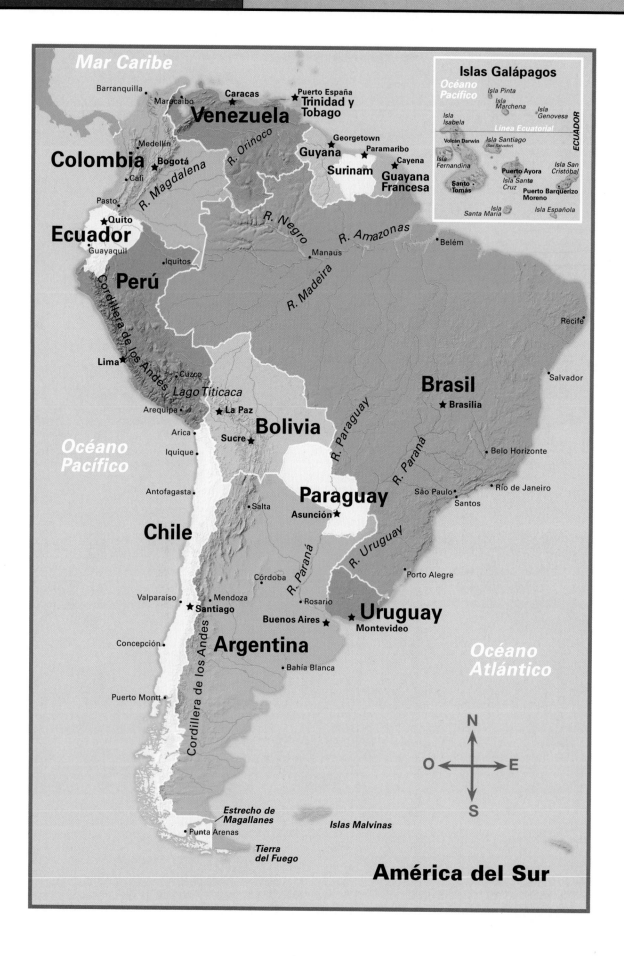

Mar Caribe

Barranquilla
Maracaibo
Caracas
Puerto España
Trinidad y Tobago
Venezuela
Medellín
Colombia
Bogotá
R. Orinoco
Georgetown
Guyana
Paramaribo
Cayena
Surinam
Guayana Francesa
Cali
R. Magdalena
Pasto
Quito
Ecuador
Guayaquil
Iquitos
R. Negro
R. Amazonas
Manaus
Belém
Perú
R. Madeira
Cordillera de los Andes
Recife
Lima
Cuzco
Lago Titicaca
Brasil
Salvador
Arequipa
La Paz
Bolivia
Brasilia
Arica
Sucre
Iquique
R. Paraguay
Belo Horizonte
Océano Pacífico
Antofagasta
Paraguay
São Paulo
Río de Janeiro
R. Paraná
Salta
Santos
Asunción
Chile
R. Paraná
R. Uruguay
Porto Alegre
Córdoba
Valparaíso
Mendoza
Rosario
Uruguay
Santiago
Buenos Aires
Montevideo
Océano Atlántico
Concepción
Argentina
Cordillera de los Andes
Bahía Blanca
Puerto Montt
N
O — E
S
Estrecho de Magallanes
Islas Malvinas
Punta Arenas
Tierra del Fuego
América del Sur

Islas Galápagos
Océano Pacífico
Isla Pinta
Isla Marchena
Isla Genovesa
Isla Isabela
Línea Ecuatorial
ECUADOR
Volcán Darwin
Isla Santiago (San Salvador)
Isla Fernandina
Puerto Ayora
Isla San Cristóbal
Isla Santa Cruz
Santo Tomás
Puerto Barquerizo Moreno
Isla Santa María
Isla Española

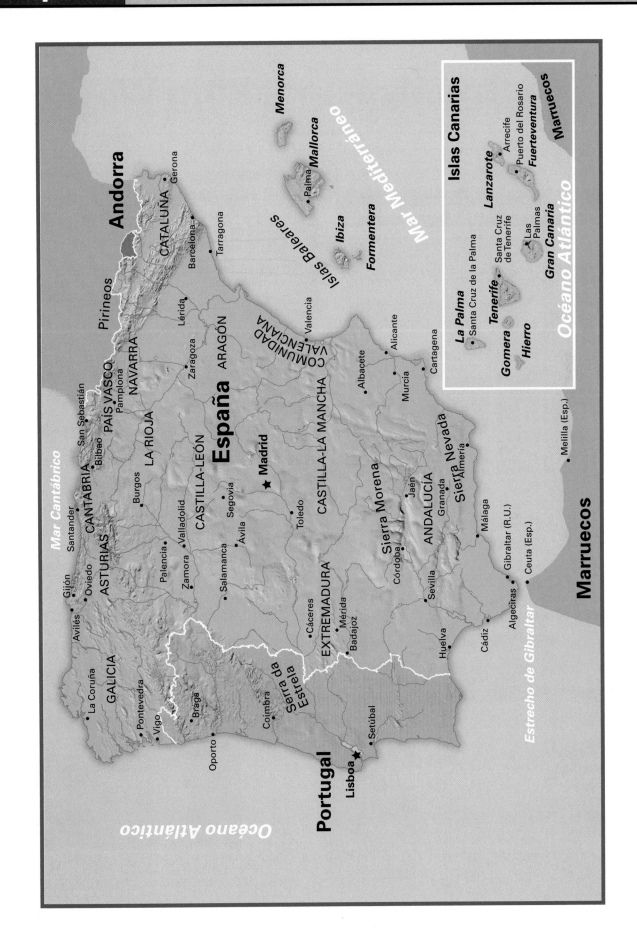

The Spanish-speaking World

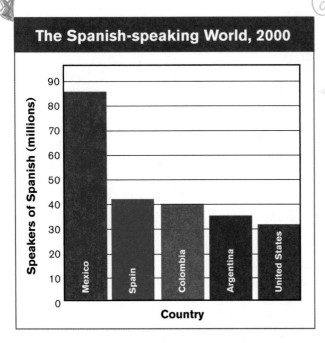

The Spanish-speaking World, 2000

Speakers of Spanish (millions)

Country

(Mexico, Spain, Colombia, Argentina, United States)

Do you know someone whose first language is Spanish? Chances are you do! Thirty-one million people living in the U.S. speak Spanish; after English, it is the second most commonly spoken language in this country. It is the official language of twenty-two countries and an official language of the European Union and United Nations.

The Growth of Spanish

Have you ever heard of a language called Castilian? It's Spanish! The Spanish language as we know it today has its origins in a dialect called Castilian (**castellano** in Spanish). Castilian developed in the 9th century in north-central Spain, in a historic provincial region known as Old Castile. Castilian gradually spread towards the central region of New Castile, where it was adopted as the main language of commerce. By the 16th century, Spanish had become the official language of Spain and eventually, the country's role in exploration, colonization, and overseas trade led to the language spreading across Central and South America, North America, the Caribbean, parts of North Africa, the Canary Islands, and the Philippines.

Spanish in the United States

1500   **1600**   **1700**

16th Century
Spanish is the official language of Spain.

1565
The Spanish arrive in Florida and found St. Augustine.

1610
The Spanish found Santa Fe, today's capital of New Mexico, the state with the most Spanish speakers in the U.S.

Spanish in the United States

Spanish came to North America in the 16th century with the Spanish who settled in St. Augustine, Florida. Spanish-speaking communities flourished in several parts of the continent over the next few centuries. Then, in 1848, in the aftermath of the Mexican-American War, Mexico lost almost half its land to the United States, including portions of modern-day Texas, New Mexico, Arizona, Colorado, California, Wyoming, Nevada, and Utah. Overnight, hundreds of thousands of Mexicans became citizens of the United States, bringing with them their rich history, language, and traditions.

This heritage, combined with that of the other Hispanic populations that have immigrated to the United States over the years, has led to the remarkable growth of Spanish around the country. After English, it is the most commonly spoken language in 43 states. More than 12 million people in California alone claim Spanish as their first or "home" language.

You've made a popular choice by choosing to take Spanish in school. Not only is Spanish found and heard almost everywhere in the United States, but it is the most commonly taught foreign language in classrooms throughout the country! Have you heard people speaking Spanish in your community? Chances are that you've come across an advertisement, menu, or magazine that is in Spanish. If you look around, you'll find that Spanish can be found in some pretty common places. For example, most ATM machines respond to users in both English and Spanish. News agencies and television stations such as CNN and Telemundo provide Spanish-language broadcasts. When you listen to the radio or download music from the Internet, some of the most popular choices are Latino artists who perform in Spanish. Federal government agencies such as the Internal Revenue Service and the Department of State provide services in both languages. Even the White House has an official Spanish-language webpage! Learning Spanish can create opportunities within your everyday life.

1800   1900   2000

1848
Mexicans who choose to stay in the U.S. after the Mexican-American War become U.S. citizens.

1959
After the Cuban Revolution, thousands of Cubans emigrate to the U.S.

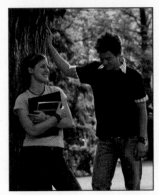

2000
Spanish is the 2nd most commonly spoken language in the U.S., with 31 million speakers.

Why Study Spanish?

Learn an International Language

There are many reasons for learning Spanish, a language that has spread to many parts of the world and has along the way embraced words and sounds of languages as diverse as Latin, Arabic, and Nahuatl. Spanish has evolved from a medieval dialect of north-central Spain into the fourth most commonly spoken language in the world. It is the second language of choice amongst most people in North America.

Understand the World Around You

Knowing Spanish can also open doors to communities within the United States, and it can broaden your understanding of the nation's history and geography. The very names Colorado, Montana, Nevada, and Florida are Spanish in origin. Just knowing their meanings can give you some insight into, of all things, the landscapes for which the states are renowned. Colorado means "colored red;" Montana means "mountain;" Nevada is derived from "snow-capped mountain;" and Florida means "flowered." You've already been speaking Spanish whenever you talk about some of these states!

State Name	Meaning in Spanish
Colorado	"colored red"
Florida	"flowered"
Montana	"mountain"
Nevada	"snow-capped mountain"

Connect with the World

Learning Spanish can change how you view the world. While you learn Spanish, you will also explore and learn about the origins, customs, art, music, and literature of people in close to two dozen countries. When you travel to a Spanish-speaking country, you'll be able to converse freely with the people you meet. And whether here in the U.S. or abroad, you'll find that speaking to people in their native language is the best way to bridge any culture gap.

Why Study Spanish?

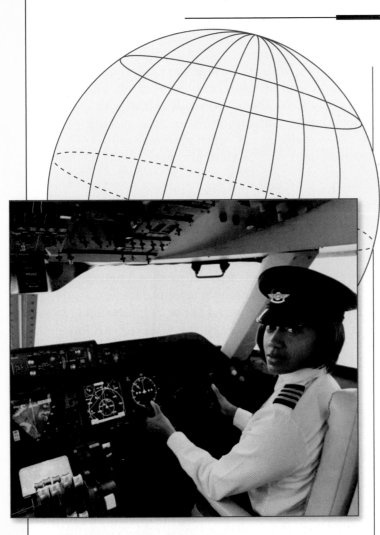

Expand Your Skills

Studying a foreign language can improve your ability to analyze and interpret information and help you succeed in many other subject areas. When you begin learning Spanish, much of your studies will focus on reading, writing, grammar, listening, and speaking skills. You'll be amazed at how the skills involved with learning how a language works can help you succeed in other areas of study. Many people who study a foreign language claim that they gained a better understanding of English and the structures it uses. Spanish can even help you understand the origins of many English words and expand your own vocabulary in English. Knowing Spanish can also help you pick up other related languages, such as Italian, Portuguese, and French. Spanish can really open doors for learning many other skills in your school career.

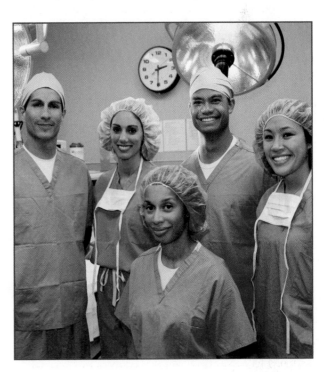

Explore Your Future

How many of you are already planning your future careers? Employers in today's global economy look for workers who know different languages and understand other cultures. Your knowledge of Spanish will make you a valuable candidate for careers abroad as well as in the United States. Doctors, nurses, social workers, hotel managers, journalists, businessmen, pilots, flight attendants, and many other kinds of professionals need to know Spanish or another foreign language to do their jobs well.

How to Learn Spanish

Start with the Basics !

As with anything you want to learn, start with the basics and remember that learning takes time! The basics are vocabulary, grammar, and culture.

Vocabulary Every new word you learn in Spanish will expand your vocabulary and ability to communicate. The more words you know, the better you can express yourself. Focus on sounds and think about ways to remember words. Use your knowledge of English and other languages to figure out the meaning of and memorize words like **conversación, teléfono, oficina, clase,** and **música.**

Grammar Grammar helps you put your new vocabulary together. By learning the rules of grammar, you can use new words correctly and speak in complete sentences. As you learn verbs and tenses, you will be able to speak about the past, present, or future, express yourself with clarity, and be able to persuade others with your opinions. Pay attention to structures and use your knowledge of English grammar to make connections with Spanish grammar.

Culture Culture provides you with a framework for what you may say or do. As you learn about the culture of Spanish-speaking communities, you'll improve your knowledge of Spanish. Think about a word like **salsa,** and how it connects to both food and music. Think about and explore customs observed at **Nochevieja** (New Year's Eve) or a **quinceañera** (a girl's fifteenth birthday party). Observe customs. Watch people greet each other or say good-bye. Listen for idioms and sayings that capture the spirit of what you want to communicate!

Teenagers celebrating a quinceañera party

Listen, Speak, Read, and Write

Listening Listen for sounds and for words you can recognize. Listen for inflections and watch for key words that signal a question such as **cómo** (*how*), **dónde** (*where*), or **qué** (*what*). Get used to the sound of Spanish. Play Spanish pop songs or watch Spanish movies. Borrow books on CD from your local library, or try to visit places in your community where Spanish is spoken. Don't worry if you don't understand every single word. If you focus on key words and phrases, you'll get the main idea. The more you listen, the more you'll understand!

Speaking Practice speaking Spanish as often as you can. As you talk, work on your pronunciation, and read aloud texts so that words and sentences flow more easily. Don't worry if you don't sound like a native speaker, or if you make some mistakes. Time and practice will help you get there. Participate actively in Spanish class. Try to speak Spanish with classmates, especially native speakers (if you know any), as often as you can.

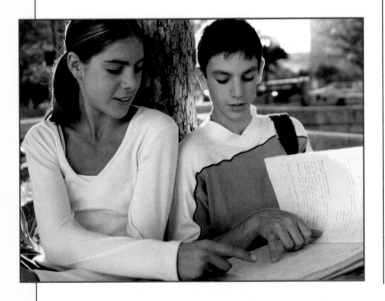

Reading Pick up a Spanish-language newspaper or a pamphlet on your way to school, read the lyrics of a song as you listen to it, or read books you've already read in English translated into Spanish. Use reading strategies that you know to understand the meaning of a text that looks unfamiliar. Look for cognates, or words that are related in English and Spanish, to guess the meaning of some words. Read as often as you can, and remember to read for fun!

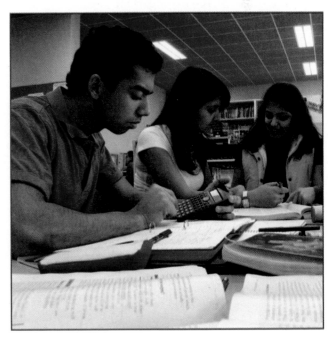

Writing It's easy to write in Spanish if you put your mind to it. And remember that Spanish spelling is phonetic, which means that once you learn the basic rules of how letters and sounds are related, you can probably become an expert speller in Spanish! Write for fun—make up poems or songs, write e-mails or instant messages to friends, or start a journal or blog in Spanish.

Tips for Learning Spanish

- **Listen** to Spanish radio shows. Write down words that you can't recognize or don't know and look up the meaning.

- **Watch** Spanish TV shows or movies. Read subtitles to help you grasp the content.

- **Read** Spanish-language newspapers, magazines, or blogs.

- **Listen** to Spanish songs that you like —anything from a Shakira song to a traditional mariachi melody. Sing along and concentrate on your pronunciation.

- **Seek** out Spanish speakers. Look for neighborhoods, markets, or cultural centers where Spanish might be spoken in your community. Greet people, ask for directions, or order from a menu at a Mexican restaurant in Spanish.

- **Pursue** language exchange opportunities (**intercambio cultural**) in your school or community. Try to join language clubs or cultural societies, and explore opportunities

Practice, practice, practice!

Seize every opportunity you find to listen, speak, read, or write Spanish. Think of it like a sport or learning a musical instrument—the more you practice, the more you will become comfortable with the language and how it works. You'll marvel at how quickly you can begin speaking Spanish and how the world that it transports you to can change your life forever!

for studying abroad or hosting a student from a Spanish-speaking country in your home or school.

- **Connect** your learning to everyday experiences. Think about naming the ingredients of your favorite dish in Spanish. Think about the origins of Spanish place names in the U.S., like Cape Canaveral and Sacramento, or of common English words like *adobe, chocolate, mustang, tornado,* and *patio.*

- **Use** mnemonics, or a memorizing device, to help you remember words. Make up a saying in English to remember the order of the days of the week in Spanish (L, M, M, J, V, S, D).

- **Visualize** words. Try to associate words with images to help you remember meanings. For example, think of a **paella** as you learn the names of different types of seafood or meat. Imagine a national park and create mental pictures of the landscape as you learn names of animals, plants, and habitats.

- **Enjoy** yourself! Try to have as much fun as you can learning Spanish. Take your knowledge beyond the classroom and find ways to make your learning experience your very own.

ICONS AND *RECURSOS* BOXES

Icons

Familiarize yourself with these icons that appear throughout **DESCUBRE**.

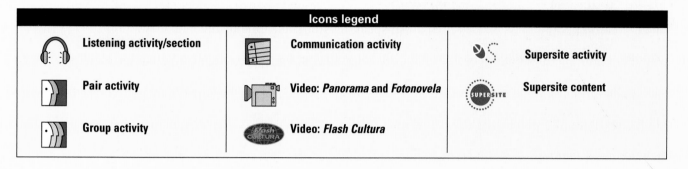

- You will see the listening icon in each lesson's **Contextos, Pronunciación, Escuchar,** and **Vocabulario** sections.

- The video icons appear in the **Fotonovela, Cultura,** and **Panorama** sections of each lesson.

- Both Supersite icons appear in every strand of every lesson. Visit descubre1.vhlcentral.com

Recursos Boxes

Recursos boxes let you know exactly what print and technology supplements you can use to reinforce and expand on every section of the lessons in your textbook. They even include page numbers when applicable.

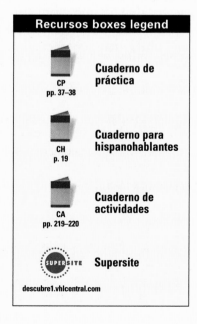

THE CAST

Here are the main characters you will meet when you watch the **DESCUBRE** video:

From Ecuador,
Inés Ayala Loor

From Spain,
María Teresa (Maite) Fuentes de Alba

From Mexico,
Alejandro (Álex) Morales Paredes

From Puerto Rico,
Javier Gómez Lozano

And, also from Ecuador,
don Francisco Castillo Moreno

FOTONOVELA VIDEO PROGRAM

Wouldn't it be great if you could travel to a Latin American country and learn the language from Spanish-speaking students? One of the best ways to learn a language is to hear it used in real-world situations. Since you might not be able to take a long trip to Latin America, we've created the next best thing: a video! The **DESCUBRE** *Fotonovela* videos will introduce you to four international students who are studying at the **Universidad de San Francisco** in Quito, Ecuador. The nine episodes, one for each lesson in your book, follow the students on a bus tour of the Ecuadorian countryside. In addition to the four students, you'll also meet Don Francisco, the tour bus driver, and a whole supporting cast of native speakers.

In most of the video episodes, the characters will share information about their home countries in a flashback format. These flashbacks give you a chance to learn about everyday life in Spain, Mexico, Puerto Rico, and different parts of Ecuador.

As you begin watching each episode, the characters will interact using the same vocabulary and grammar that you are studying in your lesson. As the episode progresses, the characters continue to use new vocabulary and grammar along with language you already know. In the **Resumen** section, one of the main characters will summarize the episode, highlighting the important grammar and vocabulary.

An abbreviated version of each episode can be found in the **Fotonovela** section in each lesson of your textbook. In this section you will read character dialogues, practice useful phrases, and learn more about culture.

PANORAMA CULTURAL
VIDEO PROGRAM

You can continue your virtual travel experience into the world of Spanish-speaking communities with the *Panorama cultural* video. You don't even need a suitcase! The video works directly with the **Panorama** section in each lesson of **DESCUBRE**. The video shows a short clip about the country featured in the lesson. The clips give you a first-hand look at the different countries. You will also notice that the Spanish narrations cover grammar and vocabulary from your lessons.

These videos will transport you to many Spanish-speaking countries, the United States, and Canada. As you watch the video segments, the images and topics will give you a first-hand look at cities, monuments, traditions, festivals, archaeological sites, and geographical wonders. You will have the opportunity to learn about a variety of cultures and perspectives that tie directly to what you are learning in **DESCUBRE**.

FLASH CULTURA
VIDEO PROGRAM

Have you ever wondered what life is like for your peers in Mexico, Argentina, or Puerto Rico? What could you have in common? Do you think about the same things? Now you can go right to the source! The entertaining *Flash cultura* video provides a humorous side to the **Cultura** section in **DESCUBRE**. Students from Mexico, Argentina, and Puerto Rico share information about their countries with each other. The similarities and differences among Spanish-speaking countries that come up through these exchanges might make you think about your own culture and values.

Useful Spanish Expressions

The following expressions will be very useful in getting you started learning Spanish. You can use them in class to check your understanding, and to ask and answer questions about the lessons. Read **En las instrucciones** ahead of time to help you understand direction lines in Spanish, as well as your teacher's instructions. Remember to practice your Spanish as often as you can!

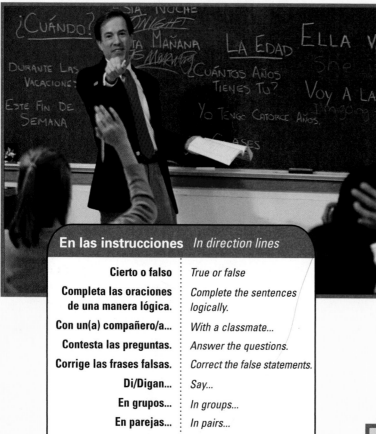

Expresiones útiles *Useful expressions*

¿Cómo se dice _____ en español?	How do you say _____ in Spanish?
¿Cómo se escribe _____?	How do you spell _____?
¿Comprende(n)?	Do you understand?
Con permiso.	Excuse me.
De acuerdo.	Okay.
De nada.	You're welcome.
¿De veras?	Really?
¿En qué página estamos?	What page are we on?
Enseguida.	Right away.
Más despacio, por favor.	Slower, please.
Muchas gracias.	Thanks a lot.
No entiendo.	I don't understand.
No sé.	I don't know.
Perdone.	Excuse me.
Pista	Clue
Por favor.	Please.
Por supuesto.	Of course.
¿Qué significa _____?	What does _____ mean?
Repite, por favor.	Please repeat.
Tengo una pregunta.	I have a question.
¿Tiene(n) alguna pregunta?	Do you have questions?
Vaya(n) a la página dos.	Go to page 2.

En las instrucciones *In direction lines*

Cierto o falso	True or false
Completa las oraciones de una manera lógica.	Complete the sentences logically.
Con un(a) compañero/a...	With a classmate...
Contesta las preguntas.	Answer the questions.
Corrige las frases falsas.	Correct the false statements.
Di/Digan...	Say...
En grupos...	In groups...
En parejas...	In pairs...
Entrevista...	Interview...
Forma oraciones completas.	Create/Make complete sentences.
Háganse preguntas.	Ask each other questions.
Haz el papel de...	Play the role of...
Haz los cambios necesarios.	Make the necessary changes.
Indica/Indiquen si las oraciones...	Indicate if the sentences...
Lee/Lean en voz alta.	Read aloud.
...que mejor completa...	...that best completes...
Toma nota...	Take note...
Tomen apuntes.	Take notes.
Túrnense...	Take turns...

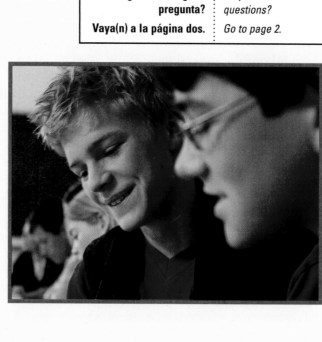

Common Names

Get started learning Spanish by using a Spanish name in class. You can choose from the lists on these pages, or you can find one yourself. How about learning the Spanish equivalent of your name? The most popular Spanish female names are Ana, Isabel, Elena, Sara, and María. The most popular male names in Spanish are Alejandro, Jorge, Juan, José, and Pedro. Is your name, or that of someone you know, in the Spanish top five?

Más nombres masculinos	Más nombres femeninos
Alfonso	Alicia
Antonio (Toni)	Beatriz (Bea, Beti, Biata)
Carlos	Blanca
César	Carolina (Carol)
Diego	Claudia
Ernesto	Diana
Felipe	Emilia
Francisco (Paco)	Irene
Guillermo	Julia
Ignacio (Nacho)	Laura
Javier (Javi)	Leonor
Leonardo	Lourdes
Luis	Lucía
Manolo	Margarita (Marga)
Marcos	Marta
Oscar (Óscar)	Noelia
Rafael (Rafa)	Paula
Sergio	Rocío
Vicente	Verónica

Los 5 nombres masculinos más populares	Los 5 nombres femeninos más populares
Alejandro	Ana
Jorge	Elena
José (Pepe)	Isabel
Juan	María
Pedro	Sara

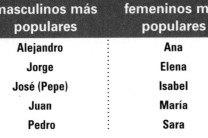

Acknowledgments

On behalf of its authors and editors, Vista Higher Learning expresses its sincere appreciation to the many instructors and teachers across the U.S. and Canada who contributed their ideas and suggestions. Their insights and detailed comments were invaluable to us as we created **DESCUBRE**.

In-depth reviewers

Patrick Brady
Tidewater Community College, VA

Christine DeGrado
Chestnut Hill College, PA

Martha L. Hughes
Georgia Southern University, GA

Aida Ramos-Sellman
Goucher College, MD

Reviewers

Kathleen Aguilar
Fort Lewis College, CO

Aleta Anderson
Grand Rapids Community College, MI

Gunnar Anderson
SUNY Potsdam, NY

Nona Anderson
Ouachita Baptist University, AR

Ken Arant
Darton College, GA

Vicki Baggia
Phillips Exeter Academy, NH

Jorge V. Bajo
Oracle Charter School, NY

Ana Basoa-McMillan
Columbia State Community
College, TN

Timothy Benson
Lake Superior College, MN

Georgia Betcher
Fayetteville Technical Community
College, NC

Teresa Borden
Columbia College, CA

Courtney Bradley
The Principia, MO

Vonna Breeze-Marti
Columbia College, CA

Christa Bucklin
University of Hartford, CT

Mary Cantu
South Texas College, TX

Christa Chatrnuch
University of Hartford, CT

Tina Christodouleas
SUNY Cortland, NY

Edwin Clark
SUNY Potsdam, NY

Donald Clymer
Eastern Mennonite University, VA

Ann Costanzi
Chestnut Hill College, PA

Patricia Crespo-Martin
Foothill College, CA

Miryam Criado
Hanover College, KY

Thomas Curtis
Madison Area Technical College, WI

Patricia S. Davis
Darton College, GA

Danion Doman
Truman State University, MO

Deborah Dubiner
Carnegie Mellon University, PA

Benjamin Earwicker
Northwest Nazarene University, ID

Deborah Edson
Tidewater Community College, VA

Matthew T. Fleming
Grand Rapids Community College, MI

Ruston Ford
Indian Hills Community College, IA

Marianne Franco
Modesto Junior College, CA

Elena García
Muskegon Community College, MI

María D. García
Fayetteville Technical Community
College, NC

Lauren Gates
East Mississippi Community
College, MS

Marta M. Gómez
Gateway Academy, MO

Danielle Gosselin
Bishop Brady High School, NH

Reviewers

Charlene Grant
Skidmore College, NY

Betsy Hance
Kennesaw State University, GA

Marti Hardy
Laurel School, OH

Dennis Harrod
Syracuse University, NY

Fanning Hearon
Brunswick School, CT

Richard Heath
Kirkwood Community College, IA

Óscar Hernández
South Texas College, TX

Yolanda Hernández
Community College of Southern
Nevada, North Las Vegas, NV

Martha L. Hughes
Georgia Southern University, GA

Martha Ince
Cushing Academy, MA

Stacy Jazan
Glendale Community College, CA

María Jiménez Smith
Tarrant County College, TX

Emory Kinder,
Columbia Prep School, NY

Marina Kozanova
Crafton Hills College, CA

Tamara Kunkel
Alice Lloyd College, KY

Anna Major
The Westminster Schools, GA

Armando Maldonado
Morgan Community College, CO

Molly Marostica Smith
Canterbury School of Florida, FL

Jesús G. Martínez
Fresno City College, CA

Laura Martínez
Centralia College, WA

Daniel Millis
Verde Valley School, AZ

Deborah Mistron
Middle Tennessee State
University, TN

Mechteld Mitchin
Village Academy, OH

Anna Montoya
Florida Institute of Technology, FL

Robert P. Moore
Loyola Blakefield Jesuit School, MD

S. Moshir
St. Bernard High School, CA

Javier Múñoz-Basols
Trinity School, NY

William Nichols
Grand Rapids Community College, MI

Bernice Nuhfer-Halten
Southern Polytechnic State
University, GA

Amanda Papanikolas
Drew School, CA

Elizabeth M. Parr
Darton College, GA

Julia E. Patiño
Dillard University, LA

Martha Pérez
Kirkwood Community College, IA

Teresa Pérez-Gamboa
University of Georgia, GA

Marion Perry
The Thacher School, CA

Molly Perry
The Thacher School, CA

Melissa Pytlak
The Canterbury School, CT

Ana F. Sache
Emporia State University, KS

Celia S. Samaniego
Cosumnes River College, CA

Virginia Sánchez-Bernardy
San Diego Mesa College, CA

Frank P. Sanfilippo
Columbia College, CA

Piedad Schor
South Kent School, CT

David Schuettler
The College of St. Scholastica, MN

Romina Self
Ankeny Christian Academy, IA

David A. Short
Indian Hills Community College, IA

Carol Snell-Feikema
South Dakota State University, SD

Matias Stebbings
Columbia Grammar
& Prep School, NY

Mary Studer Shea
Napa Valley College, CA

Cathy Swain
University of Maine, Machias, ME

Cristina Szterensus
Rock Valley College, IL

John Tavernakis
College of San Mateo, CA

David E. Tipton
Circleville Bible College, OH

Larry Thornton
Trinity College School, ON

Linda Tracy
Santa Rosa Junior College, CA

Acknowledgments

Reviewers

Beverly Turner
  Truckee Meadows Community
  College, OK

Christine Tyma DeGrado
  Chestnut Hill College, PA

Fanny Vera de Viacava
  Canterbury School, CT

Luis Viacava
  Canterbury School, CT

Maria Villalobos-Buehner
  Grand Valley State University, MI

Hector Villarreal
  South Texas College, TX

Juanita Villena-Álvarez
  University of South Carolina,
  Beaufort, SC

Marcella Anne Wendzikowski
  Villa Maria College of Buffalo, NY

Doug West
  Sage Hill School, CA

Paula Whittaker
  Bishop Brady High School, NH

Mary Zold-Herrera
  Glenbrook North High School, IL

About the Authors

José A. Blanco founded Vista Higher Learning in 1998. A native of Barranquilla, Colombia, Mr. Blanco holds degrees in Literature and Hispanic Studies from Brown University and the University of California, Santa Cruz. He has worked as a writer, editor, and translator for Houghton Mifflin and D.C. Heath and Company and has taught Spanish at the secondary and university levels. Mr. Blanco is also the co-author of several other Vista Higher Learning programs: **Panorama, Aventuras,** and **¡Viva!** at the introductory level; **Ventanas, Facetas, Enfoques, Imagina,** and **Sueña** at the intermediate level; and **Revista** at the advanced conversation level.

Philip Redwine Donley received his M.A. in Hispanic Literature from the University of Texas at Austin in 1986 and his Ph.D. in Foreign Language Education from the University of Texas at Austin in 1997. Dr. Donley taught Spanish at Austin Community College, Southwestern University, and the University of Texas at Austin. He published articles and conducted workshops about language anxiety management and the development of critical thinking skills, and was involved in research about teaching languages to the visually impaired. Dr. Donley was also the co-author of **Aventuras** and **Panorama,** two other introductory college Spanish textbook programs published by Vista Higher Learning.

About the Illustrators

Yayo, an internationally acclaimed illustrator, was born in Colombia. He has illustrated children's books, newspapers, and magazines, and has been exhibited around the world. He currently lives in Montreal, Canada.

Pere Virgili lives and works in Barcelona, Spain. His illustrations have appeared in textbooks, newspapers, and magazines throughout Spain and Europe.

Born in Caracas, Venezuela, **Hermann Mejía** studied illustration at the *Instituto de Diseño de Caracas*. Hermann currently lives and works in the United States.

Hola, ¿qué tal?

1

Communicative Goals

You will learn how to:

- Greet people in Spanish
- Say goodbye
- Identify yourself and others
- Talk about the time of day

Lesson Goals

In **Lección 1**, students will be introduced to the following:

- terms for greetings and leave-takings
- identifying where one is from
- expressions of courtesy
- greetings in the Spanish-speaking world
- the **plaza principal**
- nouns and articles (definite and indefinite)
- numbers 0–30
- present tense of **ser**
- telling time
- recognizing cognates
- reading a telephone list rich in cognates
- writing a telephone/address list in Spanish
- listening for known vocabulary
- a television commercial for MasterCard
- musician **Tito Puente**
- demographic and cultural information about Hispanics in the United States and Canada

A primera vista Have students look at the photo. Ask: *What do you think the young women are doing?* Say: *It is common in Hispanic cultures for friends to greet each other with a kiss (or two) on the cheek.* Ask: *How do you greet your friends?*

A PRIMERA VISTA

- Guess what the people in the photo are saying:
  a. Adiós b. Hola c. Salsa
- Most likely they would also say:
  a. Gracias b. Fiesta c. Buenos días
- The girls are:
  a. amigas b. chicos c. señores

INSTRUCTIONAL RESOURCES

Student Materials
Cuaderno de práctica, Cuaderno para hispanohablantes, Cuaderno de actividades
Student MAESTRO™ Supersite
(descubre1.vhlcentral.com)
MAESTRO™ e-Cuaderno

Teacher's Resource CD-ROM and in print
*Answer Keys, Audioscripts, Videoscripts
*PowerPoints
Testing Program (**Pruebas,** Test Generator, MP3 Audio Files)
Vista Higher Learning *Cancionero*
*Also available on Supersite

Teacher's MAESTRO™ Supersite
(descubre1.vhlcentral.com)
Learning Management System (Assignment Task Manager, Gradebook)
Also on DVD
Fotonovela, Flash cultura, Panorama cultural

Section Goals

In **Contextos**, students will learn and practice:
- basic greetings
- introductions
- courtesy expressions

Instructional Resources
Cuaderno de práctica, pp. 1–2
Cuaderno para hispanohablantes, pp. 1–2
Cuaderno de actividades, p. 87
e-Cuaderno
Supersite: Textbook, Vocabulary, & Audio Activity MP3 Audio Files
Supersite/TRCD/Print: *PowerPoints* (**Lección 1 Contextos** Presentation, Overheads #9, #10); Textbook Audio Script, Audio Activity Script, Answer Keys
Textbook & Audio Activity CD

Teaching Tips
- For complete lesson plans, go to **descubre1.vhlcentral.com** to access the instructor's part of the **DESCUBRE** Supersite.
- With books closed, write a few greetings, farewells, and courtesy expressions on the board, explain their meaning, and model their pronunciation. Circulate around the class, greeting students, making introductions, and encouraging responses. Then have students open their books to pages 2–3 or show *Overhead PowerPoint #9* and ask them to identify which conversations seem to be exchanges between friends and which seem more formal. Overlay *Overhead PowerPoint #10* or use the printed text to draw attention to the use of **usted** vs. **tú** in these conversations. Explain situations in which each form is appropriate.

Hola, ¿qué tal?

Buanas tardes= Good afternoon

Más vocabulario

Buenos días.	*Good morning.*
Buenas noches.	*Good evening; Good night.*
Hasta la vista.	*See you later.*
Hasta pronto.	*See you soon.*
¿Cómo se llama usted?	*What's your name? (form.)*
Le presento a...	*I would like to introduce (name) to you. (form.)*
Te presento a...	*I would like to introduce (name) to you. (fam.)*
el nombre	*name*
¿Cómo estás?	*How are you? (fam.)*
No muy bien.	*Not very well.*
¿Qué pasa?	*What's happening?; What's going on?*
por favor	*please*
De nada.	*You're welcome.*
No hay de qué.	*You're welcome.*
Lo siento.	*I'm sorry.*
Gracias.	*Thank you; Thanks.*
Muchas gracias.	*Thank you very much; Thanks a lot.*

Variación léxica

Items are presented for recognition purposes only.

Buenos días. ⟷	Buenas.
De nada. ⟷	A la orden.
Lo siento. ⟷	Perdón.
¿Qué tal? ⟷	¿Qué hubo? (*Col.*)
chau ⟷	ciao

recursos

CP	CH	CA	SUPERSITE
pp. 1–2	pp. 1–2	p. 87	descubre1.vhlcentral.com Lección 1

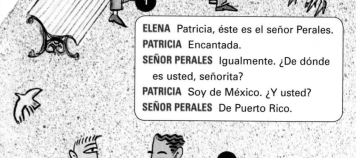

1
ELENA Patricia, éste es el señor Perales.
PATRICIA Encantada.
SEÑOR PERALES Igualmente. ¿De dónde es usted, señorita?
PATRICIA Soy de México. ¿Y usted?
SEÑOR PERALES De Puerto Rico.
2
TOMÁS ¿Qué tal, Alberto?
ALBERTO Regular. ¿Y tú?
TOMÁS Bien. ¿Qué hay de nuevo?
ALBERTO Nada.
3
SEÑOR VARGAS Buenas tardes, señora Wong. ¿Cómo está usted?
SEÑORA WONG Muy bien, gracias. ¿Y usted, señor Vargas?
SEÑOR VARGAS Bien, gracias.
SEÑORA WONG Hasta mañana, señor Vargas. Saludos a la señora Vargas.
SEÑOR VARGAS Adiós.

TEACHING OPTIONS

Extra Practice Bring in photos or magazine images of people greeting each other or saying goodbye. Ask pairs to write dialogue captions for each photo. Remind students to use formal and informal expressions as appropriate.

Small Groups Have small groups write and role-play a conversation in which older adults, children, teenagers, and young adults interact. Verify that the groups are using formal and informal expressions as appropriate. Have a few groups present their conversations to the class.

Extra Practice After calling a name, greet that student and ask a question related to the day's lesson.

Práctica

1

Escuchar Listen to each question or statement, then choose the correct response.

1. a. Muy bien, gracias.   b. Me llamo Graciela. b
2. a. Lo siento.   b. Mucho gusto. b
3. a. Soy de Puerto Rico.   b. No muy bien. a
4. a. No hay de qué.   b. Regular. a
5. a. Mucho gusto.   b. Hasta pronto. b
6. a. Nada.   b. Igualmente. a
7. a. Me llamo Guillermo Montero.   b. Muy bien, gracias. b
8. a. Buenas tardes. ¿Cómo estás?   b. El gusto es mío. a
9. a. Saludos a la Sra. Ramírez.   b. Encantada. b
10. a. Adiós.   b. Regular. b

2

Identificar You will hear a series of expressions. Identify the expression (**a**, **b**, **c**, or **d**) that does not belong in each series.

1. __c__   3. __b__
2. __a__   4. __c__

3

Escoger For each expression, write another word or phrase that expresses a similar idea.

> **modelo**
> ¿Cómo estás?   ¿Qué tal?

1. De nada. No hay de qué.   4. Te presento a Antonio. Éste es Antonio.
2. Encantado. Mucho gusto.   5. Hasta la vista. Hasta luego.
3. Adiós. Chau o Hasta luego/mañana/pronto.   6. Mucho gusto. El gusto es mío.

4

Ordenar Work with a classmate to put this scrambled conversation in order. Then act it out.

—Muy bien, gracias. Soy Rosabel.
—Soy del Ecuador. ¿Y tú?
—Mucho gusto, Rosabel.
—Hola. Me llamo Carlos. ¿Cómo estás?
—Soy de Argentina.
—Igualmente. ¿De dónde eres, Carlos?

CARLOS	Hola. Me llamo Carlos. ¿Cómo estás?
ROSABEL	Muy bien, gracias. Soy Rosabel.
CARLOS	Mucho gusto, Rosabel.
ROSABEL	Igualmente. ¿De dónde eres, Carlos?
CARLOS	Soy del Ecuador. ¿Y tú?
ROSABEL	Soy de Argentina.

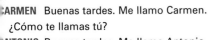
BERTA Hasta luego, Tere.
TERESA Chau, Berta. Nos vemos mañana.

CARMEN Buenas tardes. Me llamo Carmen. ¿Cómo te llamas tú?
ANTONIO Buenas tardes. Me llamo Antonio. Mucho gusto.
CARMEN El gusto es mío. ¿De dónde eres?
ANTONIO Soy de los Estados Unidos, de California.

5 Teaching Tip Have pairs
share their responses with
the class.

5 Expansion Have pairs
or small groups create
conversations that include
the expressions used in
Actividad 5. Ask volunteers
to present their conversations
to the class.

6 Teaching Tips
• Discuss the **modelo** with the
class before assigning the
activity to pairs.
• After students have
completed the activity, have
pairs role-play the corrected
mini-conversations. Ask
them to substitute their
own names and personal
information where possible.
• Have volunteers write each
mini-conversation on the
board. Work as a class
to identify and explain
any errors.

¡Lengua viva! Have students
locate examples of the titles
in **Actividad 6**. Then ask them
to create short sentences in
which they use the titles with
people they know.

5 **Completar** Work with a partner to complete these exchanges. Use expressions from the word bank.

Buenos días.	¿De dónde eres?	De nada.
¿Qué pasa?	Hasta luego.	¿Qué tal?
¿Cómo te llamas?	Encantado/a.	Muy bien, gracias.

1. **Estudiante 1:** Buenos días.
   Estudiante 2: Buenos días. ¿Qué tal?
2. **Estudiante 1:** ¿Cómo te llamas?
   Estudiante 2: Me llamo Carmen Sánchez.
3. **Estudiante 1:** ¿De dónde eres?
   Estudiante 2: De Canadá.
4. **Estudiante 1:** Te presento a Marisol.
   Estudiante 2: Encantado/a.

5. **Estudiante 1:** Gracias.
   Estudiante 2: De nada.
6. **Estudiante 1:** ¿Qué tal?
   Estudiante 2: Regular.
7. **Estudiante 1:** ¿Qué pasa?
   Estudiante 2: Nada.
8. **Estudiante 1:** ¡Hasta la vista!
   Estudiante 2: Answers will vary.

6 **Cambiar** Work with a partner to complete these exchanges.   Answers will vary.

> **modelo**
> **Estudiante 1:** ¿Qué tal?
> **Estudiante 2:** Bien. ¿Y tú?

1. **Estudiante 1:** Hasta mañana, señora Ramírez. Saludos al señor Ramírez.
   Estudiante 2: _____
2. **Estudiante 1:** ¿Qué hay de nuevo, Alberto?
   Estudiante 2: _____
3. **Estudiante 1:** Gracias, Tomás.
   Estudiante 2: _____
4. **Estudiante 1:** Miguel, ésta es la señorita Perales.
   Estudiante 2: _____
5. **Estudiante 1:** ¿De dónde eres, Antonio?
   Estudiante 2: _____
6. **Estudiante 1:** ¿Cómo se llama usted?
   Estudiante 2: _____
7. **Estudiante 1:** ¿Qué pasa?
   Estudiante 2: _____
8. **Estudiante 1:** Buenas tardes, señor. ¿Cómo está usted?
   Estudiante 2: _____

◄ **¡LENGUA VIVA!**

The titles **señor,
señora**, and **señorita**
are abbreviated
Sr., Sra., and **Srta**.
Note that these
abbreviations are
capitalized, while
the titles themselves
are not.

•••

There is no Spanish
equivalent for the
English title *Ms.;*
women are addressed
as **señora** or **señorita**.

Comunicación

7 **Diálogos** With a partner, complete and act out these conversations. Answers will vary.

Conversación 1 —Hola. Me llamo Teresa. ¿Cómo te llamas tú?
_____

—Soy de Puerto Rico. ¿Y tú?
_____

Conversación 2 _____

—Muy bien, gracias. ¿Y usted, señora López?
_____

—Hasta luego, señora. Saludos al señor López.
_____

Conversación 3 _____

—Regular. ¿Y tú?
_____

—Nada.

8 **Conversaciones** This is the first day of class. Write four short conversations based on what the people in this scene would say. Answers will vary.

9. **Situaciones** In groups of three, write and act out these situations. Answers will vary.

1. On your way out of class on the first day of school, you strike up a conversation with the two students who were sitting next to you. You find out each student's name and where he or she is from before you say goodbye and go to your next class.
2. At the next class you meet up with a friend and find out how he or she is doing. As you are talking, your friend Elena enters. Introduce her to your friend.
3. As you're leaving school, you meet your parents' friends Mrs. Sánchez and Mr. Rodríguez. You greet them and ask how each person is. As you say goodbye, you send greetings to Mrs. Rodríguez.
4. Make up and act out a real-life situation that you and your classmates can role-play.

7 **Expansion**
• Have students work in small groups to write a few mini-conversations modeled on this activity. Then ask them to copy the dialogues, omitting a few exchanges. Have groups exchange papers and fill in the blanks.
• Have students rewrite **Conversaciones 1** and **3** in the formal register and **Conversación 2** in the informal register.

8 **Teaching Tip** To simplify, have students brainstorm who the people in the illustration are and what they are talking about. Ask students which groups would be speaking to each other in the **usted** form, and which would be using the **tú** form.

9 **Teaching Tip** To challenge students, have each group pick a situation to prepare and perform. Tell groups not to memorize every word of the conversation, but rather to recreate it.

The Affective Dimension Have students rehearse the situations a few times, so that they will feel more comfortable with the material and less anxious when presenting before the class.

TEACHING OPTIONS

Extra Practice Have students circulate around the classroom and conduct unrehearsed mini-conversations in Spanish with other students, using the words and expressions that they learned on pages 2–3. Monitor students' work and offer assistance if requested.

Heritage Speakers Ask heritage speakers to role-play some of the conversations and situations in these **Comunicación** activities, modeling correct pronunciation and intonation for the class. Remind students that, just as in English, there are regional differences in the way Spanish is pronounced. Help clarify unfamiliar vocabulary as necessary.

Section Goals

In **Fotonovela**, students will:
- receive comprehensible input from free-flowing discourse
- learn functional phrases that preview lesson grammatical structures

Instructional Resources
Cuaderno de actividades, pp. 51–52
e-Cuaderno
Supersite/DVD: *Fotonovela*
Supersite/TRCD/Print:
Fotonovela Videoscript & Translation, Answer Keys

Video Synopsis **Don Francisco,** the bus driver, and **Sra. Ramos,** a representative of Ecuatur, meet the four travelers at the university. **Sra. Ramos** passes out travel documents. **Inés** and **Maite** introduce themselves, as do **Javier** and **Álex.** The travelers board the bus.

Teaching Tips
- Have students cover the captions and guess the plot based on the video stills. Record their predictions. After students have watched the video, compare their predictions to what actually happened in the episode.
- Point out that **don** is a title of respect and neither equivalent nor related to the English name *Don.* Ask if students think **Francisco** is the conductor's first or last name. (It is his first name.) Students will learn more about the titles **don** and **doña** on page 8.
- Tell students that all items in **Expresiones útiles** on page 7 are active vocabulary for which they are responsible. Model the pronunciation of each item and have the class repeat. Also, practice the **Expresiones útiles** by using them in short conversations with individual students.

¡Todos a bordo!

NATIONAL communication cultures STANDARDS

Los cuatro estudiantes, don Francisco y la Sra. Ramos se reúnen (*meet*) en la universidad.

PERSONAJES

DON FRANCISCO

SRA. RAMOS

ÁLEX

JAVIER

INÉS

MAITE

SRA. RAMOS Buenos días, chicos. Yo soy Isabel Ramos de la agencia Ecuatur.
DON FRANCISCO Y yo soy don Francisco, el conductor.

SRA. RAMOS Bueno, ¿quién es María Teresa Fuentes de Alba?
MAITE ¡Soy yo!
SRA. RAMOS Ah, bien. Aquí tienes los documentos de viaje.
MAITE Gracias.

SRA. RAMOS ¿Javier Gómez Lozano?
JAVIER Aquí... soy yo.

JAVIER ¿Qué tal? Me llamo Javier.
ÁLEX Mucho gusto, Javier. Yo soy Álex. ¿De dónde eres?
JAVIER De Puerto Rico. ¿Y tú?
ÁLEX Yo soy de México.

DON FRANCISCO Bueno, chicos, ¡todos a bordo!

INÉS Con permiso.

recursos

CA pp. 51–52

SUPERSITE
descubre1.vhlcentral.com
Lección 1

TEACHING OPTIONS

¡Todos a bordo! Have students make a three-column chart with the headings *Greetings, Self-Identification,* and *Courtesy Expressions.* Have students suggest two or three possible phrases for each category. Then play the **¡Todos a bordo!** episode once and ask students to fill in the first column with the basic greetings that they hear. Repeat this process for the second column, where they should list the expressions the characters use to identify themselves. Play the video a third time for students to jot down courtesy expressions, such as ways to say "pleased to meet you" and "excuse me."

SRA. RAMOS Y tú eres Inés Ayala Loor, ¿verdad?

INÉS Sí, yo soy Inés.

SRA. RAMOS Y tú eres Alejandro Morales Paredes, ¿no?

ÁLEX Sí, señora.

INÉS Hola. Soy Inés.

MAITE Encantada. Yo me llamo Maite. ¿De dónde eres?

INÉS Soy del Ecuador, de Portoviejo. ¿Y tú?

MAITE De España. Soy de Madrid, la capital. Oye, ¿qué hora es?

INÉS Son las diez y tres minutos.

ÁLEX Perdón.

DON FRANCISCO ¿Y los otros?

SRA. RAMOS Son todos.

DON FRANCISCO Está bien.

Expresiones útiles

Identifying yourself and others

- **¿Cómo se llama usted?**
  What's your name?
  Yo soy don Francisco, el conductor.
  I'm Don Francisco, the driver.

- **¿Cómo te llamas?**
  What's your name?
  Me llamo Javier.
  My name is Javier.

- **¿Quién es...?**
  Who is...?
  Aquí... soy yo.
  Here... that's me.

- **Tú eres..., ¿verdad?/¿no?**
  You are..., right?/no?
  Sí, señora.
  Yes, ma'am.

Saying what time it is

- **¿Qué hora es?**
  What time is it?
  Es la una.
  It's one o'clock.
  Son las dos.
  It's two o'clock.
  Son las diez y tres minutos.
  It's 10:03.

Saying "excuse me"

- **Con permiso.**
  Pardon me; Excuse me.
  (to request permission)
- **Perdón.**
  Pardon me; Excuse me.
  (to get someone's attention or to ask forgiveness)

When starting a trip

- **¡Todos a bordo!**
  All aboard!
- **¡Buen viaje!**
  Have a good trip!

Getting someone's attention

- **Oye/Oiga(n)...**
  Listen (fam./form.)...

Teaching Tip Have volunteers read individual parts of the **Fotonovela** captions aloud. Then have students work in groups of six to role-play the episode. Have one or two groups present the episode to the class.

Expresiones útiles Identify forms of the verb **ser** and point out some subject pronouns. Identify time-telling expressions. Tell students that they will learn more about these concepts in **Estructura**.

Successful Language Learning Tell students that their conversational skills will grow more quickly as they learn each lesson's **Expresiones útiles**. This feature is designed to teach phrases that will be useful in conversation, and it will also help students understand key phrases in each **Fotonovela**.

¿Qué pasó?

1 **¿Cierto o falso?** Indicate if each statement is **cierto** or **falso**. Then correct the false statements.

	Cierto	Falso	
1. Javier y Álex son pasajeros (*passengers*).	☑	○	
2. Javier Gómez Lozano es el conductor.	○	☑	Don Francisco es el conductor.
3. Inés Ayala Loor es de la agencia Ecuatur.	○	☑	Isabel Ramos es de la agencia Ecuatur.
4. Inés es del Ecuador.	☑	○	
5. Maite es de España.	☑	○	
6. Javier es de Puerto Rico.	☑	○	
7. Álex es del Ecuador.	○	☑	Álex es de México.

2 **Identificar** Indicate which person would make each statement. One name will be used twice.

1. Yo soy de México. ¿De dónde eres tú? Álex
2. ¡Atención! ¡Todos a bordo! Don Francisco
3. ¿Yo? Soy de la capital de España. Maite
4. Y yo soy del Ecuador. Inés
5. ¿Qué hora es, Inés? Maite
6. Yo soy de Puerto Rico. ¿Y tú? Javier

ÁLEX **INÉS** **MAITE**

DON FRANCISCO **JAVIER**

3 **Completar** Complete this slightly altered version of the conversation that Inés and Maite had.

INÉS   Hola. ¿Cómo te (1) __llamas__ ?
MAITE Me llamo Maite. ¿Y (2) __tú__ ?
INÉS   Inés. Mucho (3) __gusto__ .
MAITE (4) __El__ gusto es mío.
INÉS   ¿De (5) __dónde__ eres?
MAITE (6) __De__ España. ¿Y (7) __tú__ ?
INÉS   Del (8) __Ecuador__ .

4 **Conversar** Imagine that you are chatting with a traveler you just met at the airport. With a partner, prepare a conversation using these cues. *Some answers will vary.*

Estudiante 1	Estudiante 2
Say "good afternoon" to your partner and ask for his or her name.	Say hello and what your name is. Then ask what your partner's name is.
Say what your name is and that you are glad to meet your partner.	Say that the pleasure is yours.
Ask how your partner is.	Say that you're doing well, thank you.
Ask where your partner is from.	Say where you're from.
Wish your partner a good trip.	Say thank you and goodbye.

Pronunciación SUPERSITE

The Spanish alphabet

The Spanish alphabet consists of 29 letters. The Spanish letter **ñ** (**eñe**) doesn't appear in the English alphabet. The letters **k** (**ka**) and **w** (**doble ve**) are used only in words of foreign origin.

[handwritten note: See my sheet "El alphabeto español" + La Cancion + The Alphabet]

Letra	Nombre(s)	Ejemplos	Letra	Nombre(s)	Ejemplos
a	a	adiós	m	eme	mapa
b	be	bien, problema	n	ene	nacionalidad
c	ce	cosa, cero	ñ	eñe	mañana
ch	che	chico	o	o	once
d	de	diario, nada	p	pe	profesor
e	e	estudiante	q	cu	qué
f	efe	foto	r	ere	regular, señora
g	ge	gracias, Gerardo, regular	s	ese	señor
			t	te	tú
h	hache	hola	u	u	usted
i	i	igualmente	v	ve	vista, nuevo
j	jota	Javier	w	doble ve	*walkman*
k	ka, ca	kilómetro	x	equis	existir, México
l	ele	lápiz	y	i griega, ye	yo
ll	elle	llave	z	zeta, ceta	zona

El alfabeto Repeat the Spanish alphabet and example words after your instructor.

Práctica Spell these words aloud in Spanish.

1. nada
2. maleta
3. quince
4. muy
5. hombre
6. por favor
7. San Fernando
8. Estados Unidos
9. Puerto Rico
10. España
11. Javier
12. Ecuador
13. Maite
14. gracias
15. Nueva York

Refranes Read these sayings aloud.

Ver es creer.[1]

En boca cerrada no entran moscas.[2]

1 Seeing is believing. 2 Silence is golden.

recursos		
CH p. 3	CA p. 88	SUPERSITE descubre1.vhlcentral.com Lección 1

EN DETALLE

Saludos y besos en los países hispanos

In Spanish-speaking countries, kissing on the cheek is a customary way to greet friends and family members. It is common to kiss someone upon introduction, particularly in a non-business setting. Whereas North Americans maintain considerable personal space when greeting, Spaniards and Latin Americans tend to decrease interpersonal space and give one or two kisses (**besos**) on the cheek, sometimes accompanied by a handshake or a hug. In formal business settings, where associates do not know one another on a personal level, greetings entail a simple handshake.

Greeting someone with a **beso** varies according to region, gender, and context. With the exception of Argentina—where male friends and relatives lightly kiss on the cheek—men generally greet each other with a hug or warm handshake. Greetings between men and women, and between women, can differ depending on the country and context, but generally include kissing. In Spain, it is customary to give **dos besos**, starting with the right cheek first. In Latin American countries, including Mexico, Costa Rica, Colombia, and Chile, a greeting consists of a single "air kiss" on the right cheek. Peruvians also "air kiss," but strangers will simply shake hands. In Colombia, female acquaintances tend to simply pat each other on the right forearm or shoulder.

Tendencias

País	Beso	País	Beso
Argentina	💋	España	💋💋
Bolivia	💋	México	💋
Chile	💋	Paraguay	💋💋
Colombia	💋	Puerto Rico	💋
El Salvador	💋	Venezuela	💋/💋💋

ACTIVIDADES

1 **¿Cierto o falso?** Indicate whether these statements are true (**cierto**) or false (**falso**). Correct the false statements.

1. Hispanic cultures leave less interpersonal space when greeting than in the U.S. Cierto.
2. Men never greet with a kiss in Spanish-speaking countries. Falso. Argentine men can greet with a light kiss.
3. Shaking hands is not appropriate for a business setting in Latin America. Falso. In most business settings, people greet one another by shaking hands.

4. Spaniards greet with one kiss on the right cheek. Falso. They greet with one kiss on each cheek.
5. In Mexico, people greet with an "air kiss". Cierto.
6. Gender can play a role in the type of greeting given. Cierto.
7. If two women acquaintances meet in Colombia, they should exchange two kisses on the cheek. Falso. They pat one another on the right forearm or shoulder.
8. In Peru, a man and a woman meeting for the first time would probably greet each other with an "air kiss." Falso. They would probably shake hands.

ASÍ SE DICE

Saludos y despedidas

Buenas.	*Hello./Hi.*
Chao.	*Chau.*
¿Cómo te/le va?	*How are things going (for you)?*
Hasta ahora.	*See you soon.*
¿Qué hay?	*What's new?*
¿Qué onda? (Méx.);	*What's going on?*
¿Qué hubo? (Col.)	

EL MUNDO HISPANO

Parejas y amigos famosos

Here are some famous couples and friends from the Spanish-speaking world.

○ **Jennifer López** (Estados Unidos) y **Marc Anthony** (Estados Unidos/ Puerto Rico) Not long after ending her relationship with Ben Affleck, Jennifer López married salsa singer Marc Anthony.

○ **Gael García Bernal** (México) y **Diego Luna** (México) These lifelong friends both starred in the 2001 Mexican film *Y tu mamá también.*

○ **Salma Hayek** (México) y **Penélope Cruz** (España) Close friends Salma Hayek and Penélope Cruz developed their acting skills in their countries of origin before meeting in Hollywood.

PERFIL

La plaza principal

In the Spanish-speaking world, public space is treasured. Small city and town life revolves around the **plaza principal**. Often surrounded by cathedrals or municipal buildings like the **ayuntamiento** (*city hall*), the pedestrian **plaza** is designated as a central meeting place for family and friends. During warmer months, when outdoor cafés usually line the **plaza**, it is a popular spot to have a leisurely cup of coffee, chat,

La Plaza Mayor de Salamanca

and people watch. Many town festivals, or **ferias**, also take place in this space. One of the most famous town

squares is the **Plaza Mayor** in the university town of Salamanca, Spain. Students gather underneath its famous clock tower to meet up with friends or simply take a coffee break.

La Plaza de Armas, Arequipa, Perú

SUPERSITE · Conexión Internet

What are the **plazas principales** in large cities such as Mexico City and Buenos Aires?

Go to **descubre1.vhlcentral.com** to find more cultural information related to this **Cultura** section.

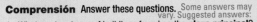
ACTIVIDADES

2 **Comprensión** Answer these questions. *Some answers may vary. Suggested answers:*

1. What are two types of buildings found on the **plaza principal**? *municipal buildings and cathedrals*
2. What are two types of events or activities common at a **plaza principal**? *meeting with friends and festivals*
3. How would Diego Luna greet his friends? *¿Qué onda?*
4. Would Salma Hayek and Jennifer López greet with one kiss or two? *one*

3 **Saludos** Role-play these greetings with a partner. Include a verbal greeting as well as a handshake, as appropriate. *Role-plays will vary according to student gender.*

1. friends in Mexico
2. business associates at a conference in Chile
3. friends in Madrid's Plaza Mayor
4. Peruvians meeting for the first time
5. relatives in Argentina

recursos

| CH p. 4 | descubre1.vhlcentral.com Lección 1 |

TEACHING OPTIONS

Cultural Activity For homework, have students use the Internet to research a famous **plaza principal** in a Spanish-speaking city or town. They should find out the **plaza**'s location in the city, when it was built, current uses, and other significant information. Encourage them to bring in a photo. Then have the students present their findings to the class.

Heritage Speakers Ask heritage speakers to describe cities and towns from their families' countries of origin. Is there a **plaza principal**? How is it used? Ask the class to think of analogous public spaces in the U.S. (Ex: a common or "town green" in small New England towns)

Section Goals

In **Estructura 1.1**, students will be introduced to:

- gender of nouns
- definite and indefinite articles

Instructional Resources

Cuaderno de práctica, p. 3
Cuaderno para hispanohablantes, pp. 5–6
Cuaderno de actividades, p. 89
e-Cuaderno
Supersite: Audio Activity MP3 Audio Files
Supersite/TRCD/Print: *PowerPoints* (**Lección 1 Estructura** Presentation); Audio Activity Script, Answer Keys
Audio Activity CD

Teaching Tips

- Write these nouns from the **Fotonovela** on the board: **agencia, conductor, documentos, universidades.** Ask volunteers what each means. Point out the different endings and introduce grammatical gender in Spanish. Explain what a noun is and give examples of people (**chicos**), places (**universidad**), things (**documentos**), and ideas (**nacionalidad**). Ask volunteers to point out which of these nouns are singular or plural and why.
- Point out that while nouns for male beings are generally masculine and those for female beings are generally feminine, grammatical gender does not necessarily correspond to the actual gender of the noun.
- Point out patterns of noun endings –o, –a; –or, –ora. Stress that –ista can refer to males or females and give additional examples: **el/la artista, el/la dentista.**

1.1 ## Nouns and articles (SUPERSITE) comparisons NATIONAL STANDARDS

Spanish nouns

ANTE TODO A noun is a word used to identify people, animals, places, things, or ideas. Unlike English, all Spanish nouns, even those that refer to non-living things, have gender; that is, they are considered either masculine or feminine. As in English, nouns in Spanish also have number, meaning that they are either singular or plural.

Nouns that refer to living things	
Masculine nouns	**Feminine nouns**
el hombre — *the man*	**la mujer** — *the woman*
ending in –o	*ending in –a*
el chico — *the boy*	**la chica** — *the girl*
el pasajero — *the (male) passenger*	**la pasajera** — *the (female) passenger*
ending in –or	*ending in –ora*
el conductor — *the (male) driver*	**la conductora** — *the (female) driver*
el profesor — *the (male) teacher*	**la profesora** — *the (female) teacher*
ending in –ista	*ending in –ista*
el turista — *the (male) tourist*	**la turista** — *the (female) tourist*

▶ As shown above, nouns that refer to males, like **el hombre,** are generally masculine, while nouns that refer to females, like **la mujer,** are generally feminine.

▶ Many nouns that refer to male beings end in **–o** or **–or**. Their corresponding feminine forms end in **–a** and **–ora**, respectively.

el conductor

la profesora

▶ The masculine and feminine forms of nouns that end in **–ista,** like **turista,** are the same, so gender is indicated by the article **el** (masculine) or **la** (feminine). Some other nouns have identical masculine and feminine forms.

el joven
the youth; the young man

la joven
the youth; the young woman

el estudiante
the (male) student

la estudiante
the (female) student

TEACHING OPTIONS

Extra Practice Write ten singular nouns on the board. Make sure the nouns represent a mix of the different types of noun endings. In a rapid-response drill, call on students to give the appropriate gender. For –ista words, accept either masculine or feminine, but clarify that both are used. You may also do this as a completely oral drill by not writing the words on the board.

Game Divide the class into teams of three or four. Bring in photos or magazine pictures showing objects or people. Hold up each photo and say the Spanish noun without the article. Call on teams to indicate the object or person's gender. Give one point for each correct answer. Deduct one point for each incorrect answer. The team with the most points at the end wins.

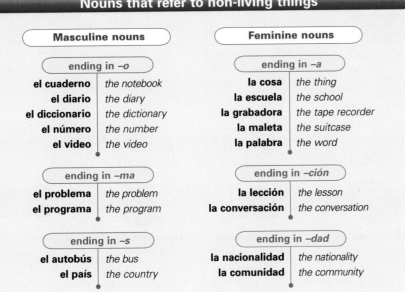

Nouns that refer to non-living things

Masculine nouns		Feminine nouns	
ending in –o		**ending in –a**	
el cuaderno	the notebook	**la cosa**	the thing
el diario	the diary	**la escuela**	the school
el diccionario	the dictionary	**la grabadora**	the tape recorder
el número	the number	**la maleta**	the suitcase
el video	the video	**la palabra**	the word
ending in –ma		**ending in –ción**	
el problema	the problem	**la lección**	the lesson
el programa	the program	**la conversación**	the conversation
ending in –s		**ending in –dad**	
el autobús	the bus	**la nacionalidad**	the nationality
el país	the country	**la comunidad**	the community

¡LENGUA VIVA!

The Spanish word for *video* can be pronounced with the stress on the **i** or the **e**. For that reason, you might see the word written with or without an accent: **video** or **vídeo**.

▶ As shown above, certain noun endings are strongly associated with a specific gender, so you can use them to determine if a noun is masculine or feminine.

▶ Because the gender of nouns that refer to non-living things cannot be determined by foolproof rules, you should memorize the gender of each noun you learn. It is helpful to memorize each noun with its corresponding article, **el** for masculine and **la** for feminine.

▶ Another reason to memorize the gender of every noun is that there are common exceptions to the rules of gender. For example, **el mapa** (*map*) and **el día** (*day*) end in **–a,** but are masculine. **La mano** (*hand*) ends in **–o,** but is feminine.

Plural of nouns

▶ In Spanish, nouns that end in a vowel form the plural by adding **–s**. Nouns that end in a consonant add **–es**. Nouns that end in **–z** change the **–z** to **–c**, then add **–es**.

el chico ⟶ los chic**os**   la nacionalida**d** ⟶ las nacionalida**des**

el diari**o** ⟶ los diari**os**   el paí**s** ⟶ los paí**ses**

el problem**a** ⟶ los problem**as**   el lápi**z** (*pencil*) ⟶ los lápi**ces**

CONSULTA

You will learn more about accent marks in **Lección 4, Pronunciación,** p. 123.

▶ In general, when a singular noun has an accent mark on the last syllable, the accent is dropped from the plural form.

la lecci**ón** ⟶ las lecci**ones**   el autob**ús** ⟶ los autob**uses**

▶ Use the masculine plural form to refer to a group that includes both males and females.

1 pasajer**o** + 2 pasajer**as** = 3 pasajer**os**   2 chic**os** + 2 chic**as** = 4 chic**os**

Teaching Tips
• Work through the list of nouns, modeling their pronunciation. Point out patterns of gender, including word endings **–ma**, **–ción**, and **–dad**. Give cognate nouns with these endings and ask students to indicate the gender. Ex: **diagrama, acción, personalidad**. Point out common exceptions to gender agreement rules for **el mapa, el día,** and **la mano.**

• Stress the addition of **–s** to nouns that end in vowels and **–es** to nouns that end in consonants. Write ten nouns on the board and ask volunteers to give the plural forms, along with the appropriate articles.

• Point to three male students and ask if the group is **los** or **las estudiantes (los)**. Next, point to three female students and ask the same question **(las)**. Then indicate a group of males and females and ask for the correct term to refer to them **(los estudiantes)**. Stress that even if a group contains 100 women and one man, the masculine plural form and article are used.

• Point out that words like **lección** and **autobús** lose the written accent in the plural form in order to keep the stress on the same syllable as in the singular noun.

The Affective Dimension
Tell students that many people feel anxious when learning grammar. Tell them that grammar will seem less intimidating if they think of it as a description of how the language works instead of a list of strict rules.

TEACHING OPTIONS

TPR Give four students each a card with a different definite article. Give the other students each a card with a noun (include a mix of masculine, feminine, singular, and plural). Have students form a circle; each student's card should be visible to others. Call out one of the nouns; that student must step forward. The student with the corresponding article has five seconds to join the noun student.

Game Divide the class into two teams, A and B. Point to a member of team A and say a singular noun. The student repeats the noun, including the correct definite article, and then spells it. Then point to a team B member, who will supply the plural form and spell it. Award one point per correct answer and deduct one point for each wrong answer. The team with the most points at the end wins.

Spanish articles

ANTE TODO As you know, English often uses definite articles (**the**) and indefinite articles (**a, an**) before nouns. Spanish also has definite and indefinite articles. Unlike English, Spanish articles vary in form because they agree in gender and number with the nouns they modify.

Definite articles

Masculine		Feminine	
SINGULAR	PLURAL	SINGULAR	PLURAL
el diccionario *the dictionary*	**los** diccionarios *the dictionaries*	**la** computadora *the computer*	**las** computadoras *the computers*

▶ Spanish has four forms that are equivalent to the English definite article *the*. You use definite articles to refer to specific nouns.

Indefinite articles

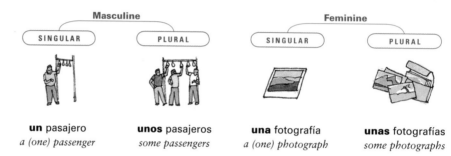

Masculine		Feminine	
SINGULAR	PLURAL	SINGULAR	PLURAL
un pasajero *a (one) passenger*	**unos** pasajeros *some passengers*	**una** fotografía *a (one) photograph*	**unas** fotografías *some photographs*

▶ Spanish has four forms that are equivalent to the English indefinite article, which according to context may mean *a, an,* or *some.* You use indefinite articles to refer to unspecified persons or things.

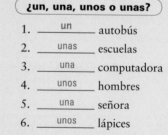

¡INTÉNTALO! Provide a definite article for each noun in the first column and an indefinite article for each noun in the second column. The first item has been done for you.

¿el, la, los o las?
1. __la__ chica
2. __el__ chico
3. __la__ maleta
4. __los__ cuadernos
5. __el__ lápiz
6. __las__ mujeres

¿un, una, unos o unas?
1. __un__ autobús
2. __unas__ escuelas
3. __una__ computadora
4. __unos__ hombres
5. __una__ señora
6. __unos__ lápices

Práctica

1 **¿Singular o plural?** If the word is singular, make it plural. If it is plural, make it singular.

1. el número los números
2. un diario unos diarios
3. la estudiante las estudiantes
4. el conductor los conductores
5. el país los países
6. las cosas la cosa
7. unos turistas un turista
8. las nacionalidades la nacionalidad
9. unas computadoras una computadora
10. los problemas el problema
11. una fotografía unas fotografías
12. los profesores el profesor
13. unas señoritas una señorita
14. el hombre los hombres
15. la grabadora las grabadoras
16. la señora las señoras

2 **Identificar** For each drawing, provide the noun with its corresponding definite and indefinite articles.

> **modelo**
> las maletas, unas maletas

1. la computadora, una computadora
2. los cuadernos, unos cuadernos

3. las mujeres, unas mujeres
4. el chico, un chico
5. la escuela, una escuela

6. las fotos, unas fotos
7. los autobuses, unos autobuses
8. el diario, un diario

Comunicación

3 **Charadas** In groups, play a game of charades. Individually, think of two nouns for each charade, for example, a boy using a computer (**un chico; una computadora**). The first person to guess correctly acts out the next charade. Answers will vary.

---

1 Expansion Reverse the activity by reading the on-page answers and having students convert the singular to plural and vice versa. Make sure they close their books. Give the nouns in random order.

2 Expansion As an additional visual excercise, bring in photos or magazine pictures that illustrate items whose names students know. Ask students to indicate the definite article and the noun. Include a mix of singular and plural nouns. Repeat the exercise with indefinite articles.

3 Teaching Tip Explain the basic rules of charades relevant to what students know at this point: (1) the student acting out the charade may not speak and (2) he or she may show the number of syllables by using fingers.

3 Expansion Split the class into two teams, with volunteers from each team acting out the charades. Give a point to each team for correctly guessing the charade. The team with the most points wins.

TEACHING OPTIONS

Video Show the *Fotonovela* episode again to offer more input on singular and plural nouns and articles. With their books closed, have students write down every noun and article that they hear. After viewing the video, ask volunteers to list the nouns and articles they heard. Explain that the **las** used when telling time refers to **las horas** (Ex: **Son las cinco = Son las cinco horas**).

Extra Practice To challenge students, slowly read a short passage from a novel, story, or poem written in Spanish, preferably one with a great number of nouns and articles. As a listening exercise, have students write down every noun and article they hear, even unfamiliar ones (the articles may cue when nouns appear).

1.2 # Numbers 0–30

see my sheet "Los números" + Lección números 17... Las matemáticas (handwritten)

Los números 0 a 30		
0 cero		
1 uno	**11** once	**21** veintiuno
2 dos	**12** doce	**22** veintidós
3 tres	**13** trece	**23** veintitrés
4 cuatro	**14** catorce	**24** veinticuatro
5 cinco	**15** quince	**25** veinticinco
6 seis	**16** dieciséis	**26** veintiséis
7 siete	**17** diecisiete	**27** veintisiete
8 ocho	**18** dieciocho	**28** veintiocho
9 nueve	**19** diecinueve	**29** veintinueve
10 diez	**20** veinte	**30** treinta

AYUDA

The numbers sixteen through nineteen can also be written as three words: **diez y seis, diez y siete…**

▶ The number **uno** (*one*) and numbers ending in **–uno**, such as **veintiuno**, have more than one form. Before masculine nouns, **uno** shortens to **un**. Before feminine nouns, **uno** changes to **una**.

un hombre → veinti**ún** hombres   **una** mujer → veinti**una** mujeres

▶ **¡Atención!** The forms **uno** and **veintiuno** are used when counting (**uno, dos, tres... veinte, veintiuno, veintidós...**). They are also used when the number *follows* a noun, even if the noun is feminine: **la lección uno**.

▶ To ask *how many people* or *things* there are, use **cuántos** before masculine nouns and **cuántas** before feminine nouns.

▶ The Spanish equivalent of both *there is* and *there are* is **hay**. Use **¿Hay...?** to ask *Is there...?* or *Are there...?* Use **no hay** to express *there is not* or *there are not*.

—**¿Cuántos** estudiantes **hay?**
How many students are there?

—**Hay** tres estudiantes en la foto.
There are three students in the photo.

—**¿Hay** chicas en la fotografía?
Are there girls in the picture?

—**Hay** cuatro chicos, y **no hay** chicas.
There are four guys, and there are no girls.

¡INTÉNTALO! Provide the Spanish words for these numbers.

1. **7** siete
2. **16** dieciséis
3. **29** veintinueve
4. **1** uno
5. **0** cero
6. **15** quince
7. **21** veintiuno
8. **9** nueve
9. **23** veintitrés
10. **11** once
11. **30** treinta
12. **4** cuatro
13. **12** doce
14. **28** veintiocho
15. **14** catorce
16. **10** diez

recursos

CP
p. 4

CH
pp. 7–8

CA
pp. 1–2, 90

SUPERSITE
descubre1.
vhlcentral.com
Lección 1

Section Goals

In **Estructura 1.2**, students will be introduced to:
• numbers 0–30
• the verb form **hay**

Instructional Resources
Cuaderno de práctica, p. 4
Cuaderno para hispanohablantes, pp. 7–8
Cuaderno de actividades, pp. 1–2, 90
e-Cuaderno
Supersite: Audio Activity MP3 Audio Files
Supersite/TRCD/Print: *PowerPoints* (**Lección 1 Estructura** Presentation); Communication Activities, Audio Activity Script, Answer Keys
Audio Activity CD

Teaching Tips

• Introduce numbers by asking students if they can count to ten in Spanish. Model the pronunciation of each number. Write individual numbers on the board and call on students at random to say the number.
• Say numbers aloud at random and have students hold up the appropriate number of fingers. Then hold up varying numbers of fingers at random and ask students to shout out the corresponding number in Spanish.
• Emphasize the variable forms of **uno** and **veintiuno**, giving examples of each. Ex: **veintiún profesores, veintiuna profesoras.**
• Ask questions like these: **¿Cuántos estudiantes hay en la clase? (Hay _____ estudiantes en la clase.)**

TEACHING OPTIONS

TPR Assign ten students a number from 0–30 and line them up in front of the class. Call out one of the numbers at random, and have the student assigned that number step forward. When two students have stepped forward, ask them to repeat their numbers. Then ask individuals to add (Say: **Suma**) or subtract (Say: **Resta**) the two numbers, giving the result in Spanish.

Game Ask students to write B-I-N-G-O across the top of a blank piece of paper. Have them draw five squares vertically under each letter and randomly fill in the squares with numbers from 0–30, without repeating any numbers. Draw numbers from a hat and call them out in Spanish. The first student to mark five in a row (horizontally, vertically, or diagonally) yells **¡Bingo!** and wins. Have the winner confirm the numbers for you in Spanish.

Práctica (SUPERSITE)

1

Contar Following the pattern, provide the missing numbers in Spanish.

1. 1, 3, 5, ..., 29   7, 9, 11, 13, 15, 17, 19, 21, 23, 25, 27
2. 2, 4, 6, ..., 30   8, 10, 12, 14, 16, 18, 20, 22, 24, 26, 28
3. 3, 6, 9, ..., 30   12, 15, 18, 21, 24, 27
4. 30, 28, 26, ..., 0   24, 22, 20, 18, 16, 14, 12, 10, 8, 6, 4, 2
5. 30, 25, 20, ..., 0   15, 10, 5
6. 28, 24, 20, ..., 0   16, 12, 8, 4

2

Resolver Solve these math problems with a partner.

AYUDA

+	→	más
−	→	menos
=	→	son

> **modelo**
>
> 5 + 3 =
> **Estudiante 1:** cinco más tres son...
> **Estudiante 2:** ocho

1. **2 + 15 =** Dos más quince son diecisiete.
2. **20 – 1 =** Veinte menos uno son diecinueve.
3. **5 + 7 =** Cinco más siete son doce.
4. **18 + 12 =** Dieciocho más doce son treinta.
5. **3 + 22 =** Tres más veintidós son veinticinco.
6. **6 – 3 =** Seis menos tres son tres.
7. **11 + 12 =** Once más doce son veintitrés.
8. **7 – 2 =** Siete menos dos son cinco.
9. **8 + 5 =** Ocho más cinco son trece.
10. **23 – 14 =** Veintitrés menos catorce son nueve.

3

¿Cuántos hay? How many persons or things are there in these drawings?

> **modelo**
>
> Hay tres maletas.

 1. _____ Hay veinte lápices.

 2. _____ Hay un hombre.

 *Chicos* 3. _____ Hay veinticinco chicos.

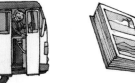 4. _____ Hay una conductora.

 5. _____ Hay cuatro fotos.

 6. _____ Hay treinta cuadernos.

 7. _____ Hay seis turistas.

 *Chicas* 8. _____ Hay diecisiete chicas.

---

1 Teaching Tips
- Before beginning the activity, make sure students know each pattern: odds (**los números impares**), evens (**los números pares**), count by threes (**contar de tres en tres**), etc.
- To simplify, write complete patterns out on the board.

1 Expansion Explain that a prime number is any number that can only be evenly divided by itself and 1. To challenge students, ask the class to list the prime numbers (**los números primos**) up to 30. Prime numbers to 30 are: 1, 2, 3, 5, 7, 11, 13, 17, 19, 23, 29.

2 Expansion Do simple multiplication and division problems. Introduce the phrases **multiplicado por** and **dividido por**. Ex: **Cinco multiplicado por cinco son...** (**veinticinco**). **Veinte dividido por cuatro son...** (**cinco**).

3 Teaching Tip Have students read the directions and the model. Cue student responses by asking questions related to the drawings. Ex: **¿Cuántos lápices hay?** (**Hay veinte lápices.**)

3 Expansion Add an additional visual aspect to this activity. Hold up or point to classroom objects and ask how many there are. Since students will not know the names of many items, a simple number or **hay** + the number will suffice to signal comprehension. Ex: —**¿Cuántos diccionarios hay aquí?** —**(Hay) Dos**.

TEACHING OPTIONS

TPR Give ten students each a card that contains a different number from 0–30. The cards should be visible to the other students. Then call out simple math problems (addition or subtraction) involving the assigned numbers. When the first two numbers are called, each student steps forward. The student whose assigned number completes the math problem then has five seconds to join them.

Extra Practice Ask questions about your school and the town or city in which it is located. Ex: **¿Cuántos profesores de español hay? ¿Cuántas escuelas secundarias hay en _____? ¿Cuántas pizzerías hay en _____?** Encourage students to guess the number. If a number exceeds 30, write that number on the board and model its pronunciation.

4 **Teaching Tip** If there are no examples of the item listed, students should say: **No hay ____.**

4 **Expansion** After completing the activity, call on individuals to give rapid responses for the same items. To challenge students, mix up the order of items.

5 **Teaching Tip** Remind students that they will be forming sentences with **hay** and a number. Give them four minutes to do the activity. You might also have students write out their answers.

5 **Expansion** After pairs have finished analyzing the drawing, call on individuals to respond. Convert the statements into questions in Spanish. Ask: **¿Cuántos chicos hay? ¿Cuántas mujeres hay?**

Teaching Tip See the Communication Activities for an additional activity to practice the material presented in this section.

Comunicación

4

En la clase With a classmate, take turns asking and answering these questions about your classroom. Answers will vary.

1. ¿Cuántos estudiantes hay?
2. ¿Cuántos profesores hay?
3. ¿Hay una computadora?
4. ¿Hay una maleta?
5. ¿Cuántos mapas hay?

6. ¿Cuántos lápices hay?
7. ¿Hay cuadernos?
8. ¿Cuántas grabadoras hay?
9. ¿Hay hombres?
10. ¿Cuántas mujeres hay?

5

Preguntas With a classmate, take turns asking and answering questions about the drawing. Talk about: Answers will vary.

1. how many children there are
2. how many women there are
3. if there are some photographs
4. if there is a boy
5. how many notebooks there are

6. if there is a bus
7. if there are tourists
8. how many pencils there are
9. if there is a man
10. how many computers there are

TEACHING OPTIONS

Pairs Have each student draw a scene similar to the one on this page. Stick figures are perfectly acceptable! Give them three minutes to draw the scene. Encourage students to include multiple numbers of particular items (**cuadernos, maletas, lápices,** etc.). Then have pairs take turns describing what is in their partner's picture.

Pairs Divide the class into pairs. Give half of the pairs magazine pictures that contain images of familiar words or cognates. Give the other half written descriptions of the pictures, using **hay**. Ex: **En la foto hay dos mujeres, un chico y una chica.** Have pairs circulate around the room to match the descriptions with the corresponding pictures.

1.3 Present tense of ser

Subject pronouns

ANTE TODO   In order to use verbs, you will need to learn about subject pronouns. A subject pronoun replaces the name or title of a person or thing and acts as the subject of a verb. In both Spanish and English, subject pronouns are divided into three groups: first person, second person, and third person.

Subject pronouns				
	SINGULAR		**PLURAL**	
FIRST PERSON	**yo**	*I*	**nosotros**	*we* (masculine)
			nosotras	*we* (feminine)
SECOND PERSON	**tú**	*you* (familiar)	**vosotros**	*you* (masc., fam.)
	usted (Ud.)	*you* (formal)	**vosotras**	*you* (fem., fam.)
			ustedes (Uds.)	*you* (form.)
THIRD PERSON	**él**	*he*	**ellos**	*they* (masc.)
	ella	*she*	**ellas**	*they* (fem.)

¡LENGUA VIVA!

In Latin America, **ustedes** is used as the plural for both **tú** and **usted**. In Spain, however, **vosotros** and **vosotras** are used as the plural of **tú**, and **ustedes** is used only as the plural of **usted**.

• • •

Usted and **ustedes** are abbreviated as **Ud.** and **Uds.**, or occasionally as **Vd.** and **Vds.**

▶ Spanish has two subject pronouns that mean *you* (singular). Use **tú** when addressing a friend, a family member, or a child you know well. Use **usted** to address a person with whom you have a formal or more distant relationship, such as a superior at work, a professor, or a person older than you.

Tú eres de Canadá, ¿verdad David?   ¿**Usted** es la profesora de español?
You are from Canada, right David?   *Are you the Spanish professor?*

▶ The masculine plural forms **nosotros**, **vosotros**, and **ellos** refer to a group of males or to a group of males and females. The feminine plural forms **nosotras**, **vosotras**, and **ellas** can refer only to groups made up exclusively of females.

nosotros, vosotros, ellos   nosotros, vosotros, ellos   nosotras, vosotras, ellas

▶ There is no Spanish equivalent of the English subject pronoun *it*. Generally *it* is not expressed in Spanish.

Es un problema.   Es una computadora.
It's a problem.   *It's a computer.*

Section Goals

In **Estructura 1.3**, students will be introduced to:
• subject pronouns
• present tense of the verb **ser**
• the use of **ser** to identify, to indicate possession, to describe origin, and to talk about professions or occupations

Instructional Resources
Cuaderno de práctica, pp. 5–6
Cuaderno para hispanohablantes, pp. 9–10
Cuaderno de actividades, p. 91
e-Cuaderno
Supersite: Audio Activity
MP3 Audio Files
Supersite/TRCD/Print:
PowerPoints (**Lección 1**
Estructura Presentation); Audio
Activity Script, Answer Keys
Audio Activity CD

Teaching Tips
• Point to yourself and say: **Yo soy profesor(a)**. Then point to a student and ask: ¿**Tú eres profesor(a) o estudiante?** (estudiante) Say: **Sí, tú eres estudiante.** Indicate the whole class and tell them: **Ustedes son estudiantes.** Once the pattern has been established, include other subject pronouns and forms of **ser** while indicating other students. Ex: **Él es..., Ella es..., Ellos son...**
• Remind students of the familiar and formal forms of address they learned in **Contextos**.
• You may want to point out that while **usted** and **ustedes** are part of the second person *you*, they use third person forms.
• While the **vosotros/as** forms are listed in verb paradigms in **DESCUBRE**, they will not be actively practiced.

TEACHING OPTIONS

Extra Practice Explain that students are to give subject pronouns based on their point of view. Ex: Point to yourself (**usted**), a female student (**ella**), everyone in the class (**nosotros**).
Extra Practice Ask students to indicate whether certain people would be addressed as **tú** or **usted**. Ex: A classmate, a friend's grandfather, a doctor, a neighbor's child.

Heritage Speakers Ask heritage speakers how they address elder members of their family, such as parents, grandparents, aunts, and uncles—whether they use **tú** or **usted**. Also ask them if they use **vosotros/as** (they typically will not unless they or their family are from Spain).

The present tense of ser

ANTE TODO In **Contextos** and **Fotonovela**, you have already used several forms of the present tense of **ser** (*to be*) to identify yourself and others and to talk about where you and others are from. **Ser** is an irregular verb, which means its forms don't follow the regular patterns that most verbs follow. You need to memorize the forms, which appear in this chart.

The verb ser (*to be*)		
SINGULAR FORMS		
yo	**soy**	*I am*
tú	**eres**	*you are* (fam.)
Ud./él/ella	**es**	*you are* (form.); *he/she is*
PLURAL FORMS		
nosotros/as	**somos**	*we are*
vosotros/as	**sois**	*you are* (fam.)
Uds./ellos/ellas	**son**	*you are* (form.); *they are*

Uses of *ser*

▶ Use **ser** to identify people and things.

—¿Quién **es** él?
Who is he?

—**Es** Javier Gómez Lozano.
He's Javier Gómez Lozano.

—¿Qué **es**?
What is it?

—**Es** un mapa de España.
It's a map of Spain.

Es Maite.

Es un autobús.

▶ **Ser** also expresses possession, with the preposition **de**. There is no Spanish equivalent of the English construction [*noun*] + 's (*Maite's*). In its place, Spanish uses [*noun*] + **de** + [*owner*].

—¿**De** quién **es**?
Whose is it?

—**Es** el diario **de** Maite.
It's Maite's diary.

—¿**De** quiénes **son**?
Whose are they?

—**Son** los lápices **de** la chica.
They are the girl's pencils.

▶ When **de** is followed by the article **el**, the two combine to form the contraction **del**. **De** does *not* contract with **la, las,** or **los**.

—**Es** la computadora **del** conductor.
It's the driver's computer.

—**Son** las maletas **del** chico.
They are the boy's suitcases.

▶ **Ser** also uses the preposition **de** to express origin.

¿De dónde eres?

Yo soy de México.

¿De dónde eres?

Yo soy de España.

—¿**De** dónde **es** Javier?
Where is Javier from?

—**Es de** Puerto Rico.
He's from Puerto Rico.

—¿**De** dónde **es** Inés?
Where is Inés from?

—**Es del** Ecuador.
She's from Ecuador.

▶ Use **ser** to express profession or occupation.

Don Francisco **es conductor.**
Don Francisco is a driver.

Yo **soy estudiante.**
I am a student.

▶ Unlike English, Spanish does not use the indefinite article (**un, una**) after **ser** when referring to professions, unless accompanied by an adjective or other description.

Marta **es** profesora.
Marta is a teacher.

Marta **es una** profesora excelente.
Marta is an excellent teacher.

Somos Perú

LanPerú

¡INTÉNTALO! Provide the correct subject pronouns and the present forms of **ser.** The first item has been done for you.

1. Gabriel	*él*	es	5. las turistas	ellas	son
2. Juan y yo	nosotros	somos	6. el chico	él	es
3. Óscar y Flora	ellos	son	7. los conductores	ellos	son
4. Adriana	ella	es	8. los señores Ruiz	ellos	son

Práctica (SUPERSITE)

Sidebar (Teacher notes)

1 Teaching Tip Review **tú** and **usted**, asking students which pronoun they would use in a formal situation and which they would use in an informal situation.

1 Expansion Once students have identified the correct subject pronouns, ask them to give the form of **ser** they would use when *addressing* each person and when *talking about* each person.

2 Expansion Give additional names of well-known Spanish speakers and ask students to tell where they are from. Have students give the country names in English if they do not know the Spanish equivalent. Ex: **¿De dónde es Andy García? (Es de Cuba.)**

3 Teaching Tips
• To simplify, before beginning the activity, guide students in identifying the objects.
• You might tell students to answer the second part of the question (**¿De quién es?**) with any answer they wish. Have students take turns asking and answering questions.

---

1 Pronombres What subject pronouns would you use to (a) talk to these people directly and (b) talk about them?

> **modelo**
> un joven tú, él

1. una chica tú, ella
2. el presidente de México Ud., él
3. tres chicas y un chico Uds., ellos
4. un estudiante tú, él
5. la señora Ochoa Ud., ella
6. dos profesoras Uds., ellas

---

2 Identidad y origen With a partner, take turns asking and answering these questions about the people indicated: **¿Quién es?/¿Quiénes son?** and **¿De dónde es?/¿De dónde son?**

> **modelo**
> Ricky Martin (Puerto Rico)
> **Estudiante 1:** ¿Quién es?   **Estudiante 1:** ¿De dónde es?
> **Estudiante 2:** Es Ricky Martin.   **Estudiante 2:** Es de Puerto Rico.

1. Enrique Iglesias (España)
   E1: ¿Quién es? E2: Es Enrique Iglesias. E1: ¿De dónde es? E2: Es de España.
2. Sammy Sosa (República Dominicana)
   E2: ¿Quién es? E1: Es Sammy Sosa. E2: ¿De dónde es? E1: Es de la República Dominicana.
3. Rebecca Lobo y Martin Sheen (Estados Unidos) E1: ¿Quiénes son? E2: Son Rebecca Lobo y Martin Sheen. E1: ¿De dónde son? E2: Son de los Estados Unidos.
4. Carlos Santana y Salma Hayek (México) E2: ¿Quiénes son? E1: Son Carlos Santana y Salma Hayek. E2: ¿De dónde son? E1: Son de México.
5. Shakira (Colombia)
   E1: ¿Quién es? E2: Es Shakira. E1: ¿De dónde es? E2: Es de Colombia.
6. Antonio Banderas y Penélope Cruz (España) E2: ¿Quiénes son? E1: Son Antonio Banderas y Penélope Cruz. E2: ¿De dónde son? E1: Son de España.
7. Edward James Olmos y Jimmy Smits (Estados Unidos) E1: ¿Quiénes son? E2: Son Edward James Olmos y Jimmy Smits. E1: ¿De dónde son? E2: Son de los Estados Unidos.
8. Gloria Estefan (Cuba) E2: ¿Quién es? E1: Es Gloria Estefan. E2: ¿De dónde es? E1: Es de Cuba.

---

3 ¿Qué es? Ask your partner what each object is and to whom it belongs.

> **modelo**
> **Estudiante 1:** ¿Qué es?   **Estudiante 1:** ¿De quién es?
> **Estudiante 2:** Es una grabadora.   **Estudiante 2:** Es del profesor.

 1.    2.  Gregorio   3.  Rafael   4.  Marisa

1. E1: ¿Qué es?
   E2: Es una maleta.
   E1: ¿De quién es?
   E2: Es de la Sra. Valdés.

2. E1: ¿Qué es?
   E2: Es un cuaderno.
   E1: ¿De quién es?
   E2: Es de Gregorio.

3. E1: ¿Qué es?
   E2: Es una computadora.
   E1: ¿De quién es?
   E2: Es de Rafael.

4. E1: ¿Qué es?
   E2: Es un diario.
   E1: ¿De quién es?
   E2: Es de Marisa.

TEACHING OPTIONS

Video Replay the *Fotonovela*, having students focus on subject pronouns and the verb **ser**. Ask them to copy down as many examples of sentences that use forms of **ser** as they can. Stop the video where appropriate to ask comprehension questions on what the characters said.

Heritage Speakers Encourage heritage speakers to describe themselves and their family briefly. Make sure they use the cognates **familia**, **mamá**, and **papá**. Call on students to report the information given. Ex: **Francisco es de la Florida. La mamá de Francisco es de España. Ella es profesora. El papá de Francisco es de Cuba. Él es dentista.**

Comunicación

4 **Preguntas** Using the items in the word bank, ask your partner questions about the ad. Be imaginative in your responses. Answers will vary.

| ¿Quién? | ¿De dónde? | ¿Cuántos? |
| ¿Qué? | ¿De quién? | ¿Cuántas? |

SOMOS ECUATURISTA, S.A.
El autobús nacional del Ecuador

- 25 autobuses en total
- 30 conductores del Ecuador
- pasajeros internacionales
- mapas de las regiones del país

¡Todos a bordo!

5 **¿Quién es?** In small groups, take turns pretending to be a person from Spain, Mexico, Puerto Rico, Cuba, or another Spanish-speaking country who is famous in these professions. Your partners will try to guess who you are. Answers will vary.

| actor *actor* | deportista *athlete* | escritor(a) *writer* |
| actriz *actress* | cantante *singer* | músico/a *musician* |

modelo

Estudiante 3: ¿Eres de Puerto Rico?
Estudiante 1: No. Soy de Colombia.
Estudiante 2: ¿Eres hombre?
Estudiante 1: Sí. Soy hombre.
Estudiante 3: ¿Eres escritor?
Estudiante 1: No. Soy actor.
Estudiante 2: ¿Eres John Leguizamo?
Estudiante 1: ¡Sí! ¡Sí!

NOTA CULTURAL

John Leguizamo was born in Bogotá, Colombia. John is best known for his work as an actor and comedian. He has appeared in movies such as *Moulin Rouge* and *Land of the Dead*. Other Hispanic celebrities: Laura Esquivel (writer from Mexico), Andy García (actor from Cuba), and Don Omar (singer from Puerto Rico).

---

4 Teaching Tip If students ask, explain that the abbreviation **S.A.** in the ad stands for **Sociedad Anónima** and is equivalent to the English abbreviation *Inc.* (*Incorporated*).

4 Expansion Ask pairs to write four true-false statements about the ad. Call on volunteers to read their sentences aloud. The class will indicate whether the statements are true (**cierto**) or false (**falso**) and correct the false statements.

5 Teaching Tips
- To simplify, have students brainstorm a list of names in the categories suggested.
- Have three students read the **modelo** aloud.

TEACHING OPTIONS

Small Groups Bring in personal photos or magazine pictures that show people. In small groups, have students invent stories about the people: who they are, where they are from, and what they do. Circulate around the room and assist with unfamiliar vocabulary as necessary, but encourage students to use terms they already know.

Game Hand out individual strips of paper with names of famous people on them. There should be several duplicates of each name. Then describe one of the famous people (**Es de ____. Es** [*profession*].), including cognate adjectives if you wish (**inteligente**, **pesimista**). The first person to stand and indicate that the name they have is the one you are describing (**¡Yo lo tengo!**) wins that round.

Section Goals

In **Estructura 1.4,** students will be introduced to:
- asking and telling time
- times of day

Instructional Resources
Cuaderno de práctica, pp. 7–8
Cuaderno para hispanohablantes, pp. 11–12
Cuaderno de actividades, pp. 3–4, 92
e-Cuaderno
Supersite: Audio Activity MP3 Audio Files
Supersite/TRCD/Print:
PowerPoints (**Lección 1 Estructura** Presentation, Overhead #11); Communication Activities, Audio Activity Script, Answer Keys
Audio Activity CD

Teaching Tips
- To prepare students for telling time, review **es** and **son** and numbers 0–30.
- Introduce **es la una** and **son las dos (tres, cuatro…).** Remind students that **las** in time constructions refers to **las horas.** Introduce **y cinco (diez, veinte…), y quince/ cuarto,** and **y treinta/media.**
- Show *Overhead PowerPoint #11,* use a paper plate clock, or any other clock where you can quickly move the hands to different positions. Display a number of different times for students to identify. Ask: **¿Qué hora es?** Concentrate on this until students are relatively comfortable with expressing the time in Spanish.
- Introduce **menos diez (cuarto, veinte…)** and explain this method of telling time in Spanish. It typically takes students longer to master this aspect of telling time. Spend about five minutes with your moveable-hands clock and ask students to state the times shown.

 1.4 **Telling time**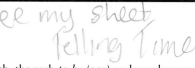

see my sheet Telling Time

ANTE TODO In both English and Spanish, the verb *to be* (**ser**) and numbers are used to tell time.

▶ To ask what time it is, use **¿Qué hora es?** When telling time, use **es + la** with **una** and **son + las** with all other hours.

Es la una.   **Son las** dos.   **Son las** seis.

▶ As in English, you express time from the hour to the half-hour in Spanish by adding minutes.

Son las cuatro **y cinco.**   Son las once **y veinte.**

▶ You may use either **y cuarto** or **y quince** to express fifteen minutes or quarter past the hour. For thirty minutes or half past the hour, you may use either **y media** or **y treinta.**

Es la una **y cuarto.**   Son las doce **y media.**   Son las nueve **y quince.**   Son las siete **y treinta.**

▶ You express time from the half-hour to the hour in Spanish by subtracting minutes or a portion of an hour from the next hour.

Es la una **menos cuarto.**   Son las tres **menos quince.**   Son las ocho **menos veinte.**   Son las tres **menos diez.**

TEACHING OPTIONS

Extra Practice Draw a large clock face on the board with numbers but without hands. Say a time and ask a volunteer to come up to the board and draw the hands to indicate that time. The rest of the class verifies that their classmate has written the correct time. Continue until several volunteers have participated.

Pairs Tell the class **tengo** means *I have.* Have pairs take turns telling each other what time their classes are this semester/ quarter. (Ex: **Tengo una clase a las…**) For each time given, the other student draws a clock face with the corresponding time. The first student verifies the time. To challenge students, give a list of course names (**las matemáticas, la biología,** etc.)

▶ To ask at what time a particular event takes place, use the phrase **¿A qué hora (...)?**
  To state at what time something takes place, use the construction **a la(s)** + *time*.

> **¿A qué hora** es la clase de biología?
> *(At) what time is biology class?*
>
> La clase es **a las dos**.
> *The class is at two o'clock.*
>
> **¿A qué hora** es la fiesta?
> *(At) what time is the party?*
>
> **A las ocho.**
> *At eight.*

▶ Here are some useful words and phrases associated with telling time.

> Son las ocho **en punto**.
> *It's 8 o'clock on the dot/sharp.*
>
> Son las nueve **de la mañana**.
> *It's 9 a.m./in the morning.*
>
> Es **el mediodía**.
> *It's noon.*
>
> Son las cuatro y cuarto **de la tarde**.
> *It's 4:15 p.m./in the afternoon.*
>
> Es **la medianoche**.
> *It's midnight.*
>
> Son las diez y media **de la noche**.
> *It's 10:30 p.m./at night.*

¡LENGUA VIVA!

Other useful expressions for telling time:

Son las doce (del día).
It is twelve o'clock (p.m.).

Son las doce (de la noche).
It is twelve o'clock (a.m.).

Oye, ¿qué hora es?

Son las diez y tres minutos.

Oiga, ¿qué hora es?

Son las diez.

¡INTÉNTALO! Practice telling time by completing these sentences. The first item has been done for you.

1. (1:00 a.m.) Es la _____una_____ de la mañana.
2. (2:50 a.m.) Son las tres _____menos_____ diez de la mañana.
3. (4:15 p.m.) Son las cuatro y _____cuarto/quince_____ de la tarde.
4. (8:30 p.m.) Son las ocho y _____media/treinta_____ de la noche.
5. (9:15 a.m.) Son las nueve y quince de la _____mañana_____.
6. (12:00 p.m.) Es el _____mediodía_____.
7. (6:00 a.m.) Son las seis de la _____mañana_____.
8. (4:05 p.m.) Son las cuatro y cinco de la _____tarde_____.
9. (12:00 a.m.) Es la _____medianoche_____.
10. (3:45 a.m.) Son las cuatro menos _____cuarto/quince_____ de la mañana.
11. (2:15 a.m.) Son las _____dos_____ y cuarto de la mañana.
12. (1:25 p.m.) Es la una y _____veinticinco_____ de la tarde.
13. (6:50 a.m.) Son las _____siete_____ menos diez de la mañana.
14. (10:40 p.m.) Son las once menos veinte de la _____noche_____.

recursos

CP
pp. 7–8

CH
pp. 11–12

CA
pp. 3–4, 92

descubre1.
vhlcentral.com
Lección 1

Teaching Tips
• Review **¿Qué hora es?** and introduce **¿A qué hora?** and make sure students know the difference between them. Ask a few questions to contrast the constructions. Ex: **¿Qué hora es? ¿A qué hora es la clase de español?** Emphasize the difference between the questions by looking at your watch as you ask **¿Qué hora es?** and shrugging your shoulders with a quizzical look when asking **¿A qué hora es?**
• Go over **en punto, mediodía,** and **medianoche.** Explain that **medio/a** means *half.*
• Go over **de la mañana/tarde/noche.** Ask students what time it is now.
• You may wish to explain that Spanish speakers tend to view times of day differently than English speakers do. In many countries, only after someone has eaten lunch does one say **Buenas tardes.** Similarly, with the evening, Spanish speakers tend to view 6:00 and even 7:00 as **de la tarde,** not **de la noche.**

¡Lengua viva! Introduce the Spanish equivalents for noon (**las doce del día**) and midnight (**las doce de la noche**).

TEACHING OPTIONS

Extra Practice Give half of the class slips of paper with clock faces depicting certain times. Give the corresponding times written out in Spanish to the other half of the class. Have students circulate around the room to match their times. To increase difficulty, include duplicates of each time with **de la mañana** or **de la tarde/noche** on the written-out times and a sun or a moon on the clock faces.

Heritage Speakers Ask heritage speakers if they generally tell time as presented in the text or if they use different constructions. Some ways Hispanics use time constructions include (1) forgoing **menos** and using a number from 31–59 and (2) asking the question **¿Qué horas son?** Stress, however, that the constructions presented in the text are the ones students should focus on.

Práctica

1 Ordenar Put these times in order, from the earliest to the latest.

a. Son las dos de la tarde. 4
b. Son las once de la mañana. 2
c. Son las siete y media de la noche. 6
d. Son las seis menos cuarto de la tarde. 5
e. Son las dos menos diez de la tarde. 3
f. Son las ocho y veintidós de la mañana. 1

2 ¿Qué hora es? Give the times shown on each clock or watch.

modelo
Son las cuatro y cuarto/quince de la tarde.

1. Son las doce y media/treinta de la tarde.
2. Es la una de la mañana.
3. Son las cinco y cuarto/quince de la tarde.
4. Son las ocho y diez de la noche.
5. Son las siete y media/treinta de la mañana.

6. Son las once menos cuarto/quince de la mañana.
7. Son las dos y doce de la tarde.
8. Son las siete y cinco de la mañana.
9. Son las cuatro menos cinco de la tarde.
10. Son las doce menos veinticinco de la noche.

3 ¿A qué hora? Ask your partner at what time these events take place. Your partner will answer according to the cues provided.

modelo
la clase de matemáticas (2:30 p.m.)
Estudiante 1: ¿A qué hora es la clase de matemáticas?
Estudiante 2: Es a las dos y media de la tarde.

1. el programa *Las cuatro amigas* (11:30 a.m.)
2. el drama *La casa de Bernarda Alba* (7:00 p.m.)
3. el programa *Las computadoras* (8:30 a.m.)
4. la clase de español (10:30 a.m.)
5. la clase de biología (9:40 a.m.)
6. la clase de historia (10:50 a.m.)
7. el partido (*game*) de béisbol (5:15 p.m.)
8. el partido de tenis (12:45 p.m.)
9. el partido de baloncesto (*basketball*) (7:45 p.m.)

1. E1: ¿A qué hora es el programa *Las cuatro amigas*?
E2: Es a las once y media/treinta de la mañana.
2. E1: ¿A qué hora es el drama *La casa de Bernarda Alba*?
E2: Es a las siete de la noche.
3. E1: ¿A qué hora es el programa *Las computadoras*?
E2: Es a las ocho y media/treinta de la mañana.
4. E1: ¿A qué hora es la clase de español?
E2: Es a las diez y media/treinta de la mañana.
5. E1: ¿A qué hora es la clase de biología?
E2: Es a las diez menos veinte de la mañana.
6. E1: ¿A qué hora es la clase de historia?
E2: Es a las once menos diez de la mañana.
7. E1: ¿A qué hora es el partido de béisbol?
E2: Es a las cinco y cuarto/quince de la tarde.
8. E1: ¿A qué hora es el partido de tenis?
E2: Es a la una menos cuarto/quince de la tarde.
9. E1: ¿A qué hora es el partido de baloncesto?
E2: Es a las ocho menos cuarto/quince de la noche.

Comunicación

4 **En la televisión** With a partner, take turns asking and answering questions about these television listings. Answers will vary.

> **modelo**
>
> **Estudiante 1:** ¿A qué hora es el documental *Las computadoras?*
> **Estudiante 2:** Es a las nueve en punto de la noche.

TV Hoy – Programación

11:00 am	Telenovela: *Cuatro viajeros y un autobús*	**5:00 pm**	Telenovela: *Tres mujeres*
12:00 pm	Película: *El cóndor* (drama)	**6:00 pm**	Noticias
2:00 pm	Telenovela: *Dos mujeres y dos hombres*	**7:00 pm**	Especial musical: *Música folklórica de México*
3:00 pm	Programa juvenil: *Fiesta*	**7:30 pm**	La naturaleza: *Jardín secreto*
3:30 pm	Telenovela: *¡Sí, sí, sí!*	**8:00 pm**	Noticiero: *Veinticuatro horas*
4:00 pm	Telenovela: *El diario de la Sra. González*	**9:00 pm**	Documental: *Las computadoras*

5 **Preguntas** With a partner, answer these questions based on your own knowledge.
Some answers will vary.
1. Son las tres de la tarde en Nueva York. ¿Qué hora es en Los Ángeles?
   Es el mediodía./Son las doce.
2. Son las ocho y media en Chicago. ¿Qué hora es en Miami?
   Son las nueve y media.
3. Son las dos menos cinco en San Francisco. ¿Qué hora es en San Antonio?
   Son las cuatro menos cinco.
4. ¿A qué hora es el programa *60 Minutes*? ¿A qué hora es el programa *Today Show*?
   Es a las siete de la noche. Es a las siete de la mañana.

6 **Más preguntas** Using the questions in the previous activity as a model, make up four questions of your own. Then, get together with a classmate and take turns asking and answering each other's questions.
Answers will vary.

Síntesis

7 **Situación** With a partner, play the roles of a student on the school newspaper interviewing the new Spanish teacher (**profesor(a) de español**) from Venezuela. Be prepared to act out the conversation for your classmates. Answers will vary.

Estudiante	**Profesor(a) de español**
Ask the teacher his/her name.	→ Ask the student his/her name.
Ask the teacher what time his/her Spanish classes are.	→ Ask the student where he/she is from.
Ask how many students are in his/her classes.	→ Ask to whom his/her tape recorder belongs.
Say thank you and goodbye.	→ Say thank you and you are pleased to meet him/her.

Recapitulación

SUPERSITE For self-scoring and diagnostics, go to **descubre1.vhlcentral.com**.

Review the grammar concepts you have learned in this lesson by completing these activities.

1 Completar Complete the charts according to the models. `14 pts.`

MASCULINO	FEMENINO
el chico	la chica
el profesor	la profesora
el amigo	la amiga
el señor	la señora
el pasajero	la pasajera
el estudiante	la estudiante
el turista	la turista
el joven	la joven

SINGULAR	PLURAL
una cosa	unas cosas
un libro	unos libros
una clase	unas clases
una lección	unas lecciones
un conductor	unos conductores
un país	unos países
un lápiz	unos lápices
un problema	unos problemas

2 En la clase Complete each conversation with the correct word. `11 pts.`

César   Beatriz

CÉSAR ¿(1) __Cuántas__ (Cuántos/Cuántas) chicas hay en la (2) __clase__ (maleta/clase)?

BEATRIZ Hay (3) __catorce__ (catorce/cuatro) [14] chicas.

CÉSAR Y, ¿(4) __cuántos__ (cuántos/cuántas) chicos hay?

BEATRIZ Hay (5) __trece__ (tres/trece) [13] chicos.

CÉSAR Entonces (*Then*), en total hay (6) __veintisiete__ (veintiséis/veintisiete) (7) __estudiantes__ (estudiantes/chicas) en la clase.

Ariana   Daniel

ARIANA ¿Tienes (*Do you have*) (8) __un__ (un/una) diccionario?

DANIEL No, pero (*but*) aquí (9) __hay__ (es/hay) uno.

ARIANA ¿De quién (10) __es__ (eres/es)?

DANIEL (11) __Es__ (Soy/Es) de Carlos.

RESUMEN GRAMATICAL

1.1 Nouns and articles *pp. 12–14*

Gender of nouns

Nouns that refer to living things

	Masculine		Feminine
-o	el chico	-a	la chica
-or	el profesor	-ora	la profesora
-ista	el turista	-ista	la turista

Nouns that refer to non-living things

	Masculine		Feminine
-o	el libro	-a	la cosa
-ma	el programa	-ción	la lección
-s	el autobús	-dad	la nacionalidad

Plural of nouns
▶ ending in vowels + *-s*   la chica → las chicas
▶ ending in consonant + *-es*   el señor → los señores
(-z → -ces   un lápiz → unos lápices)
Definite articles: el, la, los, las
Indefinite articles: un, una, unos, unas

1.2 Numbers 0–30 *p. 16*

0	cero	7	siete	14	catorce
1	uno	8	ocho	15	quince
2	dos	9	nueve	16	dieciséis
3	tres	10	diez	17	diecisiete
4	cuatro	11	once	20	veinte
5	cinco	12	doce	21	veintiuno
6	seis	13	trece	22	veintidós
				30	treinta

1.3 Present tense of *ser* *pp. 19–21*

yo	soy	nosotros/as	somos
tú	eres	vosotros/as	sois
Ud./él/ella	es	Uds./ellos/ellas	son

Section Goal
In **Recapitulación**, students will review the grammar concepts from this lesson.

Instructional Resource
Supersite

1 Teaching Tips
• Before beginning the activity, remind students that nouns ending in **-ma** tend to be masculine, despite ending in an **-a**.
• To add an auditory aspect to this activity, read aloud a masculine or feminine noun, then call on individuals to supply the other form. Do the same for plural and singular nouns. Keep a brisk pace.

1 Expansion Have students identify the corresponding definite and indefinite articles in both singular and plural forms for all of the nouns.

2 Teaching Tips
• Have students explain why they chose their answers. Ex: 1. **Cuántas** is feminine and modifies **chicas**.
• Ask students to explain the difference between **¿Tienes un diccionario?** and **¿Tienes el diccionario?** (general versus specific).

2 Expansion
• Ask students to rewrite the dialogue with information from one of their classes.
• Have volunteers ask classmates questions using possessives with **ser**. Ex: —¿De quién es esta mochila? —Es de ella.

TEACHING OPTIONS

Extra Practice To add a visual aspect to this grammar review, bring in pictures from newspapers, magazines, or the Internet of nouns that students have learned. Ask them to identify the people or objects using **ser**. As a variation, ask students questions about the photos, using **hay**. Ex: ¿Cuántos/as _____ hay en la foto?

TPR Give certain times of day and night and ask students to identify who would be awake: **vigilante** (*night watchman*), **estudiante**, or **los dos**. Have students raise their left hand for the **vigilante**, right hand for the **estudiante**, and both hands for **los dos**. Ex: **Son las cinco menos veinte de la mañana.** (left hand) **Es la medianoche.** (both hands)

3 **Presentaciones** Complete this conversation with the correct form of the verb **ser**. `6 pts.`

JUAN ¡Hola! Me llamo Juan. (1) _____Soy_____ estudiante en la clase de español.

DANIELA ¡Hola! Mucho gusto. Yo (2) _____soy_____ Daniela y ella (3) _____es_____ Mónica. ¿De dónde (4) _____eres_____ (tú), Juan?

JUAN De California. Y ustedes, ¿de dónde (5) _____son_____ ?

MÓNICA Nosotras (6) _____somos_____ de Florida.

1.4 | **Telling time** *pp. 24–25*

Es la **una**.	It's 1:00.
Son las **dos**.	It's 2:00.
Son las tres y diez.	It's 3:10.
Es la **una** y cuarto/ quince.	It's 1:15.
Son las siete y media/ treinta.	It's 7:30.
Es la **una** menos cuarto/quince.	It's 12:45.
Son las once menos veinte.	It's 10:40.
Es el mediodía/ la medianoche.	It's noon/ midnight.

---

4 **¿Qué hora es?** Write out in words the following times, indicating whether it's morning, noon, afternoon, or night. `10 pts.`

1. It's 12:00 p.m.
Es el mediodía./Son las doce del día.

2. It's 7:05 a.m.
Son las siete y cinco de la mañana.

3. It's 9:35 p.m.
Son las diez menos veinticinco de la noche.

4. It's 5:15 p.m.
Son las cinco y cuarto/quince de la tarde.

5. It's 1:30 p.m.
Es la una y media/treinta de la tarde.

5 **¡Hola!** Write five sentences introducing yourself and talking about your classes. You may want to include: your name, where you are from, who your Spanish teacher is, the time of your Spanish class, how many students are in the class, etc. `9 pts.` Answers will vary.

_____

_____

_____

_____

6 **Adivinanza** Write the missing words to complete this children's song. `2 EXTRA points!`

" ¿ _____Cuántas_____ patas°
tiene un gato°?
Una, dos, tres y
_____cuatro_____ . "

patas *legs* tiene un gato *does a cat have*

---

3 **Teaching Tip** Before beginning the activity, orally review the conjugation of **ser**.

3 **Expansion** Ask questions about the characters in the dialogue. Ex: **¿Quién es Juan? (Juan es un estudiante en la clase de español.) ¿De dónde es? (Es de California.)**

4 **Teaching Tip** Remind students to make sure they use the correct form of **ser**.

4 **Expansion** To challenge students, give them these times as items 6–10: **(6) It's 3:13 p.m., (7) It's 4:29 a.m., (8) It's 1:04 a.m., (9) It's 10:09 a.m., (10) It's 12:16 a.m.**

5 **Expansion** For further practice with **ser** and **hay**, ask students to share the time and size of their other classes. Be certain to list necessary vocabulary on the board, such as **matemáticas, ciencias, inglés,** and **historia.**

6 **Teaching Tip** Point out the word **Una** in line 3 of the song. To challenge students, have them work in pairs to come up with an explanation for why **Una** is used. (It refers to **pata** [una pata, dos patas...]).

TEACHING OPTIONS

Game Have students make a five-column, five-row chart with B-I-N-G-O written across the top of the columns. Tell them to fill in the squares at random with different times of day. (Remind them to use only full, quarter, or half hours.) Draw times from a hat and call them out in Spanish. The first student to mark five in a row (horizontally, vertically, or diagonally) yells **¡Bingo!** and wins.

Extra Practice Have students imagine they have a new penpal in a Spanish-speaking country. Ask them to write a short e-mail in which they introduce themselves, state where they are from, and give information about their class schedule. (You may want to give students the verb form **tengo** and class subjects vocabulary.) Encourage them to finish the message with questions about their penpal.

Section Goals

In **Lectura**, students will:
• learn to recognize cognates
• use prefixes and suffixes to recognize cognates
• read a telephone list rich in cognates

Instructional Resources
Cuaderno para hispanohablantes, pp. 13–14
Supersite

Estrategia Have students look at the cognates in the **Estrategia** box. Write some of the common suffix correspondences between Spanish and English on the board: **–ción/–sión** = *–tion/ –sion* (**nación, decisión**); **–ante/ –ente** = *–ant/–ent* (**importante, inteligente, elegante**); **–ia/–ía** = *–y* (**farmacia, sociología, historia**); **–dad** = *–ty* (**oportunidad, universidad**).

The Affective Dimension Tell students that reading in Spanish will be less anxiety-provoking if they follow the advice in the **Estrategia** sections, which are designed to reinforce and improve reading comprehension skills.

Examinar el texto Ask students to tell you what type of text **Teléfonos importantes** is and how they can tell. (It is a list and it contains names and telephone numbers.)

Cognados Ask students to mention any cognates they see in the phone list. Discuss the cognates and explain any discrepancies with the list of corresponding suffixes given above. Ex: **policía** = *police*, not *policy*.

Lectura

Antes de leer

Estrategia
Recognizing cognates

As you learned earlier in this lesson, cognates are words that share similar meanings and spellings in two or more languages. When reading in Spanish, it's helpful to look for cognates and use them to guess the meaning of what you're reading. But watch out for false cognates. For example, **librería** means *bookstore*, not *library*, and **embarazada** means *pregnant*, not *embarrassed*. Look at this list of Spanish words, paying special attention to prefixes and suffixes. Can you guess the meaning of each word?

importante	oportunidad
farmacia	cultura
inteligente	activo
dentista	sociología
decisión	**espectacular**
televisión	restaurante
médico	policía

Examinar el texto
Glance quickly at the reading selection and guess what type of document it is. Explain your answer.

Cognados
Read the document and make a list of the cognates you find. Guess their English equivalents, then compare your answers with those of a classmate.

recursos

| CH pp. 13–14 | descubre1.vhlcentral.com Lección 1 |

Teléfonos importantes

Policía

Médico

Dentista

Pediatra

Farmacia

Banco Central

Aerolíneas Nacionales

Cine Metro

Hora/Temperatura

Profesora Salgado (escuela)

Papá (oficina)

Gimnasio Gente Activa

Restaurante Roma

Supermercado Famoso

Librería El Inteligente

TEACHING OPTIONS

Heritage Speakers Ask heritage speakers to model reading and writing the numbers in **Teléfonos importantes**, and to discuss how digits are grouped and punctuated (periods instead of hyphens). For example, 732.5722 may be pronounced by a combination of tens (**siete, treinta y dos, cincuenta y siete, veintidós**) or hundreds and tens (**setecientos treinta y dos, cincuenta y siete, veintidós**).

Extra Practice Write some Spanish words on the board and have students name the English cognate: **democracia, actor, eficiente, nacionalidad, diferencia, guitarrista, artista, doctora, dificultad, exploración.** Then write some words with less obvious cognates: **ciencias, población, número, signo, remedio.**

54.11.11

54.36.92

54.87.11

53.14.57

54.03.06

54.90.83

54.87.40

53.45.96

53.24.81

54.15.33

54.84.99

54.36.04

53.75.44

54.77.23

54.66.04

Después de leer

¿Cierto o falso?

Indicate whether each statement is **cierto** or **falso**.
Then correct the false statements.

1. There is a child in this household.
   Cierto.

2. To renew a prescription you would dial 54.90.83.
   Falso. To renew a prescription you would dial 54.03.06.

3. If you wanted the exact time and information about the weather you'd dial 53.24.81.
   Cierto.

4. Papá probably works outdoors.
   Falso. Papá works in an office.

5. This household probably orders a lot of Chinese food.
   Falso. They probably order a lot of Italian food.

6. If you had a toothache, you would dial 54.87.11.
   Cierto.

7. You would dial 54.87.40 to make a flight reservation.
   Cierto.

8. To find out if a best-selling book were in stock, you would dial 54.66.04.
   Cierto.

9. If you needed information about aerobics classes, you would dial 54.15.33.
   Falso. If you needed information about aerobics classes, you would call Gimnasio Gente Activa at 54.36.04.

10. You would call **Cine Metro** to find out what time a movie starts.
    Cierto.

Números de teléfono

Make your own list of phone numbers like the one shown in this reading. Include emergency phone numbers as well as frequently called numbers. Use as many cognates from the reading as you can.

Section Goals

In **Escritura**, students will:
• learn to write a telephone/address list in Spanish
• integrate lesson vocabulary, including cognates and structures

Instructional Resources
Cuaderno para hispanohablantes, pp. 15–16
Supersite
Cuaderno de actividades, pp. 141–142

Tema Introduce students to standard headings (**Nombre, Teléfono, Dirección electrónica**) used in a telephone/address list. They may wish to add notes pertaining to home (**número de casa**), cellular (**número de celular/móvil**), office (**número de oficina**) phone numbers, or fax numbers (**número de fax**).

The Affective Dimension
Tell the class that they will feel less anxious about writing in a foreign language if they follow the step-by-step advice in the **Estrategia** and **Tema** sections.

Spanish Characters on the Word Processor

Macintosh
á Á, etc.   *opt + e* then *a* or *A*, etc.
ñ Ñ   *opt + n* then *n* or *N*
ü Ü   *opt + u* then *u* or *U*
¿   *opt + shift + ?*
¡   *opt + !*

PC (Windows)
á Á, etc.   *ctrl + '* then *a* or *A*, etc.
ñ Ñ   *ctrl + shift + ~* then *n* or *N*
ü Ü   *ctrl + shift + :* then *u* or *U*
¿   *ctrl + alt + shift + ?*
¡   *ctrl + alt + shift + !*

Escritura

Estrategia
Writing in Spanish

Why do we write? All writing has a purpose. For example, we may write a poem to reveal our innermost feelings, a letter to impart information, or an essay to persuade others to accept a point of view. Proficient writers are not born, however. Writing requires time, thought, effort, and a lot of practice. Here are some tips to help you write more effectively in Spanish.

DO

▸ Try to write your ideas in Spanish

▸ Use the grammar and vocabulary that you know

▸ Use your textbook for examples of style, format, and expression in Spanish

▸ Use your imagination and creativity

▸ Put yourself in your reader's place to determine if your writing is interesting

AVOID

▸ Translating your ideas from English to Spanish

▸ Simply repeating what is in the textbook or on a web page

▸ Using a dictionary until you have learned how to use foreign language dictionaries

recursos

CH pp. 15–16	CA pp. 141–142	descubre1.vhlcentral.com Lección 1

Tema
Hacer una lista

Create a telephone/address list that includes important names, numbers, and websites that will be helpful to you in your study of Spanish. Make whatever entries you can in Spanish without using a dictionary. You might want to include this information:

▸ The names, phone numbers, and e-mail addresses of at least four classmates

▸ Your teacher's name, e-mail address, and phone number

▸ Three phone numbers and e-mail addresses of locations related to your study of Spanish

▸ Five electronic resources for students of Spanish, such as international keypal sites and sites dedicated to the study of Spanish as a second language

Nombre *Sally*
Teléfono *655-8888*
Dirección electrónica *sally@uru.edu*

Nombre *Profesor José Ramón Casas*
Teléfono *655-8090*
Dirección electrónica *jrcasas@uru.edu*

Nombre *Biblioteca* *655-7000*
Dirección electrónica *library@uru.edu*

EVALUATION: Lista

Criteria	Scale
Content	1 2 3 4 5
Organization	1 2 3 4 5
Accuracy	1 2 3 4 5
Creativity	1 2 3 4 5

Scoring	
Excellent	18–20 points
Good	14–17 points
Satisfactory	10–13 points
Unsatisfactory	< 10 points

Escuchar

Estrategia

Listening for words you know

You can get the gist of a conversation by listening for words and phrases you already know.

 To help you practice this strategy, listen to the following sentence and make a list of the words you have already learned.

Preparación

Based on the photograph, what do you think Dr. Cavazos and Srta. Martínez are talking about? How would you get the gist of their conversation, based on what you know about Spanish?

Ahora escucha

Now you are going to hear Dr. Cavazos's conversation with Srta. Martínez. List the familiar words and phrases each person says.

Dr. Cavazos	Srta. Martínez
1. _____	9. _____
2. _____	10. _____
3. _____	11. _____
4. _____	12. _____
5. _____	13. _____
6. _____	14. _____
7. _____	15. _____
8. _____	16. _____

With a classmate, use your lists of familiar words as a guide to come up with a summary of what happened in the conversation.

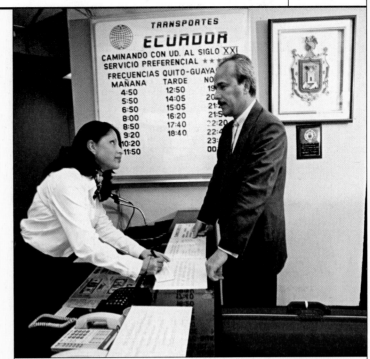

Comprensión

Identificar

Who would say the following things, Dr. Cavazos or Srta. Martínez?

1. Me llamo… Dr. Cavazos
2. De nada. Srta. Martínez
3. Gracias. Muchas gracias. Dr. Cavazos
4. Aquí tiene usted los documentos de viaje, señor. Srta. Martínez
5. Usted tiene tres maletas, ¿no? Srta. Martínez
6. Tengo dos maletas. Dr. Cavazos
7. Hola, señor. Srta. Martínez
8. ¿Viaja usted a Buenos Aires? Srta. Martínez

Contestar

1. Does this scene take place in the morning, afternoon, or evening? How do you know? The scene takes place in the morning, as indicated by **Buenos días.**
2. How many suitcases does Dr. Cavazos have? two
3. Using the words you already know to determine the context, what might the following words and expressions mean?
   - boleto
   - pasaporte
   - un viaje de ida y vuelta
   - ¡Buen viaje!

M: ¿Un viaje de ida y vuelta a Quito?
C: Sí.
M: ¿Cuántas maletas tiene usted? ¿Tres?
C: Dos.

M: Bueno, aquí tiene usted su boleto.
C: Muchas gracias, señorita.
M: No hay de qué, doctor Cavazos. ¡Buen viaje!
C: Gracias. ¡Adiós!

En pantalla

Hispanics form the largest minority group in the United States, and, by the year 2050, one in four Americans will be Hispanic. Viewership of the two major Spanish-language TV stations, **Univisión** and **Telemundo**, has skyrocketed, at times surpassing that of the four major English-language networks. With Hispanic purchasing power estimated at one trillion dollars for 2007, many companies have responded by adapting successful marketing campaigns to target a Spanish-speaking audience. Turn on a Spanish-language channel any night of the week, and you'll see ads for the world's biggest consumer brands, from soft drinks to car makers; many of these advertisements are adaptations of English-language counterparts. Bilingual ads, using English and Spanish in a way that is accessible to all viewers, are also becoming a popular alternative during events such as the Super Bowl, where advertisers want to appeal to a diverse market.

Vocabulario útil	
no tiene precio	*priceless*
naranjas	*oranges*

Emparejar

Match each item with its price according to the ad. **¡Ojo!** (*Careful!*) One of the responses will not be used.

d 1. pelota de cuero
c 2. pelotita de tenis
a 3. un kilo de naranjas

a. tres pesos
b. ocho pesos
c. doce pesos
d. treinta pesos

Un comercial

With a partner, brainstorm and write a MasterCard-like TV ad about something you consider priceless. Then read it to the class. Use as much Spanish as you can. Answers will vary.

pelota *ball* cuero *leather* Que haya *To have* ilusión *hope* después de *after*

Anuncio de MasterCard

Pelota° de cuero°...

Pelotita de tenis...

Que haya° una ilusión° después de° Diego...

recursos
descubre1.vhlcentral.com
Lección 1

SUPERSITE Conexión Internet
Go to descubre1.vhlcentral.com to watch the TV clip featured in this **En pantalla** section.

Oye cómo va

to Puente

[...]esto Antonio Puente (1923–2000) was born
[...] Puerto Rican parents in New York City.
[...]is legendary musician played the vibraphone,
[...]ves, piano, saxophone, and clarinet
[...]raordinarily well, but his specialty was the
[...]bales (*kettledrums*) and, in general, all types
[...] percussion. In the fifties, Tito Puente helped
[...]pularize Afro-Cuban and Caribbean rhythms,
[...]h as mambo, son, and cha-cha-cha, in the
[...]ited States. Later, he also recorded bossa nova,
[...]in jazz, and salsa albums. Throughout his career,
[...]nte won five Grammy awards for his albums
[...] *tributo a Beny Moré*, *On Broadway*, *Mambo*
[...]*blo*, *Goza mi timbal*, and *Mambo Birdland*.

[...]ur instructor will play the song. Listen and then
[...]nplete these activities.

[...]mprensión

[...]icate whether these statements are **cierto** or **falso**.

	Cierto	Falso
Tito Puente was born in Puerto Rico.	○	⊘
Puente helped popularize Afro-Cuban rhythms in the U.S.	⊘	○
His specialty was the saxophone.	○	⊘
Puente won three Grammy awards.	○	⊘
Carlos Santana recorded *Oye cómo va* in 1970.	⊘	○
Tito Puente has never performed with Carlos Santana.	○	⊘

[...]úsica hispana

[...]atch each musical genre with its country of origin.
[...]**jo!** (*Careful!*) One of the countries will not be used.

ranchera	c	a. España
vallenato	g	b. Estados Unidos
flamenco	a	c. México
tango	e	d. Cuba
tex-mex	b	e. Argentina
son	d	f. Guatemala
		g. Colombia

[...]goes　**mi ritmo** *my rhythm*　**pa' gozar** *to enjoy*　**mulata** *(fem.) person of [...]ed ethnic heritage*

Oye cómo va

Oye cómo va° mi ritmo°,
bueno pa' gozar°, mulata°.

Oye cómo va mi ritmo,
bueno pa' gozar, mulata.

La transculturización

Tito Puente's eclectic sound has
transcended generations and
cultures. Rocker Carlos Santana
recorded a best-selling rendition
of *Oye cómo va* in 1970. Seven
years later, Puente and Santana
performed the song together
during a live show.

Carlos Santana

recursos
SUPERSITE
descubre1.vhlcentral.com
Lección 1

Conexión Internet
Go to descubre1.vhlcentral.com to learn
more about the artist featured in this
Oye cómo va section.

Section Goals

In **Oye cómo va**, students will:
• read about **Tito Puente**
• read about **Tito Puente's** influence on **Carlos Santana**
• listen to a song by **Tito Puente**

Instructional Resources
Vista Higher Learning
Cancionero
Supersite

Antes de escuchar
• Ask students if they have heard this song before.
• Have students read the lyrics aloud. Explain that Spanish speakers frequently shorten **para** to **pa'**.
• Some students might assume that the word **mulata** has negative connotations. Explain that, in certain regions and contexts, **mulata** is used in an affectionate way. Here, the singer uses **mulata** to refer to a pretty woman.

Comprensión Have students correct the false statements.

Música hispana Encourage students to use background knowledge to complete this activity and check the answers orally as a class. Then ask students which musical genres are most familiar. Where have they heard this music? Did they enjoy it? What other Latin music do they know?

Section Goal

In **Panorama**, students will read demographic and cultural information about Hispanics in the United States and Canada.

Instructional Resources
Cuaderno de práctica, pp. 9–10
Cuaderno de actividades, pp. 69–70
e-Cuaderno
Supersite/DVD: *Panorama cultural*
Supersite/TRCD/Print: *PowerPoints* (Overhead #12); *Panorama cultural* Videoscript & Translation, Answer Keys

Teaching Tip Have students look at the map of the United States and Canada or show *Overhead PowerPoint #12.* Have volunteers read aloud the labeled cities and geographic features. Model Spanish pronunciation of names as necessary. Have students jot down as many names of places and geographic features with Hispanic origins as they can. Ask volunteers to share their lists with the class.

El país en cifras Have volunteers read the bulleted headings in **El país en cifras**. Point out cognates and clarify unfamiliar words. Explain that numerals in Spanish have a comma where English would use a decimal point (**3,5%**) and have a period where English would use a comma (**12.445.000**). Explain that **EE.UU.** is the abbreviation of **Estados Unidos**, and the doubling of the initial letters indicates plural. Model the pronunciation of **Florida** (accent on the second syllable) and point out that it is often used with an article (**la Florida**) by Spanish speakers.

¡Increíble pero cierto! Assure students that they are not expected to produce numbers greater than 30 at this point. Explain phrases such as **se estima**.

Estados Unidos

El país en cifras°

▶ **Población**° de EE.UU.: 302 millones
▶ **Población de origen hispano:** 43 millones
▶ **País de origen de hispanos en EE.UU.:**

- 19,8% otros
- 3,5% Cuba
- 9,6% Puerto Rico
- 8,6% Centroamérica y Suramérica
- 58,5% México

SOURCE: U.S. Census Bureau

▶ **Estados con la mayor° población hispana:**

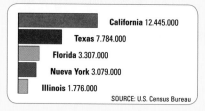

- **California** 12.445.000
- **Texas** 7.784.000
- **Florida** 3.307.000
- **Nueva York** 3.079.000
- **Illinois** 1.776.000

SOURCE: U.S. Census Bureau

Canadá

El país en cifras

▶ **Población de Canadá:** 33 millones
▶ **Población de origen hispano:** 300.000
▶ **País de origen de hispanos en Canadá:**

- 12,4% México
- 11,6% Chile
- 9% El Salvador
- 67% otros

SOURCE: Statistics Canada

▶ **Ciudades° con la mayor población hispana:**
Montreal, Toronto, Vancouver

en cifras *in figures* Población *Population* mayor *largest* Ciudades *Cities* creció *grew* cada *each* niños *children* Se estima *It is estimated* va a ser *it is going to be*

recursos

| CP pp. 9–10 | CA pp. 69–70 | descubre1.vhlcentral.com Lección 1 |

¡Increíble pero cierto!

La población hispana en los EE.UU. creció° un 3.3% entre los años 2004 (dos mil cuatro) y 2005 (dos mil cinco)—1.3 millones de personas más. Hoy, uno de cada° cinco niños° en los EE.UU. es de origen hispano. Se estima° que en el año 2050 va a ser° uno de cada cuatro.

SOURCE: U.S. Census Bureau and The Associated Press

Mission District, en San Francisco

AK   HI

CANADÁ

Vancouver   Calgary

Ottawa ★ ·M
Toronto ·
San Francisco   Chicago ·   Nueva York
Las Vegas   EE.UU.   Washington, D.★
Los Ángeles
San Diego

San Antonio   Océa Atlá

Miami

Golfo de México

MÉXICO   Mar Caribe

El Álamo, en San Antonio, Texas

TEACHING OPTIONS

Heritage Speakers Ask heritage speakers to describe the celebrations that are held in their families' countries of origin. Ask them to tell the date when the celebration takes place, the event it commemorates, and some of the particulars of the celebration. Possible celebrations: **Cinco de Mayo, Día de la Raza, Día de los Muertos, Fiesta de San Juan, Carnaval.**

Game Divide the class into teams of five. Give teams five minutes to brainstorm place names (cities, states, lakes, rivers, mountain ranges) in the United States that have Spanish origins. One team member should jot down the names in a numbered list. After five minutes, go over the names with the class, confirming the accuracy of each name. The team with the greatest number wins.

Comida • La comida mexicana

La comida° mexicana es muy popular en los Estados Unidos. Los tacos, las enchiladas, las quesadillas y los frijoles son platos° mexicanos que frecuentemente forman parte de las comidas de muchos norteamericanos. También° son populares las variaciones de la comida mexicana en los Estados Unidos... el tex-mex y el cali-mex.

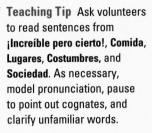

Lugares • La Pequeña Habana

La Pequeña Habana° es un barrio° de Miami, Florida, donde viven° muchos cubanoamericanos. Es un lugar° donde se encuentran° las costumbres° de la cultura cubana, los aromas y sabores° de su comida y la música salsa. La Pequeña Habana es una parte de Cuba en los Estados Unidos.

Costumbres • Desfile puertorriqueño

Cada junio desde° 1951 (mil novecientos cincuenta y uno), los puertorriqueños celebran su cultura con un desfile° en Nueva York. Es un gran espectáculo con carrozas° y música salsa, merengue y hip-hop. Muchos espectadores llevan° la bandera° de Puerto Rico en su ropa° o pintada en la cara°.

Sociedad • La influencia hispánica en Canadá

La presencia hispana en Canadá es importante en la cultura del país. En 1998 (mil novecientos noventa y ocho) se establecieron° los *Latin American Achievement Awards Canada*, para reconocer° los logros° de la comunidad en varios campos°. Dos figuras importantes de origen argentino son Alberto Manguel (novelista) y Sergio Marchi (político°). Osvaldo Núñez es un político de origen chileno. Hay grupos musicales que son parte de la cultura hispana en Canadá: Dominicanada, Bomba, Norteño y Rasca.

 ¿Qué aprendiste? Completa las frases con la información adecuada (*appropriate*).

1. Hay __43 millones__ de personas de origen hispano en los Estados Unidos.

2. Los cuatro estados con las poblaciones hispanas más grandes son (en orden) __California__, Texas, Florida y __Nueva York__.

3. Toronto, Montreal y __Vancouver__ son las tres ciudades con mayor población hispana del Canadá.

4. Las quesadillas y las enchiladas son platos __mexicanos__.

5. La Pequeña __Habana__ es un barrio de Miami.

6. En Miami hay muchas personas de origen __cubano__.

7. Cada junio se celebra en Nueva York un gran desfile para personas de origen __puertorriqueño__.

8. Dominicanada es un __grupo musical__ de Canadá.

 Conexión Internet Investiga estos temas en **descubre1.vhlcentral.com**.

1. Haz (*Make*) una lista de seis hispanos célebres de los EE.UU. o Canadá. Explica (*Explain*) por qué (*why*) son célebres.

2. Escoge (*Choose*) seis lugares en los Estados Unidos con nombres hispanos e investiga sobre el origen y el significado (*meaning*) de cada nombre.

....

comida *food* platos *dishes* También *Also* La Pequeña Habana *Little Havana* barrio *neighborhood* viven *live* lugar *place* se encuentran *are found* costumbres *customs* sabores *flavors* Cada junio desde *Each June since* desfile *parade* con carrozas *with floats* llevan *wear* bandera *flag* ropa *clothing* cara *face* se establecieron *were established* reconocer *to recognize* logros *achievements* campos *fields* político *politician*

Saludos

Hola.	Hello; Hi.
Buenos días.	Good morning.
Buenas tardes.	Good afternoon.
Buenas noches.	Good evening; Good night.

Despedidas

Adiós.	Goodbye.
Nos vemos.	See you.
Hasta luego.	See you later.
Hasta la vista.	See you later.
Hasta pronto.	See you soon.
Hasta mañana.	See you tomorrow.
Saludos a...	Greetings to...
Chau.	Bye.

¿Cómo está?

¿Cómo está usted?	How are you? (form.)
¿Cómo estás?	How are you? (fam.)
¿Qué hay de nuevo?	What's new?
¿Qué pasa?	What's happening?; What's going on?
¿Qué tal?	How are you?; How is it going?
(Muy) bien, gracias.	(Very) well, thanks.
Nada.	Nothing.
No muy bien.	Not very well.
Regular.	So-so; OK.

Expresiones de cortesía

Con permiso.	Pardon me; Excuse me.
De nada.	You're welcome.
Lo siento.	I'm sorry.
(Muchas) gracias.	Thank you (very much); Thanks (a lot).
No hay de qué.	You're welcome.
Perdón.	Pardon me; Excuse me.
por favor	please

Títulos

señor (Sr.); don	Mr.; sir
señora (Sra.); doña	Mrs.; ma'am
señorita (Srta.)	Miss

Presentaciones

¿Cómo se llama usted?	What's your name? (form.)
¿Cómo te llamas (tú)?	What's your name? (fam.)
Me llamo...	My name is...
¿Y tú?	And you? (fam.)
¿Y usted?	And you? (form.)
Mucho gusto.	Pleased to meet you.
El gusto es mío.	The pleasure is mine.
Encantado/a.	Delighted; Pleased to meet you.
Igualmente.	Likewise.
Éste/Ésta es...	This is...
Le presento a...	I would like to introduce (name) to you... (form.)
Te presento a...	I would like to introduce (name) to you... (fam.)
el nombre	name

¿De dónde es?

¿De dónde es usted?	Where are you from? (form.)
¿De dónde eres?	Where are you from? (fam.)
Soy de...	I'm from...

Palabras adicionales

¿cuánto(s)/a(s)?	how much/many?
¿de quién...?	whose...? (sing.)
¿de quiénes...?	whose...? (plural)
(no) hay	there is (not); there are (not)

Países

Ecuador	Ecuador
España	Spain
Estados Unidos (EE.UU.)	United States
México	Mexico
Puerto Rico	Puerto Rico

Verbo

ser	to be

Sustantivos

el autobús	bus
la capital	capital city
el chico	boy
la chica	girl
la computadora	computer
la comunidad	community
el/la conductor(a)	driver
la conversación	conversation
la cosa	thing
el cuaderno	notebook
el día	day
el diario	diary
el diccionario	dictionary
la escuela	school
el/la estudiante	student
la foto(grafía)	photograph
la grabadora	tape recorder
el hombre	man
el/la joven	youth; young person
el lápiz	pencil
la lección	lesson
la maleta	suitcase
la mano	hand
el mapa	map
la mujer	woman
la nacionalidad	nationality
el número	number
el país	country
la palabra	word
el/la pasajero/a	passenger
el problema	problem
el/la profesor(a)	teacher
el programa	program
el/la turista	tourist
el video	video

Numbers 0–30	See page 16.
Telling time	See pages 24–25.
Expresiones útiles	See page 7.

el mundo = the world

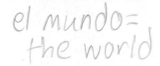

recursos

CA p. 92 | descubre1.vhlcentral.com Lección 1

En la clase

2

Communicative Goals

You will learn how to:

- Talk about your classes and school life
- Discuss everyday activities
- Ask questions in Spanish
- Describe the location of people and things

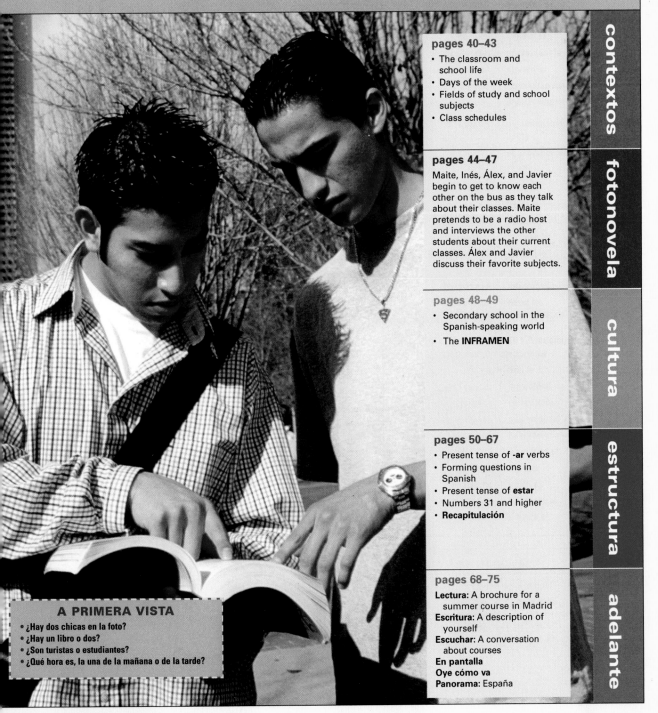

contextos

pages 40–43
- The classroom and school life
- Days of the week
- Fields of study and school subjects
- Class schedules

fotonovela

pages 44–47
Maite, Inés, Álex, and Javier begin to get to know each other on the bus as they talk about their classes. Maite pretends to be a radio host and interviews the other students about their current classes. Álex and Javier discuss their favorite subjects.

cultura

pages 48–49
- Secondary school in the Spanish-speaking world
- The INFRAMEN

estructura

pages 50–67
- Present tense of -ar verbs
- Forming questions in Spanish
- Present tense of estar
- Numbers 31 and higher
- **Recapitulación**

adelante

pages 68–75
Lectura: A brochure for a summer course in Madrid
Escritura: A description of yourself
Escuchar: A conversation about courses
En pantalla
Oye cómo va
Panorama: España

A PRIMERA VISTA
- ¿Hay dos chicas en la foto?
- ¿Hay un libro o dos?
- ¿Son turistas o estudiantes?
- ¿Qué hora es, la una de la mañana o de la tarde?

Lesson Goals

In **Lección 2**, students will be introduced to the following:
- classroom- and school-related words
- names of school courses and fields of study
- class schedules
- days of the week
- secondary school in Latin America
- the **INFRAMEN**, (El Salvador)
- present tense of regular –ar verbs
- forming negative sentences
- the verb **gustar**
- forming questions
- the present tense of **estar**
- prepositions of location
- numbers 31 and higher
- using text formats to predict content
- brainstorming and organizing ideas for writing
- writing descriptions of themselves
- listening for cognates
- a television commercial for **Jumbo**, a Chilean superstore chain
- Spanish singer **Sara Montiel**
- cultural, geographic, and economic information about Spain

A primera vista Have students look at the photo. Say: **Es una foto de dos jóvenes en la escuela.** Then ask: **¿Qué son los jóvenes? (Son estudiantes.) ¿Qué hay en la mano del chico? (Hay un diccionario/libro.)**

INSTRUCTIONAL RESOURCES

Student Materials
Cuaderno de práctica, Cuaderno para hispanohablantes, Cuaderno de actividades
Student MAESTRO™ Supersite
(descubre1.vhlcentral.com)
MAESTRO™ e-Cuaderno

Teacher's Resource CD-ROM and in print
*Answer Keys, Audioscripts, Videoscripts
*PowerPoints
Testing Program (**Pruebas,** Test Generator, MP3 Audio Files)
Vista Higher Learning *Cancionero*
*Also available on Supersite

Teacher's MAESTRO™ Supersite
(descubre1.vhlcentral.com)
Learning Management System (Assignment Task Manager, Gradebook)
Also on DVD
Fotonovela, Flash cultura, Panorama cultural

Section Goals

In **Contextos**, students will learn and practice:
- names for people, places, and things at school
- names of academic courses

Instructional Resources
Cuaderno de práctica, pp. 11–12
Cuaderno para hispanohablantes, pp. 17–18
Cuaderno de actividades, p. 93
e-Cuaderno
Supersite: Textbook, Vocabulary, & Audio Activity MP3 Audio Files
Supersite/TRCD/Print: *PowerPoints* (**Lección 2 Contextos** Presentation, Overhead #13); Textbook Audio Script, Audio Activity Script, Answer Keys
Textbook & Audio Activity CD

Teaching Tips

- Introduce vocabulary for classroom objects such as **mesa, libro, pluma, lápiz, papel**. Hold up or point to an object and say: **Es un lápiz.** Ask questions that include **¿Hay/No hay…?** and **¿Cuántos/as…?**
- Using either objects in the classroom or *Overhead PowerPoint #13,* point to items and ask questions such as: **¿Qué es? ¿Es una mesa? ¿Es un reloj?** Vary by asking: **¿Qué hay en el escritorio? ¿Qué hay en la mesa? ¿Cuántas tizas hay en la pizarra? ¿Hay una pluma en el escritorio de ____?**

Successful Language Learning Encourage students to make flash cards to help them memorize new vocabulary words.

En la clase (class)

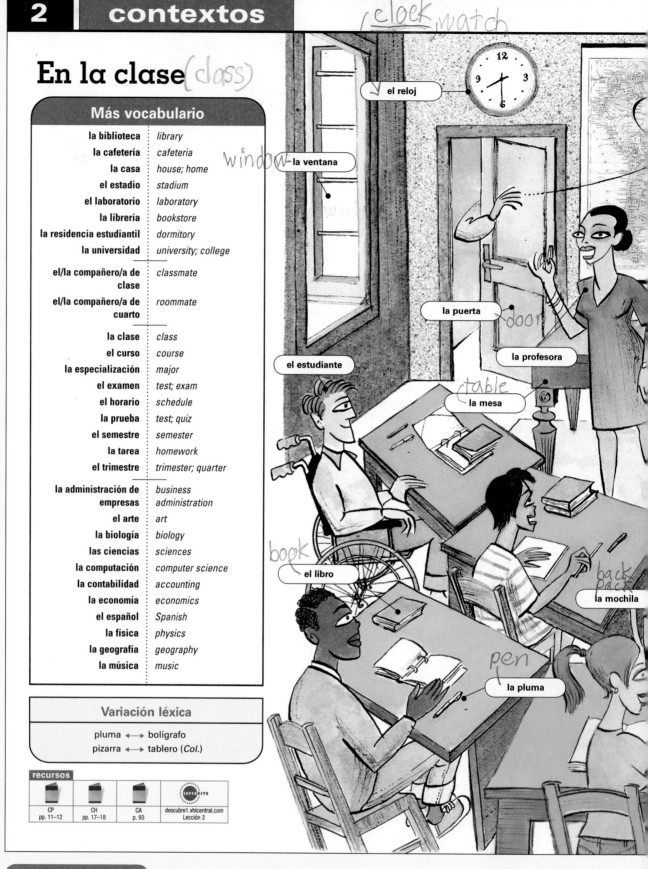

Más vocabulario

la biblioteca	*library*
la cafetería	*cafeteria*
la casa	*house; home*
el estadio	*stadium*
el laboratorio	*laboratory*
la librería	*bookstore*
la residencia estudiantil	*dormitory*
la universidad	*university; college*
el/la compañero/a de clase	*classmate*
el/la compañero/a de cuarto	*roommate*
la clase	*class*
el curso	*course*
la especialización	*major*
el examen	*test; exam*
el horario	*schedule*
la prueba	*test; quiz*
el semestre	*semester*
la tarea	*homework*
el trimestre	*trimester; quarter*
la administración de empresas	*business administration*
el arte	*art*
la biología	*biology*
las ciencias	*sciences*
la computación	*computer science*
la contabilidad	*accounting*
la economía	*economics*
el español	*Spanish*
la física	*physics*
la geografía	*geography*
la música	*music*

Variación léxica

pluma ⟷ bolígrafo
pizarra ⟷ tablero (*Col.*)

recursos

CP pp. 11–12	CH pp. 17–18	CA p. 93	SUPERSITE descubre1.vhlcentral.com Lección 2

TEACHING OPTIONS

Variación léxica Ask heritage speakers to tell the class any other terms they or their families use to talk about people, places, or things at school. Ask them to tell where these terms are used. Possible responses: **el boli, el profe, el profesorado, la asignatura, el gimnasio, el pizarrón, el salón de clases, el aula, el pupitre, el gis, el alumno.**

Game Divide the class into two teams. Then, in English, name an academic course and ask one of the teams to provide the Spanish equivalent. If the team provides the correct term, it gets a point. If not, the second team gets a chance at the same item. Alternate between teams until you have read all the course names. The team with the most points at the end wins.

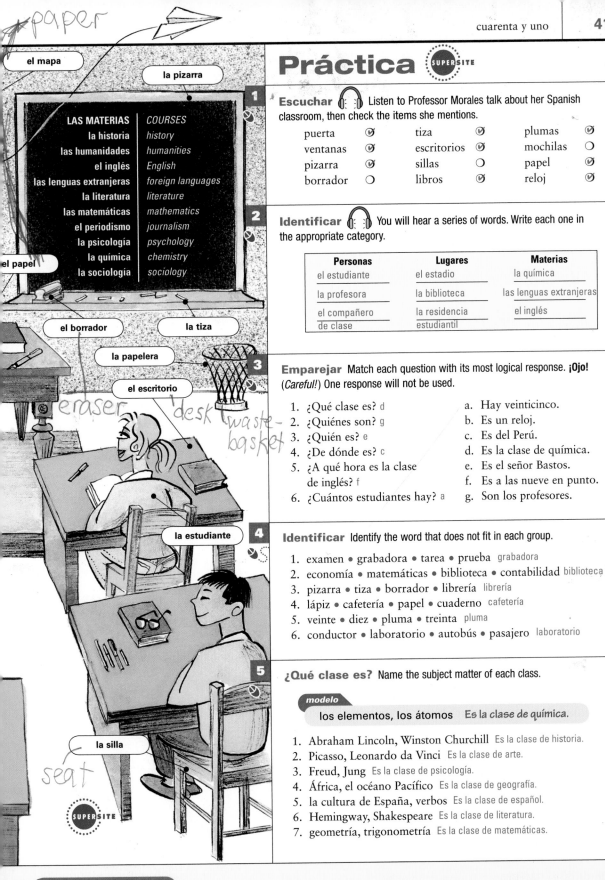

paper

el mapa

la pizarra

LAS MATERIAS	COURSES
la historia	history
las humanidades	humanities
el inglés	English
las lenguas extranjeras	foreign languages
la literatura	literature
las matemáticas	mathematics
el periodismo	journalism
la psicología	psychology
la química	chemistry
la sociología	sociology

el papel

el borrador

la tiza

la papelera

el escritorio

eraser   *desk*   *waste-basket*

la estudiante

la silla

seat

SUPERSITE

Práctica   SUPERSITE

1 **Escuchar** 🎧 Listen to Professor Morales talk about her Spanish classroom, then check the items she mentions.

puerta	☑	tiza	☑	plumas	☑
ventanas	☑	escritorios	☑	mochilas	☐
pizarra	☑	sillas	☐	papel	☑
borrador	☐	libros	☑	reloj	☑

2 **Identificar** 🎧 You will hear a series of words. Write each one in the appropriate category.

Personas	Lugares	Materias
el estudiante	el estadio	la química
la profesora	la biblioteca	las lenguas extranjeras
el compañero de clase	la residencia estudiantil	el inglés

3 **Emparejar** Match each question with its most logical response. ¡Ojo! (*Careful!*) One response will not be used.

1. ¿Qué clase es? d
2. ¿Quiénes son? g
3. ¿Quién es? e
4. ¿De dónde es? c
5. ¿A qué hora es la clase de inglés? f
6. ¿Cuántos estudiantes hay? a

a. Hay veinticinco.
b. Es un reloj.
c. Es del Perú.
d. Es la clase de química.
e. Es el señor Bastos.
f. Es a las nueve en punto.
g. Son los profesores.

4 **Identificar** Identify the word that does not fit in each group.

1. examen • grabadora • tarea • prueba   grabadora
2. economía • matemáticas • biblioteca • contabilidad   biblioteca
3. pizarra • tiza • borrador • librería   librería
4. lápiz • cafetería • papel • cuaderno   cafetería
5. veinte • diez • pluma • treinta   pluma
6. conductor • laboratorio • autobús • pasajero   laboratorio

5 **¿Qué clase es?** Name the subject matter of each class.

> **modelo**
> los elementos, los átomos   Es la clase de química.

1. Abraham Lincoln, Winston Churchill   Es la clase de historia.
2. Picasso, Leonardo da Vinci   Es la clase de arte.
3. Freud, Jung   Es la clase de psicología.
4. África, el océano Pacífico   Es la clase de geografía.
5. la cultura de España, verbos   Es la clase de español.
6. Hemingway, Shakespeare   Es la clase de literatura.
7. geometría, trigonometría   Es la clase de matemáticas.

SUPERSITE

1 **Teaching Tip** Have students check their answers by going over **Actividad 1** as a class.

1 **Script** ¿Qué hay en mi clase de español? ¡Muchas cosas! Hay una puerta y cinco ventanas. Hay una pizarra con tiza. Hay muchos escritorios para los estudiantes. En los escritorios de los estudiantes hay libros y plumas. En la mesa de la profesora hay papel. Hay un mapa y un reloj en la clase también.
Textbook Audio

2 **Teaching Tip** To simplify, have students prepare for listening by predicting a few words for each category.

2 **Script** el estudiante, la química, el estadio, las lenguas extranjeras, la profesora, la biblioteca, el inglés, el compañero de clase, la residencia estudiantil
Textbook Audio

3 **Expansion** Have student pairs ask each other the questions and answer based on your class. Ex: **1. ¿Qué clase es? (Es la clase de español.)** For items 2–4, the questioner should indicate specific people in the classroom.

4 **Expansion** Give students these word groups as items 7–9:
7. humanidades, mesa, ciencias, lenguas extranjeras (mesa)
8. papelera, casa, residencia estudiantil, biblioteca (papelera)
9. pluma, lápiz, silla, tiza (silla)

5 **Expansion** Have the class associate famous people with these fields: **periodismo, computación, humanidades**. Then have them guess the field associated with these people: Albert Einstein (**física**), Charles Darwin (**biología**).

TEACHING OPTIONS

Extra Practice Ask students what phrases or vocabulary words they associate with these items: **1. la pizarra** (Ex: **la tiza, el borrador**), **2. las ciencias** (Ex: **la biología, la física, la química, el laboratorio**), **3. el reloj** (Ex: **¿Qué hora es?, Son las…, Es la…**), **4. la biblioteca** (Ex: **los libros, los exámenes, las materias**).

Extra Practice On the board, write **¿Qué clases tomas?** and **Tomo…** Explain the meaning of these phrases and ask students to circulate around the classroom and imagine that they are meeting their classmates for the first time. Tell them to introduce themselves, find out where each person is from, and what classes they are taking. Follow up by asking individual students what their classmates are taking.

Teaching Tips
• Review the captions, explaining their meaning as you do so.

Los días de la semana

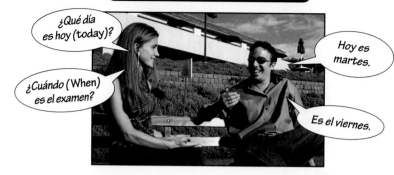

¿Qué día es hoy (today)?

Hoy es martes.

¿Cuándo (When) es el examen?

Es el viernes.

septiembre

lunes	martes	miércoles	jueves	viernes	sábado	domingo
	1	2	3	4	5	6
7	8	9	10			

6 Expansion To challenge students, ask them questions such as: **Mañana es viernes... ¿qué día fue ayer? (miércoles); Ayer fue domingo... ¿qué día es mañana? (martes)**

6 **¿Qué día es hoy?** Complete each statement with the correct day of the week.

1. Hoy es martes. Mañana es ___miércoles___. Ayer fue (*Yesterday was*) ___lunes___.
2. Ayer fue sábado. Mañana es ___lunes___. Hoy es ___domingo___.
3. Mañana es viernes. Hoy es ___jueves___. Ayer fue ___miércoles___.
4. Ayer fue domingo. Hoy es ___lunes___. Mañana es ___martes___.
5. Hoy es jueves. Ayer fue ___miércoles___. Mañana es ___viernes___.
6. Mañana es lunes. Hoy es ___domingo___. Ayer fue ___sábado___.

7 Teaching Tip To simplify, before doing this activity, have students review the list of **sustantivos** on page 38 and numbers 0–30 on page 16.

7 **Analogías** Use these words to complete the analogies. Some words will not be used.

arte	día	martes	pizarra
biblioteca	domingo	matemáticas	profesor
catorce	estudiante	mujer	reloj

1. maleta ⟷ pasajero ⊜ mochila ⟷ ___estudiante___
2. chico ⟷ chica ⊜ hombre ⟷ ___mujer___
3. pluma ⟷ papel ⊜ tiza ⟷ ___pizarra___
4. inglés ⟷ lengua ⊜ miércoles ⟷ ___día___
5. papel ⟷ cuaderno ⊜ libro ⟷ ___biblioteca___
6. quince ⟷ dieciséis ⊜ lunes ⟷ ___martes___
7. Cervantes ⟷ literatura ⊜ Dalí ⟷ ___arte___
8. autobús ⟷ conductor ⊜ clase ⟷ ___profesor___
9. los EE.UU. ⟷ mapa ⊜ hora ⟷ ___reloj___
10. veinte ⟷ veintitrés ⊜ jueves ⟷ ___domingo___

TEACHING OPTIONS

Extra Practice Have students prepare a day-planner for the upcoming week. Tell them to list each day of the week and the things they expect to do each day, including classes, homework, tests, appointments, and social events. Provide unfamiliar vocabulary as needed. Tell them to include the time each activity takes place. Have them exchange their day-planners with a partner and check each other's work for accuracy.

Game Have groups of five or six play a "word-chain" game in which the first group member says a word in Spanish (e.g., **estudiante**). The next student has to say a word that begins with the last letter of the first person's word (e.g., **español**). If a student cannot think of a word, he or she is eliminated and it is the next student's turn. The last student left in the game is the winner.

Comunicación

8 **Horario** Choose three classes to create your own class schedule, then discuss it with a classmate. Answers will vary.

materia	hora	días	profesor(a)
inglés	9:50	lunes, miércoles, viernes	Ordóñez
historia	9–10:30	martes, jueves	Dávila
biología	1:30–3	martes, jueves	Quiñones
matemáticas	2:10–3:00	lunes, miércoles, viernes	Jiménez
arte	10:40–12:10	jueves	Molina

¡ATENCIÓN!

Use **el** + [*day of the week*] when an activity occurs on a specific day and **los** + [*day of the week*] when an activity occurs regularly.

El lunes tengo un examen.
On Monday I have an exam.

Los lunes y miércoles tomo biología.
On Mondays and Wednesdays I take biology.

• • •

Except for **sábados** and **domingos**, the singular and plural forms for days of the week are the same.

modelo

Estudiante 1: Tomo (*I take*) historia los martes y jueves con (*with*) la profesora Dávila.
Estudiante 2: ¿Sí? Yo no tomo historia. Yo tomo arte los jueves con el profesor Molina.

9 **La clase** First, look around your classroom to get a mental image, then close your eyes. Your partner will then use these words or other vocabulary to ask you questions about the classroom. After you have answered six questions, switch roles. Answers will vary.

modelo

Estudiante 1: ¿Cuántas ventanas hay?
Estudiante 2: Hay cuatro ventanas.

escritorio	mochila	puerta
estudiante	pizarra	reloj
libro	profesor(a)	silla

10 **Nuevos amigos** During the first week of class, you meet a new student in the cafeteria. With a partner, prepare a conversation using these cues. Answers will vary.

Estudiante 1

Greet your new acquaintance.
Find out about him or her.
Ask about your partner's class schedule.
Say nice to meet you and goodbye.

Estudiante 2

→ Introduce yourself.
→ Tell him or her about yourself.
→ Compare your schedule to your partner's.
→ Say nice to meet you and goodbye.

---

8 **Expansion** Tell students to write their name at the top of their schedules and have pairs exchange papers with another pair. Then have them repeat the activity with the new schedules, asking and answering questions in the third person. Ex: —**¿Qué clases toma ____?** —**Los martes y jueves ____ toma biología con la profesora Quiñones.**

Successful Language Learning Remind the class that errors are a natural part of language learning. Point out that it is impossible to speak "perfectly" in any language. Emphasize that their spoken and written Spanish will improve if they make the effort to practice.

10 **Teaching Tip** To simplify, quickly review the basic greetings, courtesy expressions, and introductions taught in **Lección 1, Contextos**, pages 2–3.

10 **Expansion** Ask volunteers to introduce their new acquaintances to the class.

TEACHING OPTIONS

Groups Have students do **Actividad 10** in groups, imagining that they meet several new students in the cafeteria. Have the groups present this activity as a skit for the class. Give the groups time to prepare and rehearse, and tell them that they will be presenting it without a script or any other kind of notes.

Game Point out the **modelo** in **Actividad 8**. Have students write a few simple sentences that describe their course schedules. Ex: **Los lunes, miércoles y viernes tomo español con la profesora Morales. Los martes y jueves tomo arte con el profesor Casas.** Then collect the descriptions, shuffle them, and read them aloud. The class should guess who wrote each description.

¿Qué clases tomas?

Maite, Inés, Javier y Álex hablan de las clases.

Section Goals

In **Fotonovela**, students will:
- receive comprehensible input from free-flowing discourse
- learn functional phrases that preview lesson grammatical structures

Instructional Resources
Cuaderno de actividades,
pp. 53–54
e-Cuaderno
Supersite/DVD: *Fotonovela*
Supersite/TRCD/Print:
Fotonovela Videoscript & Translation, Answer Keys

Video Recap: Lección 1
Before doing this **Fotonovela** section, review the previous episode with this activity.
1. ¿Quiénes son Maite, Inés, Javier y Álex? (estudiantes/pasajeros/turistas) 2. ¿Cómo se llama el conductor? (don Francisco) 3. ¿Quiénes son del Ecuador? (don Francisco e Inés) 4. ¿De dónde es Maite? (España) ¿Y Álex? (México) ¿Y Javier? (Puerto Rico)

Video Synopsis While **Álex** writes an e-mail, **Maite** pretends to be a radio reporter and asks **Inés** and **Javier** a few questions about school. **Álex** is shocked that **Javier** does not like computers.

Teaching Tips
- Have students cover the **Expresiones útiles**. Then have them scan the captions under the video stills and find two phrases about classes and two phrases that express likes and dislikes.
- Ask a few basic questions that use the **Expresiones útiles**. Ex: **¿Qué clases tomas? ¿Te gusta la clase de _____?**

PERSONAJES

MAITE

INÉS

ÁLEX

JAVIER

ÁLEX Hola, Ricardo... Aquí estamos en la Mitad del Mundo. ¿Qué tal las clases en la UNAM?

MAITE Es exactamente como las fotos en los libros de geografía.

INÉS ¡Sí! ¿También tomas tú geografía?

MAITE Yo no. Yo tomo inglés y literatura. También tomo una clase de periodismo.

MAITE Muy buenos días. María Teresa Fuentes, de Radio Andina FM 93. Hoy estoy con estudiantes de la Universidad San Francisco de Quito. ¡A ver! La señorita que está cerca de la ventana... ¿Cómo te llamas y de dónde eres?

MAITE ¿En qué clase hay más chicos?

INÉS Bueno, eh... en la clase de historia.

MAITE ¿Y más chicas?

INÉS En la de sociología hay más chicas, casi un ochenta y cinco por ciento.

MAITE Y tú, joven, ¿cómo te llamas y de dónde eres?

JAVIER Me llamo Javier Gómez y soy de San Juan, Puerto Rico.

MAITE ¿Tomas muchas clases este semestre?

JAVIER Sí, tomo tres: historia y arte los lunes, miércoles y viernes y computación los martes y jueves.

MAITE ¿Te gustan las computadoras, Javier?

JAVIER No me gustan nada. Me gusta mucho más el arte... y sobre todo me gusta dibujar.

ÁLEX ¿Cómo que no? ¿No te gustan las computadoras?

recursos

CA pp. 53–54

descubre1.vhlcentral.com Lección 2

TEACHING OPTIONS

¿Qué clases tomas? Play the **¿Qué clases tomas?** segment of the *Fotonovela* and have students give you a "play-by-play" description of the action. Write their descriptions on the board. After playing the segment, give the class a moment to read the descriptions you have written on the board. Then play the

segment a second time so that students can add more details to the descriptions or consolidate information. Finally, discuss the material on the board with the class and call attention to any incorrect information. Help students prepare a brief plot summary.

INÉS Hola. Me llamo Inés Ayala Loor y soy del Ecuador... de Portoviejo.

MAITE Encantada. ¿Qué clases tomas en la universidad?

INÉS Tomo geografía, inglés, historia, sociología y arte.

MAITE Tomas muchas clases, ¿no?

INÉS Pues sí, me gusta estudiar mucho.

ÁLEX Pero si son muy interesantes, hombre.

JAVIER Sí, ¡muy interesantes!

Expresiones útiles

Talking about classes

- **¿Qué tal las clases en la UNAM?**
  How are classes going at UNAM?
- **¿También tomas tú geografía?**
  Are you also taking geography?
  No, tomo inglés y literatura.
  No, I'm taking English and literature.

- **Tomas muchas clases, ¿no?**
  You're taking lots of classes, aren't you?
  Pues sí. *Well, yes.*

- **¿En qué clase hay más chicos?**
  In which class are there more guys?
  En la clase de historia.
  In history class.

Talking about likes/dislikes

- **¿Te gusta estudiar?**
  Do you like to study?
  Sí, me gusta mucho. Pero también me gusta mirar la televisión.
  Yes, I like it a lot. But I also like to watch television.
- **¿Te gusta la clase de sociología?**
  Do you like sociology class?
  Sí, me gusta muchísimo.
  Yes, I like it very much.
- **¿Te gustan las computadoras?**
  Do you like computers?
  No, no me gustan nada.
  No, I don't like them at all.

Talking about location

- **Aquí estamos en...**
  Here we are at/in...
- **¿Dónde está la señorita?**
  Where is the young woman?
  Está cerca de la ventana.
  She's near the window.

Expressing hesitation

- **A ver...**
  Let's see...
- **Bueno...**
  Well...

Teaching Tip Have the class read through the entire **Fotonovela**, with volunteers playing the parts of **Álex, Maite, Inés,** and **Javier.**

Expresiones útiles Identify forms of **tomar** and **estar**. Point out question-forming devices and the accent marks over question words. Tell students that they will learn more about these concepts in **Estructura**. Point out that **gusta** is used when what is liked is singular, and **gustan** when what is liked is plural. A detailed discussion of the **gustar** construction (see **Estructura 2.1**, page 52) is unnecessary here.

TEACHING OPTIONS

Extra Practice Have students scan the captions and make a list of the **gustar** constructions. Then ask students to identify the phrases that best describe themselves. Repeat the exercise with the verb **tomar**.

Pairs Ask pairs to write five true-false statements based on the **¿Qué clases tomas?** captions. Then have them exchange papers with another pair, who will complete the activity and correct the false statements. Ask volunteers to read a few statements for the class, who will answer and point out the caption that contains the information.

¿Qué pasó? SUPERSITE

1 Escoger Choose the answer that best completes each sentence.

1. Maite toma (*is taking*) ___c___ en la universidad.
   a. geografía, inglés y periodismo   b. economía, periodismo y literatura
   c. periodismo, inglés y literatura

2. Inés toma sociología, geografía, ___a___.
   a. inglés, historia y arte   b. periodismo, computación y arte
   c. historia, literatura y biología

3. Javier toma ___b___ clases este semestre.
   a. cuatro   b. tres   c. dos

4. Javier toma historia y ___c___ los ___c___.
   a. computación; martes y jueves   b. arte; lunes, martes y miércoles
   c. arte; lunes, miércoles y viernes

2 Identificar Indicate which person would make each statement. The names may be used more than once.

1. Sí, me gusta estudiar. Inés
2. ¡Hola! ¿Te gustan las clases en la UNAM? Álex
3. ¿La clase de periodismo? Sí, me gusta mucho. Maite
4. Hay más chicas en la clase de sociología. Inés
5. Buenos días. Yo soy de Radio Andina FM 93. Maite
6. ¡Uf! ¡No me gustan las computadoras! Javier
7. Las computadoras son muy interesantes. Álex
8. Me gusta dibujar en la clase de arte. Javier

INÉS

JAVIER   MAITE

ÁLEX

3 Completar These sentences are similar to things said in the **Fotonovela**. Complete each sentence with the correct word(s).

la sociología	el arte	la Universidad San Francisco de Quito
la clase de historia	geografía	la Mitad del Mundo

1. Maite, Javier, Inés y yo estamos en... la Mitad del Mundo
2. Hay fotos impresionantes de la Mitad del Mundo en los libros de... geografía
3. Me llamo Maite. Estoy aquí con estudiantes de... la Universidad San Francisco de Quito
4. Hay muchos chicos en... la clase de historia
5. No me gustan las computadoras. Me gusta más... el arte

NOTA CULTURAL

In the **Fotonovela**, Álex, Maite, Javier, and Inés visit **la Mitad del Mundo** (*Midpoint of the World*), a monument north of Quito, Ecuador. It marks the line at which the equator divides the Earth's northern and southern hemispheres.

4 Preguntas personales Interview a classmate about his/her classes. Answers will vary.

1. ¿Cuántas clases tomas?
2. ¿Qué clases tomas los martes?
3. ¿Qué clases tomas los viernes?
4. ¿En qué clase hay más chicos?
5. ¿En qué clase hay más chicas?
6. ¿Te gusta la clase de español?

NATIONAL communication STANDARDS

TEACHING OPTIONS

Small Groups Have students work in small groups to create a skit in which a radio reporter asks local students where they are from, which classes they are taking, and which classes they like. Encourage students to use the phrases in **Expresiones útiles** as much as possible. Have one or two groups role-play their skit for the class.

Extra Practice Have students close their books and complete these statements with information from the **Fotonovela**. You may present the sentences orally or write them on the board. **1. Hoy estoy con dos _____ de la Universidad San Francisco de Quito. (estudiantes) 2. ¿En qué _____ hay más chicos? (clase) 3. ¿_____ te llamas y de _____ eres? (Cómo; dónde)**

Pronunciación
Spanish vowels

a **e** **i** **o** **u**

Spanish vowels are never silent; they are always pronounced in a short, crisp way without the glide sounds used in English.

Álex	**clase**	**nada**	**encantada**

The letter **a** is pronounced like the *a* in *father*, but shorter.

el	**ene**	**mesa**	**elefante**

The letter **e** is pronounced like the *e* in *they*, but shorter.

Inés	**chica**	**tiza**	**señorita**

The letter **i** sounds like the *ee* in *beet*, but shorter.

hola	**con**	**libro**	**don Francisco**

The letter **o** is pronounced like the *o* in *tone*, but shorter.

uno	**regular**	**saludos**	**gusto**

The letter **u** sounds like the *oo* in *room*, but shorter.

Práctica Practice the vowels by saying the names of these places in Spain.

Oraciones Read the sentences aloud, focusing on the vowels.

1. Hola. Me llamo Ramiro Morgado.
2. Estudio arte en la Universidad de Salamanca.
3. Tomo también literatura y contabilidad.
4. Ay, tengo clase en cinco minutos. ¡Nos vemos!

Refranes Practice the vowels by reading these sayings aloud.

AYUDA

Although **ay** and **hay** are pronounced identically, they do not have the same meaning. **¡Ay!** is an exclamation expressing pain, shock, or affliction: *Oh, dear; Woe is me!* As you learned in **Lección 1, hay** is a verb form that means *there is/are.* **Hay veinte libros.** (*There are twenty books.*)

Cada loco con su tema.²

Del dicho al hecho hay un gran trecho.¹

¹ Easier said than done. ² To each his own.

recursos		
CH p. 19	CA p. 94	descubre1.vhlcentral.com Lección 2

Section Goal

In **Pronunciación**, students will be introduced to Spanish vowels and how they are pronounced.

Instructional Resources
Cuaderno para hispanohablantes, p. 19
Cuaderno de actividades, p. 94
e-Cuaderno
Supersite: Textbook & Audio Activity MP3 Audio Files
Supersite/TRCD/Print: Textbook Audio Script; Audio Activity Script, Answer Keys
Textbook & Audio Activity CD

Teaching Tips
- Point out that the drawings above the vowels on this page indicate the approximate position of the mouth as the vowels are pronounced.
- Model the pronunciation of each vowel and have students watch the shape of your mouth. Have them repeat the vowel after you. Then go through the example words.
- To practice pure vowel sounds, teach students this chant: **A-E-I-O-U, ¡el burro sabe más que tú!**
- Pronounce a few of the example words and have the students write them on the board with their books closed.

Práctica/Oraciones/Refranes
These exercises are recorded in the *Textbook Audio*. You may want to play the audio so that students practice the pronunciation point by listening to Spanish spoken by speakers other than yourself.

TEACHING OPTIONS

Extra Practice Provide additional names of places in Spain. Have students spell each name aloud in Spanish, then ask them to pronounce each one. Avoid names that contain diphthongs. Ex: **Sevilla, Salamanca, Santander, Albacete, Gerona, Lugo, Badajoz, Tarragona, Logroño, Valladolid, Orense, Pamplona, Ibiza.**

Small Groups Have the class turn to the **Fotonovela,** pages 44–45, and work in groups of four to read all or part of the **Fotonovela** aloud, focusing on the correct pronunciation of the vowels. Circulate among the groups and, as needed, model the correct pronunciation and intonation of words and phrases.

Section Goals

In **Cultura**, students will:

• learn about high schools in different Spanish-speaking countries

• learn how Mexican students choose their program of study to determine their career or university-level studies

• read about the **Instituto Nacional Franscico Menéndez**

• read about Latin American school systems

Instructional Resources
Cuaderno para hispanohablantes, p. 20
Supersite/DVD: *Flash cultura*
Supersite/TRCD: *Flash cultura*
Videoscript & Translation

En detalle

Antes de leer Ask students about how they choose their classes, including how they decided to take Spanish. Did family, friends, or guidance counselors influence their choices? What types of courses do they plan to take in future years, and why?

Lectura

• Explain that students often choose their high school based on the programs that are offered.

• High school studies and the programs of study offered vary greatly from country to country.

• In Mexico, **preparatoria** is optional, but all students are legally required to finish **escuela secundaria**.

Después de leer Ask students what they think of the Mexican school system and how it differs from that of the U.S.

1 Expansion Give students these sentences as items 9–10:
9. Students in Mexico take courses in foreign languages every year. (**Cierto.**) 10. Students enrolled in **Ciencias Biológicas** are not expected to continue studying. (**Falso.** They usually plan to continue their studies in a university.)

La escuela secundaria

Manuel, a 15-year-old student in Mexico, is taking an intense third level course focused on **la química** (*chemistry*). This is a typical part of the studies for his grade. **Escuela secundaria** (*secondary school*), which in Mexico begins after six years of **escuela primaria** (*primary school*), has three grades for students between the ages of 12 and 15.

Students like Manuel must study courses in mathematics, science, Spanish, foreign languages (English or French), music, and more every

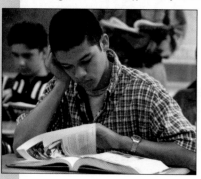

year. After that, students choose a **plan de estudio** (*program of study*) in **preparatoria,** the three years (or two, depending on the program) of school after escuela secundaria and before university studies. The program of study that students choose requires them to study specific **materias** (*subjects*) that are needed in preparation for their future career.

Some **bachilleratos** (*high school degrees*) are **terminales,** which means that when students graduate they are prepared with all of the skills and requirements to begin their field of work.

These students are not expected to continue studying. Some **modalidades** (*programs of study*) that are terminal include:

• **Educación Tecnológica Agropecuaria** (*Agriculture and Fishing*)

• **Comercio y Administración** (*Commerce,* for administrative work)

Other programs are designed for students who plan to continue their studies in a **carrera universitaria** (*college major*). Some programs that prepare students for university studies are:

• **Ciencias Biológicas**

• **Ciencias Contables Económicas y Bancarias** (*Economic and Banking Sciences*)

• **Música y Arte**

Each program has courses that are designed for a specific career. This means that although all high school students may take a mathematics course, the type of mathematics studied varies according to the needs of each degree.

La escuela y la universidad

Some Mexican high schools are designed and managed by universities as well as by the Secretary of Education. One university that directs such schools is the **Universidad Autónoma de México,** Mexico's largest university.

ACTIVIDADES

1 **¿Cierto o falso?** Indicate whether each statement is cierto or falso. Correct the false statements.

1. High schools are specialized in certain areas of study. Cierto.

2. Students in Mexico cannot study art in school. Falso. Música y arte is a **preparatoria** program of study.

3. Students do not need to complete primary school before going to escuela secundaria. Falso. Students must complete primary school as a prerequisite for **escuela secundaria**.

4. The length of high school planes de estudio in Mexico varies between two and three years. Cierto.

5. Students need to go to college to study to do administrative work. Falso. Comercio y Administración is a terminal program of study.

6. All students must take the same mathematics courses at the high school level. Falso. Mathematics courses differ depending on the program of study a student follows.

7. **La escuela secundaria** is for students from the ages of 16 to 18 years old. Falso. Escuela secundaria primarily serves students who are 12 to 15 years old, followed by the **preparatoria**.

8. All students in Mexico complete university studies. Falso. Some students do not study beyond **preparatoria**.

TEACHING OPTIONS

Small Groups In groups of three, have students discuss their favorite courses in which they are currently enrolled. Ask them to write several sentences in Spanish about why they like the course and whether or not it is a **curso electivo** (*elective*).

Cultural Activity Ask student pairs to decide whether or not they would prefer to study in a school program similar to Manuel's program in Mexico. Ask them to explain their choice based on the aspects included in the reading, such as programs of study, courses offered, and future plans. Tally their choices and make a bar graph of the results to hang in the classroom.

ASÍ SE DICE

Clases y exámenes

aprobar	to pass
el colegio/la escuela	school
la escuela secundaria/ la preparatoria (Méx.)/ el liceo (Ven.)/ el instituto (Esp.)	high school
el examen parcial	midterm exam
el horario	schedule
la matrícula	inscription (to school)
reprobar	to fail
la tarea	homework

EL MUNDO HISPANO

La escuela en Latinoamérica

○ **In Latin America**, public secondary schools are free of charge. Private schools, however, can be quite costly. At **la Escuela Campo Alegre** in Venezuela, annual tuition is more than $18,000 a year.

○ **In Argentina**, 48% of high school students go on to attend college, the highest rate in all Latin America.

○ **In Chile**, students begin the school year in March and finish in December. Of course—Chile lies south of the equator, so while it is winter in the United States, Chilean students are on their summer break!

PERFIL

El INFRAMEN

The **Instituto Nacional Francisco Menéndez (INFRAMEN)** is one of the largest public high schools in El Salvador. So it should be: it is named after General Francisco Menéndez, an ex-president of the country who was the founder of **enseñanza secundaria** (*secondary studies*) for the entire country! The 2,100 students at the INFRAMEN can choose to complete one of four kinds of diplomas: general studies, health care, tourism, and business. The institution has changed locales (and even cities) many times since it was founded in 1885 and is currently located in the capital city of San Salvador. Students at the INFRAMEN begin their school year in mid January and finish in early November.

Downtown San Salvador

SUPERSITE Conexión Internet

How do dress codes vary in schools across Latin America?

Go to **descubre1.vhlcentral.com** to find more cultural information related to this **Cultura** section.

ACTIVIDADES

2 **Comprensión** Complete these sentences.
1. The INFRAMEN was founded in ___1885___.
2. The programs of study available in the INFRAMEN are _general studies_, health care, tourism, and business
3. There are ___2,100___ students in the INFRAMEN.
4. General Francisco Menéndez was a ___president___ of El Salvador.
5. El ___horario___ is a student's schedule.

3 **¡A estudiar!** All students have classes they like and classes they don't. What are your favorite classes? Which are your least favorite? With a partner, discuss what you like and don't like about your classes and make a short list of what could be done to improve the classes you don't like.
Answers will vary.

recursos
CH p. 20 | descubre1.vhlcentral.com Lección 2

Section Goals

In **Estructura 2.1**, students will learn:

- the present tense of regular –**ar** verbs
- the formation of negative sentences
- the verb **gustar**

Instructional Resources
Cuaderno de práctica, pp. 13–14
Cuaderno para hispanohablantes, pp. 21–22
Cuaderno de actividades, p. 95
e-Cuaderno
Supersite: Audio Activity MP3 Audio Files
Supersite/TRCD/Print: *PowerPoints* (**Lección 2** *Estructura* Presentation); Audio Activity Script, Answer Keys
Audio Activity CD

Teaching Tips

- Point out that students have been using verbs and verb constructions from the start: **¿Cómo te llamas?, hay, ser,** and so forth. Ask a student: **¿Qué clases tomas?** Model student answer as **Yo tomo...** Then ask another student: **¿Qué clases toma ____? ____ toma ____.**
- Explain that, because the verb endings mark the person speaking or spoken about, subject pronouns are usually optional in Spanish.
- Remind students that **vosotros/as** forms will not be practiced actively in **DESCUBRE**.

2.1 Present tense of -ar verbs

ANTE TODO In order to talk about activities, you need to use verbs. Verbs express actions or states of being. In English and Spanish, the infinitive is the base form of the verb. In English, the infinitive is preceded by the word *to*: *to study*, *to be*. The infinitive in Spanish is a one-word form and can be recognized by its endings: **-ar, -er,** or **-ir.**

-ar verb		-er verb		-ir verb	
estudiar	*to study*	**comer**	*to eat*	**escribir**	*to write*

▶ In this lesson, you will learn the forms of regular **-ar** verbs.

The verb estudiar (to study)

SINGULAR FORMS	yo	estudi**o**	*I study*
	tú	estudi**as**	*you* (fam.) *study*
	Ud./él/ella	estudi**a**	*you* (form.) *study; he/she studies*
PLURAL FORMS	nosotros/as	estudi**amos**	*we study*
	vosotros/as	estudi**áis**	*you* (fam.) *study*
	Uds./ellos/ellas	estudi**an**	*you* (form.) *study; they study*

¿Tomas muchas clases este semestre?

Sí, tomo tres.

▶ To create the forms of most regular verbs in Spanish, drop the infinitive endings (**-ar, -er, -ir**). You then add to the stem the endings that correspond to the different subject pronouns. This diagram will help you visualize the process by which verb forms are created.

Conjugation of -ar verbs

INFINITIVE	VERB STEM	CONJUGATED FORM
estudi**ar**	estudi-	yo estudi**o**
bail**ar**	bail-	tú bail**as**
trabaj**ar**	trabaj-	nosotros trabaj**amos**

TEACHING OPTIONS

Extra Practice Do a pattern practice drill. Write an infinitive from the list of common –**ar** verbs on page 51 on the board and ask individual students to provide conjugations for the subject pronouns and names you suggest. Reverse the activity by saying a conjugated form and asking students to give the corresponding subject pronoun. Allow multiple answers for the third-person singular and plural.

Extra Practice Ask questions, using **estudiar, bailar,** and **trabajar.** Students should answer in complete sentences. Ask additional questions to get more information. Ex: —____, ¿trabajas? —Sí, trabajo. —¿Dónde trabajas? —Trabajo en ____. • —¿Quién baila los sábados? —Yo bailo los sábados. —¿Bailas merengue? • —¿Estudian ustedes mucho? —¿Quién estudia más? —¿Cuántas horas estudias los lunes? ¿Y los sábados?

Common -ar verbs

bailar	to dance	estudiar	to study
buscar	to look for	explicar	to explain
caminar	to walk	hablar	to talk; to speak
cantar	to sing	llegar	to arrive
cenar	to have dinner	llevar	to carry
comprar	to buy	mirar	to look (at); to watch
contestar	to answer	necesitar (+ *inf.*)	to need
conversar	to converse, to chat	practicar	to practice
desayunar	to have breakfast	preguntar	to ask (a question)
descansar	to rest	preparar	to prepare
desear (+ *inf.*)	to desire; to wish	regresar	to return
dibujar	to draw	terminar	to end; to finish
enseñar	to teach	tomar	to take; to drink
escuchar	to listen (to)	trabajar	to work
esperar (+ *inf.*)	to wait (for); to hope	viajar	to travel

▶ **¡Atención!** The Spanish verbs **buscar, escuchar, esperar,** and **mirar** do not need to be followed by prepositions as do their English equivalents.

Busco la tarea.
I'm looking for the homework.

Escucho la música.
I'm listening to the music.

Espero el autobús.
I'm waiting for the bus.

Miro la pizarra.
I'm looking at the blackboard.

COMPARE & CONTRAST

English uses three sets of forms to talk about the present: (1) the simple present (*Paco works*), (2) the present progressive (*Paco is working*), and (3) the emphatic present (*Paco does work*). In Spanish, the simple present can be used in all three cases.

Paco **trabaja** en la cafetería.
1. *Paco works in the cafeteria.*
2. *Paco is working in the cafeteria.*
3. *Paco does work in the cafeteria.*

In Spanish, the present tense is also sometimes used to express future action.

Marina **viaja** a Madrid mañana.
1. *Marina travels to Madrid tomorrow.*
2. *Marina will travel to Madrid tomorrow.*
3. *Marina is traveling to Madrid tomorrow.*

▶ When two verbs are used together with no change of subject, the second verb is generally in the infinitive. To make a sentence negative in Spanish, the word **no** is placed before the conjugated verb. In this case, **no** means *not*.

Deseo hablar con don Francisco.
I want to speak with Don Francisco.

Alicia **no** desea bailar ahora.
Alicia doesn't want to dance now.

Teaching Tips
• Model the pronunciation of each infinitive and have students repeat it after you.
• Model the **yo** form of several verbs, creating simple sentences about yourself (Ex: **Bailo con los amigos.**) and asking students if they do the same activities (Ex: **¿Bailas mucho con los amigos?**). Restate students' answers using the **él/ella** forms of the –ar verbs and then ask them to verify their classmates' answers.
Ex: ¿_____ baila mucho?
No, _____ no baila.
• Explain that the simple present tense in Spanish is the equivalent of the three present tense forms of English. Model sentences and give a few additional examples.
• Write additional examples of a conjugated verb followed by an infinitive on the board.
• Explain that, when answering questions negatively, **no** must be used twice. Ask questions of students that will most likely result in negative answers.
Ex: —_____, ¿bailas tango?
—No, no bailo tango.

TEACHING OPTIONS

Heritage Speakers Ask heritage speakers to use verbs from this section to create sentences about their current semester: what they are studying, if/where they work, what television programs they watch, and so on. Ask the rest of the class comprehension questions.
Extra Practice Ask students to create a two-column chart with the heads **Necesito…** and **Espero…**, and have them complete it with six things they need to do this week and six things they hope to do after the semester is over. Ex: **Necesito estudiar. Espero viajar.** Then have them interview a classmate and report back to the class.
Pairs Ask student pairs to write ten sentences, using verbs presented in this section. Point out that students can use vocabulary words from **Contextos** with these verbs.

▶ Spanish speakers often omit subject pronouns because the verb endings indicate who the subject is. In Spanish, subject pronouns are used for emphasis, clarification, or contrast.

> **Clarification/Contrast**

—¿Qué enseñan?	—**Ella** enseña arte y **él** enseña física.
What do they teach?	*She teaches art, and he teaches physics.*

> **Emphasis**

—¿Quién desea trabajar hoy?	—**Yo** no deseo trabajar hoy.
Who wants to work today?	*I don't want to work today.*

The verb gustar

▶ To express your own likes and dislikes, use the expression **me gusta** + [*singular noun*] or **me gustan** + [*plural noun*]. Never use a subject pronoun (such as **yo**) with this structure.

Me gusta la música clásica.	**Me gustan las clases** de español y biología.
I like classical music.	*I like Spanish and biology classes.*

▶ To express what you like to do, use the expression **me gusta** + [*infinitive(s)*].

Me gusta viajar.	**Me gusta cantar** y **bailar**.
I like to travel.	*I like to sing and dance.*

▶ To use the verb **gustar** with reference to another person, use the expressions **te gusta(n)** (**tú**) or a + [*name/pronoun*] **le gusta(n)** (**usted, él, ella**). To say that someone does not like something, insert the word **no** before the expression.

Te gusta la geografía.	**A Javier no le gustan las computadoras.**
You like geography.	*Javier doesn't like computers.*

▶ To use the verb **gustar** with reference to more than one person, use **nos gusta(n)** (**nosotros**) or a + [*name/pronoun*] **les gusta(n)** (**ustedes, ellos, ellas**).

Nos gusta dibujar.
We like to draw.

No **les gustan los exámenes.**
They don't like tests.

AYUDA

Use the construction a + [*name/pronoun*] to clarify to whom you are referring. This construction is not always necessary.
A Gabriela le gusta bailar.
A Sara y a Francisco les gustan los animales.

CONSULTA

For other verbs like gustar, see **Estructura 7.4**, pp. 246–247.

recursos

CP pp. 13–14

CH pp. 21–22

CA p. 95

SUPERSITE
descubre1.
vhlcentral.com
Lección 2

¡INTÉNTALO! Provide the present tense forms of these verbs. The first items have been done for you.

hablar

1. Yo _____hablo_____ español.
2. Ellos ___hablan___ español.
3. Inés ___habla___ español.
4. Nosotras ___hablamos___ español.
5. Tú ___hablas___ español.

gustar

1. ___Me gusta___ el café. (yo)
2. ¿___Te gustan___ las clases? (tú)
3. No ___le gusta___ el café. (usted)
4. No ___le gustan___ las clases. (ella)
5. No ___nos gusta___ el café. (nosotros)

Práctica   SUPERSITE

1 **Completar** Complete the conversation with the appropriate forms of the verbs.

JUAN ¡Hola, Linda! ¿Qué tal las clases?

LINDA Bien. (1)___Tomo___ (tomar) tres clases... química, biología y computación. Y tú, ¿cuántas clases (2)___tomas___ (tomar)?

JUAN (3)___Tomo___ (tomar) tres también... biología, arte y literatura. Yo (4)___tomo___ (tomar) biología a las cuatro con el profesor Cárdenas. ¿Y tú?

LINDA Lily, Alberto y yo (5)___tomamos___ (tomar) biología a las diez, con la profesora Garza.

JUAN ¿(6)___Estudian___ (estudiar) ustedes mucho?

LINDA Sí, porque hay muchos exámenes. Alberto y yo (7)___estudiamos___ (estudiar) dos horas todos los días (*every day*).

2 **Oraciones** Form sentences using the words provided. Remember to conjugate the verbs and add any other necessary words.

1. ustedes / practicar / vocabulario   Ustedes practican el vocabulario.
2. ¿preparar (tú) / tarea?   ¿Preparas la tarea?
3. clase de español / terminar / once   La clase de español termina a las once.
4. ¿qué / buscar / ustedes?   ¿Qué buscan ustedes?
5. (nosotros) buscar / computadora   Buscamos una computadora.
6. (yo) comprar / pluma   Compro una pluma.

3 **Gustos** Read what these people do. Then use the information in parentheses to tell what they like or like to do.

> **modelo**
> Álvaro enseña en la universidad. (las clases)   *Le gustan las clases.*

1. Los jóvenes desean mirar cuadros (*paintings*) de Picasso. (el arte)   Les gusta el arte.
2. Soy estudiante de economía. (estudiar)   Me gusta estudiar.
3. Tú estudias italiano y español. (las lenguas extranjeras)   Te gustan las lenguas extranjeras.
4. Ustedes no descansan los sábados. (cantar y bailar)   Les gusta cantar y bailar.
5. Nosotros buscamos una computadora. (la computación)   Nos gusta la computación.

4 **Actividades** Get together with a classmate and take turns asking each other if you do these activities. Which activities does your partner like? Which do you both like?   Answers will vary.

bailar merengue	escuchar música rock	practicar el español
cantar bien	estudiar física	conversar con amigos
dibujar en clase	mirar la televisión	viajar a Europa

> **modelo**
> tomar el autobús
> **Estudiante 1:** ¿Tomas el autobús?
> **Estudiante 2:** Sí, tomo el autobús, pero (*but*) no me gusta./ No, no tomo el autobús.

AYUDA

The Spanish **no** translates to both *no* and *not* in English. In negative answers to questions, you will need to use **no** twice:
¿Estudias geografía?
No, no estudio geografía.

TEACHING OPTIONS

5 **Teaching Tip** To challenge students, encourage them to offer additional descriptions of the drawings. Ex: **La profesora habla en clase. Hay números y letras en la pizarra.** Ask volunteers to share their descriptions with the class.

6 **Teaching Tip** You may want to split the class into two teams with volunteers from each team acting out the charades. Give points for correct guesses. Deduct points for incorrect guesses. The team with the most points at the end wins.

7 **Teaching Tip** Point out that, in addition to practicing –**ar** verbs, this activity recycles and reviews material from **Lección 1**: greetings, leave-takings, and telling time. Allow students several minutes to plan their conversation before they begin speaking.

7 **Expansion** Have volunteers role-play their conversations for the class.

Comunicación

5 **Describir** With a partner, describe what you see in the pictures using the given verbs. Then ask your partner whether or not he/she likes one of the activities.
Answers will vary.

modelo
enseñar
La profesora enseña química. ¿Te gusta la química?

1. caminar, hablar, llevar

2. buscar, descansar, estudiar

3. dibujar, cantar, escuchar

4. llevar, tomar, viajar

6 **Charadas** In groups of three students, play a game of charades using the verbs in the word bank. For example, if someone is studying, you say "**Estudias.**" The first person to guess correctly acts out the next charade. *Answers will vary.*

bailar	cantar	descansar	enseñar	mirar
caminar	conversar	dibujar	escuchar	preguntar

Síntesis

7 **Conversación** Pretend that you and a classmate are friends who have not seen each other at school for a few days. Have a conversation in which you catch up on things. Mention how you're feeling, what classes you're taking, what days and times you have classes, and which classes you like and don't like. *Answers will vary.*

TEACHING OPTIONS

Extra Practice Have students write a description of themselves made up of activities they like or do not like to do, using sentences containing **(no) me gusta…** Collect the descriptions and read them aloud. Have the class guess who wrote each description.
Game To add a visual aspect to this grammar practice, play **Concentración**. Choose eight infinitives taught in this section, and write each one on a separate card. On another eight cards, draw or paste a picture that illustrates the action of each infinitive. Randomly place the cards facedown in four rows of four. Play with even-numbered groups of students. In pairs, students select two cards. If the two cards match, the pair keeps them. If the cards do not match, students return them to their original position. The pair that finishes with the most cards wins.

2.2 Forming questions in Spanish

ANTE TODO There are three basic ways to ask questions in Spanish. Can you guess what they are by looking at the photos and photo captions on this page?

¿Dibujas mucho?

Las computadoras son muy interesantes, ¿no?

¿También tomas tú geografía?

▶ One way to form a question is to raise the pitch of your voice at the end of a declarative sentence. When writing any question in Spanish, be sure to use an upside down question mark (**¿**) at the beginning and a regular question mark (**?**) at the end of the sentence.

Statement	**Question**
Ustedes trabajan los sábados.	¿Ustedes trabajan los sábados?
You work on Saturdays.	*Do you work on Saturdays?*
Miguel busca un mapa.	¿Miguel busca un mapa?
Miguel is looking for a map.	*Is Miguel looking for a map?*

▶ You can also form a question by inverting the order of the subject and the verb of a declarative statement. The subject may even be placed at the end of the sentence.

Statement	**Question**
SUBJECT VERB	VERB SUBJECT
Ustedes trabajan los sábados.	**¿Trabajan ustedes** los sábados?
You work on Saturdays.	*Do you work on Saturdays?*
SUBJECT VERB	VERB SUBJECT
Carlota regresa a las seis.	**¿Regresa** a las seis **Carlota**?
Carlota returns at six.	*Does Carlota return at six?*

▶ Questions can also be formed by adding the tags **¿no?** or **¿verdad?** at the end of a statement.

Statement	**Question**
Ustedes trabajan los sábados.	Ustedes trabajan los sábados, **¿no?**
You work on Saturdays.	*You work on Saturdays, don't you?*
Carlota regresa a las seis.	Carlota regresa a las seis, **¿verdad?**
Carlota returns at six.	*Carlota returns at six, right?*

Teaching Tips
- Model pronunciation by asking questions. Ex: **¿Cómo estás? ¿Cuál es tu clase favorita?**
- Point out written accent marks on interrogative words.
- Explain that **¿qué?** and **¿cuál?** are not used interchangeably. The word **¿qué?** generally precedes a noun while **¿cuál?** is typically used with a verb. Compare and contrast the following: **¿Qué clase te gusta? ¿Cuál es tu clase favorita?** Write similar questions on the board but leave out the interrogative word. Ask students to tell whether **¿qué?** or **¿cuál?** is used for each.
- Point out **¿cuáles?** and **¿quiénes?** and give examples for each.
- Clarify singular/plural and masculine/feminine variants for **¿cuánto/a?** and **¿cuántos/as?** Ex: **¿Cuánta tarea hay? ¿Cuántos libros hay?**
- Model the pronunciation of example sentences, asking similar questions of students. Ex: ___, **¿dónde trabajas?** Ask other students to verify their classmates' answers. Ex: ____ **trabaja en ____.**
- Explain that the answer to the question **¿por qué?** is **porque.**
- Point out that a question such as **¿Caminan a la escuela?** has several answers: **Sí, caminamos a la escuela. No, no caminamos a la escuela. No, tomamos el autobús.**

Question words

Interrogative words

¿Adónde?	Where (to)?	**¿De dónde?**	From where?
¿Cómo?	How?	**¿Dónde?**	Where?
¿Cuál?, ¿Cuáles?	Which?; Which one(s)?	**¿Por qué?**	Why?
¿Cuándo?	When?	**¿Qué?**	What?; Which?
¿Cuánto/a?	How much?	**¿Quién?**	Who?
¿Cuántos/as?	How many?	**¿Quiénes?**	Who (plural)?

▶ To ask a question that requires more than a *yes* or *no* answer, use an interrogative word.

¿Cuál de ellos estudia en la biblioteca?
Which one of them studies in the library?

¿Cuántos estudiantes hablan español?
How many students speak Spanish?

¿Dónde trabaja Ricardo?
Where does Ricardo work?

¿Qué clases tomas?
What classes are you taking?

¿Adónde caminamos?
Where are we walking?

¿Por qué necesitas hablar con ella?
Why do you need to talk to her?

¿Quién enseña la clase de arte?
Who teaches the art class?

¿Cuánta tarea hay?
How much homework is there?

CONSULTA

You will learn more about the difference between **qué** and **cuál** in **Estructura 9.3**, p. 316.

▶ When pronouncing this type of question, the pitch of your voice falls at the end of the sentence.

¿Cómo llegas a clase?
How do you get to class?

¿Por qué necesitas estudiar?
Why do you need to study?

▶ Notice the difference between **¿por qué?**, which is written as two words and has an accent, and **porque**, which is written as one word without an accent.

¿Por qué estudias español?
Why do you study Spanish?

¡Porque es divertido!
Because it's fun!

▶ In Spanish **no** can mean both *no* and *not*. Therefore, when answering a yes/no question in the negative, you need to use **no** twice.

¿Caminan a clase?
Do you walk to class?

No, no caminamos a clase.
No, we do not walk to class.

 **¡INTÉNTALO!** Make questions out of these statements. Use intonation in column 1 and the tag **¿no?** in column 2. The first item has been done for you.

Statement	Intonation	Tag question
1. Hablas inglés.	¿Hablas inglés?	Hablas inglés, ¿no?
2. Trabajamos mañana.	¿Trabajamos mañana?	Trabajamos mañana, ¿no?
3. Ustedes desean bailar.	¿Ustedes desean bailar?	Ustedes desean bailar, ¿no?
4. Raúl estudia mucho.	¿Raúl estudia mucho?	Raúl estudia mucho, ¿no?
5. Enseño a las nueve.	¿Enseño a las nueve?	Enseño a las nueve, ¿no?
6. Luz mira la televisión.	¿Luz mira la televisión?	Luz mira la televisión, ¿no?

recursos

CP
pp. 15–16

CH
pp. 23–24

CA
p. 96

SUPERSITE
descubre1.
vhlcentral.com
Lección 2

TEACHING OPTIONS

Video Show the *Fotonovela* again to give students more input on forming questions. Stop the video where appropriate to discuss how certain questions, including tag questions, are formed. Have students focus on characters' rising and falling intonation in questions and statements.

Heritage Speakers Ask heritage speakers to give original statements and questions at random. Have the rest of the class determine whether each sentence is a statement or a question. **Pairs** Give pairs of students five minutes to write original questions using as many interrogative words as they can. Can any group come up with questions using all the interrogative words?

Práctica ⬤SUPERSITE

1 **Preguntas** Change these sentences into questions by inverting the word order.

> **modelo**
>
> Ernesto habla con su compañero de clase.
> ¿Habla Ernesto con su compañero de clase? /
> ¿Habla con su compañero de clase Ernesto?

1. La profesora Cruz prepara la prueba.
   ¿Prepara la profesora Cruz la prueba? / ¿Prepara la prueba la profesora Cruz?
2. Sandra y yo necesitamos estudiar.
   ¿Necesitamos Sandra y yo estudiar? / ¿Necesitamos estudiar Sandra y yo?
3. Los chicos practican el vocabulario.
   ¿Practican los chicos el vocabulario? / ¿Practican el vocabulario los chicos?
4. Jaime termina la tarea.
   ¿Termina Jaime la tarea? / ¿Termina la tarea Jaime?
5. Tú trabajas en la biblioteca. ¿Trabajas tú en la biblioteca? / ¿Trabajas en la biblioteca tú?

2 **Completar** Irene and Manolo are chatting in the library. Complete their conversation with
the appropriate questions. *Answers will vary.*

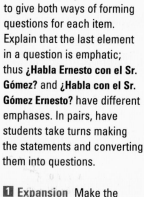

IRENE   Hola, Manolo. (1) ¿Cómo estás?/¿Qué tal?

MANOLO Bien, gracias. (2) ¿Y tú?

IRENE   Muy bien. (3) ¿Qué hora es?

MANOLO Son las nueve.

IRENE   (4) ¿Qué estudias?

MANOLO Estudio historia.

IRENE   (5) ¿Por qué?

MANOLO Porque hay un examen mañana.

IRENE   (6) ¿Te gusta la clase?

MANOLO Sí, me gusta mucho la clase.

IRENE   (7) ¿Quién enseña la clase?

MANOLO El profesor Padilla enseña la clase.

IRENE   (8) ¿Tomas psicología este semestre?

MANOLO No, no tomo psicología este semestre.

IRENE   (9) ¿A qué hora regresas a la casa?

MANOLO Regreso a la casa a las tres y media.

IRENE   (10) ¿Deseas tomar una soda?

MANOLO No, no deseo tomar soda. ¡Deseo estudiar!

3 **Dos profesores** In pairs, create a dialogue, similar to the one in **Actividad 2**, between two teachers,
señor Padilla and his colleague señora Martínez. Use question words. *Answers will vary.*

> **modelo**
>
> **Señor Padilla:** ¿Qué enseñas este semestre?
> **Señora Martínez:** Enseño dos cursos de sociología.

1 Teaching Tip Ask students
to give both ways of forming
questions for each item.
Explain that the last element
in a question is emphatic;
thus **¿Habla Ernesto con el Sr.
Gómez?** and **¿Habla con el Sr.
Gómez Ernesto?** have different
emphases. In pairs, have
students take turns making
the statements and converting
them into questions.

1 Expansion Make the
even statements negative.
Then have students add tag
questions to the statements.

2 Expansion Have pairs
of students create a similar
conversation, replacing the
answers with items that are
true for them. Then ask
volunteers to role-play their
conversations for the class.

3 Teaching Tip To prepare
students for the activity, have
them brainstorm possible
topics of conversation.

TEACHING OPTIONS

Heritage Speakers Ask students to interview heritage speakers,
whether in the class or outside. Students should prepare questions about who the person is, if they work and when/where,
what they study and why, and so forth. Have students use the
information they gather in the interviews to write a brief profile
of the person.

Large Groups Divide the class into two groups, A and B. To
each member of group A give a strip of paper with a question
on it. Ex: **¿Cuántos estudiantes hay en la clase?** Give an answer
to each member of group B. Ex: **Hay treinta estudiantes en
la clase.** Have students find their partners. Be sure that each
question has only one possible answer.

Comunicación

4   **Encuesta** Your teacher will give you a worksheet. Change the categories in the first column into questions, then use them to survey your classmates. Find at least one person for each category. Be prepared to report the results of your survey to the class.   Answers will vary.

Categorías	Nombres
1. estudiar computación	
2. tomar una clase de psicología	
3. dibujar bien	
4. cantar bien	
5. escuchar música clásica	

recursos

CA
p. 9

5   **Un juego** In groups of four or five, play a game (**un juego**) of Jeopardy.® Each person has to write two clues. Then take turns reading the clues and guessing the questions. The person who guesses correctly reads the next clue.   Answers will vary.

Es algo que...	**Es un lugar donde...**	**Es una persona que...**
It's something that...	*It's a place where...*	*It's a person that...*

modelo

Estudiante 1: Es un lugar donde estudiamos.
Estudiante 2: ¿Qué es la biblioteca?

Estudiante 1: Es algo que escuchamos.
Estudiante 2: ¿Qué es la música?

Estudiante 1: Es un director de España.
Estudiante 2: ¿Quién es Pedro Almodóvar?

Síntesis

6   **Entrevista** Imagine that you are a reporter for the school newspaper. Write five questions about student life at your school and use them to interview two classmates. Be prepared to report your findings to the class.   Answers will vary.

---

4 Teaching Tip For survey-type activities, encourage students to ask one question per person and move on. This will promote circulation throughout the room and prevent students from remaining in clusters.

4 Expansion Ask students to say the name of a classmate on their sheet. Then ask that student for more information. Ex: **¿Quién estudia computación? Ah, ¿sí? ____ estudia computación. ¿Dónde estudias computación, ____? ¿Quién es el/la profesor(a)?**

5 Expansion Play this game with the entire class. Select a few students to play the contestants and to "buzz in" their answers.

6 Teaching Tip Brainstorm ideas for interview questions and write them on the board, or have students prepare their questions as homework for an in-class interview session.

TEACHING OPTIONS

Extra Practice Have students go back to the **Fotonovela** on pages 44–45 and write as many questions as they can about what they see in the photos. Ask volunteers to share their questions as you write them on the board. Then call on individual students to answer them.

Extra Practice Prepare eight questions and answers. Write only the answers on the board in random order. Then read the questions aloud and have students identify the appropriate answer. Ex: **¿Cuándo es la clase de español?** (**Es los lunes, miércoles y viernes.**)

[2.3] Present tense of **estar**

CONSULTA

To review the forms of **ser**, see **Estructura 1.3**, pp. 19–21.

ANTE TODO In **Lección 1**, you learned how to conjugate and use the verb **ser** (*to be*). You will now learn a second verb which means *to be*, the verb **estar**. Although **estar** ends in **-ar**, it does not follow the pattern of regular **-ar** verbs. The **yo** form (**estoy**) is irregular. Also, all forms have an accented **á** except the **yo** and **nosotros/as** forms.

The verb estar (*to be*)		
SINGULAR FORMS		
yo	est**oy**	*I am*
tú	est**ás**	*you* (fam.) *are*
Ud./él/ella	est**á**	*you* (form.) *are; he/she is*
PLURAL FORMS		
nosotros/as	est**amos**	*we are*
vosotros/as	est**áis**	*you* (fam.) *are*
Uds./ellos/ellas	est**án**	*you* (form.) *are; they are*

Hola, Ricardo...
Aquí estamos en
la Mitad del
Mundo.

Inés y Maite están
en el autobús.

AYUDA

Use **la casa** to express *the house*, but **en casa** to express *at home*.

CONSULTA

To learn more about the difference between **ser** and **estar**, see **Estructura 5.3**, pp. 170–171.

COMPARE & CONTRAST

Compare the uses of the verb **estar** to those of the verb **ser**.

Uses of *estar*

Location
Estoy en casa.
I am at home.

Inés **está** al lado de Javier.
Inés is next to Javier.

Health
Álex **está** enfermo hoy.
Álex is sick today.

Well-being
—¿Cómo **estás**, Maite?
How are you, Maite?

—**Estoy** muy bien, gracias.
I'm very well, thank you.

Uses of *ser*

Identity
Hola, **soy** Maite.
Hello, I'm Maite.

Occupation
Soy estudiante.
I'm a student.

Origin
—¿**Eres** de España?
Are you from Spain?

—Sí, **soy** de España.
Yes, I'm from Spain.

Telling time
Son las cuatro.
It's four o'clock.

Section Goals

In **Estructura 2.3**, students will be introduced to:
• the present tense of **estar**
• contrasts between **ser** and **estar**
• prepositions of location used with **estar**

Instructional Resources
Cuaderno de práctica,
pp. 17–18
Cuaderno para hispanohablantes, pp. 25–26
Cuaderno de actividades, p. 97
e-Cuaderno
Supersite: Audio Activity MP3 Audio Files
Supersite/TRCD/Print:
PowerPoints (**Lección 2 Estructura** Presentation, Overhead #14); Audio Activity Script, Answer Keys
Audio Activity CD

Teaching Tips
• Emphasize that the principal distinction between **estar** and **ser** is that **estar** is generally used to express temporary conditions (**Álex está enfermo hoy.**) and **ser** is generally used to express inherent qualities (**Álex es inteligente.**)
• Students will learn to compare **ser** and **estar** formally in **Estructura 5.3**.

TEACHING OPTIONS

TPR Have students write **ser** and **estar** on separate sheets of paper. Give statements in English and have students indicate if they would use **ser** or **estar** in each by holding up the appropriate paper. Ex: *I'm at home.* (**estar**) *I'm a student.* (**ser**) *I'm tired.* (**estar**) *I'm glad.* (**estar**) *I'm generous.* (**ser**)
Extra Practice Ask students to tell where certain people are or probably are at this moment. Ex: **¿Dónde estás?** (**Estoy en la** clase.) **¿Dónde está el presidente?** (**Está en Washington, D.C.**)
Heritage Speakers Ask heritage speakers to name instances where either **ser** or **estar** may be used. They may point out more advanced uses, such as with certain adjectives: **Es aburrido** vs. **Está aburrido**. This may help to compare and contrast inherent qualities and temporary conditions.

Teaching Tips
- Explain that prepositions typically indicate where one thing or person is in relation to another thing or person: *near, far, on, between, below.*
- Point out that **estar** is used in the model sentences to indicate presence or existence in a place.
- Ask volunteers to read the captions for the video stills.
- Take a book or other object and place it in various locations in relation to your desk or a student's. Ask individual students about its location. Ex: **¿Dónde está el libro? ¿Está cerca o lejos del escritorio de ____? ¿Qué objeto está al lado/a la izquierda del libro?** Work through various locations, eliciting all of the prepositions of location.
- Ask where students are in relation to one another. Ex: **____, ¿dónde está ____? Está al lado (a la derecha/ izquierda, delante, detrás) de ____.**
- Describe students' locations in relation to each other. Ex: **Esta persona está lejos de ____. Está delante de ____. Está al lado de ____ ...** Have the class call out the student you identify. Ex: **Es ____.** Then have students describe other students' locations for a partner to guess.

▶ **Estar** is often used with certain prepositions to describe the location of a person or an object.

Prepositions often used with estar

al lado de	next to; beside	**delante de**	in front of
a la derecha de	to the right of	**detrás de**	behind
a la izquierda de	to the left of	**encima de**	on top of
en	in; on	**entre**	between; among
cerca de	near	**lejos de**	far from
con	with	**sin**	without
debajo de	below	**sobre**	on; over

La clase **está al lado de** la biblioteca.
The class is next to the library.

Los libros **están encima del** escritorio.
The books are on top of the desk.

El laboratorio **está cerca de** la clase.
The lab is near the classroom.

Maribel **está delante de** José.
Maribel is in front of José.

El estadio no **está lejos de** la librería.
The stadium isn't far from the bookstore.

El mapa **está entre** la pizarra y la puerta.
The map is between the blackboard and the door.

Los estudiantes **están en** la clase.
The students are in class.

El libro **está sobre** la mesa.
The book is on the table.

¡A ver! La señorita que está cerca de la ventana…

Aquí estoy con cuatro estudiantes de la universidad…

¡INTÉNTALO! Provide the present tense forms of **estar**. The first item has been done for you.

1. Ustedes ___están___ en la clase.
2. José ___está___ en la biblioteca.
3. Yo ___estoy___ bien, gracias.
4. Nosotras ___estamos___ en la cafetería.
5. Tú ___estás___ en el laboratorio.
6. Elena ___está___ en la librería.
7. Ellas ___están___ en la clase.
8. Ana y yo ___estamos___ en la clase.
9. ¿Cómo ___está___ usted?
10. Javier y Maribel ___están___ en el estadio.
11. Nosotros ___estamos___ en la cafetería.
12. Yo ___estoy___ en el laboratorio.
13. Carmen y María ___están___ enfermas.
14. Tú ___estás___ en la clase.

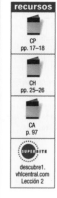

recursos

CP pp. 17–18

CH pp. 25–26

CA p. 97

descubre1. vhlcentral.com Lección 2

TEACHING OPTIONS

Extra Practice Name various places at your school and ask students to describe their location in relation to other buildings. Model sample sentences so students will know how to answer. You may wish to write **el aula de…** on the board and explain its meaning.

TPR Have students remain seated. One student holds a foam or paper ball. Then identify another student by his or her location with reference to other students. Ex: **Es la persona a la derecha de ____.** The student with the ball has to throw it to the student you described. That student must then toss the ball to the next person you identify.

Práctica SUPERSITE

1 **Completar** Daniela has just returned home from school. Complete this conversation with the appropriate forms of **ser** or **estar**.

MAMÁ   Hola, Daniela. ¿Cómo (1)___estás___?

DANIELA   Hola, mamá. (2)___Estoy___ bien. ¿Dónde (3)___está___ papá?
          ¡Ya (*Already*) (4)___son___ las seis de la noche!

MAMÁ   No (5)___está___ aquí. (6)___Está___ en la oficina.

DANIELA   Y Andrés y Margarita, ¿dónde (7)___están___ ellos?

MAMÁ   (8)___Están___ en el restaurante La Palma con Martín.

DANIELA   ¿Quién (9)___es___ Martín?

MAMÁ   (10)___Es___ un compañero de clase. (11)___Es___ de México.

DANIELA   Ah. Y el restaurante La Palma, ¿dónde (12)___está___?

MAMÁ   (13)___Está___ cerca de la Plaza Mayor, en San Modesto.

DANIELA   Gracias, mamá. Voy (*I'm going*) al restaurante. ¡Hasta pronto!

2 **Escoger** Choose the preposition that best completes each sentence.

1. La pluma está (encima de / detrás de) la mesa. encima de
2. La ventana está (a la izquierda de / debajo de) la puerta. a la izquierda de
3. La pizarra está (debajo de / delante de) los estudiantes. delante de
4. Las sillas están (encima de / detrás de) los escritorios. detrás de
5. Los estudiantes llevan los libros (en / sobre) la mochila. en
6. La biblioteca está (sobre / al lado de) la residencia estudiantil. al lado de
7. España está (cerca de / lejos de) Puerto Rico. lejos de
8. Cuba está (cerca de / lejos de) los Estados Unidos. cerca de
9. Felipe trabaja (con / en) Ricardo en la cafetería. con

3 **La librería** Imagine that you are in a bookstore and can't find various items. Ask the clerk (your partner) where the items in the drawing are located. Then switch roles. Answers will vary.

> **modelo**
> **Estudiante 1:** ¿Dónde están los diccionarios?
> **Estudiante 2:** Los diccionarios están debajo de los libros de literatura.

1 **Teaching Tips**
• To simplify, guide students in choosing **ser** or **estar** for each item.
• Ask students to explain why they chose **ser** or **estar** in each case.

1 **Expansion** Ask two volunteers to role-play the conversation for the class.

2 **Expansion**
• To challenge students, rework items 1 through 6, asking questions about items in the classroom or places at the university. Ex: ¿**Qué objeto está encima de la mesa? ¿Dónde está la ventana?**
• To add a visual aspect to this exercise, ask students to create simple illustrations that show the relationship of location in items 1–8.

3 **Teaching Tip** Using *Overhead PowerPoint #14* or the drawing in the textbook, quickly have volunteers name the objects they see in the illustration.

3 **Expansion** Assign one student the role of **vendedor(a)** and another the role of **cliente/a**. Then name one of the items in the drawing and ask the participants to create a conversation as in the activity.

TEACHING OPTIONS

Extra Practice Add a visual aspect to this grammar practice. Use a large world map (one with Spanish labels is best), *Overhead PowerPoints #1–#8*, and/or the maps in the frontmatter of this textbook. Ask students where countries and cities are in relation to each other on the map(s). Ex: ¿**Bolivia está a la derecha del Brasil? ¿Uruguay está más cerca de Chile o del Ecuador? ¿Qué país está entre Colombia y Costa Rica? ¿Está**

Puerto Rico a la izquierda de la República Dominicana?
Small Groups Have each group member think of a country or well-known location on campus and describe it with progressively more specific statements. After each statement, the other group members guess what country or location it is. Ex: **Es un país. Está en Europa. Está cerca de España. Está a la izquierda de Italia y Suiza. Es Francia.**

Comunicación

4 Teaching Tips
- Ask two volunteers to read the model aloud.
- Have students scan the days and times and ask you for any additional vocabulary.

4 Expansion After students have completed the activity, ask the same questions of selected individuals. Then expand on their answers by asking additional questions. Ex: —¿**Dónde estás los sábados a las seis de la mañana?** —**Estoy en casa.** —¿**Dónde está la casa?**

5 Expansion
- To make more challenging for students, have them create statements about the buildings' locations from the point of view of the man in the drawing.

4 ¿**Dónde estás...?** With a partner, take turns asking where you are at these times. Answers will vary.

> **modelo**
> lunes / 10:00 a.m.
> **Estudiante 1:** ¿Dónde estás los lunes a las *diez de la mañana*?
> **Estudiante 2:** Estoy en la clase de español.

1. sábados / 6:00 a.m.
2. miércoles / 9:15 a.m.
3. lunes / 11:10 a.m.
4. jueves / 12:30 a.m.
5. viernes / 2:25 p.m.
6. martes / 3:50 p.m.
7. jueves / 5:45 p.m.
8. miércoles / 8:20 p.m.

5 **La ciudad universitaria** You are visiting your older sister, who is an exchange student at a Spanish university. Tell a classmate which buildings you are looking for and ask for their location relative to where you are. Answers will vary.

> **modelo**
> **Estudiante 1:** ¿La Facultad de Medicina está lejos?
> **Estudiante 2:** No, está cerca. Está a la izquierda de la Facultad de Administración de Empresas.

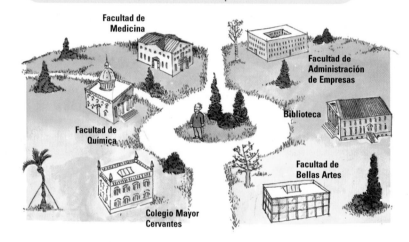

Facultad de Medicina

Facultad de Administración de Empresas

Facultad de Química

Biblioteca

Facultad de Bellas Artes

Colegio Mayor Cervantes

La Facultad (*School*) **de Filosofía y Letras** includes departments such as language, literature, philosophy, history, and linguistics. Fine arts can be studied in **la Facultad de Bellas Artes**. In Spain the business school is sometimes called **la Facultad de Administración de Empresas**. **Residencias estudiantiles** are referred to as **colegios mayores**.

Síntesis

6 Teaching Tip Remind students to jot down each interviewee's answers.

6 Expansion Call on students to share the information they obtained with the class.

6 **Entrevista** Use these questions to interview two classmates. Then switch roles. Answers will vary.

1. ¿Cómo estás?
2. ¿Dónde estamos ahora?
3. ¿Dónde está tu (*your*) padre ahora?
4. ¿Cuántos estudiantes hay en la clase de español?
5. ¿Quién(es) no está(n) en la clase hoy?
6. ¿A qué hora termina la clase hoy?
7. ¿Estudias mucho?
8. ¿Cuántas horas estudias para (*for*) una prueba?

TEACHING OPTIONS

Video Show the *Fotonovela* again to give students more input. Stop the video where appropriate to discuss how **estar** and prepositions were used and to ask comprehension questions.
Pairs Write a list of well-known monuments, places, and people on the board. Ex: **las Torres Petrona, el Space Needle y Bill Gates, las Cataratas del Niágara, Madonna** Have student pairs take turns asking each other the location of each item. Ex: —¿**Dónde están**

las Torres Petrona? —**Están en Kuala Lumpur/Malasia.**
Game Divide the class into two teams. Select a student from team A to think of an item in the classroom. Team B can ask five questions about where this item is. The first student can respond only with **sí, no, caliente** (*hot*), or **frío** (*cold*). If a team guesses the item within five tries, award a point. If not, give the other team a point. The team with the most points wins.

2.4 Numbers 31 and higher

ANTE TODO   You have already learned numbers 0–30. Now you will learn the rest of the numbers.

Numbers 31–100

▶ Numbers 31–99 follow the same basic pattern as 21–29.

	Numbers 31–100				
31	treinta y uno	40	cuarenta	50	cincuenta
32	treinta y dos	41	cuarenta y uno	51	cincuenta y uno
33	treinta y tres	42	cuarenta y dos	52	cincuenta y dos
34	treinta y cuatro	43	cuarenta y tres	60	sesenta
35	treinta y cinco	44	cuarenta y cuatro	63	sesenta y tres
36	treinta y seis	45	cuarenta y cinco	64	sesenta y cuatro
37	treinta y siete	46	cuarenta y seis	70	setenta
38	treinta y ocho	47	cuarenta y siete	80	ochenta
39	treinta y nueve	48	cuarenta y ocho	90	noventa
		49	cuarenta y nueve	100	cien, ciento

▶ **Y** is used in most numbers from **31** through **99**. Unlike numbers 21–29, these numbers must be written as three separate words.

Hay **noventa y dos** exámenes.
There are ninety-two exams.

Hay **cuarenta y dos** estudiantes.
There are forty-two students.

¿En qué clase hay más chicas?

En la de sociología… casi un ochenta y cinco por ciento.

▶ With numbers that end in **uno** (31, 41, etc.), **uno** becomes **un** before a masculine noun and **una** before a feminine noun.

Hay **treinta y un** chicos.
There are thirty-one guys.

Hay **treinta y una** chicas.
There are thirty-one girls.

▶ **Cien** is used before nouns and in counting. The words **un**, **una**, and **uno** are never used before **cien** in Spanish. **Ciento** is used for numbers over one hundred.

¿Cuántos libros hay? **Cientos.**
How many books are there? Hundreds.

Hay **cien** libros y **cien** sillas.
There are one hundred books and one hundred chairs.

Section Goal

In **Estructura 2.4**, students will be introduced to numbers 31 and higher.

Instructional Resources
Cuaderno de práctica, pp. 19–20
Cuaderno para hispanohablantes, pp. 27–28
Cuaderno de actividades, pp. 5–8, 98
e-Cuaderno
Supersite: Audio Activity MP3 Audio Files
Supersite/TRCD/Print: PowerPoints (**Lección 2 Estructura** Presentation); Communication Activities, Audio Activity Script, Answer Keys
Audio Activity CD

Teaching Tips
- Review 0–30 by having the class count with you. When you reach 30, ask individual students to count through 39. Count 40 yourself and have students continue counting through 100.
- Write on the board numbers not included in the chart: 56, 68, 72, and so forth. Ask students to say the number in Spanish.
- Drill numbers 31–100 counting in sequences of twos and threes. Point to individuals at random and have them supply the next number in the series. Keep a brisk pace.
- Emphasize that from 31 to 99, numbers are written as three words (**treinta y nueve**).
- Remind students that **uno** changes into **un** and **una**, as in **veintiún** and **veintiuna**.
- Bring in a newspaper or magazine ad that shows phone numbers and prices. Call on volunteers to read the numbers aloud.

TEACHING OPTIONS

Extra Practice Do simple math problems (addition and subtraction) with numbers 31 and higher. Include numbers 0–30 as well, for a balanced review. Remind students that **más** = *plus*, **menos** = *minus*, and **es/son** = *equals*.
Extra Practice Write the beginning of a series of numbers on the board and have students continue the sequence. Ex: **45, 50, 55,…** or **77, 80, 83, 86,…**

Heritage Speakers Add an auditory aspect to this grammar presentation. Ask heritage speakers to give the house or apartment number where they live (they do not have to give the street name). Ask them to give the addresses in tens (**1471 = catorce setenta y uno**). Have volunteers write the numbers they say on the board.

Numbers 101 and higher

▶ As shown in the chart, Spanish uses a period to indicate thousands and millions, rather than a comma as used in English.

Numbers 101 and higher			
101	ciento uno	**1.000**	mil
200	doscientos/as	**1.100**	mil cien
300	trescientos/as	**2.000**	dos mil
400	cuatrocientos/as	**5.000**	cinco mil
500	quinientos/as	**100.000**	cien mil
600	seiscientos/as	**200.000**	doscientos/as mil
700	setecientos/as	**550.000**	quinientos/as cincuenta mil
800	ochocientos/as	**1.000.000**	un millón (de)
900	novecientos/as	**8.000.000**	ocho millones (de)

▶ The numbers 200 through 999 agree in gender with the nouns they modify.

324 plum**as**   605 libr**os**
trescient**as** veinticuatro plum**as**   seiscient**os** cinco libr**os**

Hay tres mil quinient**os** libr**os** en la biblioteca.

▶ The word **mil**, which can mean *a thousand* and *one thousand*, is not usually used in the plural form when referring to numbers. **Un millón** (*a million* or *one million*), has the plural form **millones,** in which the accent is dropped.

1.000 relojes   25.000 pizarras   2.000.000 de estudiantes
mil relojes   veinticinco **mil** pizarras   dos **millones** de estudiantes

▶ To express a complex number (including years), string together its component parts.

55.422   cincuenta y cinco mil cuatrocientos veintidós

¡INTÉNTALO! Give the Spanish equivalent of each number. The first item has been done for you.

1. **102** _____ *ciento dos* _____
2. **5.000.000** __ cinco millones __
3. **201** __ doscientos uno __
4. **76** __ setenta y seis __
5. **92** __ noventa y dos __
6. **550.300** __ quinientos cincuenta mil trescientos __

7. **235** __ doscientos treinta y cinco __
8. **79** __ setenta y nueve __
9. **113** __ ciento trece __
10. **88** __ ochenta y ocho __
11. **17.123** __ diecisiete mil ciento veintitrés __
12. **497** __ cuatrocientos noventa y siete __

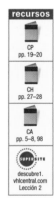

Práctica y Comunicación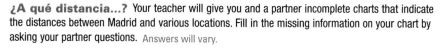

1 **Baloncesto** Provide these basketball scores in Spanish.

1. Ohio State 76, Michigan 65
2. Florida 92, Florida State 104
3. Stanford 78, UCLA 89
4. Purdue 81, Indiana 78
5. Princeton 67, Harvard 55
6. Duke 115, Virginia 121

1. setenta y seis, sesenta y cinco   3. setenta y ocho, ochenta y nueve   5. sesenta y siete, cincuenta y cinco
2. noventa y dos, ciento cuatro   4. ochenta y uno, setenta y ocho   6. ciento quince, ciento veintiuno

2 **Completar** Complete these sequences of numbers.

1. 50, 150, 250 ... 1.050 trescientos cincuenta, cuatrocientos cincuenta, quinientos cincuenta,
seiscientos cincuenta, setecientos cincuenta, ochocientos cincuenta, novecientos cincuenta
2. 5.000, 20.000, 35.000 ... 95.000
cincuenta mil, sesenta y cinco mil, ochenta mil
3. 100.000, 200.000, 300.000 ... 1.000.000
cuatrocientos mil, quinientos mil, seiscientos mil, setecientos mil, ochocientos mil, novecientos mil
4. 100.000.000, 90.000.000, 80.000.000 ... 0 setenta millones, sesenta millones,
cincuenta millones, cuarenta millones, treinta millones, veinte millones, diez millones

3 **Resolver** Read the math problems aloud and solve them.

> **modelo**
> 200 + 300 = *Doscientos más trescientos son quinientos.*

AYUDA

+ → **más**
− → **menos**
= → **son**

1. 1.000 + 753 = Mil más setecientos cincuenta y tres son mil setecientos cincuenta y tres.
2. 1.000.000 − 30.000 = Un millón menos treinta mil son novecientos setenta mil.
3. 10.000 + 555 = Diez mil más quinientos cincuenta y cinco son diez mil quinientos cincuenta y cinco.
4. 15 + 150 = Quince más ciento cincuenta son ciento sesenta y cinco.
5. 100.000 + 205.000 = Cien mil más doscientos cinco mil son trescientos cinco mil.
6. 29.000 − 10.000 = Veintinueve mil menos diez mil son diecinueve mil.

4 **Entrevista** Find out the telephone numbers and e-mail addresses of four classmates.

Answers will vary.

> **modelo**
> **Estudiante 1:** ¿Cuál es tu (your) número de teléfono?
> **Estudiante 2:** Es el 635-19-51.
> **Estudiante 1:** ¿Y tu dirección de correo electrónico?
> **Estudiante 2:** Es a-Smith-arroba-pe-ele-punto-e-de-u. (asmith@pl.edu)

AYUDA

arroba *at* (@)
punto *dot* (.)

Síntesis

recursos

CA
pp. 5–6

5 **¿A qué distancia...?** Your teacher will give you and a partner incomplete charts that indicate the distances between Madrid and various locations. Fill in the missing information on your chart by asking your partner questions. Answers will vary.

> **modelo**
> **Estudiante 1:** ¿A qué distancia está Arganda del Rey?
> **Estudiante 2:** Está a veintisiete kilómetros de Madrid.

Sidebar

1 **Expansion** In pairs, have each student write three additional basketball scores and dictate them to his or her partner, who writes them down.

2 **Teaching Tip** To simplify, have students identify the pattern of each sequence. Ex: 1. Add one hundred.

3 **Expansion** To challenge students, have them create four additional math problems for a partner to solve.

4 **Teaching Tips**
• Write your own (or an imaginary) e-mail address on the board as you pronounce it aloud.
• Point out that **el correo electrónico** means *e-mail*.
• Reassure students that, if they are uncomfortable revealing their personal information, they can invent a number and address.
• Ask volunteers to share their phone numbers and e-mail addresses. Other students write them on the board.

5 **Teaching Tips**
• Divide the class into pairs and distribute the Communication Activity worksheets that correspond to this activity. Explain that this type of exercise is called an information gap activity. In it, each partner has information that the other needs, and the way to get this information is by asking the partner questions.
• Point out and model **está a ____ de...** to express distance.
• Give students ten minutes to complete this activity.

Teaching Tip See the Communication Activities for an additional activity to practice the material presented in this section.

TEACHING OPTIONS

Small Groups In groups of three or four, ask students to think of a city or town within a 100-mile radius of your school. Have them find out the distance in miles (**Está a ____ millas de la escuela.**) and what other cities or towns are nearby (**Está cerca de...**). Then have groups read their descriptions for the class to guess.

Game Ask for two volunteers and station them at opposite ends of the board so neither one can see what the other is writing. Say a number for them to write on the board. If both students are correct, continue to give numbers until one writes an incorrect number. The winner continues on to play against another student.

66 Teacher's Annotated Edition • Lesson Two

Section Goal

In **Recapitulación**, students will review the grammar concepts from this lesson.

Instructional Resource
Supersite

1 Teaching Tips

- To simplify, ask students to identify the infinitive of the verb in each row.
- Complete this activity orally as a class. Write each form on the board as students call them out.

1 Expansion
Ask students to provide the third-person singular (**Ud./él/ella**) conjugations.

2 Expansion

- Ask students to write five more numbers above 31. Have them read the numbers to a partner, who will jot them down. Remind students to check each other's answers.
- To challenge students, have them complete the activity and then say what they can buy with that amount of money. Model the first item for the class. Ex: **Con 49 dólares, compro una mochila.**

3 Teaching Tips

- Remind students that all questions words should carry accent marks.
- Remind students that verbs in Spanish do not require subject pronouns; they are used for emphasis or clarification.

Recapitulación

SUPERSITE For self-scoring and diagnostics, go to **descubre1.vhlcentral.com.**

Review the grammar concepts you have learned in this lesson by completing these activities.

1 **Completar** Complete the chart with the correct verb forms. **12 pts.**

yo	tú	nosotros	ellas
compro	compras	compramos	compran
deseo	**deseas**	deseamos	desean
miro	miras	**miramos**	miran
pregunto	preguntas	preguntamos	**preguntan**

2 **Números** Write these numbers in Spanish. **8 pts.**

modelo
645: *seiscientos cuarenta y cinco*

1. **49:** cuarenta y nueve
2. **97:** noventa y siete
3. **113:** ciento trece
4. **632:** seiscientos treinta y dos
5. **1.781:** mil setecientos ochenta y uno
6. **3.558:** tres mil quinientos cincuenta y ocho
7. **1.006.015:** un millón seis mil quince
8. **67.224.370:** sesenta y siete millones doscientos veinticuatro mil trescientos setenta

3 **Preguntas** Write questions for these answers. **12 pts.**

1. —¿ De dónde es _____ Patricia?
—Patricia es de Colombia.
2. —¿ Quién es _____ él?
—Él es mi amigo (*friend*).
3. —¿ Cuántas lenguas hablas _____ (tú)?
—Hablo dos lenguas.
4. —¿ Qué desean (tomar) _____ (ustedes)?
—Deseamos tomar dos cafés.
5. —¿ Por qué tomas biología _____?
—Tomo biología porque me gusta.
6. —¿ Cuándo descansa Camilo _____?
—Camilo descansa por las mañanas.

RESUMEN GRAMATICAL

2.1 Present tense of -ar verbs pp. 50–52

estudiar	
estudio	estudiamos
estudias	estudiáis
estudia	estudian

The verb gustar

SINGULAR	me, te, le	**gusta**	el chocolate viajar cantar y bailar
PLURAL	nos, os, les	**gustan**	los libros

2.2 Forming questions in Spanish pp. 55–56

► ¿Ustedes trabajan los sábados?
► ¿Trabajan ustedes los sábados?
► Ustedes trabajan los sábados, ¿verdad?/¿no?

Interrogative words		
¿Adónde?	¿Cuánto/a?	¿Por qué?
¿Cómo?	¿Cuántos/as?	¿Qué?
¿Cuál/es?	¿(De) dónde?	¿Quién/es?
¿Cuándo?		

2.3 Present tense of estar pp. 59–60

► estar: estoy, estás, está, estamos, estáis, están

2.4 Numbers 31 and higher pp. 63–64

31	treinta y uno	101	ciento uno
32	treinta y dos	200	doscientos/as
	(and so on)	500	quinientos/as
40	cuarenta	700	setecientos/as
50	cincuenta	900	novecientos/as
60	sesenta	1.000	mil
70	setenta	2.000	dos mil
80	ochenta	5.100	cinco mil cien
90	noventa	100.000	cien mil
100	cien, ciento	1.000.000	un millón (de)

TEACHING OPTIONS

Pairs Have students create ten questions using the interrogative words from **Estructura 2.2.** Remind students that **¿Cuánto/a?** and **¿Cuántos/as?** should modify their corresponding nouns. Then have students exchange papers with a classmate and answer the questions. Finally, have pairs work together to review the answers. Have them write sentences using **nosotros/as** about any items they have in common.

Extra Practice On the board, write a list of landmarks (libraries, parks, churches, restaurants, hotels, and so forth) in the community. Have students create sentences describing the location of the landmarks. Ex: **El Hotel Plaza está al lado de la biblioteca. Está cerca de la catedral y delante de Sebastian's Café.**

4 **Al teléfono** Complete this telephone conversation with the correct forms of the verb **estar**. `8 pts.`

MARÍA TERESA   Hola, señora López. (1) ¿_____ Está _____
Elisa en casa?

SRA. LÓPEZ   ¿Quién es?

MARÍA TERESA   Soy María Teresa. Elisa y yo
(2) _____ estamos _____ en la misma (*same*)
clase de literatura.

SRA. LÓPEZ   ¡Ah, María Teresa! ¿Cómo (3) _____ estás _____?

MARÍA TERESA   (4) _____ Estoy _____ muy bien, gracias. Y usted, ¿cómo (5) _____ está _____?

SRA. LÓPEZ   Bien, gracias. Pues, no, Elisa no (6) _____ está _____ en casa. Ella y su hermano
(*her brother*) (7) _____ están _____ en la Biblioteca Cervantes.

MARÍA TERESA   ¿Cervantes?

SRA. LÓPEZ   Es la biblioteca que (8) _____ está _____ al lado del Café Bambú.

MARÍA TERESA   ¡Ah, sí! Gracias, señora López.

SRA. LÓPEZ   Hasta luego, María Teresa.

5 **¿Qué te gusta?** Write a paragraph of at least five sentences stating what you like and
don't like about your school. If possible, explain your likes and dislikes. `10 pts.`
Answers will vary.

> *Me gusta la clase de música porque*
> *no hay muchos exámenes. No me*
> *gusta estudiar en la cafetería...*

6 **Canción** Write the missing words to complete the beginning of a popular song by
Manu Chao. `2 EXTRA points!`

“ Me _____ gustan _____ los aviones°,
me gustas tú,
me _____ gusta _____ viajar,
me gustas tú,
me gusta la mañana,
me gustas tú. ”

aviones *airplanes*

---

4 **Expansion** Ask student pairs to write a brief phone conversation based on the one in **Actividad 4**. Have volunteers role-play their dialogues for the class.

5 **Teaching Tips**
- Before writing their paragraphs, have students brainstorm a list of words or phrases related to high school life.
- Remind students of when to use **gusta** versus **gustan**. Write a few example sentences on the board.
- Have students exchange papers with a partner to peer-edit each other's paragraphs.

6 **Teaching Tip** Point out the form **gustas** in lines 2, 4, and 6, and ask students to guess the translation of the phrase **me gustas** (*I like you*, literally, *you are pleasing to me*). Tell students that **me gustas** and **le gustas** are not used as often as their English counterparts. Most often they are used in romantic situations.

6 **Expansion** Share with students that Manu Chao is a French singer/songwriter born of Spanish parents. The founder of the group **Mano Negra**, he has also performed with the group **Radio Bemba** and as a solo artist.

TEACHING OPTIONS

Pairs Write **más, menos, multiplicado por**, and **dividido por** on the board. Model a few simple problems using numbers 31 and higher. Ex: **Cien mil trescientos menos diez mil son noventa mil trescientos. Mil dividido por veinte son cincuenta.** Then ask students to write two math problems of each type for a class-mate to solve. Have partners verify each other's work.

Extra Practice Collect the paragraphs that students wrote for **Actividad 5** and redistribute them among the class. Ask students to write a profile about the person whose paper they received, based on that person's likes and dislikes. For instance, if Kim wrote **No me gusta la clase de música**, the profile should say **Kim estudia música, pero no le gusta la clase**.

Lectura

Antes de leer

Estrategia
Predicting Content Through Formats

Recognizing the format of a document can help you to predict its content. For instance, invitations, greeting cards, and classified ads follow an easily identifiable format, which usually gives you a general idea of the information they contain. Look at the text and identify it based on its format.

	lunes	martes	miércoles	jueves	viernes
8:30	biología		biología		biología
9:00		historia		historia	
9:30	inglés		inglés		inglés
10:00					
10:30					
11:00					
12:00					
12:30					
1:00					
2:00	arte		arte		arte

If you guessed that this is a page from a student's schedule, you are correct. You can now infer that the document contains information about a student's weekly schedule, including days, times, and activities.

Cognados

With a classmate, make a list of the cognates in the document entitled *¡Español en Madrid!* and guess their English meanings. What do cognates reveal about the content of the document?

Examinar el texto

Look at the format of the document. What type of text is it? What information do you expect to find in a document of this kind?

recursos
CH pp. 29–30 | descubre1.vhlcentral.com Lección 2

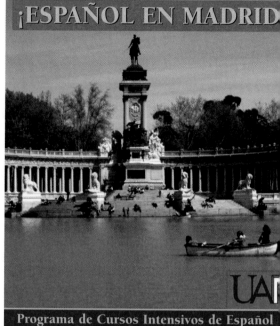

¡ESPAÑOL EN MADRID!

UA

Programa de Cursos Intensivos de Español
Universidad Autónoma de Madrid

Madrid, la capital cultural de Europa, y la UAM te ofrecen cursos intensivos de verano° para aprender° español como nunca antes°.

Después de leer
Correspondencias

Match each item in Column B with the correct word in Column A. Two items will not be used.

A
1. profesores
2. vivienda
3. Madrid
4. número de teléfono
5. Español 2
6. número de fax

B
a. (34) 91 523 4500
b. (34) 91 524 0210
c. 23 junio–30 julio
d. capital cultural de Europa
e. 23 junio–22 julio
f. especializados en enseñar español como lengua extranj
g. (34) 91 523 4623
h. familias españolas

Correspondencias Go over the answers as a class or assign pairs of students to work together to check each other's answers.

¿Dónde?
En el campus de la UAM, edificio° de la Facultad de Filosofía y Letras.

¿Quiénes son los profesores?
Son todos hablantes nativos de español especializados en enseñar el español como lengua extranjera.

¿Qué niveles se ofrecen?
Se ofrecen tres niveles° básicos:
 Español Elemental
 Español Intermedio
 Español Avanzado

Vivienda
Para estudiantes extranjeros se ofrece vivienda° con familias españolas.

¿Cuándo?
Este verano desde° el 16 de junio hasta el 10 de agosto. Los cursos tienen una duración de 6 semanas.

Cursos	Empieza°	Termina
Español 1	16 junio	22 julio
Español 2	23 junio	30 julio
Español 3	30 junio	10 agosto

Información
Para mayor información, sirvan comunicarse con la siguiente° oficina:

Universidad Autónoma de Madrid
Programa de Español como Lengua Extranjera
Ctra. Colmenar Viejo, Km. 15
28049 Madrid, ESPAÑA
Tel. (34) 91 523 4500
Fax (34) 91 523 4623
www.uam.es

verano *summer* aprender *to learn* nunca antes *never before* edificio *building* niveles *levels* vivienda *housing*
desde *from* Empieza *Begins* siguiente *following*

Cierto o falso?

Indicate whether each statement is **cierto** or **falso**. Then correct the false statements.

	Cierto	Falso
1. La Universidad Autónoma de Madrid ofrece (*offers*) cursos intensivos de italiano. Ofrece cursos intensivos de español.	○	⊘
2. La lengua nativa de los profesores del programa es el inglés. La lengua nativa de los profesores es el español.	○	⊘
3. Los cursos de español son en la Facultad de Ciencias. Son en la Facultad de Filosofía y Letras.	○	⊘
4. Los estudiantes pueden vivir (*can live*) con familias españolas.	⊘	○

	Cierto	Falso
5. La universidad que ofrece los cursos intensivos está en Salamanca. Está en Madrid.	○	⊘
6. Español 2 termina en agosto. Termina en julio.	○	⊘
7. Si deseas información sobre (*about*) los cursos intensivos de español, puedes llamar al (34) 91 523 4500.	⊘	○
8. Español 1 empieza en julio. Empieza en junio.	○	⊘

¿Cierto o falso? Give students these true-false statements as items 9–16: **9. El campus de la UAM está en la Ciudad de México. (Falso; está en Madrid.) 10. Los cursos terminan en junio. (Falso; terminan en julio y agosto.) 11. Hay un curso de español intermedio. (Cierto.) 12. Los cursos se ofrecen en el verano. (Cierto.) 13. Hay una residencia estudiantil para los estudiantes extranjeros en el campus. (Falso; hay vivienda con familias españolas para estudiantes extranjeros.) 14. Hay un número de teléfono en la universidad para más información. (Cierto) 15. Todos los profesores son hablantes nativos. (Cierto) 16. Los cursos tienen una duración de doce semanas. (Falso; tienen una duración de seis semanas.)**

TEACHING OPTIONS

Language Notes Explain that in Spanish dates are usually written in the order of day/month/year rather than month/day/year, as they are in the United States and Canada. Someone from Mexico with a birthdate of July 5, 1994, would write his or her birthdate as 5/7/94. To avoid confusion, the month is often written with a roman numeral, 5/VII/94.

Pairs Provide pairs of students with Spanish-language magazines and newspapers. Ask them to look for documents with easily recognizable formats, such as classified ads or advertisements. Ask them to use cognates and other context clues to predict the content. Then have partners present their examples and findings to the class.

Section Goals

In **Escritura**, students will:
- brainstorm and organize their ideas for writing
- write a description of themselves
- incorporate lesson vocabulary and structures

Instructional Resources
Cuaderno para hispanohablantes, pp. 31–32
Cuaderno de actividades, pp. 143–144
Supersite

Estrategia Discuss information students might want to include in a self-description. Record their suggestions in Spanish on the board. Quickly review structures students will include in their writing, such as **me gusta** and **no me gusta** as well as the first-person singular of several verbs, for example: **soy, estoy, tomo, trabajo, estudio.**

Tema Copy on the board the brief chat room description for Alicia Roberts, leaving blanks where her name, courses, and preferences appear. At the end, add the sentences **Me gusta _____.** and **No me gusta _____.** Model completing the description orally with your information and then ask volunteers to complete it with their information.

Escritura

Estrategia
Brainstorming

How do you find ideas to write about? In the early stages of writing, brainstorming can help you generate ideas on a specific topic. You should spend ten to fifteen minutes brainstorming and jotting down any ideas about the topic that occur to you. Whenever possible, try to write down your ideas in Spanish. Express your ideas in single words or phrases, and jot them down in any order. While brainstorming, don't worry about whether your ideas are good or bad. Selecting and organizing ideas should be the second stage of your writing. Remember that the more ideas you write down while you're brainstorming, the more options you'll have to choose from later when you start to organize your ideas.

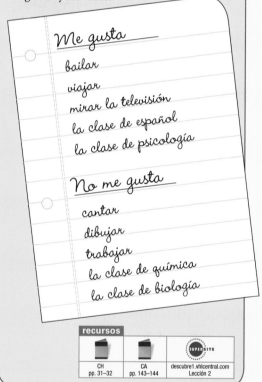

Me gusta
bailar
viajar
mirar la televisión
la clase de español
la clase de psicología

No me gusta
cantar
dibujar
trabajar
la clase de química
la clase de biología

recursos

| CH pp. 31–32 | CA pp. 143–144 | descubre1.vhlcentral.com Lección 2 |

Tema

Una descripción

Write a description of yourself to post in a chat room on a website in order to meet Spanish-speaking people. Include this information in your description:

- your name and where you are from, and a photo (optional) of yourself
- where you go to school
- the courses you are taking
- where you work if you have a job
- some of your likes and dislikes

¡Hola! Me llamo Alicia Roberts. Estudio matemáticas y economía. Me gusta dibujar, cantar y viajar.

EVALUATION: Descripción

Criteria	Scale
Content	1 2 3 4 5
Organization	1 2 3 4 5
Use of vocabulary	1 2 3 4 5
Grammatical accuracy	1 2 3 4 5

Scoring	
Excellent	18–20 points
Good	14–17 points
Satisfactory	10–13 points
Unsatisfactory	< 10 points

Escuchar

Estrategia

Listening for cognates

You already know that cognates are words that have similar spellings and meanings in two or more languages: for example, *group* and **grupo** or *stereo* and **estéreo**. Listen for cognates to increase your comprehension of spoken Spanish.

 To help you practice this strategy, you will now listen to two sentences. Make a list of all the cognates you hear.

Preparación

Based on the photograph, who do you think Armando and Julia are? What do you think they are talking about?

Ahora escucha

Now you are going to hear Armando and Julia's conversation. Make a list of the cognates they use.

Armando	Julia
clases, biología	semestre, astronomía
antropología, filosofía	geología, italiano
japonés, italiano	cálculo, hora, clase
cálculo, profesora	hora, profesora

Based on your knowledge of cognates, decide whether the following statements are **cierto** or **falso**.

	Cierto	Falso
1. Armando y Julia hablan de la familia.	○	⊙
2. Armando y Julia toman una clase de matemáticas.	⊙	○
3. Julia toma clases de ciencias.	⊙	○
4. Armando estudia lenguas extranjeras.	⊙	○
5. Julia toma una clase de religión.	○	⊙

Comprensión

Preguntas

Answer these questions about Armando and Julia's conversation.

1. ¿Qué clases toma Armando?
   Toma antropología, filosofía, japonés, italiano y cálculo.
2. ¿Qué clases toma Julia?
   Toma astronomía, geología, italiano y cálculo.

Seleccionar

Choose the answer that best completes each sentence.

1. Armando toma ____b____ clases en la universidad.
   a. cuatro b. cinco c. seis
2. Julia toma dos clases de ____c____.
   a. matemáticas b. lengua c. ciencias
3. Armando toma italiano y ____b____.
   a. astronomía b. japonés c. geología
4. Armando y Julia estudian ____c____ los martes y jueves.
   a. filosofía b. matemáticas c. italiano

Preguntas personales Answers will vary.

1. ¿Cuántas clases tomas tú este semestre?
2. ¿Qué clases tomas este semestre?
3. ¿Qué clases te gustan y qué clases no te gustan?

Section Goals

In **Escuchar**, students will:
- listen for cognates in a short audio passage
- answer questions based on the content of a recorded conversation

Instructional Resources
Supersite: Textbook MP3 Audio Files
Supersite/TRCD: Textbook Audio Script
Textbook Audio CD

Estrategia
Script 1. La democracia es una forma de gobierno. 2. A mí me gustan los conciertos, las obras de teatro y la danza.

Teaching Tip Invite students to look at the photo and describe what they see. Guide them to guess where they think **Armando** and **Julia** are and what they are talking about.

Ahora escucha
Script ARMANDO: ¡Hola, Julia! ¿Cómo estás?
JULIA: Bien. ¿Y tú, Armando?
A: Bien, gracias. ¿Qué tal tus clases?
J: Van bien.
A: ¿Tomas biología?
J: Este semestre no. Pero sí tomo astronomía y geología… los lunes, miércoles y viernes.
A: ¿Sólo dos? ¿Qué otras clases tomas?
J: Italiano y cálculo, los martes y jueves. ¿Y tú?
A: Los lunes, miércoles y viernes tomo antropología, filosofía y japonés. Los martes y jueves tomo italiano y cálculo.
J: ¿A qué hora es tu clase de italiano?
A: A las nueve, con la profesora Menotti.
J: Yo también tomo italiano los martes y jueves con la profesora Menotti, pero a las once.

En pantalla

Christmas isn't always in winter. During the months of cold weather and snow in North America, the southern hemisphere enjoys warm weather and longer days. Since Chile's summer lasts from December to February, school vacation coincides with these months. In Chile, the school year starts in early March and finishes toward the end of December. All schools, from preschools to universities, observe this scholastic calendar, with only a few days' variation between institutions.

Vocabulario útil	
quería	I wanted
pedirte	to ask you
te preocupa	it worries you
ahorrar	to save (money)
Navidad	Christmas
aprovecha	take advantage of
nuestras	our
ofertas	offers, deals
calidad	quality
no cuesta	doesn't cost

¿Qué hay?

For each item, write **sí** if it appears in the TV clip or **no** if it does not.

<u>no</u> 1. papelera   <u>no</u> 5. diccionario
<u>sí</u> 2. lápiz   <u>sí</u> 6. cuaderno
<u>sí</u> 3. mesa   <u>no</u> 7. tiza
<u>no</u> 4. computadora   <u>sí</u> 8. ventana

¿Qué quieres?

Write a list of things that you want for your next birthday. Then read it to the class so they know what to get you. Use as much Spanish as you can.
Answers will vary.

Lista de cumpleaños°

Quiero°...

cumpleaños *birthday*   Quiero *I want*   Viejito Pascuero *Santa Claus (Chile)*

Oye cómo va

Sarita Montiel

Sara Montiel was born **María Antonia Abad Fernández** in 1928 in the village of Campo de Criptana, Spain. Discovered by a producer when she was just fifteen, during the following three decades she starred in movies in Spain, Mexico, and Hollywood. Films, such as *Veracruz* (1954, with Gary Cooper and Burt Lancaster) and the classic musicals *El último cuplé* (1957) and *La violetera* (1958), elevated her to mythical status as both a singer and an actress. Her many honors include two best actress awards from Spain's prestigious **Círculo de Escritores Cinematográficos**. After retiring from the screen in the seventies, Sarita—as she is popularly known—has continued to thrive on stage and television, singing the popular **cuplés** and **boleros** that won her fame on film.

Your instructor will play the song. Listen and then complete these activities.

Comprensión

Put these statements about Sara Montiel's life in order.

6 a. Sara begins working on stage and television.

4 b. *La violetera* is released.

2 c. She appears in a movie with Gary Cooper.

5 d. She stops working in the film industry.

1 e. A producer discovers Sara at fifteen.

3 f. Sara stars in *El último cuplé*.

Interpretación

Discuss these questions with a classmate. Then share your answers with the class.

1. Do you think the singer is joyful or heartbroken? What word is used to convey this feeling? heartbroken; desesperando

2. What does the singer want? What words in the first verse suggest this? The singer wants to be with someone, as suggested by the question words **cuándo**, **cómo**, and **dónde**.

3. What answer does the singer always receive? Why do you think this is so? Quizás, quizás, quizás. Answers will vary.

4. Do you think the singer will continue in the same situation or move on? Answers will vary.

Siempre *Always* responde *you answer* quizás *maybe* así *like this* desesperando *despairing* contestando *answering* fronteras *borders*

Quizás, quizás, quizás

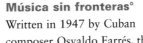

Siempre° que te pregunto
que cuándo, cómo y dónde,
tú siempre me respondes°
quizás°, quizás, quizás.

Y así° pasan los días
y yo, desesperando°,
y tú, tú contestando°
quizás, quizás, quizás.

Nat King Cole

Música sin fronteras°

Written in 1947 by Cuban composer Osvaldo Farrés, the popularity of *Quizás, quizás, quizás* has persisted over generations, with renditions existing in many languages and musical styles. Nat King Cole sang perhaps the most well-known version; other artists include Sonora Matancera, Doris Day, Xavier Cugat, Cake, and the Turkish group Athena, who made a ska-punk version. The song featured in the soundtracks for *America's Sweethearts* (2001), *La mala educación* (2004), and *Brokeback Mountain* (2005).

recursos

SUPERSITE

descubre1.vhlcentral.com
Lección 2

SUPERSITE Conexión Internet

Go to **descubre1.vhlcentral.com** to learn more about the artist featured in this **Oye cómo va** section.

Section Goals

In **Oye cómo va**, students will:
• read about **Sara Montiel**
• read about different versions of *Quizás, quizás, quizás*
• listen to a song by **Sara Montiel**

Instructional Resources
Supersite
Vista Higher Learning
Cancionero

Antes de escuchar
• Have students read the title of the song. Then have them scan the lyrics and underline any interrogative words that they recognize (**cuándo, cómo, dónde**).
• Describe the musical styles mentioned here. **Cuplés** are light songs born out of Spanish folklore. They were very popular in Spain's theaters in the nineteenth century. **Boleros** are believed to have originated in Spain, but are immensely popular in the Americas (especially Mexico and Cuba). **Boleros** usually deal with romantic or patriotic love.
• Ask students if they think the rhythm of *Quizás, quizás, quizás* will be more like a **cuplé** or a **bolero**. (It is a **bolero**.)

Comprensión After completing the activity, ask students to write three more sentences based on **Sara Montiel's** biography on separate strips of paper. Have students exchange their sentences with a partner, who will put them in chronological order.

Interpretación Have students discuss ways in which the singer mentions time. Answers might include the repeated mention of **y así pasan los días**, or questions like **¿hasta cuándo?** Why is time of importance to the singer?

TEACHING OPTIONS

Extra Practice Invite students to sing along with the recording. Then teach students two other ways to say *maybe* in Spanish: **a lo mejor** and **tal vez**. Play the song two more times, and ask students to replace **quizás** with the alternate phrases.

Cultural Activity Have pairs use the Internet or the library to research one of the other renditions of *Quizás, quizás, quizás* mentioned in **Música sin fronteras**. Ask them to compare the two versions in terms of language and musical style. Have pairs present their findings to the class.

España

El país en cifras

▶ **Área:** 504.750 km² (kilómetros cuadrados) ó 194.884 millas cuadradas°, incluyendo las islas Baleares y las islas Canarias

▶ **Población:** 43.993.000

▶ **Capital:** Madrid—5.977.000

▶ **Ciudades° principales:** Barcelona—4.998.000, Valencia—806.000, Sevilla, Zaragoza

SOURCE: Population Division, UN Secretariat

▶ **Moneda°:** euro

▶ **Idiomas°:** español o castellano, catalán, gallego, valenciano, eusquera

Regiones lingüísticas

Bandera de España

Españoles célebres

▶ **Miguel de Cervantes,** escritor° (1547–1616)
▶ **Pedro Almodóvar,** director de cine° (1949–)
▶ **Rosa Montero,** escritora y periodista° (1951–)
▶ **Fernando Alonso,** corredor de autos° (1981–)
▶ **Paz Vega,** actriz° (1976–)

millas cuadradas *square miles* Ciudades *Cities* Moneda *Currency* Idiomas *Languages* escritor *writer* cine *film* periodista *reporter* corredor de autos *racing driver* actriz *actress* pueblo *town* Cada año *Every year* Durante todo un día *All day long* se tiran *throw at each other* varias toneladas *many tons*

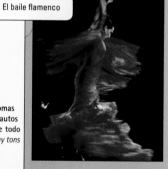

El baile flamenco

La Sagrada Familia en Barcelona

Plaza Mayor en Madrid

FRANCIA
ANDORRA
Mar Cantábrico
La Coruña
San Sebastián
Pirineos
Salamanca
Zaragoza Río Ebro
Barcelona
ESPAÑA
Madrid
Valencia
Menorca
Mallorca
Ibiza
PORTUGAL
Islas Baleares
Sevilla
Sierra Nevada
Mar Mediterráneo
Estrecho de Gibraltar
Ceuta
Melilla
MARRUECOS
OCÉANO ATLÁNTICO
EUROPA
ESPAÑA
ÁFRICA

Islas Canarias
La Palma
Lanzarote
Tenerife Gran Canaria
Gomera Fuerteventura
Hierro

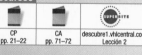

recursos

| CP pp. 21–22 | CA pp. 71–72 | descubre1.vhlcentral.com Lección 2 |

¡Increíble pero cierto!

En Buñol, un pueblo° de Valencia, la producción de tomates es un recurso económico muy importante. Cada año° se celebra el festival de *La Tomatina*. Durante todo un día°, miles de personas se tiran° tomates. Llegan turistas de todo el país, y se usan varias toneladas° de tomates.

Section Goal

In **Panorama,** students will read about the geography, culture, and economy of Spain.

Instructional Resources
Cuaderno de práctica, pp. 21–22
Cuaderno de actividades, pp. 71–72
e-Cuaderno
Supersite/DVD: *Panorama cultural*
Supersite/TRCD: *PowerPoints* (Overheads #7, #8, #15); *Panorama cultural* Videoscript & Translation, Answer Keys

Teaching Tip Show *Overhead PowerPoint #15* or have students use the map in their books to find the places mentioned. Explain that the Canary Islands are located in the Atlantic Ocean, off the northwestern coast of Africa. Point out the photos that accompany the map on this page.

El país en cifras After students have read **Idiomas,** associate the regional languages with the larger map by asking questions such as: **¿Hablan catalán en Barcelona? ¿Qué idioma hablan en Madrid?** Point out that the names of languages may be capitalized as map labels, but are not capitalized when they appear in running text.

¡Increíble pero cierto! In addition to festivals related to economic and agricultural resources, Spain has many festivals rooted in Catholic tradition. Among the most famous is **Semana Santa** (*Holy Week*) which is celebrated annually in Seville, and many other towns and cities, with great reverence and pageantry.

TEACHING OPTIONS

Heritage Speakers **Paella,** the national dish of Spain, is the ancestor of the popular Latin American dish **arroz con pollo.** Ask heritage speakers if they know of any dishes traditional in their families that have their roots in Spanish cuisine. Invite them to describe the dish to the class.

Variación léxica Tell students that they may also see the word **eusquera** spelled **euskera** and **euskara.** The letter **k** is used in Spanish only in words of foreign origin. **Euskera** is the Basque name of the Basque language, which linguists believe is unrelated to any other known language. The spelling students see on this page (**eusquera**) follows the principles of Spanish orthography. The Spanish name for *Basque* is **vascuence** or **vasco.**

Lugares • **La Universidad de Salamanca**

La Universidad de Salamanca, fundada en 1218, es la más antigua° de España. Más de 35.000 estudiantes toman clases en la universidad. La universidad está en la ciudad de Salamanca, famosa por sus edificios° históricos, tales como° los puentes° romanos y las catedrales góticas.

Economía • **La Unión Europea**

Desde° 1992 España es miembro de la Unión Europea, un grupo de países europeos que trabaja para desarrollar° una política° económica y social común en Europa. La moneda de la mayoría de países de la Unión Europea es el euro.

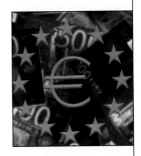

Artes • **Velázquez y el Prado**

El Prado, en Madrid, es uno de los museos más famosos del mundo°. En el Prado hay pinturas° importantes de Botticelli, de El Greco y de los españoles Goya y Velázquez. *Las meninas* es la obra° más conocida° de Diego Velázquez, pintor° oficial de la corte real° durante el siglo° XVII.

Las meninas,
Diego Velázquez, 1656

Comida • **La paella**

La paella es uno de los platos más típicos de España. Siempre se prepara° con arroz° y azafrán°, pero hay diferentes recetas°. La paella valenciana, por ejemplo, es de pollo° y conejo°, y la paella marinera es de mariscos°.

Una playa de Ibiza

¿Qué aprendiste? Completa las oraciones con la información adecuada.

1. La <u>Unión Europea</u> trabaja para desarrollar una política económica común en Europa.
2. El arroz y el azafrán son ingredientes básicos de la <u>paella</u>.
3. El Prado está en <u>Madrid</u>.
4. La universidad más antigua de España es la <u>Universidad de Salamanca</u>.
5. La ciudad de <u>Salamanca</u> es famosa por sus edificios históricos, tales como los puentes romanos.
6. El gallego es una de las lenguas oficiales de <u>España</u>.

Conexión Internet Investiga estos temas en **descubre1.vhlcentral.com.**

1. Busca (*Look for*) información sobre la Universidad de Salamanca u otra universidad española. ¿Qué cursos ofrece (*does it offer*)?
2. Busca información sobre un español o una española célebre (por ejemplo, un(a) político/a, un actor, una actriz, un(a) artista). ¿De qué parte de España es, y por qué es célebre?

....

más antigua *oldest* edificios *buildings* tales como *such as* puentes *bridges* Desde *Since* desarrollar *develop* política *policy* mundo *world* pinturas *paintings* obra *work* más conocida *best-known* pintor *painter* corte real *royal court* siglo *century* Siempre se prepara *It is always prepared* arroz *rice* azafrán *saffron* recetas *recipes* pollo *chicken* conejo *rabbit* mariscos *seafood*

La Universidad de Salamanca The University of Salamanca hosts many programs for foreign students. One of the oldest universities in Europe, Salamanca is famous for its medieval buildings and student musical societies, called **tunas**.

La Unión Europea Have students use the Internet, a newspaper, or a bank to learn the current exchange rate for euros on the international market.

Velázquez y el Prado Point out **la infanta Margarita**, the royal princess, with her attendants. The name **Las meninas** comes from the Portuguese word for "girls" used to refer to royal attendants. Reflected in the mirror are **Margarita's** parents, **los reyes Felipe IV y Mariana de Asturias**. Have students find **Velázquez** himself, standing paintbrush in hand, before an enormous canvas. You may wish to ask students to research the identity of the man in the doorway.

La paella Pairs can role-play a restaurant scene: the customer asks the waiter/waitress about the ingredients in the paella, then chooses **paella valenciana** or **paella marinera**.

Conexión Internet Students will find supporting Internet activities and links at **descubre1.vhlcentral.com**.

Teaching Tip You may want to wrap up this section by playing the *Panorama cultural* video footage for this lesson.

Variación léxica Regional cultures and languages have remained strong in Spain, despite efforts made in the past to suppress them in the name of national unity. The language that has come to be called *Spanish*, **español**, is the language of the region of north central Spain called **Castilla**. Because Spain was unified under the Kingdom of Castile at the end of the Middle Ages, the language of Castile, **castellano**, became the principal language of government, business, and literature. Even today one is likely to hear Spanish speakers refer to Spanish as **castellano** or **español**. Efforts to suppress the regional languages, though often harsh, were ineffective, and after the death of the dictator **Francisco Franco** and the return of power to regional governing bodies, the regional languages of Spain were given co-official status.

Instructional Resources
Cuaderno de actividades, p. 98
e-Cuaderno
Supersite: Textbook &
Vocabulary MP3 Audio Files
Supersite/TRCD/Print: Answer
Keys; *Testing Program*
(**Lección 2 Pruebas,** Test
Generator, Testing Program
MP3 Audio Files)
Textbook & Test Audio CD

La clase

el/la compañero/a de clase	classmate
el/la compañero/a de cuarto	roommate
el/la estudiante	student
el/la profesor(a)	teacher
el borrador	eraser
el escritorio	desk
el libro	book
el mapa	map
la mesa	table
la mochila	backpack
el papel	paper
la papelera	wastebasket
la pizarra	blackboard
la pluma	pen
la puerta	door
el reloj	clock; watch
la silla	seat
la tiza	chalk
la ventana	window
la biblioteca	library
la cafetería	cafeteria
la casa	house; home
el estadio	stadium
el laboratorio	laboratory
la librería	bookstore
la residencia estudiantil	dormitory
la universidad	university; college
la clase	class
el curso, la materia	course
la especialización	major
el examen	test; exam
el horario	schedule
la prueba	test; quiz
el semestre	semester
la tarea	homework
el trimestre	trimester; quarter

Las materias

la administración de empresas	business administration
el arte	art
la biología	biology
las ciencias	sciences
la computación	computer science
la contabilidad	accounting
la economía	economics
el español	Spanish
la física	physics
la geografía	geography
la historia	history
las humanidades	humanities
el inglés	English
las lenguas extranjeras	foreign languages
la literatura	literature
las matemáticas	mathematics
la música	music
el periodismo	journalism
la psicología	psychology
la química	chemistry
la sociología	sociology

Preposiciones

al lado de	next to; beside
a la derecha de	to the right of
a la izquierda de	to the left of
en	in; on
cerca de	near
con	with
debajo de	below; under
delante de	in front of
detrás de	behind
encima de	on top of
entre	between; among
lejos de	far from
sin	without
sobre	on; over

Palabras adicionales

¿Adónde?	Where (to)?
ahora	now
¿Cuál?, ¿Cuáles?	Which?; Which one(s)?
¿Por qué?	Why?
porque	because

Verbos

bailar	to dance
buscar	to look for
caminar	to walk
cantar	to sing
cenar	to have dinner
comprar	to buy
contestar	to answer
conversar	to converse, to chat
desayunar	to have breakfast
descansar	to rest
desear	to wish; to desire
dibujar	to draw
enseñar	to teach
escuchar la radio/ música	to listen (to) the radio/music
esperar (+ *inf.*)	to wait (for); to hope
estar	to be
estudiar	to study
explicar	to explain
gustar	to like
hablar	to talk; to speak
llegar	to arrive
llevar	to carry
mirar	to look (at); to watch
necesitar (+ *inf.*)	to need
practicar	to practice
preguntar	to ask (a question)
preparar	to prepare
regresar	to return
terminar	to end; to finish
tomar	to take; to drink
trabajar	to work
viajar	to travel

Los días de la semana

¿Cuándo?	When?
¿Qué día es hoy?	What day is it?
Hoy es...	Today is...
la semana	week
lunes	Monday
martes	Tuesday
miércoles	Wednesday
jueves	Thursday
viernes	Friday
sábado	Saturday
domingo	Sunday

Numbers 31 and higher	See pages 63–64.
Expresiones útiles	See page 45.

recursos

CA p. 98	descubre1.vhlcentral.com Lección 2

La familia

3

Communicative Goals

You will learn how to:
- Talk about your family and friends
- Describe people and things
- Express ownership

contextos

pages 78–81
- The family
- Identifying people
- Professions and occupations

fotonovela

pages 82–85
On their way to Otavalo, Maite, Inés, Álex, and Javier talk about their families. Don Francisco observes the growing friendships among the four students.

cultura

pages 86–87
- Surnames and families in the Spanish-speaking world
- Spain's Royal Family

estructura

pages 88–105
- Descriptive adjectives
- Possessive adjectives
- Present tense of -er and -ir verbs
- Present tense of tener and venir
- Recapitulación

adelante

pages 106–113
Lectura: A brief article about families
Escritura: A letter to a friend
Escuchar: A conversation between friends
En pantalla
Oye cómo va
Panorama: Ecuador

A PRIMERA VISTA
- ¿Hay cuatro personas en la foto?
- ¿Hay una mujer a la izquierda? ¿Y a la derecha?
- ¿Está el hombre al lado de la mujer?
- ¿Conversan ellos? ¿Trabajan? ¿Viajan? ¿Caminan?

Lesson Goals

In **Lección 3**, students will be introduced to the following:
- terms for family relationships
- names of various professions
- surnames and families in the Spanish-speaking world
- Spain's Royal Family
- descriptive adjectives
- possessive adjectives
- the present tense of common regular –er and –ir verbs
- the present tense of **tener** and **venir**
- context clues to unlock meaning of unfamiliar words
- using idea maps when writing
- how to write a friendly letter
- strategies for asking clarification in oral communication
- a television commercial for **Pentel**
- Ecuadorian singer **Olimpo Cárdenas**
- geographical and cultural information about Ecuador

A primera vista Here are some additional questions you can ask based on the photo: **¿Cuántas personas hay en tu familia? ¿De qué conversas con ellos? ¿Viajas mucho con ellos?**

INSTRUCTIONAL RESOURCES

Student Materials
Cuaderno de práctica, Cuaderno para hispanohablantes, Cuaderno de actividades
Student MAESTRO™ Supersite
(descubre1.vhlcentral.com)
MAESTRO™ e-Cuaderno

Teacher's Resource CD-ROM and in print
*Answer Keys, Audioscripts, Videoscripts
*PowerPoints
Testing Program (**Pruebas,** Test Generator, MP3 Audio Files)
Vista Higher Learning *Cancionero*
*Also available on Supersite

Teacher's MAESTRO™ Supersite
(descubre1.vhlcentral.com)
Learning Management System (Assignment Task Manager, Gradebook)
Also on DVD
Fotonovela, Flash cultura, Panorama cultural

La familia

La familia de José Miguel Pérez Santoro

Más vocabulario

los abuelos	grandparents
el/la bisabuelo/a	great-grandfather/great-grandmother
el/la gemelo/a	twin
el/la hermanastro/a	stepbrother/stepsister
el/la hijastro/a	stepson/stepdaughter
la madrastra	stepmother
el medio hermano/ la media hermana	half-brother/ half-sister
el padrastro	stepfather
los padres	parents
los parientes	relatives
el/la cuñado/a	brother-in-law/ sister-in-law
la nuera	daughter-in-law
el/la suegro/a	father-in-law/ mother-in-law
el yerno	son-in-law
el/la amigo/a	friend
el apellido	last name
la gente	people
el/la muchacho/a	boy/girl
el/la niño/a	child
el/la novio/a	boyfriend/girlfriend
la persona	person
el/la artista	artist
el/la ingeniero/a	engineer
el/la doctor(a), el/la médico/a	doctor; physician
el/la periodista	journalist
el/la programador(a)	computer programmer

Variación léxica

madre ⟷ mamá, mami *(colloquial)*
padre ⟷ papá, papi *(colloquial)*
muchacho/a ⟷ chico/a

recursos

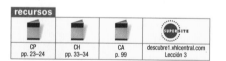

| CP pp. 23–24 | CH pp. 33–34 | CA p. 99 | descubre1.vhlcentral.com Lección 3 |

Juan Santoro Sánchez

mi abuelo (*my grandfather*)

Ernesto Santoro González

mi tío (*uncle*)
hijo (*son*) de Juan y Socorro

Marina Gutiérrez de Santoro

mi tía (*aunt*)
esposa (*wife*) de Ernesto

Silvia Socorro Santoro Gutiérrez

mi prima (*cousin*)
hija (*daughter*) de Ernesto y Marina

Héctor Manuel Santoro Gutiérrez

mi primo (*cousin*)
nieto (*grandson*) de Juan y Socorro

Carmen Santoro Gutiérrez

mi prima
hija de Ernesto y Marina

¡LENGUA VIVA!

In Spanish-speaking countries, it is common for people to go by both first name and middle name, such as **José Miguel.** You will learn more about names and naming conventions on p. 86.

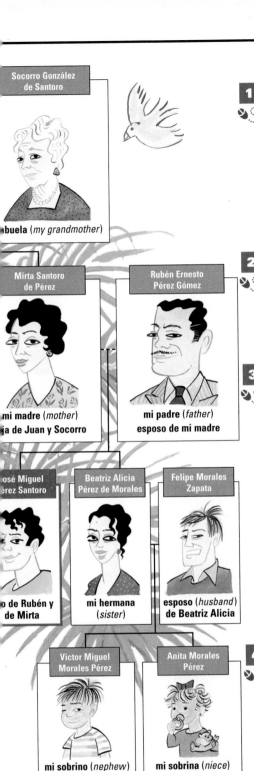

Socorro González de Santoro

...buela (*my grandmother*)

Mirta Santoro de Pérez

Rubén Ernesto Pérez Gómez

...mi madre (*mother*)
...ja de Juan y Socorro

mi padre (*father*)
esposo de mi madre

...osé Miguel ...érez Santoro

Beatriz Alicia Pérez de Morales

Felipe Morales Zapata

...o de Rubén y ...de Mirta

mi hermana (*sister*)

esposo (*husband*)
de Beatriz Alicia

Víctor Miguel Morales Pérez

Anita Morales Pérez

mi sobrino (*nephew*)
...hermano (*brother*)
de Anita

mi sobrina (*niece*)
nieta (*granddaughter*)
de mis padres

los hijos (*children*) **de Beatriz Alicia y de Felipe**

Práctica

1 Escuchar 🎧 Listen to each statement made by José Miguel Pérez Santoro, then indicate whether it is **cierto** or **falso**, based on his family tree.

	Cierto	Falso			Cierto	Falso
1.	⊘	○		6.	⊘	○
2.	⊘	○		7.	⊘	○
3.	○	⊘		8.	○	⊘
4.	⊘	○		9.	○	⊘
5.	○	⊘		10.	⊘	○

2 Personas 🎧 Indicate each word that you hear mentioned in the narration.

1. _____ cuñado   4. ✔ niño   7. _____ ingeniera
2. ✔ tía   5. ✔ esposo   8. ✔ primo
3. ✔ periodista   6. ✔ abuelos

3 Emparejar Match the letter of each phrase with the correct description. Two items will not be used.

1. Mi hermano programa las computadoras. c
2. Son los padres de mi esposo. e
3. Son los hijos de mis (*my*) tíos. h
4. Mi tía trabaja en un hospital. a
5. Es el hijo de mi madrastra y el hijastro de mi padre. b
6. Es el esposo de mi hija. l
7. Es el hijo de mi hermana. k
8. Mi primo dibuja y pinta mucho. i
9. Mi hermanastra enseña en la universidad. j
10. Mi padre trabaja con planos (*blueprints*). d

  a. Es médica.
  b. Es mi hermanastro.
  c. Es programador.
  d. Es ingeniero.
  e. Son mis suegros.
  f. Es mi novio.
  g. Es mi padrastro.
  h. Son mis primos.
  i. Es artista.
  j. Es profesora.
  k. Es mi sobrino.
  l. Es mi yerno.

4 Definiciones Define these family terms in Spanish.

modelo
hijastro Es el hijo de mi esposo/a, pero no es mi hijo.

1. abuela
2. bisabuelo
3. tío
4. parientes
5. suegra
6. cuñado
7. nietos
8. medio hermano

1. la madre de mi madre/padre
2. el abuelo de mi madre/padre
3. el hermano de mi madre/padre
4. la familia extendida
5. la madre de mi esposo/a
6. el esposo de mi hermana
7. los hijos de mis hijos
8. el hijo de mi padre/madre pero no de mi madre/padre

1 Teaching Tip To challenge students, have them correct the false statements by referring to the family tree.

1 Script 1. Beatriz Alicia es mi hermana. 2. Rubén es el abuelo de Víctor Miguel. 3. Silvia es mi sobrina. 4. Mirta y Rubén son los tíos de Héctor Manuel. 5. Anita es mi prima. 6. Ernesto es el hermano de mi madre. 7. Soy el tío de Anita. 8. Víctor Miguel es mi nieto. 9. Carmen, Beatriz Alicia y Marina son los nietos de Juan y Socorro. 10. El hijo de Juan y Socorro es el tío de Beatriz Alicia.
Textbook Audio

2 Teaching Tips
• To simplify, read through the list as a class before playing the audio. Remind students to focus only on these words as they listen.
• Tell students that the words, if they appear in the narration, will not follow the sequence in the list.

2 Script Julia y Daniel son mis abuelos. Ellos viven en Montreal con mi tía Leti, que es periodista, y con mi primo César. César es un niño muy bueno y dibuja muy bien. Hoy voy a hablar por teléfono con todos ellos y con el esposo de Leti. Él es de Canadá.
Textbook Audio

3 Expansion After students finish, ask volunteers to provide complete sentences combining elements from the numbered and lettered lists.
Ex: **Los padres de mi esposo son mis suegros. Mis primos son los hijos de mis tíos.**

4 Expansion Have student pairs write five additional definitions following the pattern of those in the activity.

5

Escoger Complete the description of each photo using words you have learned in **Contextos**. Some answers will vary.

1. La ___familia___ de Sara es muy grande.

2. Héctor y Lupita son ___novios___.

3. Alberto Díaz es ___médico___.

4. Rubén camina con su ___hijo/padre___.

5. Los dos ___hermanos___ están en el parque.

6. Don Manuel es el ___abuelo___ de Martín.

7. Elena Vargas Soto es ___artista___.

8. Irene es ___programadora___.

TEACHING OPTIONS

Extra Practice Add an additional visual aspect to this vocabulary practice. Ask students to bring in a family-related photo of their own or a photo from the Internet or a magazine. Have them write a fill-in-the-blank sentence to go with it. Working in pairs, have them guess what is happening in each other's photo and complete the sentence.

Pairs Have pairs of students create an additional sentence for each of the photos on this page. Ask one student to write sentences for the first four photos and the other student to write sentences for the remainder. Then have them exchange papers and check each other's work.

Comunicación

6   **Una familia**   With a classmate, identify the members in the family tree by asking questions about how each family member is related to Graciela Vargas García.

> **modelo**
>
> **Estudiante 1:** ¿Quién es Beatriz Pardo de Vargas?
> **Estudiante 2:** Es la abuela de Graciela.

CONSULTA

To see the cities where these family members live, look at the map in **Panorama** on p. 112.

David Vargas Olmedo — de Quito — abuelo
Beatriz Pardo de Vargas — de Ibarra — abuela

Carlos Antonio López Ríos — de Cuenca — tío
Lupe Vargas de López — de Quito — tía
Juan Vargas Pardo — de Quito — padre
María Susana García de Vargas — de Guayaquil — madre

Ernesto López Vargas — de Loja — primo
Ramón Vargas García — de Machala — hermano
Graciela Vargas García — de Machala

Now take turns asking each other these questions. Then invent three original questions.

1. ¿Cómo se llama el primo de Graciela?   Se llama Ernesto López Vargas.
2. ¿Cómo se llama la hija de David y de Beatriz?   Se llama Lupe Vargas de López.
3. ¿De dónde es María Susana?   Es de Guayaquil.
4. ¿De dónde son Ramón y Graciela?   Son de Machala.
5. ¿Cómo se llama el yerno de David y de Beatriz?   Se llama Carlos Antonio López Ríos.
6. ¿De dónde es Carlos Antonio?   Es de Cuenca.
7. ¿De dónde es Ernesto?   Es de Loja.
8. ¿Cuáles son los apellidos del sobrino de Lupe?   Son Vargas García.

7   **Preguntas personales**   With a classmate, take turns asking each other these questions.
Answers will vary.
1. ¿Cuántas personas hay en tu familia?
2. ¿Cómo se llaman tus padres? ¿De dónde son? ¿Dónde trabajan?
3. ¿Cuántos hermanos tienes? ¿Cómo se llaman? ¿Dónde estudian o trabajan?
4. ¿Cuántos primos tienes? ¿Cuáles son los apellidos de ellos? ¿Cuántos son niños y cuántos son adultos? ¿Hay más chicos o más chicas en tu familia?
5. ¿Quién es tu pariente favorito?
6. ¿Tienes novio/a? ¿Cómo se llama?

AYUDA

tu *your* (sing.)
tus *your* (plural)
mi *my* (sing.)
mis *my* (plural)
tienes *you have*
tengo *I have*

6 Teaching Tip Show *Overhead PowerPoint #17* to do this activity.

6 Expansion Model the pronunciation of the Ecuadorian cities mentioned. Ask students to locate each on the map of Ecuador, page 112. Ask students to talk about each city based on the map. Ex: **Guayaquil y Machala son ciudades de la costa del Pacífico. Quito, Loja y Cuenca son ciudades de la cordillera de los Andes. Quito es la capital del Ecuador.**

7 Expansion
• Emphasize that, for this activity and throughout the lesson, if students do not feel comfortable talking about their own families, they may refer to fictional family members or a family that they know.
• After modeling the activity with the whole class, have students circulate around the classroom asking their classmates these questions.
• Have pairs of students ask each other these questions, writing down the answers. After they have finished, ask students questions about their partner's answers. Ex: **¿Cuántas personas hay en la familia de ____? ¿Cómo se llaman los padres de ____? ¿De dónde son ellos? ¿Cuántos hermanos tiene ____?**

TEACHING OPTIONS

Extra Practice For homework, ask students to draw their own family tree or that of a fictional family. Have them label each position on the tree with the appropriate family term and the name of the family member. In class, ask students questions about the family. Ex: **¿Cómo se llama tu prima? ¿Cómo es ella? ¿Ella es estudiante? ¿Cómo se llama tu madre? ¿Quién es tu cuñado?**

TPR Start a family tree by calling on one student to stand in front of the class. Then indicate another student, telling them: ____, **eres el/la esposo/a de** (*first student*); the two should link arms. Complete the family tree by calling on students and stating their relationships. Students have five seconds to come to the front of the class and stand or kneel in the appropriate spot in the family tree.

Section Goals

In **Fotonovela**, students will:
- receive comprehensible input from free-flowing discourse
- learn functional phrases for talking about their families

Instructional Resources
Cuaderno de actividades,
pp. 55–56
e-Cuaderno
Supersite/DVD: *Fotonovela*
Supersite/TRCD/Print:
Fotonovela Videoscript &
Translation, Answer Keys

Video Recap: Lección 2
Before doing this **Fotonovela** section, review the previous one with this activity.
1. ¿Quién estudia periodismo? (Maite) 2. ¿Quién toma cinco clases? (Inés) 3. ¿En qué clase de Inés hay más chicas? (sociología) 4. ¿Cuál es la opinión de Álex con respecto a las computadoras? (Son muy interesantes.)

Video Synopsis The bus trip continues. **Maite, Inés,** and **Javier** talk about their families. As they talk, **Javier** secretly sketches **Inés**. When **Maite** discovers what he is drawing, both he and **Inés** are embarrassed. Behind the wheel, **Don Francisco** wonders what is happening.

Teaching Tips
- Ask students to read the title, glance at the video stills, and predict what they think the episode will be about.
- Work through the **Expresiones útiles** by asking students about their families. React to their responses and ask other students questions about their classmates' answers. Ex: **¿Cuántos hermanos tienes? (Sólo tengo una hermana.)** Ask another student: **¿Cuántos hermanos tiene _____? (Sólo tiene una hermana.)**

¿Es grande tu familia?

communication / cultures
NATIONAL STANDARDS

Los chicos hablan de sus familias en el autobús.

PERSONAJES

MAITE

INÉS

DON FRANCISCO

ÁLEX

JAVIER

1
MAITE Inés, ¿tienes una familia grande?
INÉS Pues, sí... mis papás, mis abuelos, cuatro hermanas y muchos tíos y primos.

2
INÉS Sólo tengo un hermano mayor, Pablo. Su esposa, Francesca, es médica. No es ecuatoriana, es italiana. Sus papás viven en Roma, creo. Vienen de visita cada año. Ah... y Pablo es periodista.
MAITE ¡Qué interesante!

3
INÉS ¿Y tú, Javier? ¿Tienes hermanos?
JAVIER No, pero aquí tengo unas fotos de mi familia.
INÉS ¡Ah! ¡Qué bien! ¡A ver!

6
INÉS ¿Y cómo es él?
JAVIER Es muy simpático. Él es viejo pero es un hombre muy trabajador.

7
MAITE Oye, Javier, ¿qué dibujas?
JAVIER ¿Eh? ¿Quién? ¿Yo? ¡Nada!
MAITE ¡Venga! ¡No seas tonto!

8
MAITE Jaaavieeer... Oye, pero ¡qué bien dibujas!
JAVIER Este... pues... ¡Sí! ¡Gracias!

recursos
CA pp. 55–56
SUPERSITE
descubre1.vhlcentral.com
Lección 3

¿Es grande tu familia? Before viewing the **¿Es grande tu familia?** segment of the **Fotonovela**, ask students to brainstorm a list of things that they think might happen in an episode in which the characters find out about each other's families. Then play the segment once without sound and have the class create a plot summary based on visual clues. Afterward, show the segment with sound and have the class correct any mistaken guesses and fill in any gaps in the plot summary they created.

Teaching Tip Ask students to read the **Fotonovela** captions in groups of five. Then ask one or two groups to role-play the conversation for the class.

Expresiones útiles Draw attention to the masculine, feminine, singular, and plural forms of descriptive adjectives and the present tense of **tener** in the video-still captions and the **Expresiones útiles**, and as they occur in your conversation with the students. Point out that this material will be formally presented in **Estructura**. Correct students when they ask for correction, but do not expect them to be able to produce the forms correctly at this time.

JAVIER ¡Aquí están!

INÉS ¡Qué alto es tu papá! Y tu mamá, ¡qué bonita!

JAVIER Mira, aquí estoy yo. Y éste es mi abuelo. Es el padre de mi mamá.

INÉS ¿Cuántos años tiene tu abuelo?

JAVIER Noventa y dos.

MAITE Álex, mira, ¿te gusta?

ÁLEX Sí, mucho. ¡Es muy bonito!

DON FRANCISCO Epa, ¿qué pasa con Inés y Javier?

Expresiones útiles

Talking about your family

- **¿Tienes una familia grande?**
  Do you have a large family?
  Sí... mis papás, mis abuelos, cuatro hermanas y muchos tíos.
  Yes... my parents, my grandparents, four sisters, and many (aunts and) uncles.
  Sólo tengo un hermano mayor/ menor.
  I only have one older/younger brother.

- **¿Tienes hermanos?**
  Do you have siblings (brothers or sisters)?
  No, soy hijo único.
  No, I'm an only (male) child.

- **Su esposa, Francesca, es médica.**
  His wife, Francesca, is a doctor.
  No es ecuatoriana, es italiana.
  She's not Ecuadorian; she's Italian.
  Pablo es periodista.
  Pablo is a journalist.
  Es el padre de mi mamá.
  He is my mother's father.

Describing people

- **¡Qué alto es tu papá!**
  How tall your father is!
- **Y tu mamá, ¡qué bonita!**
  And your mother, how pretty!

- **¿Cómo es tu abuelo?**
  What is your grandfather like?
  Es simpático.
  He's nice.
  Es viejo.
  He's old.
  Es un hombre muy trabajador.
  He's a very hard-working man.

Saying how old people are

- **¿Cuántos años tienes?**
  How old are you?
- **¿Cuántos años tiene tu abuelo?**
  How old is your grandfather?
  Noventa y dos.
  Ninety-two.

TEACHING OPTIONS

TPR As you play the *Fotonovela* segment, have students raise their right hand when they hear family-related vocabulary and their left hand when they hear a word or phrase related to professions.
Extra Practice As a preview to **Estructura 3.1**, have students scan the **Fotonovela** captions and **Expresiones útiles** and guide them in identifying the descriptive adjectives. Then ask students to rephrase the sentences so that they reflect their own family.

Ex: **No tengo una familia grande. Mi papá es alto.**
Extra Practice Have students close their books and create a two-column chart with the heads *Inés* and *Javier*. Play the first part of the *Fotonovela* episode, in which **Inés** and **Javier** talk about their families. Have students jot down the words and phrases related to family and professions that they hear in the appropriate column. Then ask them to create a simple family tree for each character.

¿Qué pasó? SUPERSITE

1 Expansion Give these true-false statements to the class as items 7–9: **7. El padre de Javier es alto. (Cierto.) 8. Javier tiene unas fotos de su familia. (Cierto.) 9. Inés es italiana. (Falso. Inés es del Ecuador.)**

1 ¿Cierto o falso? Indicate whether each sentence is **cierto** or **falso**. Correct the false statements.

	Cierto	Falso
1. Inés tiene una familia grande.	⊙	○
2. El hermano de Inés es médico.	○	⊙ Es periodista.
3. Francesca es de Italia.	⊙	○
4. Javier tiene cuatro hermanos.	○	⊙ Javier no tiene hermanos.
5. El abuelo de Javier tiene ochenta años.	○	⊙ Tiene noventa y dos años.
6. Javier habla del padre de su (*his*) padre.	○	⊙ Javier habla del padre de su madre.

2 Expansion Álex is the only student not associated with a statement. Ask the class to look at the **Fotonovela** captions and **Expresiones útiles** on pages 82–83 and invent a statement for him. Remind students not to use his exact words. Ex: **¡Qué bonito! ¡Me gusta mucho!**

2 Identificar Indicate which person would make each statement. The names may be used more than once. **¡Ojo!** One name will not be used.

ÁLEX   JAVIER

1. Tengo una familia grande. Tengo un hermano, cuatro hermanas y muchos primos. Inés
2. Mi abuelo tiene mucha energía. Trabaja mucho. Javier
3. ¿Es tu mamá? ¡Es muy bonita! Inés
4. Oye, chico... ¿qué dibujas? Maite
5. ¿Fotos de mi familia? ¡Tengo muchas! Javier
6. Mmm... Inés y Javier... ¿qué pasa con ellos? don Francisco
7. ¡Dibujas muy bien! Eres un artista excelente. Maite
8. Mmm... ¿Yo? ¡No dibujo nada! Javier

INÉS   MAITE

DON FRANCISCO

3 Expansion Have pairs who wrote about the same family exchange papers and compare their descriptions. Ask them to share the differences with the class.

3 Escribir In pairs, choose Don Francisco, Álex, or Maite and write a brief description of his or her family. Be creative! Answers will vary.

MAITE
Maite es de España. ¿Cómo es su familia?

ÁLEX
Álex es de México. ¿Cómo es su familia?

DON FRANCISCO
Don Francisco es del Ecuador. ¿Cómo es su familia?

4 Teaching Tip Model the activity for students by providing answers based on your own family.

4 Expansion Ask volunteers to share their partner's answers with the class.

4 Conversar With a partner, use these questions to talk about your families. Answers will vary.

1. ¿Cuántos años tienes?
2. ¿Tienes una familia grande?
3. ¿Tienes hermanos o hermanas?
4. ¿Cuántos años tiene tu abuelo (tu hermana, tu primo, etc.)?
5. ¿De dónde son tus padres?

AYUDA
Here are some expressions to help you talk about age.
Yo tengo... años.
I am... years old.
Mi abuelo tiene... años.
My grandfather is... years old.

TEACHING OPTIONS

Extra Practice Ask volunteers to ad-lib the **Fotonovela** episode for the class. Assure them that it is not necessary to memorize the **Fotonovela** or stick strictly to its content. They should try to get the general meaning across with the vocabulary and expressions they know, and they also should feel free to be creative. Give students time to prepare.

Small Groups Have groups of three interview each other about their families. Assign one person to be the interviewer, one the interviewee, and the third person to be the note taker. At three-minute intervals, have students switch roles. When everyone has been interviewed, have students report back to the class.

Pronunciación

Diphthongs and linking

hermano	**niña**	**cuñado**

In Spanish, **a**, **e**, and **o** are considered strong vowels. The weak vowels are **i** and **u**.

ruido	**parientes**	**periodista**

A diphthong is a combination of two weak vowels or of a strong vowel and a weak vowel. Diphthongs are pronounced as a single syllable.

mi hijo	**una clase excelente**

Two identical vowel sounds that appear together are pronounced like one long vowel.

la abuela

con Natalia	**sus sobrinos**	**las sillas**

Two identical consonants together sound like a single consonant.

es ingeniera	**mis abuelos**	**sus hijos**

A consonant at the end of a word is linked with the vowel at the beginning of the next word.

mi hermano	**su esposa**	**nuestro amigo**

A vowel at the end of a word is linked with the vowel at the beginning of the next word.

Práctica Say these words aloud, focusing on the diphthongs.

1. historia
2. nieto
3. parientes
4. novia
5. residencia
6. prueba
7. puerta
8. ciencias
9. lenguas
10. estudiar
11. izquierda
12. ecuatoriano

Oraciones Read these sentences aloud to practice diphthongs and linking words.

1. Hola. Me llamo Anita Amaral. Soy del Ecuador.
2. Somos seis en mi familia.
3. Tengo dos hermanos y una hermana.
4. Mi papá es del Ecuador y mi mamá es de España.

Refranes Read these sayings aloud to practice diphthongs and linking sounds.

Cuando una puerta se cierra, otra se abre.[1]

Hablando del rey de Roma, por la puerta se asoma.[2]

[1] When one door closes, another opens. [2] Speak of the devil and he will appear.

recursos		
CH p. 35	CA p. 100	descubre1.vhlcentral.com Lección 3

¿Cómo te llamas?

In the Spanish-speaking world, it is common to have two last names. The first last name is inherited from the father and the second from the mother. In some cases, the conjunctions **de** or **y** are used to connect the two last names. For example, in the name **Juan Martínez de Velasco**, *Martínez* is the paternal surname (**el apellido paterno**), and *Velasco* is the maternal surname (**el apellido materno**); **de** simply links the two names. This convention of using two last names (**doble apellido**) is a European tradition that Spaniards brought to the Americas and continues to be practiced in many countries, including Chile, Colombia, Mexico, Peru, and Venezuela. There are exceptions, however; in Argentina, the prevailing custom is to use only the father's last name.

When a woman marries in a country where two last names are used, legally she retains her two maiden surnames. However, socially she may take her husband's paternal surname in

Gabriel García Márquez   **Mercedes Barcha Pardo**

Rodrigo García Barcha

place of her inherited maternal surname. Therefore, now that **Mercedes Barcha Pardo** is married to Colombian writer **Gabriel García Márquez**, she could use **Mercedes Barcha García** or **Mercedes Barcha de García** in social situations, although officially her name remains **Mercedes Barcha Pardo**. (Adopting a husband's last name for social purposes, though widespread, is only legally recognized in Ecuador and Peru.)

Regardless of the surnames the mother uses, most parents do not break tradition upon naming their children; they maintain the father's first surname followed by the mother's first surname, as in the name **Rodrigo García Barcha**. However, one should note that both surnames come from the grandfathers, and therefore all **apellidos** are effectively paternal.

Hijos en la casa

In Spanish-speaking countries, family and society place very little pressure on young adults to live on one's own (**independizarse**), and children often live with their parents well into their thirties. Although reluctance to live on one's own is partly cultural, the main reason is economic—lack of job security or low wages coupled with a high cost of living make it impractical for young adults to live independently before they marry. For example, about 60% of Spaniards under 34 years of age live at home with their parents.

---

1 **¿Cierto o falso?** Indicate whether these statements are **cierto** or **falso**. Correct the false statements.

1. Most Spanish-speaking people have three last names. **Falso.** Most people have two last names.
2. Hispanic last names generally consist of the paternal last name followed by the maternal last name. **Cierto.**
3. It is common to see **de** or **y** used in a Hispanic last name. **Cierto.**
4. Someone from Argentina would most likely have two last names. **Falso.** They would use only the father's last name.

5. Generally, married women legally retain two maiden surnames. **Cierto.**
6. In social situations, a married woman often uses her husband's last name in place of her inherited paternal surname. **Falso.** She often uses it in place of her inherited maternal surname.
7. Adopting a husband's surname is only legally recognized in Peru and Ecuador. **Cierto.**
8. Hispanic last names are effectively a combination of the maternal surnames from the previous generation. **Falso.** They are a combination of the paternal surnames from the previous generation.

ASÍ SE DICE

Familia y amigos

el/la bisnieto/a	*great-grandson/daughter*
el/la chamaco/a (Méx.); el/la chamo/a (Ven.); el/la chaval(a) (Esp.)	el/la muchacho/a
el/la colega (Esp.)	el/la amigo/a
mi cuate (Méx.); mi llave (Col.); mi pana (Ven., P. Rico, Rep. Dom.)	*my pal; my buddy*
la madrina	*godmother*
el padrino	*godfather*
el/la tatarabuelo/a	*great-great-grandfather/ great-great-grandmother*

EL MUNDO HISPANO

Las familias

Although worldwide population trends show a decrease in average family size, households in many Spanish-speaking countries are still larger than their U.S. counterparts.

○ **Colombia** 5,2 personas

○ **México** 5,0 personas

○ **Argentina** 3,7 personas

○ **Uruguay** 3,2 personas

○ **España** 2,9 personas

○ **Estados Unidos** 2,6 personas

PERFIL

La familia real española

Undoubtedly, Spain's most famous family is **la familia real** (*royal*). In 1962, then-prince **Juan Carlos de Borbón**, living in exile in Italy, married Princess **Sofía** of Greece. Then, in the late 1970s, **el Rey** (*King*) **Juan Carlos** and **la Reina** (*Queen*) **Sofía** returned to Spain and helped to transition the country to democracy after a forty-year dictatorship. The royal couple, who enjoys immense public support, has three children: **las infantas** (*Princesses*) **Elena** and **Cristina**, and a son, **el príncipe** (*Prince*) **Felipe**, whose official title is **el príncipe de Asturias**. In 2004, Felipe married **Letizia Ortiz Rocasolano** (now **la princesa de Asturias**), a journalist and TV presenter. A year later, the future king and queen had their first child, **la infanta** Leonor.

SUPERSITE Conexión Internet

What role do **padrinos** and **madrinas** have in today's Hispanic family?

Go to descubre1.vhlcentral.com to find more cultural information related to this **Cultura** section.

ACTIVIDADES

2 **Comprensión** Complete these sentences.

1. Spain's royals were responsible for guiding in ___democracy___
2. In Spanish, your godmother is called ___la madrina___.
3. Princess Leonor is the ___granddaughter___ of Queen Sofía.
4. Uruguay's average household has ___3.2___ people.
5. If a Venezuelan calls you **mi pana**, you are that person's ___friend___

3 **Una familia famosa** Create a genealogical tree of a famous family, using photos or drawings labeled with names and ages. Present the family tree to a classmate and explain who the people are and their relationships to each other.
Answers will vary.

recursos	
CH p. 36	descubre1.vhlcentral.com Lección 3

Section Goals

In **Estructura 3.1**, students will learn:

- forms, agreement, and position of adjectives ending in **–o/–a**, **–e**, or a consonant
- high-frequency descriptive adjectives and some adjectives of nationality

Instructional Resources

Cuaderno de práctica, pp. 25–26
Cuaderno para hispanohablantes, pp. 37–38
Cuaderno de actividades, pp. 11–12, 101
e-Cuaderno
Supersite: Audio Activity MP3 Audio Files
Supersite/TRCD/Print: *PowerPoints* (**Lección 3 Estructura** Presentation); Communication Activities, Audio Activity Script, Answer Keys
Audio Activity CD

Teaching Tips

- Write these adjectives on the board: **ecuatoriana, alto, bonito, viejo, trabajador.** Ask volunteers to tell what each means and say whether it is masculine or feminine. Model one of the adjectives in a sentence and ask volunteers to use the others in sentences.
- Work through the discussion of adjective forms point by point, writing examples on the board. Test comprehension as you proceed by asking volunteers to supply the correct form of adjectives for nouns you suggest. Remind students that grammatical gender does not necessarily reflect actual gender.
- Drill gender by pointing to individuals and asking the class to supply the correct form. Ex: (Pointing to male student) **¿Guapo o guapa?** (Pointing to female) **¿Simpático o simpática?** Then use adjectives ending in **–e.** Point to a male and say **inteligente**, then point to a female and have students provide the correct form. Continue with plurals.

3.1 Descriptive adjectives

ANTE TODO Adjectives are words that describe people, places, and things. In Spanish, descriptive adjectives are used with the verb **ser** to point out characteristics such as nationality, size, color, shape, personality, and appearance.

Forms and agreement of adjectives

> **COMPARE & CONTRAST**
>
> In English, the forms of descriptive adjectives do not change to reflect the gender (masculine/feminine) and number (singular/plural) of the noun or pronoun they describe.
>
> *Juan is **nice**.*   *Elena is **nice**.*   *They are **nice**.*
>
> In Spanish, the forms of descriptive adjectives agree in gender and/or number with the nouns or pronouns they describe.
>
> Juan es simpátic**o**.   Elena es simpátic**a**.   Ellos son simpátic**os.**

▸ Adjectives that end in **-o** have four different forms. The feminine singular is formed by changing the **-o** to **-a**. The plural is formed by adding **-s** to the singular forms.

Masculine		Feminine	
SINGULAR	PLURAL	SINGULAR	PLURAL
el muchach**o** alt**o**	los muchach**os** alt**os**	la muchach**a** alt**a**	las muchach**as** alt**as**

Mi abuelo es muy simpático.

¡Qué alto es tu papá! Y tu mamá, ¡qué bonita!

▸ Adjectives that end in **-e** or a consonant have the same masculine and feminine forms.

Masculine		Feminine	
SINGULAR	PLURAL	SINGULAR	PLURAL
el chico inteligent**e**	los chicos inteligent**es**	la chica inteligent**e**	las chicas inteligent**es**
el examen difíc**il**	los exámenes difíc**iles**	la clase difíc**il**	las clases difíc**iles**

▸ Adjectives that end in **-or** are variable in both gender and number.

Masculine		Feminine	
SINGULAR	PLURAL	SINGULAR	PLURAL
el hombre trabajad**or**	los hombres trabajad**ores**	la mujer trabajad**ora**	las mujeres trabajad**oras**

> **TEACHING OPTIONS**
>
> **Extra Practice** Have pairs of students write sentences using adjectives such as **inteligente, alto, joven.** When they have finished, ask volunteers to dictate their sentences to you while you write them on the board. After you have written a sentence and corrected any errors, ask volunteers to suggest a sentence that uses the antonym of the adjective.
>
> **Variación léxica** Clarify that the adjective **americano/a** applies to all inhabitants of North and South America, not just citizens of the United States. Residents of the United States usually are referred to with the adjective **norteamericano/a.** In more formal contexts, such as official documents, the adjective **estadounidense** is used.

▶ Adjectives that refer to nouns of different genders use the masculine plural form.

Manuel es alt**o**.   Lola es alt**a**.   Manuel y Lola son alt**os**.

Common adjectives

alto/a	tall	**gordo/a**	fat	**moreno/a**	brunet(te)
antipático/a	unpleasant	**grande**	big; large	**mucho/a**	much; many; a lot of
bajo/a	short (in height)	**guapo/a**	handsome; good-looking	**pelirrojo/a**	red-haired
bonito/a	pretty	**importante**	important	**pequeño/a**	small
bueno/a	good	**inteligente**	intelligent	**rubio/a**	blond(e)
delgado/a	thin; slender	**interesante**	interesting	**simpático/a**	nice; likeable
difícil	hard; difficult	**joven**	young	**tonto/a**	silly; foolish
fácil	easy	**malo/a**	bad	**trabajador(a)**	hard-working
feo/a	ugly	**mismo/a**	same	**viejo/a**	old

Adjectives of nationality

▶ Unlike in English, Spanish adjectives of nationality are **not** capitalized. Proper names of countries, however, are capitalized.

Some adjectives of nationality

alemán, alemana	German	**inglés, inglesa**	English
canadiense	Canadian	**italiano/a**	Italian
chino/a	Chinese	**japonés, japonesa**	Japanese
ecuatoriano/a	Ecuadorian	**mexicano/a**	Mexican
español(a)	Spanish	**norteamericano/a**	(North) American
estadounidense	from the U.S.	**puertorriqueño/a**	Puerto Rican
francés, francesa	French	**ruso/a**	Russian

▶ Adjectives of nationality are formed like other descriptive adjectives. Those that end in -**o** form the feminine by changing the -**o** to -**a**.

chin**o** ⟶ chin**a**   mexican**o** ⟶ mexican**a**

The plural is formed by adding an -**s** to the masculine or feminine form.

chin**o** ⟶ chin**os**   mexican**a** ⟶ mexican**as**

▶ Adjectives of nationality that end in -**e** have only two forms, singular and plural.

canadiens**e** ⟶ canadiens**es**   estadounidens**e** ⟶ estadounidens**es**

▶ Adjectives of nationality that end in a consonant form the feminine by adding –**a**.

alem**án** ⟶ alem**ana**   español ⟶ español**a**
japon**és** ⟶ japon**esa**   ingl**és** ⟶ ingl**esa**

▶ Adjectives of nationality which carry an accent mark on the last syllable drop it in the feminine and plural forms.

ingl**és** ⟶ ingl**esa**   alem**án** ⟶ alem**anes**

Teaching Tips

Teaching Tips
• After describing each grammar point, practice it by asking questions like these.

Descriptive adjectives
¿Tienes amigos inteligentes? ¿Tienes amigas guapas? ¿Tomas clases difíciles? ¿Tienes compañeros trabajadores? ¿Tienes profesores simpáticos o antipáticos?

Adjectives of quantity
¿Cuántos hermanos tienes? ¿Cuántas personas hay en la clase de español? ¿Cuántas materias estudias?

Bueno/a and *malo/a*
¿Tus amigos son buenos estudiantes? ¿Tienes un buen diccionario? ¿Hoy es un mal día? ¿Tu novio es una persona mala?

Grande
¿Vives en una casa grande o pequeña? ¿Estudias en una escuela grande o pequeña?

• Ask simple questions about the **Fotonovela** characters using adjectives from this lesson. Ex: ¿Son estadounidenses los cuatro estudiantes? ¿Es simpático o antipático el conductor? ¿Las dos muchachas son altas?

Position of adjectives

▶ Descriptive adjectives and adjectives of nationality generally follow the nouns they modify.

El niño **rubio** es de España.
The blond boy is from Spain.

La mujer **española** habla inglés.
The Spanish woman speaks English.

▶ Unlike descriptive adjectives, adjectives of quantity are placed before the modified noun.

Hay **muchos** libros en la biblioteca.
There are many books in the library.

Hablo con **dos** turistas puertorriqueños.
I am talking with two Puerto Rican tourists.

▶ **Bueno/a** and **malo/a** can be placed before or after a noun. When placed before a masculine singular noun, the forms are shortened: **bueno → buen; malo → mal**.

Joaquín es un **buen** amigo.
Joaquín es un amigo **bueno.** ⟶ *Joaquín is a good friend.*

Hoy es un **mal** día.
Hoy es un día **malo.** ⟶ *Today is a bad day.*

▶ When **grande** appears before a singular noun, it is shortened to **gran,** and the meaning of the word changes: **gran** = *great* and **grande** = *big, large*.

Don Francisco es un **gran** hombre.
Don Francisco is a great man.

La familia de Inés es **grande**.
Inés' family is large.

¡INTÉNTALO! Provide the appropriate forms of the adjectives. The first item in each group has been done for you.

simpático
1. Mi hermano es _simpático_.
2. La profesora Martínez es _simpática_.
3. Rosa y Teresa son _simpáticas_.
4. Nosotros somos _simpáticos_.

alemán
1. Hans es _alemán_.
2. Mis primas son _alemanas_.
3. Marcus y yo somos _alemanes_.
4. Mi tía es _alemana_.

difícil
1. La química es _difícil_.
2. El curso es _difícil_.
3. Las pruebas son _difíciles_.
4. Los libros son _difíciles_.

guapo
1. Su esposo es _guapo_.
2. Mis sobrinas son _guapas_.
3. Los padres de ella son _guapos_.
4. Marta es _guapa_.

recursos

CP
pp. 25–26

CH
pp. 37–38

CA
pp. 11–12, 101

descubre1.
vhlcentral.com
Lección 3

Práctica SUPERSITE

1   **Emparejar** Find the words in column B that are the opposite of the words in column A. One word in B will not be used.

Marcos

Jorge

A		B
1. guapo	d	a. delgado
2. moreno	f	b. pequeño
3. alto	h	c. malo
4. gordo	a	d. feo
5. joven	e	e. viejo
6. grande	b	f. rubio
7. simpático	g	g. antipático
		h. bajo

2   **Completar** Indicate the nationalities of these people by selecting the correct adjectives and changing their forms when necessary.

1. Una persona del Ecuador es __ecuatoriana__.
2. Carlos Fuentes es un gran escritor (*writer*) de México; es __mexicano__.
3. Los habitantes de Vancouver son __canadienses__.
4. Giorgio Armani es un diseñador de modas (*fashion designer*) __italiano__.
5. Gérard Depardieu es un actor __francés__.
6. Tony Blair y Margaret Thatcher son __ingleses__.
7. Claudia Schiffer y Boris Becker son __alemanes__.
8. Los habitantes de Puerto Rico son __puertorriqueños__.

3   **Describir** Look at the drawing and describe each family member using as many adjectives as possible. *Some answers will vary.*

Carlos Romero Sandoval

Josefina Barcos de Romero

Susana Romero Barcos

Tomás Romero Barcos

Alberto Romero Pereda

1. Susana Romero Barcos es __delgada, rubia__.
2. Tomás Romero Barcos es __pelirrojo, inteligente__.
3. Los dos hermanos son __jóvenes__.
4. Josefina Barcos de Romero es __alta, bonita, rubia__.
5. Carlos Romero Sandoval es __bajo, gordo__.
6. Alberto Romero Pereda es __viejo, bajo__.
7. Tomás y su (*his*) padre son __pelirrojos__.
8. Susana y su (*her*) madre son __altas, delgadas, rubias__.

Comunicación

4 Expansion Have small groups brainstorm a list of additional famous people, places, and things. Ask them to include some plural items. Then ask the groups to exchange papers and describe the people, places, and things on the lists they receive.

4 **¿Cómo es?** With a partner, take turns describing each item on the list. Tell your partner whether you agree (**Estoy de acuerdo**) or disagree (**No estoy de acuerdo**) with the descriptions.
Answers will vary.

modelo
San Francisco
Estudiante 1: *San Francisco es una ciudad (city) muy bonita.*
Estudiante 2: *No estoy de acuerdo. Es muy fea.*

1. Nueva York
2. Jim Carrey
3. las canciones (*songs*) de Celine Dion
4. el presidente de los Estados Unidos
5. Steven Spielberg
6. la primera dama (*first lady*) de los Estados Unidos
7. el/la profesor(a) de español
8. las personas de Los Ángeles
9. las flores de primavera (*spring*)
10. mi clase de español

AYUDA
Here are some tips to help you complete the descriptions:
- **Jim Carrey es actor de cine.**
- **Celine Dion es cantante.**
- **Steven Spielberg es director de cine.**

5 Teaching Tip Have students divide a sheet of paper into two columns, labeling one **Yo** and the other **Mi amigo/a ideal** or **Mi novio/a ideal**. Have them brainstorm Spanish adjectives for each column. Ask them to rank each adjective in the second column in terms of its importance to them.

5 **Perfil personal** Write a personal profile for your school newspaper. Describe yourself and your ideal best friend. Then compare your profile with a classmate's. How are you similar and how are you different? Are you looking for the same things in a best friend?
Answers will vary.

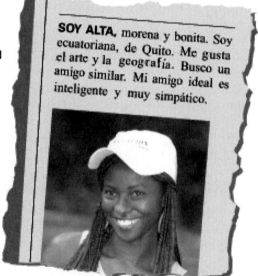

SOY ALTA, morena y bonita. Soy ecuatoriana, de Quito. Me gusta el arte y la geografía. Busco un amigo similar. Mi amigo ideal es inteligente y muy simpático.

Síntesis

6 Teaching Tips
- Divide the class into pairs and distribute the Communication Activity worksheets that correspond to this activity. Give students ten minutes to complete this activity.
- To simplify, have students brainstorm a list of adjectives for each person in their drawing, then have them proceed with the activity.

6 Expansion
- Ask questions based on the artwork. Ex: **¿Es alto el abuelo? ¿Es delgado el hijo menor?**
- Have volunteers take turns stating the differences. Then have them invent stories based on these families.

6 **Diferencias** Your teacher will give you and a partner each a drawing of a family. Find at least five more differences between your picture and your partner's. Answers will vary.

modelo
Estudiante 1: *Susana, la madre, es rubia.*
Estudiante 2: *No, la madre es morena.*

recursos
CA pp. 11–12

TEACHING OPTIONS

Heritage Speakers Ask heritage speakers to write descriptions of their extended families. Encourage them to illustrate the descriptions with a few family photos, if possible.

Extra Practice Research zodiac signs on the Internet and prepare a simple personality description for each sign, using cognates and adjectives from this lesson. Divide the class into pairs and distribute the descriptions. Have students guess their partners' sign. Ex: **—Eres aries, ¿verdad? —No, no soy aries. No soy impulsiva y no soy aventurera.**

Extra Practice For homework, have students collect several pictures of people from the Internet, magazines, or newspapers. Have them prepare a description of one of the pictures. Invite each student to display the pictures on the board and give their description orally. The class should guess which picture is being described.

3.2 Possessive adjectives

ANTE TODO Possessive adjectives, like descriptive adjectives, are words that are used to qualify people, places, or things. Possessive adjectives express the quality of ownership or possession.

Forms of possessive adjectives

SINGULAR FORMS	PLURAL FORMS	
mi	**mis**	*my*
tu	**tus**	*your* (fam.)
su	**sus**	*his, her, its, your* (form.)
nuestro/a	**nuestros/as**	*our*
vuestro/a	**vuestros/as**	*your* (fam.)
su	**sus**	*their, your* (form.)

COMPARE & CONTRAST

In English, possessive adjectives are invariable; that is, they do not agree in gender and number with the nouns they modify. Spanish possessive adjectives, however, do agree in number with the nouns they modify.

my cousin	*my cousins*	*my aunt*	*my aunts*
mi primo	**mis** primos	**mi** tía	**mis** tías

The forms **nuestro** and **vuestro** agree in both gender and number with the nouns they modify.

nuestr**o** prim**o**	nuestr**os** prim**os**	nuestr**a** tía	nuestr**as** tías

▶ Possessive adjectives are always placed before the nouns they modify.

—¿Está **tu novio** aquí?   —No, **mi novio** está en la biblioteca.
Is your boyfriend here?   *No, my boyfriend is in the library.*

AYUDA
Look at the context, focusing on nouns and pronouns, to help you determine the meaning of **su(s)**.

▶ Because **su** and **sus** have multiple meanings (*your, his, her, their, its*), you can avoid confusion by using this construction instead: [*article*] + [*noun*] + **de** + [*subject pronoun*].

sus parientes ◀
los parientes **de él/ella**   *his/her relatives*
los parientes **de Ud./Uds.**   *your relatives*
los parientes **de ellos/ellas**   *their relatives*

recursos

CP pp. 27–28

CH pp. 39–40

CA p. 102

descubre1. vhlcentral.com Lección 3

¡INTÉNTALO! Provide the appropriate form of each possessive adjective. The first item in each column has been done for you.

1. Es ___mi___ (*my*) libro.
2. ___Mi___ (*My*) familia es ecuatoriana.
3. ___Tu___ (*Your*, fam.) novio es italiano.
4. ___Nuestro___ (*Our*) profesor es español.
5. Es ___su___ (*her*) reloj.
6. Es ___tu___ (*your*, fam.) mochila.
7. Es ___su___ (*your*, form.) maleta.
8. ___Su___ (*Their*) sobrina es alemana.

1. ___Sus___ (*Her*) primos son franceses.
2. ___Nuestros___ (*Our*) primos son canadienses.
3. Son ___sus___ (*their*) lápices.
4. ___Sus___ (*Their*) nietos son japoneses.
5. Son ___nuestras___ (*our*) plumas.
6. Son ___mis___ (*my*) papeles.
7. ___Mis___ (*My*) amigas son inglesas.
8. Son ___sus___ (*his*) cuadernos.

TEACHING OPTIONS

Video Replay the *Fotonovela*, having students focus on possessive adjectives. Ask them to write down each one they hear, with the noun it modifies. Afterward, ask the class to describe the families of **Inés** and **Javier**. Remind them to use definite articles and **de** if necessary to avoid confusion with the possessive **su**.

Small Groups Give small groups three minutes to brainstorm how many words they can associate with the phrases **nuestro país, nuestro estado, nuestra universidad,** and **nuestra clase de español**. Have them model their responses for **En nuestra clase hay ____** and **Nuestro país es ____**. Have the groups share their associations with the rest of the class.

Section Goals
In **Estructura 3.2**, students will be introduced to:
• possessive adjectives
• ways of clarifying **su(s)** when the referent is ambiguous

Instructional Resources
Cuaderno de práctica, pp. 27–28
Cuaderno para hispanohablantes, pp. 39–40
Cuaderno de actividades, p. 102
e-Cuaderno
Supersite: Audio Activity MP3 Audio Files
Supersite/TRCD/Print: *PowerPoints* (**Lección 3 Estructura** Presentation); Audio Activity Script, Answer Keys
Audio Activity CD

Teaching Tips
• Introduce the concept of possessive adjectives. Hold up your book, jacket, or other personal possession and ask individuals: **¿Es tu libro? (No.)** Then, as you point to one student, ask the class: **¿Es el libro de ____? ¿Es su libro?** Link arms with another student and ask the class: **¿Es nuestro libro?** Indicate the whole class and ask: **¿Es el libro de ustedes? ¿Es su libro?** Finally, hug the object dramatically and say: **No. Es mi libro.** Ask volunteers personalized questions. Ex: **¿Es simpática tu madre?**
• Use each possessive adjective with a noun to illustrate agreement. Point out that all agree in number with the noun they modify but that only **nuestro/a** and **vuestro/a** show gender. Point out that **tú** (subject) has an accent mark; **tu** (possessive) does not.
• Ask students to give the plural or singular of possessive adjectives with nouns. Say: **Da el plural: nuestra clase. (nuestras clases)** Say: **Da el singular: mis manos. (mi mano)**
• Write **su familia** and **sus amigos** on the board and ask volunteers to supply the equivalent phrases using **de**.

Práctica

1

La familia de Manolo Complete each sentence with the correct possessive adjective. Use the subject of each sentence as a guide.

1. Me llamo Manolo, y _____mi_____ (nuestro, mi, sus) hermano es Federico.
2. ___Nuestra___ (Nuestra, Sus, Mis) madre Silvia es profesora y enseña química.
3. Ella admira a _____sus_____ (tu, nuestro, sus) estudiantes porque trabajan mucho.
4. Yo estudio en la misma escuela, pero no tomo clases con _____mi_____ (mi, nuestras, tus) madre.
5. Federico trabaja en una oficina con ___nuestro___ (mis, tu, nuestro) padre.
6. _____Su_____ (Mi, Su, Tu) oficina está en el centro de Quito.
7. Javier y Óscar son _____mis_____ (mis, mi, sus) tíos de Guayaquil.
8. ¿Y tú? ¿Cómo es _____tu_____ (mi, su, tu) familia?

2

Clarificar Clarify each sentence with a prepositional phrase. Follow the model.

> **modelo**
> Su hermana es muy bonita. (ella)
> *La hermana de ella es muy bonita.*

1. Su casa es muy grande. (ellos) _____ La casa de ellos es muy grande.
2. ¿Cómo se llama su hermano? (ellas) _____ ¿Cómo se llama el hermano de ellas?
3. Sus padres trabajan en el centro. (ella) _____ Los padres de ella trabajan en el centro.
4. Sus abuelos son muy simpáticos. (él) _____ Los abuelos de él son muy simpáticos.
5. Maribel es su prima. (ella) _____ Maribel es la prima de ella.
6. Su primo lee los libros. (ellos) _____ El primo de ellos lee los libros.

3

¿Dónde está? With a partner, imagine that you can't remember where you put some of the belongings you see in the pictures. Your partner will help you by reminding you where your things are. Take turns playing each role. Answers will vary.

CONSULTA

For a list of useful prepositions, refer to the table *Prepositions often used with estar*, in **Estructura 2.3**, p. 60.

> **modelo**
> **Estudiante 1:** ¿Dónde está mi mochila?
> **Estudiante 2:** *Tu mochila está encima del escritorio.*

1. 2. 3.

4. 5. 6.

Left margin:

1 Expansion
- Have students change the number and gender of the nouns in items 1–7. Then have them say each new sentence, changing the possessives as necessary.
- Have students respond to the question in item 8.

2 Expansion
- Change the subject pronouns in parentheses and have the class provide new answers. Then have groups of students provide new nouns and the corresponding answers.
- Give the class sentences such as **Es su libro** and have volunteers rephrase them with a clarifying prepositional phrase.

3 Teaching Tips
- Before doing the activity, quickly review **estar** by writing the present-tense forms on the board.
- Remind students that **estar** is used to indicate location.

3 Expansion Ask questions about objects that are in the classroom. Ex: **¿Dónde está mi escritorio? ¿Dónde está el libro de _____? ¿Dónde están las plumas de _____? ¿Dónde están tus lápices?**

Comunicación

4 **Describir** With a partner, take turns describing the people and places in the list. Answers will vary.

> **modelo**
>
> la biblioteca de su escuela
> *La biblioteca de nuestra escuela es muy grande. Hay muchos libros en la biblioteca. Mis amigos y yo estudiamos en la biblioteca.*

1. tu profesor favorito
2. tu profesora favorita
3. su clase de español
4. la biblioteca de su escuela
5. tus padres
6. tus abuelos
7. tu mejor (*best*) amigo
8. tu mejor amiga
9. su escuela
10. tu país de origen

5 **Una familia** In small groups, each student pretends to be a different member of the family pictured and shares that person's private thoughts about the others in the family. Make two positive comments and two negative ones. Answers will vary.

> **modelo**
>
> **Estudiante 1:** *Mi hijo Roberto es muy trabajador. Estudia mucho y siempre termina su tarea.*
> **Estudiante 2:** *Nuestra familia es difícil. Mis padres no escuchan mis opiniones.*

Síntesis

6 **Describe a tu familia** Describe your family to two classmates, using several sentences (**Mi padre es alto y moreno. Mi madre es delgada y muy bonita. Mis hermanos son...**). They will work together to try to repeat your description (**Su padre es alto y moreno. Su madre...**). If they forget any details, they will ask you questions (**¿Es alto tu hermano?**). Alternate roles until all of you have described your families. Answers will vary.

---

4 Teaching Tip Ask students to suggest a few more details to add to the **modelo**.

5 Teaching Tips
• Quickly review the descriptive adjectives on page 89. You can do this by saying an adjective and having volunteers give its opposite (**palabra opuesta**).
• Explain the activity to the class. Have students give names to the people in the photo following Hispanic naming conventions.

5 Expansion Ask a couple of groups to perform the activity for the class.

6 Teaching Tips
• Review the family vocabulary on pages 78–79.
• Explain that the class will divide into groups of three. One student will describe his or her own family (using **mi**), and then the other two will describe the first student's family to one another (using **su**) and ask for clarification as necessary (using **tu**).
• You may want to model this for the class. Before beginning, ask students to list the family members they plan to describe.

Extra Practice Have students work in small groups to prepare a description of a famous person, such as a politician, a movie star, or a sports figure, and his or her extended family. Tell them to feel free to invent family members as necessary. Have groups present their descriptions to the class.

Heritage Speakers Ask heritage speakers to describe their families' home country (**país de origen**) for the class. As they are giving their descriptions, ask them questions that elicit more information. Clarify for the class any unfamiliar words and expressions they may use.

3.3 Present tense of -er and -ir verbs

ANTE TODO In **Lección 2,** you learned how to form the present tense of regular -ar verbs. You also learned about the importance of verb forms, which change to show who is performing the action. The chart below shows the forms of verbs from two other important verb groups, -er verbs and -ir verbs.

Present tense of -er and -ir verbs		
	comer *(to eat)*	**escrib**ir *(to write)*
SINGULAR FORMS		
yo	com**o**	escrib**o**
tú	com**es**	escrib**es**
Ud./él/ella	com**e**	escrib**e**
PLURAL FORMS		
nosotros/as	com**emos**	escrib**imos**
vosotros/as	com**éis**	escrib**ís**
Uds./ellos/ellas	com**en**	escrib**en**

▶ **-Er** and **-ir** verbs have very similar endings. Study the preceding chart to detect the patterns that make it easier for you to use them to communicate in Spanish.

Inés y Javier comen.

Maite escribe.

▶ Like **-ar** verbs, the **yo** forms of **-er** and **-ir** verbs end in **-o**.

Yo com**o**.   Yo escrib**o**.

▶ Except for the **yo** form, all of the verb endings for **-er** verbs begin with **-e**.

-es	-emos	-en
-e	-éis	

▶ **-Er** and **-ir** verbs have the exact same endings, except in the **nosotros/as** and **vosotros/as** forms.

nosotros ◀ com**emos** / escrib**imos**   vosotros ◀ com**éis** / escrib**ís**

CONSULTA
To review the conjugation of **-ar** verbs, see **Estructura 2.1**, p. 50.

AYUDA
Here are some tips on learning Spanish verbs:
1) Learn to identify the stem of each verb, to which all endings attach.
2) Memorize the endings that go with each verb and verb tense.
3) As often as possible, practice using different forms of each verb in speech and writing.
4) Devote extra time to learning irregular verbs, such as **ser** and **estar**.

Common -er and -ir verbs

-er verbs	
aprender (a + *inf.*)	to learn
beber	to drink
comer	to eat
comprender	to understand
correr	to run
creer (en)	to believe (in)
deber (+ *inf.*)	should; must; ought to
leer	to read

-ir verbs	
abrir	to open
asistir (a)	to attend
compartir	to share
decidir (+ *inf.*)	to decide
describir	to describe
escribir	to write
recibir	to receive
vivir	to live

Ellos **corren** en el parque.

Él **escribe** una carta.

¡INTÉNTALO! Provide the appropriate present tense forms of these verbs. The first item in each column has been done for you.

correr
1. Graciela _corre_.
2. Tú _corres_.
3. Yo _corro_.
4. Sara y Ana _corren_.
5. Usted _corre_.
6. Ustedes _corren_.
7. La gente _corre_.
8. Marcos y yo _corremos_.

abrir
1. Ellos _abren_ la puerta.
2. Carolina _abre_ la maleta.
3. Yo _abro_ las ventanas.
4. Nosotras _abrimos_ los libros.
5. Usted _abre_ el cuaderno.
6. Tú _abres_ la ventana.
7. Ustedes _abren_ las maletas.
8. Los muchachos _abren_ los cuadernos.

aprender
1. Él _aprende_ español.
2. Maribel y yo _aprendemos_ inglés.
3. Tú _aprendes_ japonés.
4. Tú y tu hermanastra _aprenden_ francés.
5. Mi hijo _aprende_ chino.
6. Yo _aprendo_ alemán.
7. Usted _aprende_ inglés.
8. Nosotros _aprendemos_ italiano.

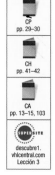

recursos

CP
pp. 29–30

CH
pp. 41–42

CA
pp. 13–15, 103

SUPERSITE
descubre1.
vhlcentral.com
Lección 3

Práctica SUPERSITE

1 Completar Complete Susana's sentences about her family with the correct forms of the verbs in parentheses. One of the verbs will remain in the infinitive.

1. Mi familia y yo ___vivimos___ (vivir) en Guayaquil.
2. Tengo muchos libros. Me gusta ___leer___ (leer).
3. Mi hermano Alfredo es muy inteligente. Alfredo ___asiste___ (asistir) a clases los lunes, miércoles y viernes.
4. Los martes y jueves Alfredo y yo ___corremos___ (correr).
5. Mis padres ___comen___ (comer) mucho.
6. Yo ___creo___ (creer) que (*that*) mis padres deben comer menos (*less*).

2 Oraciones Juan is talking about what he and his friends do after school. Form complete sentences.

> **modelo**
> yo / correr / amigos / lunes y miércoles
> *Yo corro con mis amigos los lunes y miércoles.*

1. Manuela / asistir / clase / yoga Manuela asiste a la clase de yoga.
2. Eugenio / abrir / correo electrónico (*e-mail*) Eugenio abre su correo electrónico.
3. Isabel y yo / leer / biblioteca Isabel y yo leemos en la biblioteca.
4. Sofía y Roberto / aprender / hablar / inglés Sofía y Roberto aprenden a hablar inglés.
5. tú / comer / cafetería / escuela Tú comes en la cafetería de la escuela.
6. mi novia y yo / compartir / libro de historia Mi novia y yo compartimos el libro de historia.

3 Consejos Mario teaches Japanese at a university in Quito and is spending a year in Tokyo with his family. In pairs, use the words below to say what he and/or his family members are doing or should do to adjust to life in Japan. Then, create one more sentence using a verb not in the list. Answers will vary.

> **modelo**
> recibir libros / deber practicar japonés
> **Estudiante 1:** *Mario y su esposa reciben muchos libros en japonés.*
> **Estudiante 2:** *Los hijos deben practicar japonés.*

aprender japonés	decidir explorar el país
asistir a clases	escribir listas de palabras en japonés
beber té (*tea*)	leer novelas japonesas
deber comer cosas nuevas	vivir con una familia japonesa
¿?	¿?

TEACHING OPTIONS

Pairs Have pairs of students role-play an interview with a movie star. Students can review previous lesson vocabulary lists in preparation. Give pairs sufficient time to plan and practice. When all pairs have completed the activity, ask a few of them to introduce their characters and perform the interview for the class.
TPR Add to the list of phrases in **Actividad 3**. In groups of three, have students pantomime the activities for their classmates to

guess.
Heritage Speakers Have heritage speakers brainstorm a list of things that an exchange student in a Spanish-speaking country might want to do. Have them base their list on **Actividad 3** using as many **–er/–ir** verbs as they can. Then have the rest of the class write complete sentences based on the list.

---

1 Expansion
• As a class, come up with the questions that would elicit the statements in this activity. Ex: **¿Dónde viven tú y tu familia? ¿Cuántos libros tienes? ¿Por qué tienes muchos libros? ¿Cómo es tu hermano Alfredo? ¿Cuándo asiste Alfredo a sus clases? ¿Cuándo corren ustedes? ¿Cuánto comen tus padres? ¿Cuánto deben comer tus padres?**
• Have small groups describe the family pictured here. Ask the groups to invent each person's name, using Hispanic naming conventions, and include a physical description, place of origin, and the family relationship to the other people in the photo.

2 Teaching Tip To simplify, guide students in classifying the infinitives as –**er** or –**ir**. Then help them to identify the subject for each verb and the appropriate verb ending. Finally, aid students in identifying any missing words.

2 Expansion Have pairs create two additional dehydrated sentences for another pair to write out.

3 Teaching Tip To challenge students, add these words to the list: **aprender historia japonesa, comer más *sushi*, escribir más cartas, describir sus experiencias.**

Comunicación

communication NATIONAL STANDARDS

4 **Entrevista** With a classmate, use these questions to interview each other. Be prepared to report the results of your interviews to the class. Answers will vary.

1. ¿Dónde comes al mediodía? ¿Comes mucho?
2. ¿Debes comer más (*more*) o menos (*less*)?
3. ¿Cuándo asistes a tus clases?
4. ¿Cuál es tu clase favorita? ¿Por qué?
5. ¿Dónde vives?
6. ¿Con quién vives?
7. ¿Qué cursos debes tomar el próximo (*next*) semestre?
8. ¿Lees el periódico (*newspaper*)? ¿Qué periódico lees y cuándo?
9. ¿Recibes muchas cartas (*letters*)? ¿De quién(es)?
10. ¿Escribes poemas?

recursos CA p. 15

5 **Encuesta** Your teacher will give you a worksheet. Walk around the class and ask a different classmate each question about his/her familiy members. Be prepared to report the results of your survey to the class. Answers will vary.

Actividades	Miembros de la familia
1. vivir en una casa	los padres de Juan
2. beber café	
3. correr todos los días (*every day*)	
4. comer mucho en restaurantes	
5. recibir mucho correo electrónico (*e-mail*)	
6. comprender tres lenguas	
7. deber estudiar más (*more*)	
8. leer muchos libros	

Síntesis

recursos CA pp. 13–14

communication NATIONAL STANDARDS

6 **Horario** Your teacher will give you and a partner incomplete versions of Alicia's schedule. Fill in the missing information on the schedule by talking to your partner. Be prepared to reconstruct Alicia's complete schedule with the class. Answers will vary.

modelo

Estudiante 1: A las ocho, Alicia corre.
Estudiante 2: ¡Ah, sí! (*Writes down information.*) A las nueve, ella...

4 Teaching Tips
- Tell students that one of them should complete their interview before switching roles.
- This activity is also suited to a group of three students, one of whom acts as note taker. They should switch roles at the end of each interview until each student has played all three roles.

5 Teaching Tips
- Model one or two of the questions. Then distribute the Communication Activities worksheets.
- The activity can also be done in pairs. Have students change the heading of the second column to **¿Sí o no?**

5 Expansion Go through the survey to find out how the items apply to the class. Record the results on the board. Ask: **¿Quiénes viven en una casa?**

6 Teaching Tip Divide the class into pairs and distribute the Communication Activities worksheets that correspond to this activity. Give students ten minutes to complete this activity.

6 Expansion
- Ask questions based on **Alicia's** schedule. Ex: **¿Qué hace Alicia a las nueve? (Ella desayuna.)**
- Have volunteers take turns reading aloud **Alicia's** schedule. Then have them write their own schedules using as many **–er/–ir** verbs as they can.

TEACHING OPTIONS

Small Groups Have small groups talk about their favorite classes and teachers. They should describe the classes and the teachers and indicate why they like them. They should also mention what days and times they attend each class. Ask a few volunteers to present a summary of their conversation.

Extra Practice Add an auditory aspect to this grammar practice. Use these sentences as a dictation. Read each twice, pausing after the second time for students to write. **1. Mi hermana Juana y yo asistimos a la Universidad de Quito. 2. Ella vive en la casa de mis padres y yo vivo en una residencia. 3. Juana es estudiante de literatura y lee mucho. 4. Yo estudio computación y aprendo a programar computadoras.**

Section Goals

In **Estructura 3.4**, students will:
• learn the present tense forms of **tener** and **venir**
• learn several common expressions with **tener**

Instructional Resources
Cuaderno de práctica, pp. 31–32
Cuaderno para hispanohablantes, pp. 43–44
Cuaderno de actividades, p. 104
e-Cuaderno
Supersite: Audio Activity MP3 Audio Files
Supersite/TRCD/Print: *PowerPoints* (**Lección 3** **Estructura** Presentation); Audio Activity Script, Answer Keys
Audio Activity CD

Teaching Tips
• Model **tener** by asking volunteers questions. Ex: **¿Tienes una familia grande? ¿Tienes hermanos? ¿Cuántos tíos tiene _____? ¿Tienes muchos primos?** Point out that students have been using forms of **tener** since the beginning of the lesson.
• Point out that the **yo** form of **tener** is irregular and ends in –**go**. Begin a paradigm for **tener** by writing **tengo** on the board. Ask volunteers questions that elicit **tengo** such as: **Tengo una pluma, ¿quién tiene un lápiz?**
• Write **tienes, tiene, tienen** in the paradigm. Point out that in the **tú, usted,** and **ustedes** forms, the –**e**– of the verb stem changes to –**ie**–.
• Write **tenemos** in the paradigm and point out that this form is regular.
• Follow the same procedure to present **venir**. Have students give you the **nosotros** forms of **beber** and **escribir** for comparison.

3.4 Present tense of **tener** and **venir**

ANTE TODO   The verbs **tener** (*to have*) and **venir** (*to come*) are among the most frequently used in Spanish. Because most of their forms are irregular, you will have to learn each one individually.

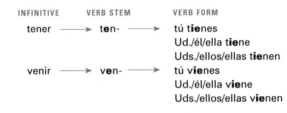

The verbs **tener** and **venir**

		tener	**venir**
SINGULAR FORMS	yo	ten**go**	ven**go**
	tú	tien**es**	vien**es**
	Ud./él/ella	tien**e**	vien**e**
PLURAL FORMS	nosotros/as	ten**emos**	ven**imos**
	vosotros/as	ten**éis**	ven**ís**
	Uds./ellos/ellas	tien**en**	vien**en**

▶ The endings are the same as those of regular **-er** and **-ir** verbs, except for the **yo** forms, which are irregular: **tengo, vengo.**

▶ In the **tú, Ud.,** and **Uds.** forms, the **e** of the stem changes to **ie** as shown below.

INFINITIVE	VERB STEM	VERB FORM
tener →	ten- →	tú ti**e**nes
		Ud./él/ella ti**e**ne
		Uds./ellos/ellas ti**e**nen
venir →	ven- →	tú vi**e**nes
		Ud./él/ella vi**e**ne
		Uds./ellos/ellas vi**e**nen

AYUDA

Use what you already know about regular **-er** and **-ir** verbs to identify the irregularities in **tener** and **venir**.

1) Which verb forms use a regular stem? Which use an irregular stem?
2) Which verb forms use the regular endings? Which use irregular endings?

¿Tienes hermanos?

Sí, tengo cuatro hermanas y un hermano mayor.

▶ The **nosotros** and **vosotros** forms are the only ones which are regular. Compare them to the forms of **comer** and **escribir** that you learned on page 96.

	tener	comer	venir	escribir
nosotros/as	ten**emos**	com**emos**	ven**imos**	escrib**imos**
vosotros/as	ten**éis**	com**éis**	ven**ís**	escrib**ís**

TEACHING OPTIONS

Pairs Have students work in pairs to create a short conversation in which they use forms of **tener, venir,** and other –**ir**/–**er** verbs they know. Tell them their conversations should involve the family and should include some descriptions of family members. Have pairs role-play their conversations for the class.

Extra Practice For further practice with the conjugation of **tener** and **venir**, first write a sentence on the board and have students say it. Then say a new subject and have students repeat the sentence, substituting the new subject and making all necessary changes. Ex: **Yo tengo una familia grande. (Ernesto y yo, usted, tú, ellos) Claudia y Pilar vienen a la clase de historia. (nosotras, Ernesto, ustedes, tú)**

Expressions with **tener**

tener... años	to be... years old	**tener (mucha) prisa**	to be in a (big) hurry
tener (mucho) calor	to be (very) hot	**tener razón**	to be right
tener (mucho) cuidado	to be (very) careful	**no tener razón**	to be wrong
tener (mucho) frío	to be (very) cold	**tener (mucha) sed**	to be (very) thirsty
tener (mucha) hambre	to be (very) hungry	**tener (mucho) sueño**	to be (very) sleepy
tener (mucho) miedo (de)	to be (very) afraid/scared (of)	**tener (mucha) suerte**	to be (very) lucky

▶ In certain idiomatic or set expressions in Spanish, you use the construction **tener** + [*noun*] to express *to be* + [*adjective*]. The chart above contains a list of the most common expressions with **tener**.

—¿**Tienen** hambre ustedes?
Are you hungry?

—Sí, y **tenemos** sed también.
Yes, and we're thirsty, too.

▶ To express an obligation, use **tener que** (*to have to*) + [*infinitive*].

—¿Qué **tienes que** estudiar hoy?
What do you have to study today?

—**Tengo que** estudiar biología.
I have to study biology.

▶ To ask people if they feel like doing something, use **tener ganas de** (*to feel like*) + [*infinitive*].

—¿**Tienes ganas de** comer?
Do you feel like eating?

—No, **tengo ganas de** dormir.
No, I feel like sleeping.

MIciudad.COM

Usted tiene que visitarnos.

¡INTÉNTALO! Provide the appropriate forms of **tener** and **venir**. The first item in each column has been done for you.

tener

1. Ellos ___tienen___ dos hermanos.
2. Yo ___tengo___ una hermana.
3. El artista ___tiene___ tres primos.
4. Nosotros ___tenemos___ diez tíos.
5. Eva y Diana ___tienen___ un sobrino.
6. Usted ___tiene___ cinco nietos.
7. Tú ___tienes___ dos hermanastras.
8. Ustedes ___tienen___ cuatro hijos.
9. Ella ___tiene___ una hija.

venir

1. Mis padres ___vienen___ de México.
2. Tú ___vienes___ de España.
3. Nosotras ___venimos___ de Cuba.
4. Pepe ___viene___ de Italia.
5. Yo ___vengo___ de Francia.
6. Ustedes ___vienen___ de Canadá.
7. Alfonso y yo ___venimos___ de Portugal.
8. Ellos ___vienen___ de Alemania.
9. Usted ___viene___ de Venezuela.

Práctica

1

Emparejar Find the phrase in column B that best matches each phrase in column A. One phrase in column B will not be used.

A		B
1. el Polo Norte	c	a. tener calor
2. una sauna	a	b. tener sed
3. la comida salada (*salty food*)	b	c. tener frío
4. una persona muy inteligente	d	d. tener razón
5. un abuelo	g	e. tener ganas de
6. una dieta	f	f. tener hambre
		g. tener 75 años

2

Completar Complete the sentences with the forms of **tener** or **venir**.

1. Hoy nosotros ___tenemos___ una reunión familiar (*family reunion*).
2. Yo ___vengo___ en autobús del aeropuerto (*airport*) de Quito.
3. Todos mis parientes ___vienen___, excepto mi tío Manolo y su esposa.
4. Ellos no ___tienen___ ganas de venir porque viven en Portoviejo.
5. Mi prima Susana y su novio no ___vienen___ hasta las ocho porque ella ___tiene___ que trabajar.
6. En las fiestas, mi hermana siempre (*always*) ___viene___ muy tarde (*late*).
7. Nosotros ___tenemos___ mucha suerte porque las reuniones son divertidas (*fun*).
8. Mi madre cree que mis sobrinos son muy simpáticos. Creo que ella ___tiene___ razón.

3

Describir Look at the drawings and describe these people using an expression with **tener**.

1. ___Tiene (mucha) prisa.___

2. ___Tiene (mucho) calor.___

3. ___Tiene veintiún años.___

4. ___Tienen (mucha) hambre.___

5. ___Tienen (mucho) frío.___

6. ___Tiene (mucha) sed.___

---

1 Teaching Tip Go over the activity with the class, reading a statement in column A and having volunteers give the corresponding phrase in column B. **Tener ganas de** does not match any items in column A. Help students think of a word or phrase that would match it. Ex: **comer una pizza, asistir a un concierto.**

1 Expansion Have pairs of students write sentences by combining elements from the two columns. Ex: **Sonia está en el Polo Norte y tiene mucho frío. José es una persona muy inteligente pero no tiene razón.**

2 Expansion Have students answer questions based on the completed sentences. Ex: **¿Qué tienen ellos hoy? ¿Cómo viene el narrador a la reunión? ¿Quién no viene?**

3 Teaching Tip Before doing this activity as a class, have students identify which picture is referred to in each of these questions. Have them answer: **La(s) persona(s) del dibujo número ____.** Ask: **¿Quién bebe agua? (6), ¿Quién asiste a una fiesta? (3), ¿Quiénes comen pizza? (4), ¿Quiénes esperan el autobús? (5), ¿Quién corre a la oficina? (1), ¿Quién hace ejercicio en una bicicleta? (2)**

3 Expansion Orally give students situations to elicit a response with a **tener** expression. Ex: **Pedro come mucho. ¿Por qué? (Porque tiene hambre.)**

TEACHING OPTIONS

Extra Practice Have students complete sentences with **tener** and **venir**. Ex: 1. Paula y Luis no tienen hambre, pero yo sí ____ mucha hambre. (tengo) 2. Mis padres vienen del Ecuador, pero mis hermanos y yo ____ de los Estados Unidos. (venimos) 3. ¿Tienes frío, Marta? Pues, Carlos y yo ____ calor. (tenemos) 4. Enrique viene de la escuela. ¿De dónde ____ tú, Angélica? (vienes) 5. ¿Ustedes tienen que trabajar hoy? Ellos no ____ que trabajar. (tienen)

Small Groups Have groups of three write nine sentences, each of which uses a different expression with **tener**, including **tener que** + [*infinitive*] and **tener ganas de** + [*infinitive*]. Ask volunteers to write some of their group's best sentences on the board. Work with the class to read the sentences and check for accuracy.

Comunicación

4 **¿Sí o no?** Using complete sentences, indicate whether these statements apply to you.

Answers will vary.

1. Mi padre tiene 50 años.
2. Mis amigos vienen a mi casa todos los días (*every day*).
3. Vengo a clase a tiempo (*on time*).
4. Tengo hambre.
5. Tengo dos computadoras.
6. Tengo sed.
7. Tengo que estudiar los domingos.
8. Tengo una familia grande.

Now interview a classmate by transforming each statement into a question. Be prepared to report the results of your interview to the class. Answers will vary.

> **modelo**
>
> **Estudiante 1:** ¿Tiene tu padre 50 años?
> **Estudiante 2:** No, no tiene 50 años. Tiene 40.

5 **Preguntas** With a classmate, ask each other these questions. Answers will vary.

1. ¿Tienes que estudiar hoy?
2. ¿Cuántos años tienes? ¿Y tus hermanos/as?
3. ¿Cuándo vienes a la clase de español?
4. ¿Cuándo vienen tus amigos a tu casa o apartamento?
5. ¿De qué tienes miedo? ¿Por qué?
6. ¿Qué tienes ganas de hacer esta noche (*tonight*)?

6 **Conversación** Use an expression with **tener** to hint at what's on your mind. Your partner will ask questions to find out why you feel that way. If your partner cannot guess what's on your mind after three attempts, tell him/her. Then switch roles. Answers will vary.

> **modelo**
>
> **Estudiante 1:** Tengo miedo.
> **Estudiante 2:** ¿Tienes que hablar en público?
> **Estudiante 1:** No.
> **Estudiante 2:** ¿Tienes un examen hoy?
> **Estudiante 1:** Sí, y no tengo tiempo para estudiar.

Síntesis

7 **Minidrama** Act out this situation with a partner: you are introducing your boyfriend/girlfriend to your extended family. To avoid any surprises before you go, talk about who is coming and what each family member is like. Switch roles. Answers will vary.

Recapitulación

SUPERSITE For self-scoring and diagnostics, go to **descubre1.vhlcentral.com**.

Review the grammar concepts you have learned in this lesson by completing these activities.

1 Adjetivos
Complete each sentence with the appropriate adjective from the list. Make all necessary changes. **6 pts.**

antipático	interesante	mexicano
difícil	joven	moreno

1. Mi tía es __mexicana__. Vive en Guadalajara.
2. Mi primo no es rubio, es __moreno__.
3. Mi novio cree que la clase no es fácil; es __difícil__.
4. Los libros son __interesantes__; me gustan mucho.
5. Mis hermanos son __antipáticos__; no tienen muchos amigos.
6. Las gemelas tienen quince años. Son __jóvenes__.

2 Completar
For each set of sentences, provide the appropriate form of the verb **tener** and the possessive adjective. Follow the model. **12 pts.**

> **modelo**
> Él _tiene_ un libro. Es _su_ libro.

1. Esteban y Julio __tienen__ una tía. Es __su__ tía.
2. Yo __tengo__ muchos amigos. Son __mis__ amigos.
3. Tú __tienes__ tres primas. Son __tus__ primas.
4. María y tú __tienen__ un hermano. Es __su__ hermano.
5. Nosotras __tenemos__ unas mochilas. Son __nuestras__ mochilas.
6. Usted __tiene__ dos sobrinos. Son __sus__ sobrinos.

3 Oraciones
Arrange the words in the correct order to form complete logical sentences. ¡Ojo! Don't forget to conjugate the verbs. **10 pts.**

1. libros / unos / tener / interesantes / tú / muy
   Tú tienes unos libros muy interesantes.
2. dos / tener / grandes / escuela / mi / cafeterías
   Mi escuela tiene dos cafeterías grandes.
3. mi / francés / ser / amigo / buen / Hugo
   Hugo es mi buen amigo francés./Mi buen amigo francés es Hugo.
4. ser / simpáticas / dos / personas / nosotras
   Nosotras somos dos personas simpáticas.
5. menores / rubios / sus / ser / hermanos
   Sus hermanos menores son rubios.

RESUMEN GRAMATICAL

3.1 Descriptive adjectives pp. 88–90

Forms and agreement of adjectives

Masculine		Feminine	
Singular	Plural	Singular	Plural
alto	altos	alta	altas
inteligente	inteligentes	inteligente	inteligentes
trabajador	trabajadores	trabajadora	trabajadoras

► Descriptive adjectives follow the noun: **el chico rubio**
► Adjectives of nationality also follow the noun: **la mujer española**
► Adjectives of quantity precede the noun: **muchos libros, dos turistas**

Note: When placed before a masculine noun, these adjectives are shortened.

bueno → buen   **malo → mal**   **grande → gran**

3.2 Possessive adjectives p. 93

Singular		Plural	
mi	nuestro/a	mis	nuestros/as
tu	vuestro/a	tus	vuestros/as
su	su	sus	sus

3.3 Present tense of -er and -ir verbs pp. 96–97

comer		escribir	
como	comemos	escribo	escribimos
comes	coméis	escribes	escribís
come	comen	escribe	escriben

3.4 Present tense of tener and venir pp. 100–101

tener		venir	
tengo	tenemos	vengo	venimos
tienes	tenéis	vienes	venís
tiene	tienen	viene	vienen

---

4 **Carta** Complete this letter with the appropriate forms of the verbs in the word list. Not all verbs will be used. **10 pts.**

abrir	correr	recibir
asistir	creer	tener
compartir	escribir	venir
comprender	leer	vivir

Hola, Ángel,

¿Qué tal? (Yo) (1) _Escribo_ esta carta (this letter) en la biblioteca. Todos los días (2) _vengo_ aquí y (3) _leo_ un buen libro. Yo (4) _creo_ que es importante leer por diversión. Mi compañero de clase no (5) _comprende_ por qué me gusta leer. Él sólo (6) _abre/lee_ los libros de texto. Pero nosotros (7) _compartimos_ unos intereses. Por ejemplo, los dos somos atléticos; por las mañanas nosotros (8) _corremos_. También nos gustan las ciencias; por las tardes (9) _asistimos_ a nuestra clase de biología. Y tú, ¿cómo estás? ¿(Tú) (10) _Tienes_ mucho trabajo?

5 **Su familia** Write a brief description of a friend's family. Describe the family members using vocabulary and structures from this lesson. Write at least five sentences. **12 pts.**
Answers will vary.

modelo

> La familia de mi amiga Gabriela es grande. Ella tiene tres hermanos y una hermana. Su hermana mayor es periodista...

6 **Proverbio** Write the missing words to complete this proverb. **2 EXTRA points!**

“Dos andares° _tiene_ **el dinero°,**
viene **despacio°**
y se va° ligero°. ”

andares *gaits* dinero *money* despacio *slowly*
se va *it leaves* ligero *fast*

---

4 Expansion
- Ask students to create sentences with the verbs not used (**recibir** and **vivir**).
- To challenge students, ask them to write a response from Ángel. Encourage them to use lesson vocabulary.
- Ask students questions using vocabulary and sentence structures from the letter. Ex: ¿**Compartes muchos intereses con tus amigos? ¿Lees en la biblioteca todos los días? ¿Crees que es importante leer aparte de las clases?**

5 Teaching Tip You may want to have students interview a classmate about his or her family.

5 Expansion
- Ask students questions about their friends' families. ¿**Tu amigo/a tiene una familia pequeña o grande? ¿Cuántos hermanos/as tiene tu amigo/a?**
- Have students choose one of their friend's family members and write a more detailed description.

6 Teaching Tips
- Have a volunteer read the proverb aloud. Help students understand the inverted word order in the first line. Explain that this is a common literary technique. Have a volunteer restate the first line in a colloquial manner (**El dinero tiene dos andares.**).
- Have students discuss their interpretation of the proverb. Ask heritage speakers if they have heard this proverb or if they know of similar ones.

TEACHING OPTIONS

Game Create two *Mad-Libs*-style paragraphs that have blanks where the nouns and descriptive adjectives should be. Underneath each blank, indicate the type of word needed. Ex: _____ (*singular, feminine adjective*) Give each pair a set of paragraphs and have them take turns asking their partner to supply the missing words. Tell them they can use any nouns or adjectives that they have learned up to this point. When students have finished, ask them to read their paragraphs aloud. Have the class vote for the funniest one.

Extra Practice Name **tener** expressions and have students say what they or family members do in that situation. Ex: **tener hambre** (**Cuando tengo hambre, como pizza. Cuando mis hermanos tienen hambre, comen en McDonald's.**); **tener prisa** (**Cuando mi padre tiene prisa, toma el autobús.**)

Lectura

Antes de leer

Estrategia

Guessing meaning from context

As you read in Spanish, you'll often come across words you haven't learned. You can guess what they mean by looking at the surrounding words and sentences. Look at the following text and guess what **tía abuela** means, based on the context.

> ¡Hola, Claudia!
>
> ¿Qué hay de nuevo?
>
> ¿Sabes qué? Ayer fui a ver a mi tía abuela, la hermana de mi abuela. Tiene 85 años pero es muy independiente. Vive en un apartamento en Quito con su prima Lorena, quien también tiene 85 años.

If you guessed *great-aunt*, you are correct, and you can conclude from this word and the format clues that this is a letter about someone's visit with his or her great-aunt.

Examinar el texto

Quickly read through the paragraphs and find two or three words you don't know. Using the context as your guide, guess what these words mean. Then glance at the paragraphs where these words appear and try to predict what the paragraphs are about.

Examinar el formato

Look at the format of the reading. What clues do the captions, photos, and layout give you about its content?

Gente··· Las familias

1. Me llamo Armando y tengo setenta años pero no me considero viejo. Tengo seis nietas y un nieto. Vivo con mi hija y tengo la oportunidad de pasar mucho tiempo con ella y con mi nieto. Por las tardes salgo a pasear° por el parque con mi nieto y por la noche le leo cuentos°.

Armando. Tiene seis nietas y un nieto.

2. Mi prima Victoria y yo nos llevamos muy bien. Estudiamos juntas° en la universidad y compartimos un apartamento. Ella es muy inteligente y me ayuda° con los estudios. Además°, es muy simpática y generosa. Si no tengo dinero°, ¡ella me lo presta!

Diana. Vive con su prima.

3. Me llamo Ramona y soy paraguaya, aunque° ahora vivo en los Estados Unidos. Tengo tres hijos, uno de nueve años, uno de doce y el mayor de quince. Es difícil a veces, pero mi esposo y yo tratamos° de ayudarlos y comprenderlos siempre°.

Ramona. Sus hijos son muy importantes para ella.

. Tengo mucha suerte.
nque mis padres están
vorciados, tengo una
milia muy unida. Tengo
s hermanos y dos
rmanas. Me gusta
blar y salir a fiestas
n ellos. Ahora tengo
vio en la universidad y él no conoce a mis
rmanos. ¡Espero que se lleven bien!

Ana María. Su familia es muy unida.

. Antes quería° tener hermanos pero ya no°
tan importante. Ser hijo único tiene muchas
ventajas°: no tengo que
compartir mis cosas
con hermanos, no hay
discusiones° y, como
soy nieto único también,
¡mis abuelos piensan°
que soy perfecto!

Fernando.
Es hijo único.

5. Como soy joven todavía°, no tengo ni esposa
hijos. Pero tengo un sobrino, el hijo de mi
ermano, que es muy especial para mí. Se llama
enjamín y tiene ocho años. Es un muchacho muy
mpático. Siempre tiene hambre y por lo tanto
amos° frecuentemente a comer hamburguesas.
os gusta también ir al cine° a ver películas
e acción.
ablamos de
do. ¡Creo que
r tío es mejor
ue ser padre!

Santiago. Ser
tío es divertido.

go a pasear *I go take a walk* cuentos *stories* juntas *together*
e ayuda *she helps me* Además *Besides* dinero *money* aunque *although*
tamos *we try* siempre *always* quería *I wanted* ya no *no longer*
ntajas *advantages* discusiones *arguments* piensan *think* todavía *still*
mos *we go* ir al cine *to go to the movies*

Después de leer

Emparejar

Glance at the paragraphs and see how the words and
phrases in column A are used in context. Then find their
definitions in column B.

A		B
1. me lo presta	d	a. the oldest
2. nos llevamos bien	h	b. movies
3. no conoce	g	c. the youngest
4. películas	b	d. loans it to me
5. mejor que	j	e. borrows it from me
6. el mayor	a	f. we see each other
		g. doesn't know
		h. we get along
		i. portraits
		j. better than

Seleccionar

Choose the sentence that best summarizes each
paragraph.

1. Párrafo 1 a
   a. Me gusta mucho ser abuelo.
   b. No hablo mucho con mi nieto.
   c. No tengo nietos.
2. Párrafo 2 c
   a. Mi prima es antipática.
   b. Mi prima no es muy trabajadora.
   c. Mi prima y yo somos muy buenas amigas.
3. Párrafo 3 a
   a. Tener hijos es un gran sacrificio pero es muy
      bonito también.
   b. No comprendo a mis hijos.
   c. Mi esposo y yo no tenemos hijos.
4. Párrafo 4 c
   a. No hablo mucho con mis hermanos.
   b. Comparto mis cosas con mis hermanos.
   c. Mis hermanos y yo somos como (*like*) amigos.
5. Párrafo 5 a
   a. Me gusta ser hijo único.
   b. Tengo hermanos y hermanas.
   c. Vivo con mis abuelos.
6. Párrafo 6 b
   a. Mi sobrino tiene diez años.
   b. Me gusta mucho ser tío.
   c. Mi esposa y yo no tenemos hijos.

Emparejar If students have
trouble inferring the meaning of
any item, help them identify the
corresponding context clues.
**1. me lo presta (si no tengo
dinero) 2. nos llevamos bien
(compartimos un apartamento)
3. no conoce (ahora tengo novio
en la universidad) 4. películas
(cine) 5. mejor que (ser tío, ser
padre) 6. el mayor (de quince)**

Seleccionar You might wish
to ask students these listening
comprehension questions.
**1. ¿Cuántos años tiene
Armando? (setenta) 2. ¿Con
quién vive Armando? (con su
hija) 3. ¿Con quién comparte
un apartamento Diana? (con
su prima Victoria) 4. ¿Cómo es
Victoria? (inteligente, simpática
y generosa) 5. ¿De dónde es
Ramona? (Es de Paraguay.)
6. ¿En qué país vive Ramona
ahora? (en los Estados Unidos)
7. ¿Cómo es la familia de Ana
María? (muy unida) 8. ¿Ana
María tiene novio? (Sí, tiene
novio.) 9. ¿Qué tiene muchas
ventajas para Fernando? (ser
hijo único) 10. ¿Qué piensan
los abuelos de Fernando?
(que es perfecto) 11. ¿Cómo se
llama el sobrino de Santiago?
(Benjamín) 12. ¿Qué tiene
Benjamín siempre? (hambre)**

Teaching Tip Encourage
students to record unfamiliar
words and phrases that
they learn in **Lectura** in their
portfolios (**carpetas**).

108

Section Goals

In **Escritura**, students will:
- learn to write a friendly letter in Spanish
- integrate vocabulary and structures taught in **Lección 3** and before

Instructional Resources
Cuaderno para hispanohablantes, pp. 47–48
Cuaderno de actividades, pp. 145–146
Supersite

Estrategia Have students create their idea maps in Spanish. Some students may find it helpful to create their idea maps with note cards. They can write each detail that would be contained in a circle on a separate card to facilitate rearrangement.

Tema
- Introduce students to the common salutations (**saludos**) and closings (**despedidas**) used in friendly letters in Spanish. Point out that the salutation **Estimado/a** is more formal than **Querido/a**, which is rather familiar. Also point out that **Un abrazo** is less familiar in Spanish than its translation *A hug* would be in English.
- Point out that **Estimado/a** and **Querido/a** are adjectives and therefore agree in gender and number with the nouns they modify. Write these salutations on the board and have students supply the correct form:
  ____ **Señora Martínez:** (Estimada)
  ____ **Allison:** (Querida)
  ____ **padres:** (Queridos)
- Point out the use of the colon (**dos puntos**). Tell students that a colon is used instead of a comma in letter salutations.

Escritura SUPERSITE

Estrategia

Using idea maps

How do you organize ideas for a first draft? Often, the organization of ideas represents the most challenging part of the process. Idea maps are useful for organizing pertinent information. Here is an example of an idea map you can use:

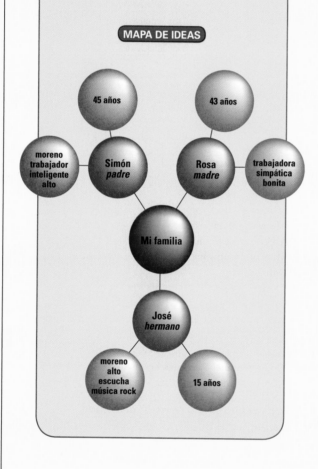

MAPA DE IDEAS

- 45 años
- 43 años
- moreno trabajador inteligente alto
- **Simón** *padre*
- **Rosa** *madre*
- trabajadora simpática bonita
- **Mi familia**
- **José** *hermano*
- moreno alto escucha música rock
- 15 años

recursos

| CH pp. 47–48 | CA pp. 145–146 | descubre1.vhlcentral.com Lección 3 |

Tema

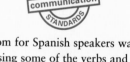
NATIONAL communication STANDARDS

Escribir una carta

A friend you met in a chat room for Spanish speakers wants to know about your family. Using some of the verbs and adjectives you have learned in this lesson, write a brief letter describing your family or an imaginary family, including:

▶ Names and relationships
▶ Physical characteristics
▶ Hobbies and interests

Here are some useful expressions for letter writing in Spanish:

Salutations

| **Estimado/a Julio/Julia:** | *Dear Julio/Julia,* |
| **Querido/a Miguel/Ana María:** | *Dear Miguel/Ana María,* |

Closings

Un abrazo,	*A hug,*
Abrazos,	*Hugs,*
Cariños,	*Much love,*
¡Hasta pronto!	*See you soon!*
¡Hasta la próxima semana!	*See you next week!*

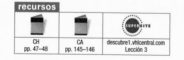

EVALUATION: Carta

Criteria	Scale
Appropriate salutations/closings	1 2 3 4 5
Appropriate details	1 2 3 4 5
Organization	1 2 3 4 5
Accuracy	1 2 3 4 5

Scoring	
Excellent	18–20 points
Good	14–17 points
Satisfactory	10–13 points
Unsatisfactory	< 10 points

Escuchar

Estrategia

Asking for repetition/Replaying the recording

Sometimes it is difficult to understand what people say, especially in a noisy environment. During a conversation, you can ask someone to repeat by saying **¿Cómo?** (*What?*) or **¿Perdón?** (*Pardon me?*). In class, you can ask your teacher to repeat by saying **Repita, por favor** (*Repeat, please*). If you don't understand a recorded activity, you can simply replay it.

 To help you practice this strategy, you will listen to a short paragraph. Ask your professor to repeat it or replay the recording, and then summarize what you heard.

Preparación

Based on the photograph, where do you think Cristina and Laura are? What do you think Laura is saying to Cristina?

Ahora escucha

Now you are going to hear Laura and Cristina's conversation. Use **R** to indicate which adjectives describe Cristina's boyfriend, Rafael. Use **E** for adjectives that describe Laura's boyfriend, Esteban. Some adjectives will not be used.

___ rubio   __E__ interesante

___ feo   ___ antipático

__R__ alto   __R__ inteligente

__E__ trabajador   __R__ moreno

__E__ un poco gordo   ___ viejo

Comprensión

Identificar

Which person would make each statement: Cristina or Laura?

	Cristina	Laura
1. Mi novio habla sólo de fútbol y de béisbol.	◉	○
2. Tengo un novio muy interesante y simpático.	○	◉
3. Mi novio es alto y moreno.	◉	○
4. Mi novio trabaja mucho.	○	◉
5. Mi amiga no tiene buena suerte con los muchachos.	○	◉
6. El novio de mi amiga es un poco gordo, pero guapo.	◉	○

¿Cierto o falso?

Indicate whether each sentence is **cierto** or **falso,** then correct the false statements.

	Cierto	Falso
1. Esteban es un chico interesante y simpático.	◉	○
2. Laura tiene mala suerte con los chicos. *Cristina tiene mala suerte con los chicos.*	○	◉
3. Rafael es muy interesante. *Esteban es muy interesante.*	○	◉
4. Laura y su novio hablan de muchas cosas.	◉	○

Section Goals

In **Escuchar**, students will:
• listen to and summarize a short paragraph
• learn strategies for asking for clarification in oral communication
• answer questions based on the content of a recorded conversation

Instructional Resources
Supersite: Textbook MP3 Audio Files
Supersite/TRCD: Textbook Audio Script
Textbook Audio CD

Estrategia

Script La familia de María Dolores es muy grande. Tiene dos hermanos y tres hermanas. Su familia vive en España. Pero la familia de Alberto es muy pequeña. No tiene hermanos ni hermanas. Alberto y sus padres viven en el Ecuador.

Teaching Tip Have students look at the photo and describe what they see. Guide them to guess where they think **Cristina** and **Laura** are and what they are talking about.

Ahora escucha

Script LAURA: ¿Qué hay de nuevo, Cristina?
CRISTINA: No mucho... sólo problemas con mi novio.
L: ¿Perdón?
C: No hay mucho de nuevo... sólo problemas con mi novio, Rafael.
L: ¿Qué les pasa?
C: Bueno, Rafael es alto y moreno... es muy guapo. Y es buena gente. Es inteligente también... pero es que no lo encuentro muy interesante.
L: ¿Cómo?
C: No es muy interesante. Sólo habla del fútbol y del béisbol. No me gusta hablar del fútbol las veinticuatro horas al día. No comprendo a los muchachos.

¿Cómo es tu novio, Laura?
L: Esteban es muy simpático. Es un poco gordo pero creo que es muy guapo. También es muy trabajador.
C: ¿Es interesante?

L: Sí. Hablamos dos o tres horas cada día. Hablamos de muchas cosas... las clases, los amigos... de todo.
C: ¡Qué bien! Siempre tengo mala suerte con los novios.

(Script continues at far left in the bottom panels.)

Introduction
To check comprehension, ask these questions. 1. Does the American concept of dating exist in the Hispanic world? (No, it is different in countries like Mexico, Spain, and Argentina.) 2. What kind of pressures might be associated with "being on a date"? (social or psychological) 3. How might one describe the beginning of a relationship in the Spanish-speaking world? (spontaneous, without labels)

Antes de ver
• Have students guess what the commercial is about, based on the video stills and captions.
• Ask students to describe the girl's expression in the first and second video stills. How does it change?
• Remind students to rely on visual cues, words from **Vocabulario útil**, and descriptive adjectives they have learned.

Preguntas To add an auditory aspect to this activity, replay the video and have students jot down the adjectives they hear. Have them state (in English) what each adjective refers to. Ex: **buena** (the young woman); **feo** (the relationship); **bonito** (the relationship).

Conversar Ask students additional questions. Ex: What advice would you give this girl? Do you think the ad is effective? Why or why not?

En pantalla

The American concept of dating does not exist in the same way in countries like Mexico, Spain, and Argentina. In the Spanish-speaking world, at the beginning of a relationship couples can go out without the social or psychological pressures and expectations of "being on a date." Relationships develop just like in the rest of the world, but perhaps in a more spontaneous manner and without insisting on labels.

Vocabulario útil

has sido	*you have been*
maravillosa	*wonderful*
conmigo	*with me*
te sorprenda	*it catches you by surprise*
quiero que me dejes	*I want you to let me*
explicarte	*explain to you*
por muy bajo que te parezca	*however low it seems to you*
lo que hago	*what I do*
Gracias por haberme querido escuchar.	*Thank you for having wanted to listen to me.*
que me dejes	*that you leave me*
haberme querido	*having loved me*
vida	*life*

Preguntas
Answer these questions.
1. Who wrote the letter to the young woman? Her boyfriend wrote her the letter.
2. What do you think she was expecting from the letter? Answers will vary.
3. How does she feel at the end of the ad? Why? Answers will vary. Sample answer: She feels satisfied, because she turned the letter into something positive for her.

Conversar
Answer these questions with a classmate. Answers will vary.
1. What is your opinion about the young woman's reaction to the letter?
2. What do you think about ending a relationship by mail?
3. What other ways do people use to break up?

algo falla *something is wrong* por eso *that's why* hay que acabar *we must break up* Sería *It would be* lo que ha sido *what has been*

Anuncio de **Pentel**

Eres una buena chica.

Pero algo falla°, por eso° hay que acabar°.

Sería° tonto convertir en feo lo que ha sido° bonito.

recursos
descubre1.vhlcentral.com
Lección 3

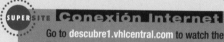
Conexión Internet
Go to descubre1.vhlcentral.com to watch the TV clip featured in this **En pantalla** section.

Oye cómo va

Olimpo Cárdenas

Ecuadorian vocalist **Olimpo Cárdenas Moreira** was born in the town of Vinces in 1919. A singer by the age of eight, at ten years old he began participating in children's music competitions in Guayaquil and Quito. In 1946 Cárdenas recorded, as a duet with Carlos Rubira Infante, the song *En las lejanías*. Of the more than fifty albums he completed during his career, six were joint endeavors with another famous Ecuadorian singer, Julio Jaramillo. Some of the songs Cárdenas made famous are *Temeridad*, *Hay que saber perder*, *Nuestro juramento*, and *Lágrimas de amor*. He often performed internationally, in countries such as Colombia, Venezuela, Mexico, and the United States. In 1991, Olimpo Cárdenas died in Tuluá, Colombia, the country where he had resided for many years.

Your instructor will play the song. Listen and then complete these activities.

Completar

Complete each sentence.

Olimpo Cárdenas started singing when he was ___eight___ years old.

He recorded _En las lejanías_ with Carlos Rubira Infante.

He visited Colombia, __Venezuela__, Mexico, and the U.S. with his music.

Cárdenas died in 1991 in __Tuluá__, Colombia.

Interpretación

Answer these questions in Spanish. Then, share your answers with a classmate. Answers will vary.

Describe the girl to whom this song is dedicated.

What do you think her relationship is with the singer?

If the girl had to reply to this song, what do you think she would say?

Chacha linda

Chacha°,
mi chacha linda°,
cómo te adoro, mi linda muchacha;
no sé° si pueda° dejar de° quererte°,
no sé si pueda dejarte de amar°.

NATIONAL STANDARDS
communication
cultures

El pasillo

Olimpo Cárdenas and Julio Jaramillo were famous for their interpretations of **pasillo**, which is considered the national music of Ecuador. **El pasillo**, a sentimental and romantic musical style, descended from the waltz and is closely related to the **bolero**.

Julio Jaramillo

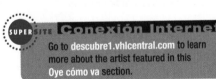

recursos
SUPERSITE
descubre1.vhlcentral.com
Lección 3

SUPERSITE Conexión Internet
Go to descubre1.vhlcentral.com to learn more about the artist featured in this **Oye cómo va** section.

chacha *short for* Muchacha linda *pretty* no sé *I don't know* si pueda *if I could* dejar de *stop* quererte *loving you* dejarte de amar *stop loving you*

TEACHING OPTIONS

El bolero One of the most popular music genres in Latin America is the **bolero**. Although its origin is debated, most agree that the form of the **bolero** sung in Latin America was born in Cuba in the late nineteenth century, and in the 1950s became an important part of Latin American popular music. **Boleros** have a unique rhythm created with guitar and percussion, and poetic lyrics, usually about romantic love. **Boleros** have given rise to other musical

genres, most notably **la bachata** in the Dominican Republic.
Small Groups Have students work in groups of three to choose another love song in Spanish. After finding the lyrics on the Internet, ask students to identify the adjectives used in the song. Are any of the adjectives common to love songs? Are any of them surprising? If time and resources permit, have groups play their song for the class.

Section Goal

In **Panorama**, students will receive comprehensible input by reading about the geography and culture of Ecuador.

Instructional Resources
Cuaderno de práctica,
pp. 33–34
Cuaderno de actividades,
pp. 73–74
e-Cuaderno
Supersite/DVD: *Panorama cultural*
Supersite/TRCD/Print:
PowerPoints (Overheads #5, #6, #18); *Panorama cultural*
Videoscript & Translation, Answer Keys

Teaching Tip Have students look at the map of Ecuador or show *Overhead PowerPoint #18.* Then have them look at the call-out photos and read the captions. Encourage students to mention anything they may know about Ecuador.

El país en cifras
- Ask students to glance at the headings. Establish the kind of information contained in each and clarify unfamiliar words. Point out that most words in the headings have an English cognate.
- Point out that in September 2000, the U.S. dollar became the official currency of Ecuador.

¡Increíble pero cierto!
Mt. St. Helens in Washington and **Cotopaxi** in Ecuador are just two of a chain of volcanoes that stretches along the entire Pacific coast of North and South America, from Mt. McKinley in Alaska to **Monte Sarmiento** in the **Tierra del Fuego** of southern Chile.

Ecuador

connections cultures — NATIONAL STANDARDS

El país en cifras

▶ **Área:** 283.560 km^2 (109.483 millas^2), *incluyendo las islas Galápagos, aproximadamente el área de Colorado*
▶ **Población:** 14.192.000
▶ **Capital:** Quito — 1.680.000
▶ **Ciudades° principales:**
Guayaquil — 2.709.000, Cuenca, Machala, Portoviejo

SOURCE: Population Division, UN Secretariat

▶ **Moneda:** dólar estadounidense
▶ **Idiomas:** español (oficial), quichua

La lengua oficial del Ecuador es el español, pero también se hablan° otras° lenguas en el país. Aproximadamente unos 4.000.000 de ecuatorianos hablan lenguas indígenas; la mayoría° de ellos habla quichua. El quichua es el dialecto ecuatoriano del quechua, la lengua de los incas.

Los indígenas del Ecuador hablan quichua.

Bandera del Ecuador

Ecuatorianos célebres

▶ **Francisco Eugenio De Santa Cruz y Espejo,** médico, periodista y patriota (1747–1795)
▶ **Juan León Mera,** novelista (1832–1894)
▶ **Eduardo Kingman,** pintor° (1913–1998)
▶ **Rosalía Arteaga,** abogada°, política y ex-vicepresidenta (1956–)

Ciudades *Cities* se hablan *are spoken* otras *other* mayoría *majority* pintor *painter* abogada *lawyer* sur *south* mundo *world* pies *feet* dos veces más alto que *twice as tall as*

Las islas Galápagos

COLOMBIA

Indígenas de Amazonas

Río Esmeraldas

Ibarra

Quito ✪

Volcán Cotopaxi

Río Napo

Portoviejo

Volcán Tungurahua

Río Daule

Río Pastaza

Guayaquil

Volcán Chimborazo

Cuenca

Cordillera de los Andes

Océano Pacífico

Machala

La ciudad de Quito y la Cordillera de los Andes

Loja

PERÚ

Catedral de Guayaquil

recursos

CP pp. 33–34

CA pp. 73–74

descubre1.vhlcentral.com Lección 3

¡Increíble pero cierto!

El volcán Cotopaxi, situado a unos 60 kilómetros al sur° de Quito, es considerado el volcán activo más alto del mundo°. Tiene una altura de 5.897 metros (19.340 pies°). Es dos veces más alto que° el monte St. Helens (2.550 metros o 9.215 pies) en el estado de Washington.

TEACHING OPTIONS

Heritage Speakers If a heritage speaker is of Ecuadorian origin or has visited Ecuador, ask him or her to prepare a short presentation about his or her experiences there. If possible, the presentation should be illustrated with photos of and articles about the country.

Language Notes Remind students that **km²** is the abbreviation for **kilómetros cuadrados** and that **millas²** is the abbreviation for **millas cuadradas.** Ask a volunteer to explain why **kilómetros** takes **cuadrados** and **millas** takes **cuadradas.**

Lugares • Las islas Galápagos

Muchas personas vienen de lejos a visitar las islas Galápagos porque son un verdadero tesoro° ecológico. Aquí Charles Darwin estudió° las especies que inspiraron° sus ideas sobre la evolución. Como las islas están lejos del continente, sus plantas y animales son únicos. Las islas son famosas por sus tortugas° gigantes.

Artes • Oswaldo Guayasamín

Oswaldo Guayasamín fue° uno de los artistas latinoamericanos más famosos del mundo. Fue escultor° y muralista. Su expresivo estilo viene del cubismo y sus temas preferidos son la injusticia y la pobreza° sufridas° por los indígenas de su país.

Madre y niño en azul, 1986, Oswaldo Guayasamín

Deportes • El *trekking*

El sistema montañoso de los Andes cruza° y divide el Ecuador en varias regiones. La Sierra, que tiene volcanes, grandes valles y una variedad increíble de plantas y animales, es perfecta para el *trekking*. Muchos turistas visitan el Ecuador cada° año para hacer° *trekking* y escalar montañas°.

Lugares • Latitud 0

Hay un monumento en el Ecuador, a unos 22 kilómetros (14 millas) de Quito, donde los visitantes están en el hemisferio norte y el hemisferio sur a la vez°. Este monumento se llama la Mitad del Mundo°, y es un destino turístico muy popular.

Explosión del volcán Tungurahua en 1999

¿Qué aprendiste? Completa las oraciones con la información correcta.
1. La ciudad más grande (*biggest*) del Ecuador es ___Guayaquil___.
2. La capital del Ecuador es ___Quito___.
3. Unos 4.000.000 de ecuatorianos hablan ___lenguas indígenas___.
4. Darwin estudió el proceso de la evolución en ___las islas Galápagos___.
5. Dos temas del arte de ___Guayasamín___ son la pobreza y la ___injusticia___.
6. Un monumento muy popular es ___la Mitad del Mundo___.
7. La Sierra es un lugar perfecto para el ___trekking___.
8. El volcán ___Cotopaxi___ es el volcán activo más alto del mundo.

Conexión Internet Investiga estos temas en **descubre1.vhlcentral.com.**

1. Busca información sobre una ciudad (*city*) del Ecuador. ¿Te gustaría (*Would you like*) visitar la ciudad? ¿Por qué?
2. Haz una lista de tres animales o plantas que viven sólo en las islas Galápagos. ¿Dónde hay animales o plantas similares?

....

verdadero tesoro *true treasure* **estudió** *studied* **inspiraron** *inspired* **tortugas** *tortoises* **fue** *was* **escultor** *sculptor* **pobreza** *poverty* **sufridas** *suffered* **cruza** *crosses* **cada** *every* **hacer** *to do* **escalar montañas** *to climb mountains* **a la vez** *at the same time* **Mitad del Mundo** *Equatorial Line Monument (lit. Midpoint of the World)*

Instructional Resources
Cuaderno de actividades, p. 104
e-Cuaderno
Supersite: Textbook &
Vocabulary MP3 Audio Files
Supersite/TRCD/Print: Answer
Keys; *Testing Program* (**Lección
3 Pruebas,** Test Generator,
Testing Program MP3 Audio
Files)
Textbook & Test Audio CD

La familia

el/la abuelo/a	grandfather/grandmother
los abuelos	grandparents
el apellido	last name
el/la bisabuelo/a	great-grandfather/great-grandmother
el/la cuñado/a	brother-in-law/sister-in-law
el/la esposo/a	husband; wife; spouse
la familia	family
el/la gemelo/a	twin
el/la hermanastro/a	stepbrother/stepsister
el/la hermano/a	brother/sister
el/la hijastro/a	stepson/stepdaughter
el/la hijo/a	son/daughter
los hijos	children
la madrastra	stepmother
la madre	mother
el/la medio/a hermano/a	half-brother/half-sister
el/la nieto/a	grandson/granddaughter
la nuera	daughter-in-law
el padrastro	stepfather
el padre	father
los padres	parents
los parientes	relatives
el/la primo/a	cousin
el/la sobrino/a	nephew/niece
el/la suegro/a	father-in-law/mother-in-law
el/la tío/a	uncle/aunt
el yerno	son-in-law

Otras personas

el/la amigo/a	friend
la gente	people
el/la muchacho/a	boy/girl
el/la niño/a	child
el/la novio/a	boyfriend/girlfriend
la persona	person

Profesiones

el/la artista	artist
el/la doctor(a), el/la médico/a	doctor; physician
el/la ingeniero/a	engineer
el/la periodista	journalist
el/la programador(a)	computer programmer

Adjetivos

alto/a	tall
antipático/a	unpleasant
bajo/a	short (in height)
bonito/a	pretty
buen, bueno/a	good
delgado/a	thin; slender
difícil	difficult; hard
fácil	easy
feo/a	ugly
gordo/a	fat
gran, grande	big; large
guapo/a	handsome; good-looking
importante	important
inteligente	intelligent
interesante	interesting
joven	young
mal, malo/a	bad
mismo/a	same
moreno/a	brunet(te)
mucho/a	much; many; a lot of
pelirrojo/a	red-haired
pequeño/a	small
rubio/a	blond(e)
simpático/a	nice; likeable
tonto/a	silly; foolish
trabajador(a)	hard-working
viejo/a	old

Nacionalidades

alemán, alemana	German
canadiense	Canadian
chino/a	Chinese
ecuatoriano/a	Ecuadorian
español(a)	Spanish
estadounidense	from the U.S.
francés, francesa	French
inglés, inglesa	English
italiano/a	Italian
japonés, japonesa	Japanese
mexicano/a	Mexican
norteamericano/a	(North) American
puertorriqueño/a	Puerto Rican
ruso/a	Russian

Verbos

abrir	to open
aprender (a + *inf.*)	to learn
asistir (a)	to attend
beber	to drink
comer	to eat
compartir	to share
comprender	to understand
correr	to run
creer (en)	to believe (in)
deber (+ *inf.*)	should; must; ought to
decidir (+ *inf.*)	to decide
describir	to describe
escribir	to write
leer	to read
recibir	to receive
tener	to have
venir	to come
vivir	to live

Possessive adjectives	See page 93.
Expressions with *tener*	See page 101.
Expresiones útiles	See page 83.

recursos

CA p. 104 | descubre1.vhlcentral.com Lección 3

Los pasatiempos

4

Communicative Goals

You will learn how to:
- Talk about pastimes, weekend activities, and sports
- Make plans and invitations

Lesson Goals

In **Lección 4**, students will be introduced to the following:
- names of sports and other pastimes
- names of places in a city
- soccer rivalries
- Cuban sprinter **Anier García** and Argentine field hockey player **Luciana Aymar**
- present tense of **ir**
- the contraction **al**
- **ir a** + [*infinitive*]
- present tense of common stem-changing verbs
- verbs with irregular **yo** forms
- predicting content by surveying graphic elements
- using a Spanish-English dictionary
- writing an events pamphlet
- listening for the gist
- a television commercial for **Totofútbol**, an electronic lottery based on soccer match results
- Mexican rock band **Café Tacuba**
- cultural, historical, economic, and geographic information about Mexico

A primera vista Here are some additional questions you can ask based on the photo: **¿Te gusta el fútbol? ¿Crees que son importantes los pasatiempos? ¿Trabajas mucho los sábados y domingos? ¿Bailas? ¿Lees? ¿Escuchas música?**

A PRIMERA VISTA
- ¿Qué son estas personas, atletas o artistas?
- ¿En qué tienen interés, en el fútbol o el tenis?
- ¿Son viejos? ¿Son delgados?
- ¿Tienen frío o calor?

INSTRUCTIONAL RESOURCES

Student Materials
Cuaderno de práctica, Cuaderno para hispanohablantes, Cuaderno de actividades
Student MAESTRO™ Supersite
(descubre1.vhlcentral.com)
MAESTRO™ e-Cuaderno

Teacher's Resource CD-ROM and in print
*Answer Keys, Audioscripts, Videoscripts
*PowerPoints
Testing Program (**Pruebas,** Test Generator, MP3 Audio Files)
Vista Higher Learning *Cancionero*
*Also available on Supersite

Teacher's MAESTRO™ Supersite
(descubre1.vhlcentral.com)
Learning Management System (Assignment Task Manager, Gradebook)
Also on DVD
Fotonovela, Flash cultura, Panorama cultural

Los pasatiempos

Más vocabulario

el béisbol	baseball
el ciclismo	cycling
el esquí (acuático)	(water) skiing
el fútbol americano	football
el golf	golf
el hockey	hockey
la natación	swimming
el tenis	tennis
el vóleibol	volleyball
el equipo	team
el parque	park
el partido	game; match
la plaza	city or town square
andar en patineta	to skateboard
bucear	to scuba dive
escalar montañas (f. pl.)	to climb mountains
esquiar	to ski
ganar	to win
ir de excursión	to go on a hike
practicar deportes (m. pl.)	to play sports
escribir una carta/ un mensaje electrónico	to write a letter/ an e-mail message
leer correo electrónico	to read e-mail
leer una revista	to read a magazine
deportivo/a	sports-related

Variación léxica

piscina ⟷ pileta (*Arg.*); alberca (*Méx.*)
baloncesto ⟷ básquetbol (*Amér. L.*)
béisbol ⟷ pelota (*P. Rico, Rep. Dom.*)

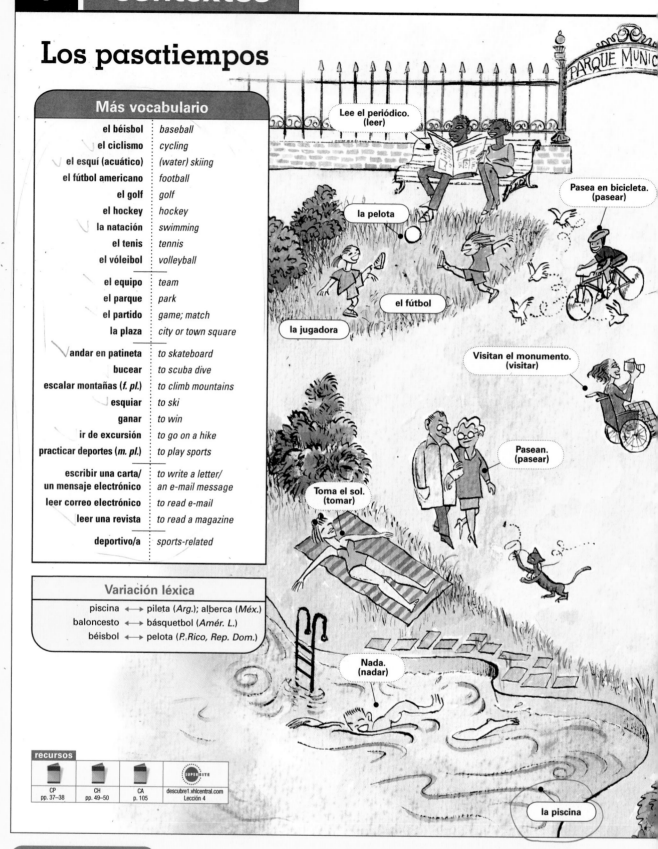

Lee el periódico. (leer)

Pasea en bicicleta. (pasear)

la pelota

el fútbol

la jugadora

Visitan el monumento. (visitar)

Pasean. (pasear)

Toma el sol. (tomar)

Nada. (nadar)

la piscina

recursos

| CP pp. 37–38 | CH pp. 49–50 | CA p. 105 | SUPERSITE descubre1.vhlcentral.com Lección 4 |

Práctica

1 **Escuchar** 🎧 Indicate the letter of the activity in Column B that best corresponds to each statement you hear. Two items in Column B will not be used.

A	B
1. __b__	a. leer correo electrónico
2. __d__	b. tomar el sol
3. __f__	c. pasear en bicicleta
4. __c__	d. ir a un partido de fútbol americano
5. __g__	e. escribir una carta
6. __h__	f. practicar muchos deportes
	g. nadar
	h. ir de excursión

2 **Ordenar** 🎧 Order these activities according to what you hear in the narration.

_5_ pasear en bicicleta		_3_ tomar el sol	
_1_ nadar		_6_ practicar deportes	
_4_ leer una revista		_2_ patinar en línea	

3 **¿Cierto o falso?** Indicate whether each statement is **cierto** or **falso** based on the illustration.

	Cierto	Falso
1. Un hombre nada en la piscina.	☑	○
2. Un hombre lee una revista. *el periódico*	○	☑
3. Un chico pasea en bicicleta.	☑	○
4. Dos muchachos esquían.	○	☑
5. Una mujer y dos niños visitan un monumento.	☑	○
6. Un hombre bucea.	○	☑
7. Hay un equipo de hockey.	○	☑
8. Una mujer toma el sol.	☑	○

4 **Clasificar** Fill in the chart below with as many terms from **Contextos** as you can. Answers will vary.

Actividades	Deportes	Personas

en línea.
(patinar)

el jugador

el baloncesto

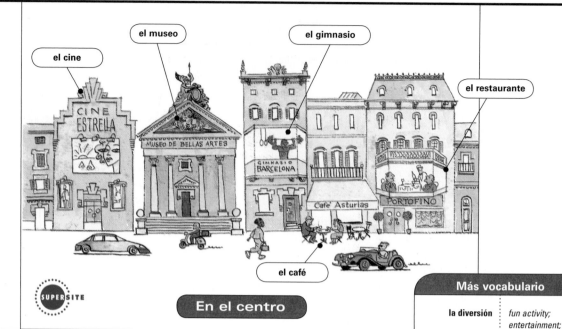

el cine   el museo   el gimnasio   el restaurante   el café

En el centro

Más vocabulario

la diversión	fun activity; entertainment; recreation
el fin de semana	weekend
el pasatiempo	pastime; hobby
los ratos libres	spare (free) time
el videojuego	video game
la iglesia	church
el lugar	place
ver películas (f. pl.)	to see movies
favorito/a	favorite

5 Identificar Identify the place where these activities would take place.

modelo
Esquiamos.
Es una montaña.

1. Tomamos una limonada.   Es un café./Es un restaurante.
2. Vemos una película.   Es un cine.
3. Nadamos y tomamos el sol.   Es una piscina./Es un parque.
4. Hay muchos monumentos.   Es un parque.
5. Comemos tacos y fajitas.   Es un restaurante.
6. Miramos pinturas (*paintings*) de Diego Rivera y Frida Kahlo.   Es un museo.
7. Hay mucho tráfico.   Es el centro.
8. Practicamos deportes.   Es un gimnasio./Es un parque.

6 Entrevista In pairs, take turns asking and answering the questions.   Answers will vary.

1. ¿Hay un café cerca de la escuela? ¿Dónde está?
2. ¿Cuál es tu restaurante favorito?
3. ¿Te gusta viajar y visitar monumentos? ¿Por qué?
4. ¿Te gusta ir al cine los fines de semana?
5. ¿Cuáles son tus películas favoritas?
6. ¿Te gusta practicar deportes?
7. ¿Cuáles son tus deportes favoritos? ¿Por qué?
8. ¿Cuáles son tus pasatiempos favoritos?

CONSULTA

To review the verb **gustar**, see **Estructura 2.1**, p. 52.

UN DÍA CON ÁNGELA

Un día inolvidable.

TEACHING OPTIONS

Extra Practice Give students five minutes to write a description of a typical weekend: what they do and where, and with whom they spend time. Circulate through the class and help with unfamiliar vocabulary. Have volunteers share their paragraphs with the class, who will decide if the weekend descriptions are "typical."

Game Have students tell a chain story. For example, one student begins with: **Es el sábado por la mañana y voy [al café].** The next student continues with: **Estoy en el café y tomo una limonada.** You may need to provide some phrases on the board: **voy a/al... , luego, después.** The story may change location; set a time limit for each response. The game ends after ten minutes.

Comunicación

7 **Preguntar** Ask a classmate what he or she does in the places mentioned below. Your classmate will respond using verbs from the word bank. Answers will vary.

beber	escribir	patinar
caminar	leer	practicar
correr	mirar	tomar
escalar	nadar	visitar

modelo

una plaza

Estudiante 1: ¿Qué haces (*do you do*) cuando estás en una plaza?

Estudiante 2: Camino por la plaza y miro a las personas.

1. una biblioteca
2. un estadio
3. una plaza
4. una piscina
5. las montañas
6. un parque
7. un café
8. un museo

8 **Conversación** Using the words and expressions provided, work with a partner to prepare a short conversation about your pastimes. Answers will vary.

¿a qué hora?	¿con quién(es)?	¿dónde?
¿cómo?	¿cuándo?	¿qué?

modelo

Estudiante 1: ¿Cuándo patinas en línea?

Estudiante 2: Patino en línea los domingos. Y tú, ¿patinas en línea?

Estudiante 1: No, no me gusta patinar en línea. Me gusta practicar el béisbol.

9 **Pasatiempos** In pairs, tell each other what pastimes three of your friends and family members enjoy. Be prepared to share with the class any pastimes they have in common. Answers will vary.

modelo

Estudiante 1: Mi hermana pasea mucho en bicicleta. Pero mis padres practican la natación. Mi hermano no nada, pero visita muchos museos.

Estudiante 2: Mi primo lee muchas revistas, pero no practica muchos deportes. Mis tíos esquían y practican el golf...

---

7 **Teaching Tip** Quickly review the verbs in the list. Make sure that students understand the meaning of **¿Qué haces… ?** Tell them that they will use this phrase throughout the activity.

7 **Expansion**
- Ask additional questions and have volunteers answer. Ex: **¿Qué haces en la casa (el apartamento)?** Suggested places: **la casa de un amigo/ una amiga, el centro, el gimnasio**.
- Have students share their responses with the class. Then have them create a table based on the responses. Ex: **En la biblioteca: yo (leo, trabajo en la computadora)**

8 **Expansion** After students have asked and answered questions, ask volunteers to report their partners' activities back to the class. The partners should verify the information.

9 **Expansion**
- Ask volunteers to share any pastimes they and their partners, friends, and families have in common. Ask for a show of hands to find out which activities are most popular and where they do them. What are the general tendencies of the class?
- In pairs, have students write sentences about the pastimes of a famous person. Then have them work with another pair, who will guess who is the famous person being described.

¡Vamos al parque!

Los estudiantes pasean por la ciudad y hablan de sus pasatiempos.

Section Goals

In **Fotonovela**, students will:
- receive comprehensible input from free-flowing discourse
- learn functional phrases for making invitations and plans, talking about pastimes, and apologizing

---

Instructional Resources
Cuaderno de actividades,
pp. 57–58
e-Cuaderno
Supersite/DVD: *Fotonovela*
Supersite/TRCD: *Fotonovela*
Videoscript & Translation,
Answer Keys

Video Recap: Lección 3
Before doing this **Fotonovela** section, review the previous episode with this activity.
1. _____ tiene una familia grande. (Inés) 2. El _____ de Javier es viejo y trabajador. (abuelo) 3. _____ no tiene hermanos. (Javier) 4. Inés tiene _____ hermanas. (cuatro)

Video Synopsis The travelers have an hour to explore the city before heading to the cabins. **Javier** and **Inés** decide to stroll around the city. **Álex** and **Maite** go to the park. While **Maite** writes postcards, **Álex** and a young man play soccer. A stray ball hits **Maite**. **Álex** and **Maite** return to the bus, and **Álex** invites her to go running with him that evening.

Teaching Tips
- Have students quickly glance over the **Fotonovela** captions and make a list of the cognates they find. Then, ask them to predict what this episode is about.
- Have students state some expressions used to talk about pastimes. Then ask a few questions. Ex: **¿Eres aficionado/a a un deporte? ¿Te gusta el fútbol?**

PERSONAJES

DON FRANCISCO

JAVIER

INÉS

ÁLEX

MAITE

JOVEN

DON FRANCISCO Tienen una hora libre. Pueden explorar la ciudad, si quieren.

JAVIER Inés, ¿quieres ir a pasear por la ciudad?
INÉS Sí, vamos.

ÁLEX ¿Por qué no vamos al parque, Maite? Podemos hablar y tomar el sol.
MAITE ¡Buena idea! También quiero escribir unas postales.

ÁLEX ¡Maite!
MAITE ¡Dios mío!

JOVEN Mil perdones. Lo siento muchísimo.
MAITE ¡No es nada! Estoy bien.

ÁLEX Ya son las dos y treinta. Debemos regresar al autobús, ¿no?
MAITE Tienes razón.
ÁLEX Oye, Maite, ¿qué vas a hacer esta noche?
MAITE No tengo planes. ¿Por qué?

recursos

CA
p. 57–58

descubre1.vhlcentral.com
Lección 4

TEACHING OPTIONS

¡Vamos al parque! Play the last half of the **¡Vamos al parque!** episode and have the class give you a description of what they saw. Write their observations on the board, pointing out any incorrect information. Repeat this process to allow the class to pick up more details of the plot. Then ask students to use the

information they have accumulated to guess what happened at the beginning of the **¡Vamos al parque!** episode. Write their guesses on the board. Then play the entire episode and, through discussion, help the class summarize the plot.

MAITE ¿Eres aficionado a los deportes, Álex?

ÁLEX Sí, me gusta mucho el fútbol. Me gusta también nadar, correr e ir de excursión a las montañas.

MAITE Yo también corro mucho.

ÁLEX Oye, Maite, ¿por qué no jugamos al fútbol con él?

MAITE Mmm... no quiero. Voy a terminar de escribir unas postales.

ÁLEX Eh, este... a veces salgo a correr por la noche. ¿Quieres venir a correr conmigo?

MAITE Sí, vamos. ¿A qué hora?

ÁLEX ¿A las seis?

MAITE Perfecto.

DON FRANCISCO Esta noche van a correr. ¡Y yo no tengo energía para pasear!

Expresiones útiles

Making invitations

- **¿Por qué no vamos al parque?**
  Why don't we go to the park?
  ¡Buena idea!
  Good idea!
- **¿Por qué no jugamos al fútbol?**
  Why don't we play soccer?
  Mmm... no quiero.
  Hmm... I don't want to.
  Lo siento, pero no puedo.
  I'm sorry, but I can't.

- **¿Quieres ir a pasear por la ciudad/ el pueblo conmigo?**
  Do you want to walk around the city/the town with me?
  Sí, vamos.
  Yes, let's go.
  Sí, si tenemos tiempo.
  Yes, if we have time.

Making plans

- **¿Qué vas a hacer esta noche?**
  What are you going to do tonight?
  No tengo planes.
  I don't have any plans.
  Voy a terminar de escribir unas postales.
  I'm going to finish writing some postcards.

Talking about pastimes

- **¿Eres aficionado/a a los deportes?**
  Are you a sports fan?
  Sí, me gustan todos los deportes.
  Yes, I like all sports.
  Sí, me gusta mucho el fútbol.
  Yes, I like soccer a lot.

- **Me gusta también nadar, correr e ir de excursión a las montañas.**
  I also like to swim, run, and go hiking in the mountains.
  Yo también corro mucho.
  I also run a lot.

Apologizing

- **Mil perdones./Lo siento muchísimo.**
  I'm so sorry.

Teaching Tip Have the class read through the entire **Fotonovela**, with volunteers playing the parts of **Don Francisco, Javier, Inés, Álex, Maite,** and the **Joven.** Have students take turns playing the roles so that more students participate.

Expresiones útiles

- Point out the written accents in the words **¿qué?, ¿por qué?,** and **también.** Explain that accents indicate a stressed syllable in a word (**también**) and remind students that all question words have accent marks. Tell students that they will learn more about word stress and accent marks in **Pronunciación.**
- Mention that **voy, vas, va,** and **vamos** are present-tense forms of the verb **ir.** Point out that **ir a** is used with an infinitive to tell what is going to happen. Ask: **¿Qué vas a hacer esta noche? ¿Por qué no vamos al parque?** Explain that **quiero, quieres,** and **siento** are forms of **querer** and **sentir,** which undergo a stem change from **e** to **ie** in certain forms. Tell students that they will learn more about these concepts in **Estructura.**

Pairs After viewing the *Fotonovela*, ask students what **Inés** and **Javier** are doing in the meantime (**pasean por la ciudad**). Have student pairs write a dialogue between **Inés** and **Javier** as they stroll through the city. Encourage them to be creative and mention at least three places that they visit on their walk. Then have pairs role-play the dialogue for the class.

TPR Go through the **Expresiones útiles** as a class. Then have students stand and form a circle. Call out a question or statement from **Expresiones útiles** (Ex: **¿Qué vas a hacer esta noche?**) and toss a foam or paper ball to a student. He or she must respond appropriately and toss the ball back to you. Ex: **Voy a mirar la televisión.** Encourage students to respond according to what is true for them.

¿Qué pasó?

1

Escoger Choose the answer that best completes each sentence.

1. Inés y Javier ___b___.
   a. toman el sol   b. pasean por la ciudad   c. corren por el parque

2. Álex desea ___a___ en el parque.
   a. hablar y tomar el sol   b. hablar y leer el periódico   c. nadar y tomar el sol

3. A Álex le gusta nadar, ___c___.
   a. jugar al fútbol y escribir postales   b. escalar montañas y esquiar
   c. ir de excursión y correr

4. A Maite le gusta ___b___.
   a. nadar y correr   b. correr y escribir postales   c. correr y jugar al fútbol

5. Maite desea ___c___.
   a. ir de excursión   b. jugar al fútbol   c. ir al parque

2

Identificar Identify the person who would make each statement.

1. No me gusta practicar el fútbol pero me gusta correr. ___Maite___

2. ¿Por qué no vamos a pasear por la ciudad? ___Javier___

3. ¿Por qué no exploran ustedes la ciudad? Tienen tiempo. ___don Francisco___

4. ¿Por qué no corres conmigo esta noche? ___Álex___

5. No voy al parque. Prefiero estar con mi amigo. ___Inés___

JAVIER

INÉS

ÁLEX

MAITE

DON FRANCISCO

3

Preguntas Answer the questions using the information from the **Fotonovela.**

1. ¿Qué desean hacer Inés y Javier? Desean pasear por la ciudad.

2. ¿Qué desea hacer Álex en el parque? Desea jugar al fútbol.

3. ¿Qué desea hacer Maite en el parque? Maite desea escribir postales./Maite desea terminar de escribir unas postales.

4. ¿Qué deciden hacer Maite y Álex esta noche? Deciden ir a correr.

4

Conversación With a partner, prepare a conversation in which you talk about pastimes and invite each other to do some activity together. Use these expressions and also look at **Expresiones útiles** on the previous page. Answers will vary.

contigo *with you*	**¿Dónde?** *Where?*	**Nos vemos a las siete.**
¿A qué hora? *(At) What time?*	**No puedo porque...** *I can't because...*	*See you at seven.*

▶ ¿Eres aficionado/a a...?   ▶ ¿Por qué no...?   ▶ ¿Qué vas a hacer esta noche?

▶ ¿Te gusta...?   ▶ ¿Quieres... conmigo?

NATIONAL communication STANDARDS

TEACHING OPTIONS

Small Groups Have the class quickly glance at frames 4–9 of the **Fotonovela.** Then have students work in groups of three to ad-lib what transpires between **Álex, Maite,** and the **Joven.** Assure them that it is not necessary to follow the **Fotonovela** word for word. Students should be creative while getting the general meaning across with the vocabulary and expressions they know.

Extra Practice Have students close their books and complete these statements with words from the **Fotonovela. 1. _____ a terminar de escribir unas postales. (Voy) 2. ¡Mil _____! Lo siento muchísimo. (perdones) 3. Inés, ¿_____ ir a pasear por la ciudad? (quieres) 4. ¿Por qué no _____ al parque, Maite? (vamos) 5. Maite, ¿qué vas a _____ esta noche? (hacer)**

Pronunciación

Word stress and accent marks

pe-lí-cu-la   **e-di-fi-cio**   **ver**   **yo**

Every Spanish syllable contains at least one vowel. When two vowels (two weak vowels or one strong and one weak) are joined in the same syllable they form a **diphthong**. A **monosyllable** is a word formed by a single syllable.

bi-blio-te-ca   **vi-si-tar**   **par-que**   **fút-bol**

The syllable of a Spanish word that is pronounced most emphatically is the "stressed" syllable.

pe-lo-ta   **pis-ci-na**   **ra-tos**   **ha-blan**

Words that end in **n**, **s**, or a **vowel** are usually stressed on the next-to-last syllable.

na-ta-ción   **pa-pá**   **in-glés**   **Jo-sé**

If words that end in **n**, **s**, or a **vowel** are stressed on the last syllable, they must carry an accent mark on the stressed syllable.

bai-lar   **es-pa-ñol**   **u-ni-ver-si-dad**   **tra-ba-ja-dor**

Words that do *not* end in **n**, **s**, or a **vowel** are usually stressed on the last syllable.

béis-bol   **lá-piz**   **ár-bol**   **Gó-mez**

If words that do *not* end in **n**, **s**, or a **vowel** are stressed on the next-to-last syllable, they must carry an accent mark on the stressed syllable.

En la unión está la fuerza.[2]

Práctica Pronounce each word, stressing the correct syllable. Then give the word stress rule for each word.

1. profesor
2. Puebla
3. ¿Cuántos?
4. Mazatlán
5. examen
6. ¿Cómo?
7. niños
8. Guadalajara
9. programador
10. México
11. están
12. geografía

Oraciones Read the conversation aloud to practice word stress.

MARINA Hola, Carlos. ¿Qué tal?
CARLOS Bien. Oye, ¿a qué hora es el partido de fútbol?
MARINA Creo que es a las siete.
CARLOS ¿Quieres ir?
MARINA Lo siento, pero no puedo. Tengo que estudiar biología.

Quien ríe de último, ríe mejor.[1]

Refranes Read these sayings aloud to practice word stress.

1 He who laughs last, laughs loudest.
2 United we stand.

recursos

CH p. 51	CA p. 106	descubre1.vhlcentral.com Lección 4

EN DETALLE

Real Madrid y Barça: rivalidad total

Soccer in Spain is a force to be reckoned with, and no two teams draw more attention than **Real Madrid** and the **Fútbol Club Barcelona.** Whether the venue is Madrid's **Santiago Bernabéu** or Barcelona's **Camp Nou,** the two cities shut down for the showdown, paralyzed by **fútbol** fever. A ticket to the actual game is always the hottest ticket in town.

The rivalry between **Real Madrid** and **Barça** is about more than soccer. As the two biggest, most powerful cities in Spain, Barcelona and Madrid are constantly compared to one another and have a natural rivalry. There is also a political component to the dynamic. Barcelona, with its distinct language and culture, has long struggled for increased autonomy from Madrid's centralized government. Under Francisco Franco's rule (1939–1975), when repression of the Catalan identity was at its height, a game between **Real Madrid** and **FC Barcelona** was wrapped up with all the symbolism of the regime versus the resistance, even though both teams suffered casualties in Spain's civil war and the subsequent Franco dictatorship.

Although the dictatorship is far behind, the momentum of all those decades of competition still transforms both cities into a frenzied, tense panic leading up to the game. Once the final score is announced, one of those cities transforms again, this time into the best party in the country.

Rivalidades del fútbol

Argentina: Boca Juniors vs River Plate
México: Águilas del América vs Chivas del Guadalajara
Chile: Colo Colo vs Universidad de Chile
Guatemala: Comunicaciones vs Municipal
Uruguay: Peñarol vs Nacional
Colombia: Millonarios vs Independiente Santa Fe

ACTIVIDADES

1 **¿Cierto o falso?** Indicate whether each statement is **cierto** or **falso.** Correct the false statements.

1. People from Spain don't like soccer. **Falso.** People from Spain like soccer very much.
2. Seville is the largest city in Spain. **Falso.** Madrid and Barcelona are the largest cities.
3. Santiago Bernabéu is a stadium in Madrid. **Cierto.**
4. The rivalry between Real Madrid and FC Barcelona is not only in soccer. **Cierto.**

5. Only the FC Barcelona team was affected by the civil war. **Falso.** Both teams were affected by the civil war.
6. Barcelona has resisted Madrid's centralized government. **Cierto.**
7. During Franco's regime, the Catalan culture thrived. **Falso.** Catalan culture was repressed during Franco's regime.
8. There are many famous rivalries between soccer teams in the Spanish-speaking world. **Cierto.**

ASÍ SE DICE

Los deportes

el/la árbitro/a	referee
el/la atleta	athlete
la bola; el balón	la pelota
el campeón/ la campeona	champion
la carrera	race
competir	to compete
empatar	to draw; to tie
la medalla	medal
el/la mejor	the best
mundial	worldwide
el torneo	tournament

EL MUNDO HISPANO

Atletas importantes

World-renowned Hispanic athletes:

○ **Rafael Nadal** (España) is one of the best tennis players in the world.

○ **Sofía Mulanovich** (Perú) was the world champion for surfing in 2004.

○ **Óscar Freire** (España) has been the cycling world champion three times.

○ **Ana Gabriela Guevara** (México) won the silver medal in the 400 meters race at the 2004 Olympic Games in Athens.

PERFILES

Anier García y Luciana Aymar

The sprinter **Anier García Ortiz** was born in Santiago de Cuba in 1976. In 2000, he won the gold medal at the Summer Olympics in Sydney for the 110-meter hurdles (**vallas**). Four years later, in Athens, Greece, he won the bronze medal for the same event.

Luciana Paula Aymar was born in 1977 in Rosario, Argentina. The International Hockey Federation named her the best female player in the world in 2001, 2004, and 2005. With the national women's field hockey team, **La Maga** (*The Magician*), as Luciana is called, won the silver medal at the Sydney Olympics in the year 2000, and a bronze medal in Athens in 2004.

Conexión Internet

¿Qué deportes son populares en los países hispanos?

Go to **descubre1.vhlcentral.com** to find more cultural information related to this **Cultura** section.

ACTIVIDADES

2 **Comprensión** Write the name of the athlete described in each sentence.

1. Es un atleta de Cuba. Anier García
2. Es una chica que practica el hockey. Luciana Aymar
3. Es un chico español al que le gusta pasear en bicicleta. Óscar Freire
4. Es una chica peruana que practica el surfing. Sofía Mulanovich

3 **¿Quién es?** Write a short paragraph describing an athlete that you like, but do not mention his or her name. What does that person look like? What sport does he/she play? Where does he/she live? Read your description to the class to see if other students can guess who the athlete is.
Answers will vary.

recursos

CH p. 52	descubre1.vhlcentral.com Lección 4

Section Goals

In **Estructura 4.1**, students will learn:
- the present tense of **ir**
- the contraction **al**
- **ir a** + [*infinitive*] to express future events
- **vamos a** to express *let's . . .*

Instructional Resources

Cuaderno de práctica, pp. 39–40
Cuaderno para hispanohablantes, pp. 53–54
Cuaderno de actividades, pp. 17–18, 21, 107
e-Cuaderno
Supersite: Audio Activity MP3 Audio Files
Supersite/TRCD/Print: *PowerPoints* (**Lección 4 Estructura** Presentation); Communication Activities, Audio Activity Script, Answer Keys
Audio Activity CD

Teaching Tips

- Write your next day's schedule on the board. Ex: **8:00— la biblioteca; 12:00—comer.** Explain what you are going to do, using the verb **ir.** Ask volunteers about their schedules, using **ir.**
- Add a visual aspect to this grammar presentation. Call on several students to come to the front of the room and create a "living map" of Latin America, calling out their country names as you position them. Point to your destination "country," and as you pantomime flying there, ask students: **¿Adónde voy? (Va a Chile.)** Once there, pantomime an activity, asking: **¿Qué voy a hacer? (Va a esquiar.)**
- Practice **vamos a** to express the idea of *let's* by asking volunteers to suggest things to do. Ex: **Tengo hambre. (Vamos a la cafetería.)**

Ayuda Point out the difference in usage between **dónde** and **adónde.** Ask: **¿Adónde va el presidente para descansar? (Va a Camp David.) ¿Dónde está Camp David? (Está en Maryland.)**

4.1 Present tense of ir

ANTE TODO The verb **ir** (*to go*) is irregular in the present tense. Note that, except for the **yo** form (**voy**) and the lack of a written accent on the **vosotros** form (**vais**), the endings are the same as those for **–ar** verbs.

The verb ir (to go)

Singular forms		Plural forms	
yo	**voy**	nosotros/as	**vamos**
tú	**vas**	vosotros/as	**vais**
Ud./él/ella	**va**	Uds./ellos/ellas	**van**

▶ **Ir** is often used with the preposition **a** (*to*). If **a** is followed by the definite article **el**, they combine to form the contraction **al**. If **a** is followed by the other definite articles (**la, las, los**), there is no contraction.

$$a + el = al$$

Voy **al** parque con Juan.
I'm going to the park with Juan.

Mis amigos van **a las** montañas.
My friends are going to the mountains.

▶ The construction **ir a** + [*infinitive*] is used to talk about actions that are going to happen in the future. It is equivalent to the English *to be going to* + [*infinitive*].

Va a leer el periódico.
He is going to read the newspaper.

Van a pasear por el pueblo.
They are going to walk around town.

Voy a escribir unas postales.

Álex y Maite van a volver al autobús.

▶ **Vamos a** + [*infinitive*] can also express the idea of *let's (do something)*.

Vamos a pasear.
Let's take a stroll.

¡Vamos a ver!
Let's see!

¡INTÉNTALO! Provide the present tense forms of **ir**. The first item has been done for you.

1. Ellos ___van___.
2. Yo ___voy___.
3. Tu novio ___va___.
4. Adela ___va___.
5. Mi prima y yo ___vamos___.
6. Tú ___vas___.
7. Ustedes ___van___.
8. Nosotros ___vamos___.
9. Usted ___va___.
10. Nosotras ___vamos___.
11. Miguel ___va___.
12. Ellas ___van___.

CONSULTA

To review the contraction **de** + **el**, see **Estructura 1.3**, pp. 20–21.

AYUDA

When asking a question that contains a form of the verb **ir**, remember to use **adónde**:

¿Adónde vas?
(To) Where are you going?

recursos

CP
pp. 39–40

CH
pp. 53–54

CA
pp. 17–18, 21, 107

descubre1.
vhlcentral.com
Lección 4

TEACHING OPTIONS

TPR Invent gestures to pantomime activities mentioned in **Lección 4**. Ex: **esquiar** (move arms and sway as if skiing), **patinar** (skate), **nadar** (move arms as if swimming). Signal individuals to gesture appropriately as you cue activities with **Vamos a…** . Keep a brisk pace.

Pairs Have students form pairs and tell them they are going on a dream date or trip. On paper strips, write varying dollar amounts, ranging from three dollars to five thousand. Have each pair draw out a dollar amount at random and tell the class what they will do with the money. Encourage creativity. Ex: **Tenemos seis dólares y vamos a McDonald's. Ella va a cenar, pero yo voy a beber agua porque no tenemos más dinero. Tenemos cinco mil dólares. Vamos a cenar a París…**

Práctica

1 **¿Adónde van?** Everyone in your neighborhood is dashing off to various places. Say where they are going.

1. la señora Castillo / el centro La señora Castillo va al centro.
2. las hermanas Gómez / la piscina Las hermanas Gómez van a la piscina.
3. tu tío y tu papá / el partido de fútbol Tu tío y tu papá van al partido de fútbol.
4. yo / el Museo de Arte Moderno (Yo) Voy al Museo de Arte Moderno.
5. nosotros / el restaurante Miramar (Nosotros) Vamos al restaurante Miramar.

2 **¿Qué van a hacer?** These sentences describe what several students in a high school hiking club are doing today. Use **ir a** + [*infinitive*] to say that they are also going to do the same activities tomorrow.

> **modelo**
>
> Martín y Rodolfo nadan en la piscina.
> **Van a nadar en la piscina mañana también.**

1. Sara lee una revista. Va a leer una revista mañana también.
2. Yo practico deportes. Voy a practicar deportes mañana también.
3. Ustedes van de excursión. Van a ir de excursión mañana también.
4. El presidente del club patina. Va a patinar mañana también.
5. Tú tomas el sol. Vas a tomar el sol mañana también.
6. Paseamos con nuestros amigos. Vamos a pasear con nuestros amigos mañana también.

3 **Preguntas** With a partner, take turns asking and answering questions about where the people are going and what they are going to do there. Some answers will vary.

> **modelo**
>
> **Estudiante 1:** ¿Adónde va Estela?
> **Estudiante 2:** Va a la Librería Sol.
> **Estudiante 1:** Va a comprar un libro.

1. Álex y Miguel
¿Adónde van Álex y Miguel?
Van al parque. Van a…

2. mi amigo ¿Adónde va
mi amigo? Va al gimnasio.
Va a…

3. tú ¿Adónde vas? Voy
al partido de tenis. Voy a…

4. los estudiantes
¿Adónde van los estudiantes?
Van al estadio. Van a…

5. profesora Torres
¿Adónde va la profesora
Torres? Va a la Biblioteca
Nacional. Va a…

6. ustedes ¿Adónde
van ustedes? Vamos a la
piscina. Vamos a…

1 **Teaching Tip** To add a visual aspect to this exercise, bring in photos of people dressed for a particular activity. As you hold up each photo, have the class say where they are going, using the verb **ir**. Ex: Show a photo of a basketball player. (**Va al gimnasio./Va a un partido.**)

1 **Expansion** After completing the activity, extend each answer with **pero** and a different name or pronoun, and have students complete the sentence. Ex: **La señora Castillo va al centro, pero el señor Castillo... (va al trabajo).**

2 **Expansion**
• Show the same photos you used for **Actividad 1** and ask students to describe what the people are going to do. Ex: **Va a jugar al baloncesto.**
• Ask students about tomorrow's activities. Ex: **¿Qué van a hacer tus amigos mañana? ¿Qué va a hacer tu padre/madre mañana?**

3 **Expansion** Ask student pairs to write a logic problem using **ir a** + [*infinitive*].
Ex: **Ángela, Laura, Tomás y Manuel van a hacer cosas diferentes. Tomás va a nadar y Laura va a comer, pero no en casa. Un chico y una chica van a ver una película. ¿Adónde van todos?** Then have pairs exchange papers to solve the problems.

4 Expansion Have students convert each dependent clause to its negative form and create a new independent clause. Ex: **Cuando no deseo descansar, voy al gimnasio.**

5 Teaching Tip Model question formation. Ex: **1. ¿Vas a comer en un restaurante chino hoy?** Then distribute the Communication Activity worksheets that correspond to this activity. Allow students five minutes to fill out the surveys.

5 Expansion After collecting the surveys, ask individuals about their plans. Ex: If someone's name appears by **ver una película de horror**, ask him or her: **¿Qué película vas a ver hoy?**

6 Teaching Tip Add a visual aspect to this activity. Ask students to use an idea map to brainstorm a trip they would like to take. Have them write **lugar** in the central circle, and in the surrounding ones: **ver, deportes, otras actividades, comida, compañeros/as.**

7 Teaching Tips
• To simplify, have students make two columns on a sheet of paper. The first one should be headed **El fin de semana tengo que…** and the other **El fin de semana deseo…** Give students a few minutes to brainstorm their activities for the weekend.
• Before students begin the last step, brainstorm a list of expressions as a class. Ex: **—¿Quieres jugar al tenis conmigo? —Lo siento, pero no puedo./Sí, vamos.**

Teaching Tip See the Communication Activities for an additional activity to practice the material presented in this section.

Comunicación

4 **Situaciones** Work with a partner and say where you and your friends go in these situations. Answers will vary.

1. Cuando deseo descansar…
2. Cuando mi mejor amigo/a tiene que estudiar…
3. Si mis compañeros de clase necesitan practicar el español…
4. Si deseo hablar con unos amigos…
5. Cuando tengo dinero (money)…
6. Cuando mis amigos y yo tenemos hambre…
7. En mis ratos libres…
8. Cuando mis amigos desean esquiar…
9. Si estoy de vacaciones…
10. Si tengo ganas de leer…

5 **Encuesta** Your teacher will give you a worksheet. Walk around the class and ask your classmates if they are going to do these activities today. Find one person to answer **Sí** and one to answer **No** for each item and note their names on the worksheet in the appropriate column. Be prepared to report your findings to the class.

Answers will vary.

modelo
Tú: ¿Vas a leer el periódico hoy?
Ana: Sí, voy a leer el periódico hoy.
Luis: No, no voy a leer el periódico hoy.

Actividades	Sí	No
1. comer en un restaurante chino		
2. leer el periódico		
3. escribir un mensaje electrónico	Ana	Luis
4. correr 20 kilómetros		
5. ver una película de horror		
6. pasear en bicicleta		

6 **Entrevista** Interview two classmates to find out where they are going and what they are going to do on their next vacation. Answers will vary.

modelo
Estudiante 1: ¿Adónde vas de vacaciones (on vacation)?
Estudiante 2: Voy a Guadalajara con mi familia.
Estudiante 1: ¿Y qué van a hacer (to do) ustedes en Guadalajara?
Estudiante 2: Vamos a visitar unos monumentos y museos.

Síntesis

7 **El fin de semana** Create a schedule with your activities for this weekend.
Answers will vary.
▶ For each day, list at least three things you have to do.
▶ For each day, list at least two things you will do for fun.
▶ Tell a classmate what your weekend schedule is like. He or she will write down what you say.
▶ Switch roles to see if you have any plans in common.
▶ Take turns asking each other to participate in some of the activities you listed.

TEACHING OPTIONS

Pairs Write these times on the board: **8:00 a.m., 12:00 p.m., 12:45 p.m., 4:00 p.m., 6:00 p.m., 10:00 p.m.** Have student pairs take turns reading a time and suggesting an appropriate activity or place. Ex: **E1: Son las ocho de la mañana. E2: Vamos a correr./Vamos al gimnasio.**

Game Divide the class into teams of three. Name a category (Ex: **lugares públicos**) and set a time limit of two minutes. The first team member will write down one answer on a piece of paper and pass it to the next person, who does the same, and so on. The team with the most words wins.
Video Show the *Fotonovela* episode again. Stop the video where appropriate to discuss how **ir** is used to express different ideas.

4.2 Stem-changing verbs: e:ie, o:ue

ANTE TODO Stem-changing verbs deviate from the normal pattern of regular verbs. In stem-changing verbs, the stressed vowel of the stem changes when the verb is conjugated.

CONSULTA

To review the present tense of regular –**ar** verbs, see **Estructura 2.1**, p. 50.

•••

To review the present tense of regular –**er** and –**ir** verbs, see **Estructura 3.3**, p. 96.

INFINITIVE	VERB STEM	STEM CHANGE	CONJUGATED FORM
empezar volver	empez- volv-	empiez- vuelv-	empiezo vuelvo

▶ In many verbs, such as **empezar** *(to begin)*, the stem vowel changes from **e** to **ie**. Note that the **nosotros/as** and **vosotros/as** forms don't have a stem change.

The verb empezar (e:ie) (*to begin*)

Singular forms		Plural forms	
yo	empiezo	nosotros/as	empezamos
tú	empiezas	vosotros/as	empezáis
Ud./él/ella	empieza	Uds./ellos/ellas	empiezan

Álex y Maite vuelven al autobús.

Álex empieza a enviar mensajes.

▶ In many other verbs, such as **volver** *(to return)*, the stem vowel changes from **o** to **ue**. The **nosotros/as** and **vosotros/as** forms have no stem change.

The verb volver (o:ue) (*to return*)

Singular forms		Plural forms	
yo	vuelvo	nosotros/as	volvemos
tú	vuelves	vosotros/as	volvéis
Ud./él/ella	vuelve	Uds./ellos/ellas	vuelven

▶ To help you identify stem-changing verbs, they will appear as follows throughout the text:

empezar (e:ie), volver (o:ue)

TEACHING OPTIONS

Extra Practice Write a pattern sentence on the board. Ex: **Ella empieza una carta.** Have students write down the model, and then dictate a list of subjects (Ex: **Maite, nosotras, don Francisco**), pausing after each one to allow students to write a complete sentence. Ask volunteers to read their sentences aloud.

Heritage Speakers Ask heritage speakers to work in pairs to write a mock interview with a Spanish-speaking celebrity such as **Ricky Martin, Salma Hayek, David Ortiz,** or **Luis Miguel,** in which they use the verbs **empezar, volver, querer,** and **recordar.** Ask them to role-play their interview for the class, who will write down the forms of **empezar, volver, querer,** and **recordar** that they hear.

Section Goals

In **Estructura 4.2**, students will be introduced to:
- present tense of stem-changing verbs: **e → ie**; **o → ue**
- common stem-changing verbs

Instructional Resources
Cuaderno de práctica, pp. 41–42
Cuaderno para hispanohablantes, pp. 55–56
Cuaderno de actividades, pp. 19–20, 108
e-Cuaderno
Supersite: Audio Activity MP3 Audio Files
Supersite/TRCD/Print: *PowerPoints* (**Lección 4 Estructura** Presentation); Communication Activities, Audio Activity Script, Answer Keys
Audio Activity CD

Teaching Tips
- Take a survey of students' habits. Ask: **¿A qué hora empiezan las clases? ¿A qué hora cierra la biblioteca?** Make a chart with students' names on the board. Ask: **¿Quiénes vuelven a casa a las seis?** Then create sentences based on the chart. Ex: **Tú vuelves a casa a las siete, pero Amanda vuelve a las seis. Daniel y yo volvemos a las cinco.**
- Copy the forms of **empezar** and **volver** on the board. Reiterate that the personal endings for the present tense of all the verbs listed in **Estructura 4.2** are the same as those for the present tense of regular –**ar**, –**er**, and –**ir** verbs.
- Explain that an easy way to remember which forms of these verbs have stem changes is to think of them as boot verbs. Draw a line around the stem-changing forms in each paradigm to show the boot-like shape.

Teaching Tips

• Write **e:ie** and **o:ue** on the board and explain that some very common verbs have these types of stem changes. Point out that all the verbs listed are conjugated like **empezar** or **volver**. Model the pronunciation of the verbs and ask students a few questions using verbs of each type. Have them answer in complete sentences. Ex: **¿A qué hora cierra la biblioteca? ¿Duermen los estudiantes tarde, por lo general? ¿Qué piensan hacer este fin de semana? ¿Quién quiere comer en un restaurante esta noche?**

• Point out the structure **jugar al** used with sports. Practice it by asking students about the sports they play. Have them answer in complete sentences. Ex: ____, **¿te gusta jugar al fútbol? Y tú, ____, ¿juegas al fútbol? ¿Prefieres jugar al fútbol o ver un partido en el estadio? ¿Cuántos juegan al tenis? ¿Qué prefieres, ____, jugar al tenis o jugar al fútbol?**

• Prepare a few dehydrated sentences. Ex: **Maite / empezar / la lección; ustedes / mostrar / los trabajos; nosotros / jugar / al fútbol.** Write them on the board one at a time, and ask students to form complete sentences based on the cues.

Common stem-changing verbs

e:ie

cerrar	*to close*
comenzar (a + *inf.***)**	*to begin*
empezar (a + *inf.***)**	*to begin*
entender	*to understand*
pensar	*to think*
perder	*to lose; to miss*
preferir (+ *inf.***)**	*to prefer*
querer (+ *inf.***)**	*to want; to love*

o:ue

almorzar	*to have lunch*
contar	*to count; to tell*
dormir	*to sleep*
encontrar	*to find*
mostrar	*to show*
poder (+ *inf.***)**	*to be able to; can*
recordar	*to remember*
volver	*to return*

▶ **Jugar** (*to play* a sport or game) is the only Spanish verb that has a **u:ue** stem change. **Jugar** is followed by **a** + [*definite article*] when the name of a sport or game is mentioned.

Oye, Maite, ¿por qué no jugamos al fútbol?

Álex y el joven juegan al fútbol.

▶ **Comenzar** and **empezar** require the preposition **a** when they are followed by an infinitive.

Comienzan a jugar a las siete.   Ana **empieza a** escribir una postal.
They begin playing at seven.   *Ana starts to write a postcard.*

▶ **Pensar** + [*infinitive*] means *to plan* or *to intend to do something.* **Pensar en** means *to think about someone* or *something.*

¿Piensan ir al gimnasio?   **¿En** qué **piensas?**
Are you planning to go to the gym?   *What are you thinking about?*

¡INTÉNTALO!   Provide the present tense forms of these verbs. The first item in each column has been done for you.

cerrar (e:ie)

1. Ustedes ___cierran___.
2. Tú ___cierras___.
3. Nosotras ___cerramos___.
4. Mi hermano ___cierra___.
5. Yo ___cierro___.
6. Usted ___cierra___.
7. Los chicos ___cierran___.
8. Ella ___cierra___.

dormir (o:ue)

1. Mi abuela no ___duerme___.
2. Yo no ___duermo___.
3. Tú no ___duermes___.
4. Mis hijos no ___duermen___.
5. Usted no ___duerme___.
6. Nosotros no ___dormimos___.
7. Él no ___duerme___.
8. Ustedes no ___duermen___.

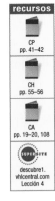

TEACHING OPTIONS

TPR Add an auditory aspect to this grammar presentation. At random, call out infinitives of regular and **e:ie** stem-changing verbs. Have students raise their hands if the verb has a stem change. Repeat for **o:ue** stem-changing verbs.
Extra Practice For additional drills of stem-changing verbs, do the **¡Inténtalo!** activity orally using infinitives other than **cerrar** and **dormir**. Keep a brisk pace.

TPR Have the class stand in a circle. As you toss a foam or paper ball to a student, call out the infinitive of a stem-changing verb, followed by a pronoun. (Ex: **querer, tú**) The student should say the appropriate verb form (**quieres**), then name a different pronoun (Ex: **usted**) and throw the ball to another student. When all subject pronouns have been covered, start over with another infinitive.

Práctica

1 Completar Complete this conversation with the appropriate forms of the verbs.
Then act it out with a partner.

PABLO Óscar, voy al centro ahora.

ÓSCAR ¿A qué hora (1)___piensas___ (pensar) volver? El partido de fútbol (2)___empieza___
(empezar) a las dos.

PABLO (3)___Vuelvo___ (Volver) a la una. (4)___Quiero___ (Querer) ver el partido.

ÓSCAR (5)¿___Recuerdas___ (Recordar) que (*that*) nuestro equipo es muy bueno?
(6)¡___Puede___ (Poder) ganar!

PABLO No, (7)___pienso___ (pensar) que va a (8)___perder___ (perder). Los jugadores de
Guadalajara son salvajes (*wild*) cuando (9)___juegan___ (jugar).

2 Preferencias With a partner, take turns asking and answering questions about what these
people want to do, using the cues provided.

> **modelo**
> Guillermo: estudiar / pasear en bicicleta
> **Estudiante 1:** ¿Quiere estudiar Guillermo?
> **Estudiante 2:** No, prefiere pasear en bicicleta.

1. tú: trabajar / dormir
¿Quieres trabajar? No, prefiero dormir.
2. ustedes: mirar la televisión / jugar al dominó
¿Quieren ustedes mirar la televisión? No, preferimos jugar al dominó.
3. tus amigos: ir de excursión / descansar
¿Quieren ir de excursión tus amigos? No, mis amigos prefieren descansar.
4. tú: comer en la cafetería / ir a un restaurante
¿Quieres comer en la cafetería? No, prefiero ir a un restaurante.
5. Elisa: ver una película / leer una revista
¿Quiere ver una película Elisa? No, prefiere leer una revista.
6. María y su hermana: tomar el sol / practicar el esquí acuático
¿Quieren tomar el sol María y su hermana? No, prefieren practicar el esquí acuático.

3 Describir Use a verb from the list to describe what these people are doing.

| almorzar | cerrar | contar | dormir | encontrar | mostrar |

1. las niñas Las niñas duermen.   2. yo (Yo) Cierro la ventana.   3. nosotros
(Nosotros) Almorzamos.

4. tú (Tú) Encuentras/Muestras
una maleta.   5. Pedro Pedro muestra una foto.   6. Teresa Teresa cuenta.

---

1 Teaching Tip Divide the
class into pairs and give them
three minutes to role-play
the conversation. Then have
partners switch roles.

1 Expansion
• To challenge students,
supply them with short-
answer prompts based on
the conversation. Ask them
to form questions that would
elicit the answers. Ex: **A las
dos.** (¿A qué hora empieza
el partido de fútbol?) Porque
quiere ver el partido. (¿Por
qué vuelve Pablo a la una?)
• Ask questions using **pensar**
+ [*infinitive*], **pensar en**, and
perder (in both senses). Ex:
**¿Qué piensas hacer mañana?
¿En qué piensas ahora?
¿Cuándo pierdes las cosas?**

2 Teaching Tip Before
dividing the class into pairs,
model the activity by reading
the **modelo** and giving other
examples in the **yo** form.
Ex: **¿Quiero descansar en casa?
No, prefiero enseñar la clase.**

2 Expansion Have students
ask each other questions of
their own using the same
pattern. Ex: —¿Quieres jugar al
baloncesto? —No, prefiero
jugar al tenis.

3 Expansion Bring in photos
or magazine pictures to extend
this activity. Choose images
that are easy to describe with
common stem-changing verbs.

TEACHING OPTIONS

TPR Brainstorm gestures for stem-changing verbs. Have
students mime the activity you mention. Tell them that only male
students should respond to **él/ellos** and only females to **ella/
ellas.** Everyone should respond to **nosotros.**
Game Arrange students in rows of five (or six if you use **vosotros**).
Give the first person in each row a piece of paper and tell the
class they should be silent while they are completing this activity.

Call out the infinitive of a stem-changing verb. The first person
writes down the **yo** form and gives the paper to the student behind,
who writes the **tú** form and passes the paper on. The last person
in the row holds up the paper and says, **¡Terminamos!** The first
team to finish the conjugation correctly gets a point. Have students
rotate positions in their row before calling out another infinitive.

Comunicación

4 **Frecuencia** In pairs, use the verbs from the list and other stem-changing verbs you know to create sentences telling your partner which activities you do daily (**todos los días**), which you do once a month (**una vez al mes**), and which you do once a year (**una vez al año**). Then switch roles. Answers will vary.

> **modelo**
>
> **Estudiante 1:** Yo recuerdo a mis abuelos todos los días.
> **Estudiante 2:** Yo pierdo uno de mis libros una vez al año.

cerrar	perder
dormir	poder
empezar	preferir
encontrar	querer
jugar	recordar
¿?	¿?

todos los días	una vez al mes	una vez al año

5 **En la televisión** Read the television listings for Saturday. In pairs, write a conversation between two siblings arguing about what to watch. Be creative and be prepared to act out your conversation for the class. Answers will vary.

> **modelo**
>
> **Hermano:** Quiero ver la Copa Mundial.
> **Hermana:** ¡No! Prefiero ver...

	13:00	14:00	15:00	16:00	17:00	18:00	19:00	20:00	21:00	22:00	23:00
7	Copa Mundial (*World Cup*) de fútbol			El tiempo libre		Fútbol internacional: Copa América: México-Argentina				Torneo de Natación	
8	Abierto (*Open*) Mexicano de Tenis: Alejandro Hernández (México) vs. Jacobo Díaz (España). Semifinales			Campeonato (*Championship*) de baloncesto: Los Correcaminos de Tampico vs. los Santos de San Luis				Aficionados al buceo		Cozumel: Aventuras	
12	Gente famosa		Amigos	Médicos jóvenes				Película: **El centro de la ciudad**		Película: **Terror en la plaza mayor**	
13	El padrastro			Periodistas en peligro (*danger*)		El esquí acuático				Patinaje artístico	
17	Biografías: La artista Frida Kahlo			Música de la semana		Entrevista del día: Miguel Indurain y su pasión por el ciclismo				Cine de la noche: **La carta misteriosa**	

NOTA CULTURAL
Miguel Indurain is a famous cyclist from Spain who has won the Tour de France bicycle race five times.

Síntesis

6 **Situación** Your teacher will give you and your partner a partially illustrated itinerary of a city tour. Complete the itineraries by asking each other questions using the verbs in the captions and vocabulary you have learned. Answers will vary.

> **modelo**
>
> **Estudiante 1:** Por la mañana, empiezan en el café.
> **Estudiante 2:** Y luego...

recursos
CA
pp. 19–20

TEACHING OPTIONS

Small Groups Have students choose their favorite pastime and work in groups of three with other students who have chosen that same activity. Have each group write six sentences about the activity, using a different stem-changing verb in each.

Pairs Ask students to write incomplete dehydrated sentences (only subjects and infinitives) about people and groups at school. Ex: **el equipo de béisbol / perder / ¿?** Then have them exchange papers with a classmate, who will form a complete sentence by conjugating the verb and inventing an appropriate ending. Ask volunteers to write sentences on the board.

Left margin (Teacher's notes):

4 Teaching Tip Model the activity by asking questions about famous people. Ex: **¿Con qué frecuencia juega al golf Tiger Woods?** Write the answers on the board.

4 Expansion After tallying results on the board, ask students to graph them. Have them refer to **Lectura**, pages 142–143, for models.

5 Teaching Tips
• Model the activity by stating two programs from the listing that you want to watch and asking the class to react.
• Remind students that the 24-hour clock is often used for schedules. Model a few of the program times. Then ask: **Quiero ver *Amigos* y mi amigo prefiere ver *La carta misteriosa*. ¿Hay un conflicto?** (No.) **¿Por qué?** (Porque *Amigos* es a las 15:00 y *La carta misteriosa* es a las 22:00.) Give students the option of answering with the 12-hour clock.

5 Expansion Have students personalize the activity by choosing their favorite programs from the list. Compare and contrast students' reasons for their choices.

6 Teaching Tip Divide the class into pairs and distribute the Communication Activities worksheets that correspond to this activity. Give students ten minutes to complete the activity.

6 Expansion
• Ask questions based on the artwork. Ex: **¿Dónde empiezan el día?** (en el café) **¿Qué pueden hacer en la plaza mayor?** (Pueden pasear.)
• Have volunteers take turns completing the information in the puzzle. Then have students invent their own stories, using stem-changing verbs, about what happens to the same group of tourists.

(4.3) # Stem-changing verbs: e:i

ANTE TODO You've already seen that many verbs in Spanish change their stem vowel when conjugated. There is a third kind of stem-vowel change in some verbs, such as **pedir** (*to ask for; to request*). In these verbs, the stressed vowel in the stem changes from **e** to **i**, as shown in the diagram.

INFINITIVE	VERB STEM	STEM CHANGE	CONJUGATED FORM
pedir ▶	ped- ▶	pid- ▶	pido

▶ As with other stem-changing verbs you have learned, there is no stem change in the **nosotros/as** or **vosotros/as** forms in the present tense.

The verb pedir (e:i) (*to ask for; to request*)

Singular forms		Plural forms	
yo	p**i**do	nosotros/as	pedimos
tú	p**i**des	vosotros/as	pedís
Ud./él/ella	p**i**de	Uds./ellos/ellas	p**i**den

▶ To help you identify verbs with the **e:i** stem change, they will appear as follows throughout the text:

digo

pedir (e:i)

▶ These are the most common **e:i** stem-changing verbs:

conseguir	⟨**decir**⟩	**repetir**	**seguir**
to get; to obtain	*to say;*	*to repeat*	*to follow; to continue;*
	to tell		*to keep (doing something)*

Pido favores cuando es necesario.
I ask for favors when it's necessary.

Javier **dice** la verdad.
Javier is telling the truth.

Sigue esperando.
He keeps waiting.

Consiguen ver buenas películas.
They get to see good movies.

▶ **¡Atención!** The verb **decir** is irregular in its **yo** form: **yo digo.**

▶ The **yo** forms of **seguir** and **conseguir** have a spelling change as well as the stem change **e→i**.

Sigo su plan.
I'm following their plan.

Consigo novelas en la librería.
I get novels at the bookstore.

¡INTÉNTALO! Provide the correct forms of the verbs.

repetir (e:i)	decir (e:i)	seguir (e: i)
1. Arturo y Eva __repiten__.	1. Yo __digo__.	1. Yo __sigo__
2. Yo __repito__.	2. Él __dice__.	2. Nosotros __seguimos__.
3. Nosotros __repetimos__.	3. Tú __dices__.	3. Tú __sigues__.
4. Julia __repite__.	4. Usted __dice__	4. Los chicos __siguen__.
5. Sofía y yo __repetimos__.	5. Ellas __dicen__.	5. Usted __sigue__.

Práctica

1 **Completar** Complete these sentences with the correct form of the verb provided.

1. Cuando mi familia pasea por la ciudad, mi madre siempre (*always*) va al café y ___pide___ (pedir) una soda.
2. Pero mi padre ___dice___ (decir) que perdemos mucho tiempo. Tiene prisa por llegar al bosque de Chapultepec.
3. Mi padre tiene suerte, porque él siempre ___consigue___ (conseguir) lo que (*that which*) desea.
4. Cuando llegamos al parque, mis hermanos y yo ___seguimos___ (seguir) conversando (*talking*) con nuestros padres.
5. Mis padres siempre ___repiten___ (repetir) la misma cosa: "Nosotros tomamos el sol aquí sin ustedes."
6. Yo siempre ___pido___ (pedir) permiso para volver a casa un poco más tarde porque me gusta mucho el parque.

2 **Combinar** Combine words from the columns to create sentences about yourself and people you know. *Answers will vary.*

A	B
yo	(no) pedir muchos favores
la gente	nunca (*never*) pedir perdón
mi mejor (*best*) amigo/a	nunca seguir las instrucciones
mi familia	siempre seguir las instrucciones
mis amigos/as	conseguir libros en Internet
mis amigos y yo	repetir el vocabulario
mis padres	
mi hermano/a	
mi profesor(a) de español	

3 **Opiniones** Work in pairs to guess how your partner completed the sentences from **Actividad 2**. If you guess incorrectly, your partner must supply the correct answer. Switch roles. *Answers will vary.*

modelo

Estudiante 1: En mi opinión, tus padres consiguen libros en Internet.
Estudiante 2: ¡No! Mi hermana consigue libros en Internet.

Comunicación

4 **Las películas** Use these questions to interview a classmate. *Answers will vary.*

1. ¿Prefieres las películas románticas, las películas de acción o las películas de horror? ¿Por qué?

2. ¿Dónde consigues información sobre (*about*) una película?

3. ¿Dónde consigues las entradas (*tickets*) para una película?

4. Para decidir qué películas vas a ver, ¿sigues las recomendaciones de tus amigos? ¿Qué dicen tus amigos en general?

5. ¿Qué cines en tu comunidad muestran las mejores (*best*) películas?

6. ¿Vas a ver una película esta semana? ¿A qué hora empieza la película?

Síntesis

5 **El cine** In pairs, first scan the ad and jot down all the stem-changing verbs. Then answer the questions. Be prepared to share your answers with the class. *Answers will vary.*

1. ¿Qué palabras indican que *Un mundo azul oscuro (Dark Blue World)* es una película dramática?

2. ¿Cuántas personas hay en el póster?

3. ¿Cómo son las personas del póster? ¿Qué relación tienen?

4. ¿Te gustan las películas como ésta (*this one*)?

5. Describe tu película favorita con los verbos de la **Lección 4.**

4 **Teaching Tips**
- Have students report to the class what their partner said. After the presentation, encourage them to ask each other questions.
- Take a class poll to find out students' film genre and local movie theater preferences.

4 **Expansion** To challenge students, write some key movie-related words on the board, such as **actor, actriz, argumento,** and **efectos especiales.** Explain how to use **mejor** and **peor** as adjectives. Have student pairs say which movies this year they think should win Oscars. Model by telling them: **Pienso que____ es la mejor película del año. Debe ganar porque…** Then ask students to nominate the year's worst. Have them share their opinions with the class.

5 **Teaching Tips**
- Write the stem-changing verbs from the ad on the board. Have students conjugate the verbs using different subjects.
- In pairs, have students use the verbs from the ad to write a dramatic dialogue.
- Go over student responses to item 5.

5 **Expansion** Tell students the gist of the love triangle in *Dark Blue World*: it is the story of two Czech pilots (Franta and Karel) who fight for the British during World War II and whose friendship is tested when they both fall in love with Susan, an Englishwoman. Ask student pairs to write a short, melodramatic dialogue between two of the characters, using verbs from this lesson. Then have them role-play the scene for the class. You may want to have the class vote for an "Oscar" for the best presentation.

4.4 Verbs with irregular **yo** forms

ANTE TODO　In Spanish, several verbs have irregular **yo** forms in the present tense. You have already seen three verbs with the **–go** ending in the **yo** form: **decir → digo**, **tener → tengo**, and **venir → vengo**.

▶ Here are some common expressions with **decir**.

decir la verdad	**decir mentiras**
to tell the truth	*to tell lies*
decir que	**decir la respuesta**
to say that	*to say the answer*

▶ The verb **hacer** is often used to ask questions about what someone does. Note that, when answering, **hacer** is frequently replaced with another, more specific, action verb.

Verbs with irregular yo forms

	hacer *(to do; to make)*	poner *(to put; to place)*	salir *(to leave)*	suponer *(to suppose)*	traer *(to bring)*
SINGULAR FORMS	**hago** haces hace	**pongo** pones pone	**salgo** sales sale	**supongo** supones supone	**traigo** traes trae
PLURAL FORMS	hacemos hacéis hacen	ponemos ponéis ponen	salimos salís salen	suponemos suponéis suponen	traemos traéis traen

¿Qué haces los fines de semana?

Salgo con mis amigos y practico deportes.

Yo no salgo, prefiero poner la televisión y ver películas.

▶ **Poner** can also mean *to turn on* a household appliance.

Carlos **pone** la radio.	María **pone** la televisión.
Carlos turns on the radio.	*María turns on the television.*

▶ **Salir de** is used to indicate that someone is leaving a particular place.

Hoy **salgo del** hospital.	**Sale de** la clase a las cuatro.
Today I leave the hospital.	*He leaves class at four.*

▶ **Salir para** is used to indicate someone's destination.

Mañana **salgo para** México.
Tomorrow I leave for Mexico.

Hoy **salen para** España.
Today they leave for Spain.

▶ **Salir con** means *to leave with someone or something*, or *to date someone.*

Alberto **sale con** su mochila.
Alberto is leaving with his backpack.

Margarita **sale con** Guillermo.
Margarita is going out with Guillermo.

The verbs ver and oír

▶ The verb **ver** (*to see*) has an irregular **yo** form. The other forms of **ver** are regular.

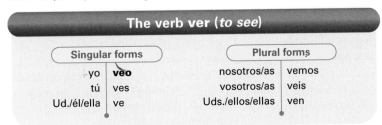

The verb ver (*to see*)			
Singular forms		**Plural forms**	
yo	**veo**	nosotros/as	vemos
tú	ves	vosotros/as	veis
Ud./él/ella	ve	Uds./ellos/ellas	ven

▶ The verb **oír** (*to hear*) has an irregular **yo** form and the spelling change **i→y** in the **tú**, **usted/él/ella** and **ustedes/ellos/ellas** forms. The **nosotros/as** and **vosotros/as** forms have an accent mark.

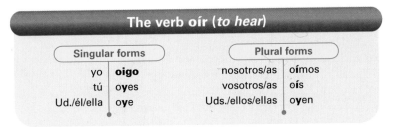

The verb oír (*to hear*)			
Singular forms		**Plural forms**	
yo	**oigo**	nosotros/as	oímos
tú	oyes	vosotros/as	oís
Ud./él/ella	oye	Uds./ellos/ellas	oyen

▶ While most commonly translated as *to hear*, **oír** is also used in contexts where English would use *to listen*.

Oigo a unas personas en la otra sala.
I hear some people in the other room.

¿**Oyes** la radio por la mañana?
Do you listen to the radio in the morning?

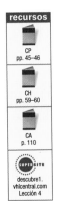

¡INTÉNTALO! Provide the appropriate forms of these verbs. The first item has been done for you.

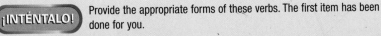

1. salir — Isabel __sale__. — Nosotros __salimos__. — Yo __salgo__.
2. ver — Yo __veo__. — Uds. __ven__. — Tú __ves__.
3. poner — Rita y yo __ponemos__. — Yo __pongo__. — Los niños __ponen__.
4. hacer — Yo __hago__. — Tú __haces__. — Ud. __hace__.
5. oír — Él __oye__. — Nosotros __oímos__. — Yo __oigo__.
6. traer — Ellas __traen__. — Yo __traigo__. — Tú __traes__.
7. suponer — Yo __supongo__. — Mi amigo __supone__. — Nosotras __suponemos__.

TEACHING OPTIONS

Extra Practice Add an auditory aspect to this grammar presentation. Call out subject pronouns and have students respond with the correct form of **ver** or **oír**. Reverse the drill by providing forms of **ver** and **oír** and asking students to give the corresponding subject pronouns.

Pairs Have student pairs create questions and ask each other about their habits. Ex: ¿**Sales a comer a restaurantes con tus amigos?** ¿**Ves la televisión en español?** ¿**Supones que una clase de matemáticas es muy difícil?** Have students record their partner's answers and be prepared to share the information with the class.

Teaching Tips

• Point out that **oír** is irregular in all forms. Write a model sentence on the board. Ex: **Ustedes oyen el programa de radio todos los viernes.** Then change the subject, and have students give the new sentence. Ex: **tú** (**Tú oyes el programa de radio todos los viernes.**)

• Call out different forms of the verbs in **Estructura 4.4** and have volunteers say the infinitive. Ex: **oyen** (**oír**). Keep a brisk pace.

• Do a chain drill. Start by writing ¿**Qué haces los sábados?** on the board. Model an appropriate answer, such as **Salgo con mis amigos.** Ask one student to respond (Ex: **Veo una película.**). The next student you call on should repeat what the first does and add on (Ex: **Cindy ve una película y yo salgo con…**). Continue until the chain becomes too long; then start with a new question. Keep a brisk pace.

• Write these phrases on the board: **ver la tele, traer un sándwich a la escuela, salir con amigos,** and **hacer yoga.** Model the question and possible answers for each phrase. Then elicit follow-up questions (Ex: ¿**Dónde ves la tele?**). Have student pairs take turns asking and answering the questions. They should be prepared to report to the class about their partners' habits.

• Explain to students that the **i → y** spelling change strengthens the **i** sound between vowels, which helps the ear identify that the verb is **oír**.

• Explain the difference between **escuchar** (*to listen*) and **oír** (*to hear*). Ex: **Escucho la radio. No oigo el perro.**

Práctica

1 **Completar** Complete this conversation with the appropriate forms of the verbs. Then act it out with a partner.

ERNESTO David, ¿qué (1)____haces____ (hacer) hoy?

DAVID Ahora estudio biología, pero esta noche (2)____salgo____ (salir) con Luisa. Vamos al cine. (3)____Dice(n)____ (Decir) que la nueva (*new*) película de Almodóvar es buena.

ERNESTO ¿Y Diana? ¿Qué (4)____hace____ (hacer) ella?

DAVID (5)____Sale____ (Salir) a comer con sus padres.

ERNESTO ¿Qué (6)____hacen____ (hacer) Andrés y Javier?

DAVID Tienen que (7)____hacer____ (hacer) las maletas. (8)____Salen____ (Salir) para Monterrey mañana.

ERNESTO Pues, ¿qué (9)____hago____ (hacer) yo?

DAVID (10)____Supongo____ (Suponer) que puedes estudiar o (11)____ver____ (ver) la televisión.

ERNESTO No quiero estudiar. Mejor (12)____pongo____ (poner) la televisión. Mi programa favorito empieza en unos minutos.

2 **Oraciones** Form sentences using the cues provided and verbs from **Estructura 4.4**.

> **modelo**
> tú / _____ / cosas / en / su lugar / antes de (*before*) / salir
> *Tú pones las cosas en su lugar antes de salir.*

1. mis amigos / _____ / conmigo / centro   Mis amigos salen conmigo al centro.
2. tú / _____ / verdad   Tú dices la verdad.
3. Alberto / _____ / música del café Pasatiempos   Alberto oye la música del café Pasatiempos.
4. yo / no / _____ / muchas películas   Yo no veo muchas películas.
5. domingo / nosotros / _____ / mucha / tarea   El domingo, nosotros hacemos mucha tarea.
6. si / yo / _____ / que / yo / querer / ir / cine / mis amigos / ir / también   Si yo digo que quiero ir al cine, mis amigos van también.

3 **Describir** Use a verb from **Estructura 4.4** to describe what these people are doing.

1. Fernán   Fernán pone la mochila en el escritorio.

2. los aficionados   Los aficionados salen del estadio.

3. yo   Yo traigo una cámara.

4. nosotros   Nosotros vemos el monumento.

5. la señora Vargas   La señora Vargas no oye bien.

6. el estudiante   El estudiante hace su tarea.

TEACHING OPTIONS

Game Ask students to write three sentences about themselves: two should be true and one should be fictional. Then, in groups of four, have students share their sentences with the group, who must decide whether that person **dice la verdad** or **dice una mentira**.

Extra Practice Have students use five of the target verbs from **Estructura 4.4** to write sentences about their habits that others may find somewhat unusual. Ex: **Traigo doce bolígrafos en la mochila. Hago la tarea en un café del centro. No pongo la televisión hasta las diez de la noche.**

Comunicación

4 Preguntas With a classmate, ask each other these questions. Answers will vary.

1. ¿Qué traes a clase?
2. ¿Quiénes traen un diccionario a clase? ¿Por qué traen un diccionario?
3. ¿A qué hora sales de tu casa por la mañana? ¿A qué hora salen tus hermanos/as o tus padres?
4. ¿Dónde pones tus libros cuando regresas de clase? ¿Siempre (*Always*) pones tus cosas en su lugar?
5. ¿Pones fotos de tu familia en tu dormitorio (*bedroom*)? ¿Quiénes son las personas que están en las fotos?
6. ¿Oyes la radio cuando estudias?
7. ¿En qué circunstancias dices mentiras?
8. ¿Haces mucha tarea los fines de semana?
9. ¿Sales con tus amigos los fines de semana? ¿A qué hora? ¿Qué hacen?
10. ¿Te gusta ver deportes en la televisión o prefieres ver otros programas? ¿Cuáles?

5 Charadas In groups, play a game of charades. Each person should think of two phrases using the verbs **hacer, oír, poner, salir, traer,** or **ver**. The first person to guess correctly acts out the next charade. Answers will vary.

6 Entrevista You are doing a market research report on lifestyles. Interview a classmate to find out when he or she goes out with the following people and what they do for entertainment. Answers will vary.
- los amigos
- el/la novio/a
- los hermanos/as
- los padres

Síntesis

7 Situación Imagine that you are speaking with a member of your family or your best friend. With a partner, prepare a conversation using these cues. Answers will vary.

Estudiante 1

Ask your partner what he or she is doing.

Say what you suppose he or she is watching.

Say no, because you are going out with friends and tell where you are going.

Say what you are going to do, and ask your partner whether he or she wants to come along.

Estudiante 2

Tell your partner that you are watching TV.

Say that you like the show _____. Ask if he or she wants to watch.

Say you think it's a good idea, and ask what your partner and his or her friends are doing there.

Say no and tell your partner what you prefer to do.

TEACHING OPTIONS

Pairs Have pairs of students role-play the perfect date. Students should write their script first, then present it to the class. Encourage students to use descriptive adjectives as well as the new verbs learned in **Estructura 4.4**.

Heritage Speakers Ask heritage speakers to make a brief oral presentation to the class about a social custom in their cultural community. Remind them to use familiar vocabulary and simple sentences.

---

4 Teaching Tip Model the activity by having volunteers answer the first two items.

4 Expansion Ask students about their classmate's responses. Ex: **¿Tu compañera trae un diccionario a clase? ¿Por qué?**

5 Teaching Tips
- Model the activity by doing a charade for the class to guess. Ex: **Pongo un lápiz en la mesa.** Then divide the class into groups of five to seven students.
- Ask each group to choose the best **charada**. Then have students present them to the class, who will guess the activities.

6 Teaching Tip Model the activity by giving a report on your lifestyle. Ex: **Salgo al cine con mis amigas. Me gusta comer en restaurantes con mi esposo. En familia vemos deportes en la televisión.** Remind students that a market researcher and the interviewee would address each other with the **usted** form of verbs.

7 Possible Conversation
E1: **¿Qué haces?**
E2: **Veo la tele.**
E1: **Supongo que ves el programa *Los Simpson*.**
E2: **Sí. Me gusta el programa. ¿Quieres ver la tele conmigo?**
E1: **No puedo. Salgo con mis amigos a la plaza.**
E2: **Buena idea. ¿Qué hacen en la plaza?**
E1: **Vamos a escuchar música y a pasear. ¿Quieres venir?**
E2: **No. Prefiero descansar.**

Recapitulación

Review the grammar concepts you have learned in this lesson by completing these activities.

1 Completar Complete the chart with the correct verb forms. **15 pts.**

Infinitive	yo	nosotros/as	ellos/as
volver	**vuelvo**	volvemos	vuelven
comenzar	comienzo	**comenzamos**	comienzan
hacer	hago	**hacemos**	**hacen**
ir	voy	vamos	van
jugar	**juego**	jugamos	juegan
repetir	repito	repetimos	**repiten**

2 Un día típico Complete the paragraph with the appropriate forms of the stem-changing verbs in the word list. Not all verbs will be used. Some may be used more than once. **10 pts.**

almorzar	ir	salir
cerrar	jugar	seguir
empezar	mostrar	ver
hacer	querer	volver

¡Hola! Me llamo Cecilia y vivo en Puerto Vallarta, México. ¿Cómo es un día típico en mi vida (*life*)? Por la mañana como con mis padres y juntos (*together*) (1)_____vemos_____ las noticias (*news*) en la televisión. A las siete y media, (yo) (2)_____salgo_____ de mi casa y tomo el autobús. Me gusta llegar temprano (*early*) a la escuela porque siempre (*always*) (3)_____veo_____ a mis amigos en la cafetería. Conversamos y planeamos lo que (4)_____queremos_____ hacer cada (*each*) día. A las ocho y cuarto, mi amiga Sandra y yo (5)_____vamos_____ al laboratorio de lenguas. La clase de francés (6)_____empieza_____ a las ocho y media. ¡Es mi clase favorita! A las doce y media (yo) (7)_____almuerzo_____ en la cafetería con mis amigos. Después (*Afterwards*), yo (8)_____sigo_____ con mis clases. Por las tardes, mis amigos (9)_____vuelven_____ a sus casas, pero yo (10)_____juego_____ al vóleibol con mi amigo Tomás.

4.1 Present tense of ir *p. 126*

yo	voy	nosotros	vamos
tú	vas	vosotros	vais
él	va	ellas	van

▶ ir a + [*infinitive*] = *to be going to* + [*infinitive*]

▶ a + el = al

▶ vamos a + [*infinitive*] = *let's* (*do something*)

4.2 Stem-changing verbs e:ie, o:ue, u:ue *pp. 129–*

	empezar	volver	jugar
yo	empiezo	vuelvo	juego
tú	empiezas	vuelves	juegas
él	empieza	vuelve	juega
nos.	empezamos	volvemos	jugamos
vos.	empezáis	volvéis	jugáis
ellas	empiezan	vuelven	juegan

▶ Other e:ie verbs: **cerrar, comenzar, entender, pensar, perder, preferir, querer**

▶ Other o:ue verbs: **almorzar, contar, dormir, encontrar, mostrar, poder, recordar**

4.3 Stem-changing verbs e:i *p. 133*

		pedir	
yo	pido	nos.	pedimos
tú	pides	vos.	pedís
él	pide	ellas	piden

▶ Other e:i verbs: **conseguir, decir, repetir, seguir**

4.4 Verbs with irregular yo forms *pp. 136–137*

hacer	poner	salir	suponer	traer
hago	pongo	salgo	supongo	traigo

▶ **ver:** veo, ves, ve, vemos, veis, ven

▶ **oír:** oigo, oyes, oye, oímos, oís, oyen

3 **Oraciones** Arrange the cues provided in the correct order to form complete sentences. Make all necessary changes. `14 pts.`

1. tarea / los / hacer / sábados / nosotros / la
   Los sábados nosotros hacemos la tarea./Nosotros hacemos la tarea los sábados.

2. en / pizza / Andrés / una / restaurante / el / pedir
   Andrés pide una pizza en el restaurante.

3. a / ? / museo / ir / ¿ / el / (tú)
   ¿(Tú) Vas al museo?

4. de / oír / amigos / bien / los / no / Elena
   Los amigos de Elena no oyen bien.

5. libros / traer / yo / clase / mis / a
   Yo traigo mis libros a clase.

6. película / ver / en / Jorge y Carlos / pensar / cine / una / el
   Jorge y Carlos piensan ver una película en el cine.

7. unos / escribir / Mariana / electrónicos / querer / mensajes
   Mariana quiere escribir unos mensajes electrónicos.

4 **Escribir** Write a short paragraph about what you do on a typical day. Use at least six of the verbs you have learned in this lesson. You can use the paragraph on the opposite page (**Actividad 2**) as a model. `11 pts.` Answers will vary.

> *Un día típico*
>
> *Hola, me llamo Julia y vivo en Vancouver, Canadá. Por la mañana, yo...*

5 **Adivinanza** Write the missing verbs to solve the rhyme. `2 EXTRA points!`

" Si no ___puedes___ dormir
y el sueño deseas,
lo vas a conseguir
si ___cuentas___ ovejas°. "

ovejas *sheep*

recursos

descubre1.vhlcentral.com
Lección 4

---

3 **Teaching Tip** To simplify, provide the first word for each sentence.

3 **Expansion** Give students these sentences as items 8–11: **8.** la / ? / ustedes / cerrar / ventana / ¿ / poder (**¿Pueden ustedes cerrar la ventana?**) **9.** cine / de / tú / las / salir / once / el / a (**Tú sales del cine a las once.**) **10.** el / conmigo / a / en / ellos / tenis / el / jugar / parque (**Ellos juegan al tenis conmigo en el parque.**) **11.** que / partido / mañana / un / decir / hay / Javier (**Javier dice que hay un partido mañana.**)

4 **Teaching Tips**
• To simplify, ask students to make a three-column chart with the headings **Por la mañana, Por la tarde,** and **Por la noche.** Have them brainstorm at least three verbs or verb phrases for each column and circle any stem-changing or irregular **yo** verbs.
• Have students exchange paragraphs with a classmate for peer editing. Ask them to underline grammatical and spelling errors.

5 **Expansion** Ask students if they ever have trouble sleeping. Have volunteers share with the class what they do when they cannot sleep.

TEACHING OPTIONS

Game Make a Bingo card of places at school or around town, such as libraries, cafeterias, movie theaters, and cafés. Give each student a card and model possible questions (Ex: for a cafeteria, **¿Almuerzas en _____?/¿Dónde almuerzas?**). Encourage them to circulate around the room, asking only one question per person; if they get an affirmative answer, they should write that person's name in the square. The first student to complete a horizontal, vertical, or diagonal row and yell **¡Bingo!** is the winner.

Heritage Speakers Ask heritage speakers if counting sheep is common advice for sleeplessness in their families. What other insomnia remedies have they heard of or practiced?

Section Goals

In **Lectura**, students will:
• learn the strategy of predicting content by surveying the graphic elements in reading matter
• read a magazine article containing graphs and charts

Instructional Resources
Cuaderno para hispanohablantes, pp. 61–62
Supersite

Estrategia Tell students that they can infer a great deal of information about the content of an article by surveying the graphic elements included in it. When students survey an article for its graphic elements, they should look for such things as:
• headlines or headings
• bylines
• photos
• photo captions
• graphs and tables

Examinar el texto Give students two minutes to take a look at the visual clues in the article and write down all the ideas the clues suggest.

Lectura

Antes de leer

Estrategia
Predicting content from visuals

When you are reading in Spanish, be sure to look for visual clues that will orient you to the content and purpose of what you are reading. Photos and illustrations, for example, will often give you a good idea of the main points that the reading covers. You may also encounter very helpful visuals that are used to summarize large amounts of data in a way that is easy to comprehend; these include bar graphs, pie charts, flow charts, lists of percentages, and other sorts of diagrams.

Examinar el texto

Take a quick look at the visual elements of the magazine article in order to generate a list of ideas about its content. Then compare your list with a classmate's. Are your lists the same or are they different? Discuss your lists and make any changes needed to produce a final list of ideas.

Contestar

Read the list of ideas you wrote in **Examinar el texto,** and look again at the visual elements of the magazine article. Then answer these questions:

1. Who is the woman in the photo, and what is her role? María Úrsula Echevarría is the author of the article.
2. What is the article about? The article is about sports in the Hispanic world.
3. What is the subject of the pie chart? The most popular sports among college students
4. What is the subject of the bar graph? Hispanic countries in world soccer championships

1. **María Úrsula Echevarría** is the author of the article.
2. The article is about sports in the Hispanic world.
3. The most popular sports
4. Hispanic countries in world soccer championships

recursos

CH pp. 61–62	descubre1.vhlcentral.com Lección 4

---

por María Úrsula Echevarría

El fútbol es el deporte más popular en el mundo° hispano, según° una encuesta° reciente realizada entre jóvenes universitarios. Mucha gente practica este deporte y tiene un equipo de fútbol favorito. Cada cuatro años se realiza la Copa Mundial°. Argentina y Uruguay han ganado° este campeonato° más de una vez°. Los aficionados siguen los partidos de fútbol en casa por tele y en muchos otros lugares como los bares, los restaurantes, los estadios y los clubes deportivos. Los jóvenes juegan al fútbol con sus amigos en parques y gimnasios.

Países hispanos en campeonatos mundiales de fútbol (1930–2002)

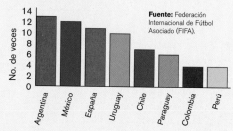

Fuente: Federación Internacional de Fútbol Asociado (FIFA).

Pero, por supuesto°, en los países de habla hispana también hay otros deportes populares. ¿Qué deporte sigue al fútbol en estos países? Bueno, ¡depende del país y de otros factores!

Después de leer

Evaluación y predicción

Which of the following sports events would be most popular among the college students surveyed? Rate them from one (most popular) to five (least popular). Which would be the most popular at your school?
Answers will vary.

_____ 1. La Copa Mundial de Fútbol
_____ 2. Los Juegos Olímpicos
_____ 3. El torneo de tenis de Wimbledon
_____ 4. La Serie Mundial de Béisbol
_____ 5. El Tour de Francia

TEACHING OPTIONS

Variación léxica Remind students that the term **fútbol** in the Hispanic world refers to soccer, and that in the English-speaking world outside of the United States and Canada, soccer is called *football*. The game called *football* here is called **fútbol americano** in the Spanish-speaking world.

Extra Practice Ask questions that require students to refer to the article. Model the use of the definite article with percentages. **¿Qué porcentaje prefiere el fútbol?** (el 69 por ciento) **¿Qué porcentaje prefiere el vóleibol?** (el 2 por ciento)

No sólo el fútbol

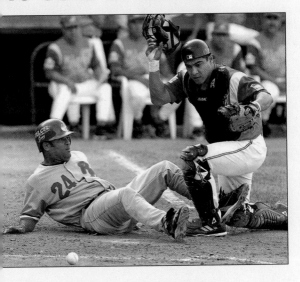

Donde el fútbol es más popular
En México el béisbol es el segundo° deporte más popular después° del fútbol. Pero en Argentina, después del fútbol, el rugby tiene mucha importancia. En Perú a la gente le gusta mucho ver partidos de vóleibol. ¿Y en España? Mucha gente prefiere el baloncesto, el tenis y el ciclismo.

En Colombia, por ejemplo, el béisbol es muy popular después del fútbol, aunque° esto varía según la región del país. En la costa del norte de Colombia, el béisbol es una pasión. Y el ciclismo también es un deporte que los colombianos siguen con mucho interés.

Donde el béisbol es más popular
En los países del Caribe, el béisbol es el deporte predominante. Éste es el caso en Puerto Rico, Cuba y la República Dominicana. Los niños empiezan a jugar cuando son muy pequeños. En Puerto Rico y la República Dominicana, la gente también quiere participar en otros deportes, como el baloncesto, o ver los partidos en la tele. Y para los espectadores aficionados del Caribe, el boxeo es número dos.

Deportes más populares

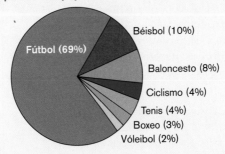

- Fútbol (69%)
- Béisbol (10%)
- Baloncesto (8%)
- Ciclismo (4%)
- Tenis (4%)
- Boxeo (3%)
- Vóleibol (2%)

mundo *world* según *according to* encuesta *survey* se realiza la Copa Mundial *the World Cup is held* han ganado *have won* campeonato *championship* más de una vez *more than once* por supuesto *of course* segundo *second* después *after* aunque *although*

¿Cierto o falso?
Indicate whether each sentence is **cierto** or **falso,** then correct the false statements.

	Cierto	Falso
1. El vóleibol es el segundo deporte más popular en México. Es el béisbol.	○	⊙
2. En España a la gente le gustan varios deportes como el baloncesto y el ciclismo.	⊙	○
3. En la costa del norte de Colombia, el tenis es una pasión. El béisbol es una pasión.	○	⊙
4. En el Caribe el deporte más popular es el béisbol.	⊙	○

Preguntas
Answer these questions in Spanish. Answers will vary.

1. ¿Dónde ven los aficionados el fútbol? Y tú, ¿cómo ves tus deportes favoritos?
2. ¿Te gusta el fútbol? ¿Por qué?
3. ¿Miras la Copa Mundial en la televisión?
4. ¿Qué deportes miras en la televisión?
5. En tu opinión, ¿cuáles son los tres deportes más populares en tu escuela? ¿En tu comunidad? ¿En los Estados Unidos?
6. ¿Qué haces en tus ratos libres?

Evaluación y predicción
Write two headings on the board: **Entre los jóvenes del mundo hispano** and **Entre los jóvenes de nuestra escuela**. Ask for a show of hands to respond to your questions about the ranking of each sporting event. Tally the reponses as you proceed. Ask: **¿Quiénes creen que entre los jóvenes hispanos la Copa Mundial de Fútbol es el evento más popular? ¿Quiénes creen que los Juegos Olímpicos son el evento más popular?** Then ask: **Entre los jóvenes de nuestra escuela, ¿quiénes de ustedes creen que la Copa Mundial de Fútbol es el evento más popular?** Briefly discuss the differences indicated by student responses.

¿Cierto o falso? After completing the activity, ask students to write an additional sentence about sports in each country or region mentioned. Ex: **El fútbol es el deporte más popular en México.**

Preguntas Give students these questions as items 7–10:
7. ¿Cuál es el deporte más popular en el mundo hispano? (el fútbol) 8. ¿En qué países es el béisbol el deporte más popular? (en los países del Caribe) 9. ¿Pueden nombrar algunos jugadores de béisbol hispanos en los Estados Unidos? (Answers will vary.)
10. ¿Participan muchos países hispanos en campeonatos mundiales de fútbol? (sí)

TEACHING OPTIONS

Pairs In pairs, have students read the article aloud and write three questions about it. Then, ask students to exchange their questions with another pair. Alternatively, you can ask pairs to read their questions to the class.

Heritage Speakers Ask heritage speakers to prepare a short presentation about soccer in their families' home countries. Encourage them to discuss how popular the sport is, what the principal teams are, and whether their country has participated in a World Cup.

Section Goals

In **Escritura**, students will:
- write a pamphlet listing sports events in their area
- integrate recreation-related vocabulary and structures taught in **Lección 4**

Instructional Resources
Cuaderno para hispanohablantes, pp. 63–64
Cuaderno de actividades, pp. 147–148
Supersite

Estrategia Explain that when students look up an English word in a Spanish-English dictionary, they will frequently find more than one definition. They must decide which one best fits the context. Discuss the meanings of *racket* that might be found in a Spanish-English dictionary and how the explanatory notes and abbreviations can be useful. Tell students that a good way to verify the meaning of a Spanish translation is to look it up and see the English translation.

Tema Discuss the three topics. You may want to introduce terms like **comité**, **guía de orientación**, **cámara de comercio**. Remind students of some common graphic features used in pamphlets: headings, lists of times and places, brief descriptions of events, and prices.

Successful Language Learning Tell students that they should resist the temptation to look up every unknown word. Advise them to guess the word's meaning based on context clues.

Escritura

Estrategia
Using a dictionary

A common mistake made by beginning language learners is to embrace the dictionary as the ultimate resource for reading, writing, and speaking. While it is true that the dictionary is a useful tool that can provide valuable information about vocabulary, using the dictionary correctly requires that you understand the elements of each entry.

If you glance at a Spanish-English dictionary, you will notice that its format is similar to that of an English dictionary. The word is listed first, usually followed by its pronunciation. Then come the definitions, organized by parts of speech. Sometimes the most frequently used definitions are listed first.

To find the best word for your needs, you should refer to the abbreviations and the explanatory notes that appear next to the entries. For example, imagine that you are writing about your pastimes. You want to write, "I want to buy a new racket for my match tomorrow," but you don't know the Spanish word for "racket." In the dictionary, you may find an entry like this:

racket s 1. alboroto; 2. raqueta (*dep.*)

The abbreviation key at the front of the dictionary says that *s* corresponds to **sustantivo** (*noun*). Then, the first word you see is **alboroto**. The definition of **alboroto** is *noise* or *racket*, so **alboroto** is probably not the word you're looking for. The second word is **raqueta**, followed by the abbreviation *dep.*, which stands for **deportes**. This indicates that the word **raqueta** is the best choice for your needs.

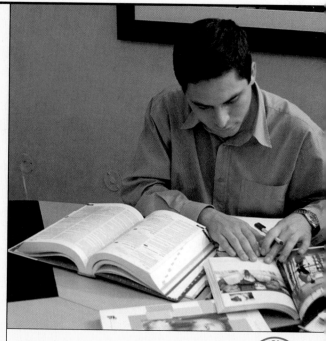

Tema

Escribir un folleto

Choose one topic.

1. You are on the Homecoming Committee at your school this year. Create a pamphlet that lists events for Friday night, Saturday, and Sunday. Include a brief description of each event and its time and location. Include activities for different age groups, since some alumni will bring their families.

2. You are on the Freshman Student Orientation Committee and are in charge of creating a pamphlet for new students describing the sports offered at your school. Write the flyer, including a variety of activities.

3. You volunteer at your community's recreation center. It is your job to market your community to potential residents. Write a brief pamphlet that describes the recreational opportunities your community provides, the areas where the activities take place, and the costs, if any. Be sure to include activities that will appeal to singles as well as couples and families; you should include activities for all age groups and for both men and women.

recursos

CH pp. 63–64	CA pp. 147–148	descubre1.vhlcentral.com Lección 4

EVALUATION: Folleto

Criteria	Scale
Appropriate details	1 2 3 4
Organization	1 2 3 4
Use of vocabulary	1 2 3 4
Grammatical accuracy	1 2 3 4
Mechanics	1 2 3 4

Scoring	
Excellent	18–20 points
Good	14–17 points
Satisfactory	10–13 points
Unsatisfactory	< 10 points

Escuchar

Estrategia

Listening for the gist

Listening for the general idea, or gist, can help you follow what someone is saying even if you can't hear or understand some of the words. When you listen for the gist, you simply try to capture the essence of what you hear without focusing on individual words.

 To help you practice this strategy, you will listen to a paragraph made up of three sentences. Jot down a brief summary of what you hear.

Preparación

[ba]sed on the photo, what do you think Anabela is [li]ke? Do you and Anabela have similar interests?

Ahora escucha

[Y]ou will hear first José talking, then Anabela. As [y]ou listen, check off each person's favorite activities.

Pasatiempos favoritos de José

1. ✔ leer el correo electrónico
2. _____ jugar al béisbol
3. ✔ ver películas de acción
4. ✔ ir al café
5. ✔ ir a partidos de béisbol
6. _____ ver películas románticas
7. ✔ dormir la siesta
8. ✔ escribir mensajes electrónicos

Pasatiempos favoritos de Anabela

9. ✔ esquiar
[1]0. ✔ nadar
[1]1. ✔ practicar el ciclismo
[1]2. ✔ jugar al golf
[1]3. _____ jugar al baloncesto
[1]4. _____ ir a ver partidos de tenis
[1]5. ✔ escalar montañas
[1]6. _____ ver televisión

Comprensión

Preguntas

Answer these questions about José's and Anabela's pastimes.

1. ¿Quién practica más deportes?
   Anabela
2. ¿Quién piensa que es importante descansar?
   José
3. ¿A qué deporte es aficionado José?
   Le gusta el béisbol.
4. ¿Por qué Anabela no practica el baloncesto?
   Ella no es alta.
5. ¿Qué películas le gustan a la novia de José?
   Le gustan las películas de romance.
6. ¿Cuál es el deporte favorito de Anabela?
   el ciclismo

Seleccionar

Which person do these statements best describe?

1. Le gusta practicar deportes. Anabela
2. Prefiere las películas de acción. José
3. Le gustan las computadoras. José
4. Le gusta nadar. Anabela
5. Siempre (*Always*) duerme una siesta por la tarde. José
6. Quiere ir de vacaciones a las montañas. Anabela

recursos

SUPERSITE

descubre1.vhlcentral.com
Lección 4

---

el tenis, el golf… bueno, en realidad todos los deportes. No, eso no es cierto—no juego al baloncesto porque no soy alta. Para

mis vacaciones quiero esquiar o escalar la montaña—depende si nieva. Suena divertido, ¿no?

En pantalla

In many Spanish-speaking countries, soccer isn't just a game; it's a way of life. Many countries have professional and amateur leagues, and soccer is even played in the streets. Every four years, during the World Cup, even those who aren't big fans of the sport find it impossible not to get swept up in "soccer fever." During the month-long Cup, passions only increase with each of the sixty-four matches played. Companies also get caught up in the soccer craze, launching ad campaigns and offering promotions with prizes ranging from commemorative glasses to all-expenses-paid trips to the World Cup venue.

Vocabulario útil

cracks	*stars, aces (sports)*
lo tuvo a Pelé de hijo	*he was a better player than Pelé (coll. expr. Peru)*
Dios me hizo	*God made me*
patito feo	*ugly duckling*
plata	*money (S. America)*
jugando	*playing*

Comprensión

Indicate whether each statement is **cierto** or **falso**.

	Cierto	Falso
1. La familia juega al baloncesto.	○	◉
2. No hay mujeres en el anuncio (*ad*).	○	◉
3. La pareja tiene cinco hijos.	○	◉
4. El hijo más joven es un mariachi.	◉	○

Conversación

With a partner, discuss these questions in Spanish. Answers will vary.

1. En el anuncio (*ad*) hay varios elementos culturales representativos de la cultura de los países hispanos. ¿Cuáles son?

2. ¿Qué otros elementos culturales de los países hispanos conocen (*do you know*)?

jugaba *used to play* cuna *crib* barriga *womb* Por eso *That's why* esperaban que yo fuera *they expected that I be* el mejor de todos *the best of all*

Anuncio de Totofútbol

Mi hermano mayor jugaba° desde la cuna°.

Mi segundo hermano, desde la barriga°.

Por eso° esperaban que yo fuera° el mejor de todos°.

recursos
SUPERSITE
descubre1.vhlcentral.com
Lección 4

SUPERSITE Conexión Internet
Go to **descubre1.vhlcentral.com** to watch the TV clip featured in this **En pantalla** section.

Oye cómo va

afé Tacuba

bén, Quique, Joselo y **Meme** have come a g way since playing rock music for fun in a age. The foursome, close friends since they at a suburban high school just outside xico City, chose the name Café Tacuba and ted playing publicly in 1989. Besides the al instruments one would expect a rock d to play—drums, bass, and electric guitar— é Tacuba incorporates more traditional ruments to produce a particular blend of k, ska, and Mexican folk rhythms. This ion of genres characterizes their distinctive le, one so diverse that some say no two songs nd alike. In addition to having recorded more n seven albums, the group has participated in ndtracks for movies like *Y tu mamá también, ir mata,* and *Amores perros.*

ur instructor will play the song. Listen and n complete these activities.

mprensión

mplete the sentences with the correct option.

Café Tacuba tiene ___c___ miembros (*members*).
a. seis   b. tres   c. cuatro

Ellos se conocieron en ___b___.
a. una casa   b. una escuela   c. un garaje

Su música es una ___b___ de diferentes géneros.
a. separación   b. fusión   c. falta (*lack*)

En la canción *Eres* el autor le canta a ___a___.
a. una mujer   b. un parque   c. una pelota

___c___ Downs es una roquera mexicana.
a. Lisa   b. Linda   c. Lila

terpretación   Answers will vary.

swer these questions in Spanish. Then, share your swers with a classmate.

¿Cómo piensas que es la mujer que inspiró (*inspired*) esta canción?

Escribe tres frases que comiencen con *Eres...* sobre una persona que tú quieres mucho.

ue *what* mundo *world* eso eres *that's what you are* pensamiento ught *dime tell me* despierto *I wake up* vida *life* le hace falta *is sing* lo único *the only thing*

Eres

Eres,
lo que° más quiero en este mundo° eso eres°,
mi pensamiento° más profundo también eres,
tan sólo dime° lo que hago, aquí me tienes.

Eres,
cuando despierto° lo primero eso eres,
lo que a mi vida° le hace falta° si no vienes,
lo único°, preciosa, que en mi mente habita hoy.

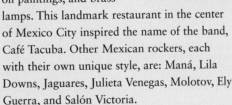

Historia y rock

Since opening in 1912, **Café de Tacuba** has maintained its colonial ambiance: ceramic tiles, oil paintings, and brass lamps. This landmark restaurant in the center of Mexico City inspired the name of the band, Café Tacuba. Other Mexican rockers, each with their own unique style, are: Maná, Lila Downs, Jaguares, Julieta Venegas, Molotov, Ely Guerra, and Salón Victoria.

recursos

descubre1.vhlcentral.com
Lección 4

SUPERSITE Conexión Internet
Go to **descubre1.vhlcentral.com** to learn more about the artist featured in this **Oye cómo va** section.

Section Goals

In **Oye cómo va**, students will:
• read about **Café Tacuba**
• listen to a song by **Café Tacuba**

Instructional Resources
Supersite
Vista Higher Learning
Cancionero

Antes de escuchar
• Have students read the song title and scan the lyrics for cognates and familiar words.
• Ask students to predict what type of song this is. Tell them to support their opinions by citing words from the lyrics.

Comprensión Have students work in pairs or groups for this activity. Ask them to explain their answers by indicating where they found the information in the text or song.

Interpretación After discussing the questions, ask volunteers to share their ideas and sentences with the class. Survey the class to find out if there is a uniform idea of what the woman is like and to whom most people dedicated their sentences.

TEACHING OPTIONS

Café Tacuba The members of **Café Tacuba** (often spelled **Café Tacvba**), who formed their band in 1989, are from Naucalpán, a municipality bordering Mexico City. As former graphic design students, **Rubén, Joselo,** and **Quique** create their own album covers.

Small Groups In groups of three, have students research another song by one of the Mexican rock artists mentioned on this page. Guide them to songs with stem-changing verbs, such as *Donde quiero estar* by **Julieta Venegas**. Ask them to compare the songs in terms of musical style and lyrics. Have each group present their song to the class.

México

El país en cifras

▶ **Área:** 1.972.550 km² (761.603 millas²), *casi° tres veces° el área de Texas*

La situación geográfica de México, al sur° de los Estados Unidos, ha influido en° la economía y la sociedad de los dos países. Una de las consecuencias es la emigración de la población mexicana al país vecino°. Hoy día, más de 20 millones de personas de ascendencia mexicana viven en los Estados Unidos.

▶ **Población:** 113.271.000

▶ **Capital:** México, D.F.—20.688.000

▶ **Ciudades principales:** Guadalajara—4.237.000, Monterrey—3.914.000, Ciudad Juárez—1.841.000, Puebla—1.801.000

SOURCE: Population Division, UN Secretariat

▶ **Moneda:** peso mexicano

▶ **Idiomas:** español (oficial), náhuatl, otras lenguas indígenas

Bandera de México

Mexicanos célebres

▶ **Benito Juárez,** héroe nacional (1806–1872)

▶ **Octavio Paz,** poeta (1914–1998)

▶ **Elena Poniatowska,** periodista y escritora (1933–)

▶ **Julio César Chávez,** boxeador (1962–)

casi *almost* veces *times* sur *south* ha influido en *has influenced* vecino *neighboring* se llenan de luz *get filled with light* flores *flowers* Muertos *Dead* se ríen *laugh* muerte *death* lo cual se refleja *which is reflected* calaveras de azúcar *sugar skulls* pan *bread* huesos *bones*

recursos

| CP pp. 47–48 | CA pp. 75–76 | descubre1.vhlcentral.com Lección 4 |

Un delfín en Baja California

Autorretrato con mono (*Self-portrait with monkey*), 1938, Frida Kahlo

ESTADOS UNIDOS

Ciudad Juárez · Río Grande · Río Bravo del Norte · Golfo de California · Baja California · Sierra Madre Oriental · Sierra Madre Occidental · Monter... · Océano Pacífico · Puerto Vallarta · Guadalajara · **Ciudad de México** · Pue... · Acapulco

Ruinas aztecas en México D.F.

Saltador en Acapulco

¡Increíble pero cierto!

Cada dos de noviembre los cementerios de México se llenan de luz°, música y flores°. El Día de Muertos° no es un evento triste; es una fiesta en honor a las personas muertas. En ese día, los mexicanos se ríen° de la muerte°, lo cual se refleja° en detalles como las calaveras de azúcar° y el pan° de muerto —pan en forma de huesos°.

Ciudades • México, D.F.

La Ciudad de México, fundada° en 1525, también se llama el D.F. o Distrito Federal. Muchos turistas e inmigrantes vienen a la ciudad porque es el centro cultural y económico del país. El crecimiento° de la población es de los más altos° del mundo. El D.F. tiene una población mayor que las de Nueva York, Madrid o París.

Artes • Diego Rivera y Frida Kahlo

Frida Kahlo y Diego Rivera eran° artistas mexicanos muy famosos. Casados° en 1929, los dos se interesaron° en las condiciones sociales de la gente indígena de su país. Puedes ver algunas° de sus obras° en el Museo de Arte Moderno de la Ciudad de México.

Historia • Los aztecas

Los aztecas dominaron° en México del siglo° XIV hasta el siglo XVI. Sus canales, puentes° y pirámides con templos religiosos eran° muy importantes. El imperio azteca terminó° cuando llegaron° los españoles en 1519, pero la presencia azteca sigue hoy. La Ciudad de México está situada en la capital azteca de Tenochtitlán, y muchos turistas van a visitar sus ruinas.

Economía • La plata

México es el mayor productor de plata° del mundo°. Estados como Zacatecas y Durango tienen ciudades fundadas cerca de los más grandes yacimientos° de plata del país. Estas ciudades fueron° en la época colonial unas de las más ricas e importantes. Hoy en día, aún° conservan mucho de su encanto° y esplendor.

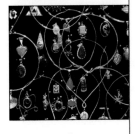

Golfo de México
Península de Yucatán
Mérida
Cancún
Bahía de Campeche
Istmo de Tehuantepec
BELICE
GUATEMALA

¿Qué aprendiste? Responde a cada pregunta con una oración completa.

1. ¿Qué lenguas hablan los mexicanos? Los mexicanos hablan español y lenguas indígenas.
2. ¿Cómo es la población del D.F. en comparación a otras ciudades? La población del D.F. es mayor.
3. ¿En qué se interesaron Frida Kahlo y Diego Rivera? Se interesaron en las condiciones sociales de la gente indígena de su país.
4. Nombra algunas de las estructuras de la arquitectura azteca. Hay canales, puentes y pirámides con templos religiosos.
5. ¿Dónde está situada la capital de México? Está situada en la capital azteca de Tenochtitlán.
6. ¿Qué estados de México tienen los mayores yacimientos de plata? Zacatecas y Durango tienen los mayores yacimientos de plata.

Conexión Internet Investiga estos temas en **descubre1.vhlcentral.com.**

1. Busca información sobre dos lugares de México. ¿Te gustaría (*Would you like*) vivir allí? ¿Por qué?
2. Busca información sobre dos artistas mexicanos. ¿Cómo se llaman sus obras más famosas?

fundada *founded* **crecimiento** *growth* **más altos** *highest* **eran** *were* **Casados** *Married* **se interesaron** *were interested in* **algunas** *some* **obras** *works* **dominaron** *dominated* **siglo** *century* **puentes** *bridges* **eran** *were* **terminó** *ended* **llegaron** *arrived* **plata** *silver* **mundo** *world* **yacimientos** *deposits* **fueron** *were* **aún** *still* **encanto** *charm*

Instructional Resources
Cuaderno de actividades, p.110
e-Cuaderno
Supersite: Textbook &
Vocabulary MP3 Audio Files
Supersite/TRCD/Print: Answer
Keys; *Testing Program*
(**Lección 4 Pruebas,** Test
Generator, Testing Program
MP3 Audio Files)
Textbook, Test Audio CD

Pasatiempos

andar en patineta	to skateboard
bucear	to scuba dive
escalar montañas (f. pl.)	to climb mountains
escribir una carta	to write a letter
escribir un mensaje electrónico	to write an e-mail message
esquiar	to ski
ganar	to win
ir de excursión	to go on a hike
leer correo electrónico	to read e-mail
leer un periódico	to read a newspaper
leer una revista	to read a magazine
nadar	to swim
pasear	to take a walk; to stroll
pasear en bicicleta	to ride a bicycle
patinar (en línea)	to (in-line) skate
practicar deportes (m. pl.)	to play sports
tomar el sol	to sunbathe
ver películas (f. pl.)	to see movies
visitar monumentos (m. pl.)	to visit monuments
la diversión	fun activity; entertainment; recreation
el fin de semana	weekend
el pasatiempo	pastime; hobby
los ratos libres	spare (free) time
el videojuego	video game

Deportes

el baloncesto	basketball
el béisbol	baseball
el ciclismo	cycling
el equipo	team
el esquí (acuático)	(water) skiing
el fútbol	soccer
el fútbol americano	football
el golf	golf
el hockey	hockey
el/la jugador(a)	player
la natación	swimming
el partido	game; match
la pelota	ball
el tenis	tennis
el vóleibol	volleyball

Adjetivos

deportivo/a	sports-related
favorito/a	favorite

Lugares

el café	café
el centro	downtown
el cine	movie theater
el gimnasio	gymnasium
la iglesia	church
el lugar	place
el museo	museum
el parque	park
la piscina	swimming pool
la plaza	city or town square
el restaurante	restaurant

Verbos

almorzar (o:ue)	to have lunch
cerrar (e:ie)	to close
comenzar (e:ie)	to begin
conseguir (e:i)	to get; to obtain
contar (o:ue)	to count; to tell
decir (e:i)	to say; to tell
dormir (o:ue)	to sleep
empezar (e:ie)	to begin
encontrar (o:ue)	to find
entender (e:ie)	to understand
hacer	to do; to make
ir	to go
jugar (u:ue)	to play
mostrar (o:ue)	to show
oír	to hear
pedir (e:i)	to ask for; to request
pensar (e:ie)	to think
pensar (+ inf.)	to intend
pensar en	to think about
perder (e:ie)	to lose; to miss
poder (o:ue)	to be able to; can
poner	to put; to place
preferir (e:ie)	to prefer
querer (e:ie)	to want; to love
recordar (o:ue)	to remember
repetir (e:i)	to repeat
salir	to leave
seguir (e:i)	to follow; to continue
suponer	to suppose
traer	to bring
ver	to see
volver (o:ue)	to return

***Decir* expressions**	See page 136.
Expresiones útiles	See page 121.

recursos

CA
p. 110

descubre1.vhlcentral.com
Lección 4

Las vacaciones

5

Communicative Goals

You will learn how to:

- **Discuss and plan a vacation**
- **Describe a hotel**
- **Talk about how you feel**
- **Talk about the seasons and the weather**

contextos

pages 152–157
- Travel and vacation
- Months of the year
- Seasons and weather
- Ordinal numbers

fotonovela

pages 158–161
After arriving in Otavalo, the students and Don Francisco check into the hotel where they will be staying. Inés and Javier then decide to explore more of the city, while Maite and Álex decide to rest before their afternoon run.

cultura

pages 162–163
- El Camino Inca
- Punta del Este

estructura

pages 164–179
- **Estar** with conditions and emotions
- The present progressive
- **Ser** and **estar**
- Direct object nouns and pronouns
- **Recapitulación**

adelante

pages 180–187
Lectura: A hotel brochure from Puerto Rico
Escritura: A tourist brochure for a hotel
Escuchar: A weather report
En pantalla
Oye cómo va
Panorama: Puerto Rico

A PRIMERA VISTA
- ¿Dónde están ellos: en una montaña o en una ciudad?
- ¿Son viejos o jóvenes?
- ¿Pasean o ven una película?

Lesson Goals

In **Lección 5**, students will be introduced to the following:
- terms for traveling and vacations
- seasons and months of the year
- weather expressions
- ordinal numbers (1st–10th)
- the **Camino Inca**
- Punta del Este, Uruguay
- **estar** with conditions and emotions
- adjectives for conditions and emotions
- present progressive of regular and irregular verbs
- comparison of the uses of **ser** and **estar**
- direct object nouns and pronouns
- personal **a**
- scanning to find specific information
- making an outline
- writing a brochure for a hotel or resort
- listening for key words
- a weather report from **TeleMadrid**
- Puerto Rican singer **Ednita Nazario**
- cultural, geographic, and historical information about Puerto Rico

A primera vista Here are some additional questions you can ask based on the photo: **¿Dónde te gusta pasar tus ratos libres? ¿Qué haces en tus ratos libres? ¿Te gusta explorar otras culturas? ¿Te gusta viajar a otros países? ¿Adónde quieres ir en las próximas vacaciones?**

INSTRUCTIONAL RESOURCES

Student Materials
Cuaderno de práctica, Cuaderno para hispanohablantes, Cuaderno de actividades
Student MAESTRO™ Supersite
(descubre1.vhlcentral.com)
MAESTRO™ e-Cuaderno

Teacher's Resource CD-ROM and in print
*Answer Keys, Audioscripts, Videoscripts
*PowerPoints
Testing Program (**Pruebas,** Test Generator, MP3 Audio Files)
Vista Higher Learning *Cancionero*
*Also available on Supersite

Teacher's MAESTRO™ Supersite
(descubre1.vhlcentral.com)
Learning Management System (Assignment Task Manager, Gradebook)
Also on DVD
Fotonovela, Flash cultura, Panorama cultural

Section Goals

In **Contextos**, students will learn and practice:

- travel- and vacation-related vocabulary
- seasons and months of the year
- weather expressions
- ordinal numbers

Instructional Resources
Cuaderno de práctica, pp. 49–50
Cuaderno para hispanohablantes, pp. 65–66
Cuaderno de actividades, pp. 23–24, 27, 111
e-Cuaderno
Supersite: Textbook, Vocabulary, & Audio Activity MP3 Audio Files
Supersite/TRCD/Print: *PowerPoints* (Lección 5 **Contextos** Presentation, Overheads #22, 23, 24); Communication Activities, Textbook Audio Script, Audio Activity Script, Answer Keys
Textbook & Audio Activity CD

Teaching Tips

- Ask: **¿A quién le gusta mucho viajar? ¿Cómo prefieres viajar?** Introduce cognates as suggestions: **¿Te gusta viajar en auto?** Write each term on the board as you say it. Ask: **¿Adónde te gusta viajar? ¿A México?** Ask students about their classmates' statements: **¿Adónde le gusta viajar a _____? ¿Cómo puede viajar?**
- Ask questions about transportation in your community. Ex: **Si quiero ir de la escuela al aeropuerto, ¿cómo puedo ir?**
- Give students two minutes to review the four scenes. Then show *Overhead PowerPoint #22* and ask questions. Ex: **¿Quién trabaja en una agencia de viajes? (el/la agente de viajes)**

Las vacaciones

Más vocabulario

la cama	bed
la habitación individual, doble	single, double room
el piso	floor (of a building)
la planta baja	ground floor
el campo	countryside
el paisaje	landscape
el equipaje	luggage
la estación de autobuses, del metro, de tren	bus, subway, train station
la llegada	arrival
el pasaje (de ida y vuelta)	(round-trip) ticket
la salida	departure; exit
acampar	to camp
estar de vacaciones	to be on vacation
hacer las maletas	to pack (one's suitcases)
hacer un viaje	to take a trip
ir de compras	to go shopping
ir de vacaciones	to go on vacation
ir en autobús (m.), auto(móvil) (m.), motocicleta (f.), taxi (m.)	to go by bus, car, motorcycle, taxi

Variación léxica

automóvil ⟷ coche (*Esp.*), carro (*Amér. L.*)
autobús ⟷ camión (*Méx.*), guagua (*P. Rico*)
motocicleta ⟷ moto (*coloquial*)

la agente de viajes
el pasaporte
Confirma una reservación. (confirmar)

En la agencia de viajes

la habitación
el ascensor
el empleado
la llave
el botones
el huésped
la huésped

En el hotel

recursos

| CP pp. 49–50 | CH pp. 65–66 | CA pp. 23–24, 27, 111 | SUPERSITE descubre1.vhlcentral.com Lección 5 |

TEACHING OPTIONS

Extra Practice Ask questions about the people, places, and activities in **Contextos**. Ex: **¿Qué actividades pueden hacer los turistas en una playa? ¿Pueden nadar? ¿Tomar el sol? ¿Sacar fotos?** Then expand questions to ask students what they specifically do at these places. **_____, ¿qué haces tú cuando vas a la playa?** Students should respond in complete sentences.

Variación léxica Point out that these are just some of the different Spanish names for vehicles. Ask heritage speakers if they are familiar with other terms. While some of these terms are mutually understood in different regions (**el coche, el carro, el auto, el automóvil**), others are specific to a region and may not be understood by others (**la guagua, el camión**). Stress that the feminine article **la** is used with the abbreviation **moto**.

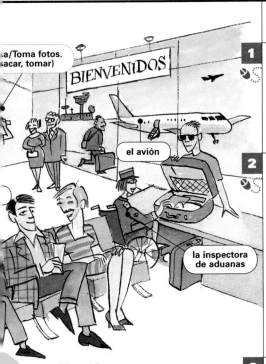

a/Toma fotos.
(sacar, tomar)

BIENVENIDOS

el avión

la inspectora de aduanas

En el aeropuerto

Pesca. (pescar)

Monta a caballo. (montar)

Va en barco.

Juegan a las cartas. (jugar)

la playa

En la playa

Práctica

1 **Escuchar** Indicate who would probably make each statement you hear. Each answer is used twice.

a. el agente de viajes   1. ___a___   4. ___b___
b. la inspectora de aduanas   2. ___a___   5. ___c___
c. un empleado del hotel   3. ___c___   6. ___b___

2 **¿Cierto o falso?** Mario and his wife, Natalia, are planning their next vacation with a travel agent. Indicate whether each statement is **cierto** or **falso** according to what you hear in the conversation.

	Cierto	Falso
1. Mario y Natalia están en Puerto Rico.	○	☒
2. Mario y Natalia quieren hacer un viaje a Puerto Rico.	☒	○
3. Natalia prefiere ir a una montaña.	○	☒
4. Mario quiere pescar en Puerto Rico.	☒	○
5. La agente de viajes va a confirmar la reservación.	☒	○

3 **Escoger** Choose the best answer for each sentence.

1. Un huésped es una persona que ___b___.
   a. toma fotos   b. está en un hotel   c. pesca en el mar
2. Abrimos la puerta con ___a___.
   a. una llave   b. un caballo   c. una llegada
3. Enrique tiene ___a___ porque va a viajar a otro (*another*) país.
   a. un pasaporte   b. una foto   c. una llegada
4. Antes de (*Before*) ir de vacaciones hay que ___c___.
   a. pescar   b. ir en tren   c. hacer las maletas
5. Nosotros vamos en ___a___ al aeropuerto.
   a. autobús   b. pasaje   c. viajero
6. Me gusta mucho ir al campo. El ___a___ es increíble.
   a. paisaje   b. pasaje   c. equipaje

4 **Analogías** Complete the analogies using the words below. Two words will not be used.

auto	huésped	mar	sacar
botones	llegada	pasaporte	tren

1. acampar → campo ⊜ pescar → mar
2. agencia de viajes → agente ⊜ hotel → botones
3. llave → habitación ⊜ pasaje → tren
4. estudiante → libro ⊜ turista → pasaporte
5. aeropuerto → viajero ⊜ hotel → huésped
6. maleta → hacer ⊜ foto → sacar

---

1 **Teaching Tip** Have students check their answers as you go over **Actividad 1** with the class.

1 **Script** 1. ¡Deben ir a Puerto Rico! Allí hay unas playas muy hermosas y pueden acampar. 2. Deben llamarme el lunes para confirmar la reservación. *Script continues on page 154.*

2 **Expansion** To challenge students, give them these true-false statements as items 6–9: **6. Mario prefiere una habitación doble. (Cierto.) 7. Natalia no quiere ir a la playa. (Falso.) 8. El hotel está en la playa. (Cierto.) 9. Mario va a montar a caballo. (Falso.)**

2 **Script** MARIO: Queremos ir de vacaciones a Puerto Rico. AGENTE: ¿Desean hacer un viaje al campo? NATALIA: Yo quiero ir a la playa. M: Pues, yo prefiero una habitación doble en un hotel con un buen paisaje. A: Puedo reservar para ustedes una habitación en el hotel San Juan que está en la playa. M: Es una buena idea, así yo voy a pescar y tú vas a montar a caballo. N: Muy bien, ¿puede confirmar la reservación? A: Claro que sí. *Textbook Audio*

3 **Expansion** Ask a volunteer to help you model making statements similar to item 1. Say: **Un turista es una persona que… (va de vacaciones).** Then ask volunteers to do the same with **una agente de viajes, un botones, una inspectora de aduanas, un empleado de hotel.**

4 **Teaching Tip** Present these items using the following formula: *Acampar* **tiene la misma relación con** *campo* **que** *pescar* **tiene con… (***mar***).**

TEACHING OPTIONS

Small Groups Have students work in groups of three to write a riddle about one of the people or objects in the **Contextos** illustrations. The group must come up with at least three descriptions of their subject. Then one of the group members reads the description to the class and asks **¿Qué soy?** Ex: **Soy un pequeño libro. Tengo una foto de una persona. Soy necesario si un viajero quiere viajar a otro país. ¿Qué soy? (Soy un pasaporte.)**

Large Groups Split the class into two evenly-numbered groups. Hand out cards at random to the members of each group. One type of card should contain a verb or verb phrase (Ex: **confirmar una reservación**). The other will contain a related noun (Ex: **el agente de viajes**). The people within the groups must find their partners.

1 Script (continued) 3. Muy bien, señor… aquí tiene la llave de su habitación. 4. Lo siento, pero tengo que abrir sus maletas. 5. Su habitación está en el piso once, señora. 6. Necesito ver su pasaporte y sus maletas, por favor. *Textbook Audio*

Teaching Tips
- Point out that the names of months are not capitalized.
- Show *Overhead PowerPoint #23* and have students look over the seasons and months of the year. Call out the names of holidays or campus events and ask students to say when they occur.
- Show *Overhead PowerPoint #24* and use magazine pictures to cover as many weather conditions from this page as possible. Begin describing one of the pictures. Then, ask volunteers questions to elicit other weather expressions. Point out the use of **mucho/a** before nouns and **muy** before adjectives.
- Drill months by calling out a month and having students name the two that follow. Ex: **abril (mayo, junio).**
- Point out the use of **primero** for the first day of the month.
- Ask volunteers to associate seasons (or months) and general weather patterns. Ex: **En invierno, hace frío/ nieva. En marzo, hace viento.**
- Review the shortened forms **buen** and **mal** before **tiempo.**
- Point out that **Llueve** and **Nieva** can also mean *It rains* and *It snows.* **Está lloviendo** and **Está nevando** emphasize *at this moment.* Students will learn more about this concept in **Estructura 5.2.**

Successful Language Learning Remind students that weather expressions are used often in conversation and that they should make a special effort to learn them.

Las estaciones y los meses del año

el invierno: **diciembre, enero, febrero**

la primavera: **marzo, abril, mayo**

el verano: **junio, julio, agosto**

el otoño: **septiembre, octubre, noviembre**

—¿Cuál es la fecha de hoy?   *What is today's date?*
—Es el primero de octubre.   *It's the first of October.*
—Es el dos de marzo.   *It's March 2nd.*
—Es el diez de noviembre.   *It's November 10th.*

El tiempo

—¿Qué tiempo hace?   *How's the weather?*
—Hace buen/mal tiempo.   *The weather is good/bad.*

Hace (mucho) calor.
It's (very) hot.

Hace (mucho) frío.
It's (very) cold.

Llueve. (llover o:ue)
It's raining.

Está lloviendo.
It's raining.

Nieva. (nevar e:ie)
It's snowing.

Está nevando.
It's snowing.

Más vocabulario

Está (muy) nublado.	*It's (very) cloudy.*
Hace fresco.	*It's cool.*
Hace (mucho) sol.	*It's (very) sunny.*
Hace (mucho) viento.	*It's (very) windy.*

TEACHING OPTIONS

Pairs Have pairs of students create sentences for each of the drawings on this page. Ask one student to write sentences for the first four drawings and the other to write sentences for the next four. When finished, ask them to check their partner's work.
TPR Introduce the question **¿Cuándo es tu cumpleaños?** and the phrase **Mi cumpleaños es…** Have students ask questions and line up according to their birthdays. Allow them five minutes to form the line.
Extra Practice Create a series of cloze sentences about the weather in a certain place. Ex: **En Puerto Rico _____ mucho calor. (hace) No _____ muy nublado cuando _____ sol. (está; hace) No _____ frío pero a veces _____ fresco. (hace; hace) Cuando _____ mal tiempo, _____ y _____ viento pero nunca _____. (hace; llueve; hace; nieva)**

5 El Hotel Regis   Label the floors of the hotel.

Números ordinales

primer (before a masculine singular noun), primero/a	first
segundo/a	second
tercer (before a masculine singular noun), tercero/a	third
cuarto/a	fourth
quinto/a	fifth
sexto/a	sixth
séptimo/a	seventh
octavo/a	eighth
noveno/a	ninth
décimo/a	tenth

a. séptimo piso
b. sexto piso
c. quinto piso
d. cuarto piso
e. tercer piso
f. segundo piso
g. primer piso
h. planta baja

6 Contestar
Look at the illustrations of the months and seasons on the previous page and answer these questions in pairs.

modelo
Estudiante 1: ¿Cuál es el primer mes de la primavera?
Estudiante 2: marzo

1. ¿Cuál es el primer mes del invierno? diciembre
2. ¿Cuál es el segundo mes de la primavera? abril
3. ¿Cuál es el tercer mes del otoño? noviembre
4. ¿Cuál es el primer mes del año? enero
5. ¿Cuál es el quinto mes del año? mayo
6. ¿Cuál es el octavo mes del año? agosto
7. ¿Cuál es el décimo mes del año? octubre
8. ¿Cuál es el segundo mes del verano? julio
9. ¿Cuál es el tercer mes del invierno? febrero
10. ¿Cuál es la cuarta estación del año? el otoño

7 Las estaciones
Name the season that applies to the description. Some answers may vary.

1. Las clases terminan. la primavera
2. Vamos a la playa. el verano
3. Acampamos. el verano
4. Nieva mucho. el invierno
5. Las clases empiezan. el otoño
6. Hace mucho calor. el verano
7. Llueve mucho. la primavera
8. Esquiamos. el invierno
9. El entrenamiento (training) de béisbol la primavera
10. Día de Acción de Gracias (Thanksgiving) el otoño

8 ¿Cuál es la fecha?   Give the dates for these holidays.

modelo
el día de San Valentín   14 de febrero

1. el día de San Patricio 17 de marzo
2. el día de Halloween 31 de octubre
3. el primer día de verano 20–23 de junio
4. el Año Nuevo primero de enero
5. mi cumpleaños (birthday) Answers will vary.
6. mi fiesta favorita Answers will vary.

TEACHING OPTIONS

TPR Ask ten volunteers to line up facing the class. Make sure students know the starting point and what number in line they are. At random, call out ordinal numbers. The student to which each ordinal number corresponds has three seconds to step forward. If they do not, they sit down and the order changes for the rest of the students further down the line. Who will be the last student(s) standing?

Game Ask four or five volunteers to come to the front of the room and hold races. (Make it difficult to reach the finish line; for example, have students hop on one foot or recite the ordinal numbers backwards.) Teach the words **llegó** and **fue** and, after each race, ask the class to summarize the results. Ex: ____ **llegó en quinto lugar.** ____ **fue la tercera persona en llegar.**

9 Teaching Tip Review weather expressions by asking students about current weather conditions around the world. Ex: ¿Hace calor en Alaska hoy? ¿Nieva en Puerto Rico?

9 Expansion Use the alternate choices in the exercise to ask students weather-related questions. Ex: No nieva en Cancún. ¿Dónde nieva?

10 Teaching Tip Point out soleado, lluvia, and nieve. Have students guess the meaning of these words based on the context. Finally, explain that soleado is an adjective and lluvia and nieve are nouns related to llover and nevar.

10 Expansion
• Ask students questions that compare and contrast the weather conditions presented in the activity or on the weather page of a Spanish-language newspaper. Ex: Cuando la temperatura está a 85 grados en Buenos Aires, ¿a cuánto está en Tokio?
• To challenge students, ask them to predict tomorrow's weather for these cities, based on the same cues. Have them use ir a + [infinitive]. Ex: En Montreal, mañana va a nevar y va a hacer mucho frío.

11 Teaching Tip Model the activity by completing the first two sentences about yourself.

---

9 **Seleccionar** Paco is talking about his family and friends. Choose the word or phrase that best completes each sentence.

1. A mis padres les gusta ir a Cancún porque (hace sol, nieva). hace sol
2. Mi primo de Kansas dice que durante (*during*) un tornado, hace mucho (sol, viento). viento
3. Mis amigos van a esquiar si (nieva, está nublado). nieva
4. Tomo el sol cuando (hace calor, llueve). hace calor
5. Nosotros vamos a ver una película si hace (buen, mal) tiempo. mal
6. Mi hermana prefiere correr cuando (hace mucho calor, hace fresco). hace fresco
7. Mis tíos van de excursión si hace (buen, mal) tiempo. buen
8. Mi padre no quiere jugar al golf si (hace fresco, llueve). llueve
9. Cuando hace mucho (sol, frío) no salgo de casa y tomo chocolate caliente (*hot*). frío
10. Hoy mi sobrino va al parque porque (está lloviendo, hace buen tiempo). hace buen tiempo

◄ **NOTA CULTURAL**
Cancún, at the tip of Mexico's Yucatán Peninsula, is a popular tourist destination for foreigners and Mexicans alike. It offers beautiful beaches and excellent opportunities for snorkeling, diving, and sailing.

10 **El clima** With a partner, take turns asking and answering questions about the weather and temperatures in these cities. Answers will vary.

> **modelo**
> **Estudiante 1:** ¿Qué tiempo hace hoy en Nueva York?
> **Estudiante 2:** Hace frío y hace viento.
> **Estudiante 1:** ¿Cuál es la temperatura máxima?
> **Estudiante 2:** Treinta y un grados (*degrees*).
> **Estudiante 1:** ¿Y la temperatura mínima?
> **Estudiante 2:** Diez grados.

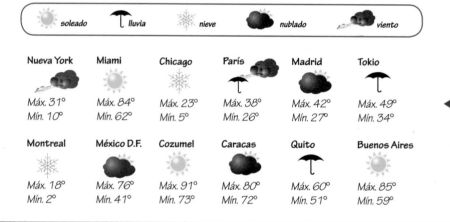

| ☀ soleado | ☂ lluvia | ❄ nieve | ☁ nublado | 🌬 viento |

Nueva York	Miami	Chicago	París	Madrid	Tokio
Máx. 31°	Máx. 84°	Máx. 23°	Máx. 38°	Máx. 42°	Máx. 49°
Mín. 10°	Mín. 62°	Mín. 5°	Mín. 26°	Mín. 27°	Mín. 34°

Montreal	México D.F.	Cozumel	Caracas	Quito	Buenos Aires
Máx. 18°	Máx. 76°	Máx. 91°	Máx. 80°	Máx. 60°	Máx. 85°
Mín. 2°	Mín. 41°	Mín. 73°	Mín. 72°	Mín. 51°	Mín. 59°

◄ **NOTA CULTURAL**
In most Spanish-speaking countries, temperatures are given in degrees Celsius. Use these formulas to convert between **grados centígrados** and **grados Fahrenheit**.
degrees C. × 9 ÷ 5 + 32 = degrees F.
degrees F. - 32 × 5 ÷ 9 = degrees C.

11 **Completar** Complete these sentences with your own ideas. Answers will vary.

1. Cuando hace sol, yo…
2. Cuando llueve, mis amigos y yo…
3. Cuando hace calor, mi familia…
4. Cuando hace viento, la gente…
5. Cuando hace frío, yo…
6. Cuando hace mal tiempo, mis amigos…
7. Cuando nieva, muchas personas…
8. Cuando está nublado, mis amigos y yo…
9. Cuando hace fresco, mis padres…
10. Cuando hace buen tiempo, mis amigos…

TEACHING OPTIONS

TPR Have volunteers mime situations that elicit weather-related vocabulary from the class. Ex: A shiver might elicit **hace frío**. **Heritage Speakers** Ask heritage speakers to talk about typical weather-dependent activities in their families' countries of origin. Refer them to **Actividad 11** as a model. Ex: **En México, cuando hace frío, la gente bebe ponche de frutas (una bebida caliente).**

Small Groups Have students form groups of two to four. Hand out cards that contain the name of a holiday or other annual event. The group must come up with at least three sentences to describe the holiday or occasion without mentioning its name. They can, however, mention the season of the year. The other groups must first guess the month and day on which the event takes place, then name the holiday or event itself.

Comunicación

12 Preguntas personales In pairs, ask each other these questions. *Answers will vary.*

1. ¿Cuál es la fecha de hoy?
2. ¿Qué estación es?
3. ¿Te gusta esta estación? ¿Por qué?
4. ¿Qué estación prefieres? ¿Por qué?
5. ¿Prefieres el mar o las montañas? ¿La playa o el campo? ¿Por qué?
6. Cuando estás de vacaciones, ¿qué haces?
7. Cuando haces un viaje, ¿qué te gusta hacer y ver?
8. ¿Piensas ir de vacaciones este verano? ¿Adónde quieres ir? ¿Por qué?
9. ¿Qué deseas ver y qué lugares quieres visitar?
10. ¿Cómo te gusta viajar? ¿En avión? ¿En motocicleta...?

13 Encuesta Your teacher will give you a worksheet. How does the weather affect what you do? Walk around the class and ask your classmates what they prefer or like to do in the weather conditions given. Note their responses on your worksheet. Be sure to personalize your survey by adding a few original questions to the list. Be prepared to report your findings to the class. *Answers will vary.*

CONSULTA

Calor and **frío** can apply to both weather and people. Use **hacer** to describe weather conditions or climate.
(**Hace frío en Santiago.** *It's cold in Santiago.*)
Use **tener** to refer to people.
(**El viajero tiene frío.** *The traveler is cold.*)
See **Estructura 3.4** p. 101.

Tiempo	Actividades
1. Hace mucho calor.	
2. Nieva.	
3. Hace buen tiempo.	
4. Hace fresco.	
5. Llueve.	
6. Está nublado.	
7. Hace mucho frío.	

14 Minidrama With two or three classmates, prepare a skit about people who are on vacation or are planning a vacation. The skit should take place in one of these areas. *Answers will vary.*

1. una agencia de viajes
2. una casa
3. un aeropuerto, una estación de tren o una estación de autobuses
4. un hotel
5. el campo o la playa

Síntesis

15 Un viaje You are planning a trip to Mexico and have many questions about your itinerary on which your partner, a travel agent, will advise you. Your teacher will give you and your partner each a sheet with different instructions for acting out the roles. *Answers will vary.*

12 Expansion Have students write the answers to questions 3–10 on a sheet of paper anonymously. Collect the papers, shuffle them, and redistribute them for pairs to guess who wrote what.

13 Teaching Tip Model the activity by asking volunteers what they enjoy doing in hot weather. Ex: **Cuando hace calor, ¿qué haces? (Nado.)** Then distribute the Communication Activities worksheets.

14 Teaching Tip To simplify, ask the class to brainstorm a list of people and topics that may be encountered in each situation. Write the lists on the board.

14 Expansion Have students judge the skits in categories such as most original, funniest, most realistic, etc.

15 Teaching Tip Divide the class into pairs and distribute the Communication Activities worksheets that correspond to this activity. Give students ten minutes to complete the activity.

15 Expansion Have pairs put together the ideal itinerary for someone else traveling to Mexico, like a classmate, a relative, someone famous, or **el/la profesor(a).**

TEACHING OPTIONS

Pairs Tell students they are part of a scientific expedition to Antarctica (**la Antártida**). Have them write a letter back home about the weather conditions and their activities there. Begin the letter for them by writing **Queridos amigos** on the board.
Game Have each student create a Bingo card with 25 squares (five rows of five). Tell them to write **GRATIS** (*FREE*) in the center square and the name of a different city in each of the other squares. Have them exchange cards. Call out different weather expressions. Ex: **Hace viento.** Students who think this description fits a city or cities on their card should mark the square with the weather condition. In order to win, a student must have marked five squares in a row and be able to give the weather condition for each one. Ex: **Hace mucho viento en Chicago.**

SUPERSITE

Section Goals

In **Fotonovela**, students will:
- receive comprehensible input from free-flowing discourse
- learn functional phrases for talking to hotel personnel and describing a hotel room

Instructional Resources
Cuaderno de actividades, pp. 59–60
e-Cuaderno
Supersite/DVD: *Fotonovela*
Supersite/TRCD/Print:
Fotonovela Videoscript & Translation, Answer Keys

Video Recap: Lección 4

Before doing this **Fotonovela** section, review the previous one with this activity.
1. **¿Qué van a hacer Inés y Javier en su hora libre? (Van a pasear por la ciudad.) 2. ¿Adónde van Maite y Álex? (Van al parque.) 3. ¿Por qué no quiere Maite jugar al fútbol? (Prefiere escribir unas postales.) 4. ¿Qué van a hacer Maite y Álex a las seis? (Van a correr.)**

Video Synopsis The travelers check in at a hotel. **Álex** and **Javier** drop by the girls' cabin. **Inés** and **Javier** decide to explore the city further. **Álex** and **Maite** decide to stay behind. **Maite** notices that **Javier** and **Inés** spend a lot of time together.

Teaching Tips
- Have the class glance over the **Fotonovela** captions and list words and phrases related to tourism and invitations.
- Ask individuals how they are today, using **cansado/a** and **aburrido/a**.
- Ask the class to describe the perfect hotel. Ex: **¿Cómo es una habitación de hotel perfecta?**

Tenemos una reservación.

communication cultures

NATIONAL STANDARDS

Don Francisco y los estudiantes llegan al hotel.

PERSONAJES

MAITE

INÉS

DON FRANCISCO

ÁLEX

JAVIER

EMPLEADA

BOTONES

1

EMPLEADA ¿En qué puedo servirles?

DON FRANCISCO Mire, yo soy Francisco Castillo Moreno y tenemos una reservación a mi nombre.

EMPLEADA Mmm… no veo su nombre aquí. No está.

2

DON FRANCISCO ¿Está segura, señorita? Quizás la reservación está a nombre de la agencia de viajes, Ecuatur.

EMPLEADA Pues sí, aquí está… dos habitaciones dobles y una individual, de la ciento uno a la ciento tres,… todas en las primeras cabañas.

DON FRANCISCO Gracias, señorita. Muy amable.

3

BOTONES Bueno, la habitación ciento dos… Por favor.

6

INÉS Oigan, yo estoy aburrida. ¿Quieren hacer algo?

JAVIER ¿Por qué no vamos a explorar la ciudad un poco más?

INÉS ¡Excelente idea! ¡Vamos!

7

MAITE No, yo no voy. Estoy cansada y quiero descansar un poco porque a las seis voy a correr con Álex.

ÁLEX Y yo quiero escribir un mensaje electrónico antes de ir a correr.

8

JAVIER Pues nosotros estamos listos, ¿verdad, Inés?

INÉS Sí, vamos.

MAITE Adiós.

INÉS Y JAVIER ¡Chau!

recursos

CA pp. 59–60

descubre1.vhlcentral.com Lección 5

TEACHING OPTIONS

Tenemos una reservación Before viewing the **Tenemos una reservación** segment of the *Fotonovela*, ask students to brainstorm a list of things that might happen in an episode in which the characters check into a hotel and decide how to spend the rest of the day. Then play the **Tenemos una**

reservación segment once without sound and have the class create a plot summary based on visual clues. Finally, show the video segment with sound and have the class correct any mistaken guesses and fill in any gaps.

ÁLEX Hola, chicas. ¿Qué están haciendo?

MAITE Estamos descansando.

JAVIER Oigan, no están nada mal las cabañas, ¿verdad?

INÉS Y todo está muy limpio y ordenado.

ÁLEX Sí, es excelente.

MAITE Y las camas son tan cómodas.

ÁLEX Bueno, nos vemos a las seis.

MAITE Sí, hasta luego.

ÁLEX Adiós.

MAITE ¿Inés y Javier? Juntos otra vez.

Expresiones útiles

Talking with hotel personnel

- **¿En qué puedo servirles?**
  How can I help you?
  Tenemos una reservación a mi nombre.
  We have a reservation in my name.
- **Mmm… no veo su nombre. No está.**
  I don't see your name. It's not here.
  ¿Está seguro/a? Quizás/Tal vez está a nombre de Ecuatur.
  Are you sure? Maybe it's under the name of Ecuatur.
- **Aquí está… dos habitaciones dobles y una individual.**
  Here it is, two double rooms and one single.
- **Aquí tienen las llaves.**
  Here are your keys.
  Gracias, señorita. Muy amable.
  Thank you, miss. You're very kind.
- **¿Dónde pongo las maletas?**
  Where do I put the suitcases?
  Allí, encima de la cama.
  There, on the bed.

Describing a hotel

- **No están nada mal las cabañas.**
  The cabins aren't bad at all.
- **Todo está muy limpio y ordenado.**
  Everything is very clean and orderly.
- **Es excelente/estupendo/ fabuloso/fenomenal.**
  It's excellent/stupendous/ fabulous/great.
- **Es increíble/magnífico/ maravilloso/perfecto.**
  It's incredible/magnificent/ marvelous/perfect.
- **Las camas son tan cómodas.**
  The beds are so comfortable.

Talking about how you feel

- **Estoy un poco aburrido/a/ cansado/a.**
  I'm a little bored/tired.

Teaching Tip Work through the scenes that correspond to video stills 1–3 with the class, asking volunteers to play each part. Have students work together in groups of four to read scenes 4–10 aloud.

Expresiones útiles Remind students that **estoy, está**, and **están** are present-tense forms of the verb **estar**, which is often used with adjectives that describe conditions and emotions. Remind students that **es** and **son** are present-tense forms of the verb **ser**, which is often used to describe the characteristics of people and things and to make generalizations. Draw students' attention to video still 4 of the **Fotonovela**. Point out that **están haciendo** and **estamos descansando** are examples of the present progressive, which is used to emphasize an action in progress. Tell students that they will learn more about these concepts in **Estructura 5.2**.

Teaching Tip To challenge students, ask them to create sentences with the unused items from the word bank.

Expansion Have students create a follow-up sentence for each item, based on the **Fotonovela**.

Expansion Tell the class to add **Maite** and the **Botones** to the list of possible answers. Then, give these statements to the class as items 6–8: **6. Yo no voy. Necesito descansar. (Maite) 7. Ah, sí. Aquí tienen ustedes las llaves. (empleada) 8. Bueno, aquí estamos… ésta es su habitación. (botones)**

Expansion After students have determined the correct order, have pairs write sentences that describe what happens chronologically between items.

Teaching Tip To simplify, have individuals prepare by brainstorming phrases for their roles.

Possible Conversation
E1: ¿Puede llevar mis maletas a mi habitación?
E2: Sí, señorita.
E1: El hotel es excelente. Me gusta muchísimo. Todo está muy limpio.
E2: Sí, es un hotel maravilloso. Bueno, aquí estamos… la habitación sesenta y ocho, una habitación individual en el sexto piso.
E1: ¿Está usted seguro? Creo que tengo la habitación número ochenta y seis.
E2: No, señorita. Usted tiene la habitación sesenta y ocho. ¿Dónde pongo las maletas?
E1: Encima de la cama. Gracias.
E2: De nada. Adiós, señorita.

¿Qué pasó?

1 Completar Complete these sentences with the correct term from the word bank.

aburrida	cansada	habitaciones individuales
la agencia de viajes	descansar	hacer las maletas
las camas	habitaciones dobles	las maletas

1. La reservación para el hotel está a nombre de _la agencia de viajes_.
2. Los estudiantes tienen dos _habitaciones dobles_.
3. Maite va a _descansar_ porque está _cansada_.
4. El botones lleva _las maletas_ a las habitaciones.
5. Las habitaciones son buenas y _las camas_ son cómodas.

2 Identificar Identify the person who would make each statement.

EMPLEADA   **ÁLEX**   **DON FRANCISCO**   **JAVIER**   **INÉS**

1. Antes de (*Before*) correr, voy a trabajar en la computadora un poco. Álex
2. Estoy aburrido. Tengo ganas de explorar la ciudad. ¿Vienes tú también? Javier
3. Lo siento mucho, señor, pero su nombre no está en la lista. empleada
4. Creo que la reservación está a mi nombre, señorita. don Francisco
5. Oye, el hotel es maravilloso, ¿no? Las habitaciones están muy limpias. Inés

CONSULTA
The meanings of some adjectives, such as **aburrido**, change depending on whether they are used with **ser** or **estar**. See **Estructura 5.3**, pp. 170–171.

3 Ordenar Place these events in the correct order.

_3_ a. Las chicas descansan en su habitación.
_5_ b. Javier e Inés deciden ir a explorar la ciudad.
_1_ c. Don Francisco habla con la empleada del hotel.
_4_ d. Javier, Maite, Inés y Álex hablan en la habitación de las chicas.
_2_ e. El botones pone las maletas en la cama.

4 Conversar With a partner, use these cues to create a conversation between a bellhop and a hotel guest in Spain. Answers will vary.

Huésped	Botones
Ask the bellhop to carry your suitcases to your room.	Say "yes, sir/ma'am/miss."
Comment that the hotel is excellent and that everything is very clean.	Agree, then point out the guest's room, a single room on the sixth floor.
Ask if the bellhop is sure. You think you have room 86.	Confirm that the guest has room 68. Ask where you should put the suitcases.
Tell the bellhop to put them on the bed and thank him or her.	Say "you're welcome" and "goodbye."

NOTA CULTURAL
As in many other European countries, a large portion of the Spanish population goes on vacation for the entire month of August. Many shops and offices close, particularly in the larger cities. Life resumes its usual pace in September.

TEACHING OPTIONS

Extra Practice Give students some true-false statements about the **Fotonovela**. Have them correct the false items. Ex: **1. Maite quiere ir a explorar la ciudad. (Falso. Maite quiere descansar.) 2. Álex y Maite van a correr a las seis. (Cierto.) 3. Las reservaciones están a nombre de Ecuatur. (Cierto.) 4. Inés no quiere explorar la ciudad porque está cansada. (Falso. Está aburrida y quiere explorar.)**

Small Groups Have students work in groups of four to prepare a skit to present to the class. In the skit, two friends check into a hotel, have a bellhop carry their suitcases to their rooms, and decide what to do for the rest of the day. Students should specify what city they are visiting, describe the hotel and their rooms, and explain what activities they want to do while they are visiting the city.

Pronunciación 🎧 (SUPERSITE)
Spanish b and v

bueno	**vóleibol**	**biblioteca**	**vivir**

There is no difference in pronunciation between the Spanish letters **b** and **v**. However, each letter can be pronounced two different ways, depending on which letters appear next to them.

bonito	**viajar**	**también**	**investigar**

B and **v** are pronounced like the English hard *b* when they appear either as the first letter of a word, at the beginning of a phrase, or after **m** or **n**.

deber	**novio**	**abril**	**cerveza**

In all other positions, **b** and **v** have a softer pronunciation, which has no equivalent in English. Unlike the hard **b**, which is produced by tightly closing the lips and stopping the flow of air, the soft **b** is produced by keeping the lips slightly open.

bola	**vela**	**Caribe**	**declive**

In both pronunciations, there is no difference in sound between **b** and **v**. The English *v* sound, produced by friction between the upper teeth and lower lip, does not exist in Spanish. Instead, the soft **b** comes from friction between the two lips.

Verónica y su esposo cantan boleros.

When **b** or **v** begins a word, its pronunciation depends on the previous word. At the beginning of a phrase or after a word that ends in **m** or **n**, it is pronounced as a hard **b**.

Benito   es de Boquerón   pero vive   en Victoria.

Words that begin with **b** or **v** are pronounced with a soft **b** if they appear immediately after a word that ends in a vowel or any consonant other than **m** or **n**.

Práctica Read these words aloud to practice the **b** and the **v**.

1. hablamos
2. trabajar
3. botones
4. van
5. contabilidad
6. bien
7. doble
8. novia
9. béisbol
10. cabaña
11. llave
12. invierno

No hay mal que por bien no venga.[1]

Hombre prevenido vale por dos.[2]

Oraciones Read these sentences aloud to practice the **b** and the **v**.

1. Vamos a Guaynabo en autobús.
2. Voy de vacaciones a la Isla Culebra.
3. Tengo una habitación individual en el octavo piso.
4. Víctor y Eva van en avión al Caribe.
5. La planta baja es bonita también.
6. ¿Qué vamos a ver en Bayamón?
7. Beatriz, la novia de Víctor, es de Arecibo, Puerto Rico.

Refranes Read these sayings aloud to practice the **b** and the **v**.

2 An ounce of prevention equals a pound of cure.
1 Every cloud has a silver lining.

recursos		
📕 CH p. 67	📕 CA p. 112	(SUPERSITE) descubre1.vhlcentral.com Lección 5

Section Goals

In **Cultura**, students will:

- read about **el Camino Inca**
- learn travel-related terms
- read about Punta del Este, Uruguay
- read about popular vacation destinations in the Spanish-speaking world

---

Instructional Resources
Cuaderno para hispanohablantes, p. 68
Supersite: *Flash cultura*
Videoscript & Translation
Supersite/DVD: *Flash cultura*

En detalle

Antes de leer Ask students what kind of travel interests them. Ex: **¿Te gusta acampar o dormir en un hotel? ¿Adónde prefieres ir: a la ciudad, a las montañas…? Cuando estás de vacaciones, ¿te gusta descansar o vivir una aventura? ¿Visitar museos o explorar ruinas?** Then ask students to predict what a tourist would see and do in the Andes.

Lectura

- Use the Inca Trail map to point out the different highlights mentioned in the reading. Explain that the map shows a four-day hike, but other options are available. Tourists can reach **Machu Picchu** by hikes of varying length or a trip by train and bus. Some opt for a helicopter ride, but those that do will not be able to see **Machu Picchu** from the air. Most tourists use the train and bus route.
- Mention that, as of 2001, it is prohibited to hike the trail without an official guide.

Después de leer Ask students if they would like to participate in a four-day hike of the Inca Trail. Why or why not?

1 Expansion Give students these true-false statements as items 9–10: 9. **Warmiwañusqua** is over 15,000 feet high. (**Falso.** It is 13,800 feet.) 10. The Incas built stone baths for water worship. (**Cierto.**)

EN DETALLE

El Camino Inca

Early in the morning, Larry rises, packs up his campsite, fills his water bottle in a stream, eats a quick breakfast, and begins his day. By tonight, the seven miles he and his group hiked yesterday to a height of 9,700 feet will seem easy; today the hikers will cover seven miles to a height of almost 14,000 feet, all the while carrying fifty-pound backpacks.

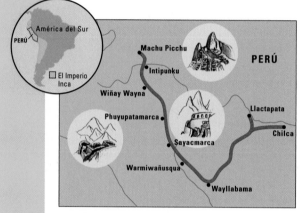

Ruta de cuatro días

While not everyone is cut out for such a rigorous trip, Larry is on the journey of a lifetime: **el Camino Inca.** Between 1438 and 1533, when the vast and powerful **Imperio Incaico** (*Incan Empire*) was at its height, the Incas built an elaborate network of **caminos** (*trails*) that traversed the Andes Mountains and converged on the empire's capital, Cuzco. Today, hundreds of thousands of tourists come to Peru annually to walk the surviving

caminos and enjoy the spectacular landscapes. The most popular trail, **el Camino Inca**, leads from Cuzco to the ancient mountain city of Machu Picchu. Many trekkers opt for a guided four-day itinerary, starting at a suspension bridge over the Urubamba River, and ending at **Intipunku** (*Sun Gate*), the entrance to Machu Picchu. Guides organize campsites and meals for travelers, as well as one night in a hostel en route.

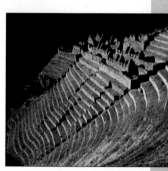

Wiñay Wayna

To preserve **el Camino Inca**, the National Cultural Institute of Peru limits the number of hikers to five hundred per day. Those who make the trip must book in advance and should be in good physical condition in order to endure altitude sickness and the terrain.

Sitios en el Camino Inca

Highlights of a four-day hike along the Inca Trail:

Warmiwañusqua (*Dead Woman's Pass*), at 13,800 feet, hiker's first taste of the Andes' extreme sun and wind

Sayacmarca (*Inaccessible Town*), fortress ruins set on a sheer cliff

Phuyupatamarca (*Town in the Clouds*), an ancient town with stone baths, probably used for water worship

Wiñay Wayna (*Forever Young*), a town named for the pink orchid native to the area, famous for its innovative agricultural terraces which transformed the mountainside into arable land

---

ACTIVIDADES

1 **¿Cierto o falso?** Indicate whether these statements are **cierto** or **falso**. Correct the false statements.

1. **El Imperio Incaico** reached its height between 1438 and 1533. Cierto.
2. Lima was the capital of the Incan Empire. **Falso.** Cuzco was the capital of the Incan Empire.
3. Hikers on **el Camino Inca** must camp out every night. **Falso.** Hikers camp out and also stay in hostels.
4. The Incas invented a series of terraces to make the rough mountain landscape suitable for farming. Cierto.

5. Along **el Camino Inca**, one can see village ruins, native orchids, and agricultural terraces. Cierto.
6. Altitude sickness is one of the challenges faced by hikers on **el Camino Inca**. Cierto.
7. At Sayacmarca, hikers can see Incan pyramids set on a sheer cliff. **Falso.** Hikers can see fortress ruins set on a sheer cliff.
8. Travelers can complete **el Camino Inca** on their own at any time. **Falso.** Travelers hike with a guide and must reserve in advance.

TEACHING OPTIONS

Small Groups If time and resources permit, bring in travel brochures or additional information about the Inca Trail from the Internet. Divide the class into groups of three. Give each group a budget and time frame and ask them to plan an itinerary in detail. Have groups present their itineraries to the class.
Extra Practice Have volunteers line up around the classroom and give each of them an index card with facts, such as location

or distinguishing features, about a particular point on the trail (**Warmiwañusqua, Sayacmarca, Phuyupatamarca, Wiñay Wayna, Machu Picchu,** and **Intipunku**). Then have the rest of the class circulate around the room and ask questions to guess the section of the trail the volunteer represents. Have students use the Inca Trail map as a reference.

ASÍ SE DICE

Viajes y turismo

el asiento del medio, del pasillo, de la ventanilla	center, aisle, window seat
el itinerario	itinerary
media pensión	breakfast and one meal included
el ómnibus (Perú)	el autobús
pensión completa	all meals included
el puente	long weekend (lit., bridge)

EL MUNDO HISPANO

Destinos populares

○ **Las playas del Parque Nacional Manuel Antonio** (Costa Rica) ofrecen° la oportunidad de nadar y luego caminar por el bosque tropical°.

○ **Teotihuacán** (México) Desde la época° de los aztecas, aquí se celebra el equinoccio de primavera en la Pirámide del Sol.

○ **Puerto Chicama** (Perú), con sus olas° de cuatro kilómetros de largo°, es un destino para surfistas expertos.

○ **Tikal** (Guatemala) Aquí puedes ver las maravillas de la selva° y ruinas de la civilización maya.

○ **Las playas de Rincón** (Puerto Rico) Son ideales para descansar y observar las ballenas°.

ofrecen *offer* bosque tropical *rainforest* Desde la época *Since the time* olas *waves* de largo *in length* selva *jungle* ballenas *whales*

PERFIL

Punta del Este

One of South America's largest and most fashionable beach resort towns is Uruguay's **Punta del Este**, a narrow strip of land containing twenty miles of pristine beaches. Its peninsular shape gives it two very different seascapes. **La Playa Mansa**, facing the bay and therefore the more protected side, has calm waters. Here, people practice water sports like swimming, water skiing, windsurfing, and diving. **La Playa Brava**, facing east, receives the Atlantic Ocean's powerful, wave-producing winds, making it popular for surfing, body boarding, and kite surfing. Besides the beaches, posh shopping, and world-famous nightlife, **Punta** offers its 600,000 yearly visitors yacht and fishing clubs, golf courses, and excursions to observe sea lions at the **Isla de Lobos** nature reserve.

SUPERSITE Conexión Internet

¿Cuáles son los sitios más populares para el turismo en Puerto Rico?

Go to descubre1.vhlcentral.com to find more cultural information related to this Cultura section.

ACTIVIDADES

2 **Comprensión** Complete the sentences.

1. En las playas de Rincón puedes ver ___ballenas___.
2. Cerca de 600.000 turistas visitan ___Punta del Este___ cada año.
3. En el avión pides el ___asiento de la ventanilla___ si te gusta ver el paisaje.
4. En Punta del Este, la gente prefiere nadar en la Playa ___Mansa___.
5. El ___ómnibus___ es un medio de transporte en el Perú.

3 **De vacaciones** Spring break is coming up, and you want to go on a short vacation with some friends. Working in a small group, decide where you will go, how you will get there, and what each of you will do. Present your trip to the class.
Answers will vary.

recursos

CH p. 68	descubre1.vhlcentral.com Lección 5

Cultura

5.1 Estar with conditions and emotions

ANTE TODO As you learned in **Lecciones 1** and **2**, the verb **estar** is used to talk about how you feel and to say where people, places, and things are located. **Estar** is also used with adjectives to talk about certain emotional and physical conditions.

▶ Use **estar** with adjectives to describe the physical condition of places and things.

La habitación **está** sucia.
The room is dirty.

La puerta **está** cerrada.
The door is closed.

▶ Use **estar** with adjectives to describe how people feel, both mentally and physically.

Estoy aburrida. ¿Quieren hacer algo?

No, estoy cansada.

▶ **¡Atención!** Two important expressions with **estar** that you can use to talk about conditions and emotions are **estar de buen humor** (*to be in a good mood*) and **estar de mal humor** (*to be in a bad mood*).

Adjectives that describe emotions and conditions

abierto/a	open	**contento/a**	happy; content	**listo/a**	ready
aburrido/a	bored	**desordenado/a**	disorderly	**nervioso/a**	nervous
alegre	happy; joyful	**enamorado/a (de)**	in love (with)	**ocupado/a**	busy
avergonzado/a	embarrassed			**ordenado/a**	orderly
cansado/a	tired	**enojado/a**	mad; angry	**preocupado/a (por)**	worried (about)
cerrado/a	closed	**equivocado/a**	wrong		
cómodo/a	comfortable	**feliz**	happy	**seguro/a**	sure
confundido/a	confused	**limpio/a**	clean	**sucio/a**	dirty
				triste	sad

¡INTÉNTALO!

Provide the present tense forms of **estar**, and choose which adjective best completes the sentence. The first item has been done for you.

1. La biblioteca ___*está*___ (cerrada / nerviosa) los domingos por la noche. *cerrada*
2. Nosotros ___*estamos*___ muy (ocupados / equivocados) todos los lunes. *ocupados*
3. Ellas ___*están*___ (alegres / confundidas) porque tienen vacaciones. *alegres*
4. Javier ___*está*___ (enamorado / ordenado) de Maribel. *enamorado*
5. Diana ___*está*___ (enojada / limpia) con su hermano. *enojada*
6. Yo ___*estoy*___ (nerviosa / abierta) por el viaje. *nerviosa*
7. La habitación siempre ___*está*___ (ordenada / segura) cuando vuelven sus padres. *ordenada*
8. Ustedes no comprenden; ___*están*___ (equivocados / tristes). *equivocados*

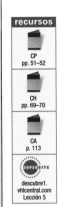

Práctica

1 **¿Cómo están?** Complete Martín's statements about how he and other people are feeling. In the first blank, fill in the correct form of **estar**. In the second blank, fill in the adjective that best fits the context. Some answers may vary.

1. Yo __estoy__ un poco __nervioso__ porque tengo un examen mañana.
2. Mi hermana Patricia __está__ muy __contenta__ porque mañana va a hacer una excursión al campo.
3. Mis hermanos Juan y José salen de la casa a las cinco de la mañana. Por la noche, siempre __están__ muy __cansados__.
4. Mi amigo Ramiro __está__ __enamorado__; su novia se llama Adela.
5. Mi papá y sus colegas __están__ muy __ocupados__ hoy. ¡Hay mucho trabajo!
6. Patricia y yo __estamos__ un poco __preocupados__ por ellos porque trabajan mucho.
7. Mi amiga Mónica __está__ un poco __triste/enojada__ porque sus amigos no pueden salir esta noche.
8. Esta clase no es muy interesante. ¿Tú __estás__ __aburrido/a__ también?

2 **Describir** Describe these people and places. Answers will vary.

1. Anabela
Está contenta.

2. Juan y Luisa
Están enojados.

3. la habitación de Teresa
Está ordenada/limpia.

4. la habitación de César
Está desordenada/sucia.

Comunicación

3 **Situaciones** With a partner, use **estar** to talk about how you feel in these situations.
Answers will vary.
1. Cuando hace sol…
2. Cuando tomas un examen…
3. Cuando estás de vacaciones…
4. Cuando tienes mucho trabajo…
5. Cuando viajas en avión…
6. Cuando estás con la familia…
7. Cuando estás en la clase de español…
8. Cuando ves una película con tu actor/actriz favorito/a…

5.2 The present progressive

ANTE TODO Both Spanish and English use the present progressive, which consists of the present tense of the verb *to be* and the present participle (the *-ing* form in English).

Hola, chicas. ¿Qué están haciendo?

Estamos descansando.

▶ Form the present progressive with the present tense of **estar** and a present participle.

FORM OF **ESTAR** + PRESENT PARTICIPLE		FORM OF **ESTAR** + PRESENT PARTICIPLE	
Estoy	**pescando.**	**Estamos**	**comiendo.**
I am	*fishing.*	*We are*	*eating.*

▶ The present participle of regular **–ar**, **–er**, and **–ir** verbs is formed as follows:

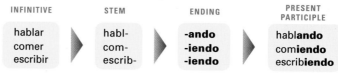

INFINITIVE	STEM	ENDING	PRESENT PARTICIPLE
hablar	habl-	-ando	hablando
comer	com-	-iendo	comiendo
escribir	escrib-	-iendo	escribiendo

▶ **¡Atención!** When the stem of an **–er** or **–ir** verb ends in a vowel, the present participle ends in **–yendo**.

INFINITIVE	STEM	ENDING	PRESENT PARTICIPLE
leer	le-	-yendo	leyendo
oír	o-	-yendo	oyendo
traer	tra-	-yendo	trayendo

▶ **Ir**, **poder**, and **venir** have irregular present participles (**yendo**, **pudiendo**, **viniendo**). Several other verbs have irregular present participles that you will need to learn.

▶ **–Ir** stem-changing verbs have a stem change in the present participle.

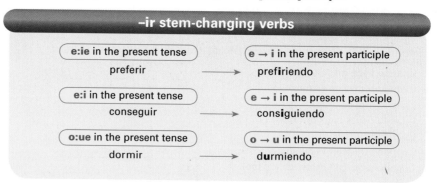

–ir stem-changing verbs

e:ie in the present tense	e → i in the present participle
preferir	prefiriendo

e:i in the present tense	e → i in the present participle
conseguir	consiguiendo

o:ue in the present tense	o → u in the present participle
dormir	durmiendo

Section Goals

In **Estructura 5.2**, students will learn:
• the present progressive of regular and irregular verbs
• the present progressive versus the simple present tense in Spanish

Instructional Resources
Cuaderno de práctica, p. 53
Cuaderno para hispanohablantes, pp. 71–72
Cuaderno de actividades, pp. 25–26, 114
e-Cuaderno
Supersite: Audio Activity MP3 Audio Files
Supersite/TRCD/Print: *PowerPoints* (**Lección 5 Estructura** Presentation, Overhead #25); Communication Activities, Audio Activity Script, Answer Keys
Audio Activity CD

Teaching Tips

• Have students read the caption under video still 4 on page 159. Focus attention on **estar** + [*present participle*] to express what is going on at that moment. Then have students describe what is happening in the rest of the episode.
• Use regular verbs to ask questions about things students are not doing. Ex: **¿Estás comiendo pizza? (No, no estoy comiendo pizza.)**
• Explain the formation of the present progressive, writing examples on the board.
• Add a visual aspect to this grammar presentation. Use photos to elicit sentences with the present progressive. Ex: **¿Qué está haciendo el hombre alto? (Está sacando fotos.)** Include present participles ending in **–yendo** as well as those with stem changes.
• Point out that the present progressive is rarely used with the verbs **ir, poder**, and **venir** since they already imply an action in progress.

TEACHING OPTIONS

TPR Divide the class into three groups. Appoint leaders and give them a list of verbs. Leaders call out a verb and a subject (Ex: **seguir/yo**), then toss a foam or paper ball to someone in the group. That student says the appropriate present progressive form of the verb (Ex: **estoy siguiendo**) and tosses the ball back. Leaders should call out all verbs on the list and toss the ball to every member of the group.

TPR Play charades. In groups of four, have students take turns miming actions for the rest of the group to guess. Ex: Student pretends to read a newspaper. (**Estás leyendo el periódico.**) For incorrect guesses, the student should respond negatively. Ex: **No, no estoy estudiando.**

COMPARE & CONTRAST

The use of the present progressive is much more restricted in Spanish than in English. In Spanish, the present progressive is mainly used to emphasize that an action is in progress at the time of speaking.

Inés **está escuchando** música latina **ahora mismo**.
Inés is listening to Latin music right now.

Álex y su amigo **todavía están jugando** al fútbol.
Álex and his friend are still playing soccer.

In English, the present progressive is often used to talk about situations and actions that occur over an extended period of time or in the future. In Spanish, the simple present tense is often used instead.

Javier **estudia** computación este semestre.
Javier is studying computer science this semester.

Inés y Maite **salen** mañana para los Estados Unidos.
Inés and Maite are leaving tomorrow for the United States.

Estamos pensando en lo mismo:

su **F**uturo

Su asesor para ganar
FIDUCOLOMBIA
Sociedad Fiduciaria S.A.

¡INTÉNTALO! Create complete sentences by putting the verbs in the present progressive. The first item has been done for you.

1. mis amigos / descansar en la playa _Mis amigos están descansando en la playa._
2. nosotros / practicar deportes _Estamos practicando deportes._
3. Carmen / comer en casa _Carmen está comiendo en casa._
4. nuestro equipo / ganar el partido _Nuestro equipo está ganando el partido._
5. yo / leer el periódico _Estoy leyendo el periódico._
6. él / pensar comprar una bicicleta _Está pensando comprar una bicicleta._
7. ustedes / jugar a las cartas _Ustedes están jugando a las cartas._
8. José y Francisco / dormir _José y Francisco están durmiendo._
9. Marisa / leer correo electrónico _Marisa está leyendo correo electrónico._
10. yo / preparar sándwiches _Estoy preparando sándwiches._
11. Carlos / tomar fotos _Carlos está tomando fotos._
12. ¿dormir / tú? _¿Estás durmiendo?_

Teaching Tips
- Discuss each point in the **Compare & Contrast** box.
- Write these statements on the board. Ask students if they would use the present or the present progressive in Spanish for each item. 1. I'm going on vacation tomorrow. 2. She's packing her suitcase right now. 3. They are fishing in Puerto Rico this week. 4. Roberto is still working. Then ask students to translate the items. (1. **Voy de vacaciones mañana. 2. Está haciendo la maleta ahora mismo. 3. Pescan en Puerto Rico esta semana. 4. Roberto todavía está trabajando.**)
- In this lesson, students learn **todavía** to mean *still* when used with the present progressive tense. You may want to point out that **todavía** also means *yet*. They will be able to use that meaning in later lessons as they learn the past tenses.
- Have students rewrite the sentences in the **¡Inténtalo!** activity using the simple present. Ask volunteers to explain how the sentences change depending on whether the verb is in the present progressive or the simple present.

TEACHING OPTIONS

Pairs Have students write eight sentences in Spanish modeled after the examples in the **Compare & Contrast** box. There should be two sentences modeled after each example. Ask students to replace the verbs with blanks. Then, have students exchange papers with a partner and complete the sentences.

Extra Practice For homework, ask students to find five photos from a magazine or create five simple drawings of people performing different activities. For each image, have them write one sentence telling what the people are doing and one describing how they feel. Ex: **Juan está trabajando. Está cansado.**

Práctica

1 Expansion Ask students comprehension questions that elicit the present progressive. Ex: ¿Quién está buscando información? (Marta y José Luis están buscando información.) ¿Qué información están buscando? (Están buscando información sobre San Juan.)

1 Completar Alfredo's Spanish class is preparing to travel to Puerto Rico. Use the present progressive of the verb in parentheses to complete Alfredo's description of what everyone is doing.

1. Yo _estoy investigando_ (investigar) la situación política de la isla (*island*).
2. La esposa del profesor _está haciendo_ (hacer) las maletas.
3. Marta y José Luis _están buscando_ (buscar) información sobre San Juan en Internet.
4. Enrique y yo _estamos leyendo_ (leer) un correo electrónico de nuestro amigo puertorriqueño.
5. Javier _está aprendiendo_ (aprender) mucho sobre la cultura puertorriqueña.
6. Y tú _estás practicando_ (practicar) el español, ¿verdad?

2 Teaching Tip Before starting the activity, show *Overhead PowerPoint #25* and ask students questions about each drawing to elicit a description of what they see. Ex: ¿Quién está en el dibujo número 5? (Samuel está en el dibujo.) ¿Dónde está Samuel? (Está en la playa.) ¿Qué más ven en el dibujo? (Vemos una silla y el mar.)

2 ¿Qué están haciendo? María and her friends are vacationing at a resort in San Juan, Puerto Rico. Complete her description of what everyone is doing right now.

CONSULTA

For more information about Puerto Rico, see **Panorama**, pp. 186–187.

1. Yo
estoy escribiendo una carta.

2. Javier
está buceando en el mar.

3. Alejandra y Rebeca
están jugando a las cartas.

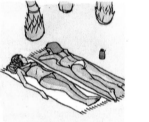
4. Celia y yo
estamos tomando el sol.

5. Samuel
está escuchando música.

6. Lorenzo
está durmiendo.

3 Teaching Tip To simplify, first read through the names in column A as a class. Point out the profession clues in the **Ayuda** box, then guide students in matching each name with an infinitive. Finally, have students form sentences.

3 Expansion Have students choose five more celebrities and write what they are doing at this moment.

3 Personajes famosos Say what these celebrities are doing right now, using the cues provided.

Answers will vary.

modelo

Celine Dion: *Celine Dion está cantando una canción ahora mismo.*

A		B	
John Grisham	Avril Lavigne	bailar	hablar
Martha Stewart	Bode Miller	cantar	hacer
James Cameron	Las New York Rockettes	correr	jugar
Venus y Serena	¿?	escribir	¿?
Williams	¿?	esquiar	¿?
Tiger Woods			

AYUDA

John Grisham: **novelas**
Martha Stewart: **televisión, negocios** (*business*)
James Cameron: **cine**
Venus y Serena Williams: **tenis**
Tiger Woods: **golf**
Avril Lavigne: **canciones**
Bode Miller: **esquí**
Las New York Rockettes: **baile**

TEACHING OPTIONS

Pairs Have students bring in personal photos (or magazine photos) from a vacation. Ask them to describe the photos to a partner. Students should explain what the weather is like, who is in the photo, what they are doing, and where they are.
Game Have the class form a circle. Appoint one student to be the starter, who will begin play by miming an action (Ex: eating) and saying what he or she is doing (Ex: **Estoy comiendo.**). In a

clockwise direction around the circle, the next student mimes the same action, says what that person is doing (____ **está comiendo.**), and then mimes and states a different action (Ex: sleeping/**Estoy durmiendo.**). Have students continue the chain until it breaks, in which case the starter changes the direction to counterclockwise. Have students see how long the chain can get in three minutes.

Comunicación

4 **Preguntar** With a partner, take turns asking each other what you are doing at these times.
Answers will vary.

> **modelo**
>
> **Estudiante 1:** ¡Hola, Andrés! Son las ocho de la mañana. ¿Qué estás haciendo?
> **Estudiante 2:** Estoy desayunando.

1. 5:00 a.m.
2. 9:30 a.m.
3. 11:00 a.m.
4. 12:00 p.m.
5. 2:00 p.m.
6. 5:00 p.m.
7. 9:00 p.m.
8. 11:30 p.m.

5 **Describir** Work with a partner and use the present progressive to describe what is going
on in this Spanish beach scene. Answers will vary.

6 **Conversar** Imagine that you and a classmate are each babysitting a group of children. With a
partner, prepare a telephone conversation using these cues. Be creative and add further comments.
Answers will vary.

Estudiante 1	**Estudiante 2**
Say hello and ask what the kids are doing.	Say hello and tell your partner that two of your kids are doing their homework. Then ask what the kids at his/her house are doing.
Tell your partner that two of your kids are running and dancing in the house.	Tell your partner that one of the kids is reading.
Tell your partner that you are tired and that two of your kids are watching TV and eating pizza.	Tell your partner that one of the kids is sleeping.
Tell your partner you have to go; the kids are playing soccer in the house.	Say goodbye and good luck (**¡Buena suerte!**).

Síntesis

recursos

CA
pp. 25–26

7 **¿Qué están haciendo?** A group of classmates is traveling to San Juan, Puerto Rico for a
week-long Spanish immersion program. The participants are running late before the flight, and you
and your partner must locate them. Your teacher will give you and your partner different handouts
that will help you do this. Answers will vary.

---

4 **Teaching Tips**
- To simplify, first have students outline their daily activities and what time they do them.
- Remind students to use **a la(s)** when expressing time.

5 **Teaching Tip** Show *Overhead PowerPoint #25* and have students do the activity with their books closed.

5 **Expansion** In pairs, have students write a conversation between two or more of the people in the drawing. Conversations should consist of at least three exchanges.

6 **Teaching Tip** To simplify, before beginning their conversation, have students prepare for their roles by brainstorming two lists: one with verbs that describe what the children are doing at home and the other with adjectives that describe how the babysitter feels.

6 **Expansion** Ask pairs to tell each other what the parents of the two sets of children are doing.

7 **Teaching Tip** Divide the class into pairs and distribute the Communication Activities worksheets that correspond to this activity. Give students ten minutes to complete the activity.

7 **Expansion** Have students work in pairs to say what each program participant is doing in flight. Ex: **Pedro está leyendo una novela.**

Section Goal

In **Estructura 5.3**, students will review and compare the uses of **ser** and **estar**.

Instructional Resources
Cuaderno de práctica,
pp. 54–55
Cuaderno para hispanohablantes, pp. 73–74
Cuaderno de actividades, p. 115
e-Cuaderno
Supersite: Audio Activity MP3
Audio Files
Supersite/TRCD/Print:
PowerPoints (**Lección 5**
Estructura Presentation,
Overhead #26); Audio Activity
Script, Answer Keys
Audio Activity CD

Teaching Tips

• Have pairs brainstorm as many uses of **ser** with examples as they can. Compile a list on the board, and repeat for **estar**.

• Divide the board or an overhead transparency into two columns. In column one, write sentences using **ser** and **estar** in random order (Ex: **Álex es de México.**). In column two, write the uses of **ser** and **estar** taught so far, also in random order (Ex: place of origin). Ask volunteers to match the sentence with its corresponding use.

• Write cloze sentences on the board. Ask students to supply the correct form of **ser** or **estar**. Ex: **Mi casa ____ lejos de aquí.** (estar, location; **está**) If either **ser** or **estar** could be used, ask students to explain how the meaning of the sentence would change.

• Contrast uses of **ser** and **estar** by talking about celebrities. Ex: **Nelly Furtado es canadiense y su familia es de origen portugués. Es bonita y delgada. Es cantante. Ella está en los Estados Unidos ahora. Está haciendo una gira de conciertos.** Pause after each sentence and have students identify the use(s). Then have volunteers create sentences about other famous people.

(5.3) Ser and estar SUPERSITE

ANTE TODO You have already learned that **ser** and **estar** both mean *to be* but are used for different purposes. These charts summarize the key differences in usage between **ser** and **estar**.

Uses of ser

1. Nationality and place of origin	Martín **es** argentino. /chino **Es** de Buenos Aires.
2. Profession or occupation	Adela **es** agente de viajes. Francisco **es** médico.
3. Characteristics of people and things . . .	José y Clara **son** simpáticos. El clima de Puerto Rico **es** agradable.
4. Generalizations.	¡**Es** fabuloso viajar! **Es** difícil estudiar a la una de la mañana.
5. Possession	**Es** la pluma de Maite. **Son** las llaves de don Francisco.
6. What something is made of	La bicicleta **es** de metal. Los pasajes **son** de papel.
7. Time and date	Hoy **es** martes. **Son** las dos. Hoy **es** el primero de julio.
8. Where or when an event takes place. .	El partido **es** en el estadio Santa Fe. La conferencia **es** a las siete.

¡ATENCIÓN!

Note that **de** is generally used after **ser** to express not only origin (**Es de Buenos Aires.**) and possession (**Es la pluma de Maite.**), but also what material something is made of (**La bicicleta es de metal.**).

Soy Francisco Castillo Moreno. Yo soy de la agencia Ecuatur.

Su nombre no está en mi lista.

Uses of estar

1. Location or spatial relationships	El aeropuerto **está** lejos de la ciudad. Tu habitación **está** en el tercer piso.
2. Health	¿Cómo **estás**? **Estoy** bien, gracias.
3. Physical states and conditions	El profesor **está** ocupado. Las ventanas **están** abiertas.
4. Emotional states	Marisa **está** feliz hoy. **Estoy** muy enojado con Javier.
5. Certain weather expressions	**Está** lloviendo. **Está** nublado.
6. Ongoing actions (progressive tenses) . .	**Estamos** estudiando para un examen. Ana **está** leyendo una novela.

TEACHING OPTIONS

Extra Practice Add an auditory aspect to this grammar presentation. Call out sentences containing forms of **ser** or **estar**. Ask students to identify the use of the verb.
Heritage Speakers Ask heritage speakers to write a postcard to a friend or family member about a vacation in Puerto Rico, incorporating as many of the uses of **ser** and **estar** as they can.

TPR Divide the class into two teams. Call out a use of **ser** or **estar**. The first member of each team runs to the board and writes a sample sentence. The first student to finish a sentence correctly earns a point for his or her team. Practice all uses of each verb and make sure each team member has at least two turns. Then tally the points to see which team wins.

Ser and estar with adjectives

▶ With many descriptive adjectives, **ser** and **estar** can both be used, but the meaning will change.

Juan **es** delgado.
Juan is thin.

Juan **está** más delgado hoy.
Juan looks thinner today.

Ana **es** nerviosa.
Ana is a nervous person.

Ana **está** nerviosa por el examen.
Ana is nervous because of the exam.

▶ In the examples above, the statements with **ser** are general observations about the inherent qualities of Juan and Ana. The statements with **estar** describe conditions that are variable.

▶ Here are some adjectives that change in meaning when used with **ser** and **estar**.

With ser	With estar
El chico **es listo**.	El chico **está listo**.
The boy is smart.	*The boy is ready.*
La profesora **es mala**.	La profesora **está mala**.
The professor is bad.	*The professor is sick.*
Jaime **es aburrido**.	Jaime **está aburrido**.
Jaime is boring.	*Jaime is bored.*
Las peras **son verdes**.	Las peras **están verdes**.
The pears are green.	*The pears are not ripe.*
El gato **es muy vivo**.	El gato **está vivo**.
The cat is very lively.	*The cat is alive.*
El puente **es seguro**.	Él no **está seguro**.
The bridge is safe.	*He's not sure.*

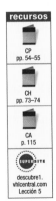

recursos

CP
pp. 54–55

CH
pp. 73–74

CA
p. 115

SUPERSITE
descubre1.
vhlcentral.com
Lección 5

¡INTÉNTALO! Form complete sentences by using the correct form of **ser** or **estar** and making any other necessary changes. The first item has been done for you.

1. Alejandra / cansado
   Alejandra está cansada.

2. ellos / pelirrojo
   Ellos son pelirrojos.

3. Carmen / alto
   Carmen es alta.

4. yo / la clase de español
   Estoy en la clase de español.

5. película / a las once
   La película es a las once.

6. hoy / viernes
   Hoy es viernes.

7. nosotras / enojado
   Nosotras estamos enojadas.

8. Antonio / médico
   Antonio es médico.

9. Romeo y Julieta / enamorado
   Romeo y Julieta están enamorados.

10. libros / de Ana
    Los libros son de Ana.

11. Marisa y Juan / estudiando
    Marisa y Juan están estudiando.

12. partido de baloncesto / gimnasio
    El partido de baloncesto es en el gimnasio.

Práctica

1 **¿Ser o estar?** Indicate whether each adjective takes **ser** or **estar**. ¡Ojo! Three of them can take both verbs.

	ser	estar			ser	estar
1. delgada	☑	☑	5. seguro		☑	☑
2. canadiense	☑	○	6. enojada		○	☑
3. enamorado	○	☑	7. importante		☑	○
4. lista	☑	☑	8. avergonzada		○	☑

2 **Completar** Complete this conversation with the appropriate forms of **ser** and **estar**.

EDUARDO ¡Hola, Ceci! ¿Cómo (1)___estás___?

CECILIA Hola, Eduardo. Bien, gracias. ¡Qué guapo (2)___estás___ hoy!

EDUARDO Gracias. (3)___Eres___ muy amable. Oye, ¿qué (4)___estás___ haciendo? (5)¿___Estás___ ocupada?

CECILIA No, sólo le (6)___estoy___ escribiendo una carta a mi prima Pilar.

EDUARDO ¿De dónde (7)___es___ ella?

CECILIA Pilar (8)___es___ del Ecuador. Su papá (9)___es___ médico en Quito. Pero ahora Pilar y su familia (10)___están___ de vacaciones en Ponce, Puerto Rico.

EDUARDO Y… ¿cómo (11)___es___ Pilar?

CECILIA (12)___Es___ muy lista. Y también (13)___es___ alta, rubia y muy bonita.

3 **Describir** With a partner, describe the people in the drawing. Your descriptions should answer the questions provided. Answers will vary.

1. ¿Quiénes son las personas?
2. ¿Dónde están?
3. ¿Cómo son?
4. ¿Cómo están?
5. ¿Qué están haciendo?
6. ¿Qué estación es?
7. ¿Qué tiempo hace?
8. ¿Quiénes están de vacaciones?

---

1 Teaching Tip Have students identify the use(s) of **ser** or **estar** for each item.

1 Expansion To challenge students, ask them to use each adjective in a sentence. If the adjective can take both verbs, have them provide two sentences.

2 Teaching Tip To simplify, ask students to point out context clues that will help them determine whether to use **ser** or **estar**. Ex: The word **hoy** in line 2 suggests that **guapo** is a variable physical state.

2 Expansion Have pairs write a continuation of the conversation and then present it to the class.

3 Teaching Tip Show *Overhead PowerPoint #26* and have students do the activity with their books closed after they have read through the questions.

3 Expansion Add another visual aspect to this grammar practice. Bring in photos or magazine pictures that show many different people performing a variety of activities. Have students use **ser** and **estar** to describe the scenes.

TEACHING OPTIONS

Extra Practice Have students write a paragraph about a close friend, including the person's physical appearance, general disposition, place of birth, birthday, and where the friend is now. Ask volunteers to share their descriptions with the class.

Pairs Ask pairs to role-play this scenario: Student A is at the beach with some friends while Student B is at home. Student A calls Student B, trying to convince him or her to come to the beach. Students should try to employ as many uses of **ser** and **estar** in their scenario as possible. After students act out the scene once, have them switch roles.

Comunicación

4 **Describir** With a classmate, take turns describing these people. First mention where each person is from. Then describe what each person is like, how each person is feeling, and what he or she is doing right now. Answers will vary.

> **modelo**
> tu compañero/a de clase
> Mi compañera de clase es de San Juan, Puerto Rico. Es muy inteligente.
> Está cansada pero está estudiando porque tiene un examen.

1. tu mejor (*best*) amigo/a
2. tus padres
3. tu profesor(a) favorito/a
4. tu vecino/a
5. tu primo/a favorito/a
6. tus abuelos

5 **Adivinar** Describe a celebrity to your partner using these questions as a guide. Don't mention the celebrity's name. Can your partner guess who you are describing? Answers will vary.

1. ¿Cómo es?
2. ¿Cómo está?
3. ¿De dónde es?
4. ¿Dónde está?
5. ¿Qué está haciendo?
6. ¿Cuál es su profesión?

6 **En el aeropuerto** In small groups, take turns using **ser** and **estar** to describe this scene at Luis Muñoz Marín International Airport. What do the people in the picture look like? How are they feeling? What are they doing? Answers will vary.

Síntesis

7 **Conversación** You and your partner are two of the characters in the drawing in **Actividad 6**. After boarding, you discover that you are sitting next to each other and must make conversation. Act out what you would say to your fellow passenger. Choose one of the pairs below or pick your own. Answers will vary.

1. Señor Villa y Elena
2. Señorita Esquivel y la señora Limón
3. Señora Villa y Luz
4. Emilio y Elena

---

4 Expansion Have pairs select two descriptions to present to the class.

5 Teaching Tip Model the activity for the class. In order to create ambiguity, you may want to tell students to use **una persona** to answer items 1, 2, and 6. Ex: **Es una persona alta…**

6 Teaching Tip Ask groups to choose a leader to moderate the activity, a secretary to record the group's description, and a proofreader to check that the written description is accurate. Then show *Overhead PowerPoint #26*. All students should take turns adding one sentence at a time to the group's description.

6 Expansion Have students pick one of the individuals pictured and write a one-paragraph description, employing as many different uses of **ser** and **estar** as possible.

7 Teaching Tips
- To simplify, first have students create a character description for the person they will be playing. Then, as a class, brainstorm topics of conversation.
- Make sure that students use **ser** and **estar**, the present progressive, and stem-changing verbs in their conversation, as well as vacation-, pastime-, and family-related vocabulary.

The Affective Dimension Encourage students to consider pair and group activities as a cooperative venture in which group members support and encourage each other.

TEACHING OPTIONS

Heritage Speakers Have heritage speakers write a television commercial for a vacation resort in the Spanish-speaking world. Ask them to employ as many uses of **ser** and **estar** as they can. If possible, after they have written the commercial, have them videotape it to show to the class.

TPR Call on a volunteer and whisper the name of a celebrity in his or her ear. The volunteer mimes actions, acts out characteristics, and uses props to elicit descriptions from the class. Ex: The volunteer points to the U.S. on a map. (**Es de los Estados Unidos.**) He or she then indicates a short, thin man. (**Es un hombre bajo y delgado.**) He or she mimes riding a bicycle. (**Está paseando en bicicleta. ¿Es Lance Armstrong?**)

5.4 Direct object nouns and pronouns

SUBJECT	VERB	DIRECT OBJECT NOUN
Álex y Javier	están tomando	fotos.
Álex and Javier	*are taking*	*photos.*

▶ A direct object noun receives the action of the verb directly and generally follows the verb. In the example above, the direct object noun answers the question *What are Álex and Javier taking?*

▶ When a direct object noun in Spanish is a person or a pet, it is preceded by the word **a**. This is called the personal **a**; there is no English equivalent for this construction.

Don Francisco visita **a** la señora Ramos.   Don Francisco visita el Hotel Prado.
Don Francisco is visiting Mrs. Ramos.   *Don Francisco is visiting the Hotel Prado.*

▶ In the first sentence above, the personal **a** is required because the direct object is a person. In the second sentence, the personal **a** is not required because the direct object is a place, not a person.

¿Dónde pongo las maletas?

Puede ponerlas encima de la cama.

Hay muchos lugares interesantes por aquí. ¿Quieren ir a verlos?

Direct object pronouns

SINGULAR		PLURAL	
me	*me*	**nos**	*us*
te	*you* (fam.)	**os**	*you* (fam.)
lo	*you* (m., form.)	**los**	*you* (m., form.)
	him; it (m.)		*them* (m.)
la	*you* (f., form.)	**las**	*you* (f., form.)
	her; it (f.)		*them* (f.)

▶ Direct object pronouns are words that replace direct object nouns. Like English, Spanish sometimes uses a direct object pronoun to avoid repeating a noun already mentioned.

	DIRECT OBJECT			DIRECT OBJECT PRONOUN	
Maribel hace	las maletas.	▶	Maribel	las	hace.
Felipe compra	el sombrero.		Felipe	lo	compra.
Vicky tiene	la llave.		Vicky	la	tiene.

Section Goals

In **Estructura 5.4**, students will study:
• direct object nouns
• the personal **a**
• direct object pronouns

Instructional Resources
Cuaderno de práctica, p. 56
Cuaderno para hispanohablantes, pp. 75–76
Cuaderno de actividades, p.116
e-Cuaderno
Supersite: Audio Activity MP3 Audio Files
Supersite/TRCD/Print: PowerPoints (Lección 5 **Estructura** Presentation); Audio Activity Script, Answer Keys
Audio Activity CD

Teaching Tips
• Ask individuals questions to elicit the personal a: **¿Visitas a tu abuela los fines de semana? ¿Llamas a tu amigo los sábados?**
• Write these sentences on the board: **—¿Quién tiene el pasaporte? —Juan lo tiene.** Underline **pasaporte** and explain that it is a direct object noun. Then underline **lo** and explain that it is the masculine singular direct object pronoun. Translate both sentences. Continue with: **—¿Quién saca fotos? —Simón las saca. —¿Quién tiene la llave? —Pilar la tiene.**
• Read this exchange aloud: **—¿Haces las maletas? —No, no hago las maletas. —¿Por qué no haces las maletas? —No hago las maletas porque las maletas no están aquí.** Ask students if the exchange sounds natural to them. Then write it on the board and ask students to use direct object pronouns to avoid repetition.
• Ask questions to elicit third-person direct object pronouns. Ex: **¿Quién ve el lápiz de Marcos? ¿Quién quiere este diccionario?**

TEACHING OPTIONS

TPR Call out a series of sentences with direct object nouns, some of which require the personal **a** and some of which do not. Ex: **Visito muchos museos. Visito a mis tíos.** Have students raise their hands if the personal **a** is used.
Extra Practice Write six sentences on the board that have direct object nouns. Use two verbs in the simple present tense,

two in the present progressive, and two using **ir a** + [*infinitive*]. Draw a line through the direct objects as students call them out. Have students state which pronouns to write to replace them. Then, draw an arrow from each pronoun to where it goes in the sentence, as indicated by students.

▶ In affirmative sentences, direct object pronouns generally appear before the conjugated verb. In negative sentences, the pronoun is placed between the word **no** and the verb.

Adela practica **el tenis**.
Adela **lo** practica.

Carmen compra **los pasajes**.
Carmen **los** compra.

Gabriela no tiene **las llaves**.
Gabriela **no las** tiene.

Diego no hace **las maletas**.
Diego **no las** hace.

▶ When the verb is an infinitive construction, such as **ir a** + [*infinitive*], the direct object pronoun can be placed before the conjugated form or attached to the infinitive.

Ellos van a escribir **unas postales**.
— Ellos **las** van a escribir.
— Ellos van a escribir**las**.

Lidia quiere ver **una película**.
— Lidia **la** quiere ver.
— Lidia quiere ver**la**.

▶ When the verb is in the present progressive, the direct object pronoun can be placed before the conjugated form or attached to the present participle. **¡Atención!** When a direct object pronoun is attached to the present participle, an accent mark is added to maintain the proper stress.

Gerardo está leyendo **la lección**.
— Gerardo **la** está leyendo.
— Gerardo está leyéndo**la**.

Toni está mirando **el partido**.
— Toni **lo** está mirando.
— Toni está mirándo**lo**.

 ¡INTÉNTALO!   Choose the correct direct object pronoun for each sentence. The first one has been done for you.

1. Tienes el libro de español. c
   a. La tienes.   b. Los tienes.   c. Lo tienes.
2. Voy a ver el partido de baloncesto. a
   a. Voy a verlo.   b. Voy a verte.   c. Voy a vernos.
3. El artista quiere dibujar a Luisa con su mamá. c
   a. Quiere dibujarme.   b. Quiere dibujarla.   c. Quiere dibujarlas.
4. Marcos busca la llave. b
   a. Me busca.   b. La busca.   c. Las busca.
5. Rita me lleva al aeropuerto y también lleva a Tomás. a
   a. Nos lleva.   b. Las lleva.   c. Te lleva.
6. Puedo oír a Gerardo y a Miguel. b
   a. Puedo oírte.   b. Puedo oírlos.   c. Puedo oírlo.
7. Quieren estudiar la gramática. c
   a. Quieren estudiarnos.   b. Quieren estudiarlo.   c. Quieren estudiarla.
8. ¿Practicas los verbos irregulares? a
   a. ¿Los practicas?   b. ¿Las practicas?   c. ¿Lo practicas?
9. Ignacio ve la película. a
   a. La ve.   b. Lo ve.   c. Las ve.
10. Sandra va a invitar a Mario a la excursión. También me va a invitar a mí. c
    a. Los va a invitar.   b. Lo va a invitar.   c. Nos va a invitar.

recursos

CP
p. 56

CH
p. 75–76

CA
p. 116

SUPERSITE
descubre1.
vhlcentral.com
Lección 5

Teaching Tips

- Elicit first- and second-person direct object pronouns by asking questions first of individual students and then groups of students. Ex: **¿Quién te invita a bailar con frecuencia? (Mi novio me invita a bailar con frecuencia.) ¿Quién te comprende? (Mi amigo me comprende.)**
- Ask questions directed at the class as a whole to elicit first-person plural direct object pronouns. Ex: **¿Quiénes los llaman los fines de semana? (Nuestros abuelos nos llaman.) ¿Quiénes los esperan después de la clase? (Los amigos nos esperan.)**
- Add a visual aspect to this grammar presentation. Use magazine pictures to practice the third-person direct object pronouns with infinitives and the present progressive. Ex: **¿Quién está practicando tenis? (Roger Federer lo está practicando./Roger Federer está practicándolo.) ¿Quién va a mirar la televisión? (El hombre pelirrojo la va a mirar./El hombre pelirrojo va a mirarla.)**
- Point out that the direct object pronoun **los** refers to both masculine and mixed groups. **Las** refers only to feminine groups.

TEACHING OPTIONS

Large Group Make a list of 20 questions requiring direct object pronouns in the answer. Arrange students in two concentric circles. Students in the center circle ask questions from the list to those in the outer circle, who answer them. When you say stop (**¡Paren!**), The outer circle moves one person to the right and the questions begin again. Continue for five minutes, then have the students in the outer circle ask the questions.

Pairs Have students write ten sentences using direct object nouns. Their sentences should also include a mixture of verbs in the present progressive, simple present, and **ir a** + [*infinitive*]. Ask students to exchange their sentences with a partner, who will rewrite them using direct object pronouns. Students should check their partner's work.

Práctica SUPERSITE

1 Teaching Tip To simplify, ask individual students to identify the direct object in each sentence before beginning the activity.

1 Sustitución Señor Vega's class is planning a trip to Costa Rica. Describe their preparations by changing the direct object nouns into direct object pronouns.

> **modelo**
> La profesora Vega tiene su pasaporte.
> La profesora Vega lo tiene.

1. Gustavo y Héctor confirman las reservaciones. Gustavo y Héctor las confirman.
2. Nosotros leemos los folletos (*brochures*). Nosotros los leemos.
3. Ana María estudia el mapa. Ana María lo estudia.
4. Yo aprendo los nombres de los monumentos de San José. Yo los aprendo.
5. Alicia escucha a la profesora. Alicia la escucha.
6. Miguel escribe las direcciones para ir al hotel. Miguel las escribe.
7. Esteban busca el pasaje. Esteban lo busca.
8. Nosotros planeamos una excursión. Nosotros la planeamos.

2 Expansion Ask questions (using direct objects) about the people in the activity to elicit **Sí/No** answers. Ex: **¿Tiene Ramón reservaciones en el hotel? (Sí, las tiene.) ¿Tiene su mochila? (No, no la tiene.)**

2 Vacaciones Ramón is going to San Juan, Puerto Rico with his friends, Javier and Marcos. Express his thoughts more succinctly using direct object pronouns.

> **modelo**
> Quiero hacer una excursión.
> Quiero hacerla./La quiero hacer.

1. Voy a hacer mi maleta. Voy a hacerla./La voy a hacer.
2. Necesitamos llevar los pasaportes. Necesitamos llevarlos./Los necesitamos llevar.
3. Marcos está pidiendo el folleto turístico. Marcos está pidiéndolo./Marcos lo está pidiendo.
4. Javier debe llamar a sus padres. Javier debe llamarlos./Javier los debe llamar.
5. Ellos esperan visitar el Viejo San Juan. Ellos esperan visitarlo./Ellos lo esperan visitar.
6. Puedo llamar a Javier por la mañana. Puedo llamarlo./Lo puedo llamar.
7. Prefiero llevar mi cámara. Prefiero llevarla./La prefiero llevar.
8. No queremos perder nuestras reservaciones de hotel. No queremos perderlas./No las queremos perder.

3 Expansion
- Ask students questions about who does what in the activity. Ex: **¿La señora Garza busca la cámara? (No, María la busca.)**
- Ask additional questions about the family's preparations, allowing students to decide who does what. Ex: **¿Quién compra una revista para leer en el avión? ¿Quién llama al taxi? ¿Quién practica el español?**

3 ¿Quién? The Garza family is preparing to go on a vacation to Puerto Rico. Based on the clues, answer the questions. Use direct object pronouns in your answers.

> **modelo**
> ¿Quién hace las reservaciones para el hotel? (el Sr. Garza)
> El Sr. Garza las hace.

1. ¿Quién compra los pasajes para el vuelo (*flight*)? (la Sra. Garza)
   La Sra. Garza los compra.
2. ¿Quién tiene que hacer las maletas de los niños? (María)
   María tiene que hacerlas./María las tiene que hacer.
3. ¿Quiénes buscan los pasaportes? (Antonio y María)
   Antonio y María los buscan.
4. ¿Quién va a confirmar las reservaciones para el hotel? (la Sra. Garza)
   La Sra. Garza va a confirmarlas./La Sra. Garza las va a confirmar.
5. ¿Quién busca la cámara? (María)
   María la busca.
6. ¿Quién compra un mapa de Puerto Rico? (Antonio) Antonio lo compra.

TEACHING OPTIONS

Pairs Have students take turns asking each other who does these activities: **leer revistas, practicar el ciclismo, ganar siempre los partidos, visitar a sus abuelos durante las vacaciones, leer el periódico, escribir cartas, escuchar a sus profesores, practicar la natación.** Ex: —**¿Quién lee revistas? —Yo las leo.**

Heritage Speakers Pair heritage speakers with other students. Ask the pairs to create a dialogue between a travel agent and client. The client would like to go to Puerto Rico and wants to know what he or she needs for the trip, how to prepare for it, and what to do once there. Have students role-play their dialogues for the class.

Comunicación

4 **Entrevista** Interview a classmate using these questions. Be sure to use direct object pronouns in your responses. Answers will vary.

1. ¿Ves mucho la televisión?
2. ¿Cuándo vas a ver tu programa favorito?
3. ¿Quién prepara la comida (*food*) en tu casa?
4. ¿Te visita mucho tu abuelo/a?
5. ¿Visitas mucho a tus abuelos?
6. ¿Nos entienden nuestros padres a nosotros?
7. ¿Cuándo ves a tus amigos/as?
8. ¿Cuándo te llaman tus amigos/as?

5 **En el aeropuerto** With a partner, take turns asking each other questions about the drawing. Use the word bank and direct object pronouns. Answers will vary.

> **modelo**
> **Estudiante 1:** ¿Quién está leyendo el libro?
> **Estudiante 2:** Susana lo está leyendo./Susana está leyéndolo.

buscar	confirmar	escribir	leer	tener	vender
comprar	encontrar	escuchar	llevar	traer	¿?

Sra. Sánchez · Orlando · Sr. López · Marta · Sr. Sánchez · Susana · Miguelito

Síntesis

6 **Adivinanzas** Play a guessing game in which you describe a person, place, or thing and your partner guesses who or what it is. Then switch roles. Each of you should give at least five descriptions. Answers will vary.

> **modelo**
> **Estudiante 1:** Lo uso para (*I use it to*) escribir en mi cuaderno.
>   No es muy grande y tiene borrador. ¿Qué es?
> **Estudiante 2:** ¿Es un lápiz?
> **Estudiante 1:** ¡Sí!

---

4 Teaching Tip Ask students to record their partner's answers. After the interviews, have students review answers in groups and report the most common responses to the class.

4 Expansion Have students write five additional questions, then continue their interviews.

5 Teaching Tip To simplify, before assigning the activity, ask individual students to identify different objects in the picture that might be used as direct objects in questions and answers.

5 Expansion
• Reverse the activity by having students say what the people are doing for a partner to guess. Ex: **Está escribiendo en su cuaderno. (Es Miguelito.)**
• Have students use **ser** and **estar** to describe the people in the drawing.

6 Teaching Tip To simplify, first have students write out their descriptions.

6 Expansion Have pairs write out five additional riddles. Have them read their riddles aloud for the rest of the class to answer.

TEACHING OPTIONS

Game Play a game of **20 Preguntas**. Divide the class into two teams. Think of an object in the room and alternate calling on teams to ask questions. Once a team knows the answer, the team captain should raise his or her hand. If right, the team gets a point. If wrong, the team loses a point. Play until one team has earned five points.

Pairs Have students create five questions that include the direct object pronouns **me, te,** and **nos**. Then have them ask their partners the questions on their list. Ex: —¿Quién te llama mucho? —Mi novia me llama mucho. —¿Quién nos escucha cuando hacemos preguntas en español? —El/La profesor(a) y los estudiantes nos escuchan.

Section Goal

In **Recapitulación**, students will review the grammar concepts from this lesson.

Instructional Resource
Supersite

---

1 Expansion Create a list of present participles and have students supply the infinitive. Ex: **durmiendo (dormir)**

2 Teaching Tip Ask students to explain why they chose **ser** or **estar** for each item.

2 Expansion Have students use **ser** and **estar** to write a brief paragraph describing **Julia's** first few days in Paris.

3 Teaching Tip To simplify, have students begin by underlining the direct object nouns and identifying the corresponding direct object pronouns.

Recapitulación

For self-scoring and diagnostics, go to **descubre1.vhlcentral.com**.

Review the grammar concepts you have learned in this lesson by completing these activities.

1 Completar Complete the chart with the correct present participle of these verbs. **8 pts.**

INFINITIVE	PRESENT PARTICIPLE	INFINITIVE	PRESENT PARTICIPLE
hacer	haciendo	**estar**	estando
acampar	acampando	**ser**	siendo
tener	teniendo	**vivir**	viviendo
venir	viniendo	**estudiar**	estudiando

2 Vacaciones en París Complete this paragraph about Julia's trip to Paris with the correct form of **ser** or **estar**. **12 pts.**

Hoy (1) __es__ (es/está) el 3 de julio y voy a París por tres semanas. (Yo) (2) __Estoy__ (Soy/Estoy) muy feliz porque voy a ver a mi mejor amiga. Ella (3) __es__ (es/está) de Puerto Rico, pero ahora (4) __está__ (es/está) viviendo en París. También (yo) (5) __estoy__ (soy/estoy) un poco nerviosa porque (6) __es__ (es/está) mi primer viaje a Francia. El vuelo (*flight*) (7) __es__ (es/está) hoy por la tarde pero ahora (8) __está__ (es/está) lloviendo. Por eso (9) __estamos__ (somos/estamos) preocupadas, porque probablemente el avión va a salir tarde. Mi equipaje ya (10) __está__ (es/está) listo. (11) __Es__ (Es/Está) tarde y me tengo que ir. ¡Va a (12) __ser__ (ser/estar) un viaje fenomenal!

3 ¿Qué hacen? Respond to these questions by indicating what people do with the items mentioned. Use direct object pronouns. **5 pts.**

> **modelo**
> ¿Qué hacen los viajeros con las vacaciones? (planear)
> Las planean.

1. ¿Qué haces tú con el libro de viajes? (leer) __Lo leo.__
2. ¿Qué hacen los turistas en la ciudad? (explorar) __La exploran.__
3. ¿Qué hace el botones con el equipaje? (llevar) __Lo lleva (a la habitación).__
4. ¿Qué hace la agente con las reservaciones? (confirmar) __Las confirma.__
5. ¿Qué hacen ustedes con los pasaportes? (mostrar) __Los mostramos.__

RESUMEN GRAMATICAL

5.1 Estar with conditions and emotions *p. 164*

▶ Yo est**oy** aburrido/a, feliz, nervioso/a.

▶ El cuarto est**á** desordenado, limpio, ordenado.

▶ Estos libros est**án** abiertos, cerrados, sucios.

5.2 The present progressive *pp. 166–167*

▶ The present progressive is formed with the present tense of **estar** plus the present participle.

Forming the present participle

infinitive	stem	ending	present participle
hablar	habl-	-ando	hablando
comer	com-	-iendo	comiendo
escribir	escrib-	-iendo	escribiendo

-ir stem-changing verbs

	infinitive	present participle
e:ie	preferir	prefiriendo
e:i	conseguir	consiguiendo
o:ue	dormir	durmiendo

▶ Irregular present participles: **yendo (ir), pudiendo (poder), viniendo (venir)**

5.3 Ser and estar *pp. 170–171*

▶ Uses of **ser**: nationality, origin, profession or occupation, characteristics, generalizations, possession, what something is made of, time and date, time and place of events

▶ Uses of **estar**: location, health, physical states and conditions, emotional states, weather expressions, ongoing actions

▶ **Ser** and **estar** can both be used with many adjectives, but the meaning will change.

Juan **es** delgado.	Juan **está** más delgado hoy.
Juan is thin.	*Juan looks thinner today.*

TEACHING OPTIONS

Extra Practice Add an auditory aspect to this grammar review. Go around the room and read a sentence with a direct object. Each student must repeat the sentence using a direct object pronoun. Ex: **María y Jennifer están comprando sus libros para la clase. (María y Jennifer los están comprando./María y Jennifer están comprándolos.)**

TPR Divide the board into two columns, with the heads **ser** and **estar**. Ask two volunteers to stand in front of each verb. The rest of the class should take turns calling out a use of **ser** or **estar**. The volunteer standing in front of the correct verb should step forward and give an example sentence. Ex: nationality or origin **(Soy norteamericano/a.)**

5.4 Direct object nouns and pronouns *pp. 174–175*

Direct object pronouns

Singular		Plural	
me	lo	nos	los
te	la	os	las

In affirmative sentences:
Adela practica el tenis. → Adela lo practica.

In negative sentences: Adela no lo practica.

With an infinitive:
Adela lo va a practicar./Adela va a practicarlo.

With the present progressive:
Adela lo está practicando./Adela está practicándolo.

---

4 Opuestos Complete these sentences with the appropriate form of the verb **estar** and an adjective with the opposite meaning of the underlined adjective. **5 pts.**

modelo
Yo estoy <u>interesado</u>, pero Susana está aburrida.

1. Las tiendas están <u>abiertas</u>, pero la agencia de viajes ___está___ ___cerrada___.
2. No me gustan las habitaciones <u>desordenadas</u>. Incluso (*Even*) mi habitación de hotel ___está___ ___ordenada___.
3. Nosotras estamos <u>tristes</u> cuando trabajamos. Hoy comienzan las vacaciones y ___estamos___ ___contentas/alegres/felices___
4. En esta ciudad los autobuses están <u>sucios</u>, pero los taxis ___están___ ___limpios___.
5. —El avión sale a las 5:30, ¿verdad? —No, estás <u>confundida</u>. Yo ___estoy___ ___seguro/a___ de que el avión sale a las 5:00.

5 En la playa Describe what these people are doing. Complete the sentences using the present progressive tense. **8 pts.**

1. El señor Camacho ___está pescando___
2. Felicia ___está yendo/paseando en barco___.
3. Leo ___está montando a caballo___.
4. Nosotros ___estamos jugando a las cartas___.

6 Antes del viaje Write a paragraph of at least six sentences describing the time right before you go on a trip. Say how you feel and what you are doing. You can use **Actividad 2** as a model. **12 pts.**

modelo
Hoy es viernes, 27 de octubre. Estoy en mi habitación...

7 Refrán Complete this Spanish saying. Refer to the translation and the drawing. **2 EXTRA points!**

¡LA CIUDAD ESTÁ MUY SUCIA!

❝Se consigue más ___haciendo___ que ___diciendo___.❞

(You can accomplish more by doing than by saying.)

---

4 Expansion Have students create three sentences about their own lives, using opposite adjectives. Ex: **Mi hermano es desordenado, pero yo soy muy ordenado.**

5 Expansion To challenge students, have them imagine these people are in a hotel. Ask students to say what they are doing. Ex: **Leo está mirando un programa sobre los caballos.**

6 Teaching Tips
• Have students exchange papers with a partner for peer editing.
• To make this activity more challenging, require students to include at least two examples each of **ser, estar**, and direct object pronouns.

7 Teaching Tip Explain the use of the impersonal **se** and explain that **Se consigue** means *You can* (as in the translation) or *One can*. Students will learn the impersonal **se** in *Descubre*, **nivel 2**.

7 Expansion To challenge students, have them work in pairs to create a short dialogue that ends with this saying. Encourage them to be creative.

TEACHING OPTIONS

TPR Prepare five anonymous descriptions of easily recognizable people, using **ser** and **estar**. Write each name on a separate card and give each student a set of cards. Read the descriptions aloud and have students hold up the corresponding name. Ex: **Es cantante y autora de libros infantiles. Es rubia y delgada. No es muy joven, pero no es vieja. Es de Michigan, pero ahora está en Inglaterra. Está enamorada de Guy Ritchie. (Madonna)**

Extra Practice Give students these items to make sentences with the present progressive. **1.** con / madre / hablar / yo / mi / estar (Yo estoy hablando con mi madre.) **2.** nuestro / equipaje / buscar / nosotros / estar (Nosotros estamos buscando nuestro equipaje.) **3.** ¿ / llover / playa / la / estar / en / ? (¿Está lloviendo en la playa?) **4.** el / Nueva York / pasaje / ella / para / comprar / estar (Ella está comprando el pasaje para Nueva York.)

Section Goals

In **Lectura**, students will:
- learn the strategy of scanning to find specific information in reading matter
- read a brochure about eco-tourism in Puerto Rico

Instructional Resources
Cuaderno para hispanohablantes, pp. 77–78
Supersite

Estrategia Explain to students that a good way to get an idea of what an article or other text is about is to scan it before reading. Scanning means running one's eyes over a text in search of specific information that can be used to infer the content of the text. Explain that scanning a text before reading it is a good way to improve Spanish reading comprehension.

The Affective Dimension Point out to students that becoming familiar with cognates will help them feel less overwhelmed when they encounter new Spanish texts.

Examinar el texto Do the activity orally as a class. Some cognates that give a clue to the content of the text are: **turismo ecológico, hotel, aire acondicionado, perfecto, Parque Nacional Foresta, Museo de Arte Nativo, Reserva, Biosfera, Santuario.** These clues should tell a reader scanning the text that it is about a hotel promoting ecotourism.

Preguntas Ask the questions orally of the class. Possible responses: 1. travel brochure 2. Puerto Rico 3. Photos of beautiful tropical beaches, bays, and forests; The document is trying to attract the reader. 4. **Hotel La Cabaña** in Lajas, Puerto Rico; attract guests

Lectura

Antes de leer

Estrategia
Scanning

Scanning involves glancing over a document in search of specific information. For example, you can scan a document to identify its format, to find cognates, to locate visual clues about the document's content, or to find specific facts. Scanning allows you to learn a great deal about a text without having to read it word for word.

Examinar el texto

Scan the reading selection for cognates and write a few of them down. Answers will vary.

1. _____   4. _____
2. _____   5. _____
3. _____   6. _____

Based on the cognates you found, what do you think this document is about?

_____

Preguntas

Read these questions. Then scan the document again to look for answers. Answers will vary.

1. What is the format of the reading selection?

2. Which place is the document about?

3. What are some of the visual cues this document provides? What do they tell you about the content of the document?

4. Who produced the document, and what do you think it is for?

recursos

CH pp. 77–78 | descubre1.vhlcentral.com Lección 5

Turismo ecológico en Puerto Rico

Hotel La Cabaña
~ Lajas, Puerto Rico ~

Habitaciones

- 40 individuales
- 15 dobles
- Teléfono/TV/Cable
- Aire acondicionado
- Restaurante (Bar)
- Piscina
- Área de juegos
- Cajero automático°

El hotel está situado en Playa Grande, un pequeño pueblo de pescadores del mar Caribe. Es el lugar perfecto para el viajero que viene de vacaciones. Las playas son seguras y limpias, ideales para tomar el sol, descansar, tomar fotografías y nadar. Está abierto los 365 días del año. Hay una rebaja° especial para estudiantes.

DIRECCIÓN: Playa Grande 406, Lajas, PR 00667, cerca del Parque Nacional Foresta.

Cajero automático *ATM* rebaja *discount*

TEACHING OPTIONS

Heritage Speakers Ask heritage speakers of Puerto Rican descent who have lived on or visited the island to prepare a short presentation about the climate, geography, or people of Puerto Rico. Ask them to illustrate their presentations with photos they have taken or illustrations from magazines, if possible.

Small Groups Have students work in groups of five to brainstorm a list of what would constitute an ideal tropical vacation for them. Each student should contribute at least one idea. Ask the group to designate one student to take notes and another to present the information to the class. When each group has its list, ask the designated presenter to share the information with the rest of the class. How do the groups differ? How are they similar?

Atracciones cercanas

Playa Grande ¿Busca la playa perfecta? Playa Grande es la playa que está buscando. Usted puede pescar, sacar fotos, nadar y pasear en bicicleta. Playa Grande es un paraíso para el turista que quiere practicar deportes acuáticos. El lugar es bonito e interesante y usted tiene muchas oportunidades para descansar y disfrutar en familia.

Valle Niebla Ir de excursión, tomar café, montar a caballo, caminar, acampar, hacer picnic. Más de 100 lugares para acampar.

Bahía Fosforescente Sacar fotos, salidas de noche, excursión en barco. Una maravillosa experiencia con peces° fosforescentes.

Arrecifes de Coral Sacar fotos, bucear, explorar. Es un lugar único en el Caribe.

Playa Vieja Tomar el sol, pasear en bicicleta, jugar a las cartas, escuchar música. Ideal para la familia.

Parque Nacional Foresta Sacar fotos, visitar el Museo de Arte Nativo, Reserva Mundial de la Biosfera.

Santuario de las Aves Sacar fotos, observar aves°, seguir rutas de excursión.

peces *fish* aves *birds*

Después de leer

Listas 🔊 S

Which of the amenities of the Hotel La Cabaña would most interest these potential guests? Explain your choices. Answers will vary.

1. dos padres con un hijo de seis años y una hija de ocho años

_____

2. un hombre y una mujer en su luna de miel (*honeymoon*)

_____

3. una persona en un viaje de negocios (*business trip*)

_____

Conversaciones 🔊 S

With a partner, take turns asking each other these questions. Answers will vary.

1. ¿Quieres visitar el Hotel La Cabaña? ¿Por qué?
2. Tienes tiempo de visitar sólo tres de las atracciones turísticas que están cerca del hotel. ¿Cuáles vas a visitar? ¿Por qué?
3. ¿Qué prefieres hacer en Valle Niebla? ¿En Playa Vieja? ¿En el Parque Nacional Foresta?

Situaciones

You have just arrived at the Hotel La Cabaña. Your classmate is the concierge. Use the phrases below to express your interests and ask for suggestions about where to go. Answers will vary.

1. montar a caballo
2. bucear
3. pasear en bicicleta
4. pescar
5. observar aves

Contestar

Answer these questions. Answers will vary.

1. ¿Quieres visitar Puerto Rico? Explica tu respuesta.

_____

2. ¿Adónde quieres ir de vacaciones el verano que viene? Explica tu respuesta.

_____

Listas

- Ask these comprehension questions. **1. ¿El Hotel La Cabaña está situado cerca de qué mar? (el mar Caribe) 2. ¿Qué playa es un paraíso para el turista? (la Playa Grande) 3. ¿Dónde puedes ver peces fosforescentes? (en la Bahía Fosforescente)**
- Encourage discussion of each of the items by asking questions such as: **En tu opinión, ¿qué tipo de atracciones buscan los padres con hijos de seis y ocho años? ¿Qué esperan de un hotel? Y una pareja en su luna de miel, ¿qué tipo de atracciones espera encontrar en un hotel? En tu opinión, ¿qué busca una persona en un viaje de negocios?**

Conversaciones Ask individuals about what their partners said. Ex: **¿Por qué (no) quiere _____ visitar el Hotel La Cabaña? ¿Qué atracciones quiere ver?** Ask other students: **Y tú, ¿quieres visitar el Parque Nacional Foresta o prefieres visitar otro lugar?**

Situaciones Give students a couple of minutes to review **Más vocabulario** on page 152 and **Expresiones útiles** on page 159. Add to the list activities such as **sacar fotos, correr, nadar,** and **ir de excursión.**

Contestar Have volunteers explain how the reading selection influenced their choice of vacation destination for next summer.

TEACHING OPTIONS

Pairs Have pairs of students work together to read the brochure aloud and write three questions about it. After they have finished, ask pairs to exchange papers with another pair, who will work together to answer them. Alternatively, you might pick pairs to read their questions to the class. Ask volunteers to answer them.

Small Groups To practice scanning written material to infer its content, bring in short, simple Spanish-language magazine or newspaper articles you have read. Have small groups scan the articles to determine what they are about. Have them write down all the clues that help them. When each group has come to a decision, ask it to present its findings to the class. Confirm the accuracy of the inferences.

Escritura ⬤SUPERSITE

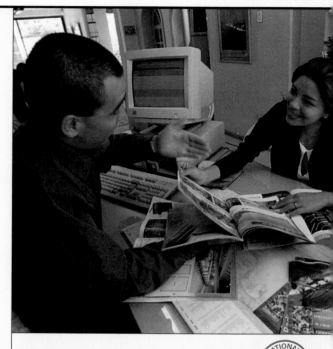

Estrategia
Making an outline

When we write to share information, an outline can serve to separate topics and subtopics, providing a framework for the presentation of data. Consider the following excerpt from an outline of the tourist brochure on pages 180–181.

IV. Descripción del sitio (con foto)
  A. Playa Grande
    1. Playas seguras y limpias
    2. Ideal para tomar el sol, descansar, tomar fotografías, nadar
  B. El hotel
    1. Abierto los 365 días del año
    2. Rebaja para estudiantes

Mapa de ideas

Idea maps can be used to create outlines. The major sections of an idea map correspond to the Roman numerals in an outline. The minor idea map sections correspond to the outline's capital letters, and so on. Consider the idea map that led to the outline above.

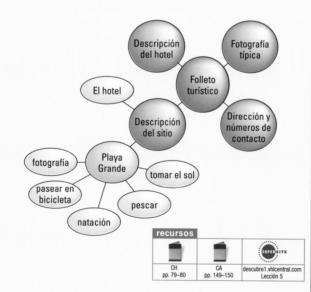

recursos

| CH pp. 79–80 | CA pp. 149–150 | descubre1.vhlcentral.com Lección 5 |

Tema

Escribir un folleto

Write a tourist brochure for a hotel or resort you have visited. If you wish, you may write about an imaginary hotel or resort. You may want to include some of this information in your brochure:

- ▸ the name of the hotel or resort
- ▸ phone and fax numbers that tourists can use to make contact
- ▸ the address of a website that tourists can consult
- ▸ an e-mail address that tourists can use to request information
- ▸ a description of the exterior of the hotel or resort
- ▸ a description of the interior of the hotel or resort, including facilities and amenities
- ▸ a description of the area around the hotel or resort, including its climate
- ▸ a listing of scenic natural attractions that are near the hotel or resort
- ▸ a listing of nearby cultural attractions
- ▸ a listing of recreational activities that tourists can pursue in the vicinity of the hotel or resort

---

EVALUATION: Folleto

Criteria	Scale
Appropriate details	1 2 3 4 5
Organization	1 2 3 4 5
Use of vocabulary	1 2 3 4 5
Grammatical accuracy	1 2 3 4 5

Scoring	
Excellent	18–20 points
Good	14–17 points
Satisfactory	10–13 points
Unsatisfactory	< 10 points

Escuchar

Estrategia

Listening for key words

By listening for key words or phrases, you can identify the subject and main ideas of what you hear, as well as some of the details.

 To practice this strategy, you will now listen to a short paragraph. As you listen, jot down the key words that help you identify the subject of the paragraph and its main ideas.

Preparación

Based on the illustration, who is Hernán Jiménez, and what is he doing? What key words might you listen for to help you understand what he is saying?

Ahora escucha

Now you are going to listen to a weather report by Hernán Jiménez. Note which phrases are correct according to the key words and phrases you hear.

Santo Domingo

1. hace sol ✔
2. va a hacer frío
3. una mañana de mal tiempo
4. va a estar nublado ✔
5. buena tarde para tomar el sol
6. buena mañana para la playa ✔

San Francisco de Macorís

1. hace frío ✔
2. hace sol
3. va a nevar
4. va a llover ✔
5. hace calor
6. mal día para excursiones ✔

recursos

SUPERSITE
descubre1.vhlcentral.com
Lección 5

Comprensión

NATIONAL
communication
STANDARDS

¿Cierto o falso?

Indicate whether each statement is **cierto** or **falso,** based on the weather report. Correct the false statements.

1. Según el meteorólogo, la temperatura en Santo Domingo es de 26 grados.
   Cierto.

2. La temperatura máxima en Santo Domingo hoy va a ser de 30 grados.
   Cierto.

3. Está lloviendo ahora en Santo Domingo.
   Falso. Hace sol.

4. En San Francisco de Macorís la temperatura mínima de hoy va a ser de 20 grados.
   Falso. La temperatura mínima va a ser de 18 grados.

5. Va a llover mucho hoy en San Francisco de Macorís.
   Cierto.

Preguntas

Answer these questions about the weather report.

1. ¿Hace viento en Santo Domingo ahora?
   Sí, hace viento en Santo Domingo.
2. ¿Está nublado en Santo Domingo ahora? No, no está nublado ahora en Santo Domingo.
3. ¿Está nevando ahora en San Francisco de Macorís? No, no está nevando ahora en San Francisco de Macorís.
4. ¿Qué tiempo hace en San Francisco de Macorís? Hace frío.

Macorís. La temperatura mínima de estas 24 horas va a ser de 18 grados. Va a llover casi todo el día. ¡No es buen día para excursiones a las montañas!

Hasta el noticiero del mediodía, me despido de ustedes. ¡Que les vaya bien!

Section Goals

In **Escuchar**, students will:
• learn the strategy of listening for key words
• listen to a short paragraph and note the key words
• answer questions based on the content of a recorded conversation

Instructional Resources
Supersite: Textbook MP3 Audio Files
Supersite/TRCD: Textbook Audio Script
Textbook Audio CD

Estrategia
Script Aquí está la foto de mis vacaciones en la playa. Ya lo sé; no debo pasar el tiempo tomando el sol. Es que vivo en una ciudad donde llueve casi todo el año y mis actividades favoritas son bucear, pescar en el mar y nadar.

Teaching Tip Have students look at the drawing and describe what they see. Guide them in saying what **Hernán Jiménez** is like and what he is doing.

Ahora escucha
Script Buenos días, queridos televidentes, les saluda el meteorólogo Hernán Jiménez, con el pronóstico del tiempo para nuestra bella isla.

Hoy, 17 de octubre, a las diez de la mañana, la temperatura en Santo Domingo es de 26 grados. Hace sol con viento del este a 10 kilómetros por hora.

En la tarde, va a estar un poco nublado con la posibilidad de lluvia. La temperatura máxima del día va a ser de 30 grados. Es una buena mañana para ir a la playa.

En las montañas hace bastante frío ahora, especialmente en el área de San Francisco de

(Script continues at far left in the bottom panels.)

Section Goals

In **En pantalla**, students will:
- read about the **Comunidad de Madrid** climate
- watch a weather report from **TeleMadrid**

Instructional Resource
Supersite: *En pantalla*
Transcript & Translation

Introduction

To check comprehension, ask these questions. 1. Into how many autonomous communities is Spain divided? (seventeen) 2. What sort of climate does the northern part of the **Comunidad de Madrid** have? (cold winters and mild summers) 3. What is the average annual temperature of the southern region of the **Comunidad de Madrid**? (14° C)

Antes de ver

- Ask students if they usually rely on weather reports. Do they watch TV, look on the Internet, or consult a newspaper? How detailed are the reports?
- Reassure students that they do not need to understand every word they hear. Tell them to rely on words from **Vocabulario útil**, visual clues, gestures, and the familiar format of weather reports.
- Remind students to pay attention to the uses of **ser** and **estar** as they watch the report.

Completar To challenge students, take away the multiple-choice answers and have them complete this activity as cloze sentences.

El reporte

- Encourage students to use the Internet to look up weather patterns of the place they have chosen.
- Have pairs present their weather reports for the class.

En pantalla

Spain is divided into seventeen autonomous communities (**comunidades autónomas**). The **Comunidad de Madrid** is located at the center of the country and is home to Spain's capital city. Although it is one of Spain's smallest communities, it encompasses two different climate regions. The northern part, which is a mountainous area, experiences very cold winters and mild summers. The rest of the community enjoys a typical Mediterranean climate, with relatively cold winters and hot summers with an average annual temperature of 14 degrees Celsius (57° F).

Vocabulario útil

acercando	*approaching*
frente	*front*
rozar	*to graze*
ha dejado	*has left*
perturbación	*disturbance*
tapan	*they cover*
deshilachadas	*frayed*
chubasco	*shower*
norte	*north*
rachas	*on and off*

Completar

Choose the correct option to complete each sentence.

1. Las nubes vienen del __c__.
   a. Pacífico   b. Mediterráneo   c. Atlántico
2. __b__ en Aranjuez.
   a. Hace sol   b. Está nublado   c. Está nevando
3. En la tarde, el __a__ va a estar más tranquilo.
   a. tiempo   b. sol   c. viento
4. El viento va a venir __b__.
   a. muy sucio   b. del norte   c. del sur (*south*)

El reporte

With a partner, choose a country or city that you like. Use the present progressive and weather expressions to write this week's weather report for the place you chose.
Answers will vary.

jornada *day* nubes *clouds* marchándose hacia el sur *heading south*

Reporte del tiempo

La jornada° está siendo tranquila.

Vamos a ver las imágenes de satélite.

... las nubes° marchándose hacia el sur°...

recursos

descubre1.vhlcentral.com
Lección 5

Conexión internet

Go to descubre1.vhlcentral.com to watch the TV clip featured in this **En pantalla** section.

TEACHING OPTIONS

Pairs Have students role-play a conversation in which a person calls a travel hotline to ask for advice on a potential vacation based on the weather. Remind students to use **ser**, **estar**, and **hacer** when describing the climates of the different destinations.

Extra Practice Brainstorm a list of activities and events with the class (a wedding, a football game, a picnic, a day at an ocean beach, a ski trip, Thanksgiving, etc.). Then ask students what the ideal weather would be in each case. Ex: **una boda (Debe hacer sol pero no debe hacer mucho calor.)**

Las vacaciones ·
ciento ochenta y cinco · · · **185**

Oye cómo va

Ednita Nazario

Puerto Rican singer and actress **Ednita Nazario** was born in 1955 in the southern city of **Ponce**. At the age of seven she recorded her first song, *Mi amor lolipop*. After a stretch of local theater appearances, Ednita formed the musical group The Kids From Ponce. While still a teenager, Ednita hosted a TV variety show (*El show de Ednita Nazario*) that gained enormous popularity not only in Puerto Rico, but throughout the Americas. Since then, Ednita has made a steady succession of hit albums and theater performances. Some of her most famous songs include *Me quedo aquí abajo*, *Eres libre*, *Más grande que grande*, and *Bajo cero*.

Your instructor will play the song. Listen and then complete these activities.

Emparejar

Match the information about Ednita Nazario. One item will not be used.

1. a band Ednita created d   a. San Juan
2. her hometown e   b. *Mi amor lolipop*
3. Ednita's first recording b c. *Más grande que grande*
4. one of her hit songs c   d. The Kids From Ponce
5. her television program f   e. Ponce
                               f. *El show de
                                  Ednita Nazario*

Emociones

With a classmate, describe Ednita's feelings in the song by completing the chart with as many adjectives and phrases as you can. Answers will vary. Sample answers:

Hoy Ednita está...	porque...
cansada aburrida, confundida, enojada, harta, nerviosa, preocupada, triste	no le gusta su situación y quiere cosas diferentes
Mañana ella va a estar...	**porque...**
alegre, con nuevas fuerzas, con nuevas ganas de vivir, contenta, de buen humor, feliz, segura, viva	va a dormir y descansar, y va a ser dueña de su destino

Cansada de estar cansada

Estoy cansada mas° no vencida°;
por esta noche voy a dormir.
Mañana es nuevo y estaré° viva
con nuevas fuerzas°, con nuevas ganas de vivir.

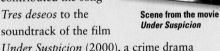
communication
cultures
NATIONAL
STANDARDS

**Scene from the movie
*Under Suspicion***

Una película en San Juan

Ednita Nazario contributed the song *Tres deseos* to the soundtrack of the film *Under Suspicion* (2000), a crime drama set in San Juan, Puerto Rico, starring Gene Hackman and Morgan Freeman. Other Puerto Rican artists whose songs appear in the movie: Millie Corretjer, José Feliciano, Vico C, Olga Tañón, Carlos Ponce, and Michael Stuart.

recursos

SUPERSITE

descubre1.vhlcentral.com
Lección 5

SUPERSITE Conexión Internet
Go to **descubre1.vhlcentral.com** to learn more about the artist featured in this *Oye cómo va* section.

mas *but* **vencida** *defeated* **estaré** *I will be* **fuerzas** *strength*

Section Goal

In **Panorama**, students will read about the geography, history, and culture of Puerto Rico.

Instructional Resources
Cuaderno de práctica, pp. 57–58
Cuaderno de actividades, pp. 77–78
e-Cuaderno
Supersite/DVD: *Panorama cultural*
Supersite/TRCD: *PowerPoints* (Overheads #3, #4, #27); *Panorama cultural* Videoscript & Translation, Answer Keys

Teaching Tip Have students look at the map of Puerto Rico or show *Overhead PowerPoint #27*. Discuss Puerto Rico's location in relation to the U.S. mainland and the other Caribbean islands. Encourage students to describe what they see in the photos on this page.

El país en cifras After reading **Puertorriqueños célebres**, ask volunteers who are familiar with these individuals to tell a little more about each. **Rita Moreno** is the only female performer to have won an Oscar, a Tony, an Emmy, and a Grammy. You might also mention novelist **Rosario Ferré**, whose *House on the Lagoon (La casa de la laguna)* gives a fictional portrait of a large part of Puerto Rican history.

¡Increíble pero cierto! The **río Camuy** caves are actually a series of karstic sinkholes, formed by water sinking into and eroding limestone. Another significant cave in this system is Clara Cave, located in the **río Camuy** Cave Park. The entrance of the 170-foot-high cave resembles the façade of a cathedral.

Puerto Rico

 NATIONAL STANDARDS connections cultures

El país en cifras

▶ **Área:** 8.959 km^2 (3.459 millas^2) menor° que el área de Connecticut
▶ **Población:** 4.060.000
Puerto Rico es una de las islas más densamente pobladas° del mundo. Más de la tercera parte de la población vive en San Juan, la capital.
▶ **Capital:** San Juan—2.758.000

SOURCE: Population Division, UN Secretariat

▶ **Ciudades principales:** Arecibo, Bayamón, Fajardo, Mayagüez, Ponce
▶ **Moneda:** dólar estadounidense
▶ **Idiomas:** español (oficial); inglés (oficial)
Aproximadamente la cuarta parte de la población puertorriqueña habla inglés. Pero, en las zonas turísticas este porcentaje es mucho más alto. El uso del inglés es obligatorio para documentos federales.

Bandera de Puerto Rico

Puertorriqueños célebres
▶ **Raúl Juliá,** actor (1940–1994)
▶ **Roberto Clemente,** beisbolista (1934–1972)
▶ **Julia de Burgos,** escritora (1914–1953)
▶ **Ricky Martin,** cantante y actor (1971–)
▶ **Rita Moreno,** actriz, cantante, bailarina (1931–)

menor *less* pobladas *populated* río subterráneo *underground river* más largo *longest* cuevas *caves* bóveda *vault* fortaleza *fort* caber *fit*

recursos		
CP pp. 57–58	CA pp. 77–78	descubre1.vhlcentral.com Lección 5

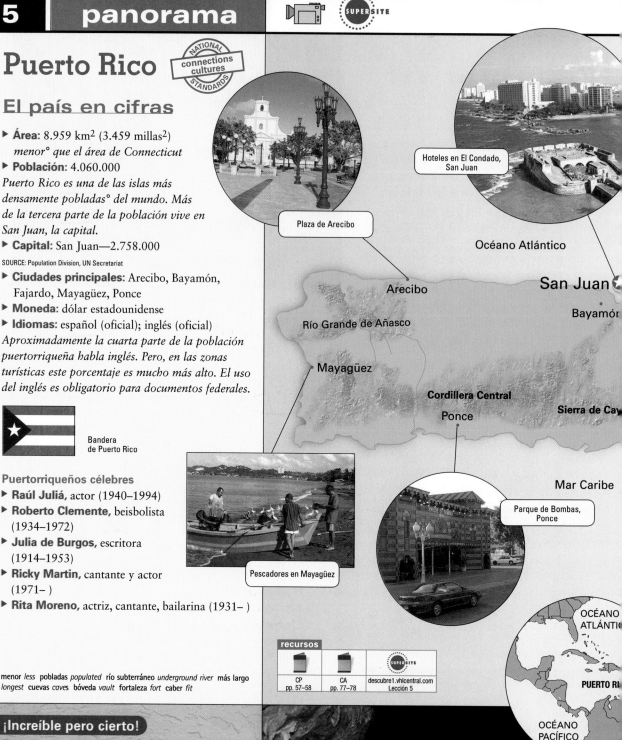
Plaza de Arecibo
Hoteles en El Condado, San Juan
Océano Atlántico
San Juan
Arecibo
Bayamón
Río Grande de Añasco
Mayagüez
Cordillera Central
Ponce
Sierra de Cay
Mar Caribe
Parque de Bombas, Ponce
Pescadores en Mayagüez
OCÉANO ATLÁNTICO
PUERTO RI
OCÉANO PACÍFICO

¡Increíble pero cierto!

El río Camuy es el tercer río subterráneo° más largo° del mundo y tiene el sistema de cuevas° más grande en el hemisferio occidental. La Cueva de los Tres Pueblos es una gigantesca bóveda°, tan grande que toda la fortaleza° del Morro puede caber° en su interior.

TEACHING OPTIONS

Heritage Speakers Encourage heritage speakers of Puerto Rican descent who have lived on the island or visited it to write a short description of their impressions. Ask them to describe people they knew or met, places they saw, and experiences they had. Ask them to think about what the most important thing they would tell a person unfamiliar with the island would be and to try to express it.

El béisbol Baseball is a popular sport in Puerto Rico, home of the Winter League. **Roberto Clemente**, a player with the Pittsburgh Pirates who died tragically in a plane crash, was the first Latino to be inducted into the Baseball Hall of Fame. He is venerated all over the island with buildings and monuments.

Lugares • El Morro

El Morro es una fortaleza que se construyó° la bahía° de San Juan desde principios del siglo° XVI hasta principios del siglo XX. Hoy día muchos turistas visitan este lugar, covertido en un museo. Es el sitio más fotografiado de Puerto Rico. La arquitectura de la fortaleza es impresionante. Tiene misteriosos túneles, oscuras mazmorras° y vistas fabulosas de la bahía.

Artes • Salsa

La salsa, este estilo musical de origen puertorriqueño y cubano, nació° en el barrio latino de la ciudad de Nueva York. Dos de los músicos de salsa más famosos son Tito Puente y Willie Colón, los dos de Nueva York. Las estrellas° de la salsa en Puerto Rico son Felipe Rodríguez y Héctor Lavoe. Hoy en día, Puerto Rico es el centro internacional de la salsa. El Gran Combo de Puerto Rico es una de las orquestas de salsa más famosas del mundo°.

Isla de Culebra

Fajardo

Isla de Vieques

Ciencias • El Observatorio de Arecibo

El Observatorio de Arecibo tiene uno de los radiotelescopios más grandes del mundo. Gracias a este telescopio, los científicos° pueden estudiar las propiedades de la Tierra°, la Luna° y otros cuerpos celestes. También pueden analizar fenómenos celestiales como los quasares y pulsares, y detectar emisiones de radio de otras galaxias, en busca de inteligencia extraterrestre.

Historia • Relación con los Estados Unidos

Puerto Rico pasó a ser° parte de los Estados Unidos después de° la guerra° de 1898 contra España y se hizo° un estado libre asociado en 1952. Los puertorriqueños, ciudadanos° estadounidenses desde° 1917, tienen representación política en el Congreso pero no votan en las elecciones presidenciales y no pagan impuestos° federales. Hay un debate entre los puertorriqueños: ¿debe la isla seguir como estado libre asociado, hacerse un estado como los otros° o volverse° independiente?

¿Qué aprendiste? Responde a las preguntas con una oración completa.
1. ¿Cuál es la moneda de Puerto Rico? La moneda de Puerto Rico es el dólar estadounidense.
2. ¿Qué idiomas se hablan (are spoken) en Puerto Rico? Se hablan español e inglés en Puerto Rico.
3. ¿Cuál es el sitio más fotografiado de Puerto Rico? El Morro es el sitio más fotografiado de Puerto Rico.
4. ¿Qué es el Gran Combo? Es una orquesta de Puerto Rico.
5. ¿Qué hacen los científicos en el Observatorio de Arecibo? Los científicos estudian la atmósfera de la Tierra y la Luna y escuchan emisiones de otras galaxias.

Conexión Internet Investiga estos temas en **descubre1.vhlcentral.com**.
1. Describe a dos puertorriqueños famosos. ¿Cómo son? ¿Qué hacen? ¿Dónde viven? ¿Por qué son célebres?
2. Busca información sobre lugares buenos para el ecoturismo en Puerto Rico. Luego presenta un informe a la clase.

proteger *protect* bahía *bay* siglo *century* mazmorras *dungeons* nació *was born* estrellas *stars* mundo *world* científicos *scientists* Tierra *Earth* Luna *Moon* pasó a ser *became* después de *after* guerra *war* se hizo *became* ciudadanos *citizens* desde *since* pagan impuestos *pay taxes* otros *others* volverse *to become*

Instructional Resources
Cuaderno de actividades, p. 116
e-Cuaderno
Supersite: Textbook &
Vocabulary MP3 Audio Files
Supersite/TRCD/Print: Answer
Keys; *Testing Program* (**Lección
5 Pruebas,** Test Generator,
Testing Program MP3 Audio
Files)
Textbook, Test Audio CD

Los viajes y las vacaciones

acampar	to camp
confirmar una reservación	to confirm a reservation
estar de vacaciones (*f. pl.*)	to be on vacation
hacer las maletas	to pack (one's suitcases)
hacer un viaje	to take a trip
ir de compras (*f. pl.*)	to go shopping
ir de vacaciones	to go on vacation
ir en autobús (*m.*), auto(móvil) (*m.*), avión (*m.*), barco (*m.*), moto(cicleta) (*f.*), taxi (*m.*)	to go by bus, car, plane, boat, motorcycle, taxi
jugar a las cartas	to play cards
montar a caballo (*m.*)	to ride a horse
pescar	to fish
sacar/tomar fotos (*f. pl.*)	to take photos
el/la agente de viajes	travel agent
el/la inspector(a) de aduanas	customs inspector
el/la viajero/a	traveler
el aeropuerto	airport
la agencia de viajes	travel agency
la cabaña	cabin
el campo	countryside
el equipaje	luggage
la estación de autobuses, del metro, de tren	bus, subway, train station
la llegada	arrival
el mar	sea
el paisaje	landscape
el pasaje (de ida y vuelta)	(round-trip) ticket
el pasaporte	passport
la playa	beach
la salida	departure; exit

El hotel

el ascensor	elevator
el/la botones	bellhop
la cama	bed
el/la empleado/a	employee
la habitación individual, doble	single, double room
el hotel	hotel
el/la huésped	guest
la llave	key
el piso	floor (of a building)
la planta baja	ground floor

Adjetivos

abierto/a	open
aburrido/a	bored; boring
alegre	happy; joyful
amable	nice; friendly
avergonzado/a	embarrassed
cansado/a	tired
cerrado/a	closed
cómodo/a	comfortable
confundido/a	confused
contento/a	happy; content
desordenado/a	disorderly
enamorado/a (de)	in love (with)
enojado/a	mad; angry
equivocado/a	wrong
feliz	happy
limpio/a	clean
listo/a	ready; smart
nervioso/a	nervous
ocupado/a	busy
ordenado/a	orderly
preocupado/a (por)	worried (about)
seguro/a	sure; safe
sucio/a	dirty
triste	sad

Los números ordinales

primer, primero/a	first
segundo/a	second
tercer, tercero/a	third
cuarto/a	fourth
quinto/a	fifth
sexto/a	sixth
séptimo/a	seventh
octavo/a	eighth
noveno/a	ninth
décimo/a	tenth

Palabras adicionales

ahora mismo	right now
el año	year
¿Cuál es la fecha (de hoy)?	What is the date (today)?
de buen/mal humor	in a good/bad mood
la estación	season
el mes	month
todavía	yet; still

Seasons, months, and dates	See page 154.
Weather expressions	See page 154.
Direct object pronouns	See page 174.
Expresiones útiles	See page 159.

recursos

CA p. 116	descubre1.vhlcentral.com Lección 5

¡De compras!

Communicative Goals

You will learn how to:

- Talk about and describe clothing
- Express preferences in a store
- Negotiate and pay for items you buy

Lesson Goals

In **Lección 6**, students will be introduced to the following:
- terms for clothing and shopping
- colors
- open-air markets
- Venezuelan clothing designer **Carolina Herrera**
- the verbs **saber** and **conocer**
- indirect object pronouns
- preterite tense of regular verbs
- demonstrative adjectives and pronouns
- skimming a text
- how to report an interview
- writing a report
- listening for linguistic cues
- a television commercial for **Galerías**, a Spanish department store
- Cuban singer **Celia Cruz**
- cultural, geographic, economic, and historical information about Cuba

A primera vista Here are some additional questions you can ask based on the photo: **¿Te gusta ir de compras? ¿Por qué? ¿Estás de buen humor cuando vas de compras? ¿Estás pensando ir de compras este fin de semana? ¿Dónde? ¿Qué compras cuando estás de vacaciones?**

A PRIMERA VISTA

- ¿Está comprando algo la mujer?
- ¿Está buscando una maleta?
- ¿Está contenta o enojada?
- ¿Cómo es la mujer?

INSTRUCTIONAL RESOURCES

Student Materials
  Cuaderno de práctica, Cuaderno para hispanohablantes, Cuaderno de actividades
Student MAESTRO™ Supersite
  (descubre1.vhlcentral.com)
MAESTRO™ e-Cuaderno

Teacher's Resource CD-ROM and in print
  *Answer Keys, Audioscripts, Videoscripts
  *PowerPoints
  Testing Program (**Pruebas**, Test Generator, MP3 Audio Files)
  Vista Higher Learning *Cancionero*
  *Also available on Supersite

Teacher's MAESTRO™ Supersite
  (descubre1.vhlcentral.com)
  Learning Management System (Assignment Task Manager, Gradebook)
  Also on DVD
  Fotonovela, Flash cultura, Panorama cultural

¡De compras!

Más vocabulario

el abrigo	*coat*
los calcetines (el calcetín)	*sock(s)*
el cinturón	*belt*
las gafas (de sol)	*(sun)glasses*
los guantes	*gloves*
el impermeable	*raincoat*
la ropa	*clothing; clothes*
la ropa interior	*underwear*
las sandalias	*sandals*
el traje	*suit*
el vestido	*dress*
los zapatos de tenis	*tennis shoes; sneakers*
el regalo	*gift*
el almacén	*department store*
el centro comercial	*shopping mall*
el mercado (al aire libre)	*(open-air) market*
el precio (fijo)	*(fixed; set) price*
la rebaja	*sale*
la tienda	*shop; store*
costar (o:ue)	*to cost*
gastar	*to spend (money)*
pagar	*to pay*
regatear	*to bargain*
vender	*to sell*
hacer juego (con)	*to match (with)*
llevar	*to wear; to take*
usar	*to wear; to use*

Variación léxica

calcetines	⟷	medias (*Amér. L.*)
cinturón	⟷	correa (*Col., Venez.*)
gafas/lentes	⟷	espejuelos (*Cuba, P.R.*), anteojos (*Arg., Chile*)
zapatos de tenis	⟷	zapatillas de deporte (*Esp.*), zapatillas (*Arg., Perú*)

recursos

CP pp. 59–60	CH pp. 81–82	CA p. 117	descubre1.vhlcentral.com Lección 6

Damas

los pantalones cortos
el traje de baño
los pantalones
la camiseta
el dependiente/el vendedor
la clienta
la camisa
el dinero en efectivo
la blusa
hacer juego
la bolsa
el suéter
la falda
las medias

Práctica

1

Escuchar Listen to Juanita and Vicente talk about what they're packing for their vacations. Indicate who is packing each item. If both are packing an item, write both names. If neither is packing an item, write an X.

1. abrigo _Vicente_
2. zapatos de tenis _Juanita, Vicente_
3. impermeable _X_
4. chaqueta _Vicente_
5. sandalias _Juanita_
6. bluejeans _Juanita, Vicente_
7. gafas de sol _Vicente_
8. camisetas _Juanita, Vicente_
9. traje de baño _Juanita_
10. botas _Vicente_
11. pantalones cortos _Juanita_
12. suéter _Vicente_

2

Lógico o ilógico Listen to Guillermo and Ana talk about vacation destinations. Indicate whether each statement is **lógico** or **ilógico**.

1. _ilógico_
2. _lógico_
3. _ilógico_
4. _lógico_

3

Completar Anita is talking about going shopping. Complete each sentence with the correct word(s), adding definite or indefinite articles when necessary.

caja	medias	tarjeta de crédito
centro comercial	par	traje de baño
dependientas	ropa	vendedores

1. Hoy voy a ir de compras al _centro comercial_.
2. Voy a ir a la tienda de ropa para mujeres. Siempre hay muchas rebajas y las _dependientas_ son muy simpáticas.
3. Necesito comprar _un par_ de zapatos.
4. Y tengo que comprar _un traje de baño_ porque el sábado voy a la playa con mis amigos.
5. También voy a comprar unas _medias_ para mi mamá.
6. Voy a pagar todo (*everything*) en _la caja_.
7. Pero hoy no tengo dinero. Voy a tener que usar mi _tarjeta de crédito_.
8. Mañana voy al mercado al aire libre. Me gusta regatear con los _vendedores_.

4

Escoger Choose the item in each group that does not belong.

1. almacén • centro comercial • mercado • (sombrero)
2. camisa • camiseta • blusa • (botas)
3. bluejeans • (bolsa) • falda • pantalones
4. abrigo • suéter • (corbata) • chaqueta
5. mercado • tienda • almacén • (cartera)
6. (pagar) • llevar • hacer juego (con) • usar
7. botas • sandalias • zapatos • (traje)
8. vender • regatear • (ropa interior) • gastar

el sombrero

un par de zapatos

los zapatos

chaqueta

la caja

la cartera

la dependienta/la vendedora

la corbata

la tarjeta de crédito

los bluejeans

la bota

Caballeros

SUPERSITE

1 Teaching Tip Have students check their answers by going over **Actividad 1** with the class.

1 Script JUANITA: Hola. Me llamo Juanita. Mi familia y yo salimos de vacaciones mañana y estoy haciendo mis maletas. Para nuestra excursión al campo ya tengo bluejeans, camisetas y zapatos de tenis. También vamos a la playa… ¡no puedo esperar! *Script continues on page 192.*

2 Teaching Tip You may want to do this activity as a TPR exercise. Have students raise their right hands if they hear a logical statement and their left hands if they hear an illogical statement.

2 Script 1. Este verano quiero ir de vacaciones a un lugar caliente, con playas y mucho, mucho sol; por eso, necesito comprar un abrigo y botas. 2. A mí me gustaría visitar Costa Rica en la estación de lluvias. Hace mucho calor, pero llueve muchísimo. Voy a necesitar mi impermeable todo el tiempo. 3. Mi lugar favorito para ir de vacaciones es Argentina en invierno. Me gusta esquiar en las montañas. No puedo ir sin mis sandalias ni mi traje de baño. 4. En mi opinión, el lugar ideal para ir de vacaciones es mi club. Allí juego mi deporte favorito, el tenis, y también asisto a fiestas elegantes. Por eso siempre llevo mis zapatos de tenis y a veces traje y corbata. *Textbook Audio*

3 Expansion Ask students to write three additional fill-in-the-blank sentences for a partner to complete.

4 Expansion Go over the answers quickly in class. After each answer, indicate why a particular item does not belong.

1 Script (continued)
Para ir a la playa necesito un traje de baño, pantalones cortos y sandalias. ¿Qué más necesito? Creo que es todo.
VICENTE: Buenos días. Soy Vicente. Estoy haciendo mis maletas porque mi familia y yo vamos a las montañas a esquiar. Los primeros dos días vamos a hacer una excursión por las montañas. Necesito zapatos de tenis, camisetas, una chaqueta y bluejeans. El tercer día vamos a esquiar. Necesito un abrigo, un suéter y botas… y gafas de sol.
Textbook Audio

Teaching Tips
• Show *Overhead PowerPoint #29* and go through the color words. Point to each drawing and ask: **¿De qué color es esta camiseta?** Ask about combinations. Ex: **Si combino rojo y azul, ¿qué color resulta? (morado)**
• Point to objects in the classroom and clothes you and students are wearing to elicit color words.
• Give dates and have students name the colors that they associate with each one. Ex: **el 14 de febrero (rojo, rosado); el 31 de octubre (negro, anaranjado)** You may want to repeat the process with brand names. Ex: **FedEx (anaranjado, morado, blanco)**
• Point out that color words are adjectives and agree in number and gender with the nouns they modify.

5 Expansion Add a visual aspect to this activity. Show magazine pictures of various products (cars, computers, etc.) and ask questions. Ex: **¿Es cara o barata esta computadora? (Es barata.)**

6 Expansion Point to students and ask others what color of clothing each is wearing. Ex: ___, ¿de qué color es la falda de ___? (Es ___.)

Los colores

amarillo/a   anaranjado/a   azul

blanco/a   gris   marrón, café   morado/a   negro/a

rojo/a   rosado/a   verde

SUPERSITE

Adjetivos

barato/a	cheap
bueno/a	good
cada	each
caro/a	expensive
corto/a	short (in length)
elegante	elegant
hermoso/a	beautiful
largo/a	long
loco/a	crazy
nuevo/a	new
otro/a	other; another
pobre	poor
rico/a	rich

5 **Contrastes** Complete each phrase with the opposite of the underlined word.

1. una corbata <u>barata</u> • unas camisas… caras
2. unas vendedoras <u>malas</u> • unos dependientes… buenos
3. un vestido <u>corto</u> • una falda… larga
4. un hombre muy <u>pobre</u> • una mujer muy… rica
5. una cartera <u>nueva</u> • un cinturón… viejo
6. unos trajes <u>hermosos</u> • unos bluejeans… feos
7. un impermeable <u>caro</u> • unos suéteres… baratos
8. unos calcetines <u>blancos</u> • unas medias… negras

CONSULTA
Like other adjectives you have seen, colors must agree in gender and number with the nouns they modify.
Ex: **las camisas verdes, el vestido amarillo.**
For a review of descriptive adjectives, see **Estructura 3.1,** pp. 88–89.

6 **Preguntas** Answer these questions with a classmate.

1. ¿De qué color es la rosa de Texas? Es amarilla.
2. ¿De qué color es la bandera (*flag*) del Canadá? Es roja y blanca.
3. ¿De qué color es la casa donde vive el presidente de los EE.UU.? Es blanca.
4. ¿De qué color es el océano Atlántico? Es azul.
5. ¿De qué color es la nieve? Es blanca.
6. ¿De qué color es el café? Es marrón./Es café.
7. ¿De qué color es el dólar de los EE.UU.? Es verde y blanco.
8. ¿De qué color es la cebra (*zebra*)? Es negra y blanca.

Pairs Ask student pairs to write a physical description of a well-known TV or cartoon character. Then have them read their descriptions for the rest of the class to guess. Ex: **Soy bajo y un poco gordo. Llevo pantalones cortos azules y una camiseta anaranjada. Tengo el pelo amarillo. También soy amarillo. ¿Quién soy? (Bart Simpson)**
Game Add a visual aspect to this vocabulary practice by playing

Concentración. On eight cards, write descriptions of clothing, including colors. Ex: **unos pantalones negros.** On another eight cards, draw pictures that match the descriptions. Shuffle the cards and place them face-down in four rows of four. In pairs, students select two cards. If the cards match, the pair keeps them. If the cards do not match, students replace them in their original position. The pair with the most cards at the end wins.

Comunicación

7 **Las maletas** With a classmate, answer these questions about the drawings.

1. ¿Qué ropa hay al lado de la maleta de Carmela?
   Hay una camiseta, unos pantalones cortos y un traje de baño.

2. ¿Qué hay en la maleta?
   Hay un sombrero y un par de sandalias.

3. ¿De qué color son las sandalias?
   Las sandalias son rojas.

4. ¿Adónde va Carmela?
   Va a la playa.

▶ 5. ¿Qué tiempo va a hacer?
   Va a hacer sol./ Va a hacer calor.

6. ¿Qué hay al lado de la maleta de Pepe?
   Hay un par de calcetines, un par de guantes, un suéter y una chaqueta.

7. ¿Qué hay en la maleta?
   Hay dos pares de pantalones.

8. ¿De qué color es el suéter?
   El suéter es rosado.

▶ 9. ¿Qué va a hacer Pepe en Bariloche?
   Va a esquiar.

10. ¿Qué tiempo va a hacer?
   Va a hacer frío./ Va a nevar.

CONSULTA

To review weather, see **Lección 5, Contextos,** p. 154.

NOTA CULTURAL

Bariloche is a popular resort for skiing in South America. Located in Argentina's Patagonia region, the town is also known for its chocolate factories and its beautiful lakes, mountains, and forests.

8 **¿Adónde van?** Imagine that you and your family are going on vacation with a classmate. Decide where you are going, then write what clothing each of you is taking. Present your lists to the class, answering these questions. Answers will vary.

- ¿Adónde van?
- ¿Qué tiempo va a hacer allí?
- ¿Qué van a hacer allí?
- ¿Qué hay en sus maletas?
- ¿De qué color es la ropa que llevan?

9 **Preferencias** Use these questions to interview a classmate. Then switch roles. Answers will vary.

1. ¿Adónde vas a comprar ropa? ¿Por qué?
2. ¿Qué tipo de ropa prefieres? ¿Por qué?
3. ¿Cuáles son tus colores favoritos?
4. En tu opinión, ¿es importante comprar ropa nueva frecuentemente? ¿Por qué?
5. ¿Gastas mucho dinero en ropa cada mes? ¿Buscas rebajas?
6. ¿Regateas cuando compras ropa? ¿Usas una tarjeta de crédito?

7 Expansion Ask volunteers what kind of clothing they take with them when they visit these places at these times: **Seattle en la primavera, la Florida en el verano, Minnesota en el invierno, San Francisco en el otoño.**

8 Teaching Tip One class period before doing this activity, assign pairs and have them discuss where they are going.

8 Expansion Have students guess where the groups are going, based on the content of the suitcases. Facilitate guessing by asking questions 2–5.

9 Expansion
- Ask students to report the findings of their interviews to the class. Ex: ____ va a **The Gap para comprar ropa porque allí la ropa no es cara. Prefiere ropa informal…**
- Have different pairs choose two famous people and explain their clothing preferences, using the questions from **Actividad 9**.

TEACHING OPTIONS

Pairs Have students form pairs and tell them they are going on a shopping spree. On paper strips, write varying dollar amounts, from ten dollars to three thousand, and distribute them. Have pairs tell what they will buy. Encourage creativity. Ex: **Tenemos quince dólares y vamos a Old Navy. Ella va a comprar medias amarillas y yo voy a comprar un sombrero en las rebajas.**

Extra Practice Add an auditory aspect to this vocabulary practice. Ask students to write an anonymous description of the article of clothing or outfit that best defines them. Collect the papers, shuffle them, and read the descriptions aloud for the class to guess.
Pairs Have pairs take turns describing classmates' clothing and guessing the person. Ex: **Esta persona usa bluejeans y una blusa marrón. Lleva sandalias blancas. (Es _____.)**

¡Qué ropa más bonita!

communication cultures NATIONAL STANDARDS

Javier e Inés van de compras al mercado.

PERSONAJES

INÉS

JAVIER

EL VENDEDOR

INÉS Javier, ¡qué ropa más bonita! A mí me gusta esa camisa blanca y azul. Debe ser de algodón. ¿Te gusta?

JAVIER Yo prefiero la camisa de la izquierda... la gris con rayas rojas. Hace juego con mis botas marrones.

INÉS Está bien, Javier. Mira, necesito comprarle un regalo a mi hermana Graciela. Acaba de empezar un nuevo trabajo...

JAVIER ¿Tal vez una bolsa?

VENDEDOR Esas bolsas son típicas de las montañas. ¿Le gusta?

INÉS Sí. Quiero comprarle una a mi hermana.

VENDEDOR Buenas tardes, joven. ¿Le puedo servir en algo?

JAVIER Sí. Voy a ir de excursión a las montañas y necesito un buen suéter.

VENDEDOR ¿Qué talla usa usted?

JAVIER Uso talla grande.

VENDEDOR Éstos son de talla grande.

JAVIER ¿Qué precio tiene ése?

VENDEDOR ¿Le gusta este suéter? Le cuesta ciento cincuenta mil sucres.

JAVIER Quiero comprarlo, pero, señor, no soy rico. ¿Ciento veinte mil sucres?

VENDEDOR Bueno, para usted... sólo ciento treinta mil sucres.

JAVIER Está bien, señor.

recursos

CA
pp. 61–62

descubre1.vhlcentral.com
Lección 6

TEACHING OPTIONS

¡Qué ropa más bonita! Photocopy the **Fotonovela** Videoscript (Supersite/TRCD/Print) and white out 7–10 words in order to create a master for a cloze activity. Distribute photocopies of the master and have students fill in the missing words as | they watch the **¡Qué ropa más bonita!** segment. You may want students to work in small groups and help each other fill in any gaps.

Teaching Tip Have students work in pairs to read the parts of **Inés** and **Javier** as they arrive at the market (captions 1–2), **Inés** bargaining with the vendor (captions 3–5), and **Javier** bargaining with the vendor (captions 6–8). Ask for volunteers to read their segment for the class.

INÉS Me gusta aquélla. ¿Cuánto cuesta?

VENDEDOR Ésa cuesta ciento sesenta mil sucres. ¡Es de muy buena calidad!

INÉS Uy, demasiado cara. Quizás otro día.

JAVIER Acabo de comprarme un suéter. Y tú, ¿qué compraste?

INÉS Compré esta bolsa para mi hermana.

INÉS También compré una camisa y un sombrero. ¿Qué tal me veo?

JAVIER ¡Guapa, muy guapa!

Expresiones útiles

Talking about clothing

- **¡Qué ropa más bonita!**
  What nice clothing!
- **Me gusta esta/esa camisa blanca de rayas negras.**
  I like this/that white shirt with black stripes.
- **Está de moda.**
  It's in fashion.
- **Debe ser de algodón/lana/seda.**
  It must be cotton/wool/silk.
- **Es de cuadros/lunares/rayas.**
  It's plaid/polka-dotted/striped.
- **Me gusta este/ese suéter.**
  I like this/that sweater.
- **Es de muy buena calidad.**
  It's very good quality.
- **¿Qué talla lleva/usa usted?**
  What size do you (form.) wear?
  Llevo/Uso talla grande.
  I wear a large.
- **¿Qué número calza usted?**
  What (shoe) size do you (form.) wear?
  Calzo el treinta y seis.
  I wear a size thirty-six.

Talking about how much things cost

- **¿Cuánto cuesta?**
  How much does it cost?
  Sólo cuesta noventa mil sucres.
  It only costs ninety thousand sucres.
  Demasiado caro/a.
  Too expensive.
  Es una ganga.
  It's a bargain.

Saying what you bought

- **¿Qué compró Ud./él/ella?**
  What did you (form.)/he/she buy?
  Compré esta bolsa para mi hermana.
  I bought this purse for my sister.
- **¿Qué compraste?**
  What did you (fam.) buy?
  Acabo de comprarme un sombrero.
  I have just bought myself a hat.

Expresiones útiles

- Point out the verb forms **compré, compraste,** and **compró.** Tell the class that these are forms of the verb **comprar** in the preterite tense, which is used to tell what happened in the past. Tell the class that **este, esta, ese,** and **esa** are examples of demonstrative adjectives, which are used to single out particular nouns. Also point out that the **me** in **Acabo de comprarme un sombrero** is an indirect object pronoun, used to tell for whom the hat was bought. Tell students that they will learn more about these concepts in **Estructura.**
- Help students with adjective placement and agreement when talking about clothing. Ask them to translate phrases such as these:
1. a white tie with gray and brown stripes (**una corbata blanca con rayas grises y marrones**) 2. black wool pants (**unos pantalones negros de lana**) 3. a yellow cotton shirt with purple polka dots (**una camisa amarilla de algodón de lunares morados**) 4. an elegant, blue plaid suit (**un traje azul elegante de cuadros**) 5. a red silk dress (**un vestido rojo de seda**) Discuss different possibilities for adjective placement and how it affects agreement. Ex: **Un vestido rojo de seda** versus **Un vestido de seda roja.**

TEACHING OPTIONS

TPR Ask students to write **clientes** and **vendedores** on separate sheets on paper. Read aloud phrases from **Expresiones útiles** and have them hold up the paper(s) that correspond(s) to the party that would say that expression. Ex: **¿Qué número calza usted? (vendedores)**

Small Groups Have the class work in small groups to write statements about the **Fotonovela.** Ask each group to exchange its statements with another group. Each group will then write out the question that would have elicited each statement.
Ex: **G1: Graciela acaba de empezar un nuevo trabajo.**
G2: ¿Quién acaba de empezar un nuevo trabajo?

1 Expansion Once all statements have been corrected, ask pairs to find the places in the episode that support their answers. Have pairs role-play the scenes for the class.

2 Expansion Give students these statements as items 7–9: 7. Pero, señor… no traigo mucho dinero. (Javier) 8. Señor, para usted… ochenta mil sucres. (el vendedor) 9. Me gusta mucho esta camisa blanca de algodón. (Inés)

3 Expansion Ask pairs to write two additional questions. Then have pairs exchange papers and answer each other's questions.

4 Possible Conversation
E1: Buenas tardes.
E2: Buenas tardes. ¿Qué desea?
E1: Estoy buscando una camisa.
E2: Pues, tengo estas camisas de algodón y estas camisas de seda. Son de muy buena calidad. ¿Cuál prefiere usted?
E1: Busco una camisa blanca o azul de algodón. Uso talla mediana.
E2: Las camisas de algodón son de talla mediana. Tengo esta camisa azul de algodón.
E1: Quiero comprarla, pero no soy rico/a. ¿Cuánto cuesta?
E2: Veinte dólares. Pero para usted... sólo quince dólares.
E1: Muy bien. La compro, pero sólo tengo trece dólares.
E2: Está bien. Muchas gracias.

Successful Language Learning Tell students to devote extra effort and attention to **Actividad 4**. This activity sums up the vocabulary and phrases that the students have learned in this lesson. In addition, this activity explores a real-life situation that travelers might encounter when visiting a Spanish-speaking country.

¿Qué pasó?

1

¿Cierto o falso? Indicate whether each sentence is **cierto** or **falso**. Correct the false statements.

	Cierto	Falso	
1. A Inés le gusta la camisa verde y amarilla.	○	⦿	A Inés le gusta la camisa blanca y azul.
2. Javier necesita comprarle un regalo a su hermana.	○	⦿	Inés necesita comprarle un regalo a su hermana.
3. Las bolsas en el mercado son típicas de las montañas.	⦿	○	
4. Javier busca un traje de baño.	○	⦿	Javier busca un suéter.

2

Identificar Provide the first initial of the person who would make each statement.

_I_ 1. ¿Te gusta el sombrero que compré?
_V_ 2. Estos suéteres son de talla grande. ¿Qué talla usa usted?
_J_ 3. ¿Por qué no compras una bolsa para Graciela?
_J_ 4. Creo que mis botas hacen juego con la camisa.
_V_ 5. Estas bolsas son excelentes, de muy buena calidad.
_I_ 6. Creo que las blusas aquí son de algodón.

INÉS

JAVIER

EL VENDEDOR

3

Completar Answer the questions using the information in the **Fotonovela**.

1. Inés quiere comprarle un regalo a su hermana. ¿Por qué? Porque su hermana acaba de empezar un nuevo trabajo.
2. ¿Cuánto cuesta la bolsa de las montañas? Cuesta ciento sesenta mil sucres.
3. ¿Por qué necesita Javier un buen suéter? Porque va de excursión a las montañas.
4. ¿Cuál es el precio final del suéter? El precio final del suéter es ciento treinta mil sucres.
5. ¿Qué compra Inés en el mercado? Inés compra una bolsa, una camisa y un sombrero.

4

Conversar With a partner, role-play a conversation between a customer and a salesperson in an open-air market. Use these expressions and also look at **Expresiones útiles** on the previous page.
Answers will vary.

¿Qué desea?	Estoy buscando...	Prefiero el/la rojo/a.
What would you like?	*I'm looking for...*	*I prefer the red one.*

Cliente/a

Say good afternoon.

Explain that you are looking for a particular item of clothing.

Discuss colors and sizes.

Ask for the price and begin bargaining.

Settle on a price and purchase the item.

Vendedor(a)

Greet the customer and ask what he/she would like.

Show him/her some items and ask what he/she prefers.

Discuss colors and sizes.

Tell him/her a price. Negotiate a price.

Accept a price and say thank you.

TEACHING OPTIONS

Extra Practice Have the class answer questions about the **Fotonovela**. Ex: 1. ¿Quién necesita una bolsa nueva para su trabajo? (Graciela, la hermana de Inés) 2. ¿Quién cree que la primera bolsa es demasiado cara? (Inés) 3. ¿Quién acaba de comprarse un suéter? (Javier)
Pairs Divide the class into pairs. Tell them to imagine that they are awards show commentators on the red carpet (la alfombra

roja). Ask each pair to choose six celebrities and write a description of their outfits. Encourage creativity, and provide additional vocabulary if needed. Then have pairs read their descriptions for the class. Ex: **Aquí estamos en la alfombra roja de los *Video Music Awards*. Ahora viene Beyoncé con Jay-Z. Ella lleva un vestido azul de seda y sandalias grises. ¡Qué ropa tan bonita! Jay-Z usa bluejeans y…**

Pronunciación
The consonants **d** and **t**

¿Dónde?   **vender**   **nadar**   **verdad**

Like **b** and **v**, the Spanish **d** can also have a hard sound or a soft sound, depending on which letters appear next to it.

Don   **dinero**   **tienda**   **falda**

At the beginning of a phrase and after **n** or **l**, the letter **d** is pronounced with a hard sound. This sound is similar to the English *d* in *dog*, but a little softer and duller. The tongue should touch the back of the upper teeth, not the roof of the mouth.

medias   **verde**   **vestido**   **huésped**

In all other positions, **d** has a soft sound. It is similar to the English *th* in *there*, but a little softer.

Don Diego no tiene el diccionario.

When **d** begins a word, its pronunciation depends on the previous word. At the beginning of a phrase or after a word that ends in **n** or **l**, it is pronounced as a hard **d**.

Doña Dolores es de la capital.

Words that begin with **d** are pronounced with a soft **d** if they appear immediately after a word that ends in a vowel or any consonant other than **n** or **l**.

traje   **pantalones**   **tarjeta**   **tienda**

When pronouncing the Spanish **t**, the tongue should touch the back of the upper teeth, not the roof of the mouth. Unlike the English *t*, no air is expelled from the mouth.

Práctica Read these phrases aloud to practice the **d** and the **t**.

1. Hasta pronto.
2. De nada.
3. Mucho gusto.
4. Lo siento.
5. No hay de qué.
6. ¿De dónde es usted?
7. ¡Todos a bordo!
8. No puedo.
9. Es estupendo.
10. No tengo computadora.
11. ¿Cuándo vienen?
12. Son las tres y media.

Oraciones Read these sentences aloud to practice the **d** and the **t**.

1. Don Teodoro tiene una tienda en un almacén en La Habana.
2. Don Teodoro vende muchos trajes, vestidos y zapatos todos los días.
3. Un día un turista, Federico Machado, entra en la tienda para comprar un par de botas.
4. Federico regatea con don Teodoro y compra las botas y también un par de sandalias.

> *En la variedad está el gusto.*[1]

Refranes Read these sayings aloud to practice the **d** and the **t**.

> *Aunque la mona se vista de seda, mona se queda.*[2]

[1] *Variety is the spice of life.*   [2] *You can't make a silk purse out of a sow's ear.*

recursos		
CH p. 83	CA p. 118	descubre1.vhlcentral.com Lección 6

EN DETALLE

Los mercados al aire libre

El Rastro

Daily or weekly mercados al aire libre in the Spanish-speaking world are an important part of commerce and culture, where locals, tourists, and vendors interact. People come to the marketplace to shop, socialize, taste local foods, and watch street performers. One can simply wander from one **puesto** (*stand*) to the next, browsing through fresh fruits and vegetables, clothing, CDs and DVDs, jewelry, tapestries, pottery, and crafts (**artesanías**). Used merchandise—such as antiques, clothing, and books—can also be found at markets.

When shoppers see an item they like, they can bargain with the vendor. Friendly bargaining is an expected ritual and usually results in lowering the price by about twenty-five percent. Occasionally vendors may give the customer a little extra quantity of the item they purchase; this free addition is known as **la ñapa**.

Many open-air markets are also tourist attractions. The market in Otavalo, Ecuador is world-famous and has taken place every Saturday since pre-Incan times. This market is well-known for the colorful textiles woven by the **otavaleños**, the indigenous people of the area. One can also find leather goods and wood carvings from nearby towns. Another popular market is **El Rastro**, held every Sunday in Madrid, Spain. Sellers set up **puestos** along the streets to display their wares, which range from local artwork and antiques to inexpensive clothing and electronics.

Mercado de Otavalo

Otros mercados famosos

Mercado	Lugar	Productos
Feria Artesanal de Recoleta	Buenos Aires, Argentina	artesanías
Mercado Central	Santiago, Chile	mariscos°, pescado°, frutas, verduras°
Tianguis Cultural del Chopo	Ciudad de México, México	ropa, música, revistas, libros, arte, artesanías
El mercado de Chichicastenango	Chichicastenango, Guatemala	frutas y verduras, flores°, cerámica, textiles

mariscos *seafood* pescado *fish* verduras *vegetables*
flores *flowers*

ACTIVIDADES

1

¿Cierto o falso? Indicate whether these statements are **cierto** or **falso**. Correct the false statements.

1. Generally, open-air markets specialize in one type of goods. Falso. They sell a variety of goods.
2. Bargaining is commonplace at outdoor markets. Cierto.
3. Only new goods can be found at open-air markets. Falso. They sell both new and used goods.
4. A Spaniard in search of antiques could search at **El Rastro.** Cierto.
5. If you are in Guatemala and want to buy ceramics, you can go to Chichicastenango. Cierto.
6. A **ñapa** is a tax on open-air market goods. Falso. A ñapa is a free addition sometimes given to customers.
7. The **otavaleños** weave colorful textiles to sell on Saturdays. Cierto.
8. Santiago's **Mercado Central** is known for books and music. Falso. It's known for seafood, fish, fruits, and vegetables.

ASÍ SE DICE

La ropa

la chamarra (Méx.)	la chaqueta
de manga corta/larga	*short/long-sleeved*
los mahones (P. Rico); el pantalón de mezclilla (Méx.); los tejanos (Esp.); los vaqueros (Arg., Cuba, Esp., Uru.)	los bluejeans
la marca	*brand*
la playera (Méx.); la remera (Arg.)	la camiseta

EL MUNDO HISPANO

Diseñadores de moda

○ **Adolfo Domínguez** (España) Su ropa tiene un estilo minimalista y práctico. Usa telas° naturales y cómodas en sus diseños.

○ **Silvia Tcherassi** (Colombia) Los colores vivos y líneas asimétricas de sus vestidos y trajes muestran influencias tropicales.

○ **Óscar de la Renta** (República Dominicana) Diseña ropa opulenta para la mujer clásica.

○ **Narciso Rodríguez** (EE.UU.) En sus diseños delicados y finos predominan los colores blanco y negro. Hizo° el vestido de boda° de Carolyn Bessette Kennedy.

telas *fabrics* Hizo *He made* boda *wedding*

PERFIL

Carolina Herrera

In 1980, at the urging of some friends, **Carolina Herrera** created a fashion collection as a "test." The Venezuelan designer received such a favorable response that within one year she moved her family from Caracas to New York City and created her own label, Carolina Herrera, Ltd.

"I love elegance and intricacy, but whether it is in a piece of clothing or a fragrance, the intricacy must appear as simplicity," Herrera once stated. She quickly found that many sophisticated women agreed; from the start, her sleek and

glamorous designs have been in constant demand. Over the years, Herrera has grown her brand into a veritable fashion empire that encompasses her fashion and bridal collections, cosmetics, perfume, and accessories that are sold around the globe.

SUPERSITE Conexión Internet

¿Qué marcas de ropa son populares en el mundo hispano?

Go to **descubre1.vhlcentral.com** to find more cultural information related to this **Cultura** section.

ACTIVIDADES

2 **Comprensión** Complete these sentences.

1. Adolfo Domínguez usa telas ___naturales___ y ___cómodas___ en su ropa.
2. Si hace fresco en el D.F., puedes llevar una ___chamarra___.
3. La diseñadora ___Carolina Herrera___ hace ropa, perfumes y más.
4. La ropa de ___Silvia Tcherassi___ muestra influencias tropicales.
5. Los ___mahones___ son una ropa casual en Puerto Rico.

3 **Mi ropa favorita** Write a brief description of your favorite article of clothing. Mention what store it is from, the brand, colors, fabric, style, etc. Then get together with a small group and take turns reading the descriptions aloud.
Answers will vary.

recursos

CH p. 84	descubre1.vhlcentral.com Lección 6

NATIONAL
comparisons
STANDARDS

Section Goals

In **Estructura 6.1**, students will learn:
- the uses of **saber** and **conocer**
- more uses of the personal **a**
- other verbs conjugated like **conocer**

Instructional Resources
Cuaderno de práctica, p. 61
Cuaderno para hispanohablantes, pp. 85–86
Cuaderno de actividades, p. 119
e-Cuaderno
Supersite: Audio Activity MP3 Audio Files
Supersite/TRCD/Print:
PowerPoints (Lección 6 **Estructura** Presentation); Audio Activity Script, Answer Keys
Audio Activity CD

Teaching Tips
- Point out the irregular **yo** forms of **saber** and **conocer**.
- Divide the board or an overhead transparency into two columns with the headings **saber** and **conocer**. In the first column, write the uses of **saber** and model them by asking individuals what they know how to do and what factual information they know. Ex: _____, **¿sabes bailar salsa? ¿Sabes mi número de teléfono?** In the second column, write the uses of **conocer** and model them by asking individuals about people and places they know. Ex: _____, **¿conoces Cuba? ¿Conoces a Anier García?**
- Further distinguish the uses of **saber** and **conocer** by making statements such as: **Sé quién es el presidente de este país, pero no lo conozco.**
- Point out that the verbs listed under **¡Atención!** are conjugated like **conocer**. Ask volunteers to provide the **yo** form of each verb.

6.1 Saber and conocer

ANTE TODO Spanish has two verbs that mean *to know*: **saber** and **conocer**. They cannot be used interchangeably. Note the irregular **yo** forms.

The verbs saber and conocer

		saber *(to know)*	conocer *(to know)*
SINGULAR FORMS	yo	sé	conozco
	tú	sabes	conoces
	Ud./él/ella	sabe	conoce
PLURAL FORMS	nosotros/as	sabemos	conocemos
	vosotros/as	sabéis	conocéis
	Uds./ellos/ellas	saben	conocen

▶ **Saber** means *to know a fact or piece(s) of information* or *to know how to do something.*

No **sé** tu número de teléfono.
I don't know your telephone number.

Mi hermana **sabe** hablar francés.
My sister knows how to speak French.

▶ **Conocer** means *to know* or *be familiar/acquainted* with a person, place, or thing.

¿**Conoces** la ciudad de Nueva York?
Do you know New York City?

No **conozco** a tu amigo Esteban.
I don't know your friend Esteban.

▶ When the direct object of **conocer** is a person or pet, the personal **a** is used.

¿Conoces La Habana?   *but*   ¿Conoces **a** Celia Cruz?
Do you know Havana?   *Do you know Celia Cruz?*

▶ **¡Atención!** These verbs are also conjugated like **conocer**.

conducir	parecer	ofrecer	traducir
to drive	*to seem*	*to offer*	*to translate*

¡INTÉNTALO! Provide the appropriate forms of these verbs. The first item in each column has been done for you.

saber

1. José no __sabe__ la hora.
2. Sara y yo __sabemos__ jugar al tenis.
3. ¿Por qué no __sabes__ tú estos verbos?
4. Mis padres __saben__ hablar japonés.
5. Yo __sé__ a qué hora es la clase.
6. Usted no __sabe__ dónde vivo.
7. Mi hermano no __sabe__ nadar.
8. Nosotros __sabemos__ muchas cosas.

conocer

1. Usted y yo __conocemos__ bien Miami.
2. ¿Tú __conoces__ a mi amigo Manuel?
3. Sergio y Taydé __conocen__ mi pueblo.
4. Emiliano __conoce__ a mis padres.
5. Yo __conozco__ muy bien el centro.
6. ¿Ustedes __conocen__ la tienda Gigante?
7. Nosotras __conocemos__ una playa hermosa.
8. ¿Usted __conoce__ a mi profesora?

recursos

CP
p. 61

CH
p. 85–86

CA
p. 119

SUPERSITE
descubre1.
vhlcentral.com
Lección 6

TEACHING OPTIONS

TPR Divide the class into two teams, **saber** and **conocer**, and have them line up. Indicate the first member of each team and call out a sentence in English that uses *to know* (Ex: We know the answer.). The team member whose verb corresponds to the English sentence has five seconds to step forward and provide the Spanish translation.

Extra Practice Ask students to jot down three things they know how to do well (**saber** + [*infinitive*] + **bien**). Collect the papers, shuffle them, and read the sentences aloud. Have the rest of the class guess who wrote the sentences.

Práctica y Comunicación

 1

Completar Indicate the correct verb for each sentence.

1. Mis hermanos (conocen/saben) conducir, pero yo no (sé/conozco).
2. —¿(Conocen/Saben) ustedes dónde está el estadio? —No, no (conocemos/sabemos).
3. —¿(Conoces/Sabes) a Cher? —Bueno, (sé/conozco) quién es, pero no la (conozco/sé).
4. Mi profesora (sabe/conoce) Cuba y también (conoce/sabe) bailar salsa.

2

Combinar Combine elements from each column to create sentences. Answers will vary.

A	B	C
Shakira	(no) conocer	Jessica Simpson
los Yankees	(no) saber	cantar y bailar
el primer ministro		La Habana Vieja
de Canadá		muchas personas importantes
mis amigos y yo		hablar dos lenguas extranjeras
tú		jugar al béisbol

3

Preguntas In pairs, ask each other these questions. Answer with complete sentences.
Answers will vary.

1. ¿Conoces a un(a) cantante famoso/a? ¿Te gusta cómo canta?
2. En tu familia, ¿quién sabe cantar? ¿Tu opinión es objetiva?
3. Tus padres, ¿conducen bien o mal? ¿Y tus hermanos mayores?
4. Si una persona no conduce muy bien, ¿le ofreces crítica constructiva?
5. ¿Cómo parece estar el/la profesor(a) hoy? ¿Y tus compañeros de clase?

4

Entrevista Jot down three things you know how to do, three people you know, and three places you are familiar with. Then, in a small group, find out what you have in common. Answers will vary.

> **modelo**
> **Estudiante 1:** ¿Conocen ustedes a David Lomas?
> **Estudiante 2:** Sí, conozco a David. Vivimos en el mismo barrio (*neighborhood*).
> **Estudiante 3:** No, no lo conozco. ¿Cómo es?

5

Anuncio In groups, read the ad and answer the questions. Answers will vary.

1. Busquen ejemplos de los verbos **saber** y **conocer**.
2. ¿Qué saben del Centro Comercial Oviedo?
3. ¿Qué pueden hacer en el Centro Comercial Oviedo?
4. ¿Conocen otros centros comerciales similares? ¿Cómo se llaman? ¿Dónde están?
5. ¿Conocen un centro comercial en otro país? ¿Cómo es?

Él sabe dónde comer
lo que más le gusta

Él sabe cómo jugar
cuatro horas seguidas

Él sabe dónde
está su regalo
de cumpleaños

Él sabe dónde divertirse

...y usted sabe dónde puede
encontrar un poco de todo.
¿Conoce algún otro lugar como éste?

Oviedo
Centro Comercial
Sabe lo que te gusta

6.2 Indirect object pronouns

ANTE TODO In **Lección 5**, you learned that a direct object receives the action of the verb directly. In contrast, an indirect object receives the action of the verb indirectly.

SUBJECT	I.O. PRONOUN	VERB	DIRECT OBJECT	INDIRECT OBJECT
Roberto	**le**	presta	cien pesos	**a Luisa**.
Roberto		*lends*	*100 pesos*	*to Luisa.*

An indirect object is a noun or pronoun that answers the question *to whom* or *for whom* an action is done. In the preceding example, the indirect object answers this question: **¿A quién le presta Roberto cien pesos?** *To whom does Roberto lend 100 pesos?*

Indirect object pronouns

Singular forms		Plural forms	
me	(to, for) *me*	**nos**	(to, for) *us*
te	(to, for) *you* (fam.)	**os**	(to, for) *you* (fam.)
le	(to, for) *you* (form.) (to, for) *him; her*	**les**	(to, for) *you* (form.) (to, for) *them*

▶ **¡Atención!** The forms of indirect object pronouns for the first and second persons (**me, te, nos, os**) are the same as the direct object pronouns. Indirect object pronouns agree in number with the corresponding nouns, but not in gender.

*Buenas tardes.
¿Le puedo servir
en algo?*

*Quiero comprarle
una a mi hermana.*

Using indirect object pronouns

▶ Spanish speakers commonly use both an indirect object pronoun and the noun to which it refers in the same sentence. This is done to emphasize and clarify to whom the pronoun refers.

I.O. PRONOUN		INDIRECT OBJECT		I.O. PRONOUN		INDIRECT OBJECT
Ella **le** vende la ropa **a Elena**.				**Les** prestamos el dinero **a Inés y a Álex**.		

▶ Indirect object pronouns are also used without the indirect object noun when the person for whom the action is being done is known.

Ana **le** presta la falda **a Elena**.
Ana lends her skirt to Elena.

También **le** presta unos bluejeans.
She also lends her a pair of blue jeans.

▶ Indirect object pronouns are usually placed before the conjugated form of the verb. In negative sentences the pronoun is placed between **no** and the conjugated verb.

Martín **me** compra un regalo.	Eva **no me** escribe cartas.
Martín buys me a gift.	*Eva doesn't write me letters.*

CONSULTA

For more information on accents, see **Lección 4, Pronunciación, p. 123.**

▶ When a conjugated verb is followed by an infinitive or the present progressive, the indirect object pronoun may be placed before the conjugated verb or attached to the infinitive or present participle. **¡Atención!** When an indirect object pronoun is attached to a present participle, an accent mark is added to maintain the proper stress.

Él no quiere **pagarte**./	Él está **escribiéndole** una postal a ella./
Él no **te** quiere pagar.	Él **le** está escribiendo una postal a ella.
He does not want to pay you.	*He is writing a postcard to her.*

▶ Because the indirect object pronouns **le** and **les** have multiple meanings, Spanish speakers often clarify to whom the pronouns refer with the preposition **a** + [*pronoun*] or **a** + [*noun*].

UNCLARIFIED STATEMENTS	CLARIFIED STATEMENTS
Yo **le** compro un abrigo.	Yo **le** compro un abrigo **a usted/él/ella**.
Ella **le** describe un libro.	Ella **le** describe un libro **a Juan**.

UNCLARIFIED STATEMENTS	CLARIFIED STATEMENTS
Él **les** vende unos sombreros.	Él **les** vende unos sombreros **a ustedes/ellos/ellas**.
Ellos **les** hablan muy claro.	Ellos **les** hablan muy claro **a los clientes**.

▶ The irregular verbs **dar** (*to give*) and **decir**, are often used with indirect object pronouns.

CONSULTA

Remember that **decir** is a stem-changing verb (e:i) with an irregular **yo** form: **digo**. To review the present tense of **decir**, see **Estructura 4.3, p. 133.**

The verb dar (*to give*)

Singular forms		Plural forms	
yo	**doy**	nosotros/as	**damos**
tú	**das**	vosotros/as	**dais**
Ud./él/ella	**da**	Uds./ellos/ellas	**dan**

Me dan una fiesta cada año.	**Te digo** la verdad.
They give (throw) me a party every year.	*I'm telling you the truth.*
Voy a **darle** consejos.	No **les digo** mentiras a mis padres.
I'm going to give her advice.	*I don't tell lies to my parents.*

recursos

CP
pp. 62–63

CH
pp. 87–88

CA
p. 120

descubre1.
vhlcentral.com
Lección 6

¡INTÉNTALO! Use the cues in parentheses to provide the indirect object pronoun for the sentence. The first item has been done for you.

1. Juan ____le____ quiere dar un regalo. (*to Elena*)
2. María ____nos____ prepara un café. (*for us*)
3. Beatriz y Felipe ____me____ escriben desde (*from*) Cuba. (*to me*)
4. Marta y yo ____les____ compramos unos guantes. (*for them*)
5. Los vendedores ____te____ venden ropa. (*to you, fam. sing.*)
6. La dependienta ____nos____ muestra los guantes. (*to us*)

Teaching Tips
- Point out that the position of indirect object pronouns in a sentence is the same as that of direct object pronouns.
- Ask individuals questions using indirect object pronouns. Ex: **¿A quién le ofreces ayuda? ¿Les das consejos a tus amigos? ¿Qué te dicen tus padres que no debes hacer? ¿Les dices mentiras a tus padres? ¿Cuándo vas a escribirles a tus abuelos?**
- After going over the **¡Inténtalo!** orally with the class, ask students which items might require clarification (items 1 and 4). Ask them what they would add to each sentence in order to clarify **le** or **les**.
- As a comprehension check, have students write answers to these questions: **1. Es el cumpleaños de tu mejor amigo. ¿Qué vas a comprarle? 2. ¿A quiénes les hablas todos los días? 3. ¿Quién te presta dinero cuando lo necesitas? 4. ¿Quién les está enseñando español a ustedes?**

TEACHING OPTIONS

Video Replay the *Fotonovela*. Ask students to note each time an indirect object pronoun is used. Point out that the pronouns used with **gustar** are indirect objects because they answer the question (*is pleasing*) *to whom*. Then, have students find each use of **le** and **les** and state to whom the pronouns refer.
Game Give each student an envelope and a sheet of paper. Ask them to write a sentence using an indirect object pronoun,

cut the paper into strips (one word per strip), shuffle them, and place them in the envelope. Then have students pass their envelopes to the person sitting behind them. Allow thirty seconds for them to decipher the sentence and write it down, before placing the shuffled strips back into the envelope and passing it on. After three minutes, the row with the most correctly deciphered sentences wins.

Práctica

1 **Completar** Fill in the correct pronouns to complete Mónica's description of her family's gift giving.

1. Juan y yo ___le___ damos una blusa a nuestra hermana Gisela.
2. Mi tía ___nos___ da a nosotros una mesa para la casa.
3. Gisela ___le___ da dos corbatas a su novio.
4. A mi mamá yo ___le___ doy un par de guantes negros.
5. A mi profesora ___le___ doy dos libros de José Martí.
6. Juan ___les___ da un regalo a mis padres.
7. Mis padres ___me___ dan a mí un traje nuevo.
8. Y a ti, yo ___te___ doy un regalo también. ¿Quieres verlo?

NOTA CULTURAL
Cuban writer and patriot **José Martí** (1853–1895) was born in **La Habana Vieja,** the old colonial center of Havana.

2 **Describir** Describe what is happening in these photos based on the cues provided.

1. escribir / mensaje electrónico Álex le escribe un mensaje electrónico (a Ricardo).

2. mostrar / fotos Javier les muestra fotos (a Inés y a Maite).

3. dar / documentos La Sra. Ramos le da los documentos (a Maite).

4. pedir / llaves Don Francisco le pide las llaves (a la empleada).

5. vender / suéter El vendedor le vende un suéter (a Javier).

6. comprar / bolsa Inés le compra una bolsa (a su hermana).

3 **Combinar** Use an item from each column and an indirect object pronoun to create logical sentences. Answers will vary.

modelo
Mis padres les dan regalos a mis primos.

A	B	C	D
yo	comprar	correo electrónico	mí
el dependiente	dar	corbata	ustedes
el profesor Arce	decir	dinero en efectivo	clienta
la vendedora	escribir	ejercicio	novia
mis padres	explicar	problemas	primos
tú	pagar	regalos	ti
nosotros/as	prestar	ropa	nosotros
¿?	vender	¿?	¿?

1 **Teaching Tip** Have students find the indirect object in each sentence.

1 **Expansion** Have students write four sentences about themselves, leaving out the indirect object pronoun. Ex: **Yo ____ doy un regalo a mis padres. Mi tío ____ compra a mí una moto.** Then have them exchange papers with a classmate and complete the sentences.

2 **Teaching Tip** Have students describe to a partner what they see in the photos. Ask them to describe not only the action, but also each person's physical appearance and clothing.

2 **Expansion** Divide the class into groups of four. Have each student pick a photo to present to the group as a verbal portrait, including an introductory sentence that sets the scene, followed by a body and conclusion. The verbal portrait should answer the questions *who, what, where, when,* and *why* with regard to what is seen in the photo. After each group member has presented his or her photo, the group chooses one to present to the class.

3 **Expansion** Have students convert three of their statements into questions, using **¿Quién?, ¿A quién?,** and **¿Qué?** Have pairs take turns asking and answering their questions. Ex: **¿Quién les vende la ropa? (el dependiente) ¿A quiénes les das regalos? (a mis primos) ¿Qué te explican tus padres? (los problemas)**

Comunicación

4 **Entrevista** Take turns with a classmate asking and answering questions using the word bank.
Answers will vary.

> **modelo**
> escribir mensajes electrónicos
> **Estudiante 1:** ¿A quién le escribes mensajes electrónicos?
> **Estudiante 2:** Le escribo mensajes electrónicos a mi hermano.

cantar	escribir mensajes electrónicos
comprar ropa	mostrar fotos de un viaje
dar una fiesta	pedir dinero
decir mentiras	preparar comida (*food*) mexicana

5 **¡Somos ricos!** You and your classmates just received a large sum of money. Now you want to spend money on your loved ones. In groups of three, discuss what each person is buying for family and friends. Answers will vary.

> **modelo**
> **Estudiante 1:** Quiero comprarle un vestido de Carolina Herrera a mi madre.
> **Estudiante 2:** Y yo voy a darles un automóvil nuevo a mis padres.
> **Estudiante 3:** Voy a comprarles una casa a mis padres, pero a mis
> amigos no les voy a dar nada.

6 **Entrevista** Use these questions to interview a classmate. Answers will vary.

1. ¿Qué tiendas, almacenes o centros comerciales prefieres?
2. ¿A quién le compras regalos cuando hay rebajas?
3. ¿A quién le prestas dinero cuando lo necesita?
4. Quiero ir de compras. ¿Cuánto dinero me puedes prestar?
5. ¿Te dan tus padres su tarjeta de crédito cuando vas de compras?

Síntesis

7 **Minidrama** With two classmates, take turns playing the roles of two shoppers and a clerk in a clothing store. The shoppers should take turns talking about the articles of clothing they want and for whom they are buying them. The clerk should recommend several items based on the shoppers' descriptions. Use these expressions and also look at **Expresiones útiles** on page 195.
Answers will vary.

> Me queda grande/pequeño.
> *It's big/small on me.*
> ¿Tiene otro color?
> *Do you have another color?*
> ¿Está en rebaja?
> *Is it on sale?*

---

4 Teaching Tips
• Have two volunteers read the model aloud. Then go through the phrases in the word bank and model question formation.
• To challenge students, have them ask follow-up questions for each item. Ex: **¿A quién le compras ropa? ¿Qué ropa le compras? ¿Dónde la compras?**

4 Expansion In groups of three, give students five minutes to brainstorm as many questions as they can using different forms of the verbs in the word bank. Invite two groups to come to the front of the class. Each group takes a turn asking the other its questions.

5 Teaching Tip Give each group a different sum of money. Remind students they have to split it equally amongst the group members.

6 Expansion Take a class survey of the answers and write the results on the board.

7 Teaching Tips
• To simplify, have students begin by brainstorming phrases for their role. Remind them that, except for dialogue *between* the two shoppers, they should use **usted** in their conversation.
• Have students rehearse their mini-dramas.
• Videotape the scenes in or outside of class.

6.3 Preterite tense of regular verbs

ANTE TODO In order to talk about events in the past, Spanish uses two simple tenses: the preterite and the imperfect. In this lesson, you will learn how to form the preterite tense, which is used to express actions or states completed in the past.

Preterite of regular -ar, -er, and -ir verbs

		-ar verbs **comprar**	-er verbs **vender**	-ir verbs **escribir**
SINGULAR FORMS	yo	compr**é** *I bought*	vend**í** *I sold*	escrib**í** *I wrote*
	tú	compr**aste**	vend**iste**	escrib**iste**
	Ud./él/ella	compr**ó**	vend**ió**	escrib**ió**
PLURAL FORMS	nosotros/as	compr**amos**	vend**imos**	escrib**imos**
	vosotros/as	compr**asteis**	vend**isteis**	escrib**isteis**
	Uds./ellos/ellas	compr**aron**	vend**ieron**	escrib**ieron**

▶ **¡Atención!** The **yo** and **Ud./él/ella** forms of all three conjugations have written accents on the last syllable to show that it is stressed.

▶ As the chart shows, the endings for regular **-er** and **-ir** verbs are identical in the preterite.

¿Qué compraste?

Compré esta bolsa.

▶ Note that the **nosotros/as** forms of regular **-ar** and **-ir** verbs in the preterite are identical to the present tense forms. Context will help you determine which tense is being used.

En invierno **compramos** ropa.
In the winter, we buy clothing.

Anoche **compramos** unos zapatos.
Last night we bought some shoes.

▶ **-Ar** and **-er** verbs that have a stem change in the present tense are regular in the preterite. They do *not* have a stem change.

	PRESENT	PRETERITE
cerrar (e:ie)	La tienda **cierra** a las seis.	La tienda **cerró** a las seis.
volver (o:ue)	Carlitos **vuelve** tarde.	Carlitos **volvió** tarde.
jugar (u:ue)	Él **juega** al fútbol.	Él **jugó** al fútbol.

▶ **¡Atención!** **-Ir** verbs that have a stem change in the present tense also have a stem change in the preterite.

CONSULTA

You will learn about the preterite of stem-changing verbs in **Estructura 8.1**, p. 274.

▶ Verbs that end in **-car**, **-gar**, and **-zar** have a spelling change in the first person singular (**yo** form) in the preterite.

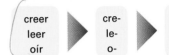

bus**car**	busc-	qu-	yo bus**qué**
lle**gar**	lleg-	gu-	yo lle**gué**
empe**zar**	empez-	c-	yo empe**cé**

▶ Except for the **yo** form, all other forms of **-car**, **-gar**, and **-zar** verbs are regular in the preterite.

▶ Three other verbs—**creer**, **leer**, and **oír**—have spelling changes in the preterite. The **i** of the verb endings of **creer**, **leer**, and **oír** carries an accent in the **yo**, **tú**, **nosotros/as**, and **vosotros/as** forms, and changes to **y** in the **Ud./él/ella** and **Uds./ellos/ellas** forms.

creer	cre-	cre**í**, cre**í**ste, cre**y**ó, cre**í**mos, cre**í**steis, cre**y**eron
leer	le-	le**í**, le**í**ste, le**y**ó, le**í**mos, le**í**steis, le**y**eron
oír	o-	o**í**, o**í**ste, o**y**ó, o**í**mos, o**í**steis, o**y**eron

▶ **Ver** is regular in the preterite, but none of its forms has an accent.

ver ⟶ vi, viste, vio, vimos, visteis, vieron

Words commonly used with the preterite

anoche	*last night*		**pasado/a** (*adj.*)	*last; past*
anteayer	*the day before*		**el año pasado**	*last year*
	yesterday		**la semana pasada**	*last week*
ayer	*yesterday*		**una vez**	*once; one time*
de repente	*suddenly*		**dos veces**	*twice; two times*
desde... hasta...	*from... until...*		**ya**	*already*

Ayer llegué a Santiago de Cuba.   **Anoche** oí un ruido extraño.
Yesterday I arrived in Santiago de Cuba.   *Last night I heard a strange noise.*

▶ **Acabar de** + [*infinitive*] is used to say that something has just occurred. Note that **acabar** is in the present tense in this construction.

Acabo de comprar una falda.   **Acabas de ir** de compras.
I just bought a skirt.   *You just went shopping.*

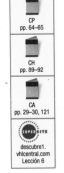

¡INTÉNTALO!   Provide the appropriate preterite forms of the verbs. The first item in each column has been done for you.

	comer	salir	comenzar	leer
1. ellas	*comieron*	*salieron*	*comenzaron*	*leyeron*
2. tú	comiste	saliste	comenzaste	leíste
3. usted	comió	salió	comenzó	leyó
4. nosotros	comimos	salimos	comenzamos	leímos
5. yo	comí	salí	comencé	leí

Teaching Tips
- Point out that verbs ending in **-car** and **-gar** are regular and have logical spelling changes in the **yo** form in order to preserve the hard **c** and **g** sounds.
- Students will learn the preterite of **dar** in **Estructura 9.1**. If you wish to present it for recognition only at this point, you can tell them that the endings are identical to **ver** in the preterite.
- Provide sentence starters using the present indicative and have students complete them in a logical manner. Ex: **Todos los días los estudiantes llegan temprano, pero anteayer… (llegaron tarde.)**
- Practice verbs with spelling changes in the preterite by asking students about things they read, heard, and saw yesterday. Ex: **¿Leíste el periódico ayer? ¿Quiénes vieron el pronóstico del tiempo? Yo oí que va a llover hoy. ¿Qué oyeron ustedes?**
- Add a visual aspect to this grammar presentation. Use magazine pictures to demonstrate **acabar de**. Ex: **¿Quién acaba de ganar? (Tiger Woods acaba de ganar.) ¿Qué acaban de ver ellos? (Acaban de ver una película.)**

TEACHING OPTIONS

Game Divide the class into teams of six and have them sit in rows. Call out the infinitive of a verb. The first person writes the preterite **yo** form on a sheet of paper and passes it to the second person, who writes the **tú** form, and so on. The sixth checks spelling. If all forms are correct, the team gets a point. Continue play, having team members rotate positions for each round. The team with the most points after six rounds wins.

Extra Practice Have students write down five things they did yesterday. Ask students questions about what they did to elicit as many different conjugations as possible. Ex: _____, ¿leíste el periódico ayer? ¿Quién más leyó el periódico ayer?... _____ y _____, ustedes dos leyeron el periódico ayer, ¿verdad? ¿Quiénes leyeron el periódico ayer?

Práctica

1

Completar Andrea is talking about what happened last weekend. Complete each sentence by choosing the correct verb and putting it in the preterite.

1. El sábado a las diez de la mañana, la profesora Mora ___asistió___ (asistir, costar, usar) a una reunión (*meeting*) de profesores.
2. A la una, yo ___llegué___ (llegar, bucear, llevar) a la tienda con mis amigos.
3. Mis amigos y yo ___compramos___ (comprar, regatear, gastar) dos o tres cosas.
4. Yo ___compré___ (costar, comprar, escribir) unos pantalones negros y mi amigo Mateo ___compró___ (gastar, pasear, comprar) una camisa azul.
5. Después, nosotros ___comimos___ (llevar, vivir, comer) cerca de un mercado.
6. A las tres, Pepe ___habló___ (hablar, pasear, nadar) con su novia por teléfono.
7. El sábado por la tarde, mi mamá ___escribió___ (escribir, beber, vivir) una carta.
8. El domingo mi tía ___decidió___ (decidir, salir, escribir) comprarme un traje.
9. A las cuatro de la tarde, mi tía ___encontró___ (beber, salir, encontrar) el traje y después nosotras ___vimos___ (acabar, ver, salir) una película.

2

Preguntas Imagine that you have a pesky friend who keeps asking you questions. Respond that you already did or have just done what he/she asks.

> **modelo**
> leer la lección
> **Estudiante 1:** ¿Leíste la lección?
> **Estudiante 2:** Sí, ya la leí./Sí, acabo de leerla.

1. escribir el correo electrónico *(emal)*
2. lavar (*to wash*) la ropa
3. oír las noticias (*news*)
4. comprar pantalones cortos
5. practicar los verbos
6. leer el artículo
7. empezar la composición
8. ver la nueva película de Almodóvar

1. E1: ¿Escribiste el correo electrónico?
   E2: Sí, ya lo escribí./Acabo de escribirlo.
2. E1: ¿Lavaste la ropa?
   E2: Sí, ya la lavé./Acabo de lavarla.
3. E1: ¿Oíste las noticias?
   E2: Sí, ya las oí./Acabo de oírlas.
4. E1: ¿Compraste pantalones cortos?
   E2: Sí, ya los compré./Acabo de comprarlos.
5. E1: ¿Practicaste los verbos?
   E2: Sí, ya los practiqué./Acabo de practicarlos.
6. E1: ¿Leíste el artículo?
   E2: Sí, ya lo leí./Acabo de leerlo.
7. E1: ¿Empezaste la composición?
   E2: Sí, ya la empecé./Acabo de empezarla.
8. E1: ¿Viste la nueva película de Almodóvar?
   E2: Sí, ya la vi./Acabo de verla.

3

¿Cuándo? Use the time expressions from the word bank to talk about when you and others did the activities listed. *Answers will vary.*

anoche	anteayer	el mes pasado	una vez
ayer	la semana pasada	el año pasado	dos veces

partner
1. mi compañero/a de clase: llegar tarde a clase
2. mi mejor (*best*) amigo/a: salir con un(a) chico/a guapo/a
3. mis padres: ver una película
4. yo: llevar un traje/vestido
5. el presidente de los EE.UU.: no escuchar a la gente *(people)*
6. mis amigos y yo: comer en un restaurante
7. ¿?: comprar algo (*something*) bueno, bonito y barato *(cheap)*

Comunicación

4 **Las vacaciones** Imagine that you took these photos on a vacation. Get together with a partner and use the pictures to tell him or her about your trip. Answers will vary.

5 **El fin de semana** Your teacher will give you and your partner different incomplete charts about what four employees at **Almacén Gigante** did last weekend. After you fill out the chart based on each other's information, you will fill out the final column about your partner.
Answers will vary.

Síntesis

6 **Conversación** With a partner, have a conversation about what you did last week, using verbs from the word bank. Don't forget to include school activities, shopping, and pastimes. Answers will vary.

acampar	comprar	hablar	tomar
asistir	correr	jugar	trabajar
bailar	escribir	leer	vender
buscar	estudiar	oír	ver
comer	gastar	pagar	viajar

4 **Teaching Tip** Have students first state where they traveled and when. Then have them identify the people in the photos, stating their names and their relationship to them and describing their personalities. Finally, students should tell what everyone did on the trip.

4 **Expansion** After completing the activity orally, have students write a paragraph about their vacation, basing their account on the photos.

5 **Teaching Tip** Divide the class into pairs and distribute the Communication Activities worksheets that correspond to this activity. Give students ten minutes to complete the activity.

5 **Expansion** Have students tell the class about any activities that both their partner and one of the **Almacén Gigante** employees did. Ex: **La señora Zapata leyó un libro y _____ también. Los dos leyeron un libro.**

6 **Teaching Tip** Have volunteers rehearse their conversation, then present it to the class.

6 **Expansion** Have volunteers report to the class what their partners did last week.

TEACHING OPTIONS

Large Group Have students stand up. Tell them to create a story chain about a student who had a very bad day. Begin the story by saying: **Ayer, Rigoberto pasó un día desastroso.** In order to sit down, students must contribute to the story. Call on a student to tell how **Rigoberto** began his day. The second person tells what happened next, and so on, until only one student remains. That person must conclude the story.

Extra Practice For homework, have students make a "to do" list at the beginning of their day. Then, ask students to return to their lists at the end of the day and write sentences stating which activities they completed. Ex: **limpiar mi habitación; No, no limpié mi habitación.**

Section Goal

In **Estructura 6.4**, students will learn to use demonstrative adjectives and pronouns.

Instructional Resources
Cuaderno de práctica,
pp. 66–68
Cuaderno para hispanohablantes, pp. 93–94
Cuaderno de actividades,
pp. 31–32, 122
e-Cuaderno
Supersite: Audio Activity MP3 Audio Files
Supersite/TRCD/Print:
PowerPoints (**Lección 6 Estructura** Presentation); Communication Activities, Audio Activity Script, Answer Keys
Audio Activity CD

Teaching Tips

- Point to the book on your desk. Say: **Este libro está en la mesa.** Point to a book on a student's desk. Say: **Ese libro está encima del escritorio de ____.** Then point to a book on the window ledge. Say: **Aquel libro está cerca de la ventana.** Repeat the procedure with **tiza, papeles,** and **plumas.**
- Point out that although the masculine singular forms **este** and **ese** do not end in –o, their plural forms end in –os: **estos, esos.**
- Hold up or point to objects and have students give the plural: **este libro, esta mochila, este traje, este zapato.** Repeat with forms of **ese** and **aquel** with other nouns.
- You may want to have students associate **este** with **aquí, ese** with **allí,** and **aquel** with **allá.**

6.4 Demonstrative adjectives and pronouns

Demonstrative adjectives (SUPERSITE)

ANTE TODO In Spanish, as in English, demonstrative adjectives are words that "demonstrate" or "point out" nouns. Demonstrative adjectives precede the nouns they modify and, like other Spanish adjectives you have studied, agree with them in gender and number. Observe these, then study the following chart.

esta camisa	**ese** vendedor	**aquellos** zapatos
this shirt	*that salesman*	*those shoes (over there)*

Demonstrative adjectives

	Singular		Plural	
	MASCULINE	FEMININE	MASCULINE	FEMININE
	este	**esta**	**estos**	**estas**	*this; these*
	ese	**esa**	**esos**	**esas**	*that; those*
	aquel	**aquella**	**aquellos**	**aquellas**	*that; those (over there)*

▶ There are three sets of demonstrative adjectives. To determine which one to use, you must establish the relationship between the speaker and the noun(s) being pointed out.

▶ The demonstrative adjectives **este, esta, estos,** and **estas** are used to point out nouns that are close to the speaker and the listener.

Me gustan estos zapatos.

▶ The demonstrative adjectives **ese, esa, esos,** and **esas** are used to point out nouns that are not close in space and time to the speaker. They may, however, be close to the listener.

Prefiero esos zapatos.

TEACHING OPTIONS

Extra Practice Hold up one or two items of clothing or classroom objects. Have students write all three forms of the demonstrative pronouns that would apply. Ex: **estos zapatos, esos zapatos, aquellos zapatos.**

Pairs Refer students to **Contextos** illustration on pages 190–191. Have them work with a partner to comment on the articles of clothing pictured. Ex: **Este suéter es bonito, ¿no? (No, ese suéter no es bonito. Es feo.) Aquella camiseta es muy cara. (Sí, aquella camiseta es cara.)**

▶ The demonstrative adjectives **aquel, aquella, aquellos,** and **aquellas** are used to point out nouns that are far away from the speaker and the listener.

Aquel auto es de mi hermana.

Demonstrative pronouns

▶ Demonstrative pronouns are identical to their corresponding demonstrative adjectives, with the exception that they carry an accent mark on the stressed vowel.

—¿Quieres comprar **este suéter**?
Do you want to buy this sweater?

—No, no quiero **éste**. Quiero **ése**.
No, I don't want this one. I want that one.

—¿Vas a leer **estas revistas**?
Are you going to read these magazines?

—Sí, voy a leer **éstas**. También voy a leer **aquéllas**.
Yes, I'm going to read these. I'll also read those (over there).

Demonstrative pronouns

Singular		Plural	
MASCULINE	FEMININE	MASCULINE	FEMININE
éste	ésta	éstos	éstas
ése	ésa	ésos	ésas
aquél	aquélla	aquéllos	aquéllas

▶ **¡Atención!** Like demonstrative adjectives, demonstrative pronouns agree in gender and number with the corresponding noun.

Este libro es de Pablito.   **Éstos** son de Juana.

▶ There are three neuter demonstrative pronouns: **esto, eso,** and **aquello.** These forms refer to unidentified or unspecified nouns, situations, ideas, and concepts. They do not change in gender or number and never carry an accent mark.

—¿Qué es **esto**?
What's this?

—**Eso** es interesante.
That's interesting.

—**Aquello** es bonito.
That's pretty.

recursos

CP
pp. 66–67

CH
pp. 93–94

CA
pp. 31–32, 122

SUPERSITE
descubre1.
vhlcentral.com
Lección 6

¡INTÉNTALO!   Provide the correct form of the demonstrative adjective for these nouns. The first item has been done for you.

1. la falda / este ___esta falda___
2. los estudiantes / este ___estos estudiantes___
3. los países / aquel ___aquellos países___
4. la ventana / ese ___esa ventana___
5. los periodistas / ese ___esos periodistas___
6. el chico / aquel ___aquel chico___
7. las sandalias / este ___estas sandalias___
8. las chicas / aquel ___aquellas chicas___

TEACHING OPTIONS

Small Groups Ask students to bring in fashion magazines. Have students work in groups of three to give their opinions about the clothing they see in the magazines. Students should tell which items they like and which they do not, using demonstrative adjectives and pronouns.

Video Have students listen for the use of demonstrative pronouns as you replay the *Fotonovela*. Ask students to write each pronoun and the noun it refers to. Then, have students look at a copy of the *Fotonovela* Videoscript (Supersite/IRCD) to see if they were correct.

Teaching Tips

• Have a volunteer stand next to you in front of the class. Place one book close to you and two more at varying distances. Say: **Necesito un libro.** Depending on the book the student hands to you, respond: **No, [éste] no. Quiero [ése].** Then place several books at each location. Say: **Necesito unos libros.** If needed, prompt the student to ask: **¿Cuáles? ¿Éstos?** Say: **No, quiero [aquéllos].** Repeat the process with pens (**plumas**) to elicit feminine forms.

• Engage students in short conversations about classroom objects and items of clothing. Ex: Pick up a student's backpack and ask him or her: **¿Es ésta mi mochila? (No, ésta es mi mochila.)** Turn to another student and ask about the same backpack: **¿Es ésa mi mochila? (No, ésa es la mochila de ____.)** Point to a student's pencil you have placed on the windowsill. Ask: **¿Es aquél tu lápiz? (No, aquél es su lápiz.)**

• Note that, since the **Real Academia Española** has determined that accents on demonstrative pronouns are only needed for clarification (Ex: **Esta mañana vendrá** versus **Ésta mañana vendrá**), students may see them without accents in some publications.

• To practice the neuter forms, write these expressions on the board: **¡Eso es fenomenal!, ¡Esto es horrible!, ¡Esto es estupendo!,** and **¿Qué es esto?** Then state situations and have students respond with one of the expressions. Ex: **1. Voy a cancelar el próximo examen. 2. La cafetería va a cerrar los lunes, miércoles y viernes. 3. Aquí te tengo un regalo.**

• Redo the ¡Inténtalo! activity, using demonstrative pronouns.

Práctica SUPERSITE

1 Cambiar
Make the singular sentences plural and the plural sentences singular.

modelo
Estas camisas son blancas.
Esta camisa es blanca.

1. Aquellos sombreros son muy elegantes. *Aquel sombrero es muy elegante.*
2. Ese abrigo es muy caro. *Esos abrigos son muy caros.*
3. Estos cinturones son hermosos. *Este cinturón es hermoso.*
4. Esos precios son muy buenos. *Ese precio es muy bueno.*
5. Estas faldas son muy cortas. *Esta falda es muy corta.*
6. ¿Quieres ir a aquel almacén? *¿Quieres ir a aquellos almacenes?*
7. Esas blusas son baratas. *Esa blusa es barata.*
8. Esta corbata hace juego con mi traje. *Estas corbatas hacen juego con mi traje.*

2 Completar
Here are some things people might say while shopping. Complete the sentences with the correct demonstrative pronouns.

1. No me gustan esos zapatos. Voy a comprar ____éstos____. (*these*)
2. ¿Vas a comprar ese traje o ____éste____? (*this one*)
3. Esta guayabera es bonita, pero prefiero ____ésa____. (*that one*)
4. Estas corbatas rojas son muy bonitas, pero ____ésas____ son fabulosas. (*those*)
5. Estos cinturones cuestan demasiado. Prefiero ____aquéllos____. (*those over there*)
6. ¿Te gustan esas botas o ____éstas____? (*these*)
7. Esa bolsa roja es bonita, pero prefiero ____aquélla____. (*that one over there*)
8. No voy a comprar estas botas; voy a comprar ____aquéllas____. (*those over there*)
9. ¿Prefieres estos pantalones o ____ésos____? (*those*)
10. Me gusta este vestido, pero voy a comprar ____ése____. (*that one*)
11. Me gusta ese almacén, pero ____aquél____ es mejor (*better*). (*that one over there*)
12. Esa blusa es bonita pero cuesta demasiado. Voy a comprar ____ésta____. (*this one*)

NOTA CULTURAL
The **guayabera** is a men's shirt typically worn in some parts of the Caribbean. Never tucked in, it is casual wear, but variations exist for more formal occasions, such as weddings, parties, or the office.

3 Describir
With your partner, look for two items in the classroom that are one of these colors: **amarillo, azul, blanco, marrón, negro, verde, rojo.** Take turns pointing them out to each other, first using demonstrative adjectives, and then demonstrative pronouns. Answers will vary.

modelo
azul
Estudiante 1: *Esta silla es azul. Aquella mochila es azul.*
Estudiante 2: *Ésta es azul. Aquélla es azul.*

Now use demonstrative adjectives and pronouns to discuss the colors of your classmates' clothing. One of you can ask a question about an article of clothing, using the wrong color. Your partner will correct you and point out that color somewhere else in the room.

modelo
Estudiante 1: *¿Esa camisa es negra?*
Estudiante 2: *No, ésa es azul. Aquélla es negra.*

---

1 Expansion To challenge students, ask them to expand each sentence with a phrase that includes a demonstrative pronoun. Ex: **Aquellos sombreros son muy elegantes, pero éstos son más baratos.**

2 Teaching Tips
• To simplify, have students identify the nouns to which the demonstrative pronouns will refer.
• As you go over the activity, write each demonstrative pronoun on the board so students may verify that they have placed the accent marks correctly.

3 Expansion Ask students to find a photo featuring different articles of clothing or to draw several articles of clothing. Have them write five statements like that of the **Estudiante 1** model in part one of this activity. Then have students exchange their statements and photo/drawing with a partner to write responses like that of the **Estudiante 2** model.

TEACHING OPTIONS

Heritage Speakers Have heritage speakers role-play a dialogue between friends shopping for clothes. Student A tries to convince the friend that the clothes he or she wants to buy are not attractive. Student A suggests other items of clothing, but the friend does not agree. Students should use as many demonstrative adjectives and pronouns as possible.
Game Divide the class into two teams. Post pictures of different versions of the same object (Ex: sedan, sports car, all-terrain vehicle) on the board. Assign each a dollar figure, but do not share the prices with the class. Team A guesses the price of each object, using demonstrative adjectives and pronouns. Team B either agrees or guesses a higher or lower price. The team that guesses the closest price, wins. Ex: **Este carro cuesta $20.000, ése cuesta $35.000 y aquél cuesta $18.000.**

Comunicación

4 **Conversación** With a classmate, use demonstrative adjectives and pronouns to ask each other questions about the people around you. Use expressions from the word bank and/or your own ideas.
Answers will vary.

¿Cómo se llama...?	¿Cuántos años tiene(n)...?
¿Cómo es (son)...?	¿A qué hora...?
¿De quién es (son)...?	¿Cuándo...?
¿De dónde es (son)...?	¿Qué clases toma(n)...?

modelo

Estudiante 1: *¿Cómo se llama esa chica?*
Estudiante 2: *Se llama Rebeca.*
Estudiante 1: *¿A qué hora llegó aquel chico a la clase?*
Estudiante 2: *A las nueve.*

5 **En una tienda** Imagine that you and a classmate are in Madrid shopping at Zara. Study the floor plan, then have a conversation about your surroundings. Use demonstrative adjectives and pronouns.
Answers will vary.

modelo

Estudiante 1: *Me gusta este suéter azul.*
Estudiante 2: *Yo prefiero aquella chaqueta.*

NOTA CULTURAL

Zara is an international company based in Spain. It manufactures clothing and accessories for men, women, and children and also markets a popular fragrance line. While Zara makes both casual and sophisticated clothing, it is better known for its trendy, classy style that appeals to young professional women.

Síntesis

6 **Diferencias** Your teacher will give you and a partner each a drawing of a store. They are almost identical, but not quite. Use demonstrative adjectives and pronouns to find seven differences.
Answers will vary.

modelo

Estudiante 1: *Aquellas gafas de sol son feas, ¿verdad?*
Estudiante 2: *No. Aquellas gafas de sol son hermosas.*

recursos

CA
pp. 31–32

---

4 **Teaching Tip** To challenge students, have both partners ask a question for each item in the word bank and at least one other question using an interrogative expression that is not included.

5 **Expansion** Divide students into groups of three to role-play a scene between a sales-person and two customers. The customers should ask about the different items of clothing pictured and the sales-person will answer. They talk about how the items fit and their cost. The customers then express their preferences and decide which items to buy.

6 **Teaching Tip** Divide the class into pairs and distribute the Communication Activities worksheets that correspond to this activity. Give students ten minutes to complete the activity.

6 **Expansion** Have pairs work together with another pair to compare the seven responses that confirmed the seven differences. Ex: **No. Aquellas gafas de sol no son feas. Aquéllas son hermosas.** Ask a few groups to share some of the sentences with the class.

TEACHING OPTIONS

Pairs Ask students to write a conversation between two people sitting at a busy sidewalk café in the city. They are watching the people who walk by, asking each other questions about what the passersby are doing, and making comments on their clothing. Students should use as many demonstrative adjectives and pronouns as possible in their conversations. Invite several pairs to present their conversation to the class.

Small Groups Ask students to bring in pictures of their families, a sports team, a group of friends, etc. Have them take turns asking about and identifying the people in the pictures.
Ex: —**¿Quién es aquella mujer? (¿Cuál?)**
—**Aquélla con la camiseta roja. (Es mi...)**

Recapitulación

Section Goal

In **Recapitulación**, students will review the grammar concepts from this lesson.

Instructional Resource
Supersite

---

1 **Teaching Tips**

- Before beginning the activity, ask students which preterite forms usually require accent marks.
- Ask a volunteer to identify which verbs have a spelling change in the preterite (**pagar, leer**).

1 **Expansion** Ask students to provide the **tú** and **nosotros** forms for these verbs.

2 **Teaching Tip** To simplify this activity, have students start by identifying each blank as a spot for an adjective or pronoun. If the blank requires an adjective, have them find the corresponding noun. If the blank calls for a pronoun, have them identify the noun it replaces.

2 **Expansion** Have two volunteers role-play the dialogue for the class.

For self-scoring and diagnostics, go to descubre1.vhlcentral.com.

Review the grammar concepts you have learned in this lesson by completing these activities.

1 **Completar** Complete the chart with the correct preterite or infinitive form of the verbs. **15 pts.**

Infinitive	yo	ella	ellos
tomar	tomé	tomó	**tomaron**
abrir	abrí	**abrió**	abrieron
comprender	comprendí	comprendió	comprendieron
leer	**leí**	leyó	leyeron
pagar	pagué	pagó	pagaron

2 **En la tienda** Look at the drawing and complete the conversation with demonstrative adjectives and pronouns. **7 pts.**

CLIENTE Buenos días, señorita. Deseo comprar (1) ____esta____ corbata.

VENDEDORA Muy bien, señor. ¿No le interesa mirar (2) ____aquellos____ trajes que están allá? Hay unos que hacen juego con la corbata.

CLIENTE (3) ____Aquéllos____ de allá son de lana, ¿no? Prefiero ver (4) ____ese____ traje marrón que está detrás de usted.

VENDEDORA Estupendo. Como puede ver, es de seda. Cuesta ciento ochenta dólares.

CLIENTE Ah… eh… no, creo que sólo voy a comprar la corbata, gracias.

VENDEDORA Bueno… si busca algo más económico, hay rebaja en (5) ____aquellos____ sombreros. Cuestan sólo treinta dólares.

CLIENTE ¡Magnífico! Me gusta (6) ____aquél____, el blanco que está arriba. Y quiero pagar todo con (7) ____esta____ tarjeta.

VENDEDORA Sí, señor. Ahora mismo le traigo el sombrero.

RESUMEN GRAMATICAL

6.1 **Saber and conocer** *p. 200*

saber	conocer
sé	conozco
sabes	conoces
sabe	conoce
sabemos	conocemos
sabéis	conocéis
saben	conocen

► **saber** = to know facts/how to do something
► **conocer** = to know a person, place, or thing

6.2 **Indirect object pronouns** *pp. 202–203*

Indirect object pronouns

Singular	Plural
me	nos
te	os
le	les

► **dar** = doy, das, da, damos, dais, dan

6.3 **Preterite tense of regular verbs** *pp. 206–207*

comprar	vender	escribir
compré	vendí	escribí
compraste	vendiste	escribiste
compró	vendió	escribió
compramos	vendimos	escribimos
comprasteis	vendisteis	escribisteis
compraron	vendieron	escribieron

Verbs with spelling changes in the preterite

► **-car**: buscar → yo busqué
► **-gar**: llegar → yo llegué
► **-zar**: empezar → yo empecé
► **creer**: creí, creíste, creyó, creímos, creísteis, creyeron
► **leer**: leí, leíste, leyó, leímos, leísteis, leyeron
► **oír**: oí, oíste, oyó, oímos, oísteis, oyeron
► **ver**: vi, viste, vio, vimos, visteis, vieron

TEACHING OPTIONS

Game Divide the class into two teams. Indicate a team member. Give an infinitive and a subject, and have the team member supply the correct preterite form. Award one point for each correct answer. Award a bonus point for correctly writing the verb on the board. The team with the most points wins.
TPR Write **presente** and **pretérito** on the board and have a volunteer stand in front of each word. Call out sentences using the present or the preterite. The student whose tense corresponds to the sentence has three seconds to step forward. Ex: **Compramos una chaqueta anteayer. (pretérito)**
Small Groups Ask students to write a description of a famous person, using **saber**, **conocer**, and one verb in the preterite. In small groups, have students read their descriptions aloud for the group to guess.

3 **¿Saber o conocer?** Complete each dialogue with the correct form of **saber** or **conocer**. **10 pts.**

1. —¿Qué ___sabes___ hacer tú?
   —(Yo) ___Sé___ jugar al fútbol.
2. —¿___Conoces___ tú esta tienda de ropa?
   —No, (yo) no la ___conozco___. ¿Es buena?
3. —¿Tus padres no ___conocen___ a tu novio?
   —No, ¡ellos no ___saben___ que tengo novio!
4. —Mi hermanastro todavía no me ___conoce___ bien.
   —Y tú, ¿lo quieres ___conocer___ a él?
5. —¿___Saben___ ustedes dónde está el mercado?
   —No, nosotros no ___conocemos___ bien esta ciudad.

6.4 Demonstrative adjectives and pronouns *pp. 210–211*

Demonstrative adjectives

	Singular		Plural
Masc.	**Fem.**	**Masc.**	**Fem.**
este	esta	estos	estas
ese	esa	esos	esas
aquel	aquella	aquellos	aquellas

Demonstrative pronouns

	Singular		Plural
Masc.	**Fem.**	**Masc.**	**Fem.**
éste	ésta	éstos	éstas
ése	ésa	ésos	ésas
aquél	aquélla	aquéllos	aquéllas

4 **Oraciones** Form complete sentences using the information provided. Use indirect object pronouns and the present tense of the verbs. **10 pts.**

1. Javier / prestar / el abrigo / a Maripili
   Javier le presta el abrigo a Maripili.
2. nosotros / vender / ropa / a los clientes
   Nosotros les vendemos ropa a los clientes.
3. el vendedor / traer / las camisetas / a mis amigos y a mí
   El vendedor nos trae las camisetas (a mis amigos y a mí).
4. yo / querer dar / consejos (*advice*) / a ti
   Yo quiero darte consejos (a ti)./Yo te quiero dar consejos (a ti).
5. ¿tú / ir a comprar / un regalo / a mí?
   ¿Tú vas a comprarme un regalo (a mí)?/¿Tú me vas a comprar un regalo (a mí)?

5 **Mi última compra** Write a short paragraph describing the last time you went shopping. Use at least four verbs in the preterite tense. **8 pts.**

> **modelo**
> El viernes pasado, busqué unos zapatos en el centro comercial...

6 **Poema** Write the missing words to complete the excerpt from the poem *Romance sonámbulo* by Federico García Lorca. **2 EXTRA points!**

> « Verde que ___te___ quiero verde.
> Verde viento. Verdes ramas°.
> El barco sobre la mar
> y el caballo en la montaña, [...]
> Verde que te quiero ___verde___ (*green*). »

ramas *branches*

3 **Teaching Tip** Ask students to explain why they chose **saber** or **conocer** in each case.

3 **Expansion** Have students choose one dialogue from this activity and write a continuation. Encourage them to use at least one more example of **saber** and **conocer**.

4 **Teaching Tips**
- Ask a volunteer to model the first sentence for the class.
- Before forming sentences, have students identify the indirect object in each item.
- Remind students of the possible placements of indirect object pronouns when using an infinitive.

4 **Expansion**
- Ask students to create three dehydrated sentences similar to those in **Actividad 4**. Have them exchange papers with a classmate and form complete sentences.
- For items 1–4, have students write questions that would elicit these statements. Ex: **1. ¿A quién le presta el abrigo Javier?/¿Qué le presta Javier a Maripili?** For item 5, have them write a response.

5 **Teaching Tip** To add a visual aspect to this activity, have students create a time line of what they did when they went shopping.

6 **Teaching Tips**
- Tell students to read through the whole excerpt before filling in the blanks.
- Have a volunteer read the excerpt aloud.

TEACHING OPTIONS

Extra Practice Add an auditory aspect to this grammar review. Read each of these sentences twice, pausing after the second time for students to write: **1. Ayer empecé a leer sobre los diseñadores hispanos. 2. Ellas buscaron unas bolsas en el mercado al aire libre. 3. El dependiente vendió cinco camisetas. 4. Nosotras oímos una explosión. 5. El joven le leyó el libro a su hermanito. 6. Raúl vio una película anoche.**

Game Divide the class into two teams. Indicate a member of each team and call out a color. The first student to find an object or article of clothing in the room, point to it, and use the correct form of a demonstrative adjective to express it earns a point for their team. Ex: **¡Aquella camiseta es morada!** The team with the most points at the end wins.

Lectura

NATIONAL communication cultures STANDARDS

Antes de leer

Estrategia
Skimming

Skimming involves quickly reading through a document to absorb its general meaning. This allows you to understand the main ideas without having to read word for word. When you skim a text, you might want to look at its title and subtitles. You might also want to read the first sentence of each paragraph.

Examinar el texto
Look at the format of the reading selection. How is it organized? What does the organization of the document tell you about its content?

Buscar cognados
Scan the reading selection to locate at least five cognates. Based on the cognates, what do you think the reading selection is about? Answers will vary.

1. _____   4. _____
2. _____   5. _____
3. _____

The reading selection is about _____.

Impresiones generales
Now skim the reading selection to understand its general meaning. Jot down your impressions. What new information did you learn about the document by skimming it? Based on all the information you now have, answer these questions in Spanish.

1. Who produced this document? un almacén
2. What is its purpose? vender ropa
3. Who is its intended audience? gente que quiere comprar ropa

recursos
CH pp. 95–96 | SUPERSITE descubre1.vhlcentral.com Lección 6

Advertisement

¡Real° Liquidación en Corona!
¡Grandes rebajas!
¡La rebaja está de moda en Corona!

SEÑORAS	CABALLEROS°
Falda larga **ROPA BONITA** Algodón. De cuadros y rayas Talla mediana **Precio especial: $8.000**	**Pantalones** **OCÉANO** Colores blanco, azul y café Ahora: $11.550 **30% de rebaja**
Blusas de seda **BAMBÚ** Seda. De cuadros y de lunares Ahora: $21.000 **40% de rebaja**	**Zapatos** **COLOR** Italianos y franceses Números del 40 al 45 **Sólo $20.000 el par**
Sandalias de playa **GINO** Números del 35 al 38 Ahora: $12.000 el par **50% de rebaja**	**Chaqueta** **CASINO** Microfibra. Colores negro, blanco y gris Tallas P-M-G-XG **Ahora: $22.500**
Carteras **ELEGANCIA** Colores anaranjado, blanco, rosado y amarillo Ahora: $15.000 **50% de rebaja**	**Traje inglés** **GALES** Modelos originales Ahora: $105.000 **30% de rebaja**
Vestido de algodón **PANAMÁ** Colores blanco, azul y verde Ahora: $18.000 **30% de rebaja**	**Ropa interior** **ATLÁNTICO** Talla mediana Colores blanco, negro, gris **40% de rebaja**

Lunes a sábado de 9 a 21 horas.
Domingo de 10 a 14 horas.

TEACHING OPTIONS

Heritage Speakers Ask heritage speakers to create an ad for one or two items of clothing. Have them use the **¡Real Liquidación en Corona!** advertisement as a model. Ask them to share their ads with the class.

Small Groups Have small groups of students work together to write a cloze paragraph about shopping for clothing, modeled on the **Completar** paragraph. Ask each group member to contribute two sentences to the paragraph. Then have the group make a clean copy, omitting several words or phrases, and writing the omitted words and phrases below the paragraph. Have groups exchange paragraphs and complete them.

Advertisement (left column)

Corona tiene las ofertas más locas
el verano!

30% 40% 50%

a tienda más elegante de la ciudad
on precios increíbles y con la tarjeta
e crédito más conveniente del mercado.

JÓVENES	NIÑOS
luejeans chicos y chicas	**Vestido de niña**
PACOS	**GIRASOL**
mericanos. Tradicional	Tallas de la 2 a la 12.
hora: $9.000 el par	De cuadros y rayas
	Ahora: $8.625
0% de rebaja	30% de rebaja
uéteres	**Pantalón deportivo de niño**
CARAMELO	**MILÁN**
lgodón y lana.	Tallas de la 4 a la 16
olores blanco, gris y negro	Ahora: $13.500
ntes°: $10.500	
hora: $6.825	30% de rebaja
olsas	**Zapatos de tenis**
LA MODERNA	**ACUARIO**
mericanas.	Números del 20 al 25
stilos variados	Ahora: $15.000 el par
ntes: $15.000	
Ahora $10.000	30% de rebaja
rajes de baño chicos	**Pantalones cortos**
y chicas	**MACARENA**
SUBMARINO	
Microfibra. Todas las tallas	Talla mediana
hora: $12.500	Ahora: $15.000
50% de rebaja	30% de rebaja
Gafas de sol	**Camisetas de algodón**
VISIÓN	**POLO**
rigen canadiense	Antes: $15.000
ntes: $23.000	Ahora: $7.500
Ahora: $14.950	50% de rebaja

or la compra de $40.000, puede llevar un regalo gratis.
- Un hermoso cinturón de señora
- Un par de calcetines
- Una corbata de seda
- Una bolsa para la playa
- Una mochila
- Unas medias

eal *Royal* Liquidación *Clearance sale* caballeros *gentlemen* Antes *Before*

Después de leer

Completar

Complete this paragraph about the reading selection with the correct forms of the words from the word bank.

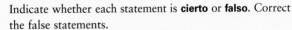

almacén	hacer juego	tarjeta de crédito
caro	increíble	tienda
dinero	pantalones	verano
falda	rebaja	zapato

En este anuncio de periódico el ___almacén___ Corona anuncia la liquidación de ___verano___ con grandes ___rebajas___ en todos los departamentos. Con muy poco ___dinero___ usted puede equipar a toda su familia. Si no tiene dinero en efectivo, puede utilizar su ___tarjeta de crédito___ y pagar luego. Para el caballero con gustos refinados, hay ___zapatos___ importados de París y Roma. La señora elegante puede encontrar blusas de seda que ___hacen juego___ con todo tipo de ___faldas/pantalones___ o ___pantalones/faldas___. Los precios de esta liquidación son realmente ___increíbles___.

¿Cierto o falso?

Indicate whether each statement is **cierto** or **falso**. Correct the false statements.

1. Hay ropa de algodón para jóvenes. **Cierto.**
2. La ropa interior tiene una rebaja del 30%. **Falso.** Tiene una rebaja del 40%.
3. El almacén Corona tiene un departamento de zapatos. **Cierto.**
4. Normalmente las sandalias cuestan $22.000 el par. **Falso.** Normalmente cuestan $24.000.
5. Cuando gastas $3.000 en la tienda, llevas un regalo gratis. **Falso.** Cuando gastas $40.000 en la tienda, llevas un regalo gratis.
6. Tienen carteras amarillas. **Cierto.**

Preguntas

Answer these questions in Spanish. Answers will vary.

1. Imagina que vas a ir a la tienda Corona. ¿Qué departamentos vas a visitar? ¿El departamento de ropa para señoras, el departamento de ropa para caballeros...?
2. ¿Qué vas a buscar en Corona?
3. ¿Hay tiendas similares a la tienda Corona en tu pueblo o ciudad? ¿Cómo se llaman? ¿Tienen muchas gangas?

(Right margin — teacher notes)

Completar Have students quickly review the lesson vocabulary on pages 190–192 and 195 before they do this activity. Make sure that they understand the meaning of **el caballero con gustos refinados.**

¿Cierto o falso? Give students these sentences as items 7–10:
**7. Las camisetas Polo no tienen una rebaja grande. (Falso. Tienen una rebaja del 50%.)
8. El almacén Corona está cerrado los domingos. (Falso. El almacén Corona está abierto de 10:00 a 14:00 los domingos.)
9. Se pueden conseguir carteras rosadas y amarillas en rebaja. (Cierto.) 10. Un señor puede comprar una chaqueta gris de talla pequeña. (Cierto.)**

Preguntas Have small groups put together an ad for a store where they shop. Have them use the **Almacén Corona** ad as a model. If two or more groups chose the same store, compare their ads in a follow-up discussion with the class.

TEACHING OPTIONS

TPR Write items of clothing on slips of paper. Divide the class into two teams. Have a member of one team draw out a slip from a hat. That team member mimes putting on the item of clothing. The other team guesses what it is. Give one point for each correct answer. The team with the most points wins. **Variación léxica** Ask heritage speakers to share phrases they know of to ask the price of items. Ex: **¿Cuánto vale?**

Game In pairs, have students play a modified version of **20 Preguntas**. Student A thinks of an item of clothing. Student B asks questions and guesses the name of the item. Student A keeps track of the number of questions and guesses. Allow partners to ask a total of ten questions and attempt to guess three times before moving on to the next item. The pair with the fewest questions overall wins.

Escritura

Estrategia

How to report an interview

There are several ways to prepare a written report about an interview. For example, you can transcribe the interview verbatim, you can simply summarize it, or you can summarize it but quote the speakers occasionally. In any event, the report should begin with an interesting title and a brief introduction, which may include the five Ws (*what, where, when, who, why*) and the H (*how*) of the interview. The report should end with an interesting conclusion. Note that when you transcribe dialogue in Spanish, you should pay careful attention to format and punctuation.

Writing dialogue in Spanish

• If you need to transcribe an interview verbatim, you can use speakers' names to indicate a change of speaker.

CARMELA	¿Qué compraste? ¿Encontraste muchas gangas?
ROBERTO	Sí, muchas. Compré un suéter, una camisa y dos corbatas. Y tú, ¿qué compraste?
CARMELA	Una blusa y una falda muy bonitas. ¿Cuánto costó tu camisa?
ROBERTO	Sólo diez dólares. ¿Cuánto costó tu blusa?
CARMELA	Veinte dólares.

• You can also use a dash (*raya*) to mark the beginning of each speaker's words.

— ¿Qué compraste?
— Un suéter y una camisa muy bonitos. Y tú, ¿encontraste muchas gangas?
— Sí... compré dos blusas, tres camisetas y un par de zapatos.
— ¡A ver!

recursos		
CH pp. 97–98	CA pp. 151–152	descubre1.vhlcentral.com Lección 6

Tema

Escribe un informe

Write a report for the school newspaper about an interview you conducted with a student about his or her shopping habits and clothing preferences. First, brainstorm a list of interview questions. Then conduct the interview using the questions below as a guide, but feel free to ask other questions as they occur to you.

Examples of questions:

▶ ¿Cuándo vas de compras?

▶ ¿Adónde vas de compras?

▶ ¿Con quién vas de compras?

▶ ¿Qué tiendas, almacenes o centros comerciales prefieres?

▶ ¿Compras ropa de catálogos o por Internet?

▶ ¿Prefieres comprar ropa cara o barata? ¿Por qué? ¿Te gusta buscar gangas?

▶ ¿Qué ropa llevas cuando vas a clase?

▶ ¿Qué ropa llevas cuando sales a bailar?

▶ ¿Qué ropa llevas cuando practicas un deporte?

▶ ¿Cuáles son tus colores favoritos? ¿Compras mucha ropa de esos colores?

▶ ¿Les das ropa a tu familia o a tus amigos/as?

EVALUATION: Informe

Criteria	Scale
Content	1 2 3 4 5
Organization	1 2 3 4 5
Accuracy	1 2 3 4 5
Creativity	1 2 3 4 5

Scoring	
Excellent	18–20 points
Good	14–17 points
Satisfactory	10–13 points
Unsatisfactory	< 10 points

Escuchar

Estrategia

Listening for linguistic cues

You can enhance your listening comprehension by listening for specific linguistic cues. For example, if you listen for the endings of conjugated verbs, or for familiar constructions, such as **acabar de** + [*infinitive*] or **ir a** + [*infinitive*], you can find out whether an event already took place, is taking place now, or will take place in the future. Verb endings also give clues about who is participating in the action.

 To practice listening for linguistic cues, you will now listen to four sentences. As you listen, note whether each sentence refers to a past, present, or future action. Also jot down the subject of each sentence.

Preparación

Based on the photograph, what do you think Marisol has recently done? What do you think Marisol and Alicia are talking about? What else can you guess about their conversation from the visual clues in the photograph?

Ahora escucha

Now you are going to hear Marisol and Alicia's conversation. Make a list of the clothing items that each person mentions. Then put a check mark after the item if the person actually purchased it.

Marisol		Alicia	
1.	pantalones ✓	1.	falda
2.	blusa ✓	2.	blusa
3.		3.	zapatos
4.		4.	cinturón

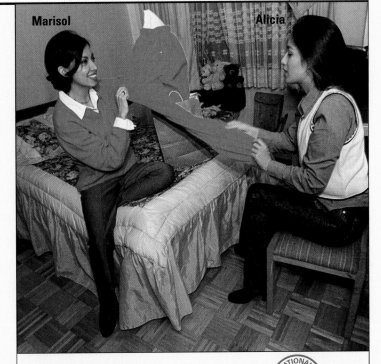

Marisol   Alicia

Comprensión

¿Cierto o falso?

Indicate whether each statement is **cierto** or **falso**. Then correct the false statements.

1. Marisol y Alicia acaban de ir de compras juntas (*together*). **Falso.** Marisol acaba de ir de compras.
2. Marisol va a comprar unos pantalones y una blusa mañana. **Falso.** Marisol ya los compró.
3. Marisol compró una blusa de cuadros. **Cierto.**
4. Alicia compró unos zapatos nuevos hoy. **Falso.** Alicia va a comprar unos zapatos nuevos.
5. Alicia y Marisol van a ir al café. **Cierto.**
6. Marisol gastó todo el dinero de la semana en ropa nueva. **Cierto.**

Preguntas

Discuss the following questions with a classmate. Be sure to explain your answers. Answers will vary.

1. ¿Crees que Alicia y Marisol son buenas amigas? ¿Por qué?
2. ¿Cuál de las dos estudiantes es más ahorradora (*frugal*)? ¿Por qué?
3. ¿Crees que a Alicia le gusta la ropa que Marisol compró?
4. ¿Crees que la moda es importante para Alicia? ¿Para Marisol? ¿Por qué?
5. ¿Es importante para ti estar a la moda? ¿Por qué?

Mi tarjeta de crédito está que no aguanta más. Y trabajé poco la semana pasada. ¡Acabo de gastar todo el dinero para la semana!
A: ¡Ay, chica! Fui al centro comercial el mes pasado y encontré unos zapatos muy, pero muy de moda. Muy caros… pero buenos. No me los compré porque no los tenían en mi número. Voy a com-

prarlos cuando lleguen más…. el vendedor me va a llamar.
M: Ajá… ¿Y va a invitarte a salir con él?
A: ¡Ay! ¡No seas así! Ven, vamos al café. Te ves muy bien y no hay que gastar eso aquí.
M: De acuerdo. Vamos.

En pantalla

In Spain, during Francisco Franco's dictatorship (1939–1975), students in public schools were required to wear uniforms. After the fall of Franco's regime and the establishment of democracy, educational authorities rejected this former policy and decided it should no longer be obligatory to wear uniforms in public schools. Today, only some private schools in Spain enforce the use of uniforms; even Catholic schools do not have anything more than a basic dress code.

Vocabulario útil	
anoraks	anoraks (Spain)
anchas	loose-fitting
vaqueros	jeans (Spain)
trencas	duffel coats (Spain)
lavables	washable
carteras	book bags (Spain)
chándals	tracksuits (Spain)
resiste	withstands
tanto como	as much as

Identificar
Check off each word that you hear in the ad.

_____ 1. camisetas   ✔ 5. chaquetas
✔ 2. hijos   _____ 6. clientas
✔ 3. zapatos   ✔ 7. lana
_____ 4. algodón   _____ 8. precio

Conversar
Work with a classmate to ask each other these questions. Use as much Spanish as you can. Answers will vary.

1. ¿Qué ropa llevas normalmente cuando vienes a la escuela?
2. ¿Y los fines de semana?
3. ¿Tienes una prenda (*garment*) favorita? ¿Cómo es?
4. ¿Qué tipo de ropa no te gusta usar? ¿Por qué?

próximo *next* Tejidos *Fabrics* resistentes *strong, tough*

Anuncio de tiendas Galerías

Presentamos la moda para el próximo° curso.

Formas geométricas y colores vivos.

Tejidos° resistentes°.

recursos
descubre1.vhlcentral.com
Lección 6

Conexión Internet
Go to descubre1.vhlcentral.com to watch the TV clip featured in this En pantalla section.

Oye cómo va

Celia Cruz

Known as the Queen of Salsa, Úrsula Hilaria Celia Caridad Cruz Alfonso (Celia Cruz) was born in Havana, Cuba, on October 21, 1924. She began singing at an early age and studied music in Havana's **Conservatorio Musical**. For many years Celia sang with the Sonora Matancera ensemble, recording over 150 songs. Then, on July 15, 1960, she left Cuba, never to return. After a stay in Mexico, Celia settled in New York City, where she recorded over fifty solo albums. Celia had an engaging stage presence, with eccentric outfits, colorful wigs, and her popular catchword, **¡Azúcar!** (*Sugar!*) Throughout her long and prolific career, Celia received numerous awards and recognitions, such as the National Endowment for the Arts, in 1994. After her cancer-related death on July 16, 2003, Celia Cruz's life was celebrated with public funerals in Miami and New York.

Your teacher will play the song. Listen and then complete these activities.

Cierto o falso?

Indicate whether each statement is **cierto** or **falso**.

	Cierto	Falso
1. Celia Cruz es cubana.	☑	○
2. Ella comenzó a cantar a los 35 años.	○	☑
3. Cantó con la Sonora Matancera.	☑	○
4. Usó ropa tradicional.	○	☑

Preguntas

Work with a partner to answer these questions.
Answers will vary.

1. ¿Creen que estos versos de la canción son ciertos? ¿Por qué?

   "Yo sólo sé que en esta vida
   el amor todo es mentira".

2. ¿Es posible estar enamorado/a de una persona y a la vez odiarla (*hate them*)? ¿Conocen a una persona en una situación como ésa?

abusó *took advantage* Sacó provecho *You took advantage* Sacó partido *You took advantage* cariño *love*

Usted abusó

Usted abusó°.
Sacó provecho° de mí, abusó.
Sacó partido° de mí, abusó.
De mi cariño° usted abusó.

Celia y la moda
Celia Cruz created a unique personal style to match her lively spirit. On stage, she favored large wigs in bright colors, over-the-top dresses, and glittery platform shoes.

recursos

SUPERSITE

descubre1.vhlcentral.com
Lección 6

SUPERSITE Conexión Internet
Go to **descubre1.vhlcentral.com** to learn more about the artist featured in this **Oye cómo va** section.

Section Goal

In **Panorama**, students will read about the geography, culture, history, and economy of Cuba.

Instructional Resources
Cuaderno de práctica, pp. 69–70
Cuaderno de actividades, pp. 79–80
e-Cuaderno
Supersite/DVD: *Panorama cultural*
Supersite/TRCD: *PowerPoints* (Overheads #3, #4, #30);
Panorama cultural Videoscript & Translation, Answer Keys

Teaching Tip Ask students to look at the map or show *Overhead PowerPoint #30*. Ask volunteers to read the captions on each call-out photo. Then discuss the photos with the class.

The Affective Dimension Some students may have strong feelings about Cuba. Encourage students to discuss their feelings.

El país en cifras
• After reading about **La Habana Vieja**, if possible, show students illustrations of this part of the city.
• Draw attention to the design and colors of the Cuban flag. Compare the Cuban flag to the Puerto Rican flag (page 186). Explain that Puerto Rico and Cuba, the last Spanish colonies in the western hemisphere, both gained their independence from Spain in 1898, in part through the intervention of the U.S.

¡Increíble pero cierto! Due to the patterns of evolution and adaptation common to islands, Cuba has many examples of unique flora and fauna. Students may wish to research other examples.

Cuba

El país en cifras

▶ **Área:** 110.860 km² (42.803 millas²), *aproximadamente el área de Pensilvania*
▶ **Población:** 11.379.000
▶ **Capital:** La Habana—2.159.000

La Habana Vieja fue declarada° Patrimonio° Cultural de la Humanidad por la UNESCO en 1982. Este distrito es uno de los lugares más fascinantes de Cuba. En La Plaza de Armas, se puede visitar el majestuoso Palacio de Capitanes Generales, que ahora es un museo. En la calle° Obispo, frecuentada por el autor Ernest Hemingway, hay hermosos cafés, clubes nocturnos y tiendas elegantes.

▶ **Ciudades principales:**
Santiago de Cuba; Camagüey; Holguín; Guantánamo
SOURCE: Population Division, UN Secretariat

▶ **Moneda:** peso cubano
▶ **Idiomas:** español (oficial)

Bandera de Cuba

Cubanos célebres
▶ **Carlos Finlay,** doctor y científico (1833–1915)
▶ **José Martí,** político y poeta (1853–1895)
▶ **Fidel Castro,** primer ministro, comandante en jefe° de las fuerzas armadas (1926–)
▶ **Zoé Valdés,** escritora (1959–)
▶ **Ibrahim Ferrer,** músico (1927–2005)

fue declarada *was declared* Patrimonio *Heritage* calle *street* comandante en jefe *commander in chief* liviano *light* colibrí abeja *bee hummingbird* ave *bird* mundo *world* miden *measure* pesan *weigh*

Fortaleza El Morro

Golfo de México

ESTADOS UNIDOS

Playa en Santiago de Cuba

Océano Atlántico

Cabaret Tropicana, famoso club de La Habana

La Habana

Cordillera de los Órganos

Isla de la Juventud

Mar Caribe

Camagü

ESTADOS UNIDOS
CUBA
OCÉANO ATLÁNTICO
OCÉANO PACÍFICO
AMÉRICA DEL SUR

Vista aérea de campos de caña de azúcar

recursos

CP pp. 69–70	CA pp. 79–80	SUPERSITE descubre1.vhlcentral.com Lección 6

¡Increíble pero cierto!
Pequeño y liviano°, el colibrí abeja° de Cuba es una de las 320 especies de colibrí, y es también el ave° más pequeña del mundo°. Menores que muchos insectos, estas aves minúsculas miden° 5 centímetros y pesan° sólo 1,95 gramos.

TEACHING OPTIONS

Variación léxica An item of clothing that you will see everywhere if you visit Cuba (or any of the other Caribbean countries) is the **guayabera**. A loose-fitting, short-sleeved shirt made of natural fibers, the **guayabera** is perfect for hot, humid climates. **Guayaberas** generally have large pockets and may be decorated with embroidery. They are worn open at the neck and never tucked in.

Extra Practice Give students two stanzas of the first poem from **José Martí's** collection *Versos sencillos*. Some students may recognize these as verses from the song *Guantanamera*.

Yo soy un hombre sincero
de donde crece la palma;
y, antes de morirme, quiero
echar mis versos del alma.

Yo vengo de todas partes,
y hacia todas partes voy;
arte soy entre las artes;
en los montes, monte soy.

Baile • **Ballet Nacional de Cuba**

La bailarina Alicia Alonso fundó el Ballet Nacional de Cuba en 1948, después de° convertirse en una estrella° internacional en el Ballet de Nueva York y en Broadway. El Ballet Nacional de Cuba es famoso en todo el mundo por su creatividad y perfección técnica.

Economía • **La caña de azúcar y el tabaco**

La caña de azúcar° es el producto agrícola° que más se cultiva en la isla y su exportación es muy importante para la economía del país. El tabaco, que se usa para fabricar los famosos puros° cubanos, es otro cultivo de mucha importancia.

Historia • **Los taínos**

Los taínos eran° una de las tres tribus indígenas que vivían° en Cuba cuando llegaron los españoles en el siglo XV. Los taínos también vivían en Puerto Rico, la República Dominicana, Haití, Trinidad, Jamaica y en partes de las Bahamas y la Florida.

Música • **Buena Vista Social Club**

En 1997 nace° el fenómeno musical conocido como *Buena Vista Social Club*. Este proyecto reúne° a un grupo de importantes músicos de Cuba, la mayoría ya mayores, con una larga trayectoria interpretando canciones clásicas del son° cubano. Ese mismo año ganaron un *Grammy*. Hoy en día estos músicos son conocidos en todo el mundo, y personas de todas las edades bailan al ritmo° de su música.

Holguín

Santiago de Cuba
Guantánamo

rra Maestra

¿Qué aprendiste? Responde a las preguntas con una oración completa.
1. ¿Quién es el líder del gobierno de Cuba? El líder del gobierno de Cuba es Fidel Castro.
2. ¿Qué autor está asociado con la Habana Vieja? Ernest Hemingway está asociado con la Habana Vieja.
3. ¿Por qué es famoso el Ballet Nacional de Cuba? Es famoso por su creatividad y perfección técnica.
4. ¿Cuáles son los dos cultivos más importantes para la economía cubana? Los cultivos más importantes son la
5. ¿Qué fabrican los cubanos con la planta del tabaco? Los cubanos fabrican puros. caña de azúcar y el tabaco.
6. ¿Quiénes son los taínos? Son una tribu indígena.
7. ¿En qué año ganó un *Grammy* el disco *Buena Vista Social Club*? Ganó un *Grammy* en 1997.

Conexión Internet Investiga estos temas en **descubre1.vhlcentral.com**.
1. Busca información sobre un(a) cubano/a célebre. ¿Por qué es célebre? ¿Qué hace? ¿Todavía vive en Cuba?
2. Busca información sobre una de las ciudades principales de Cuba. ¿Qué atracciones hay en esta ciudad?

....

después de *after* estrella *star* caña de azúcar *sugar cane* agrícola *farming* puros *cigars* eran *were* vivían *lived* nace *is born*
reúne *gets together* son *Cuban musical genre* ritmo *rhythm*

Instructional Resources
Cuaderno de actividades, p. 122
e-Cuaderno
Supersite: Textbook &
Vocabulary MP3 Audio Files
Supersite/TRCD: Answer Keys;
Testing Program (**Lección 6
Pruebas,** Test Generator,
Testing Program MP3 Audio
Files)
Textbook, Test Audio CD

La ropa

el abrigo	coat
los bluejeans	jeans
la blusa	blouse
la bolsa	purse; bag
la bota	boot
los calcetines (el calcetín)	sock(s)
la camisa	shirt
la camiseta	t-shirt
la cartera	wallet
la chaqueta	jacket
el cinturón	belt
la corbata	tie
la falda	skirt
las gafas (de sol)	(sun)glasses
los guantes	gloves
el impermeable	raincoat
las medias	pantyhose; stockings
los pantalones	pants
los pantalones cortos	shorts
la ropa	clothing; clothes
la ropa interior	underwear
las sandalias	sandals
el sombrero	hat
el suéter	sweater
el traje	suit
el traje de baño	bathing suit
el vestido	dress
los zapatos de tenis	tennis shoes, sneakers

Verbos

conducir	to drive
conocer	to know; to be acquainted with
ofrecer	to offer
parecer	to seem
saber	to know; to know how
traducir	to translate

Ir de compras

el almacén	department store
la caja	cash register
el centro comercial	shopping mall
el/la cliente/a	customer
el/la dependiente/a	clerk
el dinero	money
(en) efectivo	cash
el mercado (al aire libre)	(open-air) market
un par (de zapatos)	a pair (of shoes)
el precio (fijo)	(fixed; set) price
la rebaja	sale
el regalo	gift
la tarjeta de crédito	credit card
la tienda	shop; store
el/la vendedor(a)	salesperson
costar (o:ue)	to cost
gastar	to spend (money)
hacer juego (con)	to match (with)
llevar	to wear; to take
pagar	to pay
regatear	to bargain
usar	to wear; to use
vender	to sell

Adjetivos

barato/a	cheap
bueno/a	good
cada	each
caro/a	expensive
corto/a	short (in length)
elegante	elegant
hermoso/a	beautiful
largo/a	long
loco/a	crazy
nuevo/a	new
otro/a	other; another
pobre	poor
rico/a	rich

Los colores

el color	color
amarillo/a	yellow
anaranjado/a	orange
azul	blue
blanco/a	white
gris	gray
marrón, café	brown
morado/a	purple
negro/a	black
rojo/a	red
rosado/a	pink
verde	green

Palabras adicionales

acabar de (+ *inf.*)	to have just done something
anoche	last night
anteayer	the day before yesterday
ayer	yesterday
de repente	suddenly
desde	from
dos veces	twice; two times
hasta	until
pasado/a (*adj.*)	last; past
el año pasado	last year
la semana pasada	last week
prestar	to lend; to loan
una vez	once; one time
ya	already

Indirect object pronouns	See page 202.
Demonstrative adjectives and pronouns	See page 210.
Expresiones útiles	See page 195.

recursos

CA p. 122

descubre1.vhlcentral.com Lección 6

La rutina diaria

Communicative Goals

You will learn how to:
- Describe your daily routine
- Talk about personal hygiene
- Reassure someone —

Lesson Goals

In **Lección 7**, students will be introduced to the following:
- terms for daily routines
- reflexive verbs
- adverbs of time
- the custom of **la siesta**
- **ir de tapas** as part of a daily routine
- negative and positive expressions
- preterite of **ser** and **ir**
- verbs like **gustar**
- predicting content from the title
- sequencing events
- writing a description of a place
- listening for background information
- a television commercial for **Sedal** shampoo
- Peruvian singer **Tania Libertad**
- cultural, geographic, and historical information about Peru

A primera vista Here are some additional questions you can ask based on the photo: **¿Con quién vives? ¿Qué le dices antes de salir de casa? ¿Qué tipo de ropa llevas para ir a tus clases? ¿Les prestas esta ropa a tus amigos/as? ¿Qué ropa usaste en el verano? ¿Y en el invierno?**

A PRIMERA VISTA
- ¿Está él en casa o en una tienda?
- ¿Está contento o enojado?
- ¿Cómo es él?
- ¿Qué colores hay en la foto?

INSTRUCTIONAL RESOURCES

Student Materials
Cuaderno de práctica, Cuaderno para hispanohablantes, Cuaderno de actividades
Student MAESTRO™ Supersite
(descubre1.vhlcentral.com)
MAESTRO™ e-Cuaderno

Teacher's Resource CD-ROM and in print
*Answer Keys, Audioscripts, Videoscripts
*PowerPoints
Testing Program (**Pruebas**, Test Generator, MP3 Audio Files)
Vista Higher Learning *Cancionero*
*Also available on Supersite

Teacher's MAESTRO™ Supersite
(descubre1.vhlcentral.com)
Learning Management System (Assignment Task Manager, Gradebook)
Also on DVD
Fotonovela, Flash cultura, Panorama cultural

La rutina diaria

Section Goals

In **Contextos**, students will learn and practice:
- vocabulary to talk about daily routines
- reflexive verbs to talk about daily routines
- adverbs of time

Instructional Resources
Cuaderno de práctica, pp. 73–74
Cuaderno para hispanohablantes, pp. 99–100
Cuaderno de actividades, p. 123
e-Cuaderno
Supersite: Textbook, Vocabulary, & Audio Activity MP3 Audio Files
Supersite/TRCD/Print:
PowerPoints (**Lección 7 Contextos** Presentation, Overhead #31); Textbook Audio Script, Audio Activity Script, Answer Keys
Textbook & Audio Activity CD

Note: This is the first time students will see these instructions entirely in Spanish. Ask students to identify cognates that help them understand the instructions.

Teaching Tips
- Write **levantarse por la mañana** on the board and explain that it means *to get up in the morning.* Ask: **¿A qué hora te levantas por la mañana los lunes?** Ask another student: **¿A qué hora se levanta _____ ?** Then ask about Saturdays. Write **acostarse (o:ue)** on the board and explain that it means *to go to bed.* Follow the same procedure as for **levantarse.**
- Reflexives will only be used in the infinitive and third-person forms until **Estructura 7.1.**
- Show *Overhead PowerPoint #31* and have students refer to the scenes as you make true-false statements about them. Have them correct false statements. Ex: **Hay una chica que se peina por la noche en la habitación. (Cierto.)**
- If students ask, explain that **el pelo** is never used with **peinarse,** only with **cepillarse.**

Más vocabulario

el baño, el cuarto de baño	bathroom
el inodoro	toilet
el jabón	soap
el despertador	alarm clock
el maquillaje	makeup
la rutina diaria	daily routine
bañarse	to bathe; to take a bath
cepillarse el pelo	to brush one's hair
dormirse (o:ue)	to go to sleep; to fall asleep
lavarse la cara	to wash one's face
levantarse	to get up
maquillarse	to put on makeup
antes (de)	before
después	afterwards; then
después (de)	after
durante	during
entonces	then
luego	then
más tarde	later
por la mañana	in the morning
por la noche	at night
por la tarde	in the afternoon; in the evening
por último	finally

Variación léxica

afeitarse	⟷	rasurarse (*Méx., Amér. C.*)
ducha	⟷	regadera (*Col., Méx., Venez.*)
ducharse	⟷	bañarse (*Amér. L.*)
pantuflas	⟷	chancletas (*Méx., Col.*); zapatillas (*Esp.*)

recursos

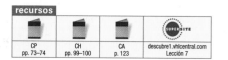

CP pp. 73–74	CH pp. 99–100	CA p. 123	SUPERSITE descubre1.vhlcentral.com Lección 7

En la habitación por la mañana

Por la mañana

TEACHING OPTIONS

TPR In groups of three, have students take turns miming actions involving daily routines. The other group members should guess the verb or verb phrase. You may want to have students use only the infinitive form at this point. Ex: A student mimes washing hands (**lavarse las manos**).

Variación léxica Ask heritage speakers if they use any of the words in **Variación léxica** and if they know of other words used to describe daily routines (Ex: **lavarse la boca/los dientes**). You may want to point out that other words for *bedroom* include **la alcoba, el aposento, el cuarto, el dormitorio,** and **la recámara.**

Se peina. (peinarse)

Se acuesta. (acostarse)

la habitación por la noche

Se lava las manos. lavarse las manos)

Se cepilla los dientes. (cepillarse los dientes)

la toalla

la pasta de dientes

tuflas

Por la noche

Práctica

1 **Escuchar** 🎧 Escucha las frases e indica si cada frase es **cierta** o **falsa**, según el dibujo.

1. _falsa_
2. _cierta_
3. _falsa_
4. _cierta_
5. _falsa_
6. _falsa_
7. _falsa_
8. _cierta_
9. _falsa_
10. _cierta_

2 **Ordenar** 🎧 Escucha la rutina diaria de Marta. Después ordena los verbos según lo que escuchaste.

_5_ a. almorzar
_2_ b. ducharse
_4_ c. peinarse
_7_ d. ver la televisión
_3_ e. desayunar
_8_ f. dormirse
_1_ g. despertarse
_6_ h. estudiar en la biblioteca

3 **Seleccionar** Selecciona la palabra que no está relacionada con cada grupo.

1. lavabo • toalla • despertador • jabón _despertador_
2. manos • antes de • después de • por último _manos_
3. acostarse • jabón • despertarse • dormirse _jabón_
4. espejo • lavabo • despertador • entonces _entonces_
5. dormirse • toalla • vestirse • levantarse _toalla_
6. pelo • cara • manos • inodoro _inodoro_
7. espejo • champú • jabón • pasta de dientes _espejo_
8. maquillarse • vestirse • peinarse • dientes _dientes_
9. baño • dormirse • despertador • acostarse _baño_
10. ducharse • luego • bañarse • lavarse _luego_

4 **Identificar** Con un(a) compañero/a, identifica las cosas que cada persona necesita. Sigue el modelo. Some answers will vary.

> **modelo**
> Jorge / lavarse la cara
> **Estudiante 1:** ¿Qué necesita Jorge para lavarse la cara?
> **Estudiante 2:** Necesita jabón y una toalla.

1. Mariana / maquillarse _maquillaje y un espejo_
2. Gerardo / despertarse _un despertador_
3. Celia / bañarse _jabón y una toalla_
4. Gabriel / ducharse _una ducha, una toalla y jabón_
5. Roberto / afeitarse _crema de afeitar_
6. Sonia / lavarse el pelo _champú y una toalla_
7. Vanesa / lavarse las manos _jabón y una toalla_
8. Manuel / vestirse _su ropa/una camiseta/unos pantalones/etc._

SUPERSITE

1 **Teaching Tip** Go over **Actividad 1** with the class. Then, have volunteers correct the false statements.

1 **Script** 1. Hay dos despertadores en la habitación de las chicas. 2. Un chico se pone crema de afeitar en la cara. 3. Una de las chicas se ducha. 4. Uno de los chicos se afeita. 5. Hay una toalla en la habitación de las chicas. 6. Una de las chicas se maquilla. 7. Las chicas están en el baño. 8. Uno de los chicos se cepilla los dientes en el baño. 9. Uno de los chicos se viste. 10. Una de las chicas se despierta. *Textbook Audio*

2 **Teaching Tip** To simplify, point out that the verbs in the list are in the infinitive form and tell students that they will hear them in conjugated (third-person singular) form. Before listening, have volunteers provide the third-person singular form of each verb.

2 **Script** Normalmente, Marta por la mañana se despierta a las siete, pero no puede levantarse hasta las siete y media. Se ducha y después se viste. Luego desayuna y se cepilla los dientes. Después, se peina y se maquilla. Entonces sale para sus clases. Después de las clases almuerza con sus amigos y por la tarde estudia en la biblioteca. Regresa a casa, cena y ve un poco la televisión. Por la noche, generalmente se acuesta a las diez y por último, se duerme. *Textbook Audio*

3 **Expansion** Go over the answers and indicate why a particular item does not belong. Ex: **El lavabo, la toalla y el jabón son para lavarse. El despertador es para despertarse.**

4 **Expansion** Have students make statements about the people's actions, then ask a question. Ex: **Jorge se lava la cara. ¿Qué necesita?**

5

La rutina de Andrés Ordena esta rutina de una manera lógica.

a. Se afeita después de cepillarse los dientes. __4__
b. Se acuesta a las once y media de la noche. __9__
c. Por último, se duerme. __10__
d. Después de afeitarse, sale para las clases. __5__
e. Asiste a todas sus clases y vuelve a su casa. __6__
f. Andrés se despierta a las seis y media de la mañana. __1__
g. Después de volver a casa, come un poco. Luego estudia en su habitación. __7__
h. Se viste y entonces se cepilla los dientes. __3__
i. Se cepilla los dientes antes de acostarse. __8__
j. Se ducha antes de vestirse. __2__

6

La rutina diaria Con un(a) compañero/a, mira los dibujos y describe lo que hacen Ángel y Lupe.
Some answers may vary.

1.

Ángel se afeita y mira la televisión.

2.

Lupe se maquilla y escucha la radio.

3.

Ángel se ducha y canta.

4.

Lupe se baña y lee.

5.

Ángel se lava la cara con jabón.

6.

Lupe se lava el pelo con champú en la ducha.

7.

Ángel se cepilla el pelo.

8.

Lupe se cepilla los dientes.

Comunicación

7 **La farmacia** Lee el anuncio y responde a las preguntas con un(a) compañero/a.
Answers will vary.

LA FARMACIA NUEVO SOL tiene todo
lo que necesitas para la vida diaria.

Esta semana tenemos grandes rebajas.

Por poco dinero puedes comprar lo que necesitas para el cuarto de baño ideal.

Para los hombres ofrecemos…
Buenas cremas de afeitar de Guapo y Máximo

Para las mujeres ofrecemos…
Nuevos maquillajes de Marisol y jabones de baño Ilusiones y Belleza

Y para todos tenemos los mejores jabones, pastas de dientes y cepillos de dientes.

¡Visita **LA FARMACIA NUEVO SOL!**
Te ofrecemos los mejores precios. Tenemos una tienda cerca de tu casa.

---

1. ¿Qué tipo de tienda es? Es una farmacia.
2. ¿Qué productos ofrecen para las mujeres? maquillajes, jabones de baño
3. ¿Qué productos ofrecen para los hombres? cremas de afeitar
4. Haz (*Make*) una lista de los verbos que asocias con los productos del anuncio.
5. ¿Dónde compras tus productos de higiene? Answers will vary.
6. ¿Tienes una tienda favorita? ¿Cuál es? Answers will vary.

Suggested answers: afeitarse, maquillarse, cepillarse los dientes

8 **Rutinas diarias** Trabajen en parejas para describir la rutina diaria de dos o tres de estas personas. Pueden usar palabras de la lista. Answers will vary.

antes (de)	entonces	primero
después (de)	luego	tarde
durante el día	por último	temprano

- un(a) maestro/a
- un(a) turista
- un hombre o una mujer de negocios (*businessman/woman*)
- un vigilante (*night watchman*)
- un(a) jubilado/a (*retired person*)
- el presidente de los Estados Unidos
- un niño de cuatro años
- Daniel Espinosa

7 **Expansion** Ask small groups to write a competing ad for another pharmacy. Have each group present its ad to the class, who will vote for the most persuasive one.

8 **Expansion** Ask volunteers to read their descriptions aloud. Ask other pairs who chose the same people if their descriptions are similar and how they differ.

TEACHING OPTIONS

Small Groups In groups of three or four, have students act out a brief skit. The situation: they are siblings who are trying to get ready for their morning classes at the same time. The problem: there is only one bathroom in the house or apartment. Have the class vote for the most original or funniest skit.

Heritage Speakers Ask heritage speakers to write paragraphs in which they describe the daily routine in their family. Have students present their paragraphs orally to the class. Verify comprehension by asking other students to relate aspects of the speaker's description.

SUPERSITE

¡Jamás me levanto temprano!

Álex y Javier hablan de sus rutinas diarias.

communication cultures
NATIONAL STANDARDS

PERSONAJES

DON FRANCISCO

ÁLEX

JAVIER

JAVIER Hola, Álex. ¿Qué estás haciendo?
ÁLEX Nada… sólo estoy leyendo mi correo electrónico. ¿Adónde fueron?

JAVIER Inés y yo fuimos a un mercado. Fue muy divertido. Mira, compré este suéter. Me encanta. No fue barato pero es chévere, ¿no?
ÁLEX Sí, es ideal para las montañas.

JAVIER ¡Qué interesantes son los mercados al aire libre! Me gustaría volver pero ya es tarde. Oye, Álex, sabes que mañana tenemos que levantarnos temprano.
ÁLEX Ningún problema.

JAVIER ¡Increíble! ¡Álex, el superhombre!
ÁLEX Oye, Javier, ¿por qué no puedes levantarte temprano?
JAVIER Es que por la noche no quiero dormir, sino dibujar y escuchar música. Por eso es difícil despertarme por la mañana.

JAVIER El autobús no sale hasta las ocho y media. ¿Vas a levantarte mañana a las seis también?
ÁLEX No, pero tengo que levantarme a las siete menos cuarto porque voy a correr.

JAVIER Ah, ya… ¿Puedes despertarme después de correr?
ÁLEX Éste es el plan para mañana. Me levanto a las siete menos cuarto y corro por treinta minutos. Vuelvo, me ducho, me visto y a las siete y media te despierto. ¿De acuerdo?
JAVIER ¡Absolutamente ninguna objeción!

recursos

CA
pp. 63–64

descubre1.vhlcentral.com
Lección 7

JAVIER ¿Seguro? Pues yo jamás me levanto temprano. Nunca oigo el despertador cuando estoy en casa y mi mamá se enoja mucho.

ÁLEX Tranquilo, Javier. Yo tengo una solución.

ÁLEX Cuando estoy en casa en la Ciudad de México, siempre me despierto a las seis en punto. Me ducho en cinco minutos y luego me cepillo los dientes. Después me afeito, me visto y ¡listo! ¡Me voy!

DON FRANCISCO Hola, chicos. Mañana salimos temprano, a las ocho y media... ni un minuto antes ni un minuto después.

ÁLEX No se preocupe, don Francisco. Todo está bajo control.

DON FRANCISCO Bueno, pues, hasta mañana.

DON FRANCISCO ¡Ay, los estudiantes! Siempre se acuestan tarde. ¡Qué vida!

Expresiones útiles

Telling where you went

- **¿Adónde fuiste/fue usted?**
  Where did you go?
  Fui a un mercado.
  I went to a market.
- **¿Adónde fueron ustedes?**
  Where did you go?
  Fuimos a un mercado. Fue divertido.
  We went to a market. It was fun.

Talking about morning routines

- **(Jamás) me levanto temprano/tarde.**
  I (never) get up early/late.
- **Nunca oigo el despertador.**
  I never hear the alarm clock.
- **Es difícil/fácil despertarme.**
  It's hard/easy to wake up.
- **Cuando estoy en casa, siempre me despierto a las seis en punto.**
  When I'm home, I always wake up at six on the dot.
- **Me ducho y luego me cepillo los dientes.**
  I take a shower and then I brush my teeth.
- **Después me afeito y me visto.**
  Afterwards, I shave and get dressed.

Reassuring someone

- **No hay problema.**
  No problem.
- **No te/se preocupes/preocupe.**
  Don't worry. (fam.)/(form.)
- **Tranquilo.**
  Don't worry.; Be cool.

Additional vocabulary

- **sino**
  but (rather)
- **Me encanta este suéter.**
  I love this sweater.
- **Me fascinó la película.**
  I liked the movie a lot.

Teaching Tip Have students get together in groups of three to role-play the episode. Have one or two groups present it to the class.

Expresiones útiles Draw attention to the verb forms **fui, fuiste, fue,** and **fuimos.** Explain that these are preterite forms of the verbs **ir** and **ser.** The context clarifies which verb is used. Then point out the phrases **me levanto, me despierto, me ducho, me cepillo, me afeito, me visto,** and **No te preocupes.** Tell the class that these are forms of the reflexive verbs **levantarse, despertarse, ducharse, cepillarse, afeitarse, vestirse,** and **preocuparse.** Also, point out the words **siempre, nunca,** and **jamás.** Explain that **siempre** is called a positive word and that the other two are called negative words. Tell students that they will learn more about these concepts in **Estructura.**

TEACHING OPTIONS

TPR Ask students to write **Javier** and **Álex** on separate pieces of paper. Read aloud statements about the characters' daily routines and have students hold up the corresponding name. Ex: **No me gusta levantarme temprano. (Javier)** Then repeat the process for tomorrow's plan. Ex: **Mañana me ducho después de correr. (Álex)**

Extra Practice Ask students to write a short description about what they think **don Francisco's** daily routine is like. Then have them get together with a classmate to find similarities and differences in their descriptions.

Pairs Ask pairs of students to work together to create six true-false sentences about the **Fotonovela.** Have pairs exchange papers and complete the activity.

¿Qué pasó?

1 **¿Cierto o falso?** Indica si lo que dicen estas oraciones es **cierto** o **falso**. Corrige las oraciones falsas.

1. Álex está mirando la televisión.
   Falso. Álex está leyendo su correo electrónico.
2. El suéter que Javier acaba de comprar es caro pero es muy bonito.
   Cierto.
3. Javier cree que el mercado es aburrido y no quiere volver.
   Falso. Javier piensa que el mercado es muy interesante.
4. El autobús va a salir mañana a las siete y media en punto.
   Falso. El autobús sale mañana a las ocho y media en punto.
5. A Javier le gusta mucho dibujar y escuchar música por la noche.
   Cierto.

2 **Identificar** Identifica quién puede decir estas oraciones. Puedes usar cada nombre más de una vez.

1. ¡Ay, los estudiantes nunca se acuestan temprano!
   don Francisco
2. ¿El despertador? ¡Jamás lo oigo por la mañana!
   Javier
3. Es fácil despertarme temprano. Y sólo necesito cinco minutos para ducharme. ___Álex___
4. Mañana vamos a salir a las ocho y media.
   Javier, don Francisco
5. Acabo de ir a un mercado fabuloso. ___Javier___
6. No se preocupe. Tenemos todo bajo control para mañana. ___Álex___

DON FRANCISCO

JAVIER

ÁLEX

3 **Ordenar** Ordena correctamente los planes que tiene Álex.

- _5_ a. Me visto.
- _2_ b. Corro por media hora.
- _6_ c. Despierto a Javier a las siete y media.
- _3_ d. Vuelvo a la habitación.
- _1_ e. Me levanto a las siete menos cuarto.
- _4_ f. Me ducho.

4 **Mi rutina** En parejas, hablen de sus rutinas de la mañana y de la noche. Indiquen a qué horas hacen las actividades más importantes. Answers will vary.

modelo

Estudiante 1: ¿Prefieres levantarte temprano o tarde?
Estudiante 2: Prefiero levantarme tarde… muy tarde.

Estudiante 1: ¿A qué hora te levantas los fines de semana?
Estudiante 2: A las once. ¿Y tú?

National comparisons standards

Pronunciación SUPERSITE
The consonant r

ropa	rutina	rico	Ramón

In Spanish, **r** has a strong trilled sound at the beginning of a word. No English words have a trill, but English speakers often produce a trill when they imitate the sound of a motor.

gustar	durante	primero	crema

In any other position, **r** has a weak sound similar to the English *tt* in *better* or the English *dd* in *ladder*. In contrast to English, the tongue touches the roof of the mouth behind the teeth.

pizarra	corro	marrón	aburrido

The letter combination **rr**, which only appears between vowels, always has a strong trilled sound.

caro	carro	pero	perro

Between vowels, the difference between the strong trilled **rr** and the weak **r** is very important, as a mispronunciation could lead to confusion between two different words.

Práctica Lee las palabras en voz alta, prestando (*paying*) atención a la pronunciación de la **r** y la **rr**.

1. Perú	4. madre	7. rubio	10. tarde
2. Rosa	5. comprar	8. reloj	11. cerrar
3. borrador	6. favor	9. Arequipa	12. despertador

Oraciones Lee las oraciones en voz alta, prestando atención a la pronunciación de la **r** y la **rr**.

1. Ramón Robles Ruiz es programador. Su esposa Rosaura es artista.
2. A Rosaura Robles le encanta regatear en el mercado.
3. Ramón nunca regatea… le aburre regatear.
4. Rosaura siempre compra cosas baratas.
5. Ramón no es rico pero prefiere comprar cosas muy caras.
6. ¡El martes Ramón compró un carro nuevo!

Refranes Lee en voz alta los refranes, prestando atención a la **r** y a la **rr**.

Perro que ladra no muerde.[1]

No se ganó Zamora en una hora.[2]

1 A dog's bark is worse than its bite.
2 Rome wasn't built in a day.

recursos		
CH p. 101	CA p. 124	SUPERSITE descubre1.vhlcentral.com Lección 7

EN DETALLE

La siesta

¿Sientes cansancio° después de comer? ¿Te cuesta° volver al trabajo° o a clase después del almuerzo? Estas sensaciones son normales. A muchas personas les gusta relajarse° después de almorzar. Este momento de descanso es **la siesta**. La siesta es popular en los países hispanos y viene de una antigua costumbre° del área del Mediterráneo. La palabra *siesta* viene del latín; es una forma corta de decir "sexta hora". La sexta hora del día es después del mediodía, el momento de más calor. Debido al° calor y al cansancio, los habitantes de España, Italia, Grecia e incluso Portugal, tienen la costumbre de dormir la siesta desde hace° más de° dos mil años. Los españoles y los portugueses llevaron la costumbre a los países americanos.

La siesta es muy importante en la cultura hispana. Muchas oficinas° y tiendas cierran dos o tres horas después del mediodía. Los empleados van a su casa, almuerzan, duermen la siesta y regresan al trabajo entre las 2:30 y las 4:30 de la tarde. Esto ocurre especialmente en Suramérica, México y España.

Los estudios científicos explican que una siesta corta después de almorzar ayuda° a trabajar más y mejor° durante la tarde. Pero, ¡cuidado! Esta siesta debe durar° sólo entre veinte y cuarenta minutos. Si dormimos más, entramos en la fase de sueño profundo y es difícil despertarse.

Hoy día, algunas empresas° de los Estados Unidos, Canadá, Japón, Inglaterra y Alemania tienen salas° especiales en las que los empleados pueden dormir la siesta.

¿Dónde duermen la siesta?

■ Costumbre Antigua
■ Costumbre Nueva

En los lugares donde la siesta es una costumbre antigua, las personas la duermen en su casa. En los países donde la siesta es una costumbre nueva, la gente duerme en sus lugares de trabajo o en centros de siesta.

Sientes cansancio *Do you feel tired* **Te cuesta** *Is it hard for you* **trabajo** *work* **relajarse** *to relax* **antigua costumbre** *old custom* **Debido al** *Because (of)* **desde hace** *for* **más de** *more than* **oficinas** *offices* **ayuda** *helps* **mejor** *better* **durar** *last* **algunas empresas** *some businesses* **salas** *rooms*

ACTIVIDADES

1 **¿Cierto o falso?** Indica si lo que dicen las oraciones es **cierto** o **falso**. Corrige la información falsa.

1. La costumbre de la siesta empezó en Asia. **Falso.** La costumbre de la siesta empezó en el área del Mediterráneo.
2. La palabra *siesta* está relacionada con la sexta hora del día. **Cierto.**
3. Los españoles y los portugueses llevaron la costumbre de la siesta a Latinoamérica. **Cierto.**
4. La siesta ayuda a trabajar más y mejor durante la tarde. **Cierto.**

5. Los horarios de trabajo de los países hispanos son los mismos que los de los Estados Unidos. **Falso.** En muchos países hispanos las oficinas y las tiendas cierran dos o tres horas después del mediodía.
6. Una siesta larga siempre es mejor que una siesta corta. **Falso.** La siesta sólo debe durar entre veinte y cuarenta minutos.
7. En los Estados Unidos, los empleados de algunas empresas pueden dormir la siesta en el trabajo. **Cierto.**
8. Es fácil despertar de un sueño profundo. **Falso.** Es difícil despertar de un sueño profundo.

ASÍ SE DICE

El cuidado personal

el aseo; el excusado; el servicio; el váter (Esp.)	el baño
el cortaúñas	*nail clippers*
el desodorante	*deodorant*
el enjuague bucal	*mouthwash*
el hilo dental/la seda dental	*dental floss*
la máquina de afeitar/ de rasurar (Méx.)	*electric razor*

EL MUNDO HISPANO

Costumbres especiales

○ **México y El Salvador** Los vendedores pasan por las calles gritando° su mercancía°: tanques de gas y flores° en México; pan y tortillas en El Salvador.

○ **Costa Rica** Para encontrar las direcciones° los costarricenses usan referencias a anécdotas, lugares o características geográficas. Por ejemplo: *200 metros norte de la Iglesia Católica, frente al° Supermercado Mi Mega.*

○ **Argentina** En El Tigre, una ciudad en una isla del Río° de la Plata, la gente usa barcos particulares°, colectivos° y barcos-taxi para ir de un lugar a otro. Todas las mañanas, un barco colectivo recoge° a los niños y los lleva a la escuela.

gritando *shouting* mercancía *merchandise* flores *flowers* direcciones *addresses* frente al *opposite* río *river* particulares *private* colectivos *collective* recoge *picks up*

PERFIL

Ir de tapas

En España, **las tapas** son pequeños platos°. **Ir de tapas** es una costumbre que consiste en comer estos platillos en bares, cafés y restaurantes. Dos tapas muy populares son la tortilla de patatas° y los calamares°. La historia de las tapas empezó cuando los dueños° de las tabernas tuvieron° la idea de servir el vaso de vino° tapado° con una rodaja° de pan°. La comida era° la "tapa"° del vaso; de ahí viene el nombre. Con la tapa, los insectos no podían° entrar en el vaso. Más tarde los dueños de las tabernas pusieron° la

tapa al lado del vaso. Luego, empezaron a servir también pequeñas porciones de platos tradicionales.

Para muchos españoles, ir de tapas con los amigos después del trabajo es una rutina diaria.

platos *dishes* tortilla de patatas *potato omelet* calamares *squid* dueños *owners* tuvieron *had* vaso de vino *glass of wine* tapado *covered* rodaja *slice* pan *bread* era *was* tapa *lid* no podían *couldn't* pusieron *put*

SUPERSITE Conexión Internet

¿Qué costumbres son populares en los países hispanos?

Go to **descubre1.vhlcentral.com** to find more cultural information related to this **Cultura** section.

ACTIVIDADES

2 Comprensión Completa las oraciones.
1. Uso _el hilo dental/la seda dental_ para limpiar (*to clean*) entre los dientes.
2. En _El Salvador_ las personas compran pan y tortillas a los vendedores que pasan por la calle.
3. Muchos españoles _van de tapas_ después del trabajo.
4. En Costa Rica usan anécdotas y lugares para dar _direcciones_.

3 ¿Qué costumbres tienes? Escribe cuatro oraciones sobre una costumbre que compartes con tus amigos o con tu familia (por ejemplo: ir al cine, ir a eventos deportivos, leer, comer juntos, etc.). Explica qué haces, cuándo lo haces y con quién. Answers will vary.

recursos

| CH p. 102 | descubre1.vhlcentral.com Lección 7 |

Section Goals

In **Estructura 7.1**, students will learn:
- the conjugation of reflexive verbs
- common reflexive verbs

Instructional Resources
Cuaderno de práctica, pp. 75–76
Cuaderno para hispanohablantes, pp. 103–104
Cuaderno de actividades, pp. 33–34, 125
e-Cuaderno
Supersite: Audio Activity MP3 Audio Files
Supersite/TRCD: *PowerPoints* (Lección 7 Estructura Presentation); Communication Activities, Audio Activity Script, Answer Keys
Audio Activity CD

Teaching Tips

- Model the first-person reflexive by talking about yourself. Ex: **Me levanto muy temprano. Me levanto a las cinco de la mañana.** Then model the second person by asking questions with a verb you have already used in the first person. Ex: **Y tú, _____, ¿a qué hora te levantas? (Me levanto a las ocho.)**

- Introduce the third person by making statements and asking questions about what a student has told you. Ex: _____ **se levanta muy tarde, ¿no? (Sí, se levanta muy tarde.)**

- Add a visual aspect to this grammar presentation. Use magazine pictures to clarify meanings between third-person singular and third-person plural forms. Ex: **Se lava las manos** and **Se lavan las manos.**

- On the board or an overhead, summarize the three possible positions for reflexive pronouns. You may want to show this visually by using an **X** to represent the reflexive pronoun: **X verbo conjugado, infinitivoX, gerundioX.** Remind students that they have already learned these positions for direct and indirect object pronouns.

7.1 Reflexive verbs

ANTE TODO A reflexive verb is used to indicate that the subject does something to or for himself or herself. In other words, it "reflects" the action of the verb back to the subject. Reflexive verbs always use reflexive pronouns.

SUBJECT · REFLEXIVE VERB

Joaquín **se ducha** por la mañana.

The verb lavarse (*to wash oneself*)

SINGULAR FORMS			
	yo	**me lavo**	*I wash (myself)*
	tú	**te lavas**	*you wash (yourself)*
	Ud.	**se lava**	*you wash (yourself)*
	él/ella	**se lava**	*he/she washes (himself/herself)*

PLURAL FORMS			
	nosotros/as	**nos lavamos**	*we wash (ourselves)*
	vosotros/as	**os laváis**	*you wash (yourselves)*
	Uds.	**se lavan**	*you wash (yourselves)*
	ellos/ellas	**se lavan**	*they wash (themselves)*

▶ The pronoun **se** attached to an infinitive identifies the verb as reflexive: **lavarse.**

▶ When a reflexive verb is conjugated, the reflexive pronoun agrees with the subject.

Me afeito.   **Te despiertas** a las siete.

Me ducho, me cepillo los dientes, me visto y ¡listo!

¡Ay, los estudiantes! Siempre se acuestan tarde.

▶ Like object pronouns, reflexive pronouns generally appear before a conjugated verb. With infinitives and present participles, they may be placed before the conjugated verb or attached to the infinitive or present participle.

Ellos **se** van a vestir.   **Nos** estamos lavando las manos.
Ellos van a vestir**se**.   Estamos lavándo**nos** las manos.
They are going to get dressed.   *We are washing our hands.*

▶ **¡Atención!** When a reflexive pronoun is attached to a present participle, an accent mark is added to maintain the original stress.

bañando ⟶ bañ**á**ndo**se**   durmiendo ⟶ durmi**é**ndo**se**

TEACHING OPTIONS

Extra Practice To provide oral practice with reflexive verbs, create sentences that follow the pattern of the sentences in the examples. Say the sentence, have students repeat it, then say a different subject, varying the gender and number. Have students then say the sentence with the new subject, changing pronouns and verbs as necessary.

Heritage Speakers Have heritage speakers describe daily routines in their families. Encourage them to use their own linguistic variation of words presented in this lesson. Ex: **regarse (e:ie)**, **pintarse**. Have heritage speakers work together to compare and contrast activities as well as lexical variations.

Common reflexive verbs

acordarse (de) (o:ue)	*to remember*	**llamarse**	*to be called; to be named*
acostarse (o:ue)	*to go to bed*		
afeitarse	*to shave*	**maquillarse**	*to put on makeup*
bañarse	*to bathe; to take a bath*	**peinarse**	*to comb one's hair*
cepillarse	*to brush*	**ponerse**	*to put on*
despedirse (de) (e:i)	*to say goodbye (to)*	**ponerse (+ adj.)**	*to become (+ adj.)*
despertarse (e:ie)	*to wake up*	**preocuparse (por)**	*to worry (about)*
dormirse (o:ue)	*to go to sleep; to fall asleep*	**probarse** (o:ue)	*to try on*
		quedarse	*to stay; to remain*
ducharse	*to shower; to take a shower*	**quitarse**	*to take off*
		secarse	*to dry (oneself)*
enojarse (con)	*to get angry (with)*	**sentarse** (e:ie)	*to sit down*
irse	*to go away; to leave*	**sentirse** (e:ie)	*to feel*
lavarse	*to wash (oneself)*	**vestirse** (e:i)	*to get dressed*
levantarse	*to get up*		

COMPARE & CONTRAST

Unlike English, a number of verbs in Spanish can be reflexive or non-reflexive. If the verb acts upon the subject, the reflexive form is used. If the verb acts upon something other than the subject, the non-reflexive form is used. Compare these sentences.

Lola **lava** los platos.

Lola **se lava** la cara.

As the preceding sentences show, reflexive verbs sometimes have different meanings than their non-reflexive counterparts. For example, **lavar** means *to wash*, while **lavarse** means *to wash oneself, to wash up.*

▶ **¡Atención!** Parts of the body or clothing are generally not referred to with possessives, but with the definite article.

La niña se quitó **los** zapatos.   Necesito cepillarme **los** dientes.

 **¡INTÉNTALO!** Indica el presente de estos verbos reflexivos. El primero de cada columna ya está conjugado.

despertarse

1. Mis hermanos *se despiertan* tarde.
2. Tú *te despiertas* tarde.
3. Nosotros *nos despertamos* tarde.
4. Benito *se despierta* tarde.
5. Yo *me despierto* tarde.

ponerse

1. Él *se pone* una chaqueta.
2. Yo *me pongo* una chaqueta.
3. Usted *se pone* una chaqueta.
4. Nosotras *nos ponemos* una chaqueta.
5. Las niñas *se ponen* una chaqueta.

Práctica SUPERSITE

1 **Nuestra rutina** La familia de Blanca sigue la misma rutina todos los días. Según Blanca, ¿qué hacen ellos?

> **modelo**
> mamá / despertarse a las 5:00
> Mamá se despierta a las cinco.

1. Roberto y yo / levantarse a las 7:00 Roberto y yo nos levantamos a las siete.
2. papá / ducharse primero y / luego afeitarse Papá se ducha primero y luego se afeita.
3. yo / lavarse la cara y / vestirse antes de tomar café Yo me lavo la cara y me visto antes de tomar café.
4. mamá / peinarse y / luego maquillarse Mamá se peina y luego se maquilla.
5. todos (nosotros) / sentarse a la mesa para comer Todos nos sentamos a la mesa para comer.
6. Roberto / cepillarse los dientes después de comer Roberto se cepilla los dientes después de comer.
7. yo / ponerse el abrigo antes de salir Yo me pongo el abrigo antes de salir.
8. nosotros / despedirse de mamá Nosotros nos despedimos de mamá.

2 **La fiesta elegante** Selecciona el verbo apropiado y completa las oraciones con la forma correcta.

1. Tú ____lavas____ (lavar / lavarse) el auto antes de ir a la fiesta.
2. Nosotros no __nos acordamos__ (acordar / acordarse) de comprar regalos.
3. Para llegar a tiempo, Raúl y Marta ____acuestan____ (acostar / acostarse) a los niños antes de irse.
4. Yo ____me siento____ (sentir / sentirse) bien hoy.
5. Mis amigos siempre ____se visten____ (vestir / vestirse) con ropa muy cara. *expensive*
6. ¿____Se prueban____ (Probar / Probarse) ustedes la ropa antes de comprarla?
7. Usted ____se preocupa____ (preocupar / preocuparse) mucho por sus amigos, ¿no?
8. En general, ____me afeito____ (afeitar / afeitarse) yo mismo, pero hoy el barbero (*barber*) me ____afeita____ (afeitar / afeitarse).

3 **Describir** Mira los dibujos y describe lo que estas personas hacen. Some answers may vary.

1. el joven El joven se quita los zapatos.

2. Carmen Carmen se duerme.

3. Juan Juan se pone la camiseta.

4. ellos Ellos se despiden.

5. Estrella Estrella se maquilla.

6. Toni Toni se enoja con el perro.

Sidebar (Teacher's notes)

1 **Teaching Tip** Before assigning the activity, review reflexive verbs by comparing and contrasting weekday and weekend routines. Ex: **¿Te levantas tarde o temprano los sábados? ¿Te acuestas tarde o temprano los domingos?**

1 **Expansion** To practice the formal register, describe situations and have students tell you what you are going to do. Ex: **Hace frío y nieva, pero necesito salir. (Usted va a ponerse el abrigo.) Acabo de levantarme. (Usted se va a lavar la cara.)**

2 **Teaching Tip** Before assigning the activity, review reflexive and non-reflexive verbs by asking questions using both forms. Ex: **¿Cuándo nos lavamos? (Nos lavamos todos los días.) ¿Cuándo lavamos el coche? (Lavamos el coche los fines de semana.)**

2 **Expansion** Ask students to write five sentence pairs contrasting reflexive and non-reflexive forms. Ex: **Me despierto a las siete. Despierto a mi hermano/a a las ocho.**

3 **Expansion**
- Repeat the activity as a pattern drill, supplying different subjects for each drawing. Ex: **Número uno, yo. (Me quito los zapatos.) Número cinco, nosotras. (Nosotras nos maquillamos.)**
- Repeat the activity using the present progressive. Ask students to provide both possible sentences. Ex: **1. El joven se está quitando los zapatos./ El joven está quitándose los zapatos.**

TEACHING OPTIONS

Extra Practice Have students figure out the morning schedule of the **Ramírez** family. Say: **El señor Ramírez se afeita antes que Alberto, pero después que Rafael. La señora Ramírez es la primera en ducharse y Montse es la última. Lolita se peina cuando su padre sale del cuarto de baño y antes que uno de** sus hermanos. Nuria se maquilla después que Lolita, pero no inmediatamente después. (Primero se ducha la señora Ramírez. Después se afeita Rafael seguido por el señor Ramírez. Después se peina Lolita. Alberto se afeita y después Nuria se maquilla. Finalmente Montse se ducha.)

Comunicación

4

Preguntas personales En parejas, túrnense para hacerse estas preguntas.   Answers will vary.

1. ¿A qué hora te levantas durante la semana?
2. ¿A qué hora te levantas los fines de semana?
3. ¿Prefieres levantarte tarde o temprano? ¿Por qué?
4. ¿Te enojas frecuentemente con tus amigos?
5. ¿Te preocupas fácilmente? ¿Qué te preocupa?
6. ¿Qué te pone contento/a?
7. ¿Qué haces cuando te sientes triste?
8. ¿Y cuando te sientes alegre?
9. ¿Te acuestas tarde o temprano durante la semana?
10. ¿A qué hora te acuestas los fines de semana?

5

Charadas En grupos, jueguen a las charadas. Cada persona debe pensar en dos frases con verbos reflexivos. La primera persona que adivina la charada dramatiza la siguiente. Answers will vary.

6

Debate En grupos, discutan este tema: ¿Quiénes necesitan más tiempo para arreglarse (*to get ready*) antes de salir, los hombres o las mujeres? Hagan una lista de las razones (*reasons*) que tienen para defender sus ideas e informen a la clase. Answers will vary.

Síntesis

7

recursos

CA
pp. 33–34

La familia ocupada Tú y tu compañero/a asisten a un programa de verano en Lima, Perú. Viven con la familia Ramos. Tu profesor(a) te va a dar la rutina incompleta que la familia sigue en las mañanas. Trabaja con tu compañero/a para completarla.   Answers will vary.

modelo
> **Estudiante 1:** ¿Qué hace el señor Ramos a las seis y cuarto?
> **Estudiante 2:** El señor Ramos se levanta.

---

4 Expansion Ask volunteers to call out some of their answers. The class should add information by speculating on the reason behind each answer. Ex: **Hablas por teléfono con tus amigos cuando te sientes triste porque ellos te comprenden muy bien.** Have the volunteer confirm or refute the speculation.

5 Expansion Ask each group to present their best **charada** to the class.

6 Teaching Tip Before assigning groups, go over some of the things men and women do to get ready to go out. Ex: **Las mujeres se maquillan. Los hombres se afeitan.** Then ask students to indicate their opinion on the question and divide the class into groups accordingly.

7 Teaching Tip Divide the class into pairs and distribute the Communication Activities worksheets that correspond to this activity. Give students ten minutes to complete this activity.

7 Expansion Ask groups of four to imagine they all live in the same house and have them put together a message board to reflect their different schedules.

Section Goals

In **Estructura 7.2**, students will learn:

- high-frequency negative and positive expressions
- the placement and use of positive and negative words

Instructional Resources
Cuaderno de práctica, pp. 77–78
Cuaderno para hispanohablantes, pp. 105–106
Cuaderno de actividades, pp. 37, 126
e-Cuaderno
Supersite: Audio Activity MP3 Audio Files
Supersite/TRCD/Print: *PowerPoints* (**Lección 7 Estructura** Presentation); Communication Activities, Audio Activity Script, Answer Keys
Audio Activity CD

Teaching Tips

- Write **alguien** and **nadie** on the board and ask questions about what students are wearing. Ex: **Hoy alguien lleva una camiseta verde. ¿Quién es? ¿Alguien lleva pantalones anaranjados?**
- Present negative words by complaining dramatically in a whining tone. Ex: **Nadie me llama por teléfono. Jamás recibo un correo electrónico de ningún estudiante. Ni mis amigos se acuerdan de mi cumpleaños.** Then smile radiantly and state the opposite. Ex: **Alguien me llama por teléfono.**
- Add a visual aspect to this grammar presentation. Use magazine pictures to compare and contrast positive and negative words. Ex: **La señora tiene algo en las manos. ¿El señor tiene algo también? No, el señor no tiene nada.**
- Have students say they do the opposite of what you do. Ex: **Yo siempre canto en la ducha. (Nosotros no cantamos nunca en la ducha.)**

7.2 Positive and negative expressions [SUPERSITE]

ANTE TODO Negative words deny the existence of people and things or contradict statements, for instance, *no one* or *nothing*. Spanish negative words have corresponding positive words, which are opposite in meaning.

Positive and negative words

Positive words		Negative words	
algo	*something; anything*	**nada**	*nothing; not anything*
alguien	*someone; somebody; anyone*	**nadie**	*no one; nobody; not anyone*
alguno/a(s), algún	*some; any*	**ninguno/a, ningún**	*no; none; not any*
o… o	*either… or*	**ni… ni**	*neither… nor*
siempre	*always*	**nunca, jamás**	*never, not ever*
también	*also; too*	**tampoco**	*neither; not either*

▶ There are two ways to form negative sentences in Spanish. You can place the negative word before the verb, or you can place **no** before the verb and the negative word after.

Nadie se levanta temprano.
No one gets up early.

No se levanta nadie temprano.
No one gets up early.

Ellos **nunca gritan**.
They never shout.

Ellos **no gritan nunca**.
They never shout.

Yo siempre me despierto a las seis en punto. ¿Y tú?

Pues yo jamás me levanto temprano. Nunca oigo el despertador.

▶ Because they refer to people, **alguien** and **nadie** are often used with the personal **a**. The personal **a** is also used before **alguno/a, algunos/as,** and **ninguno/a** when these words refer to people and they are the direct object of the verb.

—Perdón, señor, ¿busca usted **a alguien**?
—No, gracias, señorita, no busco **a nadie**.

—Tomás, ¿buscas **a alguno** de tus hermanos?
—No, mamá, no busco **a ninguno**.

▶ **¡Atención!** Before a masculine, singular noun, **alguno** and **ninguno** are shortened to **algún** and **ningún**.

—¿Tienen ustedes **algún** amigo peruano?
—No, no tenemos **ningún** amigo peruano.

AYUDA

Alguno/a, algunos/as are not always used in the same way English uses *some* or *any*. Often, **algún** is used where *a* would be used in English.

¿Tienes algún libro que hable de los incas?
Do you have a book that talks about the Incas?

Note that **ninguno/a** is rarely used in the plural.

—**¿Visitaste algunos museos?**
—**No, no visité ninguno.**

COMPARE & CONTRAST

In English, it is incorrect to use more than one negative word in a sentence. In Spanish, however, sentences frequently contain two or more negative words. Compare these Spanish and English sentences.

Nunca le escribo a **nadie**.	**No** me preocupo por **nada nunca**.
I never write to anyone.	*I do not ever worry about anything.*

As the preceding sentences show, once an English sentence contains one negative word (for example, *not* or *never*), no other negative word may be used. In Spanish, however, once a negative word is used, all other elements must be expressed in the negative if possible.

▶ Although in Spanish **pero** and **sino** both mean *but*, they are not interchangeable. **Sino** is used when the first part of a sentence is negative and the second part contradicts it. In this context, **sino** means *but rather* or *on the contrary*. In all other cases, **pero** is used to mean *but*.

Los estudiantes no se acuestan temprano **sino** tarde.	Las toallas son caras, **pero** bonitas.
The students don't go to bed early, but rather late.	*The towels are expensive, but beautiful.*
María no habla francés **sino** español.	José es inteligente, **pero** no saca buenas notas.
María doesn't speak French, but rather Spanish.	*José is intelligent but doesn't get good grades.*

 ¡INTÉNTALO!   Cambia las oraciones para que sean negativas. La primera se da como ejemplo.

1. Siempre se viste bien.
   _____Nunca_____ se viste bien.
   _____No_____ se viste bien _____nunca_____.
2. Alguien se ducha.
   _____Nadie_____ se ducha.
   _____No_____ se ducha _____nadie_____.
3. Ellas van también.
   Ellas _____tampoco_____ van.
   Ellas _____no_____ van _____tampoco_____.
4. Alguien se pone nervioso.
   _____Nadie_____ se pone nervioso.
   _____No_____ se pone nervioso _____nadie_____.
5. Tú siempre te lavas las manos.
   Tú _____nunca / jamás_____ te lavas las manos.
   Tú _no_ te lavas las manos _____nunca / jamás_____.
6. Voy a traer algo.
   _____No_____ voy a traer _____nada_____.

7. Juan se afeita también.
   Juan _____tampoco_____ se afeita.
   Juan _____no_____ se afeita _____tampoco_____.
8. Mis amigos viven en una residencia o en casa.
   Mis amigos _____no_____ viven _____ni_____ en una residencia _____ni_____ en casa.
9. La profesora hace algo en su escritorio.
   La profesora _____no_____ hace _____nada_____ en su escritorio.
10. Tú y yo vamos al mercado.
    _____Ni_____ tú _____ni_____ yo vamos al mercado.
11. Tienen un espejo en su casa.
    _____No_____ tienen _____ningún_____ espejo en su casa.
12. Algunos niños se ponen el abrigo.
    _____Ningún_____ niño se pone el abrigo.

recursos

CP
pp. 77–78

CH
pp. 105–106

CA
pp. 37,126

descubre1.
vhlcentral.com
Lección 7

Teaching Tips
- Emphasize that there is no limit to the number of negative words that can be strung together in a sentence in Spanish. Ex: **No hablo con nadie nunca de ningún problema, ni con mi familia ni con mis amigos.**
- Ask volunteers questions about their activities since the last class, reiterating the answers. Ex: **¿Quién compró algo nuevo? Sólo dos personas. Nadie más compró algo nuevo. Yo no compré nada nuevo tampoco.**
- Elicit negative responses by asking questions whose answers will clearly be negative. Ex: **¿Alguien lleva zapatos de lunares? (No, nadie lleva zapatos de lunares.) ¿Piensas comprar un barco mañana? (No, no pienso comprar ninguno/ningún barco.) ¿Tienes nietos? (No, no tengo ninguno/ningún nieto.)**
- Give examples of **pero** and **sino** using the seating of the students. Ex: _____ **se sienta al lado de _____, pero no al lado de _____. No se sienta a la izquierda de _____, sino a la derecha. _____ no se sienta al lado de la ventana, pero está cerca de la puerta.**

TEACHING OPTIONS

Video Show the **Fotonovela** again to give students more input containing positive and negative words. Stop the video where appropriate to discuss how these words are used.
Pairs Have pairs create sentences about your community using positive and negative words. Ex: **En nuestra ciudad no hay ningún mercado al aire libre. Hay algunos restaurantes de tapas. El equipo de béisbol juega bien, pero no gana muchos partidos.**

Small Groups Give small groups five minutes to write a description of **un señor muy, pero muy antipático**. Tell them to use as many positive and negative words as possible to describe what makes this person so unpleasant. Encourage exaggeration and creativity.

Práctica SUPERSITE

1 Teaching Tips
- To challenge students, ask them to change each sentence so that the opposite choice (**pero** or **sino**) would be correct. Ex: **Muchos estudiantes no quieren comer en la cafetería sino salir a comer a un restaurante local.**
- Display a magazine picture that shows a group of people involved in a specific activity. Then talk about the picture, modeling the types of constructions required in **Actividad 1**. Ex: **Todos trabajan en la oficina, pero ninguno tiene computadora.**

1 Expansion
Have pairs create four sentences, two with **sino** and two with **pero**. Have them "dehydrate" their sentences as in the **modelo** and exchange papers with another pair, who will write the complete sentences.

2 Teaching Tip
Review positive and negative words by using them in short sentences and asking volunteers to contradict your statements. Ex: **Veo a alguien en la puerta. (No, usted no ve a nadie en la puerta.) Nunca vengo a clase con el libro. (No, usted siempre viene a clase con el libro.)**

2 Expansion
After students have role-played the conversation, ask them to summarize it. **Ana María no encontró ningún regalo para Eliana. Tampoco vio a ninguna amiga en el centro comercial.**

1 ¿Pero o sino? Forma oraciones sobre estas personas usando **pero** o **sino**.

> **modelo**
> muchos estudiantes comen en la cafetería / algunos de ellos quieren salir a comer a un restaurante local.
> Muchos estudiantes comen en la cafetería, pero algunos de ellos quieren salir a comer a un restaurante local.

1. Marcos nunca se despierta temprano / siempre llega puntual a clase
   Marcos nunca se despierta temprano, pero siempre llega puntual a clase.
2. Lisa y Katarina no se acuestan temprano / muy tarde
   Lisa y Katarina no se acuestan temprano sino muy tarde.
3. Alfonso es inteligente / algunas veces es antipático
   Alfonso es inteligente, pero algunas veces es antipático.
4. los directores de la escuela no son ecuatorianos / peruanos
   Los directores de la escuela no son ecuatorianos sino peruanos.
5. no nos acordamos de comprar champú / compramos jabón
   No nos acordamos de comprar champú, pero compramos jabón.
6. Emilia no es estudiante / profesora
   Emilia no es estudiante sino profesora.
7. no quiero levantarme / tengo que ir a clase
   No quiero levantarme, pero tengo que ir a clase.
8. Miguel no se afeita por la mañana / por la noche
   Miguel no se afeita por la mañana sino por la noche.

2 Completar Completa esta conversación entre dos hermanos. Usa expresiones negativas en tus respuestas. Luego, dramatiza la conversación con un(a) compañero/a. Answers will vary.

AURELIO Ana María, ¿encontraste algún regalo para Eliana?
ANA MARÍA (1) No, no encontré ningún regalo/nada para Eliana.

AURELIO ¿Viste a alguna amiga en el centro comercial?
ANA MARÍA (2) No, no vi a ninguna amiga/ninguna/nadie en el centro comercial.

AURELIO ¿Me llamó alguien?
ANA MARÍA (3) No, nadie te llamó./No, no te llamó nadie.

AURELIO ¿Quieres ir al teatro o al cine esta noche?
ANA MARÍA (4) No, no quiero ir ni al teatro ni al cine.

AURELIO ¿No quieres salir a comer?
ANA MARÍA (5) No, no quiero salir a comer (tampoco).

AURELIO ¿Hay algo interesante en la televisión esta noche?
ANA MARÍA (6) No, no hay nada interesante en la televisión.

AURELIO ¿Tienes algún problema?
ANA MARÍA (7) No, no tengo ningún problema/ninguno.

Comunicación

3 **Opiniones** Completa estas oraciones de una manera lógica. Luego, compara tus respuestas con las de un(a) compañero/a. Answers will vary.

1. Mi habitación es _____ pero _____ .
2. Por la noche me gusta _____ pero _____ .
3. Un(a) profesor(a) ideal no es _____ sino _____ .
4. Mis amigos son _____ pero _____ .

4 **¿Qué hay?** En parejas, háganse preguntas para ver qué hay en su ciudad o pueblo: tiendas interesantes, almacenes, cines, librerías baratas, una biblioteca, una plaza central, playa, cafés, museos, una estación de tren. Sigan el modelo. Answers will vary.

> **modelo**
>
> **Estudiante 1:** ¿Hay algunas tiendas interesantes?
> **Estudiante 2:** Sí, hay una/algunas. Está(n) detrás del estadio.
>
> **Estudiante 1:** ¿Hay algún museo?
> **Estudiante 2:** No, no hay ninguno.

5 **Quejas (Complaints)** En parejas, hagan una lista de cinco quejas comunes que tienen los estudiantes. Usen expresiones negativas. Answers will vary.

> **modelo**
>
> Nadie me entiende.

Ahora hagan una lista de cinco quejas que los padres tienen de sus hijos.

> **modelo**
>
> Nunca hacen sus camas.

6 **Anuncios** En parejas, lean el anuncio y contesten las preguntas. Some answers will vary.

1. ¿Es el anuncio positivo o negativo? ¿Por qué?
   Answers will vary.
2. ¿Qué palabras indefinidas hay?
   algún, siempre, algo
3. Escriban el texto del anuncio cambiando todo
   ¡No buscas ningún producto especial? ¡Nunca hay nada para
   por expresiones negativas. nadie en las tiendas García!
4. Ahora preparen su propio (own) anuncio
   usando expresiones afirmativas y negativas.

¿Buscas algún producto especial?

¡Siempre hay algo para todos en las tiendas García!

Síntesis

7 **Encuesta** Tu profesor(a) te va a dar una hoja de actividades para hacer una encuesta. Circula por la clase y pídeles a tus compañeros que comparen las actividades que hacen durante la semana con las que hacen durante los fines de semana. Escribe las respuestas. Answers will vary.

TEACHING OPTIONS

Large Groups Write the names of four vacation spots on four slips of paper and post them in different corners of the room. Ask students to pick their vacation preference by going to one of the corners. Then, have each group produce five reasons for their choice as well as one complaint about each of the other places.

Extra Practice Have students complete this cloze activity using **pero, sino,** and **tampoco:** Yo estoy en la escuela secundaria, _____ mi hermana mayor estudia en la universidad. (pero) Ella no tiene exámenes este semestre _____ proyectos. (sino) Yo no tengo exámenes _____ . (tampoco) Sólo tengo mucha, mucha tarea.

---

3 Teaching Tip Before assigning the activity, give some personal examples using different subjects. Ex: **Mi hijo es inteligente, pero no le gusta estudiar. Mi amiga no es norteamericana, sino española.**

3 Expansion Give students these sentences as items 5–6: **5. Mis padres no son ____ sino ____. 6. Mi abuelo/a es ____ pero ____ .**

4 Teaching Tip To simplify, before beginning the activity, practice question formation for each item as a class.

4 Expansion Have pairs of students create two additional sentences about your town.

5 Expansion Divide the class into all-male and all-female groups. Then have each group make two different lists: **Quejas que tienen los hombres de las mujeres** and **Quejas que tienen las mujeres de los hombres.** After five minutes, compare and contrast the answers and perceptions.

6 Expansion Have pairs work with another pair to combine the best aspects of each of their individual ads. Then have them present the "fused" ads to the class.

7 Teaching Tip Distribute the Communication Activities worksheets that correspond to this activity.

7 Expansion Have students write five sentences using the information obtained through the **encuesta.** Ex: **1. Nadie va a la biblioteca durante el fin de semana, pero muchos vamos durante la semana. 2. No estudiamos los sábados sino los domingos.**

7.3 Preterite of **ser** and **ir** SUPERSITE

ANTE TODO In **Lección 6**, you learned how to form the preterite tense of regular **-ar**, **-er**, and **-ir** verbs. The following chart contains the preterite forms of **ser** (*to be*) and **ir** (*to go*). Since these forms are irregular, you will need to memorize them.

Preterite of **ser** and **ir**

		ser (*to be*)	**ir** (*to go*)
SINGULAR FORMS	yo	**fui**	**fui**
	tú	**fuiste**	**fuiste**
	Ud./él/ella	**fue**	**fue**
PLURAL FORMS	nosotros/as	**fuimos**	**fuimos**
	vosotros/as	**fuisteis**	**fuisteis**
	Uds./ellos/ellas	**fueron**	**fueron**

▶ Since the preterite forms of **ser** and **ir** are identical, context clarifies which of the two verbs is being used.

Él **fue** a comprar champú y jabón.
He went to buy shampoo and soap.

¿Cómo **fue** la película anoche?
How was the movie last night?

¿Adónde fueron ustedes?

Inés y yo fuimos a un mercado. Fue muy divertido.

¡INTÉNTALO! Completa las oraciones usando el pretérito de **ser** e **ir**. La primera oración de cada columna se da como ejemplo.

ir

1. Los viajeros __fueron__ a Perú.
2. Patricia __fue__ a Cuzco.
3. Tú __fuiste__ a Iquitos.
4. Gregorio y yo __fuimos__ a Lima.
5. Yo __fui__ a Trujillo.
6. Ustedes __fueron__ a Arequipa.
7. Mi padre __fue__ a Lima.
8. Nosotras __fuimos__ a Cuzco.
9. Él __fue__ a Machu Picchu.
10. Usted __fue__ a Nazca.

ser

1. Usted __fue__ muy amable.
2. Yo __fui__ muy cordial.
3. Ellos __fueron__ simpáticos.
4. Nosotros __fuimos__ muy tontos.
5. Ella __fue__ antipática.
6. Tú __fuiste__ muy generoso.
7. Ustedes __fueron__ cordiales.
8. La gente __fue__ amable.
9. Tomás y yo __fuimos__ muy felices.
10. Los profesores __fueron__ buenos.

Práctica SUPERSITE

1 **Completar** Completa estas conversaciones con la forma correcta del pretérito de **ser** o **ir**. Indica el infinitivo de cada forma verbal.

Conversación 1

RAÚL ¿Adónde (1)_____fueron/ir_____ ustedes de vacaciones?

PILAR (2)_____Fuimos/ir_____ a Perú.

RAÚL ¿Cómo (3)_____fue/ser_____ el viaje?

▶ **PILAR** ¡(4)_____Fue/ser_____ estupendo! Machu Picchu y El Callao son increíbles.

RAÚL ¿(5)_____Fue/ser_____ caro el viaje?

PILAR No, el precio (6)_____fue/ser_____ muy bajo. Sólo costó tres mil dólares.

Conversación 2

ISABEL Tina y Vicente (7)_____fueron/ser_____ novios, ¿no?

LUCÍA Sí, pero ahora no. Anoche Tina (8)_____fue/ir_____ a comer con Gregorio y la semana pasada ellos (9)_____fueron/ir_____ al partido de fútbol.

ISABEL ¿Ah sí? Javier y yo (10)_____fuimos/ir_____ al partido y no los vimos.

NOTA CULTURAL

La ciudad peruana de **El Callao**, fundada en 1537, fue por muchos años el puerto (*port*) más activo de la costa del Pacífico en Suramérica. En el siglo XVIII, una fortaleza fue construida (*built*) allí para proteger (*protect*) la ciudad de los ataques de piratas y bucaneros.

2 **Descripciones** Forma oraciones con estos elementos. Usa el pretérito. *Answers will vary.*

A	B	C	D
yo	(no) ir	a un restaurante	ayer
tú	(no) ser	en autobús	anoche
mi compañero/a		estudiante	anteayer
nosotros		muy simpático/a	la semana pasada
mis amigos		a la playa	el año pasado
ustedes		dependiente/a en una tienda	

Comunicación

3 **Preguntas** En parejas, túrnense para hacerse estas preguntas. *Answers will vary.*

1. ¿Adónde fuiste de vacaciones el año pasado? ¿Con quién fuiste?
2. ¿Cómo fueron tus vacaciones?
3. ¿Fuiste de compras la semana pasada? ¿Adónde? ¿Qué compraste?
4. ¿Fuiste al cine la semana pasada? ¿Qué película viste? ¿Cómo fue?
5. ¿Fuiste a la cafetería hoy? ¿A qué hora?
6. ¿Adónde fuiste durante el fin de semana? ¿Por qué?
7. ¿Quién fue tu profesor(a) favorito/a el año pasado? ¿Por qué?

4 **El viaje** En parejas, escriban un diálogo de un(a) viajero/a hablando con el/la agente de viajes sobre un viaje que tomó recientemente. Usen el pretérito de **ser** e **ir**. *Answers will vary.*

> **modelo**
> **Agente:** ¿Cómo fue el viaje?
> **Viajero:** El viaje fue maravilloso/horrible…

1 **Teaching Tip** Before assigning the activity, write cloze sentences on the board and ask volunteers to fill in the blanks. Ex: **¿Cómo _____ los guías turísticos durante tu viaje?** (fueron) **¿Quién _____ con Marcela al baile?** (fue)

1 **Expansion** Ask small groups to write four questions based on the conversations. Have groups exchange papers and answer the questions they receive. Then have them confirm their answers with the group who wrote the questions.

2 **Expansion** Ask a volunteer to say one of his or her sentences aloud. Point to another student, and call out an interrogative word in order to cue a question. Ex: **E1: No fui a un restaurante anoche.** Say: **¿Adónde? E2: ¿Adónde fuiste? E1: Fui al cine.**

3 **Expansion** Have pairs team up to form groups of four. Each student should report three things about his or her partner to the group.

4 **Expansion** Ask pairs to write a similar conversation within a different context (Ex: **Un día horrible**).

TEACHING OPTIONS

Small Groups Have small groups of students role-play a TV interview with astronauts who have just returned from a long stay on Mars. Have students review previous lesson vocabulary lists as necessary in preparation. Give groups sufficient time to plan and practice their skits. When all groups have completed the activity, ask a few of them to perform their role play for the class.

TPR Read aloud a series of sentences using **ser** and **ir** in the preterite. Have students raise their right hand if the verb is **ser**, and their left hand for **ir**. Ex: **Yo fui camerero a los dieciocho años.** (right hand)

Section Goals

In **Estructura 7.4**, students will learn verbs that follow the pattern of **gustar**.

Instructional Resources
Cuaderno de práctica, pp. 80–82
Cuaderno para hispanohablantes, pp. 109–110
Cuaderno de actividades, pp. 35–36, 128
e-Cuaderno
Supersite: Audio Activity MP3 Audio Files
Supersite/TRCD/Print: *PowerPoints* (**Lección 7 Estructura** Presentation); Communication Activities, Audio Activity Script, Answer Keys
Audio Activity CD

Teaching Tips

• Review the verb **gustar**. Write the headings **Gustos** and **Disgustos** on the board. Have the class brainstorm a list of likes and dislikes among high-school students including musicians, movies, clothes, or hobbies. Use the lists to form statements and questions illustrating the use of the verb **gustar**. Use different indirect object pronouns. Ex: **En general, a los estudiantes no les gustan los Beatles. A mis amigos y a mí, sí nos gustan los Beatles.**

• Use the previously generated lists of **Gustos** and **Disgustos** to present verbs like **gustar**. Ex: **A los estudiantes les aburren las películas infantiles. A mí tampoco me interesan esas películas. A muchos estudiantes les encanta la ropa de The Gap.**

7.4 ## Verbs like **gustar**

ANTE TODO   In **Lección 2**, you learned how to express preferences with **gustar**. You will now learn more about the verb **gustar** and other similar verbs. Observe these examples.

Me gusta ese champú.

> ENGLISH EQUIVALENT
> *I like that shampoo.*
> LITERAL MEANING
> *That shampoo is pleasing to me.*

¿Te gustaron las clases?

> ENGLISH EQUIVALENT
> *Did you like the classes?*
> LITERAL MEANING
> *Were the classes pleasing to you?*

▶ As the examples show, constructions with **gustar** do not have a direct equivalent in English. The literal meaning of this construction is *to be pleasing to (someone)*, and it requires the use of an indirect object pronoun.

INDIRECT OBJECT PRONOUN	SUBJECT		SUBJECT		DIRECT OBJECT
Me	**gusta**	ese champú.	*I*	*like*	*that shampoo.*

▶ In the diagram above, observe how in the Spanish sentence the object being liked (**ese champú**) is really the subject of the sentence. The person who likes the object, in turn, is an indirect object because it answers the question: *To whom is the shampoo pleasing?*

¿No te gustan las computadoras?

Me gustan mucho los parques.

▶ Other verbs in Spanish are used in the same way as **gustar**. Here is a list of the most common ones.

Verbs like **gustar**

aburrir	to bore	**importar**	to be important to; to matter
encantar	to like very much; to love (inanimate objects)	**interesar**	to be interesting to; to interest
faltar	to lack; to need	**molestar**	to bother; to annoy
fascinar	to fascinate; to like very much	**quedar**	to be left over; to fit (clothing)

¡ATENCIÓN!

Faltar expresses what is lacking or missing.
Me falta una página. *I'm missing one page.*

Quedar expresses how much of something is left.
Nos quedan tres pesos. *We have three pesos left.*

• • •

Quedar means *to fit.* It's also used to tell how something looks (on someone).
Estos zapatos me quedan bien. *These shoes fit me well.*
Esa camisa te queda muy bien. *That shirt looks good on you.*

 comparisons NATIONAL STANDARDS

TEACHING OPTIONS

Heritage Speakers Have heritage speakers compare and contrast activities they like to do with activities their parents/grandparents like to do. Encourage them to use the verb **gustar** and others that follow the same pattern.

Game Divide the class into small teams. Give a prompt including subject and object (Ex: **ella/películas de horror**). Allow teams one minute to construct a sentence using one of the verbs that follow the pattern of **gustar**. Then one member from each team will write the sentence on the board. Award one point to each team for each correct response.

▶ The forms most commonly used with **gustar** and similar verbs are the third person (singular and plural). When the object or person being liked is singular, the singular form (**gusta/molesta**, etc.) is used. When two or more objects or persons are being liked, the plural form (**gustan/molestan**, etc.) is used. Observe the following diagram:

| SINGULAR | me, te, le | ➤ | encanta interesó | ➤ | la película el concierto |
| PLURAL | nos, os, les | ➤ | importan fascinaron | ➤ | las vacaciones los museos de Lima |

▶ To express what someone likes or does not like to do, use an appropriate verb followed by an infinitive. The singular form is used even if there is more than one infinitive.

Nos molesta comer a las nueve.
It bothers us to eat at nine o'clock.

Les encanta cantar y **bailar** en las fiestas.
They love to sing and dance at parties.

▶ As you learned in **Lección 2**, the construction **a** + [*pronoun*] (**a mí, a ti, a usted, a él,** etc.) is used to clarify or to emphasize who is pleased, bored, etc. The construction **a** + [*noun*] can also be used before the indirect object pronoun to clarify or to emphasize who is pleased.

A los turistas les gustó mucho Machu Picchu.
The tourists liked Machu Picchu a lot.

A ti te gusta cenar en casa, pero **a mí** me aburre.
You like to eat dinner at home, but I get bored.

▶ **¡Atención!** **Mí** (*me*) has an accent mark to distinguish it from the possessive adjective **mi** (*my*).

¡INTÉNTALO!   Indica el pronombre del objeto indirecto y la forma del tiempo presente adecuados en cada oración. La primera oración de cada columna se da como ejemplo.

fascinar

1. A él _le fascina_ viajar.
2. A mí _me fascina_ bailar.
3. A nosotras _nos fascina_ cantar.
4. A ustedes _les fascina_ leer.
5. A ti _te fascina_ correr.
6. A Pedro _le fascina_ gritar.
7. A mis padres _les fascina_ caminar.
8. A usted _le fascina_ jugar al tenis.
9. A mi esposo y a mí _nos fascina_ dormir.
10. A Alberto _le fascina_ dibujar.
11. A todos _nos/les fascina_ opinar.
12. A Pili _le fascina_ ir de compras.

aburrir

1. A ellos _les aburren_ los deportes.
2. A ti _te aburren_ las películas.
3. A usted _le aburren_ los viajes.
4. A mí _me aburren_ las revistas.
5. A Jorge y a Luis _les aburren_ los perros.
6. A nosotros _nos aburren_ las vacaciones.
7. A ustedes _les aburren_ las fiestas.
8. A Marcela _le aburren_ los libros.
9. A mis amigos _les aburren_ los museos.
10. A ella _le aburre_ el ciclismo.
11. A Omar _le aburre_ el Internet.
12. A ti y a mí _nos aburre_ el baile.

Práctica SUPERSITE

1 Teaching Tip To simplify, have students identify the subject in each sentence before filling in the blanks.

1 Expansion Have students use the verbs in the activity to write a paragraph describing their own musical tastes.

2 Expansion Repeat the activity using the preterite. Invite students to provide additional details. Ex: **1. A Ramón le molestó el despertador ayer. 2. A nosotros nos encantó esquiar en Vail.**

3 Expansion Ask students to create two additional sentences using verbs from column B. Have students read their sentences aloud. After everyone has had a turn, ask the class how many similar or identical sentences they heard and what they were.

1 Completar Completa las oraciones con todos los elementos necesarios.

1. ____A____ Adela __le encanta__ (encantar) la música de Enrique Iglesias.
2. A ____mí____ me __interesa__ (interesar) la música de otros países.
3. A mis amigos __les encantan__ (encantar) las canciones (songs) de Maná.
4. A Juan y ____a____ Rafael no les __molesta__ (molestar) la música alta (loud).
5. ____A____ nosotros __nos fascinan__ (fascinar) los grupos de pop latino.
6. ____Al____ señor Ruiz __le interesa__ (interesar) más la música clásica.
7. A ____mí____ me __aburre__ (aburrir) la música clásica.
8. ¿A ____ti____ te __falta__ (faltar) dinero para el concierto de Carlos Santana?
9. Sí. Sólo __me quedan__ (quedar) cinco dólares.
10. ¿Cuánto dinero te __queda__ (quedar) a ____ti____?

NOTA CULTURAL

Hoy día, la música latina es popular en los EE.UU. gracias a artistas como **Shakira**, de nacionalidad colombiana, y **Enrique Iglesias**, español. Otros artistas, como **Carlos Santana** y **Gloria Estefan**, difundieron (spread) la música latina en los años 60, 70, 80 y 90.

2 Describir Mira los dibujos y describe lo que está pasando. Usa los verbos de la lista.

aburrir	faltar	molestar
encantar	interesar	quedar

1. a Ramón   A Ramón le molesta el despertador.

2. a nosotros   A nosotros nos encanta esquiar.

3. a ti   A ti no te queda bien este vestido. A ti te queda mal/grande este vestido.

4. a Sara   A Sara le interesan los libros de arte moderno.

3 Gustos Forma oraciones con los elementos de las columnas. Answers will vary.

> **modelo**
> A ti te interesan las ruinas de Machu Picchu.

A	B	C
yo	aburrir	despertarse temprano
tú	encantar	mirarse en el espejo
mi mejor amigo/a	faltar	la música rock
mis amigos y yo	fascinar	las pantuflas rosadas
Bart y Homero Simpson	interesar	la pasta de dientes con menta (mint)
Shakira	molestar	las ruinas de Machu Picchu
Antonio Banderas		los zapatos caros

TEACHING OPTIONS

TPR Have students stand and form a circle. Begin by tossing a foam or paper ball to a student, who should state a complaint using a verb like **gustar** (Ex: **Me falta dinero para comprar los libros**) and then toss the ball to another student. The next student should offer advice (Ex: **Debes pedirle dinero a tus padres**) and throw the ball to another person, who will air another complaint. Repeat the activity with positive statements (**Me fascinan las**

películas cómicas) and advice (**Debes ver My Big Fat Greek Wedding**).

Extra Practice Write sentences like these on the board. Have students copy them and draw faces (☺/☹) to indicate the feelings expressed. Ex: **1. Me encantan las enchiladas verdes. 2. Me aburren las matemáticas. 3. Me fascina la ópera italiana. 4. No me falta dinero para comprar un auto. 5. Me queda pequeño el sombrero.**

Comunicación

4 **Preguntas** En parejas, túrnense para hacer y contestar estas preguntas. Answers will vary.

1. ¿Te gusta levantarte temprano o tarde? ¿Por qué?
2. ¿Te gusta acostarte temprano o tarde? ¿Y a tus hermanos/as? *(go to bed)*
3. ¿Te gusta dormir la siesta? *(nap)*
4. A tu familia, ¿le encanta acampar o prefiere quedarse en un hotel cuando va de vacaciones? *(camp)*
5. ¿Qué te gusta hacer en el verano?
6. ¿Qué te fascina de esta escuela? ¿Qué te molesta?
7. ¿Te interesan más las ciencias o las humanidades? ¿Por qué?
8. ¿Qué cosas te molestan?

5 **Completar** Completa estas frases de una manera lógica. Answers will vary.

1. A mi novio/a le fascina(n)…
2. A mi mejor (*best*) amigo/a no le interesa(n)…
3. A mis padres les importa(n)…
4. A nosotros nos molesta(n)…
5. A mis hermanos les aburre(n)…
6. A mi compañero/a de clase le aburre(n)…
7. A los turistas les interesa(n)…
8. A los jugadores profesionales les encanta(n)…
9. A nuestro/a profesor(a) le molesta(n)…
10. A mí me importa(n)…

recursos

CA
pp. 35–36

6 **La residencia** Tú y tu compañero/a de clase son los directores de una residencia estudiantil en Perú. Su profesor(a) les va a dar a cada uno de ustedes las descripciones de cinco estudiantes. Con la información tienen que escoger quiénes van a ser compañeros de cuarto. Después, completen la lista. Answers will vary.

Síntesis

7 **Situación** Trabajen en parejas para representar los papeles de un(a) cliente/a y un(a) dependiente/a en una tienda de ropa. Usen las instrucciones como guía. Answers will vary.

Dependiente/a	Cliente/a
Saluda al/a la cliente/a y pregúntale en qué le puedes servir.	→ Saluda al/a la dependiente/a y dile (*tell him/her*) qué quieres comprar y qué colores prefieres.
Pregúntale si le interesan los estilos modernos y empieza a mostrarle la ropa.	→ Explícale que los estilos modernos te interesan. Escoge las cosas que te interesan.
Habla de los gustos del/de la cliente/a.	→ Habla de la ropa (me queda(n) bien/mal, me encanta(n)…).
Da opiniones favorables al/a la cliente/a (las botas te quedan fantásticas…).	→ Decide cuáles son las cosas que te gustan y qué vas a comprar.

TEACHING OPTIONS

Pairs Have pairs prepare short TV commercials in which they use the target verbs presented in **Estructura 7.4** to sell a particular product. Group three pairs together to present their skits.
Extra Practice Add a visual aspect to this grammar practice. Bring in magazine pictures of people enjoying or not enjoying what they are doing. Have them create sentences with verbs like **gustar**. Ex: **A los chicos no les interesa estudiar biología.**

Game Give groups of students five minutes to write a description of social life during a specific historical period, such as the French Revolution or prehistoric times, using as many of the target verbs presented in **Estructura 7.4** as possible. When finished, ask groups how many of these verbs they used in their descriptions. Have the top three read their descriptions for the class, who vote for their favorite description.

4 Expansion Take a class survey of the answers and write the results on the board. Ask volunteers to use verbs like **gustar** to summarize them.

5 Teaching Tip For items that start with **A mi(s)…** , have pairs compare their answers and then report to the class: first answers in common, then answers that differed. Ex: **A mis padres les importan los estudios, pero a los padres de ____ les importa más el dinero.**

6 Teaching Tip Divide the class into pairs and distribute the Communication Activities worksheets that correspond to this activity. Give students ten minutes to complete this activity.

6 Expansion
• Have pairs compare their matches by circulating around the classroom until they have all compared their answers with one another.
• Have pairs choose one of the students and write his or her want ad looking for a suitable roommate.

7 Teaching Tip To simplify, have students prepare for their roles by brainstorming a list of words and phrases. Remind students to use the formal register in this conversation.

7 Expansion Ask pairs to perform their conversation for the class or have them videotape it.

Recapitulación

SUPERSITE For self-scoring and diagnostics, go to descubre1.vhlcentral.com.

Completa estas actividades para repasar los conceptos de gramática que aprendiste en esta lección.

1 **Completar** Completa la tabla con la forma correcta de los verbos. *6 pts.*

yo	tú	nosotros	ellas
me levanto	te levantas	nos levantamos	se levantan
me afeito	**te afeitas**	nos afeitamos	se afeitan
me visto	te vistes	**nos vestimos**	se visten
me seco	te secas	nos secamos	**se secan**

2 **Hoy y ayer** Cambia los verbos del presente al pretérito. *5 pts.*

1. Vamos de compras hoy. _____Fuimos_____ de compras hoy.
2. Por último, voy al supermercado. Por último, _____fui_____ al supermercado.
3. Lalo es el primero en levantarse. Lalo _____fue_____ el primero en levantarse.
4. ¿Vas a tu habitación? ¿_____Fuiste_____ a tu habitación?
5. Ustedes son profesores. Ustedes _____fueron_____ profesores.

3 **Reflexivos** Completa cada conversación con la forma correcta del presente del verbo reflexivo. *11 pts.*

TOMÁS Yo siempre (1) _____me baño_____ (bañarse) antes de (2) _____acostarme_____ (acostarse). Esto me relaja porque no (3) _____me duermo_____ (dormirse) fácilmente. Y así puedo (4) _____levantarme_____ (levantarse) más tarde. Y tú, ¿cuándo (5) _____te duchas_____ (ducharse)?

LETI Pues por la mañana, para poder (6) _____despertarme_____ (despertarse).

DAVID ¿Cómo (7) _____se siente_____ (sentirse) Pepa hoy?

MARÍA Todavía está enojada.

DAVID ¿De verdad? Ella nunca (8) _____se enoja_____ (enojarse) con nadie.

BETO ¿(Nosotros) (9) _____Nos vamos_____ (Irse) de esta tienda? Estoy cansado.

SARA Pero antes vamos a (10) _____probarnos_____ (probarse) estos sombreros. Si quieres, después (nosotros) (11) _____nos sentamos_____ (sentarse) un rato.

RESUMEN GRAMATICAL

7.1 **Reflexive verbs** *pp. 236–237*

lavarse	
me lavo	nos lavamos
te lavas	os laváis
se lava	se lavan

7.2 **Positive and negative expressions** *pp. 240–2*

Positive words	Negative words
algo	nada
alguien	nadie
alguno/a(s), algún	ninguno/a, ningún
o... o	ni... ni
siempre	nunca, jamás
también	tampoco

7.3 **Preterite of ser and ir** *p. 244*

▶ The preterite of **ser** and **ir** are identical. Context will determine the meaning.

ser and ir	
fui	fuimos
fuiste	fuisteis
fue	fueron

7.4 **Verbs like gustar** *pp. 246–247*

aburrir	importar
encantar	interesar
faltar	molestar
fascinar	quedar

SINGULAR me, te, le ⟩ encanta / interesó ⟩ la película / el concierto

PLURAL nos, os, les ⟩ importan / fascinaron ⟩ las vacaciones / los museos

▶ Use the construction a + [*noun/pronoun*] to clarify the person in question.

A mí me encanta ver películas, ¿y a ti?

4 **Conversaciones** Completa cada conversación de manera lógica con palabras de la lista. No tienes que usar todas las palabras. **8 pts.**

algo	nada	ningún	siempre
alguien	nadie	nunca	también
algún	ni... ni	o... o	tampoco

1. —¿Tienes __algún__ plan para esta noche?

   —No, prefiero quedarme en casa. Hoy no quiero ver a __nadie__.

   —Yo __también__ me quedo. Estoy muy cansado.

2. —¿Puedo entrar? ¿Hay __alguien__ en el cuarto de baño?

   —Sí. Ahora mismo salgo.

3. —¿Puedes prestarme __algo__ para peinarme? No encuentro __ni__ mi cepillo (*brush*) __ni__ mi peine (*comb*).

   —Lo siento, yo __tampoco__ encuentro los míos (*mine*).

4. —¿Me prestas tu maquillaje?

   —Lo siento, no tengo. __Nunca__ me maquillo.

5 **Oraciones** Forma oraciones completas con los elementos dados (*given*). Usa el presente de los verbos. **8 pts.**

1. David y Juan / molestar / levantarse temprano   A David y a Juan les molesta levantarse temprano.
2. Lucía / encantar / las películas de terror   A Lucía le encantan las películas de terror.
3. todos (nosotros) / importar / la educación   A todos nos importa la educación.
4. tú / aburrir / ver / la televisión   A ti te aburre ver la televisión.

6 **Rutinas** Escribe seis oraciones describiendo las rutinas de dos personas que conoces. **12 pts.**

> **modelo**
>
> Mi tía se despierta temprano, pero mi primo...   Answers will vary.

7 **Adivinanza** Completa la adivinanza con las palabras que faltan y adivina la respuesta. **¡2 puntos EXTRA!**

" Cuanto más° __te seca__ (*it dries you*), más se moja°. "

¿Qué es? __La toalla__

Cuanto más *The more* se moja *it gets wet*

TEACHING OPTIONS

Game Play a game of **Diez Preguntas**. Ask a volunteer to think of a person in the class. Other students get one chance each to ask a question using positive and negative words. Ex: **¿Es alguien que siempre llega temprano a clase?**

Extra Practice Have students imagine they are a famous singer or actor. Then have them write eight sentences from the point of view of that person, using verbs like **gustar** and indefinite and negative words. Ex: **Jennifer López: Me encanta la música pop pero me aburre la música clásica. Tampoco me interesa la música *country*.** Ask volunteers to share some of their sentences and see if the rest of the class agrees with their statements.

---

4 **Expansion** Have students create four additional sentences using the remaining positive and negative words from the word bank.

5 **Teaching Tip** Remind students to use the personal **a** in their answers.

5 **Expansion** Give students these sentences as items 5–8: **5. yo / faltar / dinero (A mí me falta dinero.) 6. Pedro y yo / fascinar / cantar y bailar (A Pedro y a mí nos fascina cantar y bailar.) 7. usted / quedar / muy bien / esas gafas de sol (A usted le quedan muy bien esas gafas de sol.) 8. ¿ / ustedes / interesar / conocer / otros países / ? (¿A ustedes les interesa conocer otros países?)**

6 **Expansion** Have volunteers share their sentences with the class. Encourage classmates to ask them follow-up questions. Ex: **¿Por qué se despierta temprano tu tía?**

7 **Expansion** To challenge students, have them work in small groups to create a riddle using grammar and/or vocabulary from this lesson. Have groups share their riddles with the class.

Section Goals

In **Lectura**, students will:
- learn the strategy of predicting content from the title
- read an e-mail in Spanish

Instructional Resources
Cuaderno para hispanohablantes, pp. 111–112
Supersite

Estrategia Display or make up several cognate-rich headlines from Spanish newspapers. Ex: **Decenas de miles recuerdan la explosión atómica en Hiroshima; Lanzamiento de musicahoy.net, sitio para profesionales y aficionados a la música; Científicos anuncian que Plutón ya no es planeta.** Ask students to predict the content of each article.

Examinar el texto Survey the class to find out the most common predictions. Were most of them about a positive or negative experience?

Compartir Have students discuss how they are able to tell what the content will be by looking at the format of the text.

Cognados Discuss how scanning the text for cognates can help predict the content.

Lectura

Antes de leer

Estrategia
Predicting content from the title

Prediction is an invaluable strategy in reading for comprehension. For example, we can usually predict the content of a newspaper article from its headline. We often decide whether to read the article based on its headline. Predicting content from the title will help you increase your reading comprehension in Spanish.

Examinar el texto
Lee el título de la lectura y haz tres predicciones sobre el contenido. Escribe tus predicciones en una hoja de papel.

Compartir
Comparte tus ideas con un(a) compañero/a de clase.

Cognados
Haz una lista de seis cognados que encuentres en la lectura. Answers will vary.

1. _____
2. _____
3. _____
4. _____
5. _____
6. _____

¿Qué te dicen los cognados sobre el tema de la lectura?

recursos

CH
pp. 111–112

descubre1.vhlcentral.com
Lección 7

¡Qué día!

Anterior ▼ ⬇ Siguiente ▼ 🔺 Responder Respon a todos

Fecha: Lunes, 10 de mayo
De: Guillermo Zamora
Asunto: ¡Qué día!
Para: Lupe; Marcos; Sandra; Jorge

Hola, chicos:

La semana pasada me di cuenta° de que necesito organizar mejor° mi rutina... pero especialmente necesito prepararme mejor para los exámenes. Me falta mucha disciplina, me molesta no tener control de mi tiempo y nunca deseo repetir los eventos de la semana pasada.

El miércoles pasé todo el día y toda la noche estudiando para el examen de biología del jueves por la mañana. Me aburre la biología y no empecé a estudiar hasta el día antes del examen. El jueves a las 8, después de no dormir en toda la noche, fui exhausto al examen. Fue difícil, pero afortunadamente° me acordé de todo el material. Esa noche me acosté temprano y dormí mucho.

Me desperté a las 7, y fue extraño° ver a mi hermano, Andrés, preparándose para ir a dormir. Como° siempre se enferma° y nunca hablamos

---

TEACHING OPTIONS

Extra Practice Ask students to skim the selection and find sentences with verbs like **gustar** (**aburrir, molestar,** etc.). Have them use the **le** and **les** pronouns to rewrite the sentences and talk about **Guillermo** and **Andrés.** Ex: **A Guillermo le aburre la biología.** Encourage students to say more about the characters and what happens to them by creating additional sentences of the **gustar** type.

Heritage Speakers Ask heritage speakers if they use e-mail regularly to keep in touch with friends and family in their families' countries of origin. Ask them if they have ever used Spanish-language versions of popular web-based e-mail applications. Have them share with the class the ones they like best.

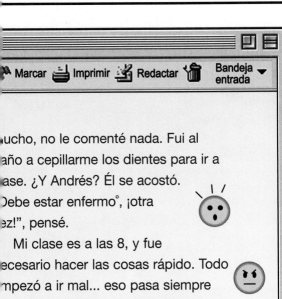

...ucho, no le comenté nada. Fui al
...año a cepillarme los dientes para ir a
...ase. ¿Y Andrés? Él se acostó.
...Debe estar enfermo°, ¡otra
...ez!", pensé.

Mi clase es a las 8, y fue
...ecesario hacer las cosas rápido. Todo
...mpezó a ir mal... eso pasa siempre
...uando uno tiene prisa. Cuando
...usqué mis cosas para el baño, no
...as encontré. Entonces me duché sin
...bón, me cepillé los dientes sin cepillo
...e dientes y me peiné con las manos.
...ampoco encontré ropa limpia, y usé
...a sucia. Rápido, tomé mis libros. ¿Y
...ndrés? Roncando°... ¡a las 7:50!

Cuando salí corriendo para la clase,
...a prisa no me permitió ver la escuela
...esierta. Cuando llegué a la clase, no
...i a nadie. No vi al profesor ni a los
...studiantes. Por último miré mi reloj,
...vi la hora. Las 8 en punto... ¡de la
...oche!

...Dormí 24 horas!

Guillermo

...e di cuenta *I realized* mejor *better* afortunadamente *fortunately*
...traño *strange* Como *Since* se enferma *he gets sick* enfermo *sick*
...oncando *Snoring*

Después de leer

Seleccionar

Selecciona la respuesta correcta.

1. ¿Quién es el/la narrador(a)? c
   a. Andrés
   b. una profesora
   c. Guillermo
2. ¿Qué le molesta al narrador? b
   a. Le molestan los exámenes de biología.
   b. Le molesta no tener control de su tiempo.
   c. Le molesta mucho organizar su rutina.
3. ¿Por qué está exhausto? c
   a. Porque fue a una fiesta la noche anterior.
   b. Porque no le gusta la biología.
   c. Porque pasó la noche anterior estudiando.
4. ¿Por qué no hay nadie en clase? a
   a. Porque es de noche.
   b. Porque todos están de vacaciones.
   c. Porque el profesor canceló la clase.
5. ¿Cómo es la relación de Guillermo y Andrés? b
   a. Son buenos amigos.
   b. No hablan mucho.
   c. Tienen una buena relación.

Ordenar

Ordena los sucesos de la narración. Utiliza los
números del 1 al 9.

a. Toma el examen de biología. 2
b. No encuentra sus cosas para el baño. 5
c. Andrés se duerme. 7
d. Pasa todo el día y toda la noche estudiando
   para un examen. 1
e. Se ducha sin jabón. 6
f. Se acuesta temprano. 3
g. Vuelve a su cuarto a las 8 de la noche. 9
h. Se despierta a las 7 y su hermano se prepara
   para dormir. 4
i. Va a clase y no hay nadie. 8

Contestar

Contesta estas preguntas. Answers will vary.

1. ¿Cómo es tu rutina diaria? ¿Muy organizada?
2. ¿Estudias mucho? ¿Cuándo empiezas a estudiar para
   los exámenes?
3. Para comunicarte con tus amigos/as, ¿prefieres
   el teléfono o el correo electrónico? ¿Por qué?

Section Goals

In **Escritura**, students will:

- learn adverbial expressions of time to clarify transitions
- write a composition with an introduction, body, and conclusion in Spanish

Instructional Resources
Cuaderno para hispanohablantes, pp. 113–114
Cuaderno de actividades, pp. 153–154
Supersite

Estrategia Discuss the importance of having an introduction (**introducción**), body (**parte principal**), and a conclusion (**conclusión**) in a narrative (**narración**). Then, as a class, read through the list of adverbs and adverbial phrases in the **Adverbios** box. Have volunteers create a sentence for each adverb or adverbial phrase listed.

Tema Read through the list of possible places with the students and have them choose the one in which they want to set their composition. Have groups of students who have chosen the same location get together and brainstorm ideas about how their daily routines would change in that place.

Escritura

Estrategia
Sequencing events

Paying strict attention to sequencing in a narrative will ensure that your writing flows logically from one part to the next.

Every composition should have an introduction, a body, and a conclusion. The introduction presents the subject, the setting, the situation, and the people involved. The main part, or the body, describes the events and people's reactions to these events. The conclusion brings the narrative to a close.

Adverbs and adverbial phrases are sometimes used as transitions between the introduction, the body, and the conclusion. Here is a list of commonly used adverbs in Spanish:

Adverbios	
además; también	*in addition; also*
al principio; en un principio	*at first*
antes (de)	*before*
después	*then*
después (de)	*after*
entonces; luego	*then*
más tarde	*later*
primero	*first*
pronto	*soon*
por fin, finalmente	*finally*
al final	*finally*

Tema

Escribe tu rutina

Imagina tu rutina diaria en uno de estos lugares:

- una isla desierta
- el Polo Norte
- un crucero° transatlántico
- un desierto

Escribe una composición en la que describes tu rutina diaria en uno de estos lugares, o en algún otro lugar interesante de tu propia° invención. Mientras planeas tu composición, considera cómo cambian algunos de los elementos más básicos de tu rutina diaria en el lugar que escogiste°. Por ejemplo, ¿dónde te acuestas en el Polo Norte? ¿Cómo te duchas en el desierto?

Usa el presente de los verbos reflexivos que conoces e incluye algunos de los adverbios de esta página para organizar la secuencia de tus actividades. Piensa también en la información que debes incluir en cada sección de la narración. Por ejemplo, en la introducción puedes hacer una descripción del lugar y de las personas que están allí, y en la conclusión puedes dar tus opiniones acerca del° lugar y de tu vida diaria allí.

recursos

CH pp. 113–114	CA pp. 153–154	descubre1.vhlcentral.com Lección 7

crucero *cruise ship* propia
your own escogiste *you chose*
acerca del *about the*

EVALUATION: Descripción

Criteria	Scale
Content	1 2 3 4 5
Organization	1 2 3 4 5
Use of vocabulary	1 2 3 4 5
Grammatical accuracy	1 2 3 4 5

Scoring	
Excellent	18–20 points
Good	14–17 points
Satisfactory	10–13 points
Unsatisfactory	< 10 points

Escuchar

Estrategia
Using background information

Once you discern the topic of a conversation, take a minute to think about what you already know about the subject. Using this background information will help you guess the meaning of unknown words or linguistic structures.

 To help you practice this strategy, you will now listen to a short paragraph. Jot down the subject of the paragraph, and then use your knowledge of the subject to listen for and write down the paragraph's main points.

reparación

gún la foto, ¿dónde están Carolina y Julián? ensa en lo que sabes de este tipo de situación. e qué van a hablar?

hora escucha

ora escucha la entrevista entre Carolina y Julián, niendo en cuenta (taking into account) lo que sabes bre este tipo de situación. Elige la información que mpleta correctamente cada oración.

. Julián es ___c___.
   a. político
   b. deportista profesional
   c. artista de cine

. El público de Julián quiere saber de ___b___.
   a. sus películas
   b. su vida
   c. su novia

. Julián habla de ___a___.
   a. sus viajes y sus rutinas
   b. sus parientes y amigos
   c. sus comidas favoritas

. Julián ___b___.
   a. se levanta y se acuesta a diferentes horas todos los días
   b. tiene una rutina diaria
   c. no quiere hablar de su vida

Comprensión

¿Cierto o falso?

Indica si las oraciones son **ciertas** o **falsas** según la información que Julián da en la entrevista.

1. Es difícil despertarme; generalmente duermo hasta las diez. Falsa
2. Pienso que mi vida no es más interesante que las vidas de ustedes. Cierta
3. Me gusta tener tiempo para pensar y meditar. Cierta
4. Nunca hago mucho ejercicio; no soy una persona activa. Falsa
5. Me fascinan las actividades tranquilas, como escribir y escuchar música clásica. Cierta
6. Los viajes me parecen aburridos. Falsa

Preguntas Answers will vary.

1. ¿Qué tiene Julián en común con otras personas de su misma profesión?
2. ¿Te parece que Julián siempre fue rico? ¿Por qué?
3. ¿Qué piensas de Julián como persona?

recursos

descubre1.vhlcentral.com
Lección 7

---

escucho un poco de música clásica. Así medito, escribo un poco y pienso sobre el día.

C: Cuando no estás filmando, ¿te quedas en casa durante el día?

J: Pues, en esos momentos, uso el tiempo libre para sentarme en casa a escribir. Pero sí tengo una rutina diaria de ejercicio. Corro unas cinco millas diarias y si hace mal tiempo voy al gimnasio.

C: Veo que eres una persona activa. Te mantienes en muy buena

forma. ¿Qué más nos puedes decir de tu vida?

J: Bueno, no puedo negar que me encanta viajar. ¡Y la elegancia de algunos hoteles es increíble! Estuve en un hotel en Londres que tiene una ducha del tamaño de un cuarto normal.

C: Ya vemos que tu vida no es nada aburrida. Qué gusto hablar contigo hoy, Julián.

J: El placer es mío. Gracias por la invitación, Carolina.

Section Goal
In **Escuchar**, students will learn the strategy of listening for background information.

Instructional Resources
Supersite: Textbook MP3 Audio Files
Supersite/TRCD: Textbook Audio Script
Textbook Audio CD

Estrategia
Script ¿Te puedes creer los precios de la ropa que venden en el mercado al aire libre? Tienen unos bluejeans muy buenos que cuestan 52 soles. Y claro, puedes regatear y los consigues todavía más baratos. Vi unos iguales en el centro comercial y son mucho más caros. ¡Cuestan 97 soles!

Teaching Tip Read the directions with the students, then have them identify the photo situation.

Ahora escucha
Script CAROLINA: Buenas tardes, queridos televidentes, y bienvenidos a "Carolina al mediodía". Tenemos el gran placer de conversar hoy con Julián Larrea, un joven actor de extraordinario talento. Bienvenido, Julián. Ya sabes que tienes muchas admiradoras entre nuestro público y más que todo quieren saber los detalles de tu vida.

JULIÁN: Buenas, Carolina, y saludos a todos. No sé qué decirles; en realidad en mi vida hay rutina, como en la vida de todos.

C: No puede ser. Me imagino que tu vida es mucho más exótica que la mía. Bueno, para comenzar, ¿a qué hora te levantas?

J: Normalmente me levanto todos los días a la misma hora, también cuando estoy de viaje filmando una película. Siempre me despierto a las 5:30. Antes de ducharme y vestirme, siempre me gusta tomar un café mientras

(Script continues at far left in the bottom panels.)

En pantalla

En algunas partes de Argentina, Uruguay, Chile y Centroamérica, las personas tienen la costumbre° de usar **vos** en lugar de **tú** al hablar o escribir. Este uso es conocido como **el voseo** y se refleja también en la manera de conjugar los verbos. El uso de **vos** como tratamiento de respeto pasó a ser° de uso coloquial a partir del° siglo° XVI.

Vocabulario útil	
rehacé	*redo* (en el voseo)
volvete	*become* (en el voseo)

Opciones

Escoge la opción correcta para cada oración.
1. El plomero (*plumber*) va a romper el __c__ del chico.
   a. cepillo   b. lavabo   c. espejo
2. El chico y la chica __b__ la primera vez que se ven.
   a. bailan   b. gritan   c. se peinan
3. Al chico __a__ conocer a la chica.
   a. le interesa   b. le molesta   c. le aburre
4. Al final __b__ rompe el espejo.
   a. la chica   b. el chico   c. el plomero

La cita (*date*)

En parejas, imaginen que los chicos del anuncio tienen una primera cita. Escriban una conversación entre ellos donde hablen sobre lo que les encanta y lo que les molesta. Después dramatícenla para la clase y decidan entre todos si los chicos son compatibles o no.
Answers will vary.

costumbre *custom* pasó a ser *became* a partir del *starting in the* siglo *century*
Acá hay... *We need to break it here.* ¿Salís? ¿Sales? (en el voseo) ¿por? *why?*

Acá hay que romper°.

—Soledad.
—Mariano.

—¿Salís°?
—Sí, ¿por°?

recursos

descubre1.vhlcentral.com
Lección 7

Conexión Internet
Go to descubre1.vhlcentral.com to watch the TV clip featured in this **En pantalla** section.

TEACHING OPTIONS

Small Groups Have groups of three work together to create their own **Sedal** shampoo commercial. Encourage them to use reflexive verbs, verbs like **gustar**, and indefinite and negative words to sell the product. Then have groups perform their commercials for the class, who will vote on the most effective ad.

Extra Practice Give students verbs in the **voseo** and ask them to identify the infinitives. Ex: **comés (comer), hablás (hablar), podés (poder), sos (ser), venís (venir), vivís (vivir)** Then ask them to provide the **vos** forms of several verbs from this lesson.

Oye cómo va

Tania Libertad

música de **Tania Libertad (Chiclayo, Perú)** no
e fronteras°. Su trabajo es apreciado en toda
inoamérica, Europa y África. Los más de°
nta álbumes que ha grabado° cuentan con°
eros tan° variados como° la salsa, el bolero
s rancheras. La música afroperuana tiene
lugar muy especial en su corazón°. El autor
rtugués José Saramago escribió: "La primera
que oí cantar a Tania Libertad, [conocí] la
oción a que puede llevarnos una voz desnuda°,
a° delante del mundo°."

profesor(a) va a poner la canción en la clase.
úchala y completa las actividades.

¿ierto o falso?

ica si lo que dice cada oración es **cierto** o **falso**.

	Cierto	Falso
La música de Tania Libertad sólo se conoce en Perú.	○	⦿
Canta sólo música afroperuana.	○	⦿
A José Saramago le fascina la música de Tania Libertad.	⦿	○
La cantante (*singer*) está muy triste porque no está su amor.	⦿	○
La cantante piensa que la historia de su amor no es importante.	○	⦿

?eguntas

sponde a las preguntas. Después comparte tus
puestas con un(a) compañero/a. Answers will vary.

. En esta canción se habla de un gran amor. ¿Qué
  crees tú que lo hace tan especial?

. Escribe los nombres de tres parejas famosas de la
  historia o la literatura.

. ¿Cuál es la historia de amor más grande que
  conoces? ¿Por qué es importante?

teras *borders* más de *more than* ha grabado *she has recorded*
tan con *include* tan... como *as... as* corazón *heart* voz desnuda
ed *voice* sola *alone* mundo *world* besos *kisses* encontraba *used to*
brindaba *used to give* amor *love* descalza *barefoot*

Historia de un amor
(a dueto con Cesária Évora)

NATIONAL communication cultures STANDARDS

Siempre fuiste la razón de mi existir;
adorarte para mí fue religión.
En tus besos° yo encontraba°
el calor que me brindaba°
el amor° y la pasión.

Fusión de culturas

La música afroperuana combina
ritmos de la música africana y la
música peruana tradicional. El instrumento
predominante de este género es el tambor.
La canción *Historia de un amor* es un
bolero adaptado al estilo afroperuano.

Cesária Évora, conocida como "la diva
descalza°", es una importante figura
musical de Cabo Verde, en la costa
africana. Es famosa por sus canciones
de *morna*, cantadas en portugués criollo.

Cesária Évora

recursos

SUPERSITE

descubre1.vhlcentral.com
Lección 7

SUPERSITE **Conexión Internet**
Go to **descubre1.vhlcentral.com** to learn
more about the artist featured in this
Oye cómo va section.

Section Goal

In **Panorama**, students will read about the geography, culture, and history of Peru.

Instructional Resources
Cuaderno de práctica, pp. 83–84
Cuaderno de actividades, pp. 81–82
e-Cuaderno
Supersite/DVD: *Panorama cultural*
Supersite/TRCD: *PowerPoints* (Overheads #5, #6, #32); *Panorama cultural* Videoscript & Translation, Answer Keys

Teaching Tip Have students look at the map of Peru or show *Overhead PowerPoint #32.* Ask them to find the **Río Amazonas** and the **Cordilleras de los Andes,** and to speculate about the types of climate found in Peru. As a mountainous country near the equator, climate varies according to elevation and ranges from tropical to arctic. Point out that well over half of the territory of Peru lies within the Amazon Basin. Encourage students to share what they know about Peru.

El país en cifras After each section, pause to ask students questions about the content. Point out that Iquitos, Peru's port city on the Amazon River, is a destination for ships that travel 2,300 miles up the Amazon from the Atlantic Ocean.

¡Increíble pero cierto! In recent years, the **El Niño** weather phenomenon has caused flooding in the deserts of southern Peru. The Peruvian government is working to preserve the **Líneas de Nazca** from further deterioration in the hope that someday scientists will discover more about their origins and meaning.

Perú

NATIONAL connections cultures STANDARDS

El país en cifras

- ▶ **Área:** 1.285.220 km² (496.224 millas²), *un poco menos que el área de Alaska*
- ▶ **Población:** 30.063.000
- ▶ **Capital:** Lima —7.590.000
- ▶ **Ciudades principales:** Arequipa —915.000, Trujillo, Chiclayo, Callao, Iquitos

SOURCE: Population Division, UN Secretariat

Iquitos es un puerto muy importante en el río Amazonas. Desde Iquitos se envían° muchos productos a otros lugares, incluyendo goma°, nueces°, madera°, arroz°, café y tabaco. Iquitos es también un destino popular para los ecoturistas que visitan la selva°.

- ▶ **Moneda:** nuevo sol
- ▶ **Idiomas:** español (oficial), quechua (oficial), aimará

Bandera del Perú

Peruanos célebres

- ▶ **Clorinda Matto de Turner,** escritora (1854–1901)
- ▶ **César Vallejo,** poeta (1892–1938)
- ▶ **Javier Pérez de Cuéllar,** diplomático (1920–)
- ▶ **Mario Vargas Llosa,** escritor (1936–)

Mario Vargas Llosa

se envían *are shipped* goma *rubber* nueces *nuts* madera *timber* arroz *rice* selva *jungle* Hace más de *More than... ago* grabó *engraved* tamaño *size*

¡Increíble pero cierto!

Hace más de° dos mil años la civilización nazca de Perú grabó° más de 2.000 kilómetros de líneas en el desierto. Los dibujos sólo son descifrables desde el aire. Uno de ellos es un cóndor del tamaño° de un estadio. Las Líneas de Nazca son uno de los grandes misterios de la humanidad.

ECUADOR
Río Putumayo
Río Napo
COLOMBI
Río Tigre
Río Pastaza
Río Amazonas
Bailando marinera norteña en Trujillo
Iquitos
Río Marañón
Cordillera Oriental de los Andes
Río Huallaga
Calle en la ciudad de Iquitos
Cordillera Central de los Andes
Chiclayo
Río Ucayali
Trujillo
Río Urubamba
Callao ☆ Lima
Fuente de la Justicia en Lima
Machu Picchu
Océano Pacífico
Cordillera Occidental de los Andes
Cuzco
La Tit
Arequipa
ESTADOS UNIDOS
OCÉANO ATLÁNT
OCÉANO PACÍFICO
AMÉRICA DEL SUR
PERÚ
Mercado indígena en Cuzco

recursos

| CP pp. 83–84 | CA pp. 81–82 | SUPERSITE descubre1.vhlcentral.com Lección 7 |

TEACHING OPTIONS

Heritage Speakers Ask heritage speakers of Peruvian origin or students who have visited Peru to make a short presentation to the class about their impressions. Encourage them to speak of the region they are from or have visited and how it differs from other regions in this vast country. If they have photographs, ask them to bring them to class to illustrate their talk.

TPR Invite students to take turns guiding the class on tours of Peru's waterways: one student gives directions, and the others follow by tracing the route on their map of Peru. For example: **Comenzamos en el río Amazonas, pasando por Iquitos hasta llegar al río Ucayali.**

Lugares • **Lima**

Lima es una ciudad moderna y antigua° a la vez°. La Iglesia de San Francisco es notable por la influencia de la arquitectura barroca colonial. También son fascinantes las exhibiciones sobre los incas en el Museo Oro del Perú y en el Museo Nacional de Antropología y Arqueología. Barranco, el barrio° bohemio de la ciudad, es famoso por su ambiente cultural y sus bares y restaurantes.

Historia • **Machu Picchu**

A 80 kilómetros al noroeste de Cuzco está Machu Picchu, una ciudad antigua del imperio inca. Está a una altitud de 2.350 metros (7.710 pies), entre dos cimas° de los Andes. Cuando los españoles llegaron al Perú, nunca encontraron Machu Picchu. En 1911, el arqueólogo norteamericano Hiram Bingham la descubrió. Todavía no se sabe ni cómo se construyó° una ciudad a esa altura, ni por qué los incas la abandonaron. Sin embargo°, esta ciudad situada en desniveles° naturales es el ejemplo más conocido de la arquitectura inca.

Artes • **La música andina**

Machu Picchu aún no existía° cuando se originó la música cautivadora° de las antiguas culturas indígenas de los Andes. La influencia española y la música africana contribuyeron a la creación de los ritmos actuales de la música andina. Dos tipos de flauta°, la quena y la antara, producen esta música tan particular. En las décadas de los sesenta y los setenta se popularizó un movimiento para preservar la música andina, y hasta° Simon y Garfunkel la incorporaron en su repertorio con la canción *El cóndor pasa*.

Economía • **Llamas y alpacas**

El Perú se conoce por sus llamas, alpacas, guanacos y vicuñas, todos ellos animales mamíferos° parientes del camello. Estos animales todavía tienen una enorme importancia en la economía del país. Dan lana para hacer ropa, mantas°, bolsas y artículos para turistas. La llama se usa también para la carga y el transporte.

 ¿Qué aprendiste? Responde a las preguntas con una oración completa.

1. ¿Qué productos envía Iquitos a otros lugares? Iquitos envía goma, nueces, madera, arroz, café y tabaco.
2. ¿Cuáles son las lenguas oficiales del Perú? Las lenguas oficiales del Perú son el español y el quechua.
3. ¿Por qué es notable la Iglesia de San Francisco en Lima? Es notable por la influencia de la arquitectura barroca colonial.
4. ¿Qué información sobre Machu Picchu no se sabe todavía? No se sabe ni cómo se construyó ni por qué la abandonaron.
5. ¿Qué son la quena y la antara? Son dos tipos de flauta.
6. ¿Qué hacen los peruanos con la lana de sus llamas y alpacas? Hacen ropa, mantas, bolsas y artículos para turistas.

 Conexión Internet Investiga estos temas en **descubre1.vhlcentral.com.**

1. Investiga la cultura incaica. ¿Cuáles son algunos de los aspectos interesantes de su cultura?
2. Busca información sobre dos artistas, escritores o músicos peruanos y presenta un breve informe a tu clase.

antigua *old* a la vez *at the same time* barrio *neighborhood* cimas *summits* se construyó *was built* Sin embargo *However* desniveles *uneven pieces of land* aún no existía *didn't exist yet* cautivadora *captivating* flauta *flute* hasta *even* mamíferos *mammalian* mantas *blankets*

Lima Lima, rich in colonial architecture, is also the home of the **Universidad de San Marcos.** Established in 1551, it is the oldest university in South America.

Los incas Another invention of the Incas were the **quipus,** clusters of knotted strings that were a means of keeping records and sending messages. A **quipu** consisted of a series of small, knotted cords attached to a larger cord. Each cord's color, place, size, and the knots it contained all had significance.

La música andina Ancient tombs belonging to pre-Columbian cultures like the Nasca and Moche have yielded instruments and other artifacts indicating that the precursors of Andean music go back at least two millenia.

Llamas y alpacas Of the camel-like animals of the Andes, only the sturdy **llama** has been domesticated as a pack animal. Its long, thick coat also provides fiber that is woven into a coarser grade of cloth. The more delicate **alpaca** and **vicuña** are raised only for their beautiful coats, used to create extremely high-quality cloth. The **guanaco** has never been domesticated.

Conexión Internet Students will find supporting Internet activities and links at **descubre1.vhlcentral.com.**

Teaching Tip You may want to wrap up this section by playing the *Panorama cultural* video footage for this lesson.

TEACHING OPTIONS

Variación léxica Some of the most familiar words to have entered Spanish from the Quechua language are the names of animals native to the Andean region, such as **el cóndor, la llama, el puma,** and **la vicuña.** These words later passed from Spanish to a number of European languages, including English. **La alpaca** comes not from Quechua, (the language of the Incas and their descendants, who inhabit most of the Andean region), but from Aymara, the language of indigenous people who live near Lake Titicaca on the Peruvian-Bolivian border. Some students may be familiar with the traditional Quechua tune, *El cóndor pasa,* which was popularized in a version by Simon and Garfunkel.

Instructional Resources
Cuaderno de actividades, p. 128
e-Cuaderno
Supersite: Textbook &
Vocabulary MP3 Audio Files
Lección 7
Supersite/TRCD: Answer Keys;
Testing Program (**Lección
7 Pruebas,** Test Generator,
Testing Program MP3
Audio Files)
Textbook, Test Audio CD

Los verbos reflexivos

acordarse (de) (o:ue)	to remember
acostarse (o:ue)	to go to bed
afeitarse	to shave
bañarse	to bathe; to take a bath
cepillarse el pelo	to brush one's hair
cepillarse los dientes	to brush one's teeth
despedirse (de) (e:i)	to say goodbye (to)
despertarse (e:ie)	to wake up
dormirse (o:ue)	to go to sleep; to fall asleep
ducharse	to shower; to take a shower
enojarse (con)	to get angry (with)
irse	to go away; to leave
lavarse la cara	to wash one's face
lavarse las manos	to wash one's hands
levantarse	to get up
llamarse	to be called; to be named
maquillarse	to put on makeup
peinarse	to comb one's hair
ponerse	to put on
ponerse (+ *adj.*)	to become (+ adj.)
preocuparse (por)	to worry (about)
probarse (o:ue)	to try on
quedarse	to stay; to remain
quitarse	to take off
secarse	to dry oneself
sentarse (e:ie)	to sit down
sentirse (e:ie)	to feel
vestirse (e:i)	to get dressed

Palabras de secuencia

antes (de)	before
después	afterwards; then
después (de)	after
durante	during
entonces	then
luego	then
más tarde	later (on)
por último	finally

Palabras afirmativas y negativas

algo	something; anything
alguien	someone; somebody; anyone
alguno/a(s), algún	some; any
jamás	never; not ever
nada	nothing; not anything
nadie	no one; nobody; not anyone
ni... ni	neither... nor
ninguno/a, ningún	no; none; not any
nunca	never; not ever
o... o	either... or
siempre	always
también	also; too
tampoco	neither; not either

En el baño

el baño, el cuarto de baño	bathroom
el champú	shampoo
la crema de afeitar	shaving cream
la ducha	shower
el espejo	mirror
el inodoro	toilet
el jabón	soap
el lavabo	sink
el maquillaje	makeup
la pasta de dientes	toothpaste
la toalla	towel

Verbos similares a gustar

aburrir	to bore
encantar	to like very much; to love (inanimate objects)
faltar	to lack; to need
fascinar	to fascinate; to like very much
importar	to be important to; to matter
interesar	to be interesting to; to interest
molestar	to bother; to annoy
quedar	to be left over; to fit (clothing)

Palabras adicionales

el despertador	alarm clock
las pantuflas	slippers
la rutina diaria	daily routine
por la mañana	in the morning
por la noche	at night
por la tarde	in the afternoon; in the evening

Expresiones útiles	See page 231.

recursos

CA
p. 128

descubre1.vhlcentral.com
Lección 7

La comida

8

Communicative Goals

You will learn how to:
- Order food in a restaurant
- Talk about and describe food

Lesson Goals

In **Lección 8**, students will be introduced to the following:
- food terms
- meal-related words
- fruits and vegetables native to the Americas
- Spanish chef **Ferrán Adrià**
- preterite of stem-changing verbs
- double object pronouns
- converting **le** and **les** to **se** with double object pronouns
- comparatives
- superlatives
- reading for the main idea
- expressing and supporting opinions
- writing a restaurant review
- taking notes while listening
- a television commercial for **Bocatta**, a Spanish sandwich shop chain
- Guatemalan singer **Shery**
- cultural, geographic, and historical information about Guatemala

A primera vista Here are some additional questions you can ask based on the photo:
¿Dónde te encanta comer? ¿Por qué? ¿Fuiste a algún lugar especial a comer la semana pasada? ¿Compras comida? ¿Dónde? ¿Quién prepara la comida en tu casa?

A PRIMERA VISTA
- ¿Dónde está ella?
- ¿Qué hace?
- ¿Es parte de su rutina diaria?
- ¿Qué colores hay en la foto?

INSTRUCTIONAL RESOURCES

Student Materials
Cuaderno de práctica, Cuaderno para hispanohablantes, Cuaderno de actividades
Student MAESTRO™ Supersite
(descubre1.vhlcentral.com)
MAESTRO™ e-Cuaderno

Teacher's Resource CD-ROM and in print
*Answer Keys, Audioscripts, Videoscripts
*PowerPoints
Testing Program (**Pruebas,** Test Generator, MP3 Audio Files)
Vista Higher Learning *Cancionero*
*Also available on Supersite

Teacher's MAESTRO™ Supersite
(descubre1.vhlcentral.com)
Learning Management System (Assignment Task Manager, Gradebook)
Also on DVD
Fotonovela, Flash cultura, Panorama cultural

Section Goals

In **Contextos**, students will learn and practice:
- food names
- meal-related vocabulary

Instructional Resources
Cuaderno de práctica, pp. 85–86
Cuaderno para hispanohablantes, pp. 115–116
Cuaderno de actividades, pp. 39–40, 129
e-Cuaderno
Supersite: Textbook, Vocabulary, & Audio Activity MP3 Audio Files
Supersite/TRCD/Print: *PowerPoints* (**Lección 8 Contextos** Presentation, Overheads #33, 34); Communication Activities, Textbook Audio Script, Audio Activity Script, Answer Keys
Textbook & Audio Activity CD

Teaching Tips

- Tell what you are going to have for lunch, writing food vocabulary on the board. Ex: **Tengo hambre y voy a preparar una hamburguesa. ¿Qué ingredientes necesito? Pues, carne de res, queso, tomates, lechuga y mayonesa. También voy a preparar una ensalada. ¿Con qué ingredientes preparo la ensalada? A ver, lechuga, tomates, zanahorias,…**
- Show *Overhead PowerPoint #33*. Ask: **¿Sí o no? ¿Hay bananas en el mercado? (Sí.) ¿Qué otras frutas hay? Y, ¿hay refrescos? (No.)** Then mention typical dishes and ask students to tell what ingredients are used to make them. Ex: **una ensalada mixta, una ensalada de fruta, un sándwich.**
- Ask students what some of their favorite foods are. Ex: **Y a ti, _____, ¿qué te gusta comer?**

La comida

Más vocabulario

el/la camarero/a	waiter/waitress
la comida	food; meal
el/la dueño/a	owner; landlord
los entremeses	hors d'oeuvres; appetizers
el menú	menu
el plato (principal)	(main) dish
la sección de (no) fumar	(non) smoking section
el agua (mineral)	(mineral) water
la bebida	drink
la cerveza	beer
la leche	milk
el refresco	soft drink
el ajo	garlic
las arvejas	peas
los cereales	cereal; grain
los frijoles	beans
el melocotón	peach
el pollo (asado)	(roast) chicken
el queso	cheese
el sándwich	sandwich
el yogur	yogurt
el aceite	oil
la margarina	margarine
la mayonesa	mayonnaise
el vinagre	vinegar
delicioso/a	delicious
sabroso/a	tasty; delicious
saber	to taste; to know
saber a	to taste like

Variación léxica

camarones ⟷ gambas (*Esp.*)

camarero ⟷ mesero (*Amér. L.*), mesonero (*Ven.*), mozo (*Arg., Chile, Urug., Perú*)

refresco ⟷ gaseosa (*Amér. C., Amér. S.*)

recursos

| CP pp. 85–86 | CH pp. 115–116 | CA pp. 39–40, 129 | descubre1.vhlcentral.com Lección 8 |

TEACHING OPTIONS

Extra Practice To review vocabulary for colors, ask students what colors these food items are: **las bananas (amarillas), las uvas (verdes o moradas), las zanahorias (anaranjadas), los tomates (rojos), los frijoles (blancos, marrones, rojos o negros), la lechuga (verde), las cebollas (blancas).**

Heritage Speakers Point out that food vocabulary varies from region to region in the Spanish-speaking world. Ask heritage speakers to share food-related terms they are familiar with. Also ask them to tell where the terms are used. Possible responses: **el guisante, el chícaro, el banano, el guineo, el cambur, el plátano, el hongo, la habichuela, el choclo, el elote, la patata, el jitomate.**

Práctica

¡LENGUA VIVA!

You learned the verb **saber** in **Lección 6**. This verb is also used to describe food.

Use **saber** + [*adjective*] to explain how something *tastes*.

Ex: **Este plato sabe dulce/rico/amargo.**
(*This dish tastes sweet/delicious/bitter.*)

Use **saber** + **a** to say what something *tastes like*.

Ex: **Sabe a ajo.**
(*It tastes like garlic.*)

Estas langostas no saben a nada.
(*These lobsters don't taste like anything./ These lobsters don't have any flavor.*)

LAS CARNES

pollo
el pavo
el jamón
la carne de res

Pescados y mariscos

la chuleta (de cerdo)
el atún
el salmón
los camarones (el camarón)
la langosta

1 Escuchar Indica si las oraciones que vas a escuchar son **ciertas** o **falsas**, según el dibujo. Después, corrige las falsas.

1. Cierta. _____
2. Falsa. El hombre compra una naranja. _____
3. Cierta. _____
4. Falsa. El pollo es una carne y la zanahoria es una verdura. _____
5. Cierta. _____
6. Falsa. El hombre y la mujer no compran vinagre. _____
7. Falsa. La naranja es una fruta. _____
8. Falsa. La chuleta de cerdo es una carne. _____
9. Falsa. El limón es una fruta y el jamón es una carne. _____
10. Cierta. _____

2 Seleccionar Paulino y Pilar van a cenar a un restaurante. Escucha la conversación y selecciona la respuesta que mejor completa cada oración.

1. Paulino le pide el ___menú___ (menú / plato) al camarero.
2. El plato del día es (atún / salmón) ___atún___.
3. Pilar ordena ___agua mineral___ (leche / agua mineral) para beber.
4. Paulino quiere un refresco de ___naranja___ (naranja / limón).
5. Paulino hoy prefiere ___la chuleta___ (el salmón / la chuleta).
6. Dicen que la carne en ese restaurante es muy ___sabrosa___ (sabrosa / mal).
7. Pilar come salmón con ___zanahorias___ (zanahorias / champiñones).

3 Identificar Identifica la palabra que no está relacionada con cada grupo.

1. champiñón • cebolla • banana • zanahoria banana
2. camarones • ajo • atún • salmón ajo
3. aceite • leche • refresco • agua mineral aceite
4. jamón • chuleta de cerdo • vinagre • carne de res vinagre
5. cerveza • lechuga • arvejas • frijoles cerveza
6. carne • pescado • mariscos • camarero camarero
7. pollo • naranja • limón • melocotón pollo
8. maíz • queso • tomate • champiñón queso

4 Completar Completa las oraciones con las palabras más lógicas.

1. ¡Me gusta mucho este plato! Sabe ___b___.
   a. feo   b. delicioso   c. antipático
2. Camarero, ¿puedo ver el ___c___, por favor?
   a. aceite   b. maíz   c. menú
3. Carlos y yo bebemos siempre agua ___b___.
   a. cómoda   b. mineral   c. principal
4. El plato del día es ___a___.
   a. el pollo asado   b. la mayonesa   c. el ajo
5. Margarita es vegetariana. Ella come ___a___.
   a. frijoles   b. chuletas   c. jamón
6. Mi hermana le da ___c___ a su niña.
   a. ajo   b. vinagre   c. yogur

SUPERSITE

1 Teaching Tip Have students check their answers by going over **Actividad 1** with the class.

1 Script 1. La langosta está cerca de los camarones. 2. El hombre compra una pera. 3. La lechuga es una verdura. 4. El pollo y la zanahoria son carnes. 5. La cebolla está cerca del maíz. 6. El hombre y la mujer compran vinagre. 7. La naranja es una verdura. 8. La chuleta de cerdo es pescado. 9. El limón y el jamón son frutas. 10. El pavo está cerca del pollo. *Textbook Audio*

2 Teaching Tip To challenge students, write the cloze sentences on the board without the choices in parentheses. Have students copy them and complete them as they listen.

2 Script PAULINO: Camarero, ¿puedo ver el menú, por favor? CAMARERO: Sí, señor. Hoy el plato del día es atún con champiñones. ¿Qué les traigo de beber? PILAR: Yo voy a beber agua mineral. PA: Para mí, un refresco de naranja, por favor. C: ¿Quieren unos entremeses? El queso es muy sabroso. PA: Sí, queremos el queso. PI: Mira, Paulino, tienen el salmón en salsa de tomate que te gusta. PA: Sí, pero hoy prefiero la chuleta de cerdo. Dicen que la carne en este restaurante sabe deliciosa. PI: Muy bien, entonces yo voy a comer el salmón en salsa de tomate y zanahorias. *Textbook Audio*

3 Expansion Have students indicate why a particular item does not belong. Ex: **El champiñón, la cebolla y la zanahoria son verduras. La banana es una fruta.**

4 Expansion Give additional statements. Ex: **Un vegetariano no come _____. (carne)**

Teaching Tips

- Involve the class in a conversation about meals. Say: **Por lo general, desayuno sólo café con leche y pan tostado, pero cuando tengo mucha hambre desayuno dos huevos y una salchicha también. ____, ¿qué desayunas tú?**

- Show *Overhead PowerPoint #34.* Say: **Mira el desayuno aquí. ¿Qué desayuna esta persona?** Then continue to **el almuerzo** and **la cena.** Have students identify the food items and participate in a conversation about their eating habits. Get them to talk about what, when, and where they eat. Say: **Yo siempre desayuno en casa, pero casi nunca almuerzo en casa. ¿A qué hora almuerzan ustedes por lo general?**

- Ask students to tell you their favorite foods to eat for each of the three meals. Ex: ____, **¿qué te gusta desayunar?** Introduce additional items such as **los espaguetis, la pasta, la pizza.**

Nota cultural Point out that in Spanish-speaking countries, **el almuerzo,** also called **la comida,** usually is the main meal of the day, consists of several courses, and is enjoyed at a leisurely pace. **La cena** is typically much lighter than **el almuerzo.**

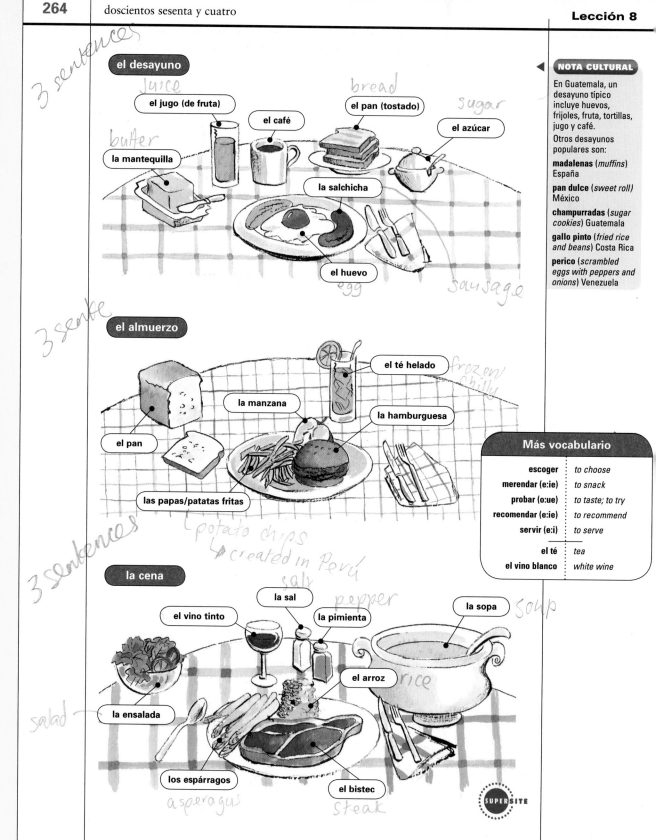

el desayuno

el jugo (de fruta) — *Juice*
el pan (tostado) — *bread*
el café
el azúcar — *sugar*
la mantequilla — *butter*
la salchicha
el huevo — *egg* / *sausage*

el almuerzo

el té helado — *frozen chilly*
la manzana
la hamburguesa
el pan
las papas/patatas fritas — *potato chips / created in Perú*

la cena

la sal — *salt*
la pimienta — *pepper*
la sopa — *soup*
el vino tinto
el arroz — *rice*
la ensalada — *salad*
los espárragos — *asperagus*
el bistec — *steak*

NOTA CULTURAL

En Guatemala, un desayuno típico incluye huevos, frijoles, fruta, tortillas, jugo y café.

Otros desayunos populares son:

madalenas (*muffins*) España

pan dulce (*sweet roll*) México

champurradas (*sugar cookies*) Guatemala

gallo pinto (*fried rice and beans*) Costa Rica

perico (*scrambled eggs with peppers and onions*) Venezuela

Más vocabulario

escoger	*to choose*
merendar (e:ie)	*to snack*
probar (o:ue)	*to taste; to try*
recomendar (e:ie)	*to recommend*
servir (e:i)	*to serve*
el té	*tea*
el vino blanco	*white wine*

SUPERSITE

TEACHING OPTIONS

Small Groups In groups of three or four, have students create a menu for a special occasion. Ask them to describe what they are going to serve for **el entremés, el plato principal,** and **bebidas.** Write **el postre** on the board and explain that it means *dessert.* Explain that in Spanish-speaking countries fresh fruit and cheese are common as dessert, but you may also want to give **el pastel** (*pie, cake*) and **el helado** (*ice cream*).

Extra Practice Add an auditory aspect to this vocabulary presentation. Prepare descriptions of five to seven different meals, with a mix of breakfasts, lunches, and dinners. As you read each description aloud, have students write down what you say as a dictation and then guess the meal it describes.

5 **Completar** Trabaja con un(a) compañero/a de clase para relacionar cada producto con el grupo alimenticio (*food group*) correcto.

> **modelo**
> <u>La carne</u> es del grupo uno.

el aceite	las bananas	los cereales	la leche
el arroz	el café	los espárragos	el pescado
el azúcar	la carne	los frijoles	el vino

1. <u>La leche</u> y el queso son del grupo cuatro.
2. <u>Los frijoles</u> son del grupo ocho.
3. <u>El pescado</u> y el pollo son del grupo tres.
4. <u>El aceite</u> es del grupo cinco.
5. <u>El azúcar</u> es del grupo dos.
6. Las manzanas y <u>las bananas</u> son del grupo siete.
7. <u>El café</u> es del grupo seis.
8. <u>Los cereales</u> son del grupo diez.
9. <u>Los espárragos</u> y los tomates son del grupo nueve.
10. El pan y <u>el arroz</u> son del grupo diez.

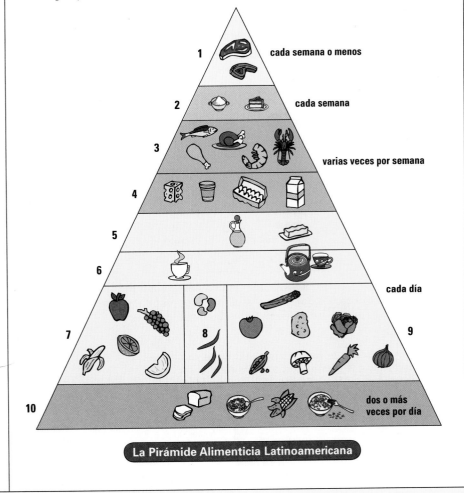

1 — cada semana o menos
2 — cada semana
3 — varias veces por semana
4
5
6
7 — cada día
8
9
10 — dos o más veces por día

La Pirámide Alimenticia Latinoamericana

5 **Teaching Tip** Ask students to compare foods at the base of the pyramid with those at the top. (The foods at the bottom of the pyramid are essential dietary requirements. As one moves closer to the top, the food items become less essential to daily requirements but help to balance out a diet.)

5 **Expansion**
- Ask additional questions about the **pirámide alimenticia**. Ask: **¿Qué se debe comer varias veces por semana? ¿Qué se debe comer todos los días? ¿Cuáles son los productos que aparecen en el grupo cuatro? ¿Y en el grupo siete?** Get students to talk about what they eat. **¿Comen ustedes carne sólo una vez a la semana o menos? ¿Qué comidas comen ustedes dos o más veces al día? ¿Toman leche todos los días?**
- Ask students if they know which food groups and food products comprise the food pyramid used in this country. If you can get a copy of one, bring it to class and have students compare similarities and differences between the dietary requirements.

TEACHING OPTIONS

Heritage Speakers Ask heritage speakers to talk about food items or dishes unique to their families' countries of origin that are not typically found in this country. Have them describe what the item looks and tastes like. If the item is a dish, they should briefly describe how to prepare it if they know how to do so.

Extra Practice Have students draw food pyramids based not on what they should eat, but on what they actually do eat as part of their diet. Encourage them to include drawings or magazine cutouts to enhance the visual presentation. Then have students present their pyramids to the class.

6 **¿Cierto o falso?** Consulta la Pirámide Alimenticia Latinoamericana de la página 265 e indica si las oraciones son **ciertas** o **falsas**. Si la oración es falsa, escribe las comidas que sí están en el grupo indicado.

> **modelo**
> El queso está en el grupo diez.
> Falsa. En ese grupo están el maíz, el pan, los cereales y el arroz.

1. La manzana, la banana, el limón y las arvejas están en el grupo siete.
   Falsa. En ese grupo están la manzana, las uvas, la banana, la naranja y el limón.
2. En el grupo cuatro están los huevos, la leche y el aceite.
   Falsa. En ese grupo están los huevos, la leche, el queso y el yogur.
3. El azúcar está en el grupo dos.
   Cierta.
4. En el grupo diez están el pan, el arroz y el maíz.
   Cierta.
5. El pollo está en el grupo uno.
   Falsa. En ese grupo están el bistec y la chuleta de cerdo.
6. En el grupo nueve están la lechuga, el tomate, las arvejas, la naranja, la papa, los espárragos y la cebolla. Falsa. En ese grupo están la lechuga, el tomate, las arvejas, la zanahoria, la papa, los espárragos, la cebolla y el champiñón.
7. El café y el té están en el mismo grupo.
   Cierta.
8. En el grupo cinco está el arroz.
   Falsa. En ese grupo están el aceite y la mantequilla.
9. El pescado, el yogur y el bistec están en el grupo tres.
   Falsa. En ese grupo están el pescado, el pollo, el pavo, los camarones y la langosta.

7 **Combinar** Combina palabras de cada columna, en cualquier (*any*) orden, para formar nueve oraciones lógicas sobre las comidas. Añade otras palabras si es necesario. Answers will vary.

> **modelo**
> La camarera nos sirve la ensalada.

A	B	C
el/la camarero/a	almorzar	la sección de no fumar
el/la dueño/a	escoger	el desayuno
mi familia	gustar	la ensalada
mi novio/a	merendar	las uvas
mis amigos y yo	pedir	el restaurante
mis padres	preferir	el jugo de naranja
mi hermano/a	probar	el refresco
el/la médico/a	recomendar	el plato
yo	servir	el arroz

8 **Un menú** En parejas, usen la Pirámide Alimenticia Latinoamericana de la página 265 para crear un menú para una cena especial. Incluyan alimentos de los diez grupos para los entremeses, los platos principales y las bebidas. Luego presenten el menú a la clase. Answers will vary.

> **modelo**
> La cena especial que vamos a preparar es deliciosa. Primero, hay dos entremeses: una ensalada César y una sopa de langosta. El plato principal es salmón con una salsa de ajo y espárragos. También vamos a servir arroz...

TEACHING OPTIONS

Extra Practice To review and practice the preterite along with food vocabulary, have students write a paragraph in which they describe what they ate up to this point today. Students should also indicate whether this meal or collection of meals represents a typical day for them. If not, they should explain why.

Small Groups In groups of three, students role-play a situation in a restaurant. Two students play the customers and the other plays the **camarero/a**. Write these sentences on the board as suggested phrases: **¿Están listos para pedir?, ¿Qué nos recomienda usted?, ¿Me trae ____, por favor?, ¿Y para empezar?, A sus órdenes, La especialidad de la casa.**

Comunicación

9 **Conversación** En grupos, contesten estas preguntas. *Answers will vary.*

1. ¿Meriendas mucho durante el día? ¿Qué comes? ¿A qué hora?
2. ¿Qué comidas te gustan más para la cena?
3. ¿A qué hora, dónde y con quién almuerzas?
4. ¿Cuáles son las comidas más (*most*) típicas de tu almuerzo?
5. ¿Desayunas? ¿Qué comes y bebes por la mañana?
6. ¿Qué comida deseas probar?
7. ¿Comes cada día comidas de los diferentes grupos de la pirámide alimenticia? ¿Cuáles son las comidas y bebidas más frecuentes en tu dieta?
8. ¿Qué comida recomiendas a tus amigos? ¿Por qué?
9. ¿Eres vegetariano/a? ¿Crees que ser vegetariano/a es una buena idea? ¿Por qué?
10. ¿Te gusta cocinar (*to cook*)? ¿Qué comidas preparas para tus amigos? ¿Para tu familia?

10 **Describir** Con dos compañeros/as de clase, describe las dos fotos, contestando estas preguntas.
Answers will vary.

▶ ¿Quiénes están en las fotos?

▶ ¿Dónde están?

▶ ¿Qué hora es?

▶ ¿Qué comen y qué beben?

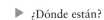

recursos

CA
pp. 39–40

11 **Crucigrama (*Crossword puzzle*)** Tu profesor(a) les va a dar a ti y a tu compañero/a un crucigrama incompleto. Tú tienes las palabras que necesita tu compañero/a y él/ella tiene las palabras que tú necesitas. Tienen que darse pistas (*clues*) para completarlo. No pueden decir la palabra necesaria; deben utilizar definiciones, ejemplos y frases. *Answers will vary.*

> **modelo**
>
> **6 vertical:** Es un condimento que normalmente viene con la sal.
>
> **2 horizontal:** Es una fruta amarilla.

9 **Expansion** Ask the same questions of individual students. Ask other students to restate what their classmates answered.

10 **Expansion** Add an additional visual aspect to this vocabulary practice. Using magazine pictures that show people in eating situations, have students describe what is going on: who the people are, what they are eating and drinking, and so forth.

11 **Teaching Tip** Divide the class into pairs and distribute the Communication Activities worksheets that correspond to this activity. Give students ten minutes to complete this activity.

11 **Expansion** Have groups create another type of word puzzle, such as a word-find, to share with the class. It should contain additional food- and meal-related vocabulary.

TEACHING OPTIONS

Small Groups In groups of two to four, ask students to prepare brief skits related to food. The skits may involve being in a market, in a restaurant, in a café, inviting people over for dinner, and so forth. Allow groups time to rehearse before performing their skits for the class, who will vote for the most creative one.

Game Play a game of continuous narration. One student begins with: **Voy a preparar** (*name of dish*) **y voy al mercado. Necesito comprar...** and names one food item. The next student then repeats the entire narration, adding another food item. Continue on with various students. When the possibilities for that particular dish are used up, have another student begin with another dish.

¿Qué tal la comida?

SUPERSITE

Don Francisco y los estudiantes van al restaurante El Cráter.

PERSONAJES

MAITE

INÉS

DON FRANCISCO

ÁLEX

JAVIER

DOÑA RITA

CAMARERO
waiter

1

JAVIER ¿Sabes dónde estamos?

INÉS Mmm, no sé. Oiga, don Francisco, ¿sabe usted dónde estamos?

DON FRANCISCO Estamos cerca de Cotacachi.

2
lunch

ÁLEX ¿Dónde vamos a almorzar, don Francisco? ¿Conoce un buen restaurante en Cotacachi?

DON FRANCISCO Pues, conozco a doña Rita Perales, la dueña del mejor restaurante de la ciudad, el restaurante El Cráter.

3

DOÑA RITA Hombre, don Paco, ¿usted por aquí?

DON FRANCISCO Sí, doña Rita... y hoy le traigo clientes. Le presento a Maite, Inés, Álex y Javier. Los llevo a las montañas para ir de excursión.

6

MAITE Voy a tomar un caldo de patas *soup* y un lomo a la plancha. *steak*

JAVIER Para mí las tortillas de maíz y el ceviche de camarón.

ÁLEX Yo también quisiera las tortillas de maíz y el ceviche. *soup*

INÉS Voy a pedir caldo de patas y lomo a la plancha.
grilled flank steak

7

DON FRANCISCO Yo quiero tortillas de maíz y una fuente de fritada, por favor. *great platter of food*

DOÑA RITA Y de tomar, les recomiendo el jugo de piña, frutilla y mora. ¿Se lo traigo a todos?

TODOS Sí, perfecto.

8

CAMARERO ¿Qué plato pidió usted?

MAITE Un caldo de patas y lomo a la plancha.

recursos

CA pp. 65–66
descubre1.vhlcentral.com Lección 8

don, doña = title of respect w/ first name

Section Goals

In **Fotonovela**, students will:
• receive comprehensible input from free-flowing discourse
• learn functional phrases that preview lesson grammatical structures

Instructional Resources
Cuaderno de actividades, pp. 65–66
e-Cuaderno
Supersite/DVD: *Fotonovela*
Supersite/TRCD: *Fotonovela*
Videoscript & Translation, Answer Keys

Video Recap: Lección 7
Before doing this **Fotonovela** section, review the previous one with this activity.
1. ¿Qué no hace Javier jamás? (Jamás se levanta temprano.) 2. ¿Qué hace Javier por la noche? (Dibuja y escucha música.) 3. ¿Qué va a hacer Álex por Javier? (Va a despertarlo.) 4. ¿Qué hace Álex por la mañana? (Se levanta, corre, se ducha y se viste.)

Video Synopsis Don Francisco takes the travelers to the **restaurante El Cráter** for lunch. The owner of the restaurant, **Doña Rita**, welcomes the group and makes recommendations about what to order. After the food is served, **Don Francisco** and **Doña Rita** plan a birthday surprise for **Maite**.

Teaching Tips
• Have the class predict the content of this episode based on its title and the video stills.
• Quickly review the predictions and ask students a few questions to help them summarize this episode.

TEACHING OPTIONS

¿Qué tal la comida? Play the first half of the **¿Qué tal la comida?** segment and have the class give you a description of what they see. Write their observations on the board, pointing out any inaccuracies. Repeat this process to allow the class to pick up more details of the plot. Then ask students to use the information they have accumulated to guess what happens in the rest of the segment. Write their predictions on the board. Then play the entire segment and, through discussion, help the class summarize the plot.

Teaching Tip Have the class read through the entire **Fotonovela**, with volunteers playing the parts of **don Francisco, Javier, Inés, Álex, Maite, doña Rita**, and the **Camarero**. Have students take turns playing the roles so that more students participate.

Expresiones útiles Point out some of the unfamiliar structures, which will be taught in detail in **Estructura**. Draw attention to the verb **pidió**. Explain that this is a form of the verb **pedir**, which has a stem change in the **Ud./él/ella** and **Uds./ellos/ellas** forms of the preterite. Have the class read the caption for video still 5, and explain that **más caro que** is an example of a comparison. Point out that in caption 9, **nos la** is an example of an indirect object pronoun and a direct object pronoun used together. Tell students that they will learn more about these concepts in **Estructura**.

DOÑA RITA ¡Bienvenidos al restaurante El Cráter! Están en muy buenas manos... don Francisco es el mejor conductor del país. Y no hay nada más bonito que nuestras montañas. Pero si van a ir de excursión deben comer bien. Vengan chicos, por aquí.

JAVIER ¿Qué nos recomienda usted?

DOÑA RITA Bueno, las tortillas de maíz son riquísimas. La especialidad de la casa es el caldo de patas... ¡tienen que probarlo! El lomo a la plancha es un poquito más caro que el caldo pero es sabrosísimo. También les recomiendo el ceviche y la fuente de fritada.

DOÑA RITA ¿Qué tal la comida? ¿Rica?

JAVIER Rica, no. ¡Riquísima!

ÁLEX Sí. ¡Y nos la sirvieron tan rápidamente!

MAITE Una comida deliciosa, gracias.

DON FRANCISCO Hoy es el cumpleaños de Maite...

DOÑA RITA ¡Ah! Tenemos unos pasteles que están como para chuparse los dedos...

Expresiones útiles

Finding out where you are

- **¿Sabe usted/Sabes dónde estamos?**
  Do you know where we are?
  Estamos cerca de Cotacachi.
  We're near Cotacachi.

Talking about people and places you're familiar with

- **¿Conoce usted/Conoces un buen restaurante en Cotacachi?**
  Do you know a good restaurant in Cotacachi?
  Sí, conozco varios.
  Yes, I know several.
- **¿Conoce/Conoces a doña Rita?**
  Do you know Doña Rita?

Ordering food

- **¿Qué le puedo traer?**
  What can I bring you?
  Voy a tomar/pedir un caldo de patas y un lomo a la plancha.
  I am going to have/to order the beef soup and grilled flank steak.
  Para mí, las tortillas de maíz y el ceviche de camarón, por favor.
  Corn tortillas and lemon-marinated shrimp for me, please.
  Yo también quisiera...
  I also would like...
  Y de tomar, el jugo de piña, frutilla y mora.
  And pineapple/strawberry/ blackberry juice to drink.
- **¿Qué plato pidió usted?**
  What did you order?
  Yo pedí un caldo de patas.
  I ordered the beef soup.

Talking about the food at a restaurant

- **¿Qué tal la comida?**
  How is the food?
  Muy rica, gracias.
  Very tasty, thanks.
  ¡Riquísima!
  Extremely delicious!

TEACHING OPTIONS

Pairs Have students work in pairs to create original mini-dialogues, using sentences in **Expresiones útiles** with other words and expressions they know. Ex: —**¿Qué tal la hamburguesa? —Perdón, pero no sabe a nada. Quisiera pedir otro plato.**

Extra Practice Photocopy the **Fotonovela** Videoscript (Supersite/TRCD) and white out words related to food, meals, and other key vocabulary in order to create a master for a cloze activity. Distribute the photocopies and have students fill in the target words as they watch the episode.

¿Qué pasó?

1 **Escoger** Escoge la respuesta que completa mejor cada oración.

1. Don Francisco lleva a los estudiantes a __c__ al restaurante de una amiga.
   a. cenar   b. desayunar   c. almorzar
2. Doña Rita es __b__.
   a. la hermana de don Francisco   b. la dueña del restaurante
   c. una camarera que trabaja en El Cráter
3. Doña Rita les recomienda a los viajeros __a__.
   a. el caldo de patas y el lomo a la plancha
   b. el bistec, las verduras frescas y el vino tinto   c. unos pasteles (*cakes*)
4. Inés va a pedir __c__.
   a. las tortillas de maíz y una fuente de fritada (*mixed grill*)
   b. el ceviche de camarón y el caldo de patas
   c. el caldo de patas y el lomo a la plancha

2 **Identificar** Indica quién puede decir estas oraciones.

1. No me gusta esperar en los restaurantes.
   ¡Qué bueno que nos sirvieron rápidamente! Álex
2. Les recomiendo la especialidad de la casa. doña Rita
3. ¡Maite y yo pedimos los mismos platos! Inés
4. Disculpe, señora… ¿qué platos recomienda usted? Javier
5. Yo conozco a una señora que tiene un restaurante
   excelente. Les va a gustar mucho. don Francisco
6. Hoy es mi cumpleaños (*birthday*). Maite

ÁLEX
INÉS
DOÑA RITA
MAITE
DON FRANCISCO
JAVIER

3 **Preguntas** Contesta estas preguntas sobre la **Fotonovela**.

1. ¿Dónde comieron don Francisco y los estudiantes?
   Comieron en el restaurante de doña Rita/El Cráter.
2. ¿Cuál es la especialidad de El Cráter?
   La especialidad de la casa es el caldo de patas.
3. ¿Qué pidió Javier? ¿Y Álex? ¿Qué tomaron todos? Javier pidió tortillas de maíz y el ceviche. Álex también pidió las tortillas de maíz y el ceviche. Todos tomaron jugo.
4. ¿Cómo son los pasteles en El Cráter?
   Los pasteles en El Cráter son sabrosísimos.

4 **En el restaurante** Answers will vary.

1. Prepara con un(a) compañero/a una conversación en la que le preguntas si conoce algún buen restaurante en tu comunidad. Tu compañero/a responde que él/ella sí conoce un restaurante que sirve una comida deliciosa. Lo/La invitas a cenar y tu compañero/a acepta. Determinan la hora para verse en el restaurante y se despiden.

2. Trabaja con un(a) compañero/a para representar los papeles de un(a) cliente/a y un(a) camarero/a en un restaurante. El/La camarero/a te pregunta qué te puede servir y tú preguntas cuál es la especialidad de la casa. El/La camarero/a te dice cuál es la especialidad y te recomienda algunos platos del menú. Tú pides entremeses, un plato principal y escoges una bebida. El/La camarero/a te sirve la comida y tú le das las gracias.

CONSULTA
To review positive words like **algún**, see **Estructura 7.2**, p. 240.

communication
NATIONAL STANDARDS

---

1 Teaching Tip Before assigning this activity, ask: **¿Qué es El Cráter? ¿Quién es doña Rita? ¿Cuáles son algunas de las comidas del menú?**

2 Teaching Tip Add an auditory aspect to this exercise. Have students close their books. Then read each item aloud and have the class guess who would have made each statement.

2 Expansion Give the class these sentences as items 7–9: **7. Les van a gustar muchísimo nuestras montañas. (doña Rita) 8. ¿Les gustó la comida? (doña Rita) 9. Para mí, las tortillas de maíz y la fuente de fritada. (don Francisco)**

3 Teaching Tip Change the questions' focus by rephrasing them. Ex: **¿Qué es El Cráter?** (Es el restaurante donde comieron don Francisco y los estudiantes.)

4 Possible Conversations
Conversation 1:
E1: Oye, María, ¿conoces un buen restaurante en esta ciudad?
E2: Sí… el restaurante El Pescador sirve comida riquísima.
E1: ¿Por qué no vamos a El Pescador esta noche?
E2: ¿A qué hora?
E1: ¿A las ocho?
E2: Perfecto.
E1: Está bien. Nos vemos a las ocho.
E2: Adiós.
Conversation 2:
E1: ¿Qué le puedo traer?
E2: Bueno, ¿cuáles son las especialidades de la casa?
E1: La especialidad de la casa es el lomo a la plancha. También le recomiendo el caldo de patas.
E2: Mmm… voy a pedir los camarones y el lomo a la plancha. De tomar, voy a pedir el jugo de piña.
E1: Gracias, señor.

TEACHING OPTIONS

Extra Practice Ask students questions about the **Fotonovela** episode. Ex: **1. ¿En qué ciudad está el restaurante El Cráter? (Cotacachi) 2. ¿Qué pidió Javier en el restaurante? (tortillas de maíz, ceviche de camarón) 3. ¿Qué pidió don Francisco? (tortillas de maíz, fuente de fritada) 4. ¿Cuándo es el cumpleaños de Maite? (hoy)**

Large Groups Have students work in groups of five or six to prepare a skit in which a family goes to a restaurant, is seated by a waitperson, examines the menu, and orders dinner. Each family member should ask a few questions about the menu and then order an entree and a drink. Have one or two groups perform the skit in front of the class.

Pronunciación SUPERSITE
ll, ñ, c, and z

pollo	**llave**	**ella**	**cebolla**

Most Spanish speakers pronounce the letter **ll** like the *y* in *yes*.

mañana	**señor**	**baño**	**niña**

The letter **ñ** is pronounced much like the *ny* in *canyon*.

café	**colombiano**	**cuando**	**rico**

Before **a**, **o**, or **u**, the Spanish **c** is pronounced like the *c* in *car*.

cereales	**delicioso**	**conducir**	**conocer**

Before **e** or **i**, the Spanish **c** is pronounced like the *s* in *sit*. (In parts of Spain, **c** before **e** or **i** is pronounced like the *th* in *think*.)

zeta	**zanahoria**	**almuerzo**	**cerveza**

The Spanish **z** is pronounced like the *s* in *sit*. (In parts of Spain, **z** is pronounced like the *th* in *think*.)

Práctica Lee las palabras en voz alta.

1. mantequilla
2. cuñado
3. aceite
4. manzana
5. español
6. cepillo
7. zapato
8. azúcar
9. quince
10. compañera
11. almorzar
12. calle

Oraciones Lee las oraciones en voz alta.

1. Mi compañero de cuarto se llama Toño Núñez. Su familia es de la ciudad de Guatemala y de Quetzaltenango.
2. Dice que la comida de su mamá es deliciosa, especialmente su pollo al champiñón y sus tortillas de maíz.
3. Creo que Toño tiene razón porque hoy cené en su casa y quiero volver mañana para cenar allí otra vez.

Refranes Lee los refranes en voz alta.

Panza llena, corazón contento.[2]

Las apariencias engañan.[1]

1 Looks can be deceiving.
2 A full belly makes a happy heart.

recursos		
CH p. 117	CA p. 130	SUPERSITE descubre1.vhlcentral.com Lección 8

Section Goals

In **Cultura**, students will:
- read about fruits and vegetables native to the Americas
- learn food-related terms
- read about Spanish chef **Ferrán Adrià**
- read about typical dishes from Peru, Spain, and Colombia

Instructional Resources
Cuaderno para hispanohablantes, p. 118
Supersite: *Flash cultura*
Videoscript & Translation
Supersite/DVD: *Flash cultura*

En detalle
Antes de leer Ask students if they can name any fruits and vegetables that are native to North America.

Lectura
- The Aztec and Maya's beverage made of cacao, chile, and other spices was far thicker and more bitter than the hot chocolate most North Americans consume today.
- Point out that many words, such as **tomate, chocolate, aguacate, tamal,** and **mole** are of Nahuatl origin, the language of the Aztecs. **Papa** comes from the Quechua word for *potato.* Explain that **salsa** is a general term for *sauce.*
- Explain that **tamales** are corn dough (usually filled with meat or cheese), which is wrapped in plant leaves or corn husks and steamed. **Arepas** are a type of thin corn cake, and **mole** is a Mexican sauce made of chile peppers, spices, and unsweetened chocolate.

Después de leer Ask students if they were surprised to learn that these foods were unknown to Europe and the rest of the world until about 500 years ago. Ask them to name dishes they would miss without these fruits and vegetables.

1 Expansion Ask students to write three additional true-false statements for a classmate to answer.

EN DETALLE

Frutas y verduras de las Américas

Imagínate una pizza sin salsa° de tomate o una hamburguesa sin papas fritas. Ahora piensa que quieres ver una película, pero las palomitas de maíz° y el chocolate no existen. ¡Qué mundo° tan insípido°! Muchas de las comidas más populares del mundo tienen ingredientes esenciales que son originarios de las Américas. Estas frutas y verduras no fueron introducidas en Europa sino hasta° el siglo° XVI.

El tomate, por ejemplo, era° usado como planta ornamental cuando llegó por primera vez a Europa porque pensaron que era venenoso°. El maíz, por su parte, era ya la base de la comida de muchos países latinoamericanos muchos siglos antes de la llegada de los españoles.

La papa fue un alimento° básico para los incas. Incluso consiguieron deshidratar las papas para almacenarlas° durante mucho tiempo. El cacao (planta con la que se hace el chocolate) fue muy importante para los aztecas y los mayas. Ellos usaron sus semillas° como moneda° y como ingrediente de diversas salsas. También las molían° para preparar una bebida, mezclándolas° con agua ¡y con chile!

El aguacate°, la guayaba°, la papaya, la piña y el maracuyá (o fruta de la pasión) son sólo algunos ejemplos de frutas originarias de las Américas que son hoy día conocidas en todo el mundo.

Mole

¿En qué alimentos encontramos estas frutas y verduras?

Tomate: pizza, ketchup, salsa de tomate, sopa de tomate

Maíz: palomitas de maíz, tamales, tortillas, arepas (Colombia y Venezuela), pan

Papa: papas fritas, frituras de papa°, puré de papas°, sopa de papas, tortilla de patatas (España)

Cacao: salsa mole (México), chocolatinas°, cereales, helados°, tartas°

Aguacate: guacamole (México), cóctel de camarones, sopa de aguacate, nachos, enchiladas hondureñas

---

salsa *sauce* palomitas de maíz *popcorn* mundo *world* insípido *flavorless* hasta *until* siglo *century* era *was* venenoso *poisonous* alimento *food* almacenarlas *to store them* semillas *seeds* moneda *currency* las molían *they used to grind them* mezclándolas *mixing them* aguacate *avocado* guayaba *guava* frituras de papa *chips* puré de papas *mashed potatoes* chocolatinas *chocolate bars* helados *ice cream* tartas *cakes*

ACTIVIDADES

1 **¿Cierto o falso?** Indica si lo que dicen estas oraciones es **cierto** o **falso.** Corrige la información falsa.

1. El tomate se introdujo a Europa como planta ornamental. **Cierto.**
2. Los aztecas y los mayas usaron las papas como moneda. **Falso.** Los aztecas y los mayas usaron las semillas de cacao como moneda.
3. Los incas sólo consiguieron almacenar las papas por poco tiempo. **Falso.** Los incas pudieron almacenar las papas por mucho tiempo.

4. En México se hace una salsa con chocolate. **Cierto.**
5. El aguacate, la guayaba, la papaya, la piña y el maracuyá son originarios de las Américas. **Cierto.**
6. Las arepas se hacen con cacao. **Falso.** Las arepas se hacen con maíz.
7. El aguacate es un ingrediente del cóctel de camarones. **Cierto.**
8. En España hacen una tortilla con papas. **Cierto.**

TEACHING OPTIONS

Game Have students make a Bingo card of fruits and vegetables mentioned on this page, with one "free" square in the middle. From a hat, draw cards with different dishes and call them out. Have students cover the square on their card that contains the fruit or vegetable used in that dish. Ex: **tortilla de patatas** (Student covers **la papa.**) The winner is the first student to fill a row (horizontally, vertically, or diagonally) and yell ¡**Bingo!**

Extra Practice Tell students to imagine they are Europeans who traveled to the Americas 500 years ago and are tasting a fruit or vegetable for the first time. Have them write a letter to a friend or family member describing the look and taste of the fruit or vegetable. Encourage them to use verbs like **gustar** in the letter. You may want to brainstorm a list of possible adjectives on the board for students to use in their descriptions.

ASÍ SE DICE

La comida

el banano (Col.), el cambur (Ven.), el guineo (Nic.), el plátano (Amér. L., Esp.)	la banana
el choclo (Amér. S.), el elote (Méx.), el jojoto (Ven.), la mazorca (Esp.)	*corncob*
las caraotas (Ven.), los porotos (Amér. S.), las habichuelas	los frijoles
el durazno	el melocotón
el jitomate (Méx.)	el tomate

EL MUNDO HISPANO

Algunos platos típicos

○ **Ceviche peruano:** Es un plato de pescado crudo° que se marina° en jugo de limón, con sal, pimienta, cebolla y ají°. Se sirve con lechuga, maíz, camote° y papa amarilla.

○ **Gazpacho andaluz:** Es una sopa fría típica del sur de España. Se hace con verduras crudas y molidas°: tomate, ají, pepino° y ajo. También lleva pan, sal, aceite y vinagre.

○ **Sancocho colombiano:** Es una sopa de pollo o de carne con plátano, maíz, zanahoria, yuca, papas, cebolla y ajo. Se sirve con arroz blanco.

crudo *raw* se marina *is marinated* ají *pepper* camote *sweet potato* molidas *mashed* pepino *cucumber*

PERFIL

Ferrán Adrià: arte en la cocina°

¿Qué haces si un amigo te invita a comer croquetas líquidas o paella de Kellogg's? ¿Piensas que es una broma°? ¡Cuidado! Puedes estar perdiendo la oportunidad de cenar en el restaurante más innovador de España: **El Bulli**.

Ferrán Adrià, el dueño de El Bulli, está entre los mejores° chefs del mundo. Su éxito° se basa en su creatividad. Adrià modifica combinaciones de ingredientes y juega con contrastes de gustos y sensaciones: frío-caliente, crudo-cocido°, dulce°-salado°... Sus platos son sorprendentes° y divertidos: cócteles en forma de espuma°, salsas servidas en tubos y sorbetes salados.

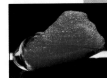

Aire de zanahorias

Adrià también creó **Fast Good** (un restaurante de comida rápida de calidad), escribe libros de cocina y participa en programas de televisión.

cocina *kitchen* broma *joke* mejores *best* éxito *success* cocido *cooked* dulce *sweet* salado *savory* sorprendentes *surprising* espuma *foam*

SUPERSITE **Conexión Internet**

¿Qué platos comen los hispanos en los Estados Unidos?

Go to **descubre1.vhlcentral.com** to find more cultural information related to this **Cultura** section.

ACTIVIDADES

2 **Comprensión** Empareja cada palabra con su definición.

1. fruta amarilla d
2. sopa típica de Colombia c
3. ingrediente del ceviche e
4. restaurante español b

a. gazpacho
b. El Bulli
c. sancocho
d. guineo
e. pescado

3 **¿Qué plato especial hay en tu región?** Escribe cuatro oraciones sobre un plato típico de tu región. Explica los ingredientes que contiene y cómo se sirve. Answers will vary.

recursos

| CH p. 118 | descubre1.vhlcentral.com Lección 8 |

Section Goal

In **Estructura 8.1**, students will be introduced to the preterite of stem-changing verbs.

Instructional Resources
Cuaderno de práctica, pp. 87–88
Cuaderno para hispanohablantes, pp. 119–120
Cuaderno de actividades, p. 131
e-Cuaderno
Supersite: Audio Activity
MP3 Audio Files
Supersite/TRCD/Print:
PowerPoints (**Lección 8**
Estructura Presentation); Audio
Activity Script, Answer Keys
Audio Activity CD

Teaching Tips

• Review present-tense forms of –ir stem-changing verbs like **pedir** and **dormir**. Also review formation of the preterite of regular –ir verbs using **escribir** and **recibir**.

• Give model sentences that use these verbs in the preterite, emphasizing stem-changing forms. Ex: **Me dormí temprano anoche, pero mi esposo/a se durmió muy tarde.**

• Ask students questions using stem-changing –ir verbs in the preterite. Ex: **¿Cuántas horas dormiste anoche?** Then have other students summarize the answers. Ex: ____ **durmió seis horas, pero** ____ **durmió ocho.** ____ **y** ____ **durmieron cinco horas.**

• Point out that **morir** means *to die* and offer sample sentences using stem-changing preterite forms of the verb. Ex: **No tengo bisabuelos. Ya murieron.**

• Other –ir verbs that change their stem vowel in the preterite are **conseguir, despedirse, divertirse, pedir, preferir, repetir, seguir, sentir, sugerir,** and **vestirse.**

8.1 Preterite of stem-changing verbs SUPERSITE

ANTE TODO As you learned in **Lección 6**, –ar and –er stem-changing verbs have no stem change in the preterite. –Ir stem-changing verbs, however, do have a stem change. Study the following chart and observe where the stem changes occur.

Preterite of –ir stem-changing verbs		
	servir (to serve)	**dormir** (to sleep)
SINGULAR FORMS		
yo	serví	dormí
tú	serviste	dormiste
Ud./él/ella	sirvió	durmió
PLURAL FORMS		
nosotros/as	servimos	dormimos
vosotros/as	servisteis	dormisteis
Uds./ellos/ellas	sirvieron	durmieron

▶ Stem-changing –ir verbs, in the preterite only, have a stem change in the third-person singular and plural forms. The stem change consists of either **e** to **i** or **o** to **u**.

(e → i) pedir: **pi**dió, **pi**dieron   (o → u) morir (*to die*): **mu**rió, **mu**rieron

Perdón, ¿quiénes pidieron las tortillas de maíz?

¿Y qué plato pidió usted?

¡INTÉNTALO! Cambia cada infinitivo al pretérito.

1. Yo _____ serví _____. (servir, dormir, pedir, preferir, repetir, seguir)
   dormí, pedí, preferí, repetí, seguí

2. Usted _____. (morir, conseguir, pedir, sentirse, despedirse, vestirse)
   murió, consiguió, pidió, se sintió, se despidió, se vistió

3. Tú _____. (conseguir, servir, morir, pedir, dormir, repetir)
   conseguiste, serviste, moriste, pediste, dormiste, repetiste

4. Ellas _____. (repetir, dormir, seguir, preferir, morir, servir)
   repitieron, durmieron, siguieron, prefirieron, murieron, sirvieron

5. Nosotros _____. (seguir, preferir, servir, vestirse, despedirse, dormirse)
   seguimos, preferimos, servimos, nos vestimos, nos despedimos, nos dormimos

6. Ustedes _____. (sentirse, vestirse, conseguir, pedir, despedirse, dormirse)
   se sintieron, se vistieron, consiguieron, pidieron, se despidieron, se durmieron

7. Él _____. (dormir, morir, preferir, repetir, seguir, pedir)
   durmió, murió, prefirió, repitió, siguió, pidió

recursos

CP
pp. 87–88

CH
pp. 119–120

CA
p. 131

SUPERSITE
descubre1.
vhlcentral.com
Lección 8

TEACHING OPTIONS

TPR Have the class stand and form a circle. Call out a name or subject pronoun and an infinitive that has a stem change in the preterite (Ex: **Miguel/seguir**). Toss a foam or paper ball to a student, who will say the correct form (Ex: **siguió**) and toss the ball back to you. Then name another pronoun and infinitive and throw the ball to another student. To challenge students, include some infinitives without a stem change in the preterite.

Pairs Ask students to work in pairs to come up with ten original sentences in which they use the **Ud./él/ella** and **Uds./ellos/ellas** preterite forms of stem-changing –ir verbs. Point out that students should try to use vocabulary items from **Contextos** in their sentences. Ask pairs to share their sentences with the class.

Práctica SUPERSITE

1 **Completar** Completa estas oraciones para describir lo que pasó anoche en el restaurante El Famoso.

1. Paula y Humberto Suárez llegaron al restaurante El Famoso a las ocho y __siguieron__ (seguir) al camarero a una mesa en la sección de no fumar.
2. El señor Suárez __pidió__ (pedir) una chuleta de cerdo.
3. La señora Suárez __prefirió__ (preferir) probar los camarones.
4. Para tomar, los dos __pidieron__ (pedir) vino tinto.
5. El camarero __repitió__ (repetir) el pedido (*the order*) para confirmarlo.
6. La comida tardó mucho (*took a long time*) en llegar y los señores Suárez __se durmieron__ (dormirse) esperando la comida.
7. A las nueve y media el camarero les __sirvió__ (servir) la comida.
8. Después de comer la chuleta, el señor Suárez __se sintió__ (sentirse) muy mal.
9. Pobre señor Suárez... ¿por qué no __pidió__ (pedir) los camarones?

2 **El camarero loco** En el restaurante La Hermosa trabaja un camarero muy loco que siempre comete muchos errores. Indica lo que los clientes pidieron y lo que el camarero les sirvió.

> **modelo**
> Armando / papas fritas
> Armando pidió papas fritas, pero el camarero le sirvió maíz.

1. nosotros / jugo de naranja   Nosotros pedimos jugo de naranja, pero el camarero nos sirvió papas.
2. Beatriz / queso   Beatriz pidió queso, pero el camarero le sirvió uvas.
3. tú / arroz   Tú pediste arroz, pero el camarero te sirvió arvejas/sopa.

4. Elena y Alejandro / atún   Elena y Alejandro pidieron atún, pero el camarero les sirvió camarones/mariscos.
5. usted / refresco   Usted pidió un refresco, pero el camarero le sirvió leche/agua.
6. yo / hamburguesa   Yo pedí una hamburguesa, pero el camarero me sirvió zanahorias.

1 **Expansion** Ask students to work in pairs to come up with an alternate ending to the narration, using stem-changing –ir verbs in the preterite. Pairs then share their endings with the class. The class can vote on the most original ending.

2 **Expansion** In pairs, students redo the activity, this time role-playing the customer and the waitperson. Model the possible interaction between the students. Ex: **E1: Perdón, pero pedí papas fritas y usted me sirvió maíz. E2: ¡Ay perdón! Le traigo papas fritas enseguida.** Have students take turns playing the role of the customer and waitperson.

TEACHING OPTIONS

Video Show the *Fotonovela* again to give students more input with stem-changing –ir verbs in the preterite. Have them write down the stem-changing forms they hear. Stop the video where appropriate to discuss how certain verbs were used and to ask comprehension questions. Ex: **¿Qué pidió Maite? ¿Cómo sirvieron la comida?**

Extra Practice Add an auditory aspect to this grammar practice. Prepare descriptions of five easily recognizable people in which you use the stem-changing forms of –ir verbs in the preterite. Write their names on the board in random order. Then read the descriptions aloud and have students match each one to the appropriate name. Ex: **Murió en un accidente de avión en 1999. También murió su esposa, Carolyn. (John F. Kennedy, Jr.)**

Comunicación

3 Expansion Have students share their sentences with the class. Ask other students comprehension questions based on what was said.

3

El almuerzo Trabajen en parejas. Túrnense para completar las oraciones de César de una manera lógica. Answers will vary.

> **modelo**
>
> Mi abuelo se despertó temprano, pero yo...
> Mi abuelo se despertó temprano, pero yo me
> desperté tarde.

1. Yo llegué al restaurante a tiempo, pero mis amigos...
2. Beatriz pidió la ensalada de frutas, pero yo...
3. Yolanda les recomendó el bistec, pero Eva y Paco...
4. Nosotros preferimos las papas fritas, pero Yolanda...
5. El camarero sirvió la carne, pero yo...
6. Beatriz y yo pedimos café, pero Yolanda y Paco...
7. Eva se sintió enferma, pero Paco y yo...
8. Nosotros repetimos el postre (*dessert*), pero Eva...
9. Ellos salieron tarde, pero yo...
10. Yo me dormí temprano, pero mi hermano...

¡LENGUA VIVA!

In Spanish, the verb **repetir** is used to express *to have a second helping* (of something).

Cuando mi mamá prepara sopa de champiñones, yo siempre repito.

When my mom makes mushroom soup, I always have a second helping.

4 Expansion To practice the formal register, have students ask you the same questions.

4

Entrevista Trabajen en parejas y túrnense para entrevistar a su compañero/a. Answers will vary.

1. ¿Te acostaste tarde o temprano anoche? ¿A qué hora te dormiste? ¿Dormiste bien?
2. ¿A qué hora te despertaste esta mañana? Y ¿a qué hora te levantaste?
3. ¿A qué hora vas a acostarte esta noche?
4. ¿Qué almorzaste ayer? ¿Quién te sirvió el almuerzo?
5. ¿Qué cenaste ayer?
6. ¿Cenaste en un restaurante recientemente? ¿Con quién?
7. ¿Qué pediste en el restaurante? ¿Qué pidieron los demás?
8. ¿Se durmió alguien en alguna de tus clases la semana pasada? ¿En qué clase?

Síntesis

5 Expansion Have groups present their description to the class in the form of a narration.

Consulta In addition to pointing out words and expressions that may signal the preterite, remind students about transition words that help to move the flow of a narration (Ex: **primero, después, luego, también**).

5

Describir En grupos, estudien la foto y las preguntas. Luego, describan la cena romántica de los señores García. Answers will vary.

▸ ¿Adónde salieron a cenar?

▸ ¿Qué pidieron?

▸ ¿Les sirvieron la comida rápidamente?

▸ ¿Les gustó la comida?

▸ ¿Cuánto costó?

▸ ¿Van a volver a este restaurante en el futuro?

▸ ¿Recomiendas el restaurante?

CONSULTA

To review words commonly associated with the preterite, such as **anoche**, see **Estructura 6.3**, p. 207.

salir = to go out / cena = dinner

TEACHING OPTIONS

Pairs In pairs, have students take turns telling each other about a memorable experience in a restaurant, whether it was someone's birthday, whether they were with family or friends, and so forth. Encourage students to take notes as their partners narrate. Then have students reveal what their partners told them.

Extra Practice Add a visual aspect to this grammar practice. As you hold up magazine pictures that show restaurant scenes, have students describe them in the past tense, using the preterite. You may want to write on the board some stem-changing –**ir** verbs that might apply to what is going on in the pictures.

8.2 Double object pronouns

ANTE TODO   In **Lecciones 5** and **6**, you learned that direct and indirect object pronouns replace nouns and that they often refer to nouns that have already been referenced. You will now learn how to use direct and indirect object pronouns together. Observe the following diagram.

Indirect Object Pronouns			Direct Object Pronouns	
me	nos	**+**	lo	los
te	os		la	las
le (se)	les (se)			

▶ When direct and indirect object pronouns are used together, the indirect object pronoun always precedes the direct object pronoun.

		DOUBLE OBJECT PRONOUNS
I.O. D.O. El camarero **me** muestra **el menú**. *The waiter shows me the menu.*	→	El camarero **me lo** muestra. *The waiter shows it to me.*
I.O. D.O. **Nos** sirven **los platos**. *They serve us the dishes.*	→	**Nos los** sirven. *They serve them to us.*
I.O. D.O. Maribel **te** pidió **una hamburguesa**. *Maribel ordered a hamburger for you.*	→	Maribel **te la** pidió. *Maribel ordered it for you.*

> *Y de tomar, les recomiendo el jugo de piña... ¿Se lo traigo a todos?*

> *Sí, perfecto.*

▶ In Spanish, two pronouns that begin with the letter **l** cannot be used together. Therefore, the indirect object pronouns **le** and **les** always change to **se** when they are used with **lo, los, la,** and **las**.

		DOUBLE OBJECT PRONOUNS
I.O. D.O. **Le** escribí **la carta**. *I wrote him the letter.*	→	**Se la** escribí. *I wrote it to him.*
I.O. D.O. **Les** sirvió **los sándwiches**. *He served them the sandwiches.*	→	**Se los** sirvió. *He served them to them.*

Section Goals

In **Estructura 8.2**, students will be introduced to:
- the use of double object pronouns
- converting **le** and **les** into **se** when used with direct object pronouns **lo, la, los,** and **las**

Instructional Resources
Cuaderno de práctica, pp. 89–90
Cuaderno para hispanohablantes, pp. 121–122
Cuaderno de actividades, pp. 41–42, 132
e-Cuaderno
Supersite: Audio Activity MP3 Audio Files
Supersite/TRCD/Print: *PowerPoints* (**Lección 8 Estructura** Presentation); Communication Activities, Audio Activity Script, Answer Keys
Audio Activity CD

Teaching Tips
- Briefly review direct object pronouns (**Estructura 5.4**) and indirect object pronouns (**Estructura 6.2**). Give sentences and have students convert objects into object pronouns. Ex: **Sara escribió la carta. (Sara la escribió.) Mis padres escribieron una carta. (yo) (Mis padres me escribieron una carta.)**
- Model additional examples for students, asking them to make the conversion with **se**. Ex: **Le pedí papas fritas. (Se las pedí.) Les servimos café. (Se lo servimos.)**
- Emphasize that, with double object pronouns, the indirect object pronoun always precedes the direct object pronoun.

TEACHING OPTIONS

Extra Practice Write six sentences on the board for students to restate using double object pronouns. Ex: **Rita les sirvió la cena a los viajeros. (Rita se la sirvió.)**
Pairs In pairs, ask students to write five sentences that contain both direct and indirect objects (not pronouns). Have them exchange papers with another pair, who will restate the sentences using double object pronouns.

Video Show the *Fotonovela* again to give students more input containing double object pronouns. Stop the video where appropriate to discuss how double object pronouns were used and to ask comprehension questions.

Estructura   **277**

▶ Because **se** has multiple meanings, Spanish speakers often clarify to whom the pronoun refers by adding **a usted, a él, a ella, a ustedes, a ellos,** or **a ellas.**

¿El sombrero? Carlos **se** lo vendió **a ella.**
The hat? Carlos sold it to her.

¿Las verduras? Ellos **se** las compran **a usted.**
The vegetables? They buy them for you.

▶ Double object pronouns are placed before a conjugated verb. With infinitives and present participles, they may be placed before the conjugated verb or attached to the end of the infinitive or present participle.

DOUBLE OBJECT PRONOUNS
Te lo voy a mostrar.

DOUBLE OBJECT PRONOUNS
Voy a mostrár**telo**.

DOUBLE OBJECT PRONOUNS
Nos las están sirviendo.

DOUBLE OBJECT PRONOUNS
Están sirviéndo**noslas**.

¿Qué tal la comida, rica?

Sí. ¡Y nos la sirvieron tan rápidamente!

▶ As you can see above, when double object pronouns are attached to an infinitive or a present participle, an accent mark is added to maintain the original stress.

¡INTÉNTALO! Escribe el pronombre de objeto directo o indirecto que falta en cada oración.

Objeto directo

1. ¿La ensalada? El camarero nos ___la___ sirvió.
2. ¿El salmón? La dueña me ___lo___ recomienda.
3. ¿La comida? Voy a preparárte___la___.
4. ¿Las bebidas? Estamos pidiéndose___las___.
5. ¿Los refrescos? Te ___los___ puedo traer ahora.
6. ¿Los platos de arroz? Van a servírnos___los___ después.

Objeto indirecto

 *bring / show*

1. —¿Puedes traerme tu plato? —No, no ___te___ lo puedo traer.
2. —¿Quieres mostrarle la carta? —Sí, voy a mostrár___se___la ahora.
3. —¿Les serviste la carne? —No, no ___se___ la serví.
4. —¿Vas a leerle el menú? —No, no ___se___ lo voy a leer.
5. —¿Me recomiendas la langosta? —Sí, ___te___ la recomiendo.
6. —¿Cuándo vas a prepararnos la cena? —___Se___ la voy a preparar en una hora.

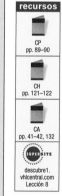

recursos

CP
pp. 89–90

CH
pp. 121–122

CA
pp. 41–42, 132

SUPERSITE
descubre1.
vhlcentral.com
Lección 8

Práctica

SUPERSITE

1 **Responder** Imagínate que trabajas de camarero/a en un restaurante. Responde a las órdenes de estos clientes usando pronombres.

You are the waiter in a restaurant. Respond to the orders of the customers using pronouns

modelo

Sra. Gómez: Una ensalada, por favor.
Sí, señora. Enseguida (Right away) se la traigo.

1. Sres. López: La mantequilla, por favor. Sí, señores. Enseguida se la traigo.
2. Srta. Rivas: Los camarones, por favor. Sí, señorita. Enseguida se los traigo.
3. Sra. Lugones: El pollo asado, por favor. Sí, señora. Enseguida se lo traigo.
4. Tus compañeros/as de clase: Café, por favor. Sí, chicos. Enseguida se lo traigo.
5. Tu profesor(a) de español: Papas fritas, por favor. Sí, profesor(a). Enseguida se las traigo.
6. Dra. González: La chuleta de cerdo, por favor. Sí, doctora. Enseguida se la traigo.
7. Tu padre: Los champiñones, por favor. Sí, papá. Enseguida te los traigo.
8. Dr. Torres: La cuenta (*check*), por favor. Sí, doctor. Enseguida se la traigo.

AYUDA

Here are some other useful expressions:
ahora mismo *right now*
inmediatamente *immediately*
¡A la orden! *At your service!*
¡Ya voy! *I'm on my way!*

dinner solve

2 **¿Quién?** La señora Cevallos está planeando una cena. Se pregunta cómo va a resolver ciertas situaciones. En parejas, túrnense para decir lo que ella está pensando. Cambien los sustantivos subrayados por pronombres de objeto directo y hagan los otros cambios necesarios.

modelo

¡No tengo carne! ¿Quién va a traerme <u>la carne</u> del supermercado? (mi esposo)
Mi esposo va a traérmela./Mi esposo me la va a traer.

1. ¡Las invitaciones! ¿Quién les manda <u>las invitaciones</u> a los invitados (*guests*)? (mi hija) Mi hija se las manda.
2. No tengo tiempo de ir a la tienda. ¿Quién me puede comprar <u>el vinagre</u>? (mi hijo) Mi hijo puede comprármelo./Mi hijo me lo puede comprar.
3. ¡Ay! No tengo suficientes platos (*plates*). ¿Quién puede prestarme <u>los platos</u> que necesito? (mi mamá) Mi mamá puede prestármelos./Mi mamá me los puede prestar.
4. Nos falta mantequilla. ¿Quién nos trae <u>la mantequilla</u>? (mi cuñada) Mi cuñada nos la trae.
5. ¡Los entremeses! ¿Quién está preparándonos <u>los entremeses</u>? (Silvia y Renata) Silvia y Renata están preparándonoslos./Silvia y Renata nos los están preparando.
6. No hay suficientes sillas. ¿Quién nos trae <u>las sillas</u> que faltan? (Héctor y Lorena) Héctor y Lorena nos las traen.
7. No tengo tiempo de pedirle el aceite a Mónica. ¿Quién puede pedirle <u>el aceite</u>? (mi hijo) Mi hijo puede pedírselo./Mi hijo se lo puede pedir.
8. ¿Quién va a servirles <u>la cena</u> a los invitados? (mis hijos) Mis hijos van a servírsela./Mis hijos se la van a servir.
9. Quiero poner buena música de fondo (*background*). ¿Quién me va a recomendar <u>la música</u>? (mi esposo) Mi esposo va a recomendármela./Mi esposo me la va a recomendar.
10. ¡Los postres! ¿Quién va a preparar <u>los postres</u> para los invitados? (Sra. Villalba) La señora Villalba va a preparáselos./La señora Villalba se los va a preparar.

1 Teaching Tip Do the activity with the whole class, selecting a student to play the role of customer and another to play the role of waiter/waitress for each item.

Ayuda Model the helpful phrases in sentences. Point out that **Ahora mismo, Inmediatamente,** and **Ya** can replace **Enseguida** in the **modelo** for **Actividad 1.**

2 Expansion
- For each item, change the subject in parentheses so that students practice different forms of the verbs.
- Add a visual aspect to this activity. Hold up magazine pictures and ask students who is doing what to or for whom. Ex: **La señora les muestra la casa a los jóvenes. Se la muestra a los jóvenes.**

TEACHING OPTIONS

Heritage Speakers Ask heritage speakers to talk about a favorite gift they received. Write **regalar** on the board and explain that it means *to give (a gift).* Have students talk about what they received, who gave it to them (**regalar**), and why. Ask the rest of the class comprehension questions.

Game Play **Concentración.** Write sentences that use double object pronouns on each of eight cards. Ex: **Óscar se las muestra.** On another eight cards, draw or paste a picture that matches each sentence. Ex: A photo of a boy showing photos to his grandparents. Place the cards face-down in four rows of four. In pairs, students select two cards. If the two cards match, the pair keeps them. If they do not match, students replace them in their original position. The pair with the most cards at the end wins.

Comunicación

3

Contestar Trabajen en parejas. Túrnense para hacer preguntas y responder a ellas usando las palabras interrogativas **¿Quién?** o **¿Cuándo?** Sigan el modelo. Answers will vary.

> **modelo**
> nos enseña español
> **Estudiante 1:** ¿Quién nos enseña español?
> **Estudiante 2:** La profesora Camacho nos lo enseña.

1. te puede explicar (*explain*) la tarea cuando no la entiendes *¿Cuándo te la puede explicar?*
2. les vende el almuerzo a los estudiantes *¿A quién se lo vende?*
3. vas a comprarme boletos (*tickets*) para un concierto *¿Para qué los voy comprar? ¿Para un concierto?*
4. te escribe mensajes electrónicos
5. nos prepara los entremeses *¿Quién nos los prepara?*
6. me vas a prestar tu computadora *¿Quién te la va a prestar?*
7. te compró esa bebida *¿Cuándo me la compró?*
8. nos va a recomendar el menú de la cafetería *¿Quién va a recomendarnoslo?*
9. le enseñó español al/a la profesor(a) *¿Quién se lo enseñó?*
10. me vas a mostrar tu casa o apartamento *¿Cuándo vas a mostrarmela?*

4

Preguntas Hazle estas preguntas a un(a) compañero/a. Answers will vary.

> **modelo**
> **Estudiante 1:** ¿Les prestas tu computadora a tus amigos?
> **Estudiante 2:** No, no se la presto a mis amigos porque no son muy responsables.

1. ¿Me prestas tu chaqueta? ¿Ya le prestaste tu chaqueta a otro/a amigo/a?
2. ¿Quién te presta dinero cuando lo necesitas?
3. ¿Les prestas dinero a tus amigos? ¿Por qué?
4. ¿Nos compras el almuerzo a mí y a los otros compañeros de clase?
5. ¿Les mandas correo electrónico a tus amigos? ¿Y a tu familia?
6. ¿Les das regalos a tus amigos? ¿Cuándo?
7. ¿Quién te va a preparar la cena esta noche?
8. ¿Quién te va a preparar el desayuno mañana?

Síntesis

5

Regalos de Navidad (*Christmas gifts*) Tu profesor(a) te va a dar a ti y a un(a) compañero/a una parte de la lista de los regalos de Navidad que Berta pidió y los regalos que sus parientes le compraron. Conversen para completar sus listas. Answers will vary.

> **modelo**
> **Estudiante 1:** ¿Qué le pidió Berta a su mamá?
> **Estudiante 2:** Le pidió una computadora. ¿Se la compró?
> **Estudiante 1:** Sí, se la compró.

3 Teaching Tips
• To simplify, begin by reading through the items and guiding students in choosing **quién** or **cuándo** for each one.
• Continue the **modelo** exchange by asking: **¿Cuándo nos lo enseña? (Nos lo enseña los lunes, miércoles, jueves y viernes.)**
• To challenge students, have them ask follow-up questions using other interrogative words.

3 Expansion Ask questions of individual students. Then ask them why they answered as they did. Students answer using double object pronouns. Ex: **¿Quién te enseña español? (Usted me lo enseña.) ¿Por qué? (Usted me lo enseña porque es profesor(a) de español.)**

4 Expansion Ask the questions of individual students. Then verify class comprehension by asking other students to repeat the information given.

5 Teaching Tip Divide the class into pairs and distribute the Communication Activities worksheets that correspond to this activity. Give students ten minutes to complete this activity.

5 Expansion With a different partner, ask pairs to make a list of the gifts they each received for their last birthday or other occasion. Then have them point to each item on their list and, using double object pronouns, tell their partner who bought it for them. Ex: **zapatos nuevos (Me los compró mi prima.)**

TEACHING OPTIONS

Heritage Speakers Ask heritage speakers if they or their families celebrate **el Día de los Reyes Magos** (The Feast of the Epiphany, January 6). Ask them to tell whether **el Día de los Reyes** is more important for them than **la Navidad**.

Large Groups Divide the class into two groups. Give each member of the first group a strip of paper with a question on it. Ex: **¿Te compró ese suéter tu novia?** Give each member of the second group the answer to one of the questions. Ex: **Sí, ella me lo compró.** Students must find their partners. Take care not to create sentences that can have more than one match.

Comparisons SUPERSITE

ANTE TODO   Spanish and English use comparisons to indicate which of two people or things has a lesser, equal, or greater degree of a quality.

Comparisons

menos interesante	**más grande**	**tan sabroso como**
less interesting	*bigger*	*as delicious as*

Comparisons of inequality

▶ Comparisons of inequality are formed by placing **más** (*more*) or **menos** (*less*) before adjectives, adverbs, and nouns and **que** (*than*) after them.

$$\textbf{más/menos} + \left[\begin{array}{c} adjective \\ adverb \\ noun \end{array}\right] + \textbf{que}$$

▶ **¡Atención!** Note that while English has a comparative form for short adjectives (*tall**er***), such forms do not exist in Spanish (**más** alto).

adjectives

Los bistecs son **más caros que** el pollo.	Estas uvas son **menos ricas que** esa pera.
Steaks are more expensive than chicken.	*These grapes are less tasty than that pear.*

adverbs

Me acuesto **más tarde que** tú.	Luis se despierta **menos temprano que** yo.
I go to bed later than you (do).	*Luis wakes up less early than I (do).*

nouns

Juan prepara **más platos que** José.	Susana come **menos carne que** Enrique.
Juan prepares more dishes than José (does).	*Susana eats less meat than Enrique (does).*

Tengo más hambre que un elefante.

El lomo a la plancha es un poquito más caro pero es sabrosísimo.

▶ When the comparison involves a numerical expression, **de** is used before the number instead of **que**.

Hay más **de** cincuenta naranjas.	Llego en menos **de** diez minutos.
There are more than fifty oranges.	*I'll be there in less than ten minutes.*

▶ With verbs, this construction is used to make comparisons of inequality.

$$\left[\ verb\ \right] + \textbf{más/menos que}$$

Mis hermanos **comen más que** yo.	Arturo **duerme menos que** su padre.
My brothers eat more than I (do).	*Arturo sleeps less than his father (does).*

TEACHING OPTIONS

Comparisons of equality

▶ This construction is used to make comparisons of equality.

tan + [*adjective / adverb*] + **como**   **tanto/a(s)** + [*singular noun / plural noun*] + **como**

¿Qué tal tu ceviche?

La comida es tan buena como en España.

▶ **¡Atención!** Note that **tanto** acts as an adjective and therefore agrees in number and gender with the noun it modifies.

Este plato es **tan rico como** aquél.
This dish is as tasty as that one (is).

Yo probé **tantos platos como** él.
I tried as many dishes as he did.

▶ **Tan** and **tanto** can also be used for emphasis, rather than to compare, with these meanings: **tan** *so*, **tanto** *so much*, **tantos/as** *so many*.

¡Tu almuerzo es **tan** grande!
Your lunch is so big!

¡Comes **tantas** manzanas!
You eat so many apples!

¡Comes **tanto**!
You eat so much!

¡Preparan **tantos** platos!
They prepare so many dishes!

▶ Comparisons of equality with verbs are formed by placing **tanto como** after the verb. Note that in this construction **tanto** does not change in number or gender.

[*verb*] + **tanto como**

Tú viajas **tanto como** mi tía.
You travel as much as my aunt (does).

Ellos hablan **tanto como** mis hermanas.
They talk as much as my sisters.

Estudiamos tanto como ustedes.
We study as much as you (do).

No **descanso tanto como** Felipe.
I don't rest as much as Felipe (does).

Irregular comparisons

▶ Some adjectives have irregular comparative forms.

Irregular comparative forms

Adjective		Comparative form	
bueno/a	good	**mejor**	better
malo/a	bad	**peor**	worse
grande	big	**mayor**	bigger
pequeño/a	small	**menor**	smaller
joven	young	**menor**	younger
viejo/a	old	**mayor**	older

CONSULTA

To review how descriptive adjectives like **bueno**, **malo**, and **grande** shorten before nouns, see **Estructura 3.1**, p. 90.

▶ When **grande** and **pequeño/a** refer to age, the irregular comparative forms, **mayor** and **menor**, are used. However, when these adjectives refer to size, the regular forms, **más grande** and **más pequeño/a**, are used.

Yo soy **menor** que tú.
I'm younger than you.

Pedí un plato **más pequeño**.
I ordered a smaller dish.

El médico es **mayor** que Isabel.
The doctor is older than Isabel.

La ensalada de Inés es **más grande** que ésa.
Inés's salad is bigger than that one.

▶ The adverbs **bien** and **mal** have the same irregular comparative forms as the adjectives **bueno/a** and **malo/a**.

Julio nada **mejor** que los otros chicos.
Julio swims better than the other boys.

Ellas cantan **peor** que las otras chicas.
They sing worse than the other girls.

recursos

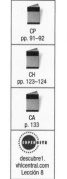

CP
pp. 91–92

CH
pp. 123–124

CA
p. 133

SUPERSITE
descubre1.
vhlcentral.com
Lección 8

¡INTÉNTALO!   Escribe el equivalente de las palabras en inglés.

1. Ernesto mira más televisión ___que___ (*than*) Alberto.
2. Tú eres ___menos___ (*less*) simpático que Federico.
3. La camarera sirve ___tanta___ (*as much*) carne como pescado.
4. Conozco ___más___ (*more*) restaurantes que tú.
5. No estudio ___tanto como___ (*as much as*) tú.
6. ¿Sabes jugar al tenis tan bien ___como___ (*as*) tu hermana?
7. ¿Puedes beber ___tantos___ (*as many*) refrescos como yo?
8. Mis amigos parecen ___tan___ (*as*) simpáticos como ustedes.

Teaching Tips
• Practice the differences between **grande—mayor** and **pequeño/a—menor** when referring to age by having two students stand. Ask E1: _____ , ¿cuántos años tienes? (E1: Tengo quince años.) Then ask E2: Y tú, _____ , ¿cuántos años tienes? (E2: Tengo dieciséis años.) Now ask the class: ¿Quién es mayor? ¿Y quién es más grande?

• Ask questions and give examples to practice irregular comparative forms. Ex: (Pointing to two students) **Lisa tiene dieciséis años y Shawn tiene diecisiete años. ¿Lisa es mayor que Shawn? (No, Lisa es menor que Shawn.)** Then ask questions about celebrities. Ex: **¿Quién canta mejor, Alicia Keys o Avril Lavigne?** Have students state their opinions in complete sentences. Ex: **Alicia Keys canta mejor que Avril Lavigne.**

TEACHING OPTIONS

Large Groups Divide the class into groups of six. Give cards with adjectives listed on this page to one group. Give cards with the corresponding irregular comparative form to another group. Students must find their partners. To avoid confusion, make duplicate cards of **mayor** and **menor**.

Pairs Write on the board the heading **Nuestra escuela vs.** [*another nearby school*]. Underneath, write a list of categories. Ex: **campus, los estudiantes, el equipo de fútbol americano.** Have pairs take turns making comparisons about the schools. Encourage them to be creative and to use a variety of comparative forms. Ex: **Los estudiantes de nuestra escuela estudian tanto como los estudiantes de** [*other school*].

Práctica SUPERSITE

1 Teaching Tip Quickly review the use of **de** before numerals in comparisons.

1 Expansion
• Ask two students a question, then have another student compare them. Ex: **¿Cuántas horas de televisión miras cada día? ¿Y tú, ____?
____ , haz una comparación.**
• Ask several pairs of students different types of questions for later comparison.
Ex: **¿Cuáles prefieres, las películas de aventuras o los dramas? ¿Estudias más para la clase de español o para la clase de matemáticas?**

2 Expansion Turn the activity statements into questions and ask them of students. Have them make up answers that involve comparisons. Ex: **¿Cómo es Mario?**

3 Teaching Tips
• Have a student read the **modelo** aloud. Emphasize that students' comparisons can begin with an element from either column A or C.
• To simplify, guide students in pairing up elements from columns A and C and brainstorming possible infinitives for each pair of elements.

1 Escoger Escoge la palabra correcta para comparar a dos hermanas muy diferentes. Haz los cambios necesarios.

1. Lucila es más alta y más bonita ___que___ Tita. (de, más, menos, que)
2. Tita es más delgada porque come ___más___ verduras que su hermana. (de, más, menos, que)
3. Lucila es más ___simpática___ que Tita porque es alegre. (listo, simpático, bajo)
4. A Tita le gusta comer en casa. Va a ___menos___ restaurantes que su hermana. (más, menos, que) Es tímida, pero activa. Hace ___más___ ejercicio (*exercise*) que su hermana. (más, tanto, menos) Todos los días toma más ___de___ cinco vasos (*glasses*) de agua mineral. (que, tan, de)
5. Lucila come muchas papas fritas y se preocupa ___menos___ que Tita por comer frutas. (de, más, menos) Son ___tan___ diferentes, pero se llevan (*they get along*) bien. (como, tan, tanto)

2 Emparejar Completa las oraciones de la columna A con información de la columna B para comparar a Mario y a Luis, los novios de Lucila y Tita.

A	B
1. Mario es ___tan interesante___ como Luis.	tantas
2. Mario viaja tanto ___como___ Luis.	diferencia
3. Luis toma ___tantas___ clases de cocina (*cooking*) como Mario.	tan interesante
4. Luis habla ___francés___ tan bien como Mario.	amigos extranjeros
5. Mario tiene tantos ___amigos extranjeros___ como Luis.	como
6. ¡Qué casualidad (*coincidence*)! Mario y Luis también son hermanos, pero no hay tanta ___diferencia___ entre ellos como entre Lucila y Tita.	francés

3 Oraciones Combina elementos de las columnas A, B y C para hacer comparaciones. Usa oraciones completas. Answers will vary.

modelo
Arnold Schwarzenegger tiene tantos autos como Jennifer Aniston.
Jennifer Aniston es menos musculosa que Arnold Schwarzenegger.

A	B	C
la comida japonesa	costar	la gente de Los Ángeles
el fútbol	saber	la música *country*
Arnold Schwarzenegger	ser	el brócoli
el pollo	tener	el presidente de los EE.UU.
la gente de Nueva York	¿?	la comida italiana
la primera dama (*lady*) de los EE.UU.		el hockey
las escuelas privadas		Jennifer Aniston
las espinacas		las escuelas públicas
la música rap		la carne de res

(handwritten notes: "food" above la comida japonesa; "Barak Obama" next to Arnold Schwarzenegger; "chicken" next to el pollo; "spinach food" next to las espinacas)

TEACHING OPTIONS

Extra Practice Add a visual aspect to this grammar practice. Using magazine pictures or drawings, show a family whose members vary widely in different aspects: age (write a number on each person that indicates how old he or she is), height, weight, and so forth. Ask students to make comparisons about that family. Give names to each family member so that the people are easier to identify.

Large Groups Divide the class into two groups. Survey each group to get information about various topics. Ex: **¿Quiénes hacen ejercicio todos los días? ¿Quiénes van al cine cada fin de semana? ¿Quiénes comen comida rápida tres veces a la semana?** Ask for a show of hands and tally the number of hands. Then have students make comparisons between the two groups based on the information given.

Comunicación

4   **Intercambiar** En parejas, hagan comparaciones sobre diferentes cosas. Pueden usar las sugerencias de la lista u otras ideas.   Answers will vary.

AYUDA

You can use these adjectives in your comparisons:

bonito/a
caro/a
elegante
interesante
inteligente

modelo

Estudiante 1: Los pollos de *Pollitos del Corral* son muy ricos.
Estudiante 2: Pues yo creo que los pollos de *Rostipollos* son tan buenos como los pollos de *Pollitos del Corral.*
Estudiante 1: Mmm… no tienen tanta mantequilla como los pollos de *Pollitos del Corral.* Tienes razón. Son muy sabrosos.

restaurantes en tu ciudad/pueblo
cafés en tu comunidad
tiendas en tu ciudad/pueblo

periódicos en tu ciudad/pueblo
revistas favoritas
libros favoritos

comidas favoritas
los profesores
las clases que toman

5   **Conversar** En grupos, túrnense para hacer comparaciones entre ustedes mismos (*yourselves*) y una persona de cada categoría de la lista.   Answers will vary.

▶ una persona de tu familia

▶ un(a) amigo/a especial

▶ un(a) persona famosa

Síntesis

6   **La familia López** En grupos, túrnense para hablar de Sara, Sabrina, Cristina, Ricardo y David y hacer comparaciones entre ellos.   Answers will vary.

Sara   Sabrina   David   Ricardo   Cristina

modelo

Estudiante 1: Sara es tan alta como Sabrina.
Estudiante 2: Sí, pero David es más alto que ellas.
Estudiante 3: En mi opinión, él es guapo también.

---

4 Expansion Ask pairs of volunteers to present one of their conversations to the class. Then survey the class to see with which of the students the class agrees more.

5 Teaching Tip Model the activity by making a few comparisons between yourself and a celebrity.

5 Expansion Ask a volunteer to share his or her comparisons. Then make comparisons between yourself and the student or yourself and the person the student mentioned. Continue to do this with different students, asking them to make similar comparisons as well.

6 Expansion Have students create a drawing of a family similar to the one on this page. Tell them not to let anyone see their drawings. Then pair students up and have them describe their drawings to one another. Each student must draw the family described by his or her partner.

TEACHING OPTIONS

Extra Practice Add an auditory aspect to this grammar practice. Prepare short descriptions of five easily recognizable people in which you compare them to other recognizable people. Write their names on the board in random order. Then read the descriptions aloud and have students match them to the appropriate name.
Ex: **Esta persona es más famosa que Enrique Iglesias pero es tan guapa como él. (Ricky Martin)**

TPR Give the same types of objects to different students but in different numbers. For example, hand out three books to one student, one book to another, and four to another. Then call on individuals to make comparisons between the students based on the number of objects they have.

8.4 Superlatives

ANTE TODO Both English and Spanish use superlatives to express the highest or lowest degree of a quality.

el/la mejor	el/la peor	la más alta
the best	*the worst*	*the tallest*

▶ This construction is used to form superlatives. Note that the noun is always preceded by a definite article and that **de** is equivalent to the English *in* or *of*.

> el/la/los/las + [*noun*] + **más/menos** + [*adjective*] + **de**

▶ The noun can be omitted if the person, place, or thing referred to is clear.

¿El restaurante El Cráter?
 Es **el más elegante** de la ciudad.
The El Cráter restaurant?
 It's the most elegant (one) in the city.

Recomiendo el pollo asado.
 Es **el más sabroso** del menú.
I recommend the roast chicken.
 It's the most delicious on the menu.

▶ Here are some irregular superlative forms.

Irregular superlatives

Adjective		Superlative form	
bueno/a	*good*	**el/la mejor**	*(the) best*
malo/a	*bad*	**el/la peor**	*(the) worst*
grande	*big*	**el/la mayor**	*(the) biggest*
pequeño/a	*small*	**el/la menor**	*(the) smallest*
joven	*young*	**el/la menor**	*(the) youngest*
viejo/a	*old*	**el/la mayor**	*(the) eldest*

▶ The absolute superlative is equivalent to *extremely, super,* or *very*. To form the absolute superlative of most adjectives and adverbs, drop the final vowel, if there is one, and add **-ísimo/a(s)**.

malo → mal- → **malísimo**
¡El bistec está **malísimo**!

mucho → much- → **muchísimo**
Comes **muchísimo**.

▶ Note these spelling changes.

rico → **riquísimo**   largo → **larguísimo**   feliz → **felicísimo**
fácil → **facilísimo**   joven → **jovencísimo**   trabajador → **trabajadorcísimo**

¡INTÉNTALO! Escribe el equivalente de las palabras en inglés.

1. Marisa es ___la más inteligente___ (*the most intelligent*) de todas.
2. Ricardo y Tomás son ___los menos aburridos___ (*the least boring*) de la fiesta.
3. Miguel y Antonio son ___los peores___ (*the worst*) estudiantes de la clase.
4. Mi profesor de biología es ___el mayor___ (*the oldest*) de la escuela.

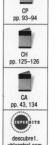

Práctica y Comunicación

1 **El más...** Responde a las preguntas afirmativamente. Usa las palabras en paréntesis.

> **modelo**
> El cuarto está sucísimo, ¿no? (casa)
> *Sí, es el más sucio de la casa.*

1. El almacén Velasco es buenísimo, ¿no? (centro comercial)   Sí, es el mejor del centro comercial.
2. La silla de tu madre es comodísima, ¿no? (casa)   Sí, es la más cómoda de la casa.
3. Ángela y Julia están nerviosísimas por el examen, ¿no? (clase)   Sí, son las más nerviosas de la clase.
4. Jorge es jovencísimo, ¿no? (mis amigos)   Sí, es el menor de mis amigos.

recursos

CA
p. 43

2 **Completar** Tu profesor(a) te va a dar una hoja de actividades con descripciones de José Valenzuela Carranza y Ana Orozco Hoffman. Completa las oraciones con las palabras de la lista. Answers will vary.

altísima	del	mejor	peor
atlética	la	menor	periodista
bajo	más	guapísimo	trabajadorcísimo
de	mayor	Orozco	Valenzuela

1. José tiene 22 años; es el ___menor___ y el más ___bajo___ de su familia. Es ___guapísimo___ y ___trabajadorcísimo___. Es el mejor ___periodista___ de la ciudad y el ___peor___ jugador de baloncesto.
2. Ana es la más ___atlética___ y ___la___ mejor jugadora de baloncesto del estado. Es la ___mayor___ de sus hermanos (tiene 28 años) y es ___altísima___. Estudió la profesión ___más___ difícil ___de___ todas: medicina.
3. Jorge es el ___mejor___ jugador de videojuegos de su familia.
4. Mauricio es el menor de la familia ___Orozco___.
5. El abuelo es el ___mayor___ de todos los miembros de la familia Valenzuela.
6. Fifí es la perra más antipática ___del___ mundo.

3 **Superlativos** Trabajen en parejas para hacer comparaciones. Usen el superlativo. Answers will vary.

> **modelo**
> Angelina Jolie, Bill Gates, Jimmy Carter
> **Estudiante 1:** *Bill Gates es el más rico de los tres.*
> **Estudiante 2:** *Sí, ¡es riquísimo! Y Jimmy Carter es el mayor de los tres.*

1. Guatemala, Argentina, España
2. Jaguar, Hummer, Mini Cooper
3. la comida mexicana, la comida francesa, la comida árabe
4. Paris Hilton, Meryl Streep, Katie Holmes
5. Ciudad de México, Buenos Aires, Nueva York
6. *Don Quijote de la Mancha, Cien años de soledad, Como agua para chocolate*
7. el fútbol americano, el golf, el béisbol
8. las películas románticas, las películas de acción, las películas cómicas

NATIONAL communication STANDARDS

1 **Expansion**
- Give these sentences to students as items 5–7: **5. Esas películas son malísimas, ¿no? (Hollywood) (Sí, son las peores de Hollywood.) 6. El centro comercial Galerías es grandísimo, ¿no? (ciudad) (Sí, es el mayor de la ciudad.) 7. Tus bisabuelos son viejísimos, ¿no? (familia) (Sí, son los mayores de mi familia.)**
- To challenge students, after they have completed the activity, have them repeat it by answering in the negative. Ex: **1. No, es el peor del centro comercial.**

2 **Teaching Tip** Distribute the Communication Activities worksheets that correspond to this activity.

2 **Expansion** In pairs, have students select a family member or a close friend and describe him or her using comparatives and superlatives. Ask volunteers to share their description with the class.

3 **Teaching Tips**
- To simplify, read through the items with students and, in English, brainstorm points of comparison between the three people or things. For item 6, briefly describe these novels for students who are not familiar with them.
- Encourage students to create as many superlatives as they can for each item. Have volunteers share their most creative statements with the class.

TEACHING OPTIONS

Extra Practice Add an auditory aspect to this grammar practice. Prepare ten superlative sentences and read them aloud slowly, pausing about thirty seconds after each sentence to allow students to write the direct opposite. Ex: **Ernesto es el menor de la familia. (Ernesto es el mayor de la familia.)**

Pairs Bring in clothing catalogs and have students work in pairs to create superlative statements about the prices of different items. Ask volunteers to share some of their statements with the class. You may want to have students review clothing-related vocabulary from **Lección 6**.

Recapitulación

For self-scoring and diagnostics, go to descubre1.vhlcentral.com.

Completa estas actividades para repasar los conceptos de gramática que aprendiste en esta lección.

1 **Completar** Completa la tabla con la forma correcta del pretérito. **9 pts.**

Infinitive	yo	usted	ellos
dormir	dormí	durmió	durmieron
servir	serví	sirvió	sirvieron
vestirse	me vestí	se vistió	se vistieron

2 **La cena** Completa la conversación con el pretérito de los verbos. **7 pts.**

PAULA ¡Hola, Daniel! ¿Qué tal el fin de semana?

DANIEL Muy bien. Marta y yo (1) conseguimos (conseguir) hacer muchas cosas, pero lo mejor fue la cena del sábado.

PAULA Ah, ¿sí? ¿Adónde fueron?

DANIEL Al restaurante Vistahermosa. Es elegante, así que (nosotros) (2) nos vestimos (vestirse) bien.

PAULA Y, ¿qué platos (3) pidieron (pedir, ustedes)?

DANIEL Yo (4) pedí (pedir) camarones y Marta (5) prefirió (preferir) el pollo. Y al final, el camarero nos (6) sirvió (servir) flan.

PAULA ¡Qué rico!

DANIEL Sí. Pero después de la cena Marta no (7) se sintió (sentirse) bien.

3 **Camareros** Genaro y Úrsula son camareros en un restaurante. Usa pronombres para completar la conversación que tienen con su jefe. **8 pts.**

JEFE Úrsula, ¿le ofreciste agua fría al cliente de la mesa 22?

ÚRSULA Sí, (1) se la ofrecí de inmediato.

JEFE Genaro, ¿los clientes de la mesa 5 te pidieron ensaladas?

GENARO Sí, (2) me las pidieron

ÚRSULA Genaro, ¿recuerdas si ya me mostraste los vinos nuevos?

GENARO Sí, ya (3) te los mostré.

JEFE Genaro, ¿van a pagarte la cuenta (*bill*) los clientes de la mesa 5?

GENARO Sí, (4) me la van a pagar/ van a pagármela ahora mismo.

RESUMEN GRAMATICAL

8.1 **Preterite of stem-changing verbs** *p. 274*

servir	dormir
serví	dormí
serviste	dormiste
sirvió	durmió
servimos	dormimos
servisteis	dormisteis
sirvieron	durmieron

8.2 **Double object pronouns** *pp. 277–278*

Indirect Object Pronouns: me, te, le (se), nos, os, les (se)
Direct Object Pronouns: lo, la, los, las

Le escribí la carta. → **Se la escribí.**

Nos van a servir los platos. → **Nos los van a servir./**
Van a servírnoslos.

8.3 **Comparisons** *pp. 281–283*

Comparisons of inequality		
más/menos +	adj., adv., n.	+ que
verb + más/menos + que		

Comparisons of equality		
tan +	adj., adv.	+ como
tanto/a(s) +	noun	+ como
verb + tanto como		

Irregular comparative forms	
bueno/a	mejor
malo/a	peor
grande	mayor
pequeño/a	menor
joven	menor
viejo/a	mayor

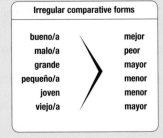

---

4 **El menú** Observa el menú y sus características. Completa las oraciones basándote en los elementos dados. Usa comparativos y superlativos. **14 pts.**

8.4 Superlatives					p. 286
el/la/ los/las +	noun	+ más/ menos +	adjective	+ de	

► Irregular superlatives follow the same pattern as irregular comparatives.

Ensaladas	*Precio*	*Calorías*
Ensalada de tomates	$9.00	170
Ensalada de mariscos	$12.99	325
Ensalada de zanahorias	$9.00	200
Platos principales		
Pollo con champiñones	$13.00	495
Cerdo con papas	$10.50	725
Atún con esparrágos	$18.95	495

1. ensalada de mariscos / otras ensaladas / costar
   La ensalada de mariscos ___cuesta más que___ las otras ensaladas.
2. pollo con champiñones / cerdo con papas / calorías
   El pollo con champiñones tiene ___menos calorías que___ el cerdo con papas.
3. atún con espárragos / pollo con champiñones / calorías
   El atún con espárragos tiene ___tantas calorías como___ el pollo con champiñones.
4. ensalada de tomates / ensalada de zanahorias / caro
   La ensalada de tomates es ___tan cara como___ la ensalada de zanahorias.
5. cerdo con papas / platos principales / caro
   El cerdo con papas es ___el menos caro de___ los platos principales.
6. ensalada de zanahorias / ensalada de tomates / costar
   La ensalada de zanahorias ___cuesta tanto como___ la ensalada de tomates.
7. ensalada de mariscos / ensaladas / caro
   La ensalada de mariscos es ___la más cara de___ las ensaladas.

5 **Dos restaurantes** ¿Cuál es el mejor restaurante que conoces? ¿Y el peor? Escribe un párrafo de por lo menos (*at least*) seis oraciones donde expliques por qué piensas así. Puedes hablar de la calidad de la comida, el ambiente, los precios, el servicio, etc. **12 pts.** Answers will vary.

6 **Adivinanza** Completa la adivinanza y adivina la respuesta. **¡2 puntos EXTRA!**

" En el campo yo nací°,
mis hermanos son
los ___ajos___ (*garlic, pl.*),
y aquél que llora° por mí
me está partiendo°
en pedazos°. **"**
¿Quién soy? ___La cebolla___

nací *was born* llora *cries* partiendo *cutting* pedazos *pieces*

4 **Teaching Tips**
• Remind students that the comparative **tanto/a** must agree in gender and number with the noun it modifies.
• To challenge students, have pairs ask each other questions about the menu using comparatives and superlatives. Ex: **¿Qué ensalada cuesta tanto como la ensalada de tomates? (La ensalada de zanahorias cuesta tanto como la ensalada de tomates.)**

5 **Teaching Tip** To help students organize their ideas, have them divide their paper into two columns: **mejor** and **peor**. Under each category, have students list the different reasons why their chosen restaurants are the best or worst.

6 **Expansion** Have students work in groups of three or four to create an original riddle related to food. Have groups read their riddles for the class to guess.

TEACHING OPTIONS

TPR Have students write a celebrity's name, a place, and a thing on separate slips of paper. Collect the papers in three envelopes, separated by category. Then divide the class into two teams. Draw out two or three slips of paper (alternate randomly) and read the terms aloud. The corresponding team member has five seconds to step forward and create a logical comparison or superlative statement.

Pairs Have pairs imagine they went to a restaurant where the server mixed up all the orders. Call on pairs to share their experiences, using **pedir** and **servir** as well as double object pronouns. Ex: **Fui a un restaurante italiano. Pedí la pasta primavera. ¡El camarero me sirvió la sopa de mariscos! ¡Y me la sirvió fría! Mi compañero pidió langosta, pero el camarero no se la sirvió. ¡Le sirvió una chuleta de cerdo!**

Lectura

 NATIONAL STANDARDS communication cultures

Antes de leer

Estrategia

Reading for the main idea

As you know, you can learn a great deal about a reading selection by looking at the format and looking for cognates, titles, and subtitles. You can skim to get the gist of the reading selection and scan it for specific information. Reading for the main idea is another useful strategy; it involves locating the topic sentences of each paragraph to determine the author's purpose for writing a particular piece. Topic sentences can provide clues about the content of each paragraph, as well as the general organization of the reading. Your choice of which reading strategies to use will depend on the style and format of each reading selection.

Examinar el texto

En esta sección tenemos dos textos diferentes. ¿Qué estrategias puedes usar para leer la crítica culinaria°? ¿Cuáles son las apropiadas para familiarizarte con el menú? Utiliza las estrategias más eficaces° para cada texto. ¿Qué tienen en común? ¿Qué tipo de comida sirven en el restaurante?

Identificar la idea principal

Lee la primera frase de cada párrafo de la crítica culinaria del restaurante **La feria del maíz**. Apunta° el tema principal de cada párrafo. Luego lee todo el primer párrafo. ¿Crees que el restaurante le gustó al autor de la crítica culinaria? ¿Por qué? Ahora lee la crítica entera. En tu opinión, ¿cuál es la idea principal de la crítica? ¿Por qué la escribió el autor? Compara tus opiniones con las de un(a) compañero/a.

recursos

CH
pp. 127–128

SUPERSITE
descubre1.vhlcentral.com
Lección 8

crítica culinaria *restaurant review*
eficaces *efficient* Apunta *Jot down*

MENÚ

Entremeses

Tortilla servida con
- Ajiaceite (chile, aceite)
- Ajicomino (chile, comino)

Pan tostado servido con
- Queso frito a la pimienta
- Salsa de ajo y mayonesa

Sopas
- Tomate
- Cebolla
- Verduras
- Pollo y huevo
- Carne de res
- Mariscos

Entradas

Tomaticán
(tomate, papas, maíz, chile, arvejas y zanahorias)

Tamales
(maíz, azúcar, ajo, cebolla)

Frijoles enchilados
(frijoles negros, carne de cerdo o de res, arroz, chile)

Chilaquil
(tortilla de maíz, queso, hierbas y chile)

Tacos
(tortillas, pollo, verduras y salsa)

Cóctel de mariscos
(camarones, langosta, vinagre, sal, pimienta, aceite)

Postres°
- Plátanos caribeños
- Cóctel de frutas al ron°
- Uvate (uvas, azúcar de caña y ron)
- Flan napolitano
- Helado° de piña y naranja
- Pastel° de yogur

Después de leer

Preguntas 🖊️

En parejas, contesten estas preguntas sobre la crítica culinaria de **La feria del maíz**.

1. ¿Quién es el dueño y chef de **La feria del maíz**?
   Ernesto Sandoval
2. ¿Qué tipo de comida se sirve en el restaurante?
   tradicional
3. ¿Cuál es el problema con el servicio?
   Se necesitan más camareros.
4. ¿Cómo es el ambiente del restaurante?
   agradable
5. ¿Qué comidas probó el autor? las tortillas, el ajiaceite, la sopa de mariscos, los tamales, los tacos de pollo y los plátanos caribeños
6. ¿Quieren ir ustedes al restaurante **La feria del maíz**? ¿Por qué? Answers will vary.

Gastronomía
Por Eduardo Fernández

23F

La feria del maíz

Sobresaliente°. En el nuevo restaurante **La feria del maíz** va a encontrar la perfecta combinación entre la comida tradicional y el encanto° de la vieja ciudad de Antigua. Ernesto Sandoval, antiguo jefe de cocina° del famoso restaurante **El fogón**, está teniendo mucho éxito° en su nueva aventura culinaria.

El gerente°, el experimentado José Sierra, controla a la perfección la calidad del servicio. El camarero que me atendió esa noche fue muy amable en todo momento. Sólo hay que comentar que,

La feria del maíz
13 calle 4-41 Zona 1
La Antigua, Guatemala
2329912

lunes a sábado
10:30am-11:30pm
domingo 10:00am-10:00pm

Comida ♟♟♟♟♟

Servicio ♟♟♟

Ambiente ♟♟♟♟

Precio ♟♟♟

debido al éxito inmediato de **La feria del maíz**, se necesitan más camareros para atender a los clientes de una forma más eficaz. En esta ocasión, el mesero se tomó unos veinte minutos

en traerme la bebida.

Afortunadamente, no me importó mucho la espera entre plato y plato, pues el ambiente es tan agradable que me sentí como en casa. El restaurante mantiene el estilo colonial de Antigua. Por dentro°, el estilo es elegante y rústico a la vez. Cuando el tiempo lo permite, se puede comer también en el patio, donde hay muchas flores.

El servicio de camareros y el ambiente agradable del local pasan a un segundo plano cuando llega la comida, de una calidad extraordinaria. Las tortillas de casa se sirven con un ajiaceite delicioso. La sopa

de mariscos es excelente, y los tamales, pues, tengo que confesar que son mejores que los de mi abuelita. También recomiendo los tacos de pollo, servidos con un mole buenísimo. De postre, don Ernesto me preparó su especialidad, unos plátanos caribeños sabrosísimos.

Los precios pueden parecer altos° para una comida tradicional, pero la calidad de los productos con que se cocinan los platos y el exquisito ambiente de **La feria del maíz** le garantizan° una experiencia inolvidable°.

Bebidas
- Cerveza negra • Chilate (bebida de maíz, chile y cacao)
- Jugos de fruta • Agua mineral • Té helado
- Vino tinto/blanco • Ron

Postres *Desserts* ron *rum* Helado *Ice cream* Pastel *Cake* Sobresaliente *Outstanding* encanto *charm* jefe de cocina *head chef* éxito *success* gerente *manager* Por dentro *Inside* altos *high* garantizan *guarantee* inolvidable *unforgettable*

Preguntas
- Have students quickly review the article before answering the questions. Suggest that pairs take turns answering them. The student who does not answer a question should find the line of text that contains the answer.
- Give students these questions as items 7–9: **7. ¿Cómo fue el camarero que atendió al crítico? (Fue muy amable, pero estaba muy ocupado con otros clientes del restaurante.) 8. ¿Cuál fue la opinión del crítico con respecto a la comida? (La encontró toda de una extraordinaria calidad.) 9. ¿Cómo son los precios de La feria del maíz? (Son altos, pero la calidad de la comida garantiza una experiencia inolvidable.)**

Un(a) guía turístico/a

Tú eres un(a) guía turístico/a en Guatemala. Estás en el restaurante **La feria del maíz** con un grupo de turistas norteamericanos. Ellos no hablan español y quieren pedir de comer, pero necesitan tu ayuda. Lee nuevamente el menú e indica qué error comete cada turista.

1. La señora Johnson es diabética y no puede comer azúcar. Pide sopa de verdura y tamales. No pide nada de postre.
   No debe pedir los tamales porque tienen azúcar.
2. Los señores Petit son vegeterianos y piden sopa de tomate, frijoles enchilados y plátanos caribeños.
   No deben pedir los frijoles enchilados porque tienen carne.

3. El señor Smith, que es alérgico al chocolate, pide tortilla servida con ajiaceite, chilaquil y chilate para beber.
   No debe pedir chilate porque tiene cacao.
4. La adorable hija del señor Smith tiene sólo cuatro años y le gustan mucho las verduras y las frutas naturales. Su papá le pide tomaticán y un cóctel de frutas.
   No debe pedir el cóctel de frutas porque tiene ron.
5. La señorita Jackson está a dieta y pide uvate, flan napolitano y helado.
   No debe pedir postres porque está a dieta.

Un(a) guía turístico/a Ask pairs to work together to check the menu and state why each customer should not order the item(s) he or she has selected.

The Affective Dimension Unfamiliar foods can be source of discomfort in travel. Tell students that by learning about the foods of a country they are going to visit they can make that part of their visit even more enjoyable.

TEACHING OPTIONS

Large Groups Ask students to review the items in **Un(a) guía turístico/a**, write a conversation, and role-play the scene involving a tour guide eating lunch in a Guatemalan restaurant with several tourists. Have them work in groups of eight to assign the following roles: **camarero, guía turístico/a, la señora Johnson, los señores Petit, el señor Smith, la hija del señor Smith**, and **la señorita Jackson.** Have groups perform their skits for the class.

Variación léxica Tell students that the adjective of place or nationality for Guatemala is **guatemalteco/a**. Guatemalans often use a more colloquial term, **chapín**, as a synonym for **guatemalteco/a**.

Escritura

Estrategia

Expressing and supporting opinions

Written reviews are just one of the many kinds of writing which require you to state your opinions. In order to convince your reader to take your opinions seriously, it is important to support them as thoroughly as possible. Details, facts, examples, and other forms of evidence are necessary. In a restaurant review, for example, it is not enough just to rate the food, service, and atmosphere. Readers will want details about the dishes you ordered, the kind of service you received, and the type of atmosphere you encountered. If you were writing a concert or album review, what kinds of details might your readers expect to find?

It is easier to include details that support your opinions if you plan ahead. Before going to a place or event that you are planning to review, write a list of questions that your readers might ask. Decide which aspects of the experience you are going to rate and list the details that will help you decide upon a rating. You can then organize these lists into a questionnaire and a rating sheet. Bring these forms with you to help you make your opinions and to remind you of the kinds of information you need to gather in order to support those opinions. Later, these forms will help you organize your review into logical categories. They can also provide the details and other evidence you need to convince your readers of your opinions.

Tema

Escribir una crítica

Escribe una crítica culinaria° sobre un restaurante local para el periódico de la escuela. Clasifica el restaurante, dándole de una a cinco estrellas°, y anota tus recomendaciones para futuros clientes del restaurante. Incluye tus opiniones acerca de°:

▶ La comida
  ¿Qué tipo de comida es? ¿Qué tipo de ingredientes usan? ¿Es de buena calidad? ¿Cuál es el mejor plato? ¿Y el peor? ¿Quién es el/la chef?

▶ El servicio
  ¿Es necesario esperar mucho para conseguir una mesa? ¿Tienen los camareros un buen conocimiento del menú? ¿Atienden° a los clientes con rapidez° y cortesía?

▶ El ambiente
  ¿Cómo es la decoración del restaurante? ¿Es el ambiente informal o elegante? ¿Hay música o algún tipo de entretenimiento°? ¿Hay un balcón? ¿Un patio?

▶ Información práctica
  ¿Cómo son los precios? ¿Se aceptan tarjetas de crédito? ¿Cuál es la dirección° y el número de teléfono? ¿Quién es el/la dueño/a? ¿El/La gerente?

crítica culinaria *restaurant review*   estrellas *stars*
acerca de *about*   Atienden *They take care of*   rapidez *speed*
entretenimiento *entertainment*   dirección *address*

EVALUATION: Crítica culinaria

Criteria	Scale
Content	1 2 3 4 5
Organization	1 2 3 4 5
Use of details to support opinions	1 2 3 4 5
Accuracy	1 2 3 4 5

Scoring	
Excellent	18–20 points
Good	14–17 points
Satisfactory	10–13 points
Unsatisfactory	< 10 points

Adelante 291

Escuchar

Estrategia

Jotting down notes as you listen

Jotting down notes while you listen to a conversation in Spanish can help you keep track of the important points or details. It will help you to focus actively on comprehension rather than on remembering what you have heard.

 To practice this strategy, you will now listen to a paragraph. Jot down the main points you hear.

Preparación

Según la foto, ¿quién es Ramón Acevedo? ¿Sobre qué crees que va a hablar?

Ahora escucha

Ahora escucha a Ramón Acevedo. Toma apuntes de las instrucciones que él da en los espacios en blanco.

Ingredientes del relleno°

carne de cerdo _____

ajo _____

papas _____

zanahorias _____

aceite _____

pimienta _____

consomé _____

Poner dentro del° pavo

sal _____

pimienta _____

relleno _____

Instrucciones para cocinar°

untarlo° con ___margarina___

cubrir° con ___papel___ de aluminio

poner en el horno° a ___325___ grados

por ___cuatro___ horas

relleno *filling*   dentro del *inside of*   cocinar *to cook*
untarlo *rub it*   cubrir *cover*   horno *oven*

En Guatemala, el pavo relleno es un plato popular para celebrar la Navidad y el Año Nuevo.

Comprensión

Seleccionar

Usa tus apuntes para seleccionar la opción correcta para completar cada oración.

1. Ramón Acevedo prepara un menú ideal para ___c___.
   a. una familia de tres personas   b. una chica y su novio
   c. una familia de once
2. Este plato es perfecto para la persona a la que le gustan ___b___.
   a. los mariscos y la langosta
   b. la carne de cerdo y las papas
   c. los espárragos y los frijoles
3. Este plato es ideal para el/la cocinero/a que ___a___.
   a. tiene mucho tiempo   b. tiene mucha prisa
   c. no tiene horno

Preguntas

En grupos de tres o cuatro, respondan a las preguntas.
Answers will vary.

1. ¿Es similar el plato que prepara Ramón Acevedo a algún plato que ustedes comen? ¿En qué es similar? ¿En qué es distinto?
2. Escriban una variación de la receta de Ramón Acevedo. Usen ingredientes interesantes. ¿Es mejor su receta que la del señor Acevedo? ¿Por qué?

recursos

descubre1.vhlcentral.com
Lección 8

pavo. Tenemos que lavarlo bien. Le ponemos sal y pimienta por dentro y le ponemos el relleno. Hay que ponerle sal y pimienta por fuera, untarlo con margarina y cubrirlo con papel de aluminio. Ya estamos listos para ponerlo en el horno a 325 grados por unas 4 horas, más o menos. Les

recomiendo un vino blanco para acompañar este plato. ¡Delicioso! Regresaremos en unos minutos después de los siguientes anuncios importantes. ¡No se vayan! Vamos a preparar unas sabrosas verduras en escabeche.

(Script continues at far left in the bottom panels.)

Section Goals

In **En pantalla**, students will:
- read about fresh foods in Spain and Latin America
- watch a television commercial for **Bocatta**, a Spanish sandwich shop chain

---

Instructional Resource
Supersite: *En pantalla*
Transcript & Translation

Introduction
To check comprehension, ask:
1. ¿Por qué usan los hispanos productos frescos más que alimentos en lata o frasco? (Los países hispanos tienen una producción muy abundante de frutas y verduras.) 2. ¿Por qué se debe preparar el gazpacho con ingredientes frescos? (Para que mantenga su sabor auténtico.)

Antes de ver
- Ask students if they like to prepare food. If so, are fresh ingredients a must?
- Have students read the title and the video captions and predict what type of food this commercial is advertising.
- Assure students that they do not need to understand every word they hear. Tell them to rely on visuals and words from **Vocabulario útil**.

Ordenar To challenge students, do not provide a list of words. Have them write down the people and food items they hear and see in the commercial.

Test Ask additional questions, such as: **¿Es importante probar nuevas comidas? ¿Qué importancia tiene la comida en la cultura de un país? ¿Qué opinan de la comida en este país? ¿Hay comidas tradicionales de nuestro país que pueden parecer "exóticas" para gente de otros países?**

En pantalla

España y la mayoría de los países de Latinoamérica tienen una producción muy abundante de frutas y verduras. Es por esto que en los hogares° hispanos se acostumbra° cocinar° con productos frescos° más que con alimentos° que vienen en latas° o frascos°. Las salsas mexicanas, el gazpacho español y el sancocho colombiano, por ejemplo, deben prepararse con ingredientes frescos para que mantengan° su sabor° auténtico.

Vocabulario útil	
Toma	Take this
aborrecido	loathed
por eso	that's why
recetas	recipes
únicas	unique
nunca has probado	you have never tasted
así	like that

Ordenar
Pon en orden lo que ves en el anuncio de televisión. No vas a usar dos elementos.

  6   a. sándwiches   2   e. abuelo
  4   b. nieto   ∅   f. pescado
  ∅   c. sal y pimienta   1   g. perro
  3   d. queso   5   h. tomates

Test
Responde a las preguntas. Después comparte tus respuestas con dos o tres compañeros/as para saber quién es el/la más arriesgado/a (*daring*). Answers will vary.
1. ¿Cuál es tu plato favorito?
2. ¿Cuál es el plato más exótico que has probado (*that you have tried*)? ¿Te gustó o no?
3. ¿Qué plato exótico te gustaría (*would you like*) probar?
4. ¿Qué plato no quieres probar nunca? ¿Por qué?

hogares *homes* se acostumbra *it is customary* cocinar *to cook* frescos *fresh* alimentos *foods* latas *cans* frascos *jars* para que mantengan *so that they keep* sabor *flavor* Lo he hecho yo *I have made it myself* necesitaba renovarse *needed to renew itself*

Anuncio de Bocatta

Lo he hecho yo°,

como mi abuelo me enseñó.

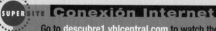

El queso necesitaba renovarse°.

recursos

descubre1.vhlcentral.com
Lección 8

Conexión Internet
Go to descubre1.vhlcentral.com to watch the TV clip featured in this **En pantalla** section.

TEACHING OPTIONS

Small Groups Play *Iron Chef:* **La clase de español**. Divide the class into groups of four. Unveil the **ingrediente secreto** (Ex: **papas**) and tell students they have five minutes to create an original recipe featuring this key ingredient. Then have groups read their recipes for the class, who will vote for their favorite one.

Cultural Comparison Have students work in pairs to compare a cooking website from Spain or Latin America with one from the U.S. or Canada. Have them consider the types of foods and format of the recipes.

Oye cómo va

Shery

Shery es una joven cantautora° guatemalteca° quien inició su camino° como artista desde muy pequeña. Ella y sus hermanos tenían° como pasatiempos cantar, bailar, aprenderse todas las canciones de la radio y hacer coreografías. Desde junio de 2005, cuando dio° su concierto debut como solista, logró° un éxito° fenomenal en su país natal. Su primer sencillo° *El amor es un fantasma*° logró mantenerse durante veintiséis semanas consecutivas entre las cuarenta canciones más escuchadas en Guatemala, un récord para una artista local. Este sencillo ganó premios° en la Competencia Internacional de Composición Unisong y en la Olimpiada Mundial de las Artes Escénicas, en Los Ángeles. Su primer álbum, que se llama igual° a su sencillo, salió a la venta° a principios° de 2007.

Tu profesor(a) va a poner la canción en la clase. Escúchala y completa las actividades.

Preguntas
Responde a las preguntas.
1. ¿Cuándo comenzó Shery a interesarse por la música? desde muy joven
2. ¿Cuándo hizo su primera presentación como solista? en 2005
3. ¿Cómo se llama su primer álbum? El amor es un fantasma
4. ¿Qué artista guatemalteco tiene más visitas que Shery en MySpace? Ricardo Arjona

La canción
En parejas, respondan a las preguntas. Answers will vary.
1. ¿De qué habla la canción?
2. ¿Creen que las palabras de la canción reflejan (*reflect*) experiencias de la vida personal de Shery?
3. ¿Con qué pueden comparar el amor?
4. ¿Les gustan las canciones de amor? ¿Por qué?
5. ¿Usan Internet para leer sobre nuevos artistas? ¿A qué artistas conocieron por ese medio?

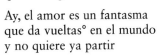

El amor es un fantasma

Ay, el amor es un fantasma,
que desgarra° mi destino,
que se niega° a morir

Ay, el amor es un fantasma
que da vueltas° en el mundo
y no quiere ya partir

Es mi herida° y cicatriz°.

Artistas hispanos en Internet
Muchos artistas hispanos tienen sus propios sitios de Internet y también cuentan con° páginas en portales° como MySpace. Estos espacios les dan la posibilidad de compartir su música con sus admiradores de forma directa. En 2006, Shery fue la segunda artista guatemalteca con más visitas en MySpace, después de Ricardo Arjona, otro famoso cantautor originario de Antigua, Guatemala.

Ricardo Arjona

recursos

descubre1.vhlcentral.com
Lección 8

SUPERSITE Conexión Internet
Go to **descubre1.vhlcentral.com** to learn more about the artist featured in this **Oye cómo va** section.

cantautora *singer-songwriter* guatemalteca *Guatemalan* camino *path* tenían *had* dio *gave* logró *she achieved* éxito *success* sencillo *single* fantasma *ghost* premios *awards* igual *the same* salió a la venta *was released* a principios *at the beginning* desgarra *tears apart* niega *refuses* da vueltas *wanders* herida *wound* cicatriz *scar* cuentan con *have* portales *sites*

Section Goals
In **Oye cómo va**, students will:
• read about **Shery**
• read about another Spanish-speaking artist who uses the Internet to promote his music
• listen to a song by **Shery**

Instructional Resources
Supersite
Vista Higher Learning *Cancionero*

Antes de escuchar
• Ask students to predict what type of song this is based on the lyrics.
• Have students read the chorus and say whether they think the artist has predominantly positive or negative views about love.

Preguntas Give students these questions as items 5–7:
5. De niños, ¿qué pasatiempos tenían Shery y sus hermanos? (cantar, bailar, aprender canciones de la radio) 6. ¿Qué éxito tuvo el primer sencillo de Shery? (Durante 26 semanas consecutivas logró mantenerse entre las cuarenta canciones más escuchadas.) 7. ¿Cuándo salió a la venta su primer álbum? (2007)

La canción Ask additional discussion questions. Ex: **¿Les gustan las canciones de amor más que las canciones sobre otros temas? ¿Quién creen que es el/la cantante hispano/a más conocido/a hoy día?**

TEACHING OPTIONS

Extra Practice Ask students to imagine that they are immigrants from a Spanish-speaking country who have recently arrived in your community. Have them draft a letter to a friend or family member back home, describing their new life in comparison with their old one. Encourage them to describe the music available here and to use as many comparatives and superlatives as they can.

Small Groups If time and resources permit, divide the class into small groups and assign each group another love song from the Spanish-speaking world. Tell them to discuss the singers' attitudes and to consider how they are reflected in the music and lyrics. Then hold a class discussion in which groups compare their songs with those of other groups.

Guatemala

NATIONAL STANDARDS connections cultures

El país en cifras

▶ **Área:** 108.890 km² (42.042 millas²), *un poco más pequeño que Tennessee*

▶ **Población:** 14.213.000

▶ **Capital:** Ciudad de Guatemala—1.103.000

▶ **Ciudades principales:** Quetzaltenango, Escuintla, Mazatenango, Puerto Barrios

SOURCE: Population Division, UN Secretariat

▶ **Moneda:** quetzal

▶ **Idiomas:** español (oficial), lenguas mayas

El español es la lengua de un 60 por ciento° de la población; el otro 40 por ciento tiene una de las lenguas mayas (cakchiquel, quiché y kekchícomo, entre otras) como lengua materna. Una palabra que las lenguas mayas tienen en común es ixim, que significa maíz, un cultivo° de mucha importancia en estas culturas.

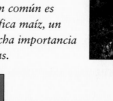
Bandera de Guatemala

Guatemaltecos célebres

▶ **Carlos Mérida,** pintor (1891–1984)

▶ **Miguel Ángel Asturias,** escritor (1899–1974)

▶ **Margarita Carrera,** poeta y ensayista (1929–)

▶ **Rigoberta Menchú Tum,** activista (1959–), premio Nobel de la Paz° en 1992

por ciento *percent* cultivo *crop* Paz *Peace* telas *fabrics* tinte *dye* aplastados *crushed* hace... destiñan *keeps the colors from running*

Vista de una calle céntrica e la Ciudad de Guatemala

ESTADOS UNIDOS
OCÉANO ATLÁNTICO
GUATEMALA
OCÉANO PACÍFICO
AMÉRICA DEL SUR

MÉXICO
Sierra de Lacandón
Río Usumacinta
Lago Petén Itzá
Río de la Pasión

Mujeres indígenas limpiando cebollas

Sierra Madre
Quetzaltenango
Lago de Atitlán
Lago de Izabal
Sierra de las Minas
Río Mot

★ Guatemala
Antigua Guatemala
Mazatenango

Iglesia de la Merced en Antigua Guatemala
EL SALVADOR

Escuintla

Océano Pacífico

recursos

| CP pp. 95–96 | CA pp. 83–84 | descubre1.vhlcentral.com Lección 8 |

¡Increíble pero cierto!

¿Qué ingrediente secreto se encuentra en las telas° tradicionales de Guatemala? ¡El mosquito! El excepcional tinte° de estas telas es producto de una combinación de flores y de mosquitos aplastados°. El insecto hace que los colores no se destiñan°. Quizás es por esto que los artesanos representan la figura del mosquito en muchas de sus telas.

TEACHING OPTIONS

Worth Noting Although the indigenous population of Guatemala is Mayan, many place names in southwestern Guatemala are in Nahuatl, the language of the Aztecs of central Mexico. In the sixteenth century, Guatemala was conquered by Spaniards who came from the Valley of Mexico after having overthrown the Aztec rulers there. The Spanish were accompanied by large numbers of Nahuatl-speaking allies, who renamed the captured Mayan strongholds with Nahuatl names. The suffix **–tenango,** which appears in many of these names, means *place with a wall,* that is, a fortified place. **Quetzaltenango,** then, means *fortified place of the quetzal bird;* **Mazatenango** means *fortified place of the deer.*

Section Goal

In **Panorama**, students will read about the geography, history, and culture of Guatemala.

Instructional Resources
Cuaderno de práctica, pp. 95–96
Cuaderno de actividades, pp. 83–84
e-Cuaderno
Supersite/DVD: *Panorama cultural*
Supersite/TRCD: *PowerPoints* (Overheads #3, #4, #35); *Panorama cultural* Videoscript & Translation, Answer Keys

Teaching Tip Have students use the map in their books or show *Overhead PowerPoint #35.* Point out that Guatemala has three main climatic regions: the tropical Pacific and Caribbean coasts, the highlands (southwest), and jungle lowlands (north). Ask volunteers to read aloud the names of the cities, mountains, and rivers of Guatemala. Point out that indigenous languages are the source of many place names.

El país en cifras As you read about the languages of Guatemala, you might point out that while some Guatemalans are monolingual in either Spanish or a Mayan language, many are bilingual, speaking an indigenous language and Spanish.

¡Increíble pero cierto! Guatemala is internationally renowned for the wealth and diversity of its textile arts. Each village has a traditional, "signature" weaving style that allows others to quickly identify where each beautiful piece comes from.

Ciudades • **Antigua Guatemala**

Antigua Guatemala fue fundada en 1543. Fue una capital de gran importancia hasta 1773, cuando un terremoto° la destruyó. Sin embargo, conserva el carácter original de su arquitectura y hoy es uno de los centros turísticos del país. Su celebración de la Semana Santa° es, para muchas personas, la más importante del hemisferio. (hemisphere)

Naturaleza • **El quetzal**

El quetzal simbolizó la libertad para los antiguos° mayas porque creían° que este pájaro° no podía° vivir en cautividad°. Hoy el quetzal es el símbolo nacional. El pájaro da su nombre a la moneda nacional y aparece también en los billetes° del país. Desafortunadamente, está en peligro° de extinción. Para su protección, el gobierno mantiene una reserva biológica especial.

Historia • **Los mayas**

Desde 1500 a.C., hasta 900 d.C., los mayas habitaron gran parte de lo que ahora es Guatemala. Su civilización fue muy avanzada. Los mayas fueron arquitectos y constructores de pirámides, templos y observatorios. También descubrieron° y usaron el cero antes que los europeos, e inventaron un calendario complejo° y preciso.

Artesanía • **La ropa tradicional**

La ropa tradicional de los guatemaltecos se llama *huipil* y muestra el amor° de la cultura maya por la naturaleza. Ellos se inspiran en las flores°, plantas y animales para crear sus diseños° de colores vivos° y formas geométricas. El diseño y los colores de cada *huipil* indican el pueblo de origen y a veces también el sexo y la edad° de la persona que lo lleva.

¿Qué aprendiste? Responde a cada pregunta con una oración completa.

1. ¿Qué significa la palabra *ixim*?
La palabra *ixim* significa maíz.
2. ¿Quién es Rigoberta Menchú?
Rigoberta Menchú es una activista de Guatemala.
3. ¿Qué pájaro representa a Guatemala?
El quetzal representa a Guatemala.
4. ¿Qué simbolizó el quetzal para los mayas?
El quetzal simbolizó la libertad para los mayas.
5. ¿Cuál es la moneda nacional de Guatemala?
La moneda nacional de Guatemala es el quetzal.
6. ¿De qué fueron arquitectos los mayas?
Los mayas fueron arquitectos de pirámides, templos y observatorios.
7. ¿Qué celebración de la Antigua Guatemala es la más importante del hemisferio para muchas personas? La celebración de la Semana Santa de la Antigua Guatemala es la más importante del hemisferio.
8. ¿Qué descubrieron los mayas antes que los europeos? Los mayas descubrieron el cero antes que los europeos.
9. ¿Qué muestra la ropa tradicional de los guatemaltecos? La ropa muestra el amor por la naturaleza.
10. ¿Qué indica un *huipil* con su diseño y sus colores? Con su diseño y colores, un *huipil* indica el pueblo de origen, el sexo y la edad de la persona.

 Conexión Internet Investiga estos temas en **descubre1.vhlcentral.com.**

1. Busca información sobre Rigoberta Menchú. ¿De dónde es? ¿Qué libros publicó? ¿Por qué es famosa?
2. Estudia un sitio arqueológico en Guatemala para aprender más sobre los mayas y prepara un breve informe para tu clase.

terremoto *earthquake* Semana Santa *Holy Week* antiguos *ancient* creían *they believed* pájaro *bird* no podía *couldn't* cautividad *captivity* los billetes *bills* peligro *danger* descubrieron *they discovered* complejo *complex* amor *love* flores *flowers* diseños *designs* vivos *bright* edad *age*

Mar Caribe

o de duras

URAS

Antigua Guatemala Students can use tour books and the Internet to learn more about **Semana Santa** celebrations in this Guatemalan city, usually referred to simply as Antigua. Also, you may want to play the *Panorama cultural* video footage for this lesson that focuses on Antigua and Chichicastenango.

El quetzal Recent conservation efforts in Guatemala, Costa Rica, and other Central American nations have focused on preserving the cloud forests (**bosques nubosos**) that are home to the **quetzal**.

Los mayas Today ethnobotanists work with Mayan traditional healers to learn about medicinal uses of plants of the region.

La ropa tradicional Many indigenous Guatemalans still wear traditional clothing richly decorated with embroidery. The **huipil** is a long, sleeveless tunic worn by women. A distinctively woven **faja**, or waist sash, identifies the town or village each woman comes from.

Conexión Internet Students will find supporting Internet activities and links at **descubre1.vhlcentral.com.**

Instructional Resources
Cuaderno de actividades, p. 134
e-Cuaderno
Supersite: Textbook, &
Vocabulary MP3 Audio Files
Supersite/TRCD: Answer Keys;
Testing Program (**Lección 8
Pruebas**, Test Generator, Testing
Program MP3 Audio Files);
Textbook, Test Audio CD

Las comidas

el/la camarero/a	waiter/waitress
la comida	food; meal
el/la dueño/a	owner; landlord
el menú	menu
la sección de (no) fumar	(non) smoking section
el almuerzo	lunch
la cena	dinner
el desayuno	breakfast
los entremeses	hors d'oeuvres; appetizers
el plato (principal)	(main) dish
delicioso/a	delicious
rico/a	tasty; delicious
sabroso/a	tasty; delicious

Las frutas

la banana	banana
las frutas	fruits
el limón	lemon
la manzana	apple
el melocotón	peach
la naranja	orange
la pera	pear
la uva	grape

Las verduras

las arvejas	peas
la cebolla	onion
el champiñón	mushroom
la ensalada	salad
los espárragos	asparagus
los frijoles	beans
la lechuga	lettuce
el maíz	corn
las papas/patatas (fritas)	(fried) potatoes; French fries
el tomate	tomato
las verduras	vegetables
la zanahoria	carrot

La carne y el pescado

el atún	tuna
el bistec	steak
los camarones	shrimp
la carne	meat
la carne de res	beef
la chuleta (de cerdo)	(pork) chop
la hamburguesa	hamburger
el jamón	ham
la langosta	lobster
los mariscos	shellfish
el pavo	turkey
el pescado	fish
el pollo (asado)	(roast) chicken
la salchicha	sausage
el salmón	salmon

Otras comidas

el aceite	oil
el ajo	garlic
el arroz	rice
el azúcar	sugar
los cereales	cereal; grains
el huevo	egg
la mantequilla	butter
la margarina	margarine
la mayonesa	mayonnaise
el pan (tostado)	(toasted) bread
la pimienta	black pepper
el queso	cheese
la sal	salt
el sándwich	sandwich
la sopa	soup
el vinagre	vinegar
el yogur	yogurt

Las bebidas

el agua (mineral)	(mineral) water
la bebida	drink
el café	coffee
la cerveza	beer
el jugo (de fruta)	(fruit) juice
la leche	milk
el refresco	soft drink
el té (helado)	(iced) tea
el vino (blanco/ tinto)	(white/red) wine

Verbos

escoger	to choose
merendar (e:ie)	to snack
morir (o:ue)	to die
pedir (e:i)	to order (food)
probar (o:ue)	to taste; to try
recomendar (e:ie)	to recommend
saber	to taste; to know
saber a	to taste like
servir (e:i)	to serve

Las comparaciones

como	like; as
más de (+ number)	more than
más... que	more ... than
menos de (+ number)	fewer than
menos... que	less ... than
tan... como	as ... as
tantos/as... como	as many... as
tanto... como	as much... as
el/la mayor	the eldest
el/la mejor	the best
el/la menor	the youngest
el/la peor	the worst
mejor	better
peor	worse

Expresiones útiles	See page 269.

recursos

CA p. 134 | descubre1.vhlcentral.com Lección 8

Las fiestas

9

Communicative Goals

You will learn how to:

- **Express congratulations**
- **Express gratitude**
- **Ask for and pay the bill at a restaurant**

Lesson Goals

In **Lección 9**, students will be introduced to the following:
- terms for parties and celebrations
- words for stages of life and interpersonal relations
- **Semana Santa** celebrations
- Chile's **Festival de Viña del Mar**
- irregular preterites
- verbs that change meaning in the preterite
- uses of **¿qué?** and **¿cuál?**
- pronouns after prepositions
- recognizing word families
- using a Venn diagram to organize information
- writing a comparative analysis
- using context to infer the meaning of unfamiliar words
- a television commercial for **Energizer**
- Chilean singer **Myriam Hernández**
- cultural, geographic, and economic information about Chile

A primera vista Here are some additional questions you can ask based on the photo: **¿Fuiste a una fiesta importante el año pasado? ¿Cuál fue la ocasión? ¿Sirvieron comida en la fiesta? ¿Qué sirvieron? En tu opinión, ¿qué fiestas son las más divertidas? ¿Por qué?**

A PRIMERA VISTA

- **¿Se conocen ellas?**
- **¿Cómo se sienten, alegres o tristes?**
- **¿Está una de las chicas más contenta que la otra?**
- **¿De qué color es su ropa, marrón o negra?**

Las fiestas

Más vocabulario

la alegría	happiness
la amistad	friendship
el amor	love
el beso	kiss
la sorpresa	surprise
el aniversario (de bodas)	(wedding) anniversary
la boda	wedding
el cumpleaños	birthday
el día de fiesta	holiday
el divorcio	divorce
el matrimonio	marriage
la Navidad	Christmas
el/la recién casado/a	newlywed
la quinceañera	young woman's fifteenth birthday celebration
cambiar (de)	to change
celebrar	to celebrate
divertirse (e:ie)	to have fun
graduarse (de/en)	to graduate (from/in)
invitar	to invite
jubilarse	to retire (from work)
nacer	to be born
odiar	to hate
pasarlo bien/mal	to have a good/bad time
reírse (e:i)	to laugh
relajarse	to relax
sorprender	to surprise
sonreír (e:i)	to smile
juntos/as	together

Variación léxica

pastel ⟷ torta (*Arg., Venez.*)
comprometerse ⟷ prometerse (*Esp.*)

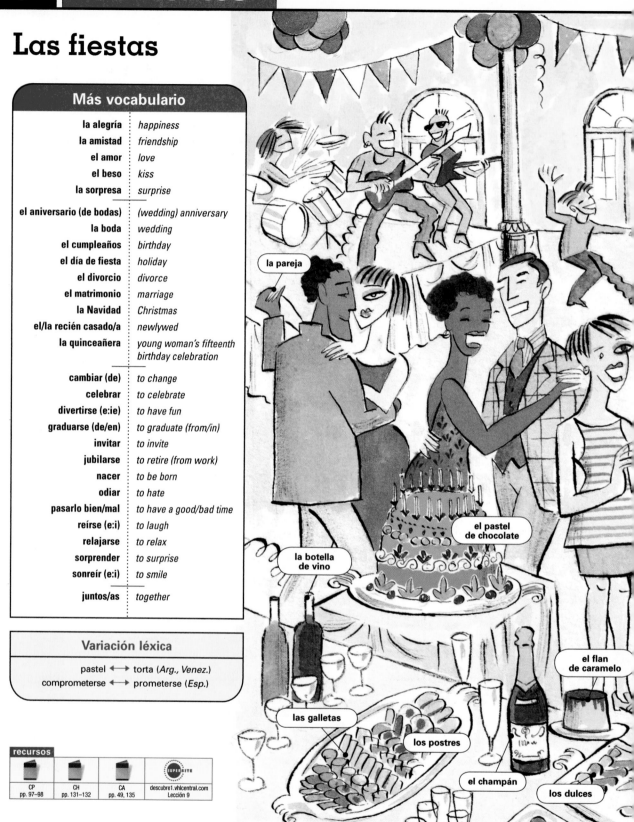

la pareja

el pastel de chocolate

la botella de vino

el flan de caramelo

las galletas

los postres

el champán

los dulces

Práctica

1 **Escuchar** Escucha la conversación e indica si las oraciones son ciertas o falsas.

1. A Silvia no le gusta mucho el chocolate. Falsa.
2. Silvia sabe que sus amigos le van a hacer una fiesta. Falsa.
3. Los amigos de Silvia le compraron un pastel de chocolate. Cierta.
4. Los amigos brindan por Silvia con refrescos. Falsa.
5. Silvia y sus amigos van a comer helado. Cierta.
6. Los amigos de Silvia le van a servir flan y galletas. Falsa.

2 **Ordenar** Escucha la narración y ordena las oraciones de acuerdo con los eventos de la vida de Beatriz.

<u>5</u> a. Beatriz se compromete con Roberto.

<u>4</u> b. Beatriz se gradúa.

<u>3</u> c. Beatriz sale con Emilio.

<u>2</u> d. Sus padres le hacen una gran fiesta.

<u>6</u> e. La pareja se casa.

<u>1</u> f. Beatriz nace en Montevideo.

3 **Emparejar** Indica la letra de la frase que mejor completa cada oración.

a. **cambió de**	d. **nos divertimos**	g. **se llevan bien**
b. **lo pasaron mal**	e. **se casaron**	h. **sonrió**
c. **nació**	f. **se jubiló**	i. **tenemos una cita**

1. María y sus compañeras de clase <u>g</u>. Son buenas amigas.
2. Pablo y yo <u>d</u> en la fiesta. Bailamos y comimos mucho.
3. Manuel y Felipe <u>b</u> en el cine. La película fue muy mala.
4. ¡Tengo una nueva sobrina! Ella <u>c</u> ayer por la mañana.
5. Mi madre <u>a</u> profesión. Ahora es artista.
6. Mi padre <u>f</u> el año pasado. Ahora no trabaja.
7. Jorge y yo <u>i</u> esta noche. Vamos a ir a un restaurante muy elegante.
8. Jaime y Laura <u>e</u> el septiembre pasado. La boda fue maravillosa.

4 **Definiciones** En parejas, definan las palabras y escriban una oración para cada ejemplo. Answers will vary.

modelo

romper (con) una pareja termina la relación
Marta rompió con su novio.

1. regalar — dar un regalo
2. helado — una comida fría y dulce
3. pareja — dos personas enamoradas
4. invitado — una persona que va a una fiesta
5. casarse — ellos deciden estar juntos para siempre
6. pasarlo bien — divertirse
7. sorpresa — la persona no sabe lo que va a pasar
8. quinceañera — la fiesta de cumpleaños de una chica de 15 años

Relaciones personales

casarse (con)	to get married (to)
comprometerse (con)	to get engaged (to)
divorciarse (de)	to get divorced (from)
enamorarse (de)	to fall in love (with)
llevarse bien/mal (con)	to get along well/badly (with)
romper (con)	to break up (with)
salir (con)	to go out (with); to date
separarse (de)	to separate (from)
tener una cita	to have a date; to have an appointment

brindar

el invitado

el helado

---

1 Teaching Tip Have students check their answers by going over **Actividad 1** with the class.

1 Script E1: ¿Estamos listos, amigos? E2: Creo que sí. Aquí tenemos el pastel y el helado… E3: De chocolate, espero. Ustedes saben cómo le encanta a Silvia el chocolate… E2: Por supuesto, el chocolate para Silvia. Bueno, un pastel de chocolate, el helado…
Script continues on page 302.

2 Teaching Tip Before listening, point out that although the items are in the present tense, students will hear a mix of present indicative and preterite in the audio.

2 Script Beatriz García nace en Montevideo, Uruguay. Siempre celebra su cumpleaños con pastel y helado. Para su cumpleaños número veinte, sus padres la sorprendieron y le organizaron una gran fiesta. Beatriz se divirtió muchísimo y conoció a Emilio, un chico muy simpático. Después de varias citas, Beatriz rompió con Emilio porque no fueron compatibles. Luego de dos años Beatriz conoció a Roberto en su fiesta de graduación y se enamoraron. En Navidad se comprometieron y celebraron su matrimonio un año más tarde, al que asistieron más de cien invitados. Los recién casados son muy felices juntos y ya están planeando otra gran fiesta para celebrar su primer aniversario de bodas. *Textbook Audio*

3 Expansion Have students write three cloze sentences based on the drawing on pages 300–301 for a partner to complete.

4 Expansion Ask students questions using verbs from the **Relaciones personales** box. Ex: **¿Con quién te llevas mal?**

TEACHING OPTIONS

Heritage Speakers Ask heritage speakers about some Hispanic holidays or other celebrations that they or their families typically celebrate, such as **el Día de los Reyes Magos, el día del santo, la quinceañera, el Cinco de Mayo,** and **el Día de los Muertos.** Ask speakers to elaborate on what the celebrations are like: who attends, what they eat and drink, why those days are celebrated, and so forth.

Game Play **Concentración**. Write vocabulary items that pertain to parties and celebrations on each of eight cards. On another eight cards, draw or paste a picture that matches each description. Place the cards facedown in four rows of four. In pairs, students select two cards. If the two cards match, the pair keeps them. If the two cards do not match, students replace them in their original position. The pair with the most cards at the end wins.

Las etapas de la vida de Sergio

el nacimiento

la niñez

la adolescencia

la juventud

la madurez

la vejez

Más vocabulario	
la edad	age
el estado civil	marital status
las etapas de la vida	the stages of life
la muerte	death
casado/a	married
divorciado/a	divorced
separado/a	separated
soltero/a	single
viudo/a	widower/widow

5 **Las etapas de la vida** Identifica las etapas de la vida que se describen en estas oraciones.

1. Mi abuela se jubiló y se mudó (*moved*) a Viña del Mar. la vejez
2. Mi padre trabaja para una compañía grande en Santiago. la madurez
3. ¿Viste a mi nuevo sobrino en el hospital? Es precioso y ¡tan pequeño! el nacimiento
4. Mi abuelo murió este año. la muerte
5. Mi hermana se enamoró de un chico nuevo en la escuela. la adolescencia
6. Mi hermana pequeña juega con muñecas (*dolls*). la niñez

6 **Cambiar** Tu hermano/a menor no entiende nada de las etapas de la vida y las relaciones personales. En parejas, túrnense para decir que las afirmaciones son falsas y corríjanlas (*correct them*), cambiando las expresiones subrayadas (*underlined*).

> **modelo**
> **Estudiante 1:** La <u>niñez</u> es cuando trabajamos mucho.
> **Estudiante 2:** No, *te equivocas (you're wrong)*. La madurez es cuando trabajamos mucho.

1. <u>El nacimiento</u> es el fin de la vida. La muerte
2. <u>La juventud</u> es la etapa cuando nos jubilamos. La vejez
3. A los sesenta y cinco años, muchas personas <u>comienzan a trabajar.</u> se jubilan
4. Julián y nuestra prima <u>se divorcian</u> mañana. se casan
5. Mamá <u>odia</u> a su hermana. quiere / se lleva bien con
6. El abuelo murió, por eso la abuela es <u>separada</u>. viuda
7. Cuando te gradúas de la universidad, estás en la etapa de <u>la adolescencia</u>. la juventud
8. Mi tío nunca se casó; es <u>viudo</u>. soltero

Comunicación

7 **Una cena especial** Planea con dos compañeros/as una cena para celebrar la graduación de tu hermano/a mayor de la escuela secundaria. Recuerda incluir la siguiente información. Answers will vary.

1. ¿Qué tipo de cena es? ¿Dónde va a ser? ¿Cuándo va a ser?
2. ¿A cuántas personas piensan invitar? ¿A quiénes van a invitar?
3. ¿Van a pedir un menú especial? ¿Qué van a comer?
4. ¿Cuánto dinero piensan gastar? ¿Cómo van a compartir los gastos?
5. ¿Qué van a hacer todos durante la fiesta?

recursos

CA
p. 49

8 **Encuesta** Tu profesor(a) va a darte una hoja. Haz las preguntas de la hoja a dos o tres compañeros/as de clase para saber qué actitudes tienen en sus relaciones personales. Luego comparte los resultados de la encuesta con la clase y comenta tus conclusiones.
Answers will vary.

Preguntas	Nombres	Actitudes
1. ¿Te importa la amistad? ¿Por qué?		
2. ¿Es mejor tener un(a) buen(a) amigo/a o muchos/as amigos/as?		
3. ¿Cuáles son las características que buscas en tus amigos/as?		
4. ¿Tienes novio/a? ¿A qué edad es posible enamorarse?		
5. ¿Deben las parejas hacer todo juntos? ¿Deben tener las mismas opiniones? ¿Por qué?		

¡LENGUA VIVA!

While a **buen(a) amigo/a** is a *good friend*, the term **amigo/a íntimo/a** refers to a *close friend*, or a very good friend, without any romantic overtones.

9 **Minidrama** En parejas, consulten la ilustración en la página 302, y luego, usando las palabras de la lista, preparen un minidrama para representar las etapas de la vida de Sergio. Pueden ser creativos e inventar más información sobre su vida. Answers will vary.

amor	celebrar	enamorarse	romper
boda	comprometerse	graduarse	salir
cambiar	cumpleaños	jubilarse	separarse
casarse	divorciarse	nacer	tener una cita

¡Feliz cumpleaños, Maite!

Don Francisco y los estudiantes celebran el cumpleaños de Maite en el restaurante El Cráter.

PERSONAJES

 MAITE

 INÉS

 DON FRANCISCO

 ÁLEX

 JAVIER

 DOÑA RITA

 CAMARERO

INÉS A mí me encantan los dulces. Maite, ¿tú qué vas a pedir?

MAITE Ay, no sé. Todo parece tan delicioso. Quizás el pastel de chocolate.

JAVIER Para mí el pastel de chocolate con helado. Me encanta el chocolate. Y tú, Álex, ¿qué vas a pedir?

ÁLEX Generalmente prefiero la fruta, pero hoy creo que voy a probar el pastel de chocolate.

DON FRANCISCO Yo siempre tomo un flan y un café.

DOÑA RITA ¡Feliz cumpleaños, Maite!

INÉS ¿Hoy es tu cumpleaños, Maite?

MAITE Sí, el 22 de junio. Y parece que vamos a celebrarlo.

TODOS MENOS MAITE ¡Felicidades!

ÁLEX Yo también acabo de cumplir los veintitrés años.

MAITE ¿Cuándo?

ÁLEX El cuatro de mayo.

DOÑA RITA Aquí tienen un flan, pastel de chocolate con helado... y una botella de vino para dar alegría.

MAITE ¡Qué sorpresa! ¡No sé qué decir! Muchísimas gracias.

DON FRANCISCO El conductor no puede tomar vino. Doña Rita, gracias por todo. ¿Puede traernos la cuenta?

DOÑA RITA Enseguida, Paco.

recursos

CA pp. 67–68

descubre1.vhlcentral.com Lección 9

Section Goals

In **Fotonovela**, students will:
• receive comprehensible input from free-flowing discourse
• learn functional phrases that preview lesson grammatical structures

Instructional Resources
Cuaderno de actividades,
pp. 67–68
e-Cuaderno
Supersite/DVD: *Fotonovela*
Supersite/TRCD: *Fotonovela*
Videoscript & Translation,
Answer Keys

Video Recap: Lección 8
Before doing this **Fotonovela** section, review the previous one with this activity.
1. ¿Quién es doña Rita Perales? (la dueña del restaurante El Cráter) 2. ¿Qué platos sirven en El Cráter? (tortillas de maíz, caldo de patas, lomo a la plancha, ceviche, fuente de fritada, pasteles) 3. ¿Qué opinión tienen los estudiantes de la comida? (Es riquísima.) 4. ¿Cuál es la ocasión especial ese día? (el cumpleaños de Maite)

Video Synopsis While the travelers are looking at the dessert menu, **Doña Rita** and the waiter bring in some flan, a cake, and some wine to celebrate **Maite's** birthday. The group leaves **Doña Rita** a nice tip, thanks her, and says goodbye.

Teaching Tip Have students read the first line of dialogue in each caption and guess what happens in this episode.

TEACHING OPTIONS

¡Feliz cumpleaños, Maite! Ask students to brainstorm a list of things that might happen during a surprise birthday party. Then play the **¡Feliz cumpleaños, Maite!** episode once, asking students to take notes about what they see and hear. After viewing, have students use their notes to tell you what happened in this episode. Then play the segment again to allow students to refine their notes. Repeat the discussion process and guide the class to an accurate summary of the plot.

Teaching Tip Go through the **Fotonovela**, asking volunteers to read the various parts.

MAITE ¡Gracias! Pero, ¿quién le dijo que es mi cumpleaños?

DOÑA RITA Lo supe por don Francisco.

ÁLEX Ayer te lo pregunté, ¡y no quisiste decírmelo! ¿Eh? ¡Qué mala eres!

JAVIER ¿Cuántos años cumples?

MAITE Veintitrés.

INÉS Creo que debemos dejar una buena propina. ¿Qué les parece?

MAITE Sí, vamos a darle una buena propina a la señora Perales. Es simpatiquísima.

DON FRANCISCO Gracias una vez más. Siempre lo paso muy bien aquí.

MAITE Muchísimas gracias, señora Perales. Por la comida, por la sorpresa y por ser tan amable con nosotros.

Expresiones útiles

Celebrating a birthday party

- **¡Feliz cumpleaños!**
  Happy birthday!
- **¡Felicidades!/¡Felicitaciones!**
  Congratulations!

- **¿Quién le dijo que es mi cumpleaños?**
  Who told you (form.) *that it's my birthday?*
  Lo supe por don Francisco.
  I found out through Don Francisco.

- **¿Cuántos años cumples/ cumple Ud.?**
  How old are you now?
  Veintitrés.
  Twenty-three.

Asking for and getting the bill

- **¿Puede traernos la cuenta?**
  Can you bring us the bill?
- **La cuenta, por favor.**
  The bill, please.
  Enseguida, señor/señora/señorita.
  Right away, sir/ma'am/miss.

Expressing gratitude

- **¡(Muchas) gracias!**
  Thank you (very much)!
- **Muchísimas gracias.**
  Thank you very, very much.
- **Gracias por todo.**
  Thanks for everything.
- **Gracias una vez más.**
  Thanks again. (lit. Thanks one more time.)

Leaving a tip

- **Creo que debemos dejar una buena propina. ¿Qué les parece?**
  I think we should leave a good tip. What do you guys think?
  Sí, vamos a darle/dejarle una buena propina.
  Yes, let's give her/leave her a good tip.

Expresiones útiles Draw attention to the forms **dijo** and **supe**. Explain that these are irregular preterite forms of the verbs **decir** and **saber**. Point out the phrase **no quisiste decírmelo** under video still 5 of the **Fotonovela**. Explain that **quisiste** is an irregular preterite form of the verb **querer**. Tell the class that **no querer** in the preterite means *to refuse*. Tell students that they will learn more about these concepts in **Estructura**.

TEACHING OPTIONS

Pairs Have pairs research birthday traditions from the Spanish-speaking world on the Internet. They may research traditional gifts, songs, superstitions, decorations, **quinceañeras,** or other significant features of birthdays. Have pairs create a short presentation for the class. Encourage them to bring in photos and other visuals.

Game Divide the class into two teams, A and B. Give a member from team A a card with the name of an item from the **Fotonovela** or **Expresiones útiles** (Ex: **helado, propina**). He or she has thirty seconds to draw the item, while team A has to guess what it is. Award one point per correct answer. If team A cannot guess the item within the time limit, team B may try to "steal" the point.

306 Teacher's Annotated Edition • Lesson Nine

¿Qué pasó? SUPERSITE

1 Completar Completa las oraciones con la información correcta, según la **Fotonovela**.

1. De postre, don Francisco siempre pide ___un café y un flan___.
2. A Javier le encanta ___el chocolate___.
3. Álex cumplió los ___veintitrés___ años ___el cuatro de mayo___.
4. Hoy Álex quiere tomar algo diferente. De postre, quiere pedir ___un pastel de chocolate___.
5. Los estudiantes le van a dejar ___una buena propina___ a doña Rita.

2 Identificar Identifica quién puede decir estas oraciones.

1. Gracias, doña Rita, pero no puedo tomar vino. don Francisco
2. ¡Qué simpática es doña Rita! Fue tan amable conmigo. Maite
3. A mí me encantan los dulces y los pasteles, ¡especialmente si son de chocolate! Javier
4. Mi amigo acaba de informarme que hoy es el cumpleaños de Maite. doña Rita
5. ¿Tienen algún postre de fruta? Los postres de fruta son los mejores. Álex
6. Me parece una buena idea dejarle una buena propina a la dueña. ¿Qué piensan ustedes? Inés

JAVIER   **ÁLEX**

INÉS   **MAITE**
DON FRANCISCO   **DOÑA RITA**

NOTA CULTURAL

En los países hispanos los camareros no dependen tanto de **las propinas** como en los EE.UU. Por eso, en estos países no es común dejar propina, pero siempre es buena idea dejar una buena propina cuando el grupo es grande o el servicio es excepcional.

3 Seleccionar Selecciona algunas de las opciones de la lista para completar las oraciones.

el amor	la cuenta	la galleta	la quinceañera
el beso	día de fiesta	pedir	¡Qué sorpresa!
celebrar	el divorcio	un postre	una sorpresa

1. Maite no sabe que van a celebrar su cumpleaños porque es ___una sorpresa___.
2. Después de una cena o un almuerzo, es normal pedir ___un postre/la cuenta___.
3. Inés y Maite no saben exactamente lo que van a ___pedir___ de postre.
4. Después de comer en un restaurante, tienes que pagar ___la cuenta___.
5. Una pareja de enamorados nunca piensa en ___el divorcio___.
6. Hoy no trabajamos porque es un ___día de fiesta___.

CONSULTA

En algunos países hispanos, el cumpleaños número quince de una chica se celebra haciendo una **quinceañera**. Ésta es una fiesta en su honor y en la que es "presentada" a la sociedad. Para conocer más sobre este tema, ve a **Lectura**, p. 323.

4 Un cumpleaños Trabajen en grupos para representar una conversación en la que uno/a de ustedes está celebrando su cumpleaños en un restaurante.

- Una persona le desea feliz cumpleaños a su compañero/a y le pregunta cuántos años cumple.
- Cada persona del grupo le pide al/a la camarero/a un postre y algo de beber.
- Después de terminar los postres, una persona pide la cuenta.
- Otra persona habla de dejar una propina.
- El amigo que no cumple años dice que quiere pagar la cuenta.
- El/La que cumple años les da las gracias por todo.

Sidebar (left column)

1 Expansion Have students work in pairs or small groups and write questions that would have elicited these statements.

2 Teaching Tip Before doing this activity, ask these questions: **¿A quién le gusta mucho la fruta?** (a Álex) **¿A quién le gusta muchísimo el chocolate?** (a Javier) **¿Quién no puede tomar vino?** (don Francisco)

2 Expansion Give these sentences to students as items 7–8: **7. ¡No lo puedo creer! ¿Pastel de chocolate y flan para mí?** (Maite) **8. ¿Mi cumpleaños? Es el cuatro de mayo.** (Álex)

3 Teaching Tip Before doing this activity, have the class review the vocabulary on pages 300–301.

3 Expansion Have pairs create additional sentences with the leftover items from the word bank.

4 Possible Conversation
E1: ¡Feliz cumpleaños! ¿Cuántos años cumples hoy?
E2: ¡Muchas gracias! Cumplo dieciséis.
E3: Buenas noches. ¿En qué les puedo servir?
E1: Quisiera el pastel de chocolate y un café, por favor.
E2: Voy a pedir un pastel de chocolate con helado, y de tomar, un café.
[LATER...]
E1: Señorita, ¿puede traernos la cuenta?
E3: Enseguida, señor.
E2: La camarera fue muy amable. Debemos dejarle una buena propina, ¿no crees?
E1: Sí. Y yo quiero pagar la cuenta, porque es tu cumpleaños.
E2: Gracias por todo...

TEACHING OPTIONS

Extra Practice Ask a group of volunteers to ad-lib the **Fotonovela** episode for the class. Assure them that it is not necessary to memorize the episode or stick strictly to its content. They should try to get the general meaning across with the vocabulary and expressions they know, and they should also feel free to be creative.

Pairs Have students work in pairs to tell each other about celebrations in their families. Remind them to use as many expressions as possible from the **Expresiones útiles** on page 305, as well as the vocabulary on pages 300–301. Follow up by asking a few students to describe celebrations in their partners' families.

Pronunciación

The letters h, j, and g

helado	**h**ombre	**h**ola	**h**ermosa

The Spanish **h** is always silent.

José	**j**ubilarse	de**j**ar	pare**j**a

The letter **j** is pronounced much like the English *h* in *his*.

a**g**encia	**g**eneral	**G**il	**G**isela

The letter **g** can be pronounced three different ways. Before **e** or **i**, the letter **g** is pronounced much like the English *h*.

Gustavo, **g**racias por llamar el domin**g**o.

At the beginning of a phrase or after the letter **n**, the Spanish **g** is pronounced like the English *g* in *girl*.

Me **g**radué en a**g**osto.

In any other position, the Spanish **g** has a somewhat softer sound.

Guerra	conse**gui**r	**gua**ntes	a**gua**

In the combinations **gue** and **gui**, the **g** has a hard sound and the **u** is silent. In the combination **gua**, the **g** has a hard sound and the **u** is pronounced like the English *w*.

Práctica Lee las palabras en voz alta, prestando atención a la **h**, la **j** y la **g**.

1. hamburguesa	5. geografía	9. seguir	13. Jorge
2. jugar	6. magnífico	10. gracias	14. tengo
3. oreja	7. espejo	11. hijo	15. ahora
4. guapa	8. hago	12. galleta	16. guantes

Oraciones Lee las oraciones en voz alta, prestando atención a la **h**, la **j** y la **g**.

1. Hola. Me llamo Gustavo Hinojosa Lugones y vivo en Santiago de Chile.
2. Tengo una familia grande; somos tres hermanos y tres hermanas.
3. Voy a graduarme en mayo.
4. Para celebrar mi graduación mis padres van a regalarme un viaje a Egipto.
5. ¡Qué generosos son!

Refranes Lee los refranes en voz alta, prestando atención a la **h**, la **j** y la **g**.

A la larga, lo más dulce amarga.[1]

El hábito no hace al monje.[2]

1 Too much of a good thing. 2 The clothes don't make the man.

recursos		
CH p. 133	CA p. 136	descubre1.vhlcentral.com Lección 9

Section Goal

In **Pronunciación**, students will be introduced to the pronunciation of **h**, **j**, and **g**.

Instructional Resources
Cuaderno para hispanohablantes, p. 133
Cuaderno de actividades, p. 136
e-Cuaderno
Supersite: Textbook & Audio Activity MP3 Audio Files
Lección 9
Supersite/TRCD: Textbook Audio Script; Audio Activity Script, Answer Keys
Textbook & Audio Activity CD

Teaching Tips
- Ask the class how the Spanish **h** is pronounced. Ask volunteers to pronounce the example words. Contrast the pronunciations of the English *hotel* and the Spanish **hotel**.
- Explain that **j** is pronounced much like the English *h*.
- Draw attention to the fact that the letter **g** is pronounced like the English *h* before **e** or **i**. Write the example words on the board and ask volunteers to pronounce them.
- Point out that the letter **g** is pronounced like the English *g* in *good* at the beginning of a phrase or after the letter **n**.
- Tell the class that in the combinations **gue** and **gui**, **g** has a hard sound and **u** is not pronounced. Explain that in the combinations **gua** and **guo**, the **u** sounds like the English *w*.

Práctica/Oraciones/Refranes
These exercises are recorded in the *Textbook Audio*. You may want to play the audio so that students practice the pronunciation point by listening to Spanish spoken by speakers other than yourself.

TEACHING OPTIONS

Extra Practice Write the names of these Chilean cities on the board and ask for a volunteer to pronounce each one: **Santiago, Antofagasta, Rancagua, Coihaique.** Repeat the process with the names of these Chilean writers: **Alberto Blest Gana, Vicente Huidobro, Gabriela Mistral, Juan Modesto Castro.**

Pairs Have students work in pairs to read aloud the sentences in **Actividad 2, Identificar**, page 306. Encourage students to help their partners if they have trouble pronouncing a particular word.

EN DETALLE

Semana Santa: vacaciones y tradición

¿Te imaginas pasar veinticuatro horas tocando un tambor° entre miles de personas? Así es como mucha gente celebra el Viernes Santo° en el pequeño pueblo de **Calanda**, España. De todas las celebraciones hispanas, la **Semana Santa°** es una de las más espectaculares y únicas.

Procesión en Sevilla, España

Semana Santa es la semana antes de Pascua°, una celebración religiosa que conmemora la Pasión de Jesucristo. Generalmente, la gente tiene unos días de vacaciones en esta semana. Algunas personas aprovechan° estos días para viajar, pero otras prefieren participar en las tradicionales celebraciones religiosas en las calles. En **Antigua**, Guatemala, hacen alfombras° de flores° y altares; también organizan Vía Crucis° y danzas. En las famosas procesiones y desfiles° religiosos de **Sevilla**, España, los fieles°

sacan a las calles imágenes religiosas. Las imágenes van encima de plataformas ricamente decoradas con abundantes flores y velas°. En la procesión, los penitentes llevan túnicas y unos sombreros cónicos que les cubren° la cara°. En sus manos llevan faroles° o velas encendidas.

Si visitas algún país hispano durante la Semana Santa, debes asistir a un desfile. Las playas pueden esperar hasta la semana siguiente.

Alfombra de flores en Antigua, Guatemala

Otras celebraciones famosas
Ayacucho, Perú: Además de alfombras de flores y procesiones, aquí hay una antigua tradición llamada "quema de la chamiza"°.
Iztapalapa, Ciudad de México: Es famoso el Vía Crucis del cerro° de la Estrella. Es una representación del recorrido° de Jesucristo con la cruz°.
Popayán, Colombia: En las procesiones "chiquitas" los niños llevan imágenes que son copias pequeñas de las que llevan los mayores.

tocando un tambor *playing a drum* Viernes Santo *Good Friday* Semana Santa *Holy Week* Pascua *Easter Sunday* aprovechan *take advantage of* alfombras *carpets* flores *flowers* Vía Crucis *Stations of the Cross* desfiles *parades* fieles *faithful* velas *candles* cubren *cover* cara *face* faroles *lamps* quema de la chamiza *burning of brushwood* cerro *hill* recorrido *route* cruz *cross*

ACTIVIDADES

1 **¿Cierto o falso?** Indica si lo que dicen estas oraciones es cierto o falso. Corrige la información falsa.

1. La Semana Santa se celebra después de Pascua. **Falso.** La Semana Santa es la semana antes de Pascua.
2. En los países hispanos, las personas tienen días libres durante la Semana Santa. **Cierto.**
3. En los países hispanos, todas las personas asisten a las celebraciones religiosas. **Falso.** Algunas personas aprovechan estos días para viajar.
4. En los países hispanos, las celebraciones se hacen en las calles. **Cierto.**
5. El Vía Crucis de Iztapalapa es en el interior de una iglesia. **Falso.** Es en el cerro de la Estrella.
6. En Antigua y en Ayacucho es típico hacer alfombras de flores en Semana Santa. **Cierto.**
7. Las procesiones "chiquitas" son famosas en Sevilla, España. **Falso.** Son famosas en Popayán, Colombia.
8. En Sevilla, sacan imágenes religiosas a las calles. **Cierto.**

ASÍ SE DICE
Fiestas y celebraciones

la despedida de soltero/a	*bachelor(ette) party*
el día feriado/festivo	el día de fiesta
disfrutar	*to enjoy*
festejar	celebrar
los fuegos artificiales	*fireworks*
pasarlo en grande	divertirse mucho
la vela	*candle*

EL MUNDO HISPANO
Celebraciones latinoamericanas

○ **Oruro, Bolivia** Durante el carnaval de Oruro se realiza la famosa Diablada, una antigua danza° que muestra la lucha° entre el bien y el mal: ángeles contra° demonios.

○ **Panchimalco, El Salvador** La primera semana de mayo, Panchimalco se cubre de flores y de color. También hacen el Desfile de las palmas° y bailan danzas antiguas.

○ **Quito, Ecuador** El mes de agosto es el Mes de las Artes. Danza, teatro, música, cine, artesanías° y otros eventos culturales inundan la ciudad.

○ **San Pedro Sula, Honduras** En junio se celebra la Feria Juniana. Hay comida típica, bailes, desfiles, conciertos, rodeos, exposiciones ganaderas° y eventos deportivos y culturales.

134 danza *dance* lucha *fight* contra *versus* palmas *palm leaves* artesanías *handcrafts* exposiciones ganaderas *cattle shows*

PERFIL
Festival de Viña del Mar

En 1959 unos estudiantes de **Viña del Mar,** Chile, celebraron una fiesta en una casa de campo conocida como la Quinta Vergara donde hubo° un espectáculo° musical. En 1960 repitieron el evento. Asistió tanta gente que muchos vieron el espectáculo parados° o sentados en el suelo°. Algunos se subieron a los árboles°.

Años después, se convirtió en el **Festival Internacional de la Canción**. Este evento se celebra en febrero, en el mismo lugar donde empezó. ¡Pero ahora nadie necesita subirse a un árbol para verlo! Hay un anfiteatro con capacidad para quince mil personas.

En el festival hay concursos° musicales y conciertos de artistas famosos como Daddy Yankee y Paulina Rubio.

Daddy Yankee

hubo *there was* espectáculo *show* parados *standing* suelo *floor* se subieron a los árboles *climbed trees* concursos *competitions*

SUPERSITE Conexión Internet

¿Qué celebraciones hispanas hay en los Estados Unidos y en Canadá?

Go to descubre1.vhlcentral.com to find more cultural information related to this **Cultura** section.

ACTIVIDADES

2 Comprensión Responde a las preguntas.
1. ¿Cuántas personas pueden asistir al Festival de Viña del Mar hoy día? quince mil
2. ¿Qué es la Diablada? Es una antigua danza que muestra la lucha entre el bien y el mal.
3. ¿Qué celebran en Quito en agosto? Celebran el Mes de las Artes.
4. Nombra dos atracciones en la Feria Juniana de San Pedro Sula. Answers will vary.
5. ¿Qué es la Quinta Vergara? una casa de campo donde empezó el Festival de Viña del Mar

3 ¿Cuál es tu celebración favorita? Escribe un pequeño párrafo sobre la celebración que más te gusta de tu comunidad. Explica cómo se llama, cuándo ocurre y cómo es. Answers will vary.

recursos

CH p. 134 | descubre1.vhlcentral.com Lección 9

Section Goal

In **Estructura 9.1**, students will be introduced to the irregular preterites of several common verbs.

Instructional Resources
Cuaderno de práctica,
pp. 99–100
*Cuaderno para
hispanohablantes,* pp. 135–138
Cuaderno de actividades,
pp. 50, 137
e-Cuaderno
Supersite: Audio Activity MP3
Audio Files
Supersite/TRCD/Print:
PowerPoints (Lección 9
Estructura Presentation);
Communication Activities, Audio
Activity Script, Answer Keys
Audio Activity CD

Teaching Tips

• Quickly review the present tense of a stem-changing verb such as **pedir**. Write the paradigm on the board and ask volunteers to point out the stem-changing forms.

• Work through the preterite paradigms of **tener**, **venir**, and **decir**, modeling the pronunciation.

• Add a visual aspect to this grammar presentation. Use magazine pictures to ask about social events in the past. Ex: **¿Con quién vino este chico a la fiesta? (Vino con esa chica rubia.) ¿Qué se puso esta señora para ir a la boda? (Se puso un sombrero.)**

• Write the preterite paradigm for **estar** on the board. Then erase the initial **es-** for each form and point out that the preterite of **estar** and **tener** are identical except for the initial **es-**.

9.1 Irregular preterites [SUPERSITE]

ANTE TODO You already know that the verbs **ir** and **ser** are irregular in the preterite. You will now learn other verbs whose preterite forms are also irregular.

		tener (u-stem)	venir (i-stem)	decir (j-stem)
SINGULAR FORMS	yo	tuve	vine	dije
	tú	tuviste	viniste	dijiste
	Ud./él/ella	tuvo	vino	dijo
PLURAL FORMS	nosotros/as	tuvimos	vinimos	dijimos
	vosotros/as	tuvisteis	vinisteis	dijisteis
	Uds./ellos/ellas	tuvieron	vinieron	dijeron

*Preterite of **tener**, **venir**, and **decir***

▶ **¡Atención!** The endings of these verbs are the regular preterite endings of **–er/–ir** verbs, except for the **yo** and **usted** forms. Note that these two endings are unaccented.

▶ These verbs observe similar stem changes to **tener, venir,** and **decir**.

INFINITIVE	U-STEM	PRETERITE FORMS
poder	pud-	pude, pudiste, pudo, pudimos, pudisteis, pudieron
poner	pus-	puse, pusiste, puso, pusimos, pusisteis, pusieron
saber	sup-	supe, supiste, supo, supimos, supisteis, supieron
estar	estuv-	estuve, estuviste, estuvo, estuvimos, estuvisteis, estuvieron

INFINITIVE	I-STEM	PRETERITE FORMS
querer	quis-	quise, quisiste, quiso, quisimos, quisisteis, quisieron
hacer	hic-	hice, hiciste, hizo, hicimos, hicisteis, hicieron

INFINITIVE	J-STEM	PRETERITE FORMS
traer	traj-	traje, trajiste, trajo, trajimos, trajisteis, trajeron
conducir	conduj-	conduje, condujiste, condujo, condujimos, condujisteis, condujeron
traducir	traduj-	traduje, tradujiste, tradujo, tradujimos, tradujisteis, tradujeron

▶ **¡Atención!** Most verbs that end in **–cir** are **j**-stem verbs in the preterite. For example, **producir → produje, produjiste,** etc.

> **Produjimos** un documental sobre los accidentes en la casa.
> *We produced a documentary about accidents in the home.*

▶ Notice that the preterites with **j**-stems omit the letter **i** in the **ustedes/ellos/ellas** form.

> Mis amigos **trajeron** comida a la fiesta.   Ellos **dijeron** la verdad.

The preterite of dar

	SINGULAR FORMS			PLURAL FORMS	
yo	d**i**		nosotros/as	d**imos**	
tú	d**iste**		vosotros/as	d**isteis**	
Ud./él/ella	d**io**		Uds./ellos/ellas	d**ieron**	

▶ The endings for **dar** are the same as the regular preterite endings for **–er** and **–ir** verbs, except that there are no accent marks.

La camarera me **dio** el menú.
The waitress gave me the menu.

Le **di** a Juan algunos consejos.
I gave Juan some advice.

Los invitados le **dieron** un regalo.
The guests gave him/her a gift.

Nosotros **dimos** una gran fiesta.
We gave a great party.

▶ The preterite of **hay** (*inf.* **haber**) is **hubo** (*there was; there were*).

Doña Rita les dio una botella de vino a los viajeros.

Hubo una fiesta en el restaurante El Cráter.

¡INTÉNTALO! Escribe la forma correcta del pretérito de cada verbo que está entre paréntesis.

1. (querer) tú _quisiste_
2. (decir) usted _dijo_
3. (hacer) nosotras _hicimos_
4. (traer) yo _traje_
5. (conducir) ellas _condujeron_
6. (estar) ella _estuvo_
7. (tener) tú _tuviste_
8. (dar) ella y yo _dimos_
9. (traducir) yo _traduje_
10. (haber) ayer _hubo_
11. (saber) usted _supo_
12. (poner) ellos _pusieron_
13. (venir) yo _vine_
14. (poder) tú _pudiste_
15. (querer) ustedes _quisieron_
16. (estar) nosotros _estuvimos_
17. (decir) tú _dijiste_
18. (saber) ellos _supieron_
19. (hacer) él _hizo_
20. (poner) yo _puse_
21. (traer) nosotras _trajimos_
22. (tener) yo _tuve_
23. (dar) tú _diste_
24. (poder) ustedes _pudieron_

Teaching Tips

- Use the preterite forms of all these verbs by talking about what you did in the recent past and then asking students questions that involve them in a conversation about what they did in the recent past. You may want to avoid the preterite of **poder, saber,** and **querer** for the moment. Ex: **El sábado pasado tuve que ir a la fiesta de cumpleaños de mi sobrina. Cumplió siete años. Le di un bonito regalo. ____, ¿tuviste que ir a una fiesta el sábado? ¿No? Pues, ¿qué hiciste el sábado?**

- Point out that **dar** has the same preterite endings as **ver**.

- Drill the preterite of **dar** by asking students about what they gave their family members for their last birthdays or other special occasion. Ex: **¿Qué le diste a tu hermano para su cumpleaños?** Then ask what other family members gave them. Ex: **¿Qué te dio tu padre? ¿Y tu madre?**

- In a dramatically offended tone, say: **Di una fiesta el sábado. Los invité a todos ustedes y ¡no vino nadie!** Complain about all the work you did to prepare for the party. Ex: **Limpié toda la casa, preparé tortilla española, fui al supermercado y compré refrescos, puse la mesa con platos bonitos, puse música salsa...** Then write **¿Por qué no viniste a mi fiesta?** and **Lo siento, profesor(a), no pude venir a su fiesta porque tuve que...** on the board and give students ten seconds to write a creative excuse. Have volunteers read their excuses aloud. Ex: **Lo siento, profesor, no pude venir a su fiesta porque tuve que lavarme el pelo.**

TEACHING OPTIONS

Video Show the *Fotonovela* again to give students more input containing irregular preterite forms. Stop the video where appropriate to discuss how certain verbs were used and to ask comprehension questions.

Extra Practice Have students write down six things they brought to class today. Then have them circulate around the room, asking other students if they also brought those items (**¿Trajiste tus llaves a clase hoy?**). When they find a student that answers **sí,** they ask that student to sign his or her name next to that item (**Firma aquí, por favor.**). Can students get signatures for all the items they brought to class?

Práctica SUPERSITE

1 Completar Completa estas oraciones con el pretérito de los verbos entre paréntesis.

1. El sábado ____hubo____ (haber) una fiesta sorpresa para Elsa en mi casa.
2. Sofía ____hizo____ (hacer) un pastel para la fiesta y Miguel ____trajo____ (traer) un flan.
3. Los amigos y parientes de Elsa ____vinieron____ (venir) y ____trajeron____ (traer) regalos.
4. El hermano de Elsa no ____vino____ (venir) porque ____tuvo____ (tener) que trabajar.
5. Su tía María Dolores tampoco ____pudo____ (poder) venir.
6. Cuando Elsa abrió la puerta, todos gritaron: "¡Feliz cumpleaños!" y su esposo le ____dio____ (dar) un beso.
7. Al final de la fiesta, todos ____dijeron____ (decir) que se divirtieron mucho.
8. La historia (*story*) le ____dio____ (dar) a Elsa tanta risa (*laughter*) que no ____pudo____ (poder) dejar de reírse (*stop laughing*) durante toda la noche.

2 Describir En parejas, usen verbos de la lista para describir lo que estas personas hicieron. Deben dar por lo menos dos oraciones por cada dibujo. Answers will vary.

dar	hacer	tener	traer
estar	poner	traducir	venir

1. el señor López

2. Norma

3. anoche nosotros

4. Roberto y Elena

Comunicación

3 **Preguntas** En parejas, túrnense para hacerse y responder a estas preguntas. Answers will vary.

1. ¿Fuiste a una fiesta de cumpleaños el año pasado? ¿De quién?
2. ¿Quiénes fueron a la fiesta?
3. ¿Quién condujo el auto?
4. ¿Cómo estuvo la fiesta?
5. ¿Quién llevó regalos, bebidas o comida? ¿Llevaste algo especial?
6. ¿Hubo comida? ¿Quién la hizo?
7. ¿Qué regalo diste tú? ¿Qué otros regalos dieron los invitados?
8. ¿Cuántos invitados hubo en la fiesta?
9. ¿Qué tipo de música hubo?
10. ¿Qué dijeron los invitados de la fiesta?

recursos
CA p. 50

4 **Encuesta** Tu profesor(a) va a darte una hoja de actividades. Para cada una de las actividades de la lista, encuentra a alguien que hizo esa actividad en el tiempo indicado. Answers will vary.

modelo

traer dulces a clase
Estudiante 1: ¿Trajiste dulces a clase?
Estudiante 2: Sí, traje galletas y helado a la fiesta del fin del semestre.

Actividades	Nombres
1. ponerse un disfraz (*costume*) de Halloween	
2. traer dulces a clase	
3. conducir su auto a clase	
4. estar en la biblioteca ayer	
5. dar un regalo a alguien ayer	
6. poder levantarse temprano esta mañana	
7. hacer un viaje a un país hispano en el verano	
8. tener una cita anoche	
9. ir a una fiesta el fin de semana pasado	
10. tener que trabajar el sábado pasado	

NOTA CULTURAL

Halloween es una fiesta que también se celebra en algunos países hispanos, como México, por su proximidad con los Estados Unidos, pero no es parte de la cultura hispana. El Día de todos los Santos (1 de noviembre) y el Día de los Muertos (2 de noviembre) sí son celebraciones muy arraigadas (*deeply rooted*) entre los hispanos.

Síntesis

5 **Conversación** En parejas, preparen una conversación en la que uno/a de ustedes va a visitar a su hermano/a para explicarle por qué no fue a su fiesta de graduación y para saber cómo estuvo la fiesta. Incluyan esta información en la conversación: Answers will vary.

- cuál fue el menú
- quiénes vinieron a la fiesta y quiénes no pudieron venir
- quiénes prepararon la comida o trajeron algo
- si él/ella tuvo que preparar algo
- lo que la gente hizo antes y después de comer
- cómo lo pasaron, bien o mal

3 Teaching Tip Instead of having students take turns, ask them to go through all the questions with their partners, writing down the information the partners give them. Later, have them write a third-person description about their partners' experiences.

3 Expansion To practice the formal register, call on different students to ask you the questions in the activity. Ex: **¿Fue usted a una fiesta de cumpleaños el año pasado? (Sí, fui a la fiesta de cumpleaños de Lisa.)**

4 Teaching Tip Distribute the Communication Activities worksheets. Point out that to get information, students must form questions using the **tú** forms of the infinitives. Ex: **¿Trajiste dulces a clase?**

4 Expansion Write items 1–10 on the board and ask for a show of hands for each item. Ex: **¿Quién trajo dulces a clase?** Write tally marks next to each item to find out which activity was the most popular.

5 Expansion Have pairs work in groups of four to write a paragraph combining the most interesting or unusual aspects of each pair's conversation. Ask a group representative to read the paragraph to the class, who will vote for the most creative or funniest paragraph.

TEACHING OPTIONS

Extra Practice Ask students to write a brief composition on the **Fotonovela** from this lesson. Students should write about where the characters went, what they did, who ordered what, what they said to each other, and so forth. (Note: Students should stick to completed actions in the past [preterite]. The use of the imperfect for narrating a story will not be presented until **Descubre,** Level 2.)

Large Groups Divide the class into two groups. Give each member of the first group a strip of paper with a question. Ex: **¿Quién me trajo el pastel de cumpleaños?** Give each member of the second group a strip of paper with the answer to that question. Ex: **Marta te lo trajo.** Students must find their partners.

Section Goal

In **Estructura 9.2**, students will be introduced to verbs that change meaning in the preterite tense.

Instructional Resources
Cuaderno de práctica, p. 101
Cuaderno para hispanohablantes, pp. 139–140
Cuaderno de actividades, p. 138
e-Cuaderno
Supersite: Audio Activity MP3 Audio Files
Supersite/TRCD/Print:
PowerPoints (**Lección 9** **Estructura** Presentation); Audio Activity Script, Answer Keys
Audio Activity CD

Teaching Tip
• Introduce the preterite of **conocer**. Say: **Ahora los conozco a ustedes muy bien. Pero me acuerdo del día en que los conocí. ¿Ustedes se acuerdan del día en que nos conocimos?** Ask volunteers to compare and contrast the meanings of **conocer** in your example.
• Stress the meaning of **poder** in the preterite by giving both affirmative (*to manage; to succeed*) and negative (*to try and fail*) examples. Ex: **Pude leer todas sus composiciones anoche, pero no pude leer las composiciones de la otra clase.**
• Stress the meaning of **querer** in the preterite by giving both affirmative (*to try*) and negative (*to refuse*) examples. Ex: **Quisimos ver una película el sábado, pero no quise ver ninguna película violenta.**

9.2 Verbs that change meaning in the preterite

ANTE TODO The verbs **conocer, saber, poder,** and **querer** change meanings when used in the preterite. Because of this, each of them corresponds to more than one verb in English, depending on its tense.

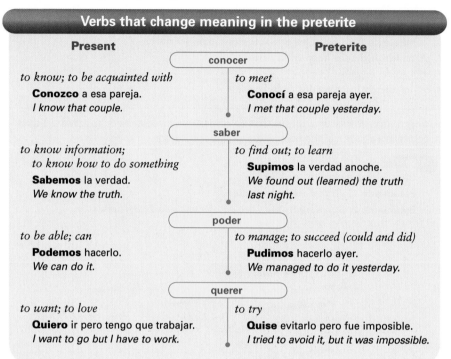

Verbs that change meaning in the preterite

Present	Preterite
conocer	
to know; to be acquainted with	*to meet*
Conozco a esa pareja.	**Conocí** a esa pareja ayer.
I know that couple.	*I met that couple yesterday.*
saber	
to know information; to know how to do something	*to find out; to learn*
	Supimos la verdad anoche.
Sabemos la verdad.	*We found out (learned) the truth*
We know the truth.	*last night.*
poder	
to be able; can	*to manage; to succeed (could and did)*
Podemos hacerlo.	**Pudimos** hacerlo ayer.
We can do it.	*We managed to do it yesterday.*
querer	
to want; to love	*to try*
Quiero ir pero tengo que trabajar.	**Quise** evitarlo pero fue imposible.
I want to go but I have to work.	*I tried to avoid it, but it was impossible.*

¡ATENCIÓN!

In the preterite, the verbs **poder** and **querer** have different meanings when they are used in affirmative or negative sentences.

pude *I succeeded*
no pude *I failed (to)*
quise *I tried (to)*
no quise *I refused (to)*

 **¡INTÉNTALO!** Elige la respuesta más lógica.

1. Yo no hice lo que me pidieron mis padres. ¡Tengo mis principios! a
   a. No quise hacerlo. b. No supe hacerlo.

2. Hablamos por primera vez con Nuria y Ana en la boda. a
   a. Las conocimos en la boda. b. Las supimos en la boda.

3. Por fin hablé con mi hermano después de llamarlo siete veces. b
   a. No quise hablar con él. b. Pude hablar con él.

4. Josefina se acostó para relajarse. Se durmió inmediatamente. a
   a. Pudo relajarse. b. No pudo relajarse.

5. Después de mucho buscar, encontraste la definición en el diccionario. b
   a. No supiste la respuesta. b. Supiste la respuesta.

6. Las chicas fueron a la fiesta. Cantaron y bailaron mucho. a
   a. Ellas pudieron divertirse. b. Ellas no supieron divertirse.

recursos

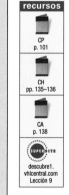

CP
p. 101

CH
pp. 135–136

CA
p. 138

descubre1.
vhlcentral.com
Lección 9

TEACHING OPTIONS

Extra Practice Prepare sentences using **conocer, saber, poder,** and **querer** in the present tense that will be logical when converted into the preterite. Have students convert them and explain how the meanings of the sentences change. Ex: **Sé la fecha de la fiesta. (Supe la fecha de la fiesta.)**

Heritage Speakers Ask heritage speakers to talk about one of these situations in the past: (1) when they found out there was no Santa Claus (**saber**), (2) when they met their best friend (**conocer**), or (3) something they tried to do but could not (**querer/no poder**). Verify student comprehension by asking other students to relate what was said.

Práctica

1 **Carlos y Eva** Forma oraciones con los siguientes elementos. Usa el pretérito y haz todos los cambios necesarios. Al final, inventa la razón del divorcio de Carlos y Eva.

1. anoche / mi esposa y yo / saber / que / Carlos y Eva / divorciarse
   Anoche mi esposa y yo supimos que Carlos y Eva se divorciaron.

▶ 2. los / conocer / viaje / isla de Pascua
   Los conocimos en un viaje a la isla de Pascua.

3. no / poder / hablar / mucho / con / ellos / ese día
   No pudimos hablar mucho con ellos ese día.

4. pero / ellos / ser / simpático / y / nosotros / hacer planes / vernos / con más / frecuencia
   Pero ellos fueron simpáticos y nosotros hicimos planes para vernos con más frecuencia.

5. yo / poder / encontrar / su / número / teléfono / páginas / amarillo
   Yo pude encontrar su número de teléfono en las páginas amarillas.

6. (yo) querer / llamar / les / ese día / pero / no / tener / tiempo
   Quise llamarles ese día pero no tuve tiempo.

7. cuando / los / llamar / nosotros / poder / hablar / Eva
   Cuando los llamé, nosotros pudimos hablar con Eva.

8. nosotros / saber / razón / divorcio / después / hablar / ella
   Nosotros supimos la razón del divorcio después de hablar con ella.

NOTA CULTURAL

La isla de Pascua es un remoto territorio chileno situado en el océano Pacífico Sur. Sus inmensas estatuas son uno de los mayores misterios del mundo: nadie sabe cómo o por qué se construyeron. Para más información, véase **Panorama**, p. 329.

2 **Completar** Completa estas frases de una manera lógica. Answers will vary.

1. Ayer mi compañero/a de clase supo…
2. Esta mañana no pude…
3. Conocí a mi mejor amigo/a en…
4. Mis padres no quisieron…
5. Mi mejor amigo/a no pudo…
6. Mi novio/a y yo nos conocimos en…
7. La semana pasada supe…
8. Ayer mis amigos quisieron…

Comunicación

3 **Telenovela** (*Soap opera*) En parejas, escriban el diálogo para una escena de una telenovela. La escena trata de una situación amorosa entre tres personas: Mirta, Daniel y Raúl. Usen el pretérito de **conocer, poder, querer** y **saber** en su diálogo. Answers will vary.

PASIÓN · SUSPENSO   AVENTURA · DECEPCIÓN
LA MUJER DOBLE

Síntesis

4 **Conversación** En una hoja de papel, escribe dos listas: las cosas que hiciste durante el fin de semana y las cosas que quisiste hacer pero no pudiste. Luego, compara tu lista con la de un(a) compañero/a, y expliquen por qué no pudieron hacer esas cosas. Answers will vary.

NATIONAL communication STANDARDS
NATIONAL communication STANDARDS

1 **Expansion**
• In pairs, students create five additional dehydrated sentences for their partner to complete, using the verbs **conocer, saber, poder,** and **querer.** After pairs have finished, ask volunteers to share some of their dehydrated sentences. Write them on the board and have the rest of the class "hydrate" them.
• To challenge students, have pairs use preterite forms of **conocer, saber, poder,** and **querer** to role-play **Carlos** and **Eva** explaining their separate versions of the divorce to their friends.

2 **Teaching Tip** Before assigning the activity, share with the class some recent things you found out, tried to do but could not, or the names of people you met, inviting students to respond.

3 **Teaching Tip** Point out that unlike their U.S. counterparts, Hispanic soap operas run for a limited period of time, like a miniseries.

4 **Expansion** Have pairs repeat the activity, this time describing another person. Ask students to share their descriptions with the class, who will guess the person being described.

TEACHING OPTIONS

Video Show the *Fotonovela* again to give students more input modeling verbs that change meaning in the preterite. Stop the video where appropriate to discuss how certain verbs were used and to ask comprehension questions.

Pairs In pairs, have students write three sentences using verbs that change meaning in the preterite. Two of the sentences should be true and the third should be false. Their partner has to guess which of the sentences is the false one.

Section Goals

In **Estructura 9.3**, students will review:
- the uses of **¿qué?** and **¿cuál?**
- interrogative words and phrases

Instructional Resources
Cuaderno de práctica, p. 102
Cuaderno para hispanohablantes, pp. 141–142
Cuaderno de actividades, pp. 45–46, 139
e-Cuaderno
Supersite: Audio Activity MP3 Audio Files
Supersite/TRCD/Print: *PowerPoints* (Lección 9 **Estructura** Presentation); Communication Activities, Audio Activity Script, Answer Keys
Audio Activity CD

Teaching Tips

- Review the question words **¿qué?** and **¿cuál?** Write incomplete questions on the board and ask students which interrogative word best completes each sentence.
- Point out that while both question words mean *what?* or *which?*, **¿qué?** is used with a noun, whereas **¿cuál?** is used with a verb. Ex: **¿Qué clase te gusta más? ¿Cuál es tu clase favorita?**
- Review the chart of interrogative words and phrases. Ask students personalized questions and invite them to ask you questions. Ex: **¿Cuál es tu película favorita?** (*Como agua para chocolate*) **¿Qué director es su favorito?** (Pedro Almodóvar)
- Give students pairs of questions and have them explain the difference in meaning. Ex: **¿Qué es tu número de teléfono? ¿Cuál es tu número de teléfono?** Emphasize that the first question would be asked by someone who has no idea what a phone number is (asking for a definition) and, in the second question, someone wants to know *which* number (out of all the phone numbers in the world) is yours.

9.3 ¿Qué? and ¿cuál? (SUPERSITE)

ANTE TODO You've already learned how to use interrogative words and phrases. As you know, **¿qué?** and **¿cuál?** or **¿cuáles?** mean *what?* or *which?* However, they are not interchangeable.

▶ **¿Qué?** is used to ask for a definition or an explanation.

¿Qué es el flan?	**¿Qué** estudias?
What is flan?	*What do you study?*

▶ **¿Cuál(es)?** is used when there is a choice among several possibilities.

¿Cuál de los dos prefieres, las galletas o el helado?	**¿Cuáles** son tus medias, las negras o las blancas?
Which of these (two) do you prefer, cookies or ice cream?	*Which ones are your socks, the black ones or the white ones?*

▶ **¿Cuál?** cannot be used before a noun; in this case, **¿qué?** is used.

¿Qué sorpresa te dieron tus amigos?	**¿Qué** colores te gustan?
What surprise did your friends give you?	*What colors do you like?*

▶ **¿Qué?** used before a noun has the same meaning as **¿cuál?**

¿Qué regalo te gusta?	**¿Qué dulces** quieren ustedes?
What (Which) gift do you like?	*What (Which) sweets do you want?*

Review of interrogative words and phrases

¿a qué hora?	at what time?		**¿cuánto/a?**	how much?
¿adónde?	(to) where?		**¿cuántos/as?**	how many?
¿cómo?	how?		**¿de dónde?**	from where?
¿cuál(es)?	what?; which?		**¿dónde?**	where?
¿cuándo?	when?		**¿qué?**	what?; which?
			¿quién(es)?	who?

¡INTÉNTALO! Completa las preguntas con **¿qué?** o **¿cuál(es)?**, según el contexto.

1. ¿ _Cuál_ de los dos te gusta más?
2. ¿ _Cuál_ es tu teléfono?
3. ¿ _Qué_ tipo de pastel pediste?
4. ¿ _Qué_ es una quinceañera?
5. ¿ _Qué_ haces ahora?
6. ¿ _Cuáles_ son tus platos favoritos?
7. ¿ _Qué_ bebidas te gustan más?
8. ¿ _Qué_ es esto?
9. ¿ _Cuál_ es el mejor?
10. ¿ _Cuál_ es tu opinión?

11. ¿ _Qué_ fiestas celebras tú?
12. ¿ _Qué_ regalo prefieres?
13. ¿ _Cuál_ es tu helado favorito?
14. ¿ _Qué_ pones en la mesa?
15. ¿ _Qué_ restaurante prefieres?
16. ¿ _Qué_ estudiantes estudian más?
17. ¿ _Qué_ quieres comer esta noche?
18. ¿ _Cuál_ es la sorpresa mañana?
19. ¿ _Qué_ postre prefieres?
20. ¿ _Qué_ opinas?

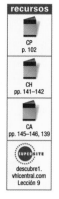

recursos

CP
p. 102

CH
pp. 141–142

CA
pp. 145–146, 139

SUPERSITE
descubre1.
vhlcentral.com
Lección 9

TEACHING OPTIONS

Extra Practice Ask questions of individual students, using **¿qué?** and **¿cuál?** Make sure a portion of the questions are general and information-seeking in nature (**¿qué?**). Ex: **¿Qué es una guitarra? ¿Qué es un elefante?** This is also a good way for students to practice circumlocution (**Es algo que...**).
Pairs Ask students to write one question using each of the interrogative words or phrases in the chart on this page. Then

have them ask those questions of a partner, who must answer in complete sentences.
TPR Divide the class into two teams, **qué** and **cuál**, and have them line up. Indicate the first member of each team and call out a question in English that uses *what* or *which*. Ex: What is your favorite ice cream? The first team member who steps forward and can provide a correct Spanish translation earns a point for his or her team.

Práctica

1 **Completar** Tu clase de español va a crear un sitio web. Completa estas preguntas con palabras interrogativas. Luego, con un(a) compañero/a, hagan y contesten las preguntas para obtener la información para el sitio web.

1. ¿____Cuál____ es la fecha de tu cumpleaños?
2. ¿____Dónde____ naciste?
3. ¿____Cuál____ es tu estado civil?
4. ¿__Cómo/Cuándo/Dónde__ te relajas?
5. ¿____Quién____ es tu mejor amigo/a?
6. ¿____Qué____ cosas te hacen reír?
7. ¿____Qué____ postres te gustan? ¿____Cuál____ te gusta más?
8. ¿____Qué____ problemas tuviste en la primera cita con alguien?

Comunicación

2 **Una invitación** En parejas, lean esta invitación. Luego, túrnense para hacer y contestar preguntas con **qué** y **cuál** basadas en la información de la invitación. Answers will vary.

> **modelo**
>
> **Estudiante 1:** ¿Cuál es el nombre del padre de la novia?
> **Estudiante 2:** Su nombre es Fernando Sandoval Valera.

> Fernando Sandoval Valera   Lorenzo Vásquez Amaral
> Isabel Arzipe de Sandoval   Elena Soto de Vásquez
>
> tienen el agrado de invitarlos
> a la boda de sus hijos
>
> María Luisa y José Antonio
>
> La ceremonia religiosa tendrá lugar
> el sábado 10 de junio a las dos de la tarde
> en el Templo de Santo Domingo
> (Calle Santo Domingo, 961).
>
> Después de la ceremonia sírvanse pasar a la recepción en el salón
> de baile del Hotel Metrópoli (Sotero del Río, 465).

3 **Quinceañera** Trabaja con un(a) compañero/a. Uno/a de ustedes es el/la director(a) del salón de fiestas "Renacimiento". La otra persona es el padre/la madre de Ana María, quien quiere hacer la fiesta de quinceañera de su hija sin gastar más de $25 por invitado. Su profesor(a) va a darles la información necesaria para confirmar la reservación. Answers will vary.

recursos
CA
pp. 45–46

> **modelo**
>
> **Estudiante 1:** ¿Cuánto cuestan los entremeses?
> **Estudiante 2:** Depende. Puede escoger champiñones por 50 centavos o camarones por dos dólares.
> **Estudiante 1:** ¡Uf! A mi hija le gustan los camarones, pero son muy caros.
> **Estudiante 2:** Bueno, también puede escoger quesos por un dólar por invitado.

Section Goals

In **Estructura 9.4**, students will be introduced to:
- pronouns as objects of prepositions
- the preposition-pronoun combinations **conmigo** and **contigo**

Instructional Resources
Cuaderno de práctica,
pp. 103–104
Cuaderno para hispanohablantes, p. 143
Cuaderno de actividades,
pp. 47–48, 140
e-Cuaderno
Supersite: Audio Activity MP3 Audio Files
Supersite/TRCD/Print:
PowerPoints (**Lección 9**
Estructura Presentation);
Communication Activities, Audio Activity Script, Answer Keys
Audio Activity CD

Teaching Tips

- Review the chart "Prepositions often used with **estar**" in **Estructura 2.3**. Use prepositional pronouns as you describe yourself and others in relation to people and things. Say: **¿Quién está delante de mí? Sí, ____ está delante de mí. ¿Y quién está detrás de ella? Sí, ____ está detrás de ella.**

- Ask students which pronouns they recognize and which are new. Ask the class to deduce the rules for pronouns after prepositions.

- Point out that students have been using these pronouns with the preposition **a** since **Lección 2**, when they learned the verb **gustar**.

- Practice **conmigo** and **contigo** by making invitations and having students decline.
Ex: ____, **¿quieres ir conmigo al museo? (No, no quiero ir contigo.)** In a sad tone, say: **Nadie quiere ir conmigo a ningún lado.**

9.4 Pronouns after prepositions

ANTE TODO In Spanish, as in English, the object of a preposition is the noun or pronoun that follows the preposition. Observe the following diagram.

PREPOSITION	NOUN	PREPOSITION	PRONOUN
La sopa es para	Alicia	y para	él.

Prepositional pronouns

	Singular			Plural	
preposition +	**mí**	me	**nosotros/as**	us
	ti	you (fam.)	**vosotros/as**	you (fam.)
	Ud.	you (form.)	**Uds.**	you (form.)
	él	him	**ellos**	them (m.)
	ella	her	**ellas**	them (f.)

▶ Note that, except for **mí** and **ti**, these pronouns are the same as the subject pronouns. **¡Atención! Mí** (*me*) has an accent mark to distinguish it from the possessive adjective **mi** (*my*).

▶ The preposition **con** combines with **mí** and **ti** to form **conmigo** and **contigo,** respectively.

—¿Quieres venir **conmigo** a Concepción?
Do you want to come with me to Concepción?

—Sí, gracias, me gustaría ir **contigo.**
Yes, thanks, I would like to go with you.

▶ The preposition **entre** is followed by **tú** and **yo** instead of **ti** and **mí.**

Papá va a sentarse **entre tú y yo**.
Dad is going to sit between you and me.

CONSULTA

For more prepositions, refer to **Estructura 2.3,** p. 60.

¡INTÉNTALO! Completa estas oraciones con las preposiciones y los pronombres apropiados.

1. *(with him)* No quiero ir ___con él___.
2. *(for her)* Las galletas son ___para ella___.
3. *(for me)* Los mariscos son ___para mí___.
4. *(with you, pl. form.)* Preferimos estar ___con ustedes___.
5. *(with you, sing. fam.)* Me gusta salir ___contigo___.
6. *(with me)* ¿Por qué no quieres tener una cita ___conmigo___?
7. *(for her)* La cuenta es ___para ella___.
8. *(for them, m.)* La habitación es muy pequeña ___para ellos___.
9. *(with them, f.)* Anoche celebré la Navidad ___con ellas___.
10. *(for you, sing. fam.)* Este beso es ___para ti___.
11. *(with you, sing. fam.)* Nunca me aburro ___contigo___.
12. *(with you, pl. form.)* ¡Qué bien que vamos ___con ustedes___!
13. *(for you, sing. fam.)* ___Para ti___ la vida es muy fácil.
14. *(for them, f.)* ___Para ellas___ no hay sorpresas.

recursos

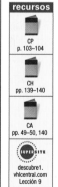

CP
p. 103–104

CH
pp. 139–140

CA
pp. 49–50, 140

descubre1.
vhlcentral.com
Lección 9

TEACHING OPTIONS

Extra Practice Describe someone in the classroom using prepositions of location, without saying the student's name. Ex: **Esta persona está entre la ventana y ____ . Y está enfrente de mí.** The rest of the class has to guess the person being described. Once students have this model, ask individuals to create similar descriptions so that their classmates may guess who is being described.

Game Divide the class into two teams. One student from the first team chooses an item in the classroom and writes it down. Call on five students from the other team to ask questions about the item's location. Ex: **¿Está cerca de mí?** The first student can respond with **sí, no, caliente,** or **frío.** If a team guesses the item within five tries, give them a point. If not, give the other team a point. The team with the most points wins.

Práctica SUPERSITE

1 **Completar** David sale con sus amigos a comer. Para saber quién come qué, lee el mensaje electrónico que David le envió (*sent*) a Cecilia dos días después y completa el diálogo en el restaurante con los pronombres apropiados.

> **modelo**
>
> **Camarero:** Los camarones en salsa verde, ¿para quién son?
> **David:** Son para _____ella_____.

NOTA CULTURAL

Las machas a la parmesana es un plato muy típico de Chile. Se prepara con machas, un tipo de almeja (*clam*) que se encuentra en Suramérica. Las machas a la parmesana se hacen con queso parmesano, limón, sal, pimienta y mantequilla, y luego se ponen en el horno (*oven*).

| Para: Cecilia | Asunto: El menú |

```
Hola, Cecilia:
¿Recuerdas la comida del viernes? Quiero repetir el menú en
mi casa el miércoles. Ahora voy a escribir lo que comimos,
luego me dices si falta algún plato. Yo pedí el filete de
pescado y Maribel camarones en salsa verde. Tatiana pidió
un plato grandísimo de machas a la parmesana. Diana y Silvia
pidieron langostas, ¿te acuerdas? Y tú, ¿qué pediste? Ah, sí,
un bistec grande con papas. Héctor también pidió un bistec,
pero más pequeño. Miguel pidió pollo y agua mineral para
todos. Y la profesora comió ensalada verde porque está a
dieta. ¿Falta algo? Espero tu mensaje. Hasta pronto. David.
```

CAMARERO	El filete de pescado, ¿para quién es?
DAVID	Es para (1)___mí___.
CAMARERO	Aquí está. ¿Y las machas a la parmesana y las langostas?
DAVID	Las machas son para (2)___ella___.
SILVIA Y DIANA	Las langostas son para (3)___nosotras___.
CAMARERO	Tengo un bistec grande...
DAVID	Cecilia, es para (4)___ti___, ¿no es cierto? Y el bistec más pequeño es para (5)___él___.
CAMARERO	¿Y la botella de agua mineral?
MIGUEL	Es para todos (6)___nosotros___, y el pollo es para (7)___mí___.
CAMARERO	(*a la profesora*) Entonces la ensalada verde es para (8)___usted___.

Comunicación

2 **Compartir** Tu profesor(a) va a darte una hoja de actividades en la que hay un dibujo. En parejas, hagan preguntas para saber dónde está cada una de las personas en el dibujo. Ustedes tienen dos versiones diferentes de la ilustración. Al final deben saber dónde está cada persona.

recursos

CA
pp. 47–48

AYUDA

Here are some other useful prepositions: **al lado de, debajo de, a la derecha de, a la izquierda de, cerca de, lejos de, delante de, detrás de, entre.**

> **modelo**
>
> **Estudiante 1:** ¿Quién está al lado de Óscar?
> **Estudiante 2:** Alfredo está al lado de él.

Alfredo	Dolores	Graciela	Raúl
Sra. Blanco	Enrique	Leonor	Rubén
Carlos	Sra. Gómez	Óscar	Yolanda

1 **Teaching Tips**
• Remind students that they are to fill in the blanks with prepositional pronouns, not names of the characters in the conversation.
• To simplify, have students begin by scanning the e-mail message. On the board, list the people who ate at the restaurant (starting with the sender of the e-mail and its recipient). Then guide students in matching each name with the dish ordered. Have students refer to the list as they complete the dialogue.

1 **Expansion** In small groups, have students play the roles of the people mentioned in the e-mail message. Ex: **E1: ¿Para quién son los camarones? E2: Son para mí. E1: ¿Y el bistec? E2: Es para él.**

2 **Teaching Tip** Divide the class into pairs and distribute the Communication Activities worksheets that correspond to this activity. Give students ten minutes to complete this activity.

2 **Expansion**
• Using both versions of the drawing as a guide, ask questions of the class to find out where the people are. Ex: **¿Quién sabe dónde está la señora Blanco?**
• Verify that all students labeled the characters correctly by suggesting changes to the drawing and using prepositions to ask about their new locations. Ex: **Yolanda y Carlos cambian de lugar. ¿Quién está al lado de Yolanda ahora? (Rubén)**

TEACHING OPTIONS

Video Show the ***Fotonovela*** again to give students more input containing prepositional pronouns. Stop the video where appropriate to discuss how certain pronouns were used and to ask comprehension questions.

Large Groups Divide the class into two groups. Give group A cards that contain an activity (Ex: **jugar al baloncesto**) and give group B cards that contain a place (Ex: **el gimnasio**). Have students circulate around the room to find places that match their activities. Ex: **E1: Voy a jugar al baloncesto. ¿Puedo ir contigo? E2: Pues, yo voy al museo. No puedes ir conmigo.** or **Voy al gimnasio. Sí, puedes ir conmigo.**

Recapitulación

For self-scoring and diagnostics, go to **descubre1.vhlcentral.com.**

Completa estas actividades para repasar los conceptos de gramática que aprendiste en esta lección.

1 **Completar** Completa la tabla con el pretérito de los verbos. **9 pts.**

Infinitive	yo	ella	nosotros
conducir	conduje	condujo	condujimos
hacer	hice	hizo	hicimos
saber	supe	supo	supimos

2 **Mi fiesta** Completa este mensaje electrónico con el pretérito de los verbos de la lista. Vas a usar cada verbo sólo una vez. **10 pts.**

dar	haber	tener
decir	hacer	traer
estar	poder	venir
	poner	

Hola, Omar:

Como tú no (1) ___pudiste___ venir a mi fiesta de cumpleaños,
quiero contarte cómo fue. El día de mi cumpleaños muy
temprano por la mañana mis hermanos me (2) ___dieron___ una
gran sorpresa: ellos (3) ___pusieron___ un regalo delante de la puerta
de mi habitación: ¡una bicicleta roja preciosa! Mi madre nos
preparó un desayuno riquísimo. Después de desayunar, mis
hermanos y yo (4) ___tuvimos___ que limpiar toda la casa, así que
(*therefore*) no (5) ___hubo___ más celebración hasta la tarde. A las
seis y media (nosotros) (6) ___hicimos___ una barbacoa en el patio
de la casa. Todos los invitados (7) ___trajeron___ bebidas y regalos.
(8) ___Vinieron___ todos mis amigos, excepto tú, ¡qué pena! :-(
La fiesta (9) ___estuvo___ muy animada hasta las diez de la noche,
cuando mis padres (10) ___dijeron___ que los vecinos (*neighbors*)
iban a (*were going to*) protestar y entonces todos se fueron a
sus casas.

Tu amigo,
Andrés

RESUMEN GRAMATICAL

9.1 **Irregular preterites** *pp. 310–311*

u-stem	estar poder poner saber tener	estuv- pud- pus- sup- tuv-	
i-stem	hacer querer venir	hic- quis- vin-	-e, -iste, -o, -imos, -isteis, -(i)eron
j-stem	conducir decir traducir traer	conduj- dij- traduj- traj-	

► Preterite of dar: di, diste, dio, dimos, disteis, dieron
► Preterite of hay (*inf.* haber): hubo

9.2 **Verbs that change meaning in the preterite** *p.*

Present	Preterite
conocer	
to know; to be acquainted with	to meet
saber	
to know info.; to know how to do something	to find out; to learn
poder	
to be able; can	to manage; to succeed
querer	
to want; to love	to try

9.3 **¿Qué? and ¿cuál?** *p. 316*

► Use ¿qué? to ask for a definition or an explanation.
► Use ¿cuál(es)? when there is a choice among several possibilities.
► ¿Cuál? cannot be used before a noun; use ¿qué? instead.
► ¿Qué? used before a noun has the same meaning as ¿cuál?

Section Goal

In **Recapitulación**, students will review the grammar concepts from this lesson.

Instructional Resource
Supersite

1 **Teaching Tip** Ask students to identify which verb changes meaning in the preterite.

1 **Expansion**
• To challenge students, ask them to provide the **tú** and **ustedes** forms of the verbs.
• Have students provide the conjugations of **conocer, dar,** and **venir.**

2 **Teaching Tip** To simplify, have students identify the subject of each verb before filling in the blanks.

2 **Expansion** Have students work in pairs to write a response e-mail from **Omar**. Tell them to use the preterite tense to ask for more details about the party. Ex: **¿Qué más tuviste que hacer para preparar la fiesta? ¿Qué regalos te dieron tus amigos?**

TEACHING OPTIONS

TPR Have students stand and form a circle. Call out an infinitive from **Resumen gramatical** and a subject pronoun (Ex: **poder/nosotros**) and toss a foam or paper ball to a student, who will give the correct preterite form (Ex: **pudimos**). He or she then tosses the ball to another student, who must use the verb correctly in a sentence before throwing the ball back to you. Ex: **No pudimos comprar los regalos.**

Small Groups Tell small groups to imagine that one of them has received an anonymous birthday gift from a secret admirer. Have them create a dialogue in which friends ask questions about the gift and the potential admirer. Students must use at least two irregular preterites, two examples of **¿qué?** or **¿cuál?,** and three pronouns after prepositions.

3 Teaching Tip To challenge students, ask them to explain why they chose the preterite or present tense in each case.

3 ¿Presente o pretérito? Escoge la forma correcta de los verbos entre paréntesis. **6 pts.**

1. Después de muchos intentos (*tries*), (podemos/**pudimos**) hacer una piñata.
2. —¿Conoces a Pepe?
   —Sí, lo (conozco/**conocí**) en tu fiesta.
3. Como no es de aquí, Cristina no (**sabe**/supo) mucho de las celebraciones locales.
4. Yo no (**quiero**/quise) ir a un restaurante grande, pero tú decides.
5. Ellos (quieren/**quisieron**) darme una sorpresa, pero Nina me lo dijo todo.
6. Mañana se terminan las clases; por fin (**podemos**/pudimos) divertirnos.

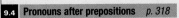

9.4	**Pronouns after prepositions**	*p. 318*

Prepositional pronouns

	Singular	Plural
	mí	nosotros/as
	ti	vosotros/as
Preposition +	Ud.	Uds.
	él	ellos
	ella	ellas

► Exceptions: **conmigo, contigo, entre tú y yo**

4 Preguntas Escribe una pregunta para cada respuesta con los elementos dados. Empieza con **qué**, **cuál** o **cuáles** de acuerdo con el contexto y haz los cambios necesarios. **8 pts.**

1. —¿? / pastel / querer —Quiero el pastel de chocolate. 1. ¿Qué pastel quieres?
2. —¿? / ser / flan —El flan es un postre típico español. 2. ¿Qué es el flan?
3. —¿? / ser / restaurante favorito —Mis restaurantes favoritos son Dalí y Jaleo. 3. ¿Cuáles son tus restaurantes favoritos?
4. —¿? / ser / dirección electrónica —Mi dirección electrónica es paco@email.com. 4. ¿Cuáles tu dirección electrónica?

5 ¿Dónde me siento? Completa la conversación con los pronombres apropiados. **7 pts.**

JUAN A ver, te voy a decir dónde te vas a sentar. Manuel, ¿ves esa silla? Es para ___ti___. Y esa otra silla es para tu novia, que todavía no está aquí.

MANUEL Muy bien, yo la reservo para ___ella___.

HUGO ¿Y esta silla es para ___mí___?

JUAN No, Hugo. No es para ___ti___. Es para Carmina, que viene con Julio.

HUGO No, Carmina y Julio no pueden venir. Hablé con ___ellos___ y me lo dijeron.

JUAN Pues ellos se lo pierden (*it's their loss*). ¡Más comida para ___nosotros___ (*us*)!

CAMARERO Aquí tienen el menú. Les doy un minuto y enseguida estoy con ___ustedes___.

6 Cumpleaños feliz Escribe cinco oraciones describiendo cómo celebraste tu último cumpleaños. Usa el pretérito y los pronombres que aprendiste en esta lección. **10 pts.**   Answers will vary.

7 Poema Completa este fragmento del poema *Elegía nocturna* de Carlos Pellicer con el pretérito de los verbos indicados. **¡2 puntos EXTRA!**

> **❝ Ay de mi corazón°** que nadie
> ___quiso___ (querer) tomar de entre mis
> manos desoladas.
> Tú ___viniste___ (venir) a mirar sus
> llamaradas° y le miraste
> arder° claro° y sereno. **❞**

corazón *heart* llamaradas *flames* arder *to burn* claro *clear*

4 Expansion Give students these answers as items 5–8:
5. —¿? / libro / comprar —Voy a comprar el libro de viajes. (¿Qué libro vas a comprar?)
6. —¿? / ser / última película / ver —Vi la película *Volver*. (¿Cuál fue la última película que viste?) 7. —¿? / ser / número de la suerte —Mi número de la suerte es el ocho. (¿Cuál es tu número de la suerte?) 8. —¿? / ser / nacimiento —El nacimiento es la primera etapa de la vida. (¿Qué es el nacimiento?)

5 Expansion Have four volunteers role-play the dialogue for the class.

6 Teaching Tip To simplify, have students make an idea map to help them organize their ideas. In the center circle, have them write **Mi último cumpleaños**. Help them brainstorm labels for the surrounding circles, such as **lugar, invitados, regalos,** etc. You also may want to provide a list of infinitives that students may use in their descriptions.

7 Teaching Tip You may want to point out the example of **leísmo** in line 5 (**le miraste**). Explain that some Spanish speakers tend to use **le** or **les** as direct object pronouns. In this case, **le** replaces the direct object pronoun **lo**, which refers to **mi corazón**.

7 Poema Mexican poet Carlos Pellicer mixes in his works the splendor of nature with the most intimate emotions. Some of his most important works are *Práctica de vuelo, Hora de junio,* and *Camino*. Also a museologist, he helped create the **Museo Casa de Frida Kahlo** and the **Anahuacalli**, which exhibits pre-Hispanic art donated by Diego Rivera.

TEACHING OPTIONS

TPR Divide the class into two teams and have them line up. Indicate the first member of each team and call out a sentence. Ex: **Me gusta el color gris.** The first student to reach the board and write a corresponding question using the proper interrogative form earns a point for his or her team. Ex: **¿Qué color te gusta?** or **¿Cuál es tu color preferido?** The team with the most points at the end wins.
Pairs Add a visual aspect to this grammar review. Have pairs choose a photo of a person from a magazine and invent an imaginary list of the ten most important things that happened to that person in his or her lifetime. Tell them to use at least four preterites from this lesson. Ex: **Conoció al presidente de los Estados Unidos. Ganó la lotería y le dio todo el dinero a su mejor amigo.** Have pairs present their photos and lists to the class, who will ask follow-up questions. Ex: **¿Por qué le dio todo el dinero a un amigo?**

In **Lectura**, students will:
- learn to use word families to infer meaning in context
- read content-rich texts

Estrategia Write **conocer** on the board, reminding students of the meaning *to know, be familiar with*. Next to it, write **conocimiento** and **conocido**. Tell students that recognizing the family relationship between a known word and unfamiliar words can help them infer the meaning of the words they do not yet know. Guide students to see that **conocimiento** is a noun meaning *knowledge, familiarity* and **conocido** is an adjective form of the verb meaning *known* or *well-known*.

Examinar el texto Have students scan the text for clues to its contents. Ask volunteers to tell what kind of text it is and how they know. Headlines (**titulares**), photos, and layout (**composición de la página**) reveal that it is the society news (**notas de sociedad**) in a newspaper.

Raíces Have students fill in the rest of the chart after they have read **Vida social**.

Lectura

Antes de leer

Estrategia
Recognizing word families

Recognizing root words can help you guess the meaning of words in context, ensuring better comprehension of a reading selection. Using this strategy will enrich your Spanish vocabulary as you will see below.

Examinar el texto

Familiarízate con el texto usando las estrategias de lectura más efectivas para ti. ¿Qué tipo de documento es? ¿De qué tratan° las cuatro secciones del documento? Explica tus respuestas.

Raíces°

Completa el siguiente cuadro° para ampliar tu vocabulario. Usa palabras de la lectura de esta lección y el vocabulario de las lecciones anteriores. ¿Qué significan las palabras que escribiste en el cuadro? Answers will vary.

Verbo	Sustantivos	Otras formas
1. agradecer	agradecimiento/ gracias	agradecido
2. estudiar	estudiante *student*	estudiado *studied*
3. celebrar *to celebrate*	celebración *celebration*	celebrado
4. bailar *to dance*	baile	bailable *danceable*
5. bautizar	bautismo *baptism*	bautizado *baptized*

CH pp. 144–145 | descubre1.vhlcentral.com Lección 9

¿De qué tratan...? *What are... about?*
Raíces *Roots* cuadro *chart*

Vida social

Matrimonio
Espinoza Álvarez-Reyes Salazar

El día sábado 17 de junio de 2007 a las 19 horas, se celebró el matrimonio de Silvia Reyes y Carlos Espinoza en la catedral de Santiago. La ceremonia fue oficiada por el pastor Federico Salas y participaron los padres de los novios, el señor Jorge Espinoza y señora, y el señor José Alfredo

Reyes y señora. Después de la ceremonia, los padres de los recién casados ofrecieron una fiesta bailable en el restaurante La Misión.

Bautismo

José María recibió el bautismo el 26 de junio de 2007.

Sus padres, don Roberto Lagos Moreno y doña María Angélica Sánchez, compartieron la alegría de la fiesta con todos sus parientes y amigos. La ceremonia religiosa tuvo lugar° en la catedral de Aguas Blancas. Después de la ceremonia, padres, parientes y amigos celebraron una fiesta en la residencia de la familia Lagos.

Heritage Speakers Ask heritage speakers to share with the class other terms they use to refer to various types of celebrations. Possible responses: wedding: **boda, casamiento**; graduation: **graduación, promoción**; baptism: **bautizo**; birthday: **cumpleaños, día del santo**.

Extra Practice Here are some related words of which at least one form will be familiar to students. Guide them to recognize the relationship between words and meanings. **idea, ideal, idealismo, idealizar, idear, ideario, idealista** • **conservar, conservación, conserva, conservador** • **bueno, bondad, bondadoso, bonito** • **habla, hablador, hablar, hablante, hablado**

Fiesta quinceañera

El doctor don Amador Larenas Fernández y la señora Felisa Vera de Larenas celebraron los quince años de su hija Ana Ester junto a sus parientes y amigos. La quinceañera° reside en la ciudad de Valparaíso y es estudiante del Colegio Francés. La fiesta de presentación en sociedad de la señorita Ana Ester fue el día viernes 2 de mayo a las 19 horas, en el Club Español. Entre los invitados especiales asistieron el alcalde° de la ciudad, don Pedro Castedo, y su esposa. La música estuvo a cargo de la Orquesta Americana. ¡Feliz cumpleaños le deseamos a la señorita Ana Ester en su fiesta bailable!

Expresión de gracias
Carmen Godoy Tapia

Agradecemos° sinceramente a todas las personas que nos acompañaron en el último adiós a nuestra preciada esposa, madre, abuela y tía, la señora Carmen Godoy Tapia. El funeral tuvo lugar el día 28 de junio de 2007 en la ciudad de Viña del Mar. La vida de Carmen Godoy fue un ejemplo de trabajo, amistad, alegría y amor para todos nosotros. La familia agradece de todo corazón° su asistencia° al funeral a todos los parientes y amigos. Su esposo, hijos y familia.

tuvo lugar *took place* quinceañera *fifteen year-old girl* alcalde *mayor*
agradecemos *We thank* de todo corazón *sincerely* asistencia *attendance*

Después de leer

Corregir 🔊💻

Escribe estos comentarios otra vez para corregir la información errónea.

1. El alcalde y su esposa asistieron a la boda de Silvia y Carlos. El alcalde y su esposa asistieron a la fiesta de quinceañera de Ana Ester.

2. Todos los anuncios° describen eventos felices. Tres de los anuncios tratan de eventos felices. Uno trata de una muerte.

3. Ana Ester Larenas cumple dieciséis años. Ana Ester Larenas cumple quince años.

4. Roberto Lagos y María Angélica Sánchez son hermanos. Roberto Lagos y María Angélica Sánchez están casados/son esposos.

5. Carmen Godoy Tapia les dio las gracias a las personas que asistieron al funeral. La familia de Carmen Godoy Tapia les dio las gracias a las personas que asistieron al funeral.

Identificar 🔊💻

Escribe los nombres de las personas descritas°.

1. Dejó viudo a su esposo en junio de 2006. Carmen Godoy Tapia

2. Sus padres y todos los invitados brindaron por él, pero él no entendió por qué. José María

3. El Club Español les presentó una cuenta considerable para pagar. don Amador Larenas Fernández y doña Felisa Vera de Larenas

4. Unió a los novios en santo matrimonio. el pastor Federico Salas

5. La celebración de su cumpleaños marcó el comienzo de su vida adulta. Ana Ester

Un anuncio

Trabaja con dos o tres compañeros/as de clase e inventen un anuncio breve sobre una celebración importante. Esta celebración puede ser una graduación, un cumpleaños o una gran fiesta en la que ustedes participan. Incluyan la siguiente información. Answers will vary.

1. nombres de los participantes
2. la fecha, la hora y el lugar
3. qué se celebra
4. otros detalles de interés

anuncios *announcements* descritas *described*

Teaching Tip You may want to discuss other aspects of **quinceañera** celebrations. Point out that a **quinceañera** has elements of a Sweet Sixteen or bat mitzvah, an American prom, and a wedding. For example, often there is a church ceremony followed by a reception with a catered dinner, live music or DJ, and dancing. The birthday girl may have a court made up of **damas de honor** and **chambelanes**. In some cases, the girl may wear flat shoes at the church mass and at the reception, to symbolize her transition into adulthood, her father will change the shoes to heels. Ask students if they have seen elements related to this celebration in North America, such as Hallmark cards, **quinceañera** Barbie dolls, or the 2006 film *Quinceañera*.

Corregir Ask volunteers to correct each false statement and point out the location in the text where they found the correct answer.

Identificar
• If students have trouble inferring the meaning of any word or phrase, help them identify the corresponding context clues.
• Have pairs write one question for each of the five items and exchange them with another pair, who will answer the questions.

Un anuncio
• Provide students with examples of announcements from Spanish-language newspapers to analyze and use as models.
• Have heritage speakers work with students who are being exposed to Spanish for the first time. When students have finished writing, ask them to read their announcements aloud. Have students combine the articles to create their own **Vida social** page for a class newspaper.

TEACHING OPTIONS

Extra Practice Have pairs visit the website of a small Spanish-speaking newspaper, such as *El Heraldo* (Colombia), *El Informador* (Mexico), or *El Norte* (Mexico). Tell them to look for sections called **Gente, Sociedad,** or **Sociales.** Have them print the photos and present the events to the class, using the preterite tense and vocabulary from this lesson.

Game Have students describe the people mentioned in the announcements they wrote for the above activity **Un anuncio**; their classmates will guess the event they are describing.

Section Goals

In **Escritura**, students will:
- create a Venn diagram to organize information
- learn words and phrases that signal similarity and difference
- write a comparative analysis

Instructional Resources
Cuaderno para hispanohablantes, pp. 146–147
Cuaderno de actividades, pp. 157–158
Supersite

Estrategia Explain that a graphic organizer, such as a Venn diagram, is a useful way to record information and visually organize details to be compared and contrasted in a comparative analysis. On the board, draw a Venn diagram with the headings **La boda de mi hermano, El bautismo de mi sobrina,** and the subheadings **Diferencias** and **Similitudes**. Tell students they are going to complete a Venn diagram to compare two celebrations. Discuss with the class how these events are alike and how they are different, using some of the terms to signal similarities and differences.

Tema Explain to students that to write a comparative analysis, they will need to use words or phrases that signal similarities (**similitudes**) and differences (**diferencias**). Model the pronunciation of the words and expressions under **Escribir una composición**. Then have volunteers use them in sentences to express the similarities and differences listed in the Venn diagram.

Escritura

Estrategia

Planning and writing a comparative analysis

Writing any kind of comparative analysis requires careful planning. Venn diagrams are useful for organizing your ideas visually before comparing and contrasting people, places, objects, events, or issues. To create a Venn diagram, draw two circles that overlap and label the top of each circle. List the differences between the two elements in the outer rings of the two circles, then list their similarities where the two circles overlap. Review the following example.

Diferencias y similitudes

Boda de Silvia Reyes y Carlos Espinoza

Diferencias:
1. Primero hay una celebración religiosa.
2. Se celebra en un restaurante.

Similitudes:
1. Las dos fiestas se celebran por la noche.
2. Las dos fiestas son bailables.

Quinceañera de Ana Ester Larenas Vera

Diferencias:
1. Se celebra en un club.
2. Vienen invitados especiales.

La lista de palabras y expresiones a la derecha puede ayudarte a escribir este tipo de ensayo (*essay*).

recursos		
CH pp. 146–147	CA pp. 157–158	descubre1.vhlcentral.com Lección 9

Tema

Escribir una composición

Compara una celebración familiar (como una boda, una fiesta de cumpleaños o una graduación) a la que tú asististe recientemente, con otro tipo de celebración. Utiliza palabras y expresiones de esta lista.

Para expresar similitudes

además; también	*in addition; also*
al igual que	*the same as*
como	*as; like*
de la misma manera	*in the same manner (way)*
del mismo modo	*in the same manner (way)*
tan + [*adjetivo*] + como	*as + [adjective] + as*
tanto/a(s) + [*sustantivo*] + como	*as many/much + [noun] + as*

Para expresar diferencias

a diferencia de	*unlike*
a pesar de	*in spite of*
aunque	*although*
en cambio	*on the other hand*
más/menos... que	*more/less . . . than*
no obstante	*nevertheless; however*
por otro lado	*on the other hand*
por el contrario	*on the contrary*
sin embargo	*nevertheless; however*

EVALUATION: Composición

Criteria	Scale
Content	1 2 3 4
Organization	1 2 3 4
Use of comparisons/contrasts	1 2 3 4
Use of vocabulary	1 2 3 4
Accuracy	1 2 3 4

Scoring	
Excellent	18–20 points
Good	14–17 points
Satisfactory	10–13 points
Unsatisfactory	< 10 points

Escuchar

Estrategia

Guessing the meaning of words through context

When you hear an unfamiliar word, you can often guess its meaning by listening to the words and phrases around it.

 To practice this strategy, you will now listen to a paragraph. Jot down the unfamiliar words that you hear. Then listen to the paragraph again and jot down the word or words that are the most useful clues to the meaning of each unfamiliar word.

Preparación

Lee la invitación. ¿De qué crees que van a hablar Rosa y Josefina?

Ahora escucha

Ahora escucha la conversación entre Josefina y Rosa. Cuando oigas una de las palabras de la columna A, usa el contexto para identificar el sinónimo o la definición en la columna B.

A	B
_d_ festejar	a. conmemoración religiosa de una muerte
_c_ dicha	b. tolera
_h_ bien parecido	c. suerte
_g_ finge (fingir)	d. celebrar
_b_ soporta (soportar)	e. me divertí
_e_ yo lo disfruté (disfrutar)	f. horror
	g. crea una ficción
	h. guapo

---

*Margarita Robles de García
y Roberto García Olmos*

*Piden su presencia en la celebración
del décimo aniversario de bodas
el día 13 de marzo de 2007
con una misa en la Iglesia Virgen del Coromoto
a las 6:30*

*seguida por cena y baile
en el restaurante El Campanero,
Calle Principal, Las Mercedes
a las 8:30*

Comprensión

¿Cierto o falso?

Lee cada oración e indica si lo que dice es **cierto** o **falso**. Corrige las oraciones falsas.

1. No invitaron a mucha gente a la fiesta de Margarita y Roberto porque ellos no conocen a muchas personas.
   Falso. Fueron muchos invitados.
2. Algunos fueron a la fiesta con pareja y otros fueron sin compañero/a. **Cierto.**
3. Margarita y Roberto decidieron celebrar el décimo aniversario porque no tuvieron ninguna celebración en su matrimonio. **Falso.** Celebraron el décimo aniversario porque les gustan las fiestas.
4. A Rosa y a Josefina les parece interesante Rafael. **Cierto.**
5. Josefina se divirtió mucho en la fiesta porque bailó toda la noche con Rafael. **Falso.** Josefina se divirtió mucho pero bailó con otros, no con Rafael.

Preguntas   Answers will vary.

1. ¿Son solteras Rosa y Josefina? ¿Cómo lo sabes?
2. ¿Tienen las chicas una amistad de mucho tiempo con la pareja que celebra su aniversario? ¿Cómo lo sabes?

¿no? Quise bailar con él pero no me sacó a bailar.
R: Hablas de Rafael. Es muy bien parecido; ¡ese pelo...! Estuve hablando con él después del brindis. Me dijo que no le gusta ni el champán ni el vino; él finge tomar cuando

brindan porque no lo soporta. No te sacó a bailar porque él y Susana estaban juntos en la fiesta.
J: De todos modos, aun sin Rafael, bailé toda la noche. Lo pasé muy, pero muy bien.

Section Goals

In **Escuchar**, students will:
• use context to infer meaning of unfamiliar words
• answer questions based on a recorded conversation

Instructional Resources
Supersite: Textbook MP3 Audio Files
Supersite/TRCD: Textbook Audio Script
Textbook Audio CD

Estrategia
Script Hoy mi sobrino Gabriel cumplió seis años. Antes de la fiesta, ayudé a mi hermana a decorar la sala con globos de todos los colores, pero ¡qué bulla después!, cuando los niños se pusieron a estallarlos todos. El pastel de cumpleaños estaba riquísimo y cuando Gabriel sopló las velas, apagó las seis. Los otros niños le regalaron un montón de juguetes, y nos divertimos mucho.

Ahora escucha
Script JOSEFINA: Rosa, ¿te divertiste anoche en la fiesta?
ROSA: Sí, me divertí más en el aniversario que en la boda. ¡La fiesta estuvo fenomenal! Fue buena idea festejar el aniversario en un restaurante. Así todos pudieron relajarse.
J: En parte, yo lo disfruté porque son una pareja tan linda; qué dicha que estén tan enamorados después de diez años de matrimonio. Me gustaría tener una relación como la de ellos. Y también saberlo celebrar con tanta alegría. ¡Pero qué cantidad de comida y bebida!
R: Es verdad que Margarita y Roberto exageran un poco con sus fiestas, pero son de la clase de gente que le gusta celebrar los eventos de la vida. Y como tienen tantas amistades y dos familias tan grandes....
J: Oye, Rosa, hablando de familia, ¿llegaste a conocer al cuñado de Magali? Es soltero,

(Script continues at far left in the bottom panels.)

En pantalla

En México existe una franja° de tierra° a lo largo de° toda la costa del país que es considerada parte del territorio público federal. Esta área abarca° aproximadamente cincuenta metros a partir de° la línea del mar. Sin embargo°, existe la posibilidad de que los propietarios de la tierra que está al lado de la zona federal puedan pedir una concesión. Así pueden utilizar el área adyacente a su propiedad, por ejemplo, para hacer un festival musical o una fiesta privada. Casos similares ocurren en otros países hispanos.

Vocabulario útil

conejo	*bunny*
pila	*battery*

Opciones
Elige la opción correcta.
1. El chico está comprando en __b__.
   a. una farmacia   b. un supermercado   c. un almacén
2. Él imagina __a__ en la playa.
   a. una fiesta   b. un examen   c. un almuerzo
3. El chico de la guitarra canta __b__.
   a. bien   b. mal   c. fabulosamente bien
4. Al final (*At the end*), el chico __a__ compra las pilas.
   a. sí   b. no   c. nunca

Fiesta
Trabajen en grupos de tres. Imaginen que van a organizar una fiesta en la playa. Escriban una invitación electrónica para invitar a sus amigos a la fiesta. Describan los planes que tienen para la fiesta y díganles a sus amigos qué tiene que traer cada uno.
Answers will vary.

franja *strip* tierra *land* a lo largo de *along* abarca *covers* a partir de *from* Sin embargo *However* ¿Y si no compraras... *And what if you didn't buy...?* cómpralas *buy them*

Anuncio de Energizer

¿Y si no compraras° las *Energizer Max*?

Hey, no se preocupen.

Sí, mejor cómpralas°.

recursos

descubre1.vhlcentral.com
Lección 9

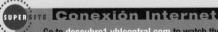

SUPERSITE Conexión Internet
Go to descubre1.vhlcentral.com to watch the TV clip featured in this *En pantalla* section.

Oye cómo va

Myriam Hernández

La actriz° y cantante° **Myriam Hernández** nació en Chile y empezó su carrera a los diez años cuando ganó un festival estudiantil. Más tarde, trabajó en la telenovela *De cara al mañana*. Desde 1988, año en que salió a la venta° su primer álbum, su éxito° se extendió por toda Latinoamérica y los Estados Unidos. En 1989 su canción *El hombre que yo amo* fue incluida en la lista *Hot Latin* de la revista *Billboard*. También se ha presentado° en escenarios° como el Madison Square Garden en Nueva York y el Festival de Viña del Mar, en Chile.

Tu profesor(a) va a poner la canción en la clase. Escúchala y completa las actividades.

Emparejar

Indica qué elemento del segundo grupo está relacionado con cada elemento del primer grupo.

<u> d </u> 1. lugar donde nació Myriam Hernández
<u> f </u> 2. telenovela en la que trabajó
<u> e </u> 3. año en que salió a la venta su primer álbum
<u> c </u> 4. canción incluida en la lista *Hot Latin*

a. Festival de Viña del Mar	d. Chile
b. 1986	e. 1988
c. *El hombre que yo amo*	f. *De cara al mañana*

Preguntas

En parejas, respondan a las preguntas. Answers will vary.

1. ¿Creen que la cantante está triste o feliz? ¿Cómo lo saben?
2. ¿Es el amor el motor del universo? ¿Por qué?
3. Completen estos versos con sus propias (*your own*) ideas. Tomen la canción de Myriam Hernández como modelo.

> Quiero cantarle a _____
> en tres o cuatro versos;
> cantarle porque _____,
> porque _____.

actriz *actress* cantante *singer* salió a la venta *was released* éxito *success* se ha presentado *she has performed* escenarios *stages* hallar *to find* soledad *loneliness* alma *soul* volar *fly*

Quiero cantarle al amor

Quiero cantarle al amor
porque me supo hallar°.
Quiero cantarle al amor,
que me vino a buscar.
Se llevó mi soledad°
y a cambio me dejó
su fantasía en el alma°.
Quiero cantarle al amor,
que me dio libertad.
Quiero cantarle al amor
porque me hizo volar°.
Se llevó mi soledad
y a cambio me dejó
su fantasía en el alma.

Discografía selecta

1990 *Dos*
1998 *Todo el amor*
2000 *+ y más*
2001 *El amor en concierto*
2004 *Huellas*

recursos

descubre1.vhlcentral.com
Lección 9

SUPERSITE **Conexión Internet**

Go to **descubre1.vhlcentral.com** to learn more about the artist featured in this **Oye cómo va** section.

Section Goals

In **Oye cómo va**, students will:
• read about **Myriam Hernández**
• listen to a song by **Myriam Hernández**

Instructional Resources
Supersite
Vista Higher Learning *Cancionero*

Antes de escuchar
• Have students read the title of the song and scan the lyrics for cognates and familiar words.
• Ask students to predict what type of song this is. They should support their opinion by citing words from the lyrics.
• Tell students to listen for irregular preterite verb forms and jot them down as you play the song.

Emparejar Ask additional comprehension questions: **¿Cómo empezó la carrera de Myriam Hernández? (Ganó un festival estudiantil a los diez años.) ¿Tuvo éxito su primer álbum? (Sí, tuvo éxito en Latinoamérica y en los Estados Unidos.) ¿En qué revista se encuentra la lista *Hot Latin*? (Se encuentra en la revista *Billboard*.)**

Preguntas
• Have volunteers give examples of the different ways love is described in the song.
• Play the song a second time. Then ask: **¿A quién canta esta canción? ¿Cómo lo saben? ¿Creen que esta canción le da esperanza a una persona que está buscando pareja? ¿Por qué?**

TEACHING OPTIONS

Extra Practice Have students imagine that their best friend has just been dumped by his or her significant other. Ask students to write an e-mail to cheer up their friend. Encourage them to use the song lyrics as the inspiration for their message. Have students exchange papers with a classmate for peer editing.

Pairs Ask pairs to think of a movie in which this song might be featured. Pairs should support their decision by giving a movie synopsis and the scene where they think the song should be featured. Have pairs share their ideas with the class.

Chile

connections cultures NATIONAL STANDARDS

El país en cifras

▶ **Área:** 756.950 km^2 (292.259 millas^2), *dos veces el área de Montana*
▶ **Población:** 17.134.000 *Aproximadamente el 80 por ciento de la población del país es urbana.*
▶ **Capital:** Santiago de Chile—5.982.000
▶ **Ciudades principales:** Concepción, Viña del Mar, Valparaíso, Temuco

SOURCE: Population Division, UN Secretariat

▶ **Moneda:** peso chileno
▶ **Idiomas:** español (oficial), mapuche

Bandera de Chile

Chilenos célebres

▶ **Bernardo O'Higgins,** militar° y héroe nacional (1778–1842)
▶ **Gabriela Mistral,** Premio Nobel de Literatura, 1945; poeta y diplomática (1889–1957)
▶ **Pablo Neruda,** Premio Nobel de Literatura, 1971; poeta (1904–1973)
▶ **Isabel Allende,** novelista (1942–)

Pablo Neruda

militar *soldier* terremoto *earthquake* heridas *wounded* hogar *home*

PERÚ

Pampa del Tamarugal

Cordillera de los Andes

Palacio de la Moneda en Santiago

BOLIVIA

Una calle de Santiago

Vista de la costa de Viña del Mar

Océano Pacífico

Viña del Mar Valparaíso

Santiago de Chile

ARGENTINA

Concepción

Temuco

Pescadores de Valparaíso

Una celebración en Temuco

Lago Buenos Aires

Océano Atlántico

Punta Arenas

recursos

Estrecho de Magallanes

Isla Grande de Tierra del Fuego

| CP pp. 105–106 | CA pp. 85–86 | descubre1.vhlcentral.com Lección 9 |

¡Increíble pero cierto!

El terremoto° de mayor intensidad registrado tuvo lugar en Chile el 22 de mayo de 1960. Registró una intensidad récord de 9.5 en la escala de Richter. Murieron 2.000 personas, 3.000 resultaron heridas° y 2.000.000 perdieron su hogar°. La geografía del país se modificó notablemente.

Lugares • La isla de Pascua

La isla de Pascuaº recibió ese nombre porque los exploradores holandesesº llegaron a la isla por primera vez el día de Pascua de 1722. Ahora es parte del territorio de Chile. La isla de Pascua es famosa por los *moai*, estatuas enormes que representan personas con rasgosº muy exagerados. Estas estatuas las construyeron los *rapa nui*, los antiguos habitantes de la zona. Todavía no se sabe mucho sobre los *rapa nui*, ni tampoco se sabe por qué decidieron abandonar la isla.

Deportes • Los deportes de invierno

Hay muchos lugares para practicar los deportes de invierno en Chile porque las montañas nevadas de los Andes ocupan gran parte del país. El Parque Nacional de Villarrica, por ejemplo, situado al pie de un volcán y junto aº un lago, es un sitio popular para el esquí y el *snowboard*. Para los que prefieren deportes más extremos, el centro de esquí Valle Nevado organiza excursiones para practicar el heliesquí.

Ciencias • Astronomía

Los observatorios chilenos, situados en los Andes, son lugares excelentes para las observaciones astronómicas. Científicosº de todo el mundo van a Chile para estudiar las estrellasº y otros cuerpos celestes. Hoy día Chile está construyendo nuevos observatorios y telescopios para mejorar las imágenes del universo.

Economía • El vino

La producción de vino comenzó en Chile en el sigloº XVI. Ahora la industria del vino constituye una parte importante de la actividad agrícola del país y la exportación de sus productos está subiendoº cada vez más. Los vinos chilenos reciben el aprecio internacional por su gran variedad y su precio moderado.

 ¿Qué aprendiste? Responde a cada pregunta con una oración completa.

1. ¿Qué porcentaje (*percentage*) de la población chilena es urbana?
   El 80 por ciento de la población chilena es urbana.

2. ¿Qué son los *moai*? ¿Dónde están? Los *moai* son estatuas enormes. Están en la isla de Pascua.

3. ¿Qué deporte extremo ofrece el centro de esquí Valle Nevado?
   Ofrece la práctica del heliesquí.

4. ¿Por qué van a Chile científicos de todo el mundo? Porque los observatorios chilenos son excelentes para las observaciones astronómicas.

5. ¿Cuándo comenzó la producción de vino en Chile?
   Comenzó en el siglo XVI.

6. ¿Por qué reciben los vinos chilenos el aprecio internacional? Lo reciben por su variedad y su precio moderado.

 Conexión Internet Investiga estos temas en **descubre1.vhlcentral.com.**

1. Busca información sobre Pablo Neruda e Isabel Allende. ¿Dónde y cuándo nacieron? ¿Cuáles son algunas de sus obras (*works*)? ¿Cuáles son algunos de los temas de sus obras?

2. Busca información sobre sitios donde los chilenos y los turistas practican deportes de invierno en Chile. Selecciona un sitio y descríbeselo a tu clase.

....

La isla de Pascua *Easter Island* holandeses *Dutch* rasgos *features* junto a *beside* Científicos *Scientists* estrellas *stars* siglo *century* subiendo *increasing*

Instructional Resources
Cuaderno de actividades, p. 140
e-Cuaderno
Supersite: Textbook &
Vocabulary MP3 Audio Files
Supersite/TRCD: Answer Keys;
Testing Program (**Lección**
9 Pruebas, Test Generator,
Testing Program MP3
Audio Files)
Textbook, Test Audio CD

Las celebraciones

el aniversario (de bodas)	(wedding) anniversary
la boda	wedding
el cumpleaños	birthday
el día de fiesta	holiday
la fiesta	party
el/la invitado/a	guest
la Navidad	Christmas
la quinceañera	young woman's fifteenth birthday celebration
la sorpresa	surprise
brindar	to toast (drink)
celebrar	to celebrate
divertirse (e:ie)	to have fun
invitar	to invite
pasarlo bien/mal	to have a good/bad time
regalar	to give (a gift)
reírse (e:i)	to laugh
relajarse	to relax
sonreír (e:i)	to smile
sorprender	to surprise

Los postres y otras comidas

la botella (de vino)	bottle (of wine)
el champán	champagne
los dulces	sweets; candy
el flan (de caramelo)	baked (caramel) custard
la galleta	cookie
el helado	ice cream
el pastel (de chocolate)	(chocolate) cake; pie
el postre	dessert

Las relaciones personales

la amistad	friendship
el amor	love
el divorcio	divorce
el estado civil	marital status
el matrimonio	marriage
la pareja	(married) couple; partner
el/la recién casado/a	newlywed
casarse (con)	to get married (to)
comprometerse (con)	to get engaged (to)
divorciarse (de)	to get divorced (from)
enamorarse (de)	to fall in love (with)
llevarse bien/mal (con)	to get along well/ badly (with)
odiar	to hate
romper (con)	to break up (with)
salir (con)	to go out (with); to date
separarse (de)	to separate (from)
tener una cita	to have a date; to have an appointment
casado/a	married
divorciado/a	divorced
juntos/as	together
separado/a	separated
soltero/a	single
viudo/a	widower/widow

Las etapas de la vida

la adolescencia	adolescence
la edad	age
el estado civil	marital status
las etapas de la vida	the stages of life
la juventud	youth
la madurez	maturity; middle age
la muerte	death
el nacimiento	birth
la niñez	childhood
la vejez	old age
cambiar (de)	to change
graduarse (de/en)	to graduate (from/in)
jubilarse	to retire (from work)
nacer	to be born

Palabras adicionales

la alegría	happiness
el beso	kiss
conmigo	with me
contigo	with you

Expresiones útiles	See page 305.

recursos

CA
p. 140

descubre1.vhlcentral.com
Lección 9

Glossary of Grammatical Terms

ADJECTIVE A word that modifies, or describes, a noun or pronoun.

muchos libros	un hombre **rico**
many books	*a rich man*
las mujeres **altas**	
the tall women	

Demonstrative adjective An adjective that specifies which noun a speaker is referring to.

esta fiesta	**ese** chico
this party	*that boy*
aquellas flores	
those flowers	

Possessive adjective An adjective that indicates ownership or possession.

mi mejor vestido	Éste es **mi** hermano.
my best dress	*This is my brother.*

Stressed possessive adjective A possessive adjective that emphasizes the owner or possessor.

Es un libro **mío.**
It's my book./It's a book of mine.

Es amiga **tuya**; yo no la conozco.
She's a friend of yours; I don't know her.

ADVERB A word that modifies, or describes, a verb, adjective, or other adverb.

Pancho escribe **rápidamente.**
Pancho writes quickly.

Este cuadro es **muy** bonito.
This picture is very pretty.

ARTICLE A word that points out a noun in either a specific or a non-specific way.

Definite article An article that points out a noun in a specific way.

el libro	**la** maleta
the book	*the suitcase*
los diccionarios	**las** palabras
the dictionaries	*the words*

Indefinite article An article that points out a noun in a general, non-specific way.

un lápiz	**una** computadora
a pencil	*a computer*
unos pájaros	**unas** escuelas
some birds	*some schools*

CLAUSE A group of words that contains both a conjugated verb and a subject, either expressed or implied.

Main (or Independent) clause A clause that can stand alone as a complete sentence.

Pienso ir a cenar pronto.
I plan to go to dinner soon.

Subordinate (or Dependent) clause A clause that does not express a complete thought and therefore cannot stand alone as a sentence.

Trabajo en la cafetería **porque necesito dinero para la escuela.**
I work in the cafeteria because I need money for school.

COMPARATIVE A construction used with an adjective or adverb to express a comparison between two people, places, or things.

Este programa es **más interesante que** el otro.
This program is more interesting than the other one.

Tomás no es **tan alto como** Alberto.
Tomás is not as tall as Alberto.

CONJUGATION A set of the forms of a verb for a specific tense or mood or the process by which these verb forms are presented.

Preterite conjugation of **cantar:**

canté	cantamos
cantaste	cantasteis
cantó	cantaron

CONJUNCTION A word used to connect words, clauses, or phrases.

Susana es de Cuba **y** Pedro es de España.
Susana is from Cuba and Pedro is from Spain.

No quiero estudiar **pero** tengo que hacerlo.
I don't want to study, but I have to.

CONTRACTION The joining of two words into one. The only contractions in Spanish are **al** and **del**.

Mi hermano fue **al** concierto ayer.
*My brother went **to the** concert yesterday.*

Saqué dinero **del** banco.
*I took money **from the** bank.*

DIRECT OBJECT A noun or pronoun that directly receives the action of the verb.

Tomás lee **el libro.**   **La** pagó ayer.
*Tomás reads **the book.**   She paid **it** yesterday.*

GENDER The grammatical categorizing of certain kinds of words, such as nouns and pronouns, as masculine, feminine, or neuter.

Masculine
articles **el, un**
pronouns **él, lo, mío, éste, ése, aquél**
adjective **simpático**

Feminine
articles **la, una**
pronouns **ella, la, mía, ésta, ésa, aquélla**
adjective **simpática**

IMPERSONAL EXPRESSION A third-person expression with no expressed or specific subject.

Es muy importante.   **Llueve** mucho.
It's very important.   *It's raining hard.*

Aquí **se habla** español.
*Spanish **is spoken** here.*

INDIRECT OBJECT A noun or pronoun that receives the action of the verb indirectly; the object, often a living being, to or for whom an action is performed.

Eduardo **le** dio un libro **a Linda.**
*Eduardo gave a book **to Linda.***

La profesora **me** dio una C en el examen.
*The professor gave **me** a C on the test.*

INFINITIVE The basic form of a verb. Infinitives in Spanish end in **-ar, -er,** or **-ir.**

hablar   correr   abrir
to speak   *to run*   *to open*

INTERROGATIVE An adjective or pronoun used to ask a question.

¿Quién habla?   **¿Cuántos** compraste?
Who is speaking?   *How many did you buy?*

¿Qué piensas hacer hoy?
What do you plan to do today?

INVERSION Changing the word order of a sentence, often to form a question.

Statement: Elena pagó la cuenta del restaurante.

Inversion: ¿Pagó Elena la cuenta del restaurante?

MOOD A grammatical distinction of verbs that indicates whether the verb is intended to make a statement or command or to express a doubt, emotion, or condition contrary to fact.

Imperative mood Verb forms used to make commands.

Di la verdad.   **Caminen** ustedes conmigo.
Tell the truth.   *Walk with me.*

¡Comamos ahora!
Let's eat now!

Indicative mood Verb forms used to state facts, actions, and states considered to be real.

Sé que **tienes** el dinero.
*I know that **you have** the money.*

Subjunctive mood Verb forms used principally in subordinate (dependent) clauses to express wishes, desires, emotions, doubts, and certain conditions, such as contrary-to-fact situations.

Prefieren que **hables** en español.
*They prefer that **you speak** in Spanish.*

Dudo que Luis **tenga** el dinero necesario.
*I doubt that Luis **has** the necessary money.*

NOUN A word that identifies people, animals, places, things, and ideas.

hombre   gato
man   *cat*

México   casa
Mexico   *house*

libertad   libro
freedom   *book*

NUMBER A grammatical term that refers to singular or plural. Nouns in Spanish and English have number. Other parts of a sentence, such as adjectives, articles, and verbs, can also have number.

Singular	Plural
una cosa	**unas** cosas
a thing	*some things*
el profesor	**los** profesores
the professor	*the professors*

NUMBERS Words that represent amounts.

Cardinal numbers Words that show specific amounts.

cinco minutos
five minutes

el año **dos mil siete**
the year 2007

Ordinal numbers Words that indicate the order of a noun in a series.

el **cuarto** jugador	la **décima** hora
*the **fourth** player*	*the **tenth** hour*

PAST PARTICIPLE A past form of the verb used in compound tenses. The past participle may also be used as an adjective, but it must then agree in number and gender with the word it modifies.

Han **buscado** por todas partes.
*They have **searched** everywhere.*

Yo no había **estudiado** para el examen.
*I hadn't **studied** for the exam.*

Hay una **ventana abierta** en la sala.
*There is an **open window** in the living room.*

PERSON The form of the verb or pronoun that indicates the speaker, the one spoken to, or the one spoken about. In Spanish, as in English, there are three persons: first, second, and third.

Person	Singular	Plural
1st	**yo** *I*	**nosotros/as** *we*
2nd	**tú, Ud.** *you*	**vosotros/as, Uds.** *you*
3rd	**él, ella** *he, she*	**ellos, ellas** *they*

PREPOSITION A word or words that describe(s) the relationship, most often in time or space, between two other words.

Anita es **de** California.
*Anita is **from** California.*

La chaqueta está **en** el carro.
*The jacket is **in** the car.*

Marta se peinó **antes de** salir.
*Marta combed her hair **before** going out.*

PRESENT PARTICIPLE In English, a verb form that ends in *-ing*. In Spanish, the present participle ends in **-ndo**, and is often used with **estar** to form a progressive tense.

Mi hermana está **hablando** por teléfono ahora mismo.
*My sister is **talking** on the phone right now.*

PRONOUN A word that takes the place of a noun or nouns.

Demonstrative pronoun A pronoun that takes the place of a specific noun.

Quiero **ésta**.
*I want **this one**.*

¿Vas a comprar **ése**?
*Are you going to buy **that one**?*

Juan prefirió **aquéllos**.
*Juan preferred **those** (over there).*

Object pronoun A pronoun that functions as a direct or indirect object of the verb.

Te digo la verdad.
*I'm telling **you** the truth.*

Me lo trajo Juan.
*Juan brought **it to me**.*

Reflexive pronoun A pronoun that indicates that the action of a verb is performed by the subject on itself. These pronouns are often expressed in English with *-self: myself, yourself,* etc.

Yo **me bañé** antes de salir.
*I **bathed** (**myself**) before going out.*

Elena **se acostó** a las once y media.
*Elena **went to bed** at eleven-thirty.*

Relative pronoun A pronoun that connects a subordinate clause to a main clause.

El chico **que** nos escribió viene a visitar mañana.
*The boy **who** wrote us is coming to visit tomorrow.*

Ya sé **lo que** tenemos que hacer.
*I already know **what** we have to do.*

Subject pronoun A pronoun that replaces the name or title of a person or thing, and acts as the subject of a verb.

Tú debes estudiar más.
***You** should study more.*

Él llegó primero.
***He** arrived first.*

SUBJECT A noun or pronoun that performs the action of a verb and is often implied by the verb.

María va al supermercado.
***María** goes to the supermarket.*

(Ellos) Trabajan mucho.
***They** work hard.*

Esos **libros** son muy caros.
*Those **books** are very expensive.*

SUPERLATIVE A word or construction used with an adjective or adverb to express the highest or lowest degree of a specific quality among three or more people, places, or things.

De todas mis clases, ésta es la **más interesante**.
*Of all my classes, this is the **most interesting**.*

Raúl es el **menos simpático** de los chicos.
*Raúl is the **least pleasant** of the boys.*

TENSE A set of verb forms that indicates the time of an action or state: past, present, or future.

Compound tense A two-word tense made up of an auxiliary verb and a present or past participle. In Spanish, there are two auxiliary verbs: **estar** and **haber**.

En este momento, **estoy estudiando**.
*At this time, **I am studying**.*

El paquete no **ha llegado** todavía.
*The package **has not arrived** yet.*

Simple tense A tense expressed by a single verb form.

María **estaba** mal anoche.
*María **was** ill last night.*

Juana **hablará** con su mamá mañana.
*Juana **will speak** with her mom tomorrow.*

VERB A word that expresses actions or states-of-being.

Auxiliary verb A verb used with a present or past participle to form a compound tense. **Haber** is the most commonly used auxiliary verb in Spanish.

Los chicos **han** visto los elefantes.
*The children **have** seen the elephants.*

Espero que **hayas** comido.
*I hope you **have** eaten.*

Reflexive verb A verb that describes an action performed by the subject on itself and is always used with a reflexive pronoun.

Me compré un carro nuevo.
*I **bought myself** a new car.*

Pedro y Adela **se levantan** muy temprano.
*Pedro and Adela **get (themselves) up** very early.*

Spelling-change verb A verb that undergoes a predictable change in spelling, in order to reflect its actual pronunciation in the various conjugations.

practicar	c→qu	practico	practiqué
dirigir	g→j	dirigí	dirijo
almorzar	z→c	almorzó	almorcé

Stem-changing verb A verb whose stem vowel undergoes one or more predictable changes in the various conjugations.

entender (i:ie)	entiendo
pedir (e:i)	piden
dormir (o:ue, u)	duermo, durmieron

Apéndice B

Verb Conjugation Tables

The verb lists

The list of verbs below and the model verb tables that start on page 338 show you how to conjugate every verb taught in **DESCUBRE**. Each verb in the list is followed by a model verb conjugated according to the same pattern. The number in parentheses indicates where in the verb tables you can find the conjugated forms of the model verb. If you want to find out how to conjugate **divertirse**, for example, look up number 33, **sentir**, the model for verbs that follow the e:ie stem-change pattern.

How to use the verb tables

In the tables you will find the infinitive, present and past participles, and all the simple forms of each model verb. The formation of the compound tenses of any verb can be inferred from the table of compound tenses, pages 338–339, either by combining the past participle of the verb with a conjugated form of **haber** or by combining the present participle with a conjugated form of **estar**.

abrazar (z:c) like cruzar (37)

abrir like vivir (3) *except* past participle is abierto

aburrir(se) like vivir (3)

acabar de like hablar (1)

acampar like hablar (1)

acompañar like hablar (1)

aconsejar like hablar (1)

acordarse (o:ue) like contar (24)

acostarse (o:ue) like contar (24)

adelgazar (z:c) like cruzar (37)

afeitarse like hablar (1)

ahorrar like hablar (1)

alegrarse like hablar (1)

aliviar like hablar (1)

almorzar (o:ue) like contar (24) *except* (z:c)

alquilar like hablar (1)

andar like hablar (1) *except* preterite stem is anduv-

anunciar like hablar (1)

apagar (g:gu) like llegar (41)

aplaudir like vivir (3)

apreciar like hablar (1)

aprender like comer (2)

apurarse like hablar (1)

arrancar (c:qu) like tocar (43)

arreglar like hablar (1)

asistir like vivir (3)

aumentar like hablar (1)

ayudar(se) like hablar (1)

bailar like hablar (1)

bajar(se) like hablar (1)

bañarse like hablar (1)

barrer like comer (2)

beber like comer (2)

besar(se) like hablar (1)

borrar like hablar (1)

brindar like hablar (1)

bucear like hablar (1)

buscar (c:qu) like tocar (43)

caber (4)

caer(se) (5)

calentarse (e:ie) like pensar (30)

calzar (z:c) like cruzar (37)

cambiar like hablar (1)

caminar like hablar (1)

cantar like hablar (1)

casarse like hablar (1)

cazar (z:c) like cruzar(37)

celebrar like hablar (1)

cenar like hablar (1)

cepillarse like hablar (1)

cerrar (e:ie) like pensar (30)

cobrar like hablar (1)

cocinar like hablar (1)

comenzar (e:ie) (z:c) like empezar (26)

comer (2)

compartir like vivir (3)

comprar like hablar (1)

comprender like comer (2)

comprometerse like comer (2)

comunicarse (c:qu) like tocar (43)

conducir (c:zc) (6)

confirmar like hablar (1)

conocer (c:zc) (35)

conseguir (e:i) (gu:g) like seguir (32)

conservar like hablar (1)

consumir like vivir (3)

contaminar like hablar (1)

contar (o:ue) (24)

controlar like hablar (1)

correr like comer (2)

costar (o:ue) like contar (24)

creer (y) (36)

cruzar (z:c) (37)

cubrir like vivir (3) *except* past participle is cubierto

cuidar like hablar (1)

cumplir like vivir (3)

dañar like hablar (1)

dar (7)

deber like comer (2)

decidir like vivir (3)

decir (e:i) (8)

declarar like hablar (1)

dejar like hablar (1)

depositar like hablar (1)

desarrollar like hablar (1)

desayunar like hablar (1)

descansar like hablar (1)

descargar (g:gu) like llegar (41)

describir like vivir (3) *except* past participle is descrito

descubrir like vivir (3) *except* past participle is descubierto

desear like hablar (1)

despedirse (e:i) like pedir (29)

despertarse (e:ie) like pensar (30)

destruir (y) (38)

dibujar like hablar (1)

dirigir like vivir (3) *except* (g:j)

disfrutar like hablar (1)

divertirse (e:ie) like sentir (33)

divorciarse like hablar (1)

doblar like hablar (1)

doler (o:ue) like volver (34) *except* past participle is regular

dormir(se) (o:ue) (25)

ducharse like hablar (1)

dudar like hablar (1)

durar like hablar (1)

echar like hablar (1)

elegir (e:i) like pedir (29) *except* (g:j)

emitir like vivir (3)

empezar (e:ie) (z:c) (26)

enamorarse like hablar (1)

encantar like hablar (1)

encontrar(se) (o:ue) like contar (24)

enfermarse like hablar (1)

engordar like hablar (1)

enojarse like hablar (1)

enseñar like hablar (1)

ensuciar like hablar (1)

entender (e:ie) (27)

entrenarse like hablar (1)

entrevistar like hablar (1)

enviar (envío) (39)

escalar like hablar (1)

escoger (g:j) like proteger (42)

escribir like vivir (3) except past participle is escrito

escuchar like hablar (1)

esculpir like vivir (3)

esperar like hablar (1)

esquiar (esquío) like enviar (39)

establecer (c:zc) like conocer (35)

estacionar like hablar (1)

estar (9)

estornudar like hablar (1)

estudiar like hablar (1)

evitar like hablar (1)

explicar (c:qu) like tocar (43)

explorar like hablar (1)

faltar like hablar (1)

fascinar like hablar (1)

firmar like hablar (1)

fumar like hablar (1)

funcionar like hablar (1)

ganar like hablar (1)

gastar like hablar (1)

grabar like hablar (1)

graduarse (gradúo) (40)

guardar like hablar (1)

gustar like hablar (1)

haber (hay) (10)

hablar (1)

hacer (11)

importar like hablar (1)

imprimir like vivir (3)

informar like hablar (1)

insistir like vivir (3)

interesar like hablar (1)

invertir (e:ie) like sentir (33)

invitar like hablar (1)

ir(se) (12)

jubilarse like hablar (1)

jugar (u:ue) (g:gu) (28)

lastimarse like hablar (1)

lavar(se) like hablar (1)

leer (y) like creer (36)

levantar(se) like hablar (1)

limpiar like hablar (1)

llamar(se) like hablar (1)

llegar (g:gu) (41)

llenar like hablar (1)

llevar(se) like hablar (1)

llover (o:ue) like volver (34) except past participle is regular

luchar like hablar (1)

mandar like hablar (1)

manejar like hablar (1)

mantener(se) like tener (20)

maquillarse like hablar (1)

mejorar like hablar (1)

merendar (e:ie) like pensar (30)

mirar like hablar (1)

molestar like hablar (1)

montar like hablar (1)

morir (o:ue) like dormir (25) except past participle is muerto

mostrar (o:ue) like contar (24)

mudarse like hablar (1)

nacer (c:zc) like conocer (35)

nadar like hablar (1)

navegar (g:gu) like llegar (41)

necesitar like hablar (1)

negar (e:ie) like pensar (30) except (g:gu)

nevar (e:ie) like pensar (30)

obedecer (c:zc) like conocer (35)

obtener like tener (20)

ocurrir like vivir (3)

odiar like hablar (1)

ofrecer (c:zc) like conocer (35)

oír (y) (13)

olvidar like hablar (1)

pagar (g:gu) like llegar (41)

parar like hablar (1)

parecer (c:zc) like conocer (35)

pasar like hablar (1)

pasear like hablar (1)

patinar like hablar (1)

pedir (e:i) (29)

peinarse like hablar (1)

pensar (e:ie) (30)

perder (e:ie) like entender (27)

pescar (c:qu) like tocar (43)

pintar like hablar (1)

planchar like hablar (1)

poder (o:ue) (14)

poner(se) (15)

practicar (c:qu) like tocar (43)

preferir (e:ie) like sentir (33)

preguntar like hablar (1)

preocuparse like hablar (1)

preparar like hablar (1)

presentar like hablar (1)

prestar like hablar (1)

probar(se) (o:ue) like contar (24)

prohibir like vivir (3)

proteger (g:j) (42)

publicar (c:qu) like tocar (43)

quedar(se) like hablar (1)

quemar like hablar (1)

querer (e:ie) (16)

quitar(se) like hablar (1)

recetar like hablar (1)

recibir like vivir (3)

reciclar like hablar (1)

recoger (g:j) like proteger (42)

recomendar (e:ie) like pensar (30)

recordar (o:ue) like contar (24)

reducir (c:zc) like conducir (6)

regalar like hablar (1)

regatear like hablar (1)

regresar like hablar (1)

reír(se) (e:i) (31)

relajarse like hablar (1)

renunciar like hablar (1)

repetir (e:i) like pedir (29)

resolver (o:ue) like volver (34)

respirar like hablar (1)

revisar like hablar (1)

rogar (o:ue) like contar (24) except (g:gu)

romper(se) like comer (2) except past participle is roto

saber (17)

sacar (c:qu) like tocar (43)

sacudir like vivir (3)

salir (18)

saludar(se) like hablar (1)

secar(se) (c:q) like tocar (43)

seguir (e:i) (32)

sentarse (e:ie) like pensar (30)

sentir(se) (e:ie) (33)

separarse like hablar (1)

ser (19)

servir (e:i) like pedir (29)

solicitar like hablar (1)

sonar (o:ue) like contar (24)

sonreír (e:i) like reír(se) (31)

sorprender like comer (2)

subir like vivir (3)

sudar like hablar (1)

sufrir like vivir (3)

sugerir (e:ie) like sentir (33)

suponer like poner (15)

temer like comer (2)

tener (20)

terminar like hablar (1)

tocar (c:qu) (43)

tomar like hablar (1)

torcerse (o:ue) like volver (34) except (c:z) and past participle is regular; e.g. yo tuerzo

toser like comer (2)

trabajar like hablar (1)

traducir (c:zc) like conducir (6)

traer (21)

transmitir like vivir (3)

tratar like hablar (1)

usar like hablar (1)

vender like comer (2)

venir (22)

ver (23)

vestirse (e:i) like pedir (29)

viajar like hablar (1)

visitar like hablar (1)

vivir (3)

volver (o:ue) (34)

votar like hablar (1)

Regular verbs: simple tenses

Infinitive	INDICATIVE					SUBJUNCTIVE		IMPERATIVE
	Present	Imperfect	Preterite	Future	Conditional	Present	Past	
1 hablar **Participles:** hablando hablado	hablo hablas habla hablamos habláis hablan	hablaba hablabas hablaba hablábamos hablabais hablaban	hablé hablaste habló hablamos hablasteis hablaron	hablaré hablarás hablará hablaremos hablaréis hablarán	hablaría hablarías hablaría hablaríamos hablaríais hablarían	hable hables hable hablemos habléis hablen	hablara hablaras hablara habláramos hablarais hablaran	habla tú (no hables) hable Ud. hablemos hablad (no habléis) hablen Uds.
2 comer **Participles:** comiendo comido	como comes come comemos coméis comen	comía comías comía comíamos comíais comían	comí comiste comió comimos comisteis comieron	comeré comerás comerá comeremos comeréis comerán	comería comerías comería comeríamos comeríais comerían	coma comas coma comamos comáis coman	comiera comieras comiera comiéramos comierais comieran	come tú (no comas) coma Ud. comamos comed (no comáis) coman Uds.
3 vivir **Participles:** viviendo vivido	vivo vives vive vivimos vivís viven	vivía vivías vivía vivíamos vivíais vivían	viví viviste vivió vivimos vivisteis vivieron	viviré vivirás vivirá viviremos viviréis vivirán	viviría vivirías viviría viviríamos viviríais vivirían	viva vivas viva vivamos viváis vivan	viviera vivieras viviera viviéramos vivierais vivieran	vive tú (no vivas) viva Ud. vivamos vivid (no viváis) vivan Uds.

All verbs: compound tenses

PERFECT TENSES

INDICATIVE				SUBJUNCTIVE	
Present Perfect	Past Perfect	Future Perfect	Conditional Perfect	Present Perfect	Past Perfect
he has ha hemos habéis han	había habías había habíamos habíais habían	habré habrás habrá habremos habréis habrán	habría habrías habría habríamos habríais habrían	haya hayas haya hayamos hayáis hayan	hubiera hubieras hubiera hubiéramos hubierais hubieran
hablado comido vivido	hablado comido vivido	hablado comido vivido	hablado comido vivido	hablado comido vivido	hablado comido vivido

PROGRESSIVE TENSES

INDICATIVE				SUBJUNCTIVE	
Present Progressive	Past Progressive	Future Progressive	Conditional Progressive	Present Progressive	Past Progressive
estoy	estaba	estaré	estaría	esté	estuviera
estás	estabas	estarás	estarías	estés	estuvieras
está hablando	estaba hablando	estará hablando	estaría hablando	esté hablando	estuviera hablando
estamos comiendo	estábamos comiendo	estaremos comiendo	estaríamos comiendo	estemos comiendo	estuviéramos comiendo
estáis viviendo	estabais viviendo	estaréis viviendo	estaríais viviendo	estéis viviendo	estuvierais viviendo
están	estaban	estarán	estarían	estén	estuvieran

Irregular verbs

Infinitive	INDICATIVE					SUBJUNCTIVE		IMPERATIVE
	Present	Imperfect	Preterite	Future	Conditional	Present	Past	
4 caber	**quepo**	cabía	**cupe**	**cabré**	**cabría**	**quepa**	**cupiera**	
	cabes	cabías	**cupiste**	**cabrás**	**cabrías**	**quepas**	**cupieras**	cabe tú (no **quepas**)
Participles:	cabe	cabía	**cupo**	**cabrá**	**cabría**	**quepa**	**cupiera**	**quepa** Ud.
cabiendo	cabemos	cabíamos	**cupimos**	**cabremos**	**cabríamos**	**quepamos**	**cupiéramos**	**quepamos**
cabido	cabéis	cabíais	**cupisteis**	**cabréis**	**cabríais**	**quepáis**	**cupierais**	cabed (no **quepáis**)
	caben	cabían	**cupieron**	**cabrán**	**cabrían**	**quepan**	**cupieran**	**quepan** Uds.
5 caer(se)	**caigo**	caía	caí	caeré	caería	**caiga**	**cayera**	
	caes	caías	**caíste**	caerás	caerías	**caigas**	**cayeras**	cae tú (no **caigas**)
Participles:	cae	caía	**cayó**	caerá	caería	**caiga**	**cayera**	**caiga** Ud.
cayendo	caemos	caíamos	**caímos**	caeremos	caeríamos	**caigamos**	**cayéramos**	**caigamos**
caído	caéis	caíais	**caísteis**	caeréis	caeríais	**caigáis**	**cayerais**	caed (no **caigáis**)
	caen	caían	**cayeron**	caerán	caerían	**caigan**	**cayeran**	**caigan** Uds.
6 conducir	**conduzco**	conducía	**conduje**	conduciré	conduciría	**conduzca**	**condujera**	
(c:zc)	conduces	conducías	**condujiste**	conducirás	conducirías	**conduzcas**	**condujeras**	conduce tú (no **conduzcas**)
Participles:	conduce	conducía	**condujo**	conducirá	conduciría	**conduzca**	**condujera**	**conduzca** Ud.
conduciendo	conducimos	conducíamos	**condujimos**	conduciremos	conduciríamos	**conduzcamos**	**condujéramos**	**conduzcamos**
conducido	conducís	conducíais	**condujisteis**	conduciréis	conduciríais	**conduzcáis**	**condujerais**	conducid (no **conduzcáis**)
	conducen	conducían	**condujeron**	conducirán	conducirían	**conduzcan**	**condujeran**	**conduzcan** Uds.

7. dar — Participles: dando, dado

	INDICATIVE					SUBJUNCTIVE		IMPERATIVE
	Present	Imperfect	Preterite	Future	Conditional	Present	Past	
	doy	daba	di	daré	daría	dé	diera	
	das	dabas	diste	darás	darías	des	dieras	da tú (no des)
	da	daba	dio	dará	daría	dé	diera	dé Ud.
	damos	dábamos	dimos	daremos	daríamos	demos	diéramos	demos
	dais	dabais	disteis	daréis	daríais	deis	dierais	dad (no deis)
	dan	daban	dieron	darán	darían	den	dieran	den Uds.

8. decir (e:i) — Participles: diciendo, dicho

	INDICATIVE					SUBJUNCTIVE		IMPERATIVE
	Present	Imperfect	Preterite	Future	Conditional	Present	Past	
	digo	decía	dije	diré	diría	diga	dijera	
	dices	decías	dijiste	dirás	dirías	digas	dijeras	di tú (no digas)
	dice	decía	dijo	dirá	diría	diga	dijera	diga Ud.
	decimos	decíamos	dijimos	diremos	diríamos	digamos	dijéramos	digamos
	decís	decíais	dijisteis	diréis	diríais	digáis	dijerais	decid (no digáis)
	dicen	decían	dijeron	dirán	dirían	digan	dijeran	digan Uds.

9. estar — Participles: estando, estado

	INDICATIVE					SUBJUNCTIVE		IMPERATIVE
	Present	Imperfect	Preterite	Future	Conditional	Present	Past	
	estoy	estaba	estuve	estaré	estaría	esté	estuviera	
	estás	estabas	estuviste	estarás	estarías	estés	estuvieras	está tú (no estés)
	está	estaba	estuvo	estará	estaría	esté	estuviera	esté Ud.
	estamos	estábamos	estuvimos	estaremos	estaríamos	estemos	estuviéramos	estemos
	estáis	estabais	estuvisteis	estaréis	estaríais	estéis	estuvierais	estad (no estéis)
	están	estaban	estuvieron	estarán	estarían	estén	estuvieran	estén Uds.

10. haber — Participles: habiendo, habido

	INDICATIVE					SUBJUNCTIVE		IMPERATIVE
	Present	Imperfect	Preterite	Future	Conditional	Present	Past	
	he	había	hube	habré	habría	haya	hubiera	
	has	habías	hubiste	habrás	habrías	hayas	hubieras	
	ha	había	hubo	habrá	habría	haya	hubiera	
	hemos	habíamos	hubimos	habremos	habríamos	hayamos	hubiéramos	
	habéis	habíais	hubisteis	habréis	habríais	hayáis	hubierais	
	han	habían	hubieron	habrán	habrían	hayan	hubieran	

11. hacer — Participles: haciendo, hecho

	INDICATIVE					SUBJUNCTIVE		IMPERATIVE
	Present	Imperfect	Preterite	Future	Conditional	Present	Past	
	hago	hacía	hice	haré	haría	haga	hiciera	
	haces	hacías	hiciste	harás	harías	hagas	hicieras	haz tú (no hagas)
	hace	hacía	hizo	hará	haría	haga	hiciera	haga Ud.
	hacemos	hacíamos	hicimos	haremos	haríamos	hagamos	hiciéramos	hagamos
	hacéis	hacíais	hicisteis	haréis	haríais	hagáis	hicierais	haced (no hagáis)
	hacen	hacían	hicieron	harán	harían	hagan	hicieran	hagan Uds.

12. ir — Participles: yendo, ido

	INDICATIVE					SUBJUNCTIVE		IMPERATIVE
	Present	Imperfect	Preterite	Future	Conditional	Present	Past	
	voy	iba	fui	iré	iría	vaya	fuera	
	vas	ibas	fuiste	irás	irías	vayas	fueras	ve tú (no vayas)
	va	iba	fue	irá	iría	vaya	fuera	vaya Ud.
	vamos	íbamos	fuimos	iremos	iríamos	vayamos	fuéramos	vamos (no vayamos)
	vais	ibais	fuisteis	iréis	iríais	vayáis	fuerais	id (no vayáis)
	van	iban	fueron	irán	irían	vayan	fueran	vayan Uds.

13. oír (y) — Participles: oyendo, oído

	INDICATIVE					SUBJUNCTIVE		IMPERATIVE
	Present	Imperfect	Preterite	Future	Conditional	Present	Past	
	oigo	oía	oí	oiré	oiría	oiga	oyera	
	oyes	oías	oíste	oirás	oirías	oigas	oyeras	oye tú (no oigas)
	oye	oía	oyó	oirá	oiría	oiga	oyera	oiga Ud.
	oímos	oíamos	oímos	oiremos	oiríamos	oigamos	oyéramos	oigamos
	oís	oíais	oísteis	oiréis	oiríais	oigáis	oyerais	oíd (no oigáis)
	oyen	oían	oyeron	oirán	oirían	oigan	oyeran	oigan Uds.

Infinitive	INDICATIVE					SUBJUNCTIVE		IMPERATIVE
	Present	Imperfect	Preterite	Future	Conditional	Present	Past	

14 poder (o:ue)
Participles: pudiendo, podido

	Present	Imperfect	Preterite	Future	Conditional	Present	Past	Imperative
	puedo	podía	pude	podré	podría	pueda	pudiera	
	puedes	podías	pudiste	podrás	podrías	puedas	pudieras	puede tú (no puedas)
	puede	podía	pudo	podrá	podría	pueda	pudiera	pueda Ud.
	podemos	podíamos	pudimos	podremos	podríamos	podamos	pudiéramos	podamos
	podéis	podíais	pudisteis	podréis	podríais	podáis	pudierais	poded (no podáis)
	pueden	podían	pudieron	podrán	podrían	puedan	pudieran	puedan Uds.

15 poner
Participles: poniendo, puesto

	Present	Imperfect	Preterite	Future	Conditional	Present	Past	Imperative
	pongo	ponía	puse	pondré	pondría	ponga	pusiera	
	pones	ponías	pusiste	pondrás	pondrías	pongas	pusieras	pon tú (no pongas)
	pone	ponía	puso	pondrá	pondría	ponga	pusiera	ponga Ud.
	ponemos	poníamos	pusimos	pondremos	pondríamos	pongamos	pusiéramos	pongamos
	ponéis	poníais	pusisteis	pondréis	pondríais	pongáis	pusierais	poned (no pongáis)
	ponen	ponían	pusieron	pondrán	pondrían	pongan	pusieran	pongan Uds.

16 querer (e:ie)
Participles: queriendo, querido

	Present	Imperfect	Preterite	Future	Conditional	Present	Past	Imperative
	quiero	quería	quise	querré	querría	quiera	quisiera	
	quieres	querías	quisiste	querrás	querrías	quieras	quisieras	quiere tú (no quieras)
	quiere	quería	quiso	querrá	querría	quiera	quisiera	quiera Ud.
	queremos	queríamos	quisimos	querremos	querríamos	queramos	quisiéramos	queramos
	queréis	queríais	quisisteis	querréis	querríais	queráis	quisierais	quered (no queráis)
	quieren	querían	quisieron	querrán	querrían	quieran	quisieran	quieran Uds.

17 saber
Participles: sabiendo, sabido

	Present	Imperfect	Preterite	Future	Conditional	Present	Past	Imperative
	sé	sabía	supe	sabré	sabría	sepa	supiera	
	sabes	sabías	supiste	sabrás	sabrías	sepas	supieras	sabe tú (no sepas)
	sabe	sabía	supo	sabrá	sabría	sepa	supiera	sepa Ud.
	sabemos	sabíamos	supimos	sabremos	sabríamos	sepamos	supiéramos	sepamos
	sabéis	sabíais	supisteis	sabréis	sabríais	sepáis	supierais	sabed (no sepáis)
	saben	sabían	supieron	sabrán	sabrían	sepan	supieran	sepan Uds.

18 salir
Participles: saliendo, salido

	Present	Imperfect	Preterite	Future	Conditional	Present	Past	Imperative
	salgo	salía	salí	saldré	saldría	salga	saliera	
	sales	salías	saliste	saldrás	saldrías	salgas	salieras	sal tú (no salgas)
	sale	salía	salió	saldrá	saldría	salga	saliera	salga Ud.
	salimos	salíamos	salimos	saldremos	saldríamos	salgamos	saliéramos	salgamos
	salís	salíais	salisteis	saldréis	saldríais	salgáis	salierais	salid (no salgáis)
	salen	salían	salieron	saldrán	saldrían	salgan	salieran	salgan Uds.

19 ser
Participles: siendo, sido

	Present	Imperfect	Preterite	Future	Conditional	Present	Past	Imperative
	soy	era	fui	seré	sería	sea	fuera	
	eres	eras	fuiste	serás	serías	seas	fueras	sé tú (no seas)
	es	era	fue	será	sería	sea	fuera	sea Ud.
	somos	éramos	fuimos	seremos	seríamos	seamos	fuéramos	seamos
	sois	erais	fuisteis	seréis	seríais	seáis	fuerais	sed (no seáis)
	son	eran	fueron	serán	serían	sean	fueran	sean Uds.

20 tener
Participles: teniendo, tenido

	Present	Imperfect	Preterite	Future	Conditional	Present	Past	Imperative
	tengo	tenía	tuve	tendré	tendría	tenga	tuviera	
	tienes	tenías	tuviste	tendrás	tendrías	tengas	tuvieras	ten tú (no tengas)
	tiene	tenía	tuvo	tendrá	tendría	tenga	tuviera	tenga Ud.
	tenemos	teníamos	tuvimos	tendremos	tendríamos	tengamos	tuviéramos	tengamos
	tenéis	teníais	tuvisteis	tendréis	tendríais	tengáis	tuvierais	tened (no tengáis)
	tienen	tenían	tuvieron	tendrán	tendrían	tengan	tuvieran	tengan Uds.

21. traer — Participles: trayendo, traído

Infinitive	INDICATIVE					SUBJUNCTIVE		IMPERATIVE
	Present	Imperfect	Preterite	Future	Conditional	Present	Past	
traer	traigo	traía	traje	traeré	traería	traiga	trajera	
	traes	traías	trajiste	traerás	traerías	traigas	trajeras	trae tú (no traigas)
	trae	traía	trajo	traerá	traería	traiga	trajera	traiga Ud.
	traemos	traíamos	trajimos	traeremos	traeríamos	traigamos	trajéramos	traigamos
	traéis	traíais	trajisteis	traeréis	traeríais	traigáis	trajerais	traed (no traigáis)
	traen	traían	trajeron	traerán	traerían	traigan	trajeran	traigan Uds.

22. venir — Participles: viniendo, venido

Infinitive	INDICATIVE					SUBJUNCTIVE		IMPERATIVE
	Present	Imperfect	Preterite	Future	Conditional	Present	Past	
venir	vengo	venía	vine	vendré	vendría	venga	viniera	
	vienes	venías	viniste	vendrás	vendrías	vengas	vinieras	ven tú (no vengas)
	viene	venía	vino	vendrá	vendría	venga	viniera	venga Ud.
	venimos	veníamos	vinimos	vendremos	vendríamos	vengamos	viniéramos	vengamos
	venís	veníais	vinisteis	vendréis	vendríais	vengáis	vinierais	venid (no vengáis)
	vienen	venían	vinieron	vendrán	vendrían	vengan	vinieran	vengan Uds.

23. ver — Participles: viendo, visto

Infinitive	INDICATIVE					SUBJUNCTIVE		IMPERATIVE
	Present	Imperfect	Preterite	Future	Conditional	Present	Past	
ver	veo	veía	vi	veré	vería	vea	viera	
	ves	veías	viste	verás	verías	veas	vieras	ve tú (no veas)
	ve	veía	vio	verá	vería	vea	viera	vea Ud.
	vemos	veíamos	vimos	veremos	veríamos	veamos	viéramos	veamos
	veis	veíais	visteis	veréis	veríais	veáis	vierais	ved (no veáis)
	ven	veían	vieron	verán	verían	vean	vieran	vean Uds.

Stem-changing verbs

24. contar (o:ue) — Participles: contando, contado

Infinitive	INDICATIVE					SUBJUNCTIVE		IMPERATIVE
	Present	Imperfect	Preterite	Future	Conditional	Present	Past	
contar (o:ue)	cuento	contaba	conté	contaré	contaría	cuente	contara	
	cuentas	contabas	contaste	contarás	contarías	cuentes	contaras	cuenta tú (no cuentes)
	cuenta	contaba	contó	contará	contaría	cuente	contara	cuente Ud.
	contamos	contábamos	contamos	contaremos	contaríamos	contemos	contáramos	contemos
	contáis	contabais	contasteis	contaréis	contaríais	contéis	contarais	contad (no contéis)
	cuentan	contaban	contaron	contarán	contarían	cuenten	contaran	cuenten Uds.

25. dormir (o:ue) — Participles: durmiendo, dormido

Infinitive	INDICATIVE					SUBJUNCTIVE		IMPERATIVE
	Present	Imperfect	Preterite	Future	Conditional	Present	Past	
dormir (o:ue)	duermo	dormía	dormí	dormiré	dormiría	duerma	durmiera	
	duermes	dormías	dormiste	dormirás	dormirías	duermas	durmieras	duerme tú (no duermas)
	duerme	dormía	durmió	dormirá	dormiría	duerma	durmiera	duerma Ud.
	dormimos	dormíamos	dormimos	dormiremos	dormiríamos	durmamos	durmiéramos	durmamos
	dormís	dormíais	dormisteis	dormiréis	dormiríais	durmáis	durmierais	dormid (no durmáis)
	duermen	dormían	durmieron	dormirán	dormirían	duerman	durmieran	duerman Uds.

26. empezar (e:ie) (z:c) — Participles: empezando, empezado

Infinitive	INDICATIVE					SUBJUNCTIVE		IMPERATIVE
	Present	Imperfect	Preterite	Future	Conditional	Present	Past	
empezar (e:ie) (z:c)	empiezo	empezaba	empecé	empezaré	empezaría	empiece	empezara	
	empiezas	empezabas	empezaste	empezarás	empezarías	empieces	empezaras	empieza tú (no empieces)
	empieza	empezaba	empezó	empezará	empezaría	empiece	empezara	empiece Ud.
	empezamos	empezábamos	empezamos	empezaremos	empezaríamos	empecemos	empezáramos	empecemos
	empezáis	empezabais	empezasteis	empezaréis	empezaríais	empecéis	empezarais	empezad (no empecéis)
	empiezan	empezaban	empezaron	empezarán	empezarían	empiecen	empezaran	empiecen Uds.

Infinitive	INDICATIVE					SUBJUNCTIVE		IMPERATIVE
	Present	Imperfect	Preterite	Future	Conditional	Present	Past	
27 entender (e:ie) Participles: entendiendo entendido	entiendo entiendes entiende entendemos entendéis entienden	entendía entendías entendía entendíamos entendíais entendían	entendí entendiste entendió entendimos entendisteis entendieron	entenderé entenderás entenderá entenderemos entenderéis entenderán	entendería entenderías entendería entenderíamos entenderíais entenderían	entienda entiendas entienda entendamos entendáis entiendan	entendiera entendieras entendiera entendiéramos entendierais entendieran	entiende tú (no entiendas) entienda Ud. entendamos entended (no entendáis) entiendan Uds.
28 jugar (u:ue) (g:gu) Participles: jugando jugado	juego juegas juega jugamos jugáis juegan	jugaba jugabas jugaba jugábamos jugabais jugaban	jugué jugaste jugó jugamos jugasteis jugaron	jugaré jugarás jugará jugaremos jugaréis jugarán	jugaría jugarías jugaría jugaríamos jugaríais jugarían	juegue juegues juegue juguemos juguéis jueguen	jugara jugaras jugara jugáramos jugarais jugaran	juega tú (no juegues) juegue Ud. juguemos jugad (no juguéis) jueguen Uds.
29 pedir (e:i) Participles: pidiendo pedido	pido pides pide pedimos pedís piden	pedía pedías pedía pedíamos pedíais pedían	pedí pediste pidió pedimos pedisteis pidieron	pediré pedirás pedirá pediremos pediréis pedirán	pediría pedirías pediría pediríamos pediríais pedirían	pida pidas pida pidamos pidáis pidan	pidiera pidieras pidiera pidiéramos pidierais pidieran	pide tú (no pidas) pida Ud. pidamos pedid (no pidáis) pidan Uds.
30 pensar (e:ie) Participles: pensando pensado	pienso piensas piensa pensamos pensáis piensan	pensaba pensabas pensaba pensábamos pensabais pensaban	pensé pensaste pensó pensamos pensasteis pensaron	pensaré pensarás pensará pensaremos pensaréis pensarán	pensaría pensarías pensaría pensaríamos pensaríais pensarían	piense pienses piense pensemos penséis piensen	pensara pensaras pensara pensáramos pensarais pensaran	piensa tú (no pienses) piense Ud. pensemos pensad (no penséis) piensen Uds.
31 reír (e:i) Participles: riendo reído	río ríes ríe reímos reís ríen	reía reías reía reíamos reíais reían	reí reíste rió reímos reísteis rieron	reiré reirás reirá reiremos reiréis reirán	reiría reirías reiría reiríamos reiríais reirían	ría rías ría riamos riáis rían	riera rieras riera riéramos rierais rieran	ríe tú (no rías) ría Ud. riamos reíd (no riáis) rían Uds.
32 seguir (e:i) (gu:g) Participles: siguiendo seguido	sigo sigues sigue seguimos seguís siguen	seguía seguías seguía seguíamos seguíais seguían	seguí seguiste siguió seguimos seguisteis siguieron	seguiré seguirás seguirá seguiremos seguiréis seguirán	seguiría seguirías seguiría seguiríamos seguiríais seguirían	siga sigas siga sigamos sigáis sigan	siguiera siguieras siguiera siguiéramos siguierais siguieran	sigue tú (no sigas) siga Ud. sigamos seguid (no sigáis) sigan Uds.
33 sentir (e:ie) Participles: sintiendo sentido	siento sientes siente sentimos sentís sienten	sentía sentías sentía sentíamos sentíais sentían	sentí sentiste sintió sentimos sentisteis sintieron	sentiré sentirás sentirá sentiremos sentiréis sentirán	sentiría sentirías sentiría sentiríamos sentiríais sentirían	sienta sientas sienta sintamos sintáis sientan	sintiera sintieras sintiera sintiéramos sintierais sintieran	siente tú (no sientas) sienta Ud. sintamos sentid (no sintáis) sientan Uds.

34 volver (o:ue)
Participles: volviendo, vuelto

Infinitive	INDICATIVE					SUBJUNCTIVE		IMPERATIVE
	Present	Imperfect	Preterite	Future	Conditional	Present	Past	
	vuelvo	volvía	volví	volveré	volvería	vuelva	volviera	
	vuelves	volvías	volviste	volverás	volverías	vuelvas	volvieras	vuelve tú (no vuelvas)
	vuelve	volvía	volvió	volverá	volvería	vuelva	volviera	vuelva Ud.
	volvemos	volvíamos	volvimos	volveremos	volveríamos	volvamos	volviéramos	volvamos
	volvéis	volvíais	volvisteis	volveréis	volveríais	volváis	volvierais	volved (no volváis)
	vuelven	volvían	volvieron	volverán	volverían	vuelvan	volvieran	vuelvan Uds.

Verbs with spelling changes only

35 conocer (c:zc)
Participles: conociendo, conocido

Infinitive	INDICATIVE					SUBJUNCTIVE		IMPERATIVE
	Present	Imperfect	Preterite	Future	Conditional	Present	Past	
	conozco	conocía	conocí	conoceré	conocería	conozca	conociera	
	conoces	conocías	conociste	conocerás	conocerías	conozcas	conocieras	conoce tú (no conozcas)
	conoce	conocía	conoció	conocerá	conocería	conozca	conociera	conozca Ud.
	conocemos	conocíamos	conocimos	conoceremos	conoceríamos	conozcamos	conociéramos	conozcamos
	conocéis	conocíais	conocisteis	conoceréis	conoceríais	conozcáis	conocierais	conoced (no conozcáis)
	conocen	conocían	conocieron	conocerán	conocerían	conozcan	conocieran	conozcan Uds.

36 creer (y)
Participles: creyendo, creído

Infinitive	INDICATIVE					SUBJUNCTIVE		IMPERATIVE
	Present	Imperfect	Preterite	Future	Conditional	Present	Past	
	creo	creía	creí	creeré	creería	crea	creyera	
	crees	creías	creíste	creerás	creerías	creas	creyeras	cree tú (no creas)
	cree	creía	creyó	creerá	creería	crea	creyera	crea Ud.
	creemos	creíamos	creímos	creeremos	creeríamos	creamos	creyéramos	creamos
	creéis	creíais	creísteis	creeréis	creeríais	creáis	creyerais	creed (no creáis)
	creen	creían	creyeron	creerán	creerían	crean	creyeran	crean Uds.

37 cruzar (z:c)
Participles: cruzando, cruzado

Infinitive	INDICATIVE					SUBJUNCTIVE		IMPERATIVE
	Present	Imperfect	Preterite	Future	Conditional	Present	Past	
	cruzo	cruzaba	crucé	cruzaré	cruzaría	cruce	cruzara	
	cruzas	cruzabas	cruzaste	cruzarás	cruzarías	cruces	cruzaras	cruza tú (no cruces)
	cruza	cruzaba	cruzó	cruzará	cruzaría	cruce	cruzara	cruce Ud.
	cruzamos	cruzábamos	cruzamos	cruzaremos	cruzaríamos	crucemos	cruzáramos	crucemos
	cruzáis	cruzabais	cruzasteis	cruzaréis	cruzaríais	crucéis	cruzarais	cruzad (no crucéis)
	cruzan	cruzaban	cruzaron	cruzarán	cruzarían	crucen	cruzaran	crucen Uds.

38 destruir (y)
Participles: destruyendo, destruido

Infinitive	INDICATIVE					SUBJUNCTIVE		IMPERATIVE
	Present	Imperfect	Preterite	Future	Conditional	Present	Past	
	destruyo	destruía	destruí	destruiré	destruiría	destruya	destruyera	
	destruyes	destruías	destruiste	destruirás	destruirías	destruyas	destruyeras	destruye tú (no destruyas)
	destruye	destruía	destruyó	destruirá	destruiría	destruya	destruyera	destruya Ud.
	destruimos	destruíamos	destruimos	destruiremos	destruiríamos	destruyamos	destruyéramos	destruyamos
	destruís	destruíais	destruisteis	destruiréis	destruiríais	destruyáis	destruyerais	destruid (no destruyáis)
	destruyen	destruían	destruyeron	destruirán	destruirían	destruyan	destruyeran	destruyan Uds.

39 enviar (envío)
Participles: enviando, enviado

Infinitive	INDICATIVE					SUBJUNCTIVE		IMPERATIVE
	Present	Imperfect	Preterite	Future	Conditional	Present	Past	
	envío	enviaba	envié	enviaré	enviaría	envíe	enviara	
	envías	enviabas	enviaste	enviarás	enviarías	envíes	enviaras	envía tú (no envíes)
	envía	enviaba	envió	enviará	enviaría	envíe	enviara	envíe Ud.
	enviamos	enviábamos	enviamos	enviaremos	enviaríamos	enviemos	enviáramos	enviemos
	enviáis	enviabais	enviasteis	enviaréis	enviaríais	enviéis	enviarais	enviad (no enviéis)
	envían	enviaban	enviaron	enviarán	enviarían	envíen	enviaran	envíen Uds.

	INDICATIVE					SUBJUNCTIVE		IMPERATIVE
Infinitive	Present	Imperfect	Preterite	Future	Conditional	Present	Past	
40 graduarse (gradúo)	gradúo	graduaba	gradué	graduaré	graduaría	gradúe	graduara	
	gradúas	graduabas	graduaste	graduarás	graduarías	gradúes	graduaras	gradúa tú (no gradúes)
	gradúa	graduaba	graduó	graduará	graduaría	gradúe	graduara	gradúe Ud.
Participles:	graduamos	graduábamos	graduamos	graduaremos	graduaríamos	graduemos	graduáramos	graduemos
graduando	graduáis	graduabais	graduasteis	graduaréis	graduaríais	graduéis	graduarais	graduad (no graduéis)
graduado	gradúan	graduaban	graduaron	graduarán	graduarían	gradúen	graduaran	gradúen Uds.
41 llegar (g:gu)	llego	llegaba	llegué	llegaré	llegaría	llegue	llegara	
	llegas	llegabas	llegaste	llegarás	llegarías	llegues	llegaras	llega tú (no llegues)
	llega	llegaba	llegó	llegará	llegaría	llegue	llegara	llegue Ud.
Participles:	llegamos	llegábamos	llegamos	llegaremos	llegaríamos	lleguemos	llegáramos	lleguemos
llegando	llegáis	llegabais	llegasteis	llegaréis	llegaríais	lleguéis	llegarais	llegad (no lleguéis)
llegado	llegan	llegaban	llegaron	llegarán	llegarían	lleguen	llegaran	lleguen Uds.
42 proteger (g:j)	protejo	protegía	protegí	protegeré	protegería	proteja	protegiera	
	proteges	protegías	protegiste	protegerás	protegerías	protejas	protegieras	protege tú (no protejas)
	protege	protegía	protegió	protegerá	protegería	proteja	protegiera	proteja Ud.
Participles:	protegemos	protegíamos	protegimos	protegeremos	protegeríamos	protejamos	protegiéramos	protejamos
protegiendo	protegéis	protegíais	protegisteis	protegeréis	protegeríais	protejáis	protegierais	proteged (no protejáis)
protegido	protegen	protegían	protegieron	protegerán	protegerían	protejan	protegieran	protejan Uds.
43 tocar (c:qu)	toco	tocaba	toqué	tocaré	tocaría	toque	tocara	
	tocas	tocabas	tocaste	tocarás	tocarías	toques	tocaras	toca tú (no toques)
	toca	tocaba	tocó	tocará	tocaría	toque	tocara	toque Ud.
Participles:	tocamos	tocábamos	tocamos	tocaremos	tocaríamos	toquemos	tocáramos	toquemos
tocando	tocáis	tocabais	tocasteis	tocaréis	tocaríais	toquéis	tocarais	tocad (no toquéis)
tocado	tocan	tocaban	tocaron	tocarán	tocarían	toquen	tocaran	toquen Uds.

Guide to Vocabulary

Contents of the glossary

This glossary contains the words and expressions listed on the **Vocabulario** page found at the end of each lesson in **DESCUBRE** as well as other useful vocabulary. The number following an entry indicates the lesson where the word or expression was introduced.

Abbreviations used in this glossary

adj.	adjective	*f.*	feminine	*m.*	masculine	*prep.*	preposition
adv.	adverb	*fam.*	familiar	*n.*	noun	*pron.*	pronoun
art.	article	*form.*	formal	*obj.*	object	*ref.*	reflexive
conj.	conjunction	*indef.*	indefinite	*p.p.*	past participle	*sing.*	singular
def.	definite	*interj.*	interjection	*pl.*	plural	*sub.*	subject
d.o.	direct object	*i.o.*	indirect object	*poss.*	possessive	*v.*	verb

Note on alphabetization

For purposes of alphabetization, **ch** and **ll** are not treated as separate letters, but **ñ** still follows **n**.

Spanish-English

A

a *prep.* at; to 1.1
  a bordo aboard 1.1
  a la derecha to the right 1.2
  a la izquierda to the left 1.2
  a la plancha grilled 1.8
  a la(s) + *time* at + *time* 1.1
  a nombre de in the name of 1.5
  ¿A qué hora...? At what time...? 1.1
  a ver let's see 1.2
abeja *f.* bee
abierto/a *adj.* open 1.5
abrazo *m.* hug
abrigo *m.* coat 1.6
abril *m.* April 1.5
abrir *v.* to open 1.3
abuelo/a *m., f.* grandfather; grandmother 1.3
abuelos *pl.* grandparents 1.3
aburrido/a *adj.* bored; boring 1.5
aburrir *v.* to bore 1.7
acabar de (+ *inf.***)** *v.* to have just (*done something*) 1.6
acampar *v.* to camp 1.5
aceite *m.* oil 1.8
acordarse (de) (o:ue) *v.* to remember 1.7
acostarse (o:ue) *v.* to go to bed 1.7
acuático/a *adj.* aquatic 1.4
adicional *adj.* additional
adiós *m.* good-bye 1.1
adjetivo *m.* adjective
administración de empresas *f.* business administration 1.2

adolescencia *f.* adolescence 1.9
¿adónde? *adv.* where (to)? (*destination*) 1.2
aduana *f.* customs 1.5
aeropuerto *m.* airport 1.5
afeitarse *v.* to shave 1.7
aficionado/a *adj.* fan 1.4
afirmativo/a *adj.* affirmative
agencia de viajes *f.* travel agency 1.5
agente de viajes *m., f.* travel agent 1.5
agosto *m.* August 1.5
agradable *adj.* pleasant
agua *f.* water 1.8
  agua mineral mineral water 1.8
ahora *adv.* now 1.2
  ahora mismo right now 1.5
aire *m.* air 1.5
ajo *m.* garlic 1.8
al (*contraction of* **a + el**) 1.2
  al aire libre open-air 1.6
  al lado de beside 1.2
alegre *adj.* happy; joyful 1.5
alegría *f.* happiness 1.9
alemán, alemana *adj.* German 1.3
algo *pron.* something; anything 1.7
algodón *m.* cotton 1.6
alguien *pron.* someone; somebody; anyone 1.7
algún, alguno/a(s) *adj.* any; some 1.7
alimento *m.* food
alimentación *f.* diet
allí *adv.* there 1.5
almacén *m.* department store 1.6
almorzar (o:ue) *v.* to have lunch 1.4
almuerzo *m.* lunch 1.8

alto/a *adj.* tall 1.3
amable *adj.* nice; friendly 1.5
amarillo/a *adj.* yellow 1.6
amigo/a *m., f.* friend 1.3
amistad *f.* friendship 1.9
amor *m.* love 1.9
anaranjado/a *adj.* orange 1.6
andar *v.* **en patineta** to skateboard 1.4
aniversario (de bodas) *m.* (wedding) anniversary 1.9
anoche *adv.* last night 1.6
anteayer *adv.* the day before yesterday 1.6
antes *adv.* before 1.7
  antes de *prep.* before 1.7
antipático/a *adj.* unpleasant 1.3
año *m.* year 1.5
  año pasado last year 1.6
aparato *m.* appliance
apellido *m.* last name 1.3
aprender (a + *inf.***)** *v.* to learn 1.3
aquel, aquella *adj.* that 1.6
aquél, aquélla *pron.* that 1.6
aquello *neuter pron.* that; that thing; that fact 1.6
aquellos/as *pl. adj.* those (over there) 1.6
aquéllos/as *pl. pron.* those (ones) (over there) 1.6
aquí *adv.* here 1.1
  Aquí está... Here it is... 1.5
  Aquí estamos en... Here we are at/in... 1.2
arriba *adv.* up
arroz *m.* rice 1.8
arte *m.* art 1.2
artista *m., f.* artist 1.3
arveja *m.* pea 1.8
asado/a *adj.* roast 1.8

ascensor *m.* elevator 1.5
así así so-so
asistir (a) *v.* to attend 1.3
atún *m.* tuna 1.8
aunque although
autobús *m.* bus 1.1
automático/a *adj.* automatic
auto(móvil) *m.* auto(mobile) 1.5
avenida *f.* avenue
avergonzado/a *adj.*
  embarrassed 1.5
avión *m.* airplane 1.5
¡Ay! *interj.* Oh!
  ¡Ay, qué dolor! Oh, what
  pain!
ayer *adv.* yesterday 1.6
azúcar *m.* sugar 1.8
azul *adj.* blue 1.6

B

bailar *v.* to dance 1.2
bajo/a *adj.* short (*in height*) 1.3
bajo control under control 1.7
baloncesto *m.* basketball 1.4
banana *f.* banana 1.8
bandera *f.* flag
bañarse *v.* to bathe;
  to take a bath 1.7
baño *m.* bathroom 1.7
barato/a *adj.* cheap 1.6
barco *m.* boat 1.5
beber *v.* to drink 1.3
bebida *f.* drink 1.8
béisbol *m.* baseball 1.4
beso *m.* kiss 1.9
biblioteca *f.* library 1.2
bicicleta *f.* bicycle 1.4
bien *adj., adv.* well 1.1
billete *m.* paper money; ticket
billón *m.* trillion
biología *f.* biology 1.2
bisabuelo/a *m.* great-grandfather;
  great-grandmother 1.3
bistec *m.* steak 1.8
bizcocho *m.* biscuit
blanco/a *adj.* white 1.6
bluejeans *m., pl.* jeans 1.6
blusa *f.* blouse 1.6
boda *f.* wedding 1.9
bolsa *f.* purse, bag 1.6
bonito/a *adj.* pretty 1.3
borrador *m.* eraser 1.2
bota *f.* boot 1.6
botella *f.* bottle 1.9
  botella de vino bottle of
  wine 1.9
botones *m., f. sing* bellhop 1.5
brindar *v.* to toast (*drink*) 1.9
bucear *v.* to scuba dive 1.4
bueno *adv.* well 1.2
buen, bueno/a *adj.* good 1.3,
  1.6
  ¡Buen viaje! Have a good
  trip! 1.1

Buena idea. Good idea. 1.4
Buenas noches. Good
  evening.; Good night. 1.1
Buenas tardes. Good
  afternoon. 1.1
buenísimo extremely good
¿Bueno? Hello. (*on telephone*)
Buenos días. Good morning.
  1.1
bulevar *m.* boulevard
buscar *v.* to look for 1.2

C

caballo *m.* horse 1.5
cabaña *f.* cabin 1.5
cada *adj.* each 1.6
café *m.* café 1.4;
  adj. brown 1.6;
  m. coffee 1.8
cafetería *f.* cafeteria 1.2
caja *f.* cash register 1.6
calcetín (calcetines) *m.*
  sock(s) 1.6
caldo *m.* soup 1.8
  caldo de patas *m.* beef
  soup 1.8
calidad *f.* quality 1.6
calor *m.* heat 1.4
calzar *v.* to take size... shoes 1.6
cama *f.* bed 1.5
camarero/a *m., f.* waiter/
  waitress 1.8
camarón *m.* shrimp 1.8
cambiar (de) *v.* to change 1.9
cambio *m.* **de moneda** currency
  exchange
caminar *v.* to walk 1.2
camino *m.* road
camión *m* truck; bus
camisa *f.* shirt 1.6
camiseta *f.* t-shirt 1.6
campo *m.* countryside 1.5
canadiense *adj.* Canadian 1.3
cansado/a *adj.* tired 1.5
cantar *v.* to sing 1.2
capital *f.* capital city 1.1
cara *f.* face 1.7
caramelo *m.* caramel 1.9
carne *f.* meat 1.8
  carne de res *f.* beef 1.8
caro/a *adj.* expensive 1.6
carta *f.* letter 1.4; (*playing*)
  card 1.5
cartera *f.* wallet 1.6
casa *f.* house; home 1.2
casado/a *adj.* married 1.9
casarse (con) *v.* to get married
  (to) 1.9
catorce *adj.* fourteen 1.1
cebolla *f.* onion 1.8
celebrar *v.* to celebrate 1.9
cena *f.* dinner 1.8
cenar *v.* to have dinner 1.2

centro *m.* downtown 1.4
  centro comercial shopping
  mall 1.6
cepillarse los dientes/el pelo
  v. to brush one's teeth/one's hair
  1.7
cerca de *prep.* near 1.2
cerdo *m.* pork 1.8
cereales *m., pl.* cereal;
  grains 1.8
cero *m.* zero 1.1
cerrado/a *adj.* closed 1.5
cerrar (e:ie) *v.* to close 1.4
cerveza *f.* beer 1.8
ceviche *m.* marinated fish
  dish 1.8
  ceviche de camarón *m.*
  lemon-marinated shrimp 1.8
chaleco *m.* vest
champán *m.* champagne 1.9
champiñón *m.* mushroom 1.8
champú *m.* shampoo 1.7
chaqueta *f.* jacket 1.6
chau *fam. interj.* bye 1.1
chévere *adj., fam.* terrific
chico/a *m., f.* boy; girl 1.1
chino/a *adj.* Chinese 1.3
chocar (con) *v.* to run into
chocolate *m.* chocolate 1.9
chuleta *f.* chop (*food*) 1.8
  chuleta de cerdo *f.* pork
  chop 1.8
cibercafé *m.* cybercafé
ciclismo *m.* cycling 1.4
cien(to) *n., adj.* one hundred 1.2
ciencia *f.* science 1.2
cinco *n., adj.* five 1.1
cincuenta *n., adj.* fifty 1.2
cine *m.* movie theater 1.4
cinta *f.* (audio)tape
cinturón *m.* belt 1.6
cita *f.* date; appointment 1.9
ciudad *f.* city 1.4
clase *f.* class 1.2
cliente/a *m., f.* customer 1.6
color *m.* color 1.6
comenzar (e:ie) *v.* to begin 1.4
comer *v.* to eat 1.3
comida *f.* food; meal 1.8
como *prep., conj.* like; as 1.8
¿cómo? *adv.* what?; how? 1.1
  ¿Cómo es...? What's...
  like? 1.3
  ¿Cómo está usted? *form.*
  How are you? 1.1
  ¿Cómo estás? *fam.* How are
  you? 1.1
  **¿Cómo se llama
  (usted)?** *form.* What's your
  name? 1.1
  ¿Cómo te llamas (tú)? *fam.*
  What's your name? 1.1
cómodo/a *adj.* comfortable 1.5
compañero/a de clase *m., f.*
  classmate 1.2

compañero/a de cuarto *m., f.* roommate 1.2
compartir *v.* to share 1.3
comprar *v.* to buy 1.2
compras *f., pl.* purchases 1.5
  ir de compras to go shopping 1.5
comprender *v.* to understand 1.3
comprobar (o:ue) *v.* to check
comprometerse (con) *v.* to get engaged (to) 1.9
computación *f.* computer science 1.2
computadora *f.* computer 1.1
comunidad *f.* community 1.1
con *prep.* with 1.2
  Con permiso. Pardon me.; Excuse me. 1.1
concordar (o:ue) *v.* to agree
conducir *v.* to drive 1.6
conductor(a) *m., f.* driver 1.1
confirmar *v.* to confirm 1.5
  confirmar *v.* **una reservación** *f.* to confirm a reservation 1.5
confundido/a *adj.* confused 1.5
conmigo *pron.* with me 1.4, 1.9
conocer *v.* to know; to be acquainted with 1.6
conocido/a *adj.; p.p.* known
conseguir (e:i) *v.* to get; to obtain 1.4
consejo *m.* advice
construir *v.* to build
contabilidad *f.* accounting 1.2
contar (o:ue) *v.* to count; to tell 1.4
contento/a *adj.* happy; content 1.5
contestar *v.* to answer 1.2
contigo *fam. pron.* with you 1.9
control *m.* control 1.7
conversación *f.* conversation 1.1
conversar *v.* to converse, to chat 1.2
corbata *f.* tie 1.6
correo electrónico *m.* e-mail 1.4
correr *v.* to run 1.3
cortesía *f.* courtesy
corto/a *adj.* short (in length) 1.6
cosa *f.* thing 1.1
costar (o:ue) *f.* to cost 1.6
creer (en) *v.* to believe (in) 1.3
crema de afeitar *f.* shaving cream 1.7
cuaderno *m.* notebook 1.1
¿cuál(es)? *pron.* which?; which one(s)? 1.2

¿Cuál es la fecha de hoy? What is today's date? 1.5
cuando *conj.* when 1.7
  ¿cuándo? *adv.* when? 1.2
¿cuánto(s)/a(s)? *adj.* how much/how many? 1.1
  ¿Cuánto cuesta...? How much does... cost? 1.6
  ¿Cuántos años tienes? How old are you? 1.3
cuarenta *n., adj.* forty 1.2
cuarto *m.* room 1.2; 1.7
  cuarto de baño *m.* bathroom 1.7
cuarto/a *n., adj.* fourth 1.5
  menos cuarto quarter to (time)
  y cuarto quarter after (time) 1.1
cuatro *n., adj.* four 1.1
cuatrocientos/as *n., adj.* four hundred 1.2
cubierto *p.p.* covered
cubiertos *m., pl.* silverware
cubrir *v.* to cover
cuenta *f.* bill 1.9
cuidado *m.* care 1.3
cumpleaños *m., sing.* birthday 1.9
cumplir años *v.* to have a birthday 1.9
cuñado/a *m., f.* brother-in-law; sister-in-law 1.3
curso *m.* course 1.2

D

dar *v.* to give 1.6, 1.9
  dar un consejo *v.* to give advice
de *prep.* of; from 1.1
  ¿De dónde eres? *fam.* Where are you from? 1.1
  ¿De dónde es usted? *form.* Where are you from? 1.1
  ¿de quién...? whose...? *sing.* 1.1
  ¿de quiénes...? whose...? *pl.* 1.1
  de algodón (made) of cotton 1.6
  de buen humor in a good mood 1.5
  de compras shopping 1.5
  de cuadros plaid 1.6
  de excursión hiking 1.4
  de hecho in fact
  de ida y vuelta roundtrip 1.5
  de la mañana in the morning; A.M. 1.1
  de la noche in the evening; at night; P.M. 1.1
  de la tarde in the afternoon; in the early evening; P.M. 1.1

  de lana (made) of wool 1.6
  de lunares polka-dotted 1.6
  de mal humor in a bad mood 1.5
  de moda in fashion 1.6
  De nada. You're welcome. 1.1
  de rayas striped 1.6
  de repente *adv.* suddenly 1.6
  de seda (made) of silk 1.6
debajo de *prep.* below; under 1.2
deber (+ *inf.*) *v.* should; must; ought to 1.3
  Debe ser... It must be... 1.6
decidir (+ *inf.*) *v.* to decide 1.3
décimo/a *adj.* tenth 1.5
decir (e:i) *v.* to say; to tell 1.4, 1.9
  decir la respuesta to say the answer 1.4
  decir la verdad to tell the truth 1.4
  decir mentiras to tell lies 1.4
  decir que to say that 1.4
dejar una propina *v.* to leave a tip 1.9
del (contraction of **de + el**) of the; from the
delante de *prep.* in front of 1.2
delgado/a *adj.* thin; slender 1.3
delicioso/a *adj.* delicious 1.8
demás *adj.* the rest
demasiado *adj., adv.* too much 1.6
dependiente/a *m., f.* clerk 1.6
deporte *m.* sport 1.4
deportista *m.* sports person
deportivo/a *adj.* sports-related 1.4
derecha *f.* right 1.2
  a la derecha de to the right of 1.2
derecho *adj.* straight (ahead)
desayunar *v.* to have breakfast 1.2
desayuno *m.* breakfast 1.8
descansar *v.* to rest 1.2
describir *v.* to describe 1.3
desde *prep.* from 1.6
desear *v.* to wish; to desire 1.2
desordenado/a *adj.* disorderly 1.5
despedida *f.* farewell; good-bye
despedirse (de) (e:i) *v.* to say good-bye (to) 1.7
despejado/a *adj.* clear (weather)
despertador *m.* alarm clock 1.7
despertarse (e:ie) *v.* to wake up 1.7
después *adv.* afterwards; then 1.7
  después de *prep.* after 1.7
detrás de *prep.* behind 1.2

día *m.* day **1.1**
día de fiesta holiday **1.9**
diario/a *adj.* daily **1.7**
diccionario *m.* dictionary **1.1**
diciembre *m.* December **1.5**
diecinueve *n., adj.* nineteen **1.1**
dieciocho *n., adj.* eighteen **1.1**
dieciséis *n., adj.* sixteen **1.1**
diecisiete *n., adj.* seventeen **1.1**
diente *m.* tooth **1.7**
diez *n., adj.* ten **1.1**
difícil *adj.* difficult; hard **1.3**
dinero *m.* money **1.6**
diseño *m.* design
diversión *f.* fun activity;
  entertainment; recreation **1.4**
divertido/a *adj.* fun **1.7**
divertirse (e:ie) *v.* to have
  fun **1.9**
divorciado/a *adj.* divorced **1.9**
divorciarse (de) *v.* to get
  divorced (from) **1.9**
divorcio *m.* divorce **1.9**
doble *adj.* double
doce *n., adj.* twelve **1.1**
doctor(a) *m., f.* doctor **1.3**
documentos de viaje *m.,*
  pl. travel documents
domingo *m.* Sunday **1.2**
don/doña title of respect used
  with a person's first name **1.1**
donde *prep.* where
  ¿dónde? *adv.* where? **1.1**
  ¿Dónde está...? Where
    is...? **1.2**
dormir (o:ue) *v.* to sleep **1.4**
dormirse (o:ue) *v.* to go to sleep;
  to fall asleep **1.7**
dos *n., adj.* two **1.1**
  dos veces *f.* twice; two
    times **1.6**
doscientos/as *n., adj.* two
  hundred **1.2**
ducha *f.* shower **1.7**
ducharse *v.* to shower; to take a
  shower **1.7**
dueño/a *m., f.* owner;
  landlord **1.8**
dulces *m., pl.* sweets; candy **1.9**
durante *prep.* during **1.7**

E

e *conj.* (used instead of *y* before
  words beginning with *i* and *hi*)
  and **1.4**
economía *f.* economics **1.2**
Ecuador *m.* Ecuador **1.1**
ecuatoriano/a *adj.* Ecuadorian
  1.3
edad *f.* age **1.9**
(en) efectivo *m.* cash **1.6**
el *m., sing., def. art.* the **1.1**
él *sub. pron.* he **1.1**; *pron., obj.*
  of prep. him **1.9**

elegante *adj.* elegant **1.6**
ella *sub. pron.* she **1.1**; *pron.,*
  obj. of prep. her **1.9**
ellos/as *sub. pron.* they **1.1**;
  pron., obj. of prep. them **1.9**
emocionante *adj.* exciting
empezar (e:ie) *v.* to begin **1.4**
empleado/a *m., f.* employee **1.5**
en *prep.* in; on; at **1.2**
  en casa at home **1.7**
  en línea in-line **1.4**
  en mi nombre in my name
  en punto on the dot; exactly;
    sharp (*time*) **1.1**
  en qué in what; how **1.2**
  ¿En qué puedo servirles?
    How can I help you? **1.5**
enamorado/a (de) *adj.* in love
  (with) **1.9**
enamorarse (de) *v.* to fall in love
  (with) **1.9**
encantado/a *adj.* delighted;
  pleased to meet you **1.1**
encantar *v.* to like very much; to
  love (*inanimate objects*) **1.7**
encima de *prep.* on top of **1.2**
encontrar (o:ue) *v.* to find **1.4**
enero *m.* January **1.5**
enojado/a *adj.* mad; angry **1.5**
enojarse (con) *v.* to get angry
  (with) **1.7**
ensalada *f.* salad **1.8**
enseguida *adv.* right away **1.9**
enseñar *v.* to teach **1.2**
entender (e:ie) *v.* to understand
  1.4
entonces *adv.* then **1.7**
entre *prep.* between; among **1.2**
entremeses *m., pl.* hors
  d'oeuvres; appetizers **1.8**
equipaje *m.* luggage **1.5**
equipo *m.* team **1.4**
equivocado/a *adj.* wrong **1.5**
eres *fam.* you are **1.1**
es he/she/it is **1.1**
  Es de... He/She is from... **1.1**
  Es la una. It's one o'clock. **1.1**
esa(s) *f., adj.* that; those **1.6**
ésa(s) *f., pron.* those (ones) **1.6**
escalar *v.* to climb **1.4**
  escalar montañas *v.* to climb
    mountains **1.4**
escoger *v.* to choose **1.8**
escribir *v.* to write **1.3**
  escribir un mensaje
    electrónico to write an
    e-mail message **1.4**
  escribir una carta to write a
    letter **1.4**
  escribir una postal to write a
    postcard **1.4**
escritorio *m.* desk **1.2**
escuchar *v.* to listen (to) **1.2**
  escuchar la radio to listen
    to the radio **1.2**

escuchar música to listen to
  music **1.2**
escuela *f.* school **1.1**
ese *m., sing., adj.* that **1.6**
ése *m., sing., pron.* that
  (one) **1.6**
eso *neuter pron.* that;
  that thing **1.6**
esos *m., pl., adj.* those **1.6**
ésos *m., pl., pron.* those
  (ones) **1.6**
España *f.* Spain **1.1**
español *m.* Spanish (language)
  1.2
español(a) *adj.* Spanish **1.3**
espárragos *m., pl.* asparagus
  1.8
especialización *f.* major **1.2**
espejo *m.* mirror **1.7**
esperar (+ inf.) *v.* to wait (for); to
  hope **1.2**
esposo/a *m., f.* husband; wife;
  spouse **1.3**
esquí (acuático) *m.* (water)
  skiing **1.4**
esquiar *v.* to ski **1.4**
está he/she/it is, you are **1.2**
  Está (muy) despejado. It's
    (very) clear. (*weather*)
  Está lloviendo. It's raining.
    1.5
  Está nevando. It's snowing.
    1.5
  Está (muy) nublado. It's
    (very) cloudy. (*weather*) **1.5**
esta(s) *f., adj.* this; these **1.6**
  esta noche tonight **1.4**
ésta(s) *f., pron.* this (one); these
  (ones) **1.6**
  Ésta es... *f.* This is...
    (*introducing someone*) **1.1**
estación *f.* station; season **1.5**
  estación de autobuses
    bus station **1.5**
  estación del metro subway
    station **1.5**
  estación de tren train
    station **1.5**
estadio *m.* stadium **1.2**
estado civil *m.* marital status
  1.9
Estados Unidos *m.* (EE.UU.;
  E.U.) United States **1.1**
estadounidense *adj.* from the
  United States **1.3**
estampado/a *adj.* print
estar *v.* to be **1.2**
  estar aburrido/a to be
    bored **1.5**
  estar bajo control to be
    under control **1.7**
  estar de moda to be in
    fashion **1.6**
  estar de vacaciones to be
    on vacation **1.5**

estar seguro/a to be sure **1.5**

   No está nada mal. It's not bad at all. **1.5**

este *m., sing., adj.* this **1.6**

éste *m., sing., pron.* this (one) **1.6**

   Éste es... *m.* This is... (*introducing someone*) **1.1**

estilo *m.* style

esto *neuter pron.* this; this thing **1.6**

estos *m., pl., adj.* these **1.6**

éstos *m., pl., pron.* these (ones) **1.6**

estudiante *m., f.* student **1.1, 1.2**

estudiantil *adj.* student **1.2**

estudiar *v.* to study **1.2**

estupendo/a *adj.* stupendous **1.5**

etapa *f.* stage **1.9**

examen *m.* test; exam **1.2**

excelente *adj.* excellent **1.5**

excursión *f.* hike; tour; excursion

excursionista *m., f.* hiker

explicar *v.* to explain **1.2**

explorar *v.* to explore

expresión *f.* expression

F

fabuloso/a *adj.* fabulous **1.5**

fácil *adj.* easy **1.3**

falda *f.* skirt **1.6**

faltar *v.* to lack; to need **1.7**

familia *f.* family **1.3**

fascinar *v.* to fascinate **1.7**

favorito/a *adj.* favorite **1.4**

febrero *m.* February **1.5**

fecha *f.* date **1.5**

feliz *adj.* happy **1.5**

   ¡Feliz cumpleaños! Happy birthday! **1.9**

   ¡Felicidades! Congratulations! (*for an event such as a birthday or anniversary*) **1.9**

   ¡Felicitaciones! Congratulations! (*for an event such as an engagement or a good grade on a test*) **1.9**

fenomenal *adj.* great, phenomenal **1.5**

feo/a *adj.* ugly **1.3**

fiesta *f.* party **1.9**

fijo/a *adj.* fixed, set **1.6**

fin *m.* end **1.4**

   fin de semana weekend **1.4**

física *f.* physics **1.2**

flan (de caramelo) *m.* baked (caramel) custard **1.9**

folleto *m.* brochure

foto(grafía) *f.* photograph **1.1**

francés, francesa *adj.* French **1.3**

frenos *m., pl.* brakes

fresco/a *adj.* cool **1.5**

frijoles *m., pl.* beans **1.8**

frío/a *adj.* cold **1.5**

frito/a *adj.* fried **1.8**

fruta *f.* fruit **1.8**

frutilla *f.* strawberry **1.8**

fuente de fritada *f.* platter of fried food

fuera *adv.* outside

fútbol *m.* soccer **1.4**

fútbol americano *m.* football **1.4**

G

gafas (de sol) *f., pl.* (sun)glasses **1.6**

gafas (oscuras) *f., pl.* (sun)glasses

galleta *f.* cookie **1.9**

ganar *v.* to win **1.4**

ganga *f.* bargain **1.6**

gastar *v.* to spend (*money*) **1.6**

gemelo/a *m., f.* twin **1.3**

gente *f.* people **1.3**

geografía *f.* geography **1.2**

gimnasio *m.* gymnasium **1.4**

golf *m.* golf **1.4**

gordo/a *adj.* fat **1.3**

grabadora *f.* tape recorder **1.1**

gracias *f., pl.* thank you; thanks **1.1**

   Gracias por todo. Thanks for everything. **1.9**

   Gracias una vez más. Thanks again. **1.9**

graduarse (de/en) *v.* to graduate (from/in) **1.9**

gran, grande *adj.* big; large **1.3**

grillo *m.* cricket

gris *adj.* gray **1.6**

gritar *v.* to scream **1.7**

guantes *m., pl.* gloves **1.6**

guapo/a *adj.* handsome; good-looking **1.3**

guía *m., f.* guide

gustar *v.* to be pleasing to; to like **1.2**

   Me gustaría... I would like...

gusto *m.* pleasure

   El gusto es mío. The pleasure is mine. **1.1**

   Mucho gusto. Pleased to meet you. **1.1**

H

habitación *f.* room **1.5**

   habitación doble double room **1.5**

   habitación individual single room **1.5**

hablar *v.* to talk; to speak **1.2**

hacer *v.* to do; to make **1.4**

   Hace buen tiempo. The weather is good. **1.5**

   Hace (mucho) calor. It's (very) hot. (*weather*) **1.5**

   Hace fresco. It's cool. (*weather*) **1.5**

   Hace (mucho) frío. It's very cold. (*weather*) **1.5**

   Hace mal tiempo. The weather is bad. **1.5**

   Hace (mucho) sol. It's (very) sunny. (*weather*) **1.5**

   Hace (mucho) viento. It's (very) windy. (*weather*) **1.5**

   hacer juego (con) to match (with) **1.6**

   hacer las maletas to pack (one's) suitcases **1.5**

   hacer turismo to go sightseeing

   hacer un viaje to take a trip **1.5**

   hacer una excursión to go on a hike; to go on a tour

hambre *f.* hunger **1.3**

hamburguesa *f.* hamburger **1.8**

hasta *prep.* until **1.6;** toward

   Hasta la vista. See you later. **1.1**

   Hasta luego. See you later. **1.1**

   Hasta mañana. See you tomorrow. **1.1**

   Hasta pronto. See you soon. **1.1**

hay *v.* there is; there are **1.1**

   Hay (mucha) contaminación. It's (very) smoggy.

   Hay (mucha) niebla. It's (very) foggy.

   No hay de qué. You're welcome. **1.1**

helado/a *adj.* iced **1.8**

helado *m.* ice cream **1.9**

hermanastro/a *m., f.* stepbrother; stepsister **1.3**

hermano/a *m., f.* brother; sister **1.3**

hermano/a mayor/menor *m., f.* older/younger brother/ sister **1.3**

hermanos *m., pl.* siblings (brothers and sisters) **1.3**

hermoso/a *adj.* beautiful **1.6**

hijastro/a *m., f.* stepson; stepdaughter **1.3**

hijo/a *m., f.* son; daughter **1.3**

   hijo/a único/a *m., f.* only child **1.3**

hijos *m., pl.* children **1.3**

historia *f.* history **1.2**

hockey *m.* hockey **1.4**

hola *interj.* hello; hi 1.1
hombre *m.* man 1.1
hora *f.* hour 1.1; the time
horario *m.* schedule 1.2
hotel *m.* hotel 1.5
hoy *adv.* today 1.2
  hoy día *adv.* nowadays
  Hoy es... Today is... 1.2
huésped *m., f.* guest 1.5
huevo *m.* egg 1.8
humanidades *f., pl.* humanities
  1.2

I

ida *f.* one way (*travel*)
idea *f.* idea 1.4
iglesia *f.* church 1.4
igualmente *adv.* likewise 1.1
impermeable *m.* raincoat 1.6
importante *adj.* important 1.3
importar *v.* to be important to;
  to matter 1.7
increíble *adj.* incredible 1.5
individual *adj.* private
  (*room*) 1.5
ingeniero/a *m., f.* engineer 1.3
inglés *m.* English (*language*)
  1.2
inglés, inglesa *adj.* English 1.3
inodoro *m.* toilet 1.7
inspector(a) de aduanas *m.,*
  f. customs inspector 1.5
inteligente *adj.* intelligent 1.3
intercambiar *v.* to exchange
interesante *adj.* interesting 1.3
interesar *v.* to be interesting to;
  to interest 1.7
invierno *m.* winter 1.5
invitado/a *m., f.* guest (*at a*
  function) 1.9
invitar *v.* to invite 1.9
ir *v.* to go 1.4
  ir a (+ *inf.*) to be going to *do*
    something 1.4
  ir de compras to go shopping
    1.5
  ir de excursión (a las
    montañas) to go for a hike
    (in the mountains) 1.4
  ir de pesca to go fishing
  ir de vacaciones to go on
    vacation 1.5
  ir en autobús to go by
    bus 1.5
  ir en auto(móvil) to go by
    car 1.5
  ir en avión to go by plane
    1.5
  ir en barco to go by boat
    1.5
  ir en metro to go by subway
  ir en motocicleta to go by
    motorcycle 1.5

ir en taxi to go by taxi 1.5
ir en tren to go by train
irse *v.* to go away; to leave 1.7
italiano/a *adj.* Italian 1.3
izquierdo/a *adj.* left 1.2
  a la izquierda de to the left
    of 1.2

J

jabón *m.* soap 1.7
jamás *adv.* never; not ever 1.7
jamón *m.* ham 1.8
japonés, japonesa *adj.*
  Japanese 1.3
joven *adj.* young 1.3
joven *m., f.* youth; young
  person 1.1
jubilarse *v.* to retire (*from*
  work) 1.9
juego *m.* game
jueves *m., sing.* Thursday 1.2
jugador(a) *m., f.* player 1.4
jugar (u:ue) *v.* to play 1.4
  jugar a las cartas to play
    cards 1.5
jugo *m.* juice 1.8
  jugo de fruta *m.* fruit
    juice 1.8
julio *m.* July 1.5
junio *m.* June 1.5
juntos/as *adj.* together 1.9
juventud *f.* youth 1.9

L

la *f., sing., def. art.* the 1.1
la *f., sing., d.o. pron.* her, it;
  form. you 1.5
laboratorio *m.* laboratory 1.2
lana *f.* wool 1.6
langosta *f.* lobster 1.8
lápiz *m.* pencil 1.1
largo/a *adj.* long 1.6
las *f., pl., def. art.* the 1.1
las *f., pl., d.o. pron.* them; *form.*
  you 1.5
lavabo *m.* sink 1.7
lavarse *v.* to wash oneself 1.7
  lavarse la cara to wash one's
    face 1.7
  lavarse las manos to wash
    one's hands 1.7
le *sing., i.o. pron.* to/for him,
  her; *form.* you 1.6
  Le presento a... *form.* I
    would like to introduce... to
    you. 1.1
lección *f.* lesson 1.1
leche *f.* milk 1.8
lechuga *f.* lettuce 1.8
leer *v.* to read 1.3
  leer correo electrónico to
    read e-mail 1.4

leer un periódico to read a
  newspaper 1.4
leer una revista to read a
  magazine 1.4
lejos de *prep.* far from 1.2
lengua *f.* language 1.2
  lenguas extranjeras *f.,*
    pl. foreign languages 1.2
lentes (de sol) (sun)glasses
lentes de contacto *m., pl.*
  contact lenses
les *pl., i.o. pron.* to/for them;
  form. you 1.6
levantarse *v.* to get up 1.7
libre *adj.* free 1.4
librería *f.* bookstore 1.2
libro *m.* book 1.2
limón *m.* lemon 1.8
limpio/a *adj.* clean 1.5
línea *f.* line 1.4
listo/a *adj.* ready; smart 1.5
literatura *f.* literature 1.2
llamarse *v.* to be called; to be
  named 1.7
llave *f.* key 1.5
llegada *f.* arrival 1.5
llegar *v.* to arrive 1.2
llevar *v.* to carry 1.2;
  to wear; to take 1.6
  llevarse bien/mal (con) to get
    along well/badly (with) 1.9
llover (o:ue) *v.* to rain 1.5
  Llueve. It's raining. 1.5
lo *m., sing., d.o. pron.* him, it;
  form. you 1.5
  Lo siento. I'm sorry. 1.1
  Lo siento muchísimo. I'm
    so sorry. 1.4
loco/a *adj.* crazy 1.6
lomo a la plancha *m.* grilled
  flank steak 1.8
los *m., pl., def. art.* the 1.1
los *m., pl., d.o. pron.* them;
  form. you 1.5
luego *adv.* then 1.7;
  adv. later 1.1
lugar *m.* place 1.4
lunares *m.* polka dots 1.6
lunes *m., sing.* Monday 1.2

M

madrastra *f.* stepmother 1.3
madre *f.* mother 1.3
madurez *f.* maturity; middle
  age 1.9
magnífico/a *adj.* magnificent
  1.5
maíz *m.* corn 1.8
mal, malo/a *adj.* bad 1.3
maleta *f.* suitcase 1.1
mamá *f.* mom 1.3
mano *f.* hand 1.1
  ¡Manos arriba! Hands up!

mantequilla *f.* butter **1.8**
manzana *f.* apple **1.8**
mañana *f.* morning, A.M. **1.1**; tomorrow **1.1**
mapa *m.* map **1.2**
maquillaje *m.* makeup **1.7**
maquillarse *v.* to put on makeup **1.7**
mar *m.* sea **1.5**
maravilloso/a *adj.* marvelous **1.5**
margarina *f.* margarine **1.8**
mariscos *m., pl.* shellfish **1.8**
marrón *adj.* brown **1.6**
martes *m., sing.* Tuesday **1.2**
marzo *m.* March **1.5**
más *pron.* more **1.2**
  más de (+ *number*) more than **1.8**
  más tarde later (on) **1.7**
  más... que more... than **1.8**
matemáticas *f., pl.* mathematics **1.2**
materia *f.* course **1.2**
matrimonio *m.* marriage **1.9**
mayo *m.* May **1.5**
mayonesa *f.* mayonnaise **1.8**
mayor *adj.* older **1.3**
  el/la mayor *adj.* the eldest **1.8**; the oldest
me *sing., d.o. pron.* me **1.5**; *sing. i.o. pron.* to/for me **1.6**
  Me gusta... I like... **1.2**
  No me gustan nada. I don't like them at all. **1.2**
  Me llamo... My name is... **1.1**
  Me muero por... I'm dying to (for)...
mediano/a *adj.* medium
medianoche *f.* midnight **1.1**
medias *f., pl.* pantyhose, stockings **1.6**
médico/a *m., f.* doctor **1.3**
medio/a *adj.* half **1.3**
  medio/a hermano/a *m., f.* half-brother; half-sister **1.3**
  mediodía *m.* noon **1.1**
  y media thirty minutes past the hour (*time*) **1.1**
mejor *adj.* better **1.8**
  el/la mejor *adj.* the best **1.8**
melocotón *m.* peach **1.8**
menor *adj.* younger **1.3**
  el/la menor *adj.* the youngest **1.8**
menos *adv.* less
  menos cuarto..., menos quince... quarter to... (*time*) **1.1**
  menos de (+ *number*) fewer than **1.8**
  menos... que less... than **1.8**

mensaje electrónico *m.* e-mail message **1.4**
mentira *f.* lie **1.4**
menú *m.* menu **1.8**
mercado *m.* market **1.6**
  mercado al aire libre *m.* open-air market **1.6**
merendar (e:ie) *v.* to snack **1.8**; to have an afternoon snack
mes *m.* month **1.5**
mesa *f.* table **1.2**
metro *m.* subway **1.5**
mexicano/a *adj.* Mexican **1.3**
México *m.* Mexico **1.1**
mí *pron., obj. of prep.* me **1.9**
mi(s) *poss. adj.* my **1.3**
miedo *m.* fear **1.3**
miércoles *m., sing.* Wednesday **1.2**
mil *m.* one thousand **1.2**
  Mil perdones. I'm so sorry. (*lit.* A thousand pardons.) **1.4**
mil millones *m.* billion
millón *m.* million **1.2**
millones (de) *m.* millions (of)
minuto *m.* minute **1.1**
mirar *v.* to look (at); to watch **1.2**
  mirar (la) televisión to watch television **1.2**
mismo/a *adj.* same **1.3**
mochila *f.* backpack **1.2**
moda *f.* fashion **1.6**
módem *m.* modem
molestar *v.* to bother; to annoy **1.7**
montaña *f.* mountain **1.4**
montar a caballo *v.* to ride a horse **1.5**
monumento *m.* monument **1.4**
mora *f.* blackberry **1.8**
morado/a *adj.* purple **1.6**
moreno/a *adj.* brunet(te) **1.3**
morir (o:ue) *v.* to die **1.8**
mostrar (o:ue) *v.* to show **1.4**
motocicleta *f.* motorcycle **1.5**
motor *m.* motor
muchacho/a *m., f.* boy; girl **1.3**
mucho/a *adj., adv.* a lot of; much **1.2**; many **1.3**
  (Muchas) gracias. Thank you (very much).; Thanks (a lot). **1.1**
  Muchísimas gracias. Thank you very, very much. **1.9**
  Mucho gusto. Pleased to meet you. **1.1**
muchísimo very much **1.2**
muela *f.* tooth; molar
muerte *f.* death **1.9**
mujer *f.* woman **1.1**

mujer policía *f.* female police officer
multa *f.* fine
mundial *adj.* worldwide
municipal *adj.* municipal
museo *m.* museum **1.4**
música *f.* music **1.2**
muy *adv.* very **1.1**
  Muy amable. That's very kind of you. **1.5**
  (Muy) bien, gracias. (Very) well, thanks. **1.1**

N

nacer *v.* to be born **1.9**
nacimiento *m.* birth **1.9**
nacionalidad *f.* nationality **1.1**
nada *pron., adv.* nothing **1.1**; not anything **1.7**
  nada mal not bad at all **1.5**
nadar *v.* to swim **1.4**
nadie *pron.* no one, nobody, not anyone **1.7**
naranja *f.* orange **1.8**
natación *f.* swimming **1.4**
Navidad *f.* Christmas **1.9**
necesitar (+ *inf.*) *v.* to need **1.2**
negativo/a *adj.* negative
negro/a *adj.* black **1.6**
nervioso/a *adj.* nervous **1.5**
nevar (e:ie) *v.* to snow **1.5**
  Nieva. It's snowing. **1.5**
ni... ni neither... nor **1.7**
niebla *f.* fog
nieto/a *m., f.* grandson; granddaughter **1.3**
nieve *f.* snow
ningún, ninguno/a(s) *adj., pron.* no; none; not any **1.7**
  ningún problema no problem
niñez *f.* childhood **1.9**
niño/a *m., f.* child **1.3**
no *adv.* no; not **1.1**
  ¿no? right? **1.1**
  No está nada mal. It's not bad at all. **1.5**
  no estar de acuerdo to disagree
  No estoy seguro. I'm not sure.
  no hay there is not; there are not **1.1**
  No hay de qué. You're welcome. **1.1**
  No hay problema. No problem. **1.7**
  No me gustan nada. I don't like them at all. **1.2**
  no muy bien not very well **1.1**
  No quiero. I don't want to. **1.4**

No sé. I don't know.

No se preocupe. *(form.)*
  Don't worry. **1.7**

No te preocupes. *(fam.)*
  Don't worry. **1.7**

no tener razón to be
  wrong **1.3**

noche *f.* night **1.1**

nombre *m.* name **1.1**

norteamericano/a *adj.* (North)
  American **1.3**

nos *pl., d.o. pron.* us **1.5**;
  pl., i.o. pron. to/for us **1.6**

  Nos vemos. See you. **1.1**

nosotros/as *sub. pron.* we **1.1**;
  pron., obj. of prep. us **1.9**

novecientos/as *n., adj.* nine
  hundred **1.2**

noveno/a *n., adj.* ninth **1.5**

noventa *n., adj.* ninety **1.2**

noviembre *m.* November **1.5**

novio/a *m., f.* boyfriend/
  girlfriend **1.3**

nublado/a *adj.* cloudy **1.5**

  Está (muy) nublado. It's
  very cloudy. **1.5**

nuera *f.* daughter-in-law **1.3**

nuestro(s)/a(s) *poss. adj.*
  our **1.3**

nueve *n., adj.* nine **1.1**

nuevo/a *adj.* new **1.6**

número *m.* number **1.1**;
  (shoe) size **1.6**

nunca *adv.* never; not ever **1.7**

O

o *conj.* or **1.7**

  o... o; either... or **1.7**

océano *m.* ocean

ochenta *n., adj.* eighty **1.2**

ocho *n., adj.* eight **1.1**

ochocientos/as *n., adj.* eight
  hundred **1.2**

octavo/a *n., adj.* eighth **1.5**

octubre *m.* October **1.5**

ocupado/a *adj.* busy **1.5**

odiar *v.* to hate **1.9**

ofrecer *v.* to offer **1.6**

oír *v.* to hear **1.4**

  Oiga./Oigan. *form., sing./pl.*
  Listen. *(in conversation)* **1.1**

  Oye. *fam., sing.* Listen. *(in
  conversation)* **1.1**

once *n., adj.* eleven **1.1**

ordenado/a *adj.* orderly **1.5**

ordinal *adj.* ordinal (number)

ortografía *f.* spelling

ortográfico/a *adj.* spelling

os *fam., pl., d.o. pron.* you **1.5**;
  fam., pl., i.o. pron. to/for you
  1.6

otoño *m.* autumn **1.5**

otro/a *adj.* other; another **1.6**

  otra vez again

P

padrastro *m.* stepfather **1.3**

padre *m.* father **1.3**

  padres *m., pl.* parents **1.3**

pagar *v.* to pay **1.6**, **1.9**

  pagar la cuenta to pay the
  bill **1.9**

país *m.* country **1.1**

paisaje *m.* landscape **1.5**

palabra *f.* word **1.1**

pan *m.* bread **1.8**

  pan tostado *m.* toasted
  bread **1.8**

pantalones *m., pl.* pants **1.6**

  pantalones cortos *m., pl.*
  shorts **1.6**

pantuflas *f., pl.* slippers **1.7**

papa *f.* potato **1.8**

  papas fritas *f., pl.* fried
  potatoes; French fries **1.8**

papá *m.* dad **1.3**

  papás *m., pl.* parents **1.3**

papel *m.* paper **1.2**

papelera *f.* wastebasket **1.2**

par *m.* pair **1.6**

  par de zapatos *m.* pair of
  shoes **1.6**

parecer *v.* to seem **1.6**

pareja *f.* (married) couple; partner
  1.9

parientes *m., pl.* relatives **1.3**

parque *m.* park **1.4**

párrafo *m.* paragraph

partido *m.* game; match
  (sports) **1.4**

pasado/a *adj.* last; past **1.6**

  pasado *p.p.* passed

pasaje *m.* ticket **1.5**

  pasaje de ida y vuelta *m.*
  roundtrip ticket **1.5**

pasajero/a *m., f.* passenger **1.1**

pasaporte *m.* passport **1.5**

pasar *v.* to go through **1.5**

  pasar por la aduana to go
  through customs

  pasar tiempo to spend time

  pasarlo bien/mal to have a
  good/bad time **1.9**

pasatiempo *m.* pastime;
  hobby **1.4**

pasear *v.* to take a walk; to
  stroll **1.4**

  pasear en bicicleta to ride a
  bicycle **1.4**

  pasear por to walk around
  1.4

pasta *f.* **de dientes**
  toothpaste **1.7**

pastel *m.* cake; pie **1.9**

  pastel de chocolate *m.*
  chocolate cake **1.9**

  pastel de cumpleaños *m.*
  birthday cake

patata *f.* potato **1.8**

patatas fritas *f., pl.* fried
  potatoes; French fries **1.8**

patinar (en línea) *v.* to (in-line)
  skate **1.4**

patineta *f.* skateboard **1.4**

pavo *m.* turkey **1.8**

pedir (e:i) *v.* to ask for;
  to request **1.4**; to order
  (food) **1.8**

peinarse *v.* to comb one's
  hair **1.7**

película *f.* movie **1.4**

pelirrojo/a *adj.* red-haired **1.3**

pelo *m.* hair **1.7**

pelota *f.* ball **1.4**

pensar (e:ie) *v.* to think **1.4**

  pensar (+ inf.) *v.* to intend
  to; to plan to (*do something*)
  1.4

  pensar en *v.* to think about
  1.4

pensión *f.* boardinghouse

peor *adj.* worse **1.8**

  el/la peor *adj.* the worst **1.8**

pequeño/a *adj.* small **1.3**

pera *f.* pear **1.8**

perder (e:ie) *v.* to lose; to miss
  1.4

Perdón. Pardon me.; Excuse me.
  1.1

perezoso/a *adj.* lazy

perfecto/a *adj.* perfect **1.5**

periódico *m.* newspaper **1.4**

periodismo *m.* journalism **1.2**

periodista *m., f.* journalist **1.3**

permiso *m.* permission

pero *conj.* but **1.2**

persona *f.* person **1.3**

pesca *f.* fishing

pescado *m.* fish *(cooked)* **1.8**

pescador(a) *m., f.* fisherman/
  fisherwoman

pescar *v.* to fish **1.5**

pimienta *f.* black pepper **1.8**

piña *f.* pineapple **1.8**

piscina *f.* swimming pool **1.4**

piso *m.* floor (*of a building*) **1.5**

pizarra *f.* blackboard **1.2**

planes *m., pl.* plans **1.4**

planta baja *f.* ground floor **1.5**

plato *m.* dish (*in a meal*) **1.8**

  plato principal *m.* main
  dish **1.8**

playa *f.* beach **1.5**

plaza *f.* city or town square **1.4**

pluma *f.* pen **1.2**

pobre *adj.* poor **1.6**

pobreza *f.* poverty

poco/a *adj.* little; few **1.5**

poder (o:ue) *v.* to be able to;
  can **1.4**

pollo *m.* chicken **1.8**

  pollo asado *m.* roast chicken
  1.8

ponchar *v.* to go flat

poner *v.* to put; to place **1.4**
ponerse (+ adj.) *v.* to become
  (+ *adj.*) **1.7**; to put on **1.7**
por *prep.* in exchange for; for;
  by; in; through; around; along;
  during; because of; on account
  of; on behalf of; in search of;
  by way of
  por avión   by plane
  por favor   please **1.1**
  por la mañana   in the
    morning **1.7**
  por la noche   at night **1.7**
  por la tarde   in the
    afternoon **1.7**
  ¿por qué?   why? **1.2**
  por teléfono   by phone; on
    the phone
  por último   finally **1.7**
porque *conj.* because **1.2**
posesivo/a *adj.* possessive **1.3**
postal *f.* postcard **1.4**
postre *m.* dessert **1.9**
practicar *v.* to practice **1.2**
  practicar deportes *m., pl.* to
    play sports **1.4**
precio (fijo) *m.* (fixed; set)
  price **1.6**
preferir (e:ie) *v.* to prefer **1.4**
pregunta *f.* question
preguntar *v.* to ask (*a question*)
  1.2
preocupado/a (por) *adj.* worried
  (about) **1.5**
preocuparse (por) *v.* to worry
  (about) **1.7**
preparar *v.* to prepare **1.2**
preposición *f.* preposition
presentación *f.* introduction
presentar *v.* to introduce
  Le presento a...   I would like
    to introduce (*name*) to you.
    (*form.*) **1.1**
  Te presento a...   I would like
    to introduce (*name*) to you.
    (*fam.*) **1.1**
prestado/a *adj.* borrowed
prestar *v.* to lend; to loan **1.6**
primavera *f.* spring **1.5**
primer, primero/a *adj.* first
  1.5
primo/a *m., f.* cousin **1.3**
principal *adj.* main **1.8**
prisa *f.* haste **1.3**
probar (o:ue) *v.* to taste; to
  try **1.8**
probarse (o:ue) *v.* to try
  on **1.7**
problema *m.* problem **1.1**
profesión *f.* profession **1.3**
profesor(a) *m., f.* teacher
  1.1, **1.2**
programa *m.* **1.1**
programador(a) *m., f.* computer
  programmer **1.3**

pronombre *m.* pronoun
propina *f.* tip **1.9**
prueba *f.* test; quiz **1.2**
psicología *f.* psychology **1.2**
pueblo *m.* town **1.4**
puerta *f.* door **1.2**
Puerto Rico *m.* Puerto Rico **1.1**
puertorriqueño/a *adj.* Puerto
  Rican **1.3**
pues *conj.* well **1.2**

               Q

que *conj.* that; which
  ¡Qué...!   How...! **1.3**
  ¡Qué dolor!   What pain!
  ¡Qué ropa más bonita!
    What pretty clothes! **1.6**
  ¡Qué sorpresa!   What a
    surprise!
  ¿qué? *pron.* what? **1.1**
  ¿Qué día es hoy?   What day
    is it? **1.2**
  ¿Qué hay de nuevo?   What's
    new? **1.1**
  ¿Qué hora es?   What time
    is it? **1.1**
  ¿Qué les parece?   What do
    you (*pl.*) think?
  ¿Qué pasa?   What's happening?;
    What's going on? **1.1**
  ¿Qué precio tiene?   What is
    the price?
  ¿Qué tal...?   How are you?;
    How is it going? **1.1**; How
    is/are...? **1.2**
  ¿Qué talla lleva/usa?   What
    size do you wear? (*form.*) **1.6**
  ¿Qué tiempo hace?   How's
    the weather? **1.5**
  ¿En qué...?   In which...? **1.2**
quedar *v.* to be left over; to fit
  (*clothing*) **1.7**
quedarse *v.* to stay; to remain
  1.7
querer (e:ie) *v.* to want; to
  love **1.4**
queso *m.* cheese **1.8**
quien(es) *pron.* who; whom
  ¿Quién es...?   Who is...? **1.1**
  ¿quién(es)? *pron.* who?;
    whom? **1.1**
química *f.* chemistry **1.2**
quince *n., adj.* fifteen **1.1**
  menos quince   quarter to
    (*time*) **1.1**
  y quince   quarter after
    (*time*) **1.1**
quinceañera *f.* young woman's
  fifteenth birthday celebration;
  fifteen-year old girl **1.9**
quinientos/as *n., adj.* five
  hundred **1.2**
quinto/a *n., adj.* fifth **1.5**

quitarse *v.* to take off **1.7**
quizás *adv.* maybe **1.5**

               R

radio *f.* radio (*medium*) **1.2**
  radio *m.* radio (*set*) **1.2**
ratos libres *m., pl.* spare (*free*)
  time **1.4**
raya *f.* stripe **1.6**
razón *f.* reason **1.3**
rebaja *f.* sale **1.6**
recibir *v.* to receive **1.3**
recién casado/a *m., f.* newlywed
  1.9
recomendar (e:ie) *v.* to
  recommend **1.8**
recordar (o:ue) *v.* to remember
  1.4
recorrer *v.* to tour an area
refresco *m.* soft drink **1.8**
regalar *v.* to give (a gift) **1.9**
regalo *m.* gift **1.6**
regatear *v.* to bargain **1.6**
regresar *v.* to return **1.2**
regular *adj.* so-so; OK **1.1**
reírse (e:i) *v.* to laugh **1.9**
relaciones *f., pl.* relationships
relajarse *v.* to relax **1.9**
reloj *m.* clock; watch **1.2**
repetir (e:i) *v.* to repeat **1.4**
residencia estudiantil *f.*
  dormitory **1.2**
respuesta *f.* answer
restaurante *m.* restaurant **1.4**
revista *f.* magazine **1.4**
rico/a *adj.* rich **1.6**; tasty;
  delicious **1.8**
riquísimo/a *adj.* extremely
  delicious **1.8**
rojo/a *adj.* red **1.6**
romper (con) *v.* to break up
  (with) **1.9**
ropa *f.* clothing; clothes **1.6**
  ropa interior *f.* underwear **1.6**
rosado/a *adj.* pink **1.6**
rubio/a *adj.* blond(e) **1.3**
ruso/a *adj.* Russian **1.3**
rutina *f.* routine **1.7**
  rutina diaria *f.* daily routine
    1.7

               S

sábado *m.* Saturday **1.2**
saber *v.* to know; to know
  how **1.6**; to taste **1.8**
  saber a   to taste like **1.8**
sabrosísimo/a *adj.* extremely
  delicious **1.8**
sabroso/a *adj.* tasty; delicious
  1.8
sacar *v.* to take out

sacar fotos   to take photos **1.5**
sal *f.* salt **1.8**
salchicha *f.* sausage **1.8**
salida *f.* departure; exit **1.5**
salir *v.* to leave **1.4**; to go out
  salir (con)   to go out (with); to date **1.9**
  salir de   to leave from
  salir para   to leave for *(a place)*
salmón *m.* salmon **1.8**
saludo *m.* greeting **1.1**
  saludos a...   greetings to... **1.1**
sandalia *f.* sandal **1.6**
sandía *f.* watermelon
sándwich *m.* sandwich **1.8**
se *ref. pron.* himself, herself, itself; *form.* yourself, themselves, yourselves **1.7**
secarse *v.* to dry oneself **1.7**
sección de (no) fumar *f.* (non) smoking section **1.8**
secuencia *f.* sequence
sed *f.* thirst **1.3**
seda *f.* silk **1.6**
seguir (e:i) *v.* to follow; to continue **1.4**
según *prep.* according to
segundo/a *n., adj.* second **1.5**
seguro/a *adj.* sure; safe **1.5**
seis *n., adj.* six **1.1**
seiscientos/as *n., adj.* six hundred **1.2**
semana *f.* week **1.2**
  fin *m.* **de semana**   weekend **1.4**
  semana *f.* **pasada** last week **1.6**
semestre *m.* semester **1.2**
sentarse (e:ie) *v.* to sit down **1.7**
sentir(se) (e:ie) *v.* to feel **1.7**
señor (Sr.) *m.* Mr.; sir **1.1**
señora (Sra.) *f.* Mrs.; ma'am **1.1**
señorita (Srta.) *f.* Miss **1.1**
separado/a *adj.* separated **1.9**
separarse (de) *v.* to separate (from) **1.9**
septiembre *m.* September **1.5**
séptimo/a *adj.* seventh **1.5**
ser *v.* to be **1.1**
  ser aficionado/a (a)   to be a fan (of) **1.4**
serio/a *adj.* serious
servir (e:i) *v.* to serve **1.8**; to help **1.5**
sesenta *n., adj.* sixty **1.2**
setecientos/as *n., adj.* seven hundred **1.2**
setenta *n., adj.* seventy **1.2**
sexto/a *n., adj.* sixth **1.5**
sí *adv.* yes **1.1**
si *conj.* if **1.4**

siempre *adv.* always **1.7**
siete *n., adj.* seven **1.1**
silla *f.* seat **1.2**
similar *adj.* similar
simpático/a *adj.* nice; likeable **1.3**
sin *prep.* without **1.2**
  sin duda   without a doubt
  sin embargo   however
sino *conj.* but (rather) **1.7**
situado/a *adj., p.p.* located
sobre *prep.* on; over **1.2**
sobrino/a *m., f.* nephew; niece **1.3**
sociología *f.* sociology **1.2**
sol *m.* sun **1.4; 1.5**
soleado/a *adj.* sunny
sólo *adv.* only **1.3**
solo *adj.* alone
soltero/a *adj.* single **1.9**
sombrero *m.* hat **1.6**
Son las dos.   It's two o'clock. **1.1**
sonreír (e:i) *v.* to smile **1.9**
sopa *f.* soup **1.8**
sorprender *v.* to surprise **1.9**
sorpresa *f.* surprise **1.9**
soy   I am **1.1**
  Soy yo.   That's me. **1.1**
  Soy de...   I'm from... **1.1**
su(s) *poss. adj.* his, her, its; *form.* your, their **1.3**
sucio/a *adj.* dirty **1.5**
sucre *m.* former Ecuadorian currency **1.6**
suegro/a *m., f.* father-in-law; mother-in-law **1.3**
sueño *m.* sleep **1.3**
suerte *f.* luck **1.3**
suéter *m.* sweater **1.6**
suponer *v.* to suppose **1.4**
sustantivo *m.* noun

T

tal vez *adv.* maybe **1.5**
talla *f.* size **1.6**
  talla grande *f.* large **1.6**
también *adv.* also; too **1.2; 1.7**
tampoco *adv.* neither; not either **1.7**
tan *adv.* so **1.5**
  tan... como   as... as **1.8**
tanto *adv.* so much
  tanto... como   as much... as **1.8**
  tantos/as... como   as many... as **1.8**
tarde *adv.* late **1.7**
tarde *f.* afternoon; evening; P.M. **1.1**
tarea *f.* homework **1.2**
tarjeta *f.* card
  tarjeta de crédito *f.* credit card **1.6**

tarjeta postal *f.* postcard **1.4**
taxi *m.* taxi **1.5**
te *sing., fam., d.o. pron.* you **1.5**; *sing., fam., i.o. pron.* to/for you **1.6**
  Te presento a... *fam.* I would like to introduce... to you. **1.1**
  ¿Te gusta(n)... ? Do you like... ? **1.2**
té *m.* tea **1.8**
té helado *m.* iced tea **1.8**
televisión *f.* television **1.2**
temprano *adv.* early **1.7**
tener *v.* to have **1.3**
  tener... años   to be... years old **1.3**
  Tengo... años.   I'm... years old. **1.3**
  tener (mucho) calor   to be (very) hot **1.3**
  tener (mucho) cuidado   to be (very) careful **1.3**
  tener (mucho) frío   to be (very) cold **1.3**
  tener ganas de (+ *inf.*)   to feel like *(doing something)* **1.3**
  tener (mucha) hambre   to be (very) hungry **1.3**
  tener (mucho) miedo (de)   to be (very) afraid (of); to be (very) scared (of) **1.3**
  tener miedo (de) que   to be afraid that
  tener planes   to have plans **1.4**
  tener (mucha) prisa   to be in a (big) hurry **1.3**
  tener que (+ *inf.*) *v.* to have to *(do something)* **1.3**
  tener razón   to be right **1.3**
  tener (mucha) sed   to be (very) thirsty **1.3**
  tener (mucho) sueño   to be (very) sleepy **1.3**
  tener (mucha) suerte *f.* to be (very) lucky **1.3**
  tener tiempo   to have time **1.4**
  tener una cita   to have a date; to have an appointment **1.9**
tenis *m.* tennis **1.4**
tercer, tercero/a *n., adj.* third **1.5**
terminar *v.* to end; to finish **1.2**
  terminar de (+ *inf.*) *v.* to finish *(doing something)* **1.4**
ti *pron., obj. of prep., fam.* you **1.9**
tiempo *m.* time **1.4**; weather **1.5**
  tiempo libre   free time
tienda *f.* shop; store **1.6**
  tienda de campaña   tent
tinto/a *adj.* red (wine) **1.8**

tío/a *m., f.* uncle; aunt 1.3
tíos *m.* aunts and uncles 1.3
título *m.* title
tiza *f.* chalk 1.2
toalla *f.* towel 1.7
todavía *adv.* yet; still 1.5
todo *m.* everything 1.5
　Todo está bajo control. Everything is under control. 1.7
todo(s)/a(s) *adj.* all; whole 1.4
todos *m., pl.* all of us; everybody; everyone
　¡Todos a bordo! All aboard! 1.1
tomar *v.* to take; to drink 1.2
　tomar clases to take classes 1.2
　tomar el sol to sunbathe 1.4
　tomar en cuenta to take into account
　tomar fotos to take photos 1.5
tomate *m.* tomato 1.8
tonto/a *adj.* silly; foolish 1.3
tortilla *f.* tortilla 1.8
　tortilla de maíz corn tortilla 1.8
tostado/a *adj.* toasted 1.8
trabajador(a) *adj.* hard-working 1.3
trabajar *v.* to work 1.2
traducir *v.* to translate 1.6
traer *v.* to bring 1.4
traje *m.* suit 1.6
　traje de baño *m.* bathing suit 1.6
tranquilo/a *adj.* calm
　Tranquilo. Don't worry.; Be cool. 1.7
trece *n., adj.* thirteen 1.1
treinta *n., adj.* thirty 1.1, 1.2
　y treinta thirty minutes past the hour (*time*) 1.1
tren *m.* train 1.5
tres *n., adj.* three 1.1
trescientos/as *n., adj.* three hundred 1.2
trimestre *m.* trimester; quarter 1.2
triste *adj.* sad 1.5
tú *fam. sub. pron.* you 1.1
　Tú eres... You are... 1.1
tu(s) *fam. poss. adj.* your 1.3
turismo *m.* tourism 1.5
turista *m., f.* tourist 1.1
turístico/a *adj.* touristic

U

Ud. *form. sing.* you 1.1
Uds. *form., pl.* you 1.1
último/a *adj.* last

un, uno/a *indef. art.* a, an; one 1.1
　uno/a *m., f., sing. pron.* one 1.1
　a la una at one o'clock 1.1
　una vez *adv.* once; one time 1.6
　una vez más one more time 1.9
　unos/as *m., f., pl. indef. art.* some; *pron.* some 1.1
único/a *adj.* only 1.3
universidad *f.* university; college 1.2
usar *v.* to wear; to use 1.6
usted (Ud.) *form. sing.* you 1.1
　ustedes (Uds.) *form., pl.* you 1.1
útil *adj.* useful
uva *f.* grape 1.8

V

vacaciones *f. pl.* vacation 1.5
vamos let's go 1.4
varios/as *adj., pl.* various; several 1.8
veces *f., pl.* times 1.6
veinte *n., adj.* twenty 1.1
veinticinco *n., adj.* twenty-five 1.1
veinticuatro *n., adj.* twenty-four 1.1
veintidós *n., adj.* twenty-two 1.1
veintinueve *n., adj.* twenty-nine 1.1
veintiocho *n., adj.* twenty-eight 1.1
veintiséis *n., adj.* twenty-six 1.1
veintisiete *n., adj.* twenty-seven 1.1
veintitrés *n., adj.* twenty-three 1.1
veintiún, veintiuno/a *n., adj.* twenty-one 1.1
vejez *f.* old age 1.9
vendedor(a) *m., f.* salesperson 1.6
vender *v.* to sell 1.6
venir *v.* to come 1.3
ventana *f.* window 1.2
ver *v.* to see 1.4
　a ver let's see 1.2
　ver películas to see movies 1.4
verano *m.* summer 1.5
verbo *m.* verb
verdad *f.* truth
　¿verdad? right? 1.1
verde *adj.* green 1.6
verduras *f., pl.* vegetables 1.8

vestido *m.* dress 1.6
vestirse (e:i) *v.* to get dressed 1.7
vez *f.* time 1.6
viajar *v.* to travel 1.2
viaje *m.* trip 1.5
viajero/a *m., f.* traveler 1.5
vida *f.* life 1.9
video *m.* video 1.1
videojuego *m.* video game 1.4
viejo/a *adj.* old 1.3
viento *m.* wind 1.5
viernes *m., sing.* Friday 1.2
vinagre *m.* vinegar 1.8
vino *m.* wine 1.8
　vino blanco *m.* white wine 1.8
　vino tinto *m.* red wine 1.8
visitar *v.* to visit 1.4
　visitar monumentos to visit monuments 1.4
viudo/a *adj.* widower; widow 1.9
vivir *v.* to live 1.3
vivo/a *adj.* bright; lively; living
vóleibol *m.* volleyball 1.4
volver (o:ue) *v.* to return 1.4
vos *pron.* you
vosotros/as *pron., form., pl.* you 1.1
vuelta *f.* return trip
vuestro(s)/a(s) *form., poss. adj.* your 1.3

W

walkman *m.* walkman

Y

y *conj.* and 1.1
　y cuarto quarter after (*time*) 1.1
　y media half-past (*time*) 1.1
　y quince quarter after (*time*) 1.1
　y treinta thirty (minutes past the hour) 1.1
　¿Y tú? *fam.* And you? 1.1
　¿Y usted? *form.* And you? 1.1
ya *adv.* already 1.6
yerno *m.* son-in-law 1.3
yo *sub. pron.* I 1.1
　Yo soy... I'm... 1.1
yogur *m.* yogurt 1.8

Z

zanahoria *f.* carrot 1.8
zapatos *m., pl.* shoes
　zapatos de tenis tennis shoes, sneakers 1.6

English-Spanish

A

a **un/a** *m., f., sing.; indef. art.* 1.1
A.M. **mañana** *f.* 1.1
able: be able to **poder (o:ue)** *v.*
   1.4
aboard **a bordo** 1.1
accounting **contabilidad** *f.* 1.2
acquainted: be acquainted with
   conocer *v.* 1.6
additional **adicional** *adj.*
adjective **adjetivo** *m.*
adolescence **adolescencia** *f.* 1.9
advice **consejo** *m.* 1.6
   give advice **dar consejos** 1.6
affirmative **afirmativo/a** *adj.*
afraid: be (very) afraid (of) **tener**
   (mucho) miedo (de) 1.3
   be afraid that **tener miedo**
     (de) que
after **después de** *prep.* 1.7
afternoon **tarde** *f.* 1.1
afterward **después** *adv.* 1.7
again **otra vez**
age **edad** *f.* 1.9
agree **concordar (o:ue)** *v.*
airplane **avión** *m.* 1.5
airport **aeropuerto** *m.* 1.5
alarm clock **despertador** *m.* 1.7
all **todo(s)/a(s)** *adj.* 1.4
   All aboard! **¡Todos a**
     bordo! 1.1
   all of us **todos** 1.1
   all over the world **en todo el**
     mundo
alleviate **aliviar** *v.*
alone **solo/a** *adj.*
already **ya** *adv.* 1.6
also **también** *adv.* 1.2; 1.7
although *conj.* **aunque**
always **siempre** *adv.* 1.7
American (North)
   norteamericano/a *adj.* 1.3
among **entre** *prep.* 1.2
amusement **diversión** *f.*
and **y** 1.1, **e** (before words
   beginning with *i* or *hi*) 1.4
   And you? **¿Y tú?** *fam.* 1.1;
     ¿Y usted? *form.* 1.1
angry **enojado/a** *adj.* 1.5
   get angry (with) **enojarse** *v.*
     (con) 1.7
anniversary **aniversario** *m.* 1.9
   (wedding) anniversary
     aniversario *m.* **(de bodas)** 1.9
annoy **molestar** *v.* 1.7
another **otro/a** *adj.* 1.6
answer **contestar** *v.* 1.2;
   respuesta *f.*
any **algún, alguno/a(s)** *adj.* 1.7
anyone **alguien** *pron.* 1.7
anything **algo** *pron.* 1.7

appear **parecer** *v.*
appetizers **entremeses** *m.,*
   pl. 1.8
apple **manzana** *f.* 1.8
appointment **cita** *f.* 1.9
   have an appointment **tener** *v.*
     una cita 1.9
April **abril** *m.* 1.5
aquatic **acuático/a** *adj.*
arrival **llegada** *f.* 1.5
arrive **llegar** *v.* 1.2
art **arte** *m.* 1.2
artist **artista** *m., f.* 1.3
as **como** 1.8
   as... as **tan... como** 1.8
   as many... as **tantos/as...**
     como 1.8
   as much... as **tanto... como**
     1.8
ask (a question) **preguntar**
   v. 1.2
   ask for **pedir (e:i)** *v.* 1.4
asparagus **espárragos** *m.,*
   pl. 1.8
at **a** *prep.* 1.1; **en** *prep.* 1.2
   at + *time* **a la(s)** + *time* 1.1
   at home **en casa** 1.7
   at night **por la noche** 1.7
   At what time...? **¿A qué**
     hora...? 1.1
attend **asistir (a)** *v.* 1.3
attract **atraer** *v.* 1.4
August **agosto** *m.* 1.5
aunt **tía** *f.* 1.3
   aunts and uncles **tíos** *m.,*
     pl. 1.3
automatic **automático/a** *adj.*
automobile **automóvil** *m.* 1.5
autumn **otoño** *m.* 1.5
avenue **avenida** *f.*

B

backpack **mochila** *f.* 1.2
bad **mal, malo/a** *adj.* 1.3
   It's not at all bad. **No está**
     nada mal. 1.5
bag **bolsa** *f.* 1.6
ball **pelota** *f.* 1.4
banana **banana** *f.* 1.8
bargain **ganga** *f.* 1.6; **regatear**
   v. 1.6
baseball (*game*) **béisbol** *m.* 1.4
basketball (*game*) **baloncesto**
   m. 1.4
bathe **bañarse** *v.* 1.7
bathing suit **traje** *m.* **de baño** 1.6
bathroom **baño** *m.* 1.7;
   cuarto de baño *m.* 1.7
be **ser** *v.* 1.1; **estar** *v.* 1.2
   be... years old **tener...**
     años 1.3
beach **playa** *f.* 1.5
beans **frijoles** *m., pl.* 1.8
beautiful **hermoso/a** *adj.* 1.6

because **porque** *conj.* 1.2
become (+ *adj.*) **ponerse (+ *adj.*)**
   1.7; **convertirse (e:ie)** *v.*
bed **cama** *f.* 1.5
   go to bed **acostarse (o:ue)**
     v. 1.7
beef **carne de res** *f.* 1.8
   beef soup **caldo** *m.* **de patas**
     1.8
before **antes** *adv.* 1.7;
   antes de *prep.* 1.7
begin **comenzar (e:ie)** *v.* 1.4;
   empezar (e:ie) *v.* 1.4
behind **detrás de** *prep.* 1.2
believe (in) **creer** *v.* **(en)** 1.3
bellhop **botones** *m., f. sing.* 1.5
below **debajo de** *prep.* 1.2
belt **cinturón** *m.* 1.6
beside **al lado de** *prep.* 1.2
best **mejor** *adj.*
   the best **el/la mejor** *adj.* 1.8
better **mejor** *adj.* 1.8
between **entre** *prep.* 1.2
bicycle **bicicleta** *f.* 1.4
big **gran, grande** *adj.* 1.3
bill **cuenta** *f.* 1.9
billion *m.* **mil millones**
biology **biología** *f.* 1.2
birth **nacimiento** *m.* 1.9
birthday **cumpleaños** *m.,*
   sing. 1.9
   have a birthday **cumplir** *v.*
     años 1.9
biscuit **bizcocho** *m.*
black **negro/a** *adj.* 1.6
blackberry **mora** *f.* 1.8
blackboard **pizarra** *f.* 1.2
blond(e) **rubio/a** *adj.* 1.3
blouse **blusa** *f.* 1.6
blue **azul** *adj.* 1.6
boardinghouse **pensión** *f.*
boat **barco** *m.* 1.5
book **libro** *m.* 1.2
bookstore **librería** *f.* 1.2
boot **bota** *f.* 1.6
bore **aburrir** *v.* 1.7
bored **aburrido/a** *adj.* 1.5
   be bored **estar** *v.* **aburrido/a**
     1.5
boring **aburrido/a** *adj.* 1.5
born: be born **nacer** *v.* 1.9
borrowed **prestado/a** *adj.*
bother **molestar** *v.* 1.7
bottle **botella** *f.* 1.9
bottom **fondo** *m.*
boulevard **bulevar** *m.*
boy **chico** *m.* 1.1; **muchacho**
   m. 1.3
boyfriend **novio** *m.* 1.3
brakes **frenos** *m., pl.*
bread **pan** *m.* 1.8
break up (with) **romper** *v.*
   (con) 1.9
breakfast **desayuno** *m.* 1.2, 1.8
   have breakfast **desayunar**
     v. 1.2

bring **traer** v. 1.4
brochure **folleto** m.
brother **hermano** m. 1.3
  brothers and sisters **hermanos**
    m., pl. 1.3
brother-in-law **cuñado** m. 1.3
brown **café** adj. 1.6;
  marrón adj. 1.6
brunet(te) **moreno/a** adj. 1.3
brush **cepillar** v. 1.7
  brush one's hair **cepillarse el**
    pelo 1.7
  brush one's teeth **cepillarse los**
    dientes 1.7
build **construir** v. 1.4
bus **autobús** m. 1.1
  bus station **estación** f. **de**
    autobuses 1.5
business administration
  administración f. **de**
  empresas 1.2
busy **ocupado/a** adj. 1.5
but **pero** conj. 1.2; (rather) **sino**
  conj. (in negative sentences) 1.7
butter **mantequilla** f. 1.8
buy **comprar** v. 1.2
by plane **en avión** 1.5
bye **chau** interj. fam. 1.1

C

cabin **cabaña** f. 1.5
café **café** m. 1.4
cafeteria **cafetería** f. 1.2
cake **pastel** m. 1.9
  chocolate cake **pastel de**
    chocolate m. 1.9
call **llamar** v.
  call on the phone **llamar por**
    teléfono
  be called **llamarse** v. 1.7
camp **acampar** v. 1.5
can **poder (o:ue)** v. 1.4
Canadian **canadiense** adj. 1.3
candy **dulces** m., pl. 1.9
capital city **capital** f. 1.1
car **auto(móvil)** m. 1.5
caramel **caramelo** m. 1.9
card **tarjeta** f.;
  (playing) **carta** f. 1.5
care **cuidado** m. 1.3
careful: be (very) careful **tener** v.
  (mucho) **cuidado** 1.3
carrot **zanahoria** f. 1.8
carry **llevar** v. 1.2
cash **(en) efectivo** 1.6
cash register **caja** f. 1.6
cashier **cajero/a** m., f.
celebrate **celebrar** v. 1.9
celebration **celebración** f.
  young woman's fifteenth
    birthday celebration
    quinceañera f. 1.9
cereal **cereales** m., pl. 1.8
chalk **tiza** f. 1.2

champagne **champán** m. 1.9
change **cambiar** v. **(de)** 1.9
chat **conversar** v. 1.2
chauffeur **conductor(a)** m.,
  f. 1.1
cheap **barato/a** adj. 1.6
cheese **queso** m. 1.8
chemistry **química** f. 1.2
chicken **pollo** m. 1.8
child **niño/a** m., f. 1.3
childhood **niñez** f. 1.9
children **hijos** m., pl. 1.3
Chinese **chino/a** adj. 1.3
chocolate **chocolate** m. 1.9
  chocolate cake **pastel** m. **de**
    chocolate 1.9
choose **escoger** v. 1.8
chop (food) **chuleta** f. 1.8
Christmas **Navidad** f. 1.9
church **iglesia** f. 1.4
city **ciudad** f. 1.4
class **clase** f. 1.2
  take classes **tomar clases** 1.2
classmate **compañero/a** m., f. **de**
  clase 1.2
clean **limpio/a** adj. 1.5
clear (weather) **despejado/a** adj.
  It's (very) clear. (weather)
    Está (muy) despejado.
clerk **dependiente/a** m., f. 1.6
climb **escalar** v. 1.4
  climb mountains **escalar**
    montañas 1.4
clock **reloj** m. 1.2
close **cerrar (e:ie)** v. 1.4
closed **cerrado/a** adj. 1.5
clothes **ropa** f. 1.6
clothing **ropa** f. 1.6
cloudy **nublado/a** adj. 1.5
  It's (very) cloudy. **Está (muy)**
    nublado. 1.5
coat **abrigo** m. 1.6
coffee **café** m. 1.8
cold **frío** m. 1.5;
  be (feel) (very) cold **tener**
    (mucho) frío 1.3
  It's (very) cold. (weather) **Hace**
    (mucho) frío. 1.5
college **universidad** f. 1.2
color **color** m. 1.6
comb one's hair **peinarse** v. 1.7
come **venir** v. 1.3
comfortable **cómodo/a** adj. 1.5
community **comunidad** f. 1.1
comparison **comparación** f.
computer **computadora** f. 1.1
  computer disc **disco** m.
  computer programmer
    programador(a) m., f. 1.3
  computer science **computación**
    f. 1.2
confirm **confirmar** v. 1.5
  confirm a reservation **confirmar**
    una reservación 1.5
confused **confundido/a** adj. 1.5

Congratulations! (for an event such
  as a birthday or anniversary)
  ¡Felicidades! f. pl. 1.9; (for
  an event such as an engagement
  or a good grade on a test)
  ¡Felicitaciones! f. pl. 1.9
contamination **contaminación** f.
content **contento/a** adj. 1.5
continue **seguir (e:i)** v. 1.4
control **control** m.
  be under control **estar bajo**
    control 1.7
conversation **conversación** f. 1.1
converse **conversar** v. 1.2
cookie **galleta** f. 1.9
cool **fresco/a** adj. 1.5
  Be cool. **Tranquilo.** 1.7
  It's cool. (weather) **Hace**
    fresco. 1.5
corn **maíz** m. 1.8
cost **costar (o:ue)** v. 1.6
cotton **algodón** f. 1.6
  (made of) cotton **de**
    algodón 1.6
count (on) **contar (o:ue)** v.
  (con) 1.4
country (nation) **país** m. 1.1
countryside **campo** m. 1.5
couple (married) **pareja** f. 1.9
course **curso** m. 1.2; **materia**
  f. 1.2
courtesy **cortesía** f.
cousin **primo/a** m., f. 1.3
cover **cubrir** v.
covered **cubierto** p.p.
crazy **loco/a** adj. 1.6
create **crear** v.
credit **crédito** m. 1.6
  credit card **tarjeta** f. **de**
    crédito 1.6
currency exchange **cambio** m. **de**
  moneda
custard (baked) **flan** m. 1.9
custom **costumbre** f. 1.1
customer **cliente/a** m., f. 1.6
customs **aduana** f. 1.5
  customs inspector **inspector(a)**
    m., f. **de aduanas** 1.5
cycling **ciclismo** m. 1.4

D

dad **papá** m. 1.3
daily **diario/a** adj. 1.7
  daily routine **rutina** f. **diaria**
    1.7
dance **bailar** v. 1.2
date (appointment) **cita** f. 1.9;
  (calendar) **fecha** f. 1.5;
  (someone) **salir** v. **con**
    (alguien) 1.9
  have a date **tener una**
    cita 1.9
daughter **hija** f. 1.3
daughter-in-law **nuera** f. 1.3

day **día** *m.* 1.1
   day before yesterday
      anteayer *adv.* **1.6**
death **muerte** *f.* 1.9
December **diciembre** *m.* 1.5
decide **decidir** *v.* (+ *inf.*) 1.3
delicious **delicioso/a** *adj.* 1.8;
   rico/a *adj.* 1.8; **sabroso/a**
   adj. **1.8**
delighted **encantado/a** *adj.* 1.1
department store **almacén** *m.* 1.6
departure **salida** *f.* 1.5
describe **describir** *v.* 1.3
design **diseño** *m.*
desire **desear** *v.* 1.2
desk **escritorio** *m.* 1.2
dessert **postre** *m.* 1.9
diary **diario** *m.* 1.1
dictionary **diccionario** *m.* 1.1
die **morir (o:ue)** *v.* 1.8
difficult **difícil** *adj.* 1.3
dinner **cena** *f.* 1.2, 1.8
   have dinner **cenar** *v.* 1.2
dirty **ensuciar** *v.*; **sucio/a**
   adj. 1.5
disagree **no estar de acuerdo**
dish **plato** *m.* 1.8
   main dish *m.* **plato principal**
   1.8
disk **disco** *m.*
disorderly **desordenado/a**
   adj. 1.5
dive **bucear** *v.* 1.4
divorce **divorcio** *m.* 1.9
divorced **divorciado/a** *adj.* 1.9
   get divorced (from) **divorciarse**
   v. (**de**) 1.9
do **hacer** *v.* 1.4
   (I) don't want to. **No quiero.**
   1.4
doctor **doctor(a)** *m.*, *f.* 1.3;
   médico/a *m.*, *f.* 1.3
domestic **doméstico/a** *adj.*
   domestic appliance
   electrodoméstico *m.*
door **puerta** *f.* 1.2
dormitory **residencia** *f.*
   estudiantil 1.2
double **doble** *adj.* 1.5
   double room **habitación** *f.*
   doble 1.5
Down with... ! **¡Abajo el/la... !**
downtown **centro** *m.* 1.4
draw **dibujar** *v.* 1.2
dress **vestido** *m.* 1.6
   get dressed **vestirse (e:i)** *v.*
   1.7
drink **beber** *v.* 1.3; **tomar**
   v. 1.2
   bebida *f.* 1.8
drive **conducir** *v.* 1.6
driver **conductor(a)** *m.*, *f.* 1.1
dry oneself **secarse** *v.* 1.7
during **durante** *prep.* 1.7

E

each **cada** *adj.* 1.6
eagle **águila** *f.*
early **temprano** *adv.* 1.7
ease **aliviar** *v.*
easy **fácil** *adj.* 1.3
eat **comer** *v.* *1.3*
economics **economía** *f.* 1.2
Ecuador **Ecuador** *m.* 1.1
Ecuadorian **ecuatoriano/a**
   adj. 1.3
effective **eficaz** *adj.*
egg **huevo** *m.* 1.8
eight **ocho** *n.*, *adj.* 1.1
eight hundred **ochocientos/as**
   n., *adj.* 1.2
eighteen **dieciocho** *n.*, *adj.* 1.1
eighth **octavo/a** *adj.* 1.5
eighty **ochenta** *n.*, *adj.* 1.2
either... or **o... o** *conj.* 1.7
eldest **el/la mayor** *adj.* 1.8
elegant **elegante** *adj.* 1.6
elevator **ascensor** *m.* 1.5
eleven **once** *n.*, *adj.* 1.1
e-mail **correo** *m.* **electrónico**
   1.4
   e-mail message **mensaje** *m.*
   electrónico 1.4
   read e-mail **leer** *v.* **el correo**
   electrónico 1.4
embarrassed **avergonzado/a**
   adj. 1.5
employee **empleado/a** *m.*, *f.* 1.5
end **fin** *m.* 1.4; **terminar** *v.* 1.2
engaged: get engaged (to)
   comprometerse *v.* (**con**) 1.9
engineer **ingeniero/a** *m.*, *f.* 1.3
English (*language*) **inglés** *m.* 1.2;
   inglés, inglesa *adj.* 1.3
entertainment **diversión** *f.* 1.4
eraser **borrador** *m.* 1.2
establish **establecer** *v.*
evening **tarde** *f.* 1.1
everybody **todos** *m.*, *pl.*
everything **todo** *m.* 1.5
   Everything is under control.
   Todo está bajo control. 1.7
exactly **en punto** 1.1
exam **examen** *m.* 1.2
excellent **excelente** *adj.* 1.5
exciting **emocionante** *adj.*
excursion **excursión** *f.*
excuse **disculpar** *v.*
   Excuse me. (*May I?*) **Con**
   permiso. 1.1; (*I beg your*
   pardon.) **Perdón.** 1.1
exit **salida** *f.* 1.5
expensive **caro/a** *adj.* 1.6
explain **explicar** *v.* 1.2
explore **explorar** *v.*
expression **expresión** *f.*
extremely delicious **riquísimo/a**
   adj. 1.8

F

fabulous **fabuloso/a** *adj.* 1.5
face **cara** *f.* 1.7
fact: in fact **de hecho**
fall (*season*) **otoño** *m.* 1.5
fall: fall asleep **dormirse (o:ue)**
   v. 1.7
   fall in love (with) **enamorarse**
   v. (**de**) 1.9
family **familia** *f.* 1.3
fan **aficionado/a** *adj.* 1.4
   be a fan (of) **ser aficionado/a**
   (**a**) 1.4
far from **lejos de** *prep.* 1.2
farewell **despedida** *f.*
fascinate **fascinar** *v.* 1.7
fashion **moda** *f.* 1.6
   be in fashion **estar de**
   moda 1.6
fast **rápido/a** *adj.*
fat **gordo/a** *adj.* 1.3
father **padre** *m.* 1.3
father-in-law **suegro** *m.* 1.3
favorite **favorito/a** *adj.* 1.4
fear **miedo** *m.* 1.3
February **febrero** *m.* 1.5
feel **sentir(se) (e:ie)** *v.* 1.7
   feel like (*doing something*)
   tener ganas de (+ *inf.*) 1.3
few **pocos/as** *adj.*, *pl.*
   fewer than **menos de**
   (+ *number*) 1.8
field: major field of study
   especialización *f.*
fifteen *n.*, *adj.* **quince** 1.1
   fifteen-year-old girl
   quinceañera *f.* 1.9
   young woman's fifteenth
   birthday celebration
   quinceañera *f.* 1.9
fifth **quinto/a** *n.*, *adj.* 1.5
fifty **cincuenta** *n.*, *adj.* 1.2
figure (*number*) **cifra** *f.*
finally **por último** 1.7
find **encontrar (o:ue)** *v.* 1.4
   find (each other) **encontrar(se)**
   v.
fine **multa** *f.*
finish **terminar** *v.* 1.2
   finish (*doing something*)
   terminar *v.* **de** (+ *inf.*) 1.4
first **primer, primero/a** *n.*,
   adj. 1.5
fish (*food*) **pescado** *m.* 1.8
fisherman **pescador** *m.*
fisherwoman **pescadora** *f.*
fishing **pesca** *f.* 1.5
fit (*clothing*) **quedar** *v.* 1.7
five **cinco** *n.*, *adj.* 1.1
five hundred **quinientos/as** *n.*,
   adj. 1.2
fixed **fijo/a** *adj.* 1.6
flag **bandera** *f.*
flank steak **lomo** *m.* 1.8

floor (*of a building*) **piso** *m.* 1.5
  ground floor **planta** *f.* **baja** 1.5
  top floor **planta** *f.* **alta** 1.5
fog **niebla** *f.*
follow **seguir (e:i)** *v.* 1.4
food **comida** *f.* 1.8; **alimento** *m.*
foolish **tonto/a** *adj.* 1.3
football **fútbol** *m.*
  americano 1.4
for me **para mí** 1.8
forbid **prohibir** *v.*
foreign languages **lenguas**
  f. pl. **extranjeras** 1.2
forty **cuarenta** *n., adj.* 1.2
four **cuatro** *n., adj.* 1.1
four hundred **cuatrocientos/as**
  n., adj. 1.2
fourteen **catorce** *n., adj.* 1.1
fourth **cuarto/a** *n., adj.* 1.5
free **libre** *adj.* 1.4
  free time **tiempo libre;**
  ratos libres 1.4
French **francés, francesa**
  adj. 1.3
French fries **papas** *f., pl.*
  fritas 1.8; **patatas** *f., pl.*
  fritas 1.8
Friday **viernes** *m., sing.* 1.2
fried **frito/a** *adj.* 1.8
  fried potatoes **papas** *f., pl.*
  fritas 1.8; **patatas** *f., pl.*
  fritas 1.8
friend **amigo/a** *m., f.* 1.3
friendly **amable** *adj.* 1.5
friendship **amistad** *f.* 1.9
from **de** *prep.* 1.1; **desde**
  prep. 1.6
  from the United States
  estadounidense *adj.* 1.3
  He/She/It is from... **Es de....**
  1.1
  I'm from... **Soy de...** 1.1
fruit **fruta** *f.* 1.8
  fruit juice **jugo** *m.* **de**
  fruta 1.8
fun **divertido/a** *adj.* 1.7
  fun activity **diversión** *f.* 1.4
  have fun **divertirse (e:ie)**
  v. 1.9
function **funcionar** *v.*

G

game **juego** *m.*; (*match*)
  partido *m.* 1.4
garlic **ajo** *m.* 1.8
geography **geografía** *f.* 1.2
German **alemán, alemana**
  adj. 1.3
get **conseguir (e:i)** *v.* 1.4
  get along well/badly (with)
  llevarse bien/mal (con)
  1.9
  get up **levantarse** *v.* 1.7
gift **regalo** *m.* 1.6

girl **chica** *f.* 1.1;
  muchacha *f.* 1.3
girlfriend **novia** *f.* 1.3
give **dar** *v.* 1.6, 1.9;
  (*as a gift*) **regalar** 1.9
glasses **gafas** *f., pl.* 1.6
  sunglasses **gafas** *f., pl.*
  de sol 1.6
gloves **guantes** *m., pl.* 1.6
go **ir** *v.* 1.4
  go away **irse** 1.7
  go by boat **ir en barco** 1.5
  go by bus **ir en autobús** 1.5
  go by car **ir en auto(móvil)**
  1.5
  go by motorcycle **ir en**
  motocicleta 1.5
  go by taxi **ir en taxi** 1.5
  go down; **bajar(se)** *v.*
  go on a hike (in the mountains)
  ir de excursión (a las
  montañas) 1.4
  go out **salir** *v.* 1.9
  go out (with) **salir** *v.* **(con)**
  1.9
  go up **subir** *v.*
  Let's go. **Vamos.** 1.4
  be going to (*do something*) **ir a**
  (+ inf.) 1.4
golf **golf** *m.* 1.4
good **buen, bueno/a** *adj.*
  1.3, 1.6
  Good afternoon. **Buenas**
  tardes. 1.1
  Good evening. **Buenas**
  noches. 1.1
  Good idea. **Buena idea.** 1.4
  Good morning. **Buenos**
  días. 1.1
  Good night. **Buenas**
  noches. 1.1
good-bye **adiós** *m.* 1.1
  say good-bye (to) **despedirse**
  v. **(de) (e:i)** 1.7
good-looking **guapo/a** *adj.* 1.3
graduate (from/in) **graduarse** *v.*
  (de/en) 1.9
grains **cereales** *m., pl.* 1.8
granddaughter **nieta** *f.* 1.3
grandfather **abuelo** *m.* 1.3
grandmother **abuela** *f.* 1.3
grandparents **abuelos** *m. pl.* 1.3
grandson **nieto** *m.* 1.3
grape **uva** *f.* 1.8
gray **gris** *adj.* 1.6
great **fenomenal** *adj.* 1.5
great-grandfather **bisabuelo**
  m. 1.3
great-grandmother **bisabuela**
  f. 1.3
green **verde** *adj.* 1.6
greeting **saludo** *m.* 1.1
  Greetings to... **Saludos a...**
  1.1
grilled (*food*) **a la plancha** 1.8

grilled flank steak **lomo** *m.* **a**
  la plancha 1.8
ground floor **planta baja** *f.* 1.5
guest (at a house/hotel) **huésped**
  m., f. 1.5; (*invited to a func-*
  tion) **invitado/a** *m., f.* 1.9
gymnasium **gimnasio** *m.* 1.4

H

hair **pelo** *m.* 1.7
half **medio/a** *adj.* 1.3
  half-past... (*time*) ...**y**
  media 1.1
half-brother **medio hermano**
  1.3
half-sister **media hermana** 1.3
ham **jamón** *m.* 1.8
hamburger **hamburguesa** *f.* 1.8
hand **mano** *f.* 1.1
  Hands up! **¡Manos arriba!**
handsome **guapo/a** *adj.* 1.3
happiness **alegría** *v.* 1.9
happy **alegre** *adj.* 1.5;
  contento/a *adj.* 1.5; **feliz**
  adj. 1.5
  Happy birthday! **¡Feliz**
  cumpleaños! 1.9
hard **difícil** *adj.* 1.3
hard-working **trabajador(a)**
  adj. 1.3
haste **prisa** *f.* 1.3
hat **sombrero** *m.* 1.6
hate **odiar** *v.* 1.9
have **tener** *v.* 1.3
  Have a good trip! **¡Buen**
  viaje! 1.1
  have time **tener tiempo** 1.4
  have to (*do something*) **tener**
  que (+ inf.) 1.3; **deber**
  (+ inf.)
he **él** *sub. pron.* 1.1
hear **oír** *v.* 1.4
heat **calor** *m.* 1.5
Hello. **Hola.** 1.1
help **servir (e:i)** *v.* 1.5
her **su(s)** *poss. adj.* 1.3;
  la *f., sing., d.o. pron.* 1.5
  to/for her **le** *f., sing., i.o.*
  pron. 1.6
here **aquí** *adv.* 1.1
  Here it is. **Aquí está.** 1.5
  Here we are at/in... **Aquí**
  estamos en... 1.2
Hi. **Hola.** 1.1
hike **excursión** *f.* 1.4
  go on a hike **hacer una**
  excursión 1.5; **ir de**
  excursión 1.4
hiker **excursionista** *m., f.*
hiking **de excursión** 1.4
him **lo** *m., sing., d.o. pron.* 1.5
  to/for him **le** *m., sing., i.o.*
  pron. 1.6
his **su(s)** *poss. adj.* 1.3

history **historia** f. 1.2
hobby **pasatiempo** m. 1.4
hockey **hockey** m. 1.4
holiday **día** m. **de fiesta** 1.9
home **casa** f. 1.2
homework **tarea** f. 1.2
hope **esperar** v. (+ inf.) 1.2
hors d'oeuvres **entremeses** m.,
   pl. 1.8
horse **caballo** m. 1.5
hot: be (feel) (very) hot **tener**
   (mucho) calor 1.3
   It's (very) hot **Hace (mucho)**
     calor 1.5
hotel **hotel** m. 1.5
hour **hora** f. 1.1
house **casa** f. 1.2
How... ! **¡Qué... !** 1.3
   how? **¿cómo?** adv. 1.1
   How are you? **¿Qué tal?** 1.1
   How are you? **¿Cómo estás?**
     fam. 1.1
   How are you? **¿Cómo está**
     usted? form. 1.1
   How can I help you? **¿En qué**
     puedo servirles? 1.5
   How is it going? **¿Qué**
     tal? 1.1
   How is/are...? **¿Qué**
     tal...? 1.2
   How much/many?
     ¿Cuánto(s)/a(s)? 1.1
   How much does... cost?
     ¿Cuánto cuesta...? 1.6
   How old are you? **¿Cuántos**
     años tienes? fam. 1.3
however **sin embargo**
humanities **humanidades** f.,
   pl. 1.2
hundred **cien, ciento** n., adj. 1.2
hunger **hambre** f. 1.3
hungry: be (very) hungry **tener** v.
   (mucha) hambre 1.3
hurry
   be in a (big) hurry **tener** v.
     (mucha) prisa 1.3
husband **esposo** m. 1.3

I

I **Yo** sub. pron. 1.1
   I am... **Yo soy...** 1.1
ice cream **helado** m. 1.9
iced **helado/a** adj. 1.8
   iced tea **té** m. **helado** 1.8
idea **idea** f. 1.4
if **si** conj. 1.4
important **importante** adj. 1.3
   be important to **importar** v.
     1.7
in **en** prep. 1.2
   in a bad mood **de mal**
     humor 1.5
   in a good mood **de buen**
     humor 1.5

in front of **delante de** prep. 1.2
   in love (with) **enamorado/a**
     (de) 1.5
   in the afternoon **de la tarde**
     1.1; **por la tarde** 1.7
   in the direction of **para**
     prep. 1.1
   in the early evening **de la**
     tarde 1.1
   in the evening **de la noche**
     1.1; **por la tarde** 1.7
   in the morning **de la mañana**
     1.1; **por la mañana** 1.7
incredible **increíble** adj. 1.5
inside **dentro** adv.
intelligent **inteligente** adj. 1.3
intend to **pensar** v. (+ inf.) 1.4
interest **interesar** v. 1.7
interesting **interesante** adj. 1.3
   be interesting to **interesar** v. 1.7
introduction **presentación** f.
   I would like to introduce (name)
     to you. **Le presento a...**
     form. 1.1; **Te presento a...**
     fam. 1.1
invite **invitar** v. 1.9
it **lo/la** sing., d.o., pron. 1.5
   It's me. **Soy yo.** 1.1
Italian **italiano/a** adj. 1.3
its **su(s)** poss. adj. 1.3

J

jacket **chaqueta** f. 1.6
January **enero** m. 1.5
Japanese **japonés, japonesa**
   adj. 1.3
jeans **bluejeans** m., pl. 1.6
jog **correr** v.
journalism **periodismo** m. 1.2
journalist **periodista** m., f. 1.3
joy **alegría** f. 1.9
   give joy **dar** v. **alegría** 1.9
joyful **alegre** adj. 1.5
juice **jugo** m. 1.8
July **julio** m. 1.5
June **junio** m. 1.5
just **apenas** adv.
   have just (done something)
     acabar de (+ inf.) 1.6

K

key **llave** f. 1.5
kind: That's very kind of
   you. **Muy amable.** 1.5
kiss **beso** m. 1.9
know **saber** v. 1.6;
   conocer v. 1.6
   know how **saber** v. 1.6

L

laboratory **laboratorio** m. 1.2

lack **faltar** v. 1.7
landlord **dueño/a** m., f. 1.8
landscape **paisaje** m. 1.5
language **lengua** f. 1.2
large **grande** adj. 1.3;
   (clothing size) **talla**
     grande 1.6
last **pasado/a** adj. 1.6;
   último/a adj.
   last name **apellido** m. 1.3
   last night **anoche** adv. 1.6
   last week **semana** f. **pasada**
     1.6
   last year **año** m. **pasado** 1.6
late **tarde** adv. 1.7
later (on) **más tarde** 1.7
   See you later. **Hasta la vista.**
     1.1; **Hasta luego.** 1.1
laugh **reírse (e:i)** v. 1.9
lazy **perezoso/a** adj.
learn **aprender** v. (a + inf.) 1.3
leave **salir** v. 1.4; **irse** v. 1.7
   leave a tip **dejar una**
     propina 1.9
   leave for (a place) **salir para**
   leave from **salir de**
left **izquierdo/a** adj. 1.2
   be left over **quedar** v. 1.7
   to the left of **a la izquierda**
     de 1.2
lemon **limón** m. 1.8
lend **prestar** v. 1.6
less **menos** adv.
   less... than **menos... que** 1.8
   less than **menos de** (+ number)
     1.8
lesson **lección** f. 1.1
let's see **a ver** 1.2
letter **carta** f. 1.4
lettuce **lechuga** f. 1.8
library **biblioteca** f. 1.2
lie **mentira** f. 1.4
life **vida** f. 1.9
like **como** prep. 1.8;
   gustar v. 1.2
   Do you like...? **¿Te**
     gusta(n)...? 1.2
   I don't like them at all. **No me**
     gustan nada. 1.2
   I like... **Me gusta(n)...** 1.2
   like very much **encantar** v.;
     fascinar v. 1.7
likeable **simpático/a** adj. 1.3
likewise **igualmente** adv. 1.1
line **línea** f. 1.4
listen (to) **escuchar** v. 1.2
   Listen! (command) **¡Oye!** fam.,
     sing. 1.1; **¡Oiga/Oigan!**
     form., sing./pl. 1.1
   listen to music **escuchar**
     música 1.2
   listen (to) the radio **escuchar**
     la radio 1.2
literature **literatura** f. 1.2
little (quantity) **poco/a** adj. 1.5

live **vivir** *v.* 1.3
loan **prestar** *v.* 1.6
lobster **langosta** *f.* 1.8
long **largo/a** *adj.* 1.6
look (at) **mirar** *v.* 1.2
  look for **buscar** *v.* 1.2
lose **perder (e:ie)** *v.* 1.4
lot of, a **mucho/a** *adj.* 1.2, 1.3
love (*another person*) **querer
(e:ie)** *v.* 1.4; (*inanimate objects*)
encantar *v.* 1.7; **amor** *m.*
1.9
  in love **enamorado/a** *adj.* 1.5
luck **suerte** *f.* 1.3
lucky: be (very) lucky **tener
(mucha) suerte** 1.3
luggage **equipaje** *m.* 1.5
lunch **almuerzo** *m.* 1.8
  have lunch **almorzar (o:ue)** *v.*
1.4

M

ma'am **señora (Sra.)** *f.* 1.1
mad **enojado/a** *adj.* 1.5
magazine **revista** *f.* 1.4
magnificent **magnífico/a**
  adj. 1.5
main **principal** *adj.* 1.8
major **especialización** *f.* 1.2
make **hacer** *v.* 1.4
makeup **maquillaje** *m.* 1.7
  put on makeup **maquillarse**
  v. 1.7
man **hombre** *m.* 1.1
many **mucho/a** *adj.* 1.3
map **mapa** *m.* 1.2
March **marzo** *m.* 1.5
margarine **margarina** *f.* 1.8
marinated fish **ceviche** *m.* 1.8
  lemon-marinated shrimp
  ceviche *m.* **de camarón** 1.8
marital status **estado** *m.*
  civil 1.9
market **mercado** *m.* 1.6
  open-air market **mercado al
  aire libre** 1.6
marriage **matrimonio** *m.* 1.9
married **casado/a** *adj.* 1.9
  get married (to) **casarse** *v.*
  (con) 1.9
marvelous **maravilloso/a**
  adj. 1.5
match (*sports*) **partido** *m.* 1.4
  match (with) **hacer** *v.* **juego
  (con)** 1.6
mathematics **matemáticas**
  f., pl. 1.2
matter **importar** *v.* 1.7
maturity **madurez** *f.* 1.9
May **mayo** *m.* 1.5
maybe **tal vez** *adv.* 1.5; **quizás**
  adv. 1.5
mayonnaise **mayonesa** *f.* 1.8

me **me** *sing., d.o. pron.* 1.5; *mí
pron., obj. of prep.* 1.9
  to/for me **me** *sing., i.o.
pron.* 1.6
meal **comida** *f.* 1.8
meat **carne** *f.* 1.8
medium **mediano/a** *adj.*
meet (*each other*) **conocer(se)** *v.*
1.8
menu **menú** *m.* 1.8
Mexican **mexicano/a** *adj.* 1.3
Mexico **México** *m.* 1.1
middle age **madurez** *f.* 1.9
midnight **medianoche** *f.* 1.1
milk **leche** *f.* 1.8
million **millón** *m.* 1.2
  million of **millón de** *m.* 1.2
mineral water **agua** *f.*
  mineral 1.8
minute **minuto** *m.* 1.1
mirror **espejo** *m.* 1.7
Miss **señorita (Srta.)** *f.* 1.1
miss **perder (e:ie)** *v.* 1.4
mistaken **equivocado/a** *adj.*
modem **módem** *m.*
mom **mamá** *f.* 1.3
Monday **lunes** *m., sing.* 1.2
money **dinero** *m.* 1.6
month **mes** *m.* 1.5
monument **monumento** *m.* 1.4
more **más** 1.2
  more... than **más... que** 1.8
  more than **más de
  (+ *number*)** 1.8
morning **mañana** *f.* 1.1
mother **madre** *f.* 1.3
mother-in-law **suegra** *f.* 1.3
motor **motor** *m.*
motorcycle **motocicleta** *f.* 1.5
mountain **montaña** *f.* 1.4
movie **película** *f.* 1.4
movie theater **cine** *m.* 1.4
Mr. **señor (Sr.); don** *m.* 1.1
Mrs. **señora (Sra.); doña** *f.* 1.1
much **mucho/a** *adj.* 1.2, 1.3
  very much **muchísimo/a**
  adj. 1.2
municipal **municipal** *adj. m., f.*
museum **museo** *m.* 1.4
mushroom **champiñón** *m.* 1.8
music **música** *f.* 1.2
must **deber** *v.* (+ *inf.*) 1.3
  It must be... **Debe ser...** 1.6
my **mi(s)** *poss. adj.* 1.3

N

name **nombre** *m.* 1.1
  be named **llamarse** *v.* 1.7
  in the name of **a nombre
  de** 1.5
  last name *m.* **apellido**
  My name is... **Me
  llamo...** 1.1
nationality **nacionalidad** *f.* 1.1

near **cerca de** *prep.* 1.2
need **faltar** *v.* 1.7; **necesitar** *v.*
  (+ *inf.*) 1.2
negative **negativo/a** *adj.*
neither **tampoco** *adv.* 1.7
neither... nor **ni... ni** *conj.* 1.7
nephew **sobrino** *m.* 1.3
nervous **nervioso/a** *adj.* 1.5
never **nunca** *adv.* 1.7;
  jamás *adv.* 1.7
new **nuevo/a** *adj.* 1.6
newlywed **recién casado/a**
  m., f. 1.9
newspaper **periódico** *m.* 1.4
next to **al lado de** *prep.* 1.2
nice **simpático/a** *adj.* 1.3;
  amable *adj.* 1.5
niece **sobrina** *f.* 1.3
night **noche** *f.* 1.1
nine **nueve** *n., adj.* 1.1
nine hundred
  novecientos/as *n., adj.* 1.2
nineteen **diecinueve** *n., adj.* 1.1
ninety **noventa** *n., adj.* 1.2
ninth **noveno/a** *n., adj.* 1.5
no **no** *adv.* 1.1; **ningún,
ninguno/a(s)** *adj.* 1.7
  no one **nadie** *pron.* 1.7
  No problem. **No hay
  problema.** 1.7
nobody **nadie** *pron.* 1.7
none **ningún, ninguno/a(s)**
  pron. 1.7
noon **mediodía** *m.* 1.1
nor **ni** *conj.* 1.7
not **no** 1.1
  not any **ningún, ninguno/a(s)**
  adj. 1.7
  not anyone **nadie** *pron.* 1.7
  not anything **nada** *pron.* 1.7
  not bad at all **nada mal** 1.5
  not either **tampoco** *adv.* 1.7
  not ever **nunca** *adv.* 1.7;
  jamás *adv.* 1.7
  Not very well. **No muy
  bien.** 1.1
notebook **cuaderno** *m.* 1.1
nothing **nada** *pron.* 1.1; 1.7
noun **sustantivo** *m.*
November **noviembre** *m.* 1.5
now **ahora** *adv.* 1.2
nowadays **hoy día** *adv.*
number **número** *m.* 1.1

O

obtain **conseguir (e:i)** *v.* 1.4
o'clock: It's... o'clock. **Son
  las...** 1.1
  It's one o'clock. **Es la una.** 1.1
October **octubre** *m.* 1.5
of **de** *prep.* 1.1
offer **ofrecer** *v.* 1.6
Oh! **¡Ay!**
oil **aceite** *m.* 1.8

OK **regular** *adj.* 1.1
  It's okay. **Está bien.**
old **viejo/a** *adj.* 1.3
old age **vejez** *f.* 1.9
older **mayor** *adj.* 1.3
  older brother/sister **hermano/a**
  mayor *m., f.* 1.3
oldest **el/la mayor** *adj.* 1.8
on **en** *prep.* 1.2; **sobre** *prep.* 1.2
  on the dot **en punto** 1.1
  on top of **encima de** 1.2
once **una vez** 1.6
one **un, uno/a** *m., f., sing.*
  pron. 1.1
  one hundred **cien(to)** *n., adj.*
  1.2
  one million **un millón** *m.* 1.2
  one more time **una vez más**
  1.9
  one thousand **mil** *n., adj.* 1.2
  one time **una vez** 1.6
onion **cebolla** *f.* 1.8
only **sólo** *adv.* 1.3; **único/a**
  adj. 1.3
  only child **hijo/a único/a**
  m., f. 1.3
open **abierto/a** *adj.* 1.5;
  abrir *v.* 1.3
open-air **al aire libre** 1.6
or **o** *conj.* 1.7
orange **anaranjado/a** *adj.* 1.6;
  naranja *f.* 1.8
order *(food)* **pedir (e:i)** *v.* 1.8
orderly **ordenado/a** *adj.* 1.5
ordinal *(numbers)* **ordinal** *adj.*
other **otro/a** *adj.* 1.6
ought to **deber** *v.* **(+ *inf.*)** 1.3
our **nuestro(s)/a(s)** *poss. adj.*
  1.3
over **sobre** *prep.* 1.2
owner **dueño/a** *m., f.* 1.8

P

P.M. **tarde** *f.* 1.1
pack *(one's suitcases)* **hacer** *v.* **las**
  maletas 1.5
pair **par** *m.* 1.6
  pair of shoes **par de**
  zapatos *m.* 1.6
pants **pantalones** *m., pl.* 1.6
pantyhose **medias** *f., pl.* 1.6
paper **papel** *m.* 1.2
Pardon me. *(May I?)* **Con**
  permiso. 1.1; *(Excuse me.)*
  Pardon me. **Perdón.** 1.1
parents **padres** *m., pl.* 1.3;
  papás *m., pl.* 1.3
park **parque** *m.* 1.4
partner *(one of a married couple)*
  pareja *f.* 1.9
party **fiesta** *f.* 1.9
passed **pasado/a** *adj., p.p.*
passenger **pasajero/a** *m., f.* 1.1
passport **pasaporte** *m.* 1.5

past **pasado/a** *adj.* 1.6
pastime **pasatiempo** *m.* 1.4
pay **pagar** *v.* 1.6
  pay the bill **pagar la**
  cuenta 1.9
pea **arveja** *m.* 1.8
peach **melocotón** *m.* 1.8
pear **pera** *f.* 1.8
pen **pluma** *f.* 1.2
pencil **lápiz** *m.* 1.1
people **gente** *f.* 1.3
pepper *(black)* **pimienta** *f.* 1.8
perfect **perfecto/a** *adj.* 1.5
perhaps **quizás** *adv.*; **tal vez** *adv.*
permission **permiso** *m.*
person **persona** *f.* 1.3
phenomenal **fenomenal** *adj.* 1.5
photograph **foto(grafía)** *f.* 1.1
physician **doctor(a)** *m., f.*,
  médico/a *m., f.* 1.3
physics **física** *f. sing.* 1.2
pie **pastel** *m.* 1.9
pineapple **piña** *f.* 1.8
pink **rosado/a** *adj.* 1.6
place **lugar** *m.* 1.4; **poner**
  v. 1.4
plaid **de cuadros** 1.6
plans **planes** *m., pl.* 1.4
  have plans **tener planes** 1.4
play **jugar (u:ue)** *v.* 1.4; *(cards)*
  jugar a (las cartas) 1.5
  play sports **practicar**
  deportes 1.4
player **jugador(a)** *m., f.* 1.4
pleasant **agradable** *adj.*
please **por favor** 1.1
  Pleased to meet you. **Mucho**
  gusto. 1.1; **Encantado/a.**
  adj. 1.1
pleasing: be pleasing to **gustar**
  v. 1.7
pleasure **gusto** *m.* 1.1
  The pleasure is mine. **El gusto**
  es mío. 1.1
polka-dotted **de lunares** 1.6
pool **piscina** *f.* 1.4
poor **pobre** *adj.* 1.6
pork **cerdo** *m.* 1.8
  pork chop **chuleta** *f.* **de**
  cerdo 1.8
possessive **posesivo/a** *adj.* 1.3
postcard **postal** *f.* 1.4
potato **papa** *f.* 1.8;
  patata *f.* 1.8
practice **practicar** *v.* 1.2
prefer **preferir (e:ie)** *v.* 1.4
prepare **preparar** *v.* 1.2
preposition **preposición** *f.*
pretty **bonito/a** *adj.* 1.3
price **precio** *m.* 1.6
  (fixed, set) price **precio** *m.*
  fijo 1.6
print **estampado/a** *adj*
private *(room)* **individual** *adj.*
problem **problema** *m.* 1.1

profession **profesión** *f.* 1.3
professor **profesor(a)** *m., f.*
program **programa** *m.* 1.1
programmer **programador(a)**
  m., f. 1.3
pronoun **pronombre** *m.*
psychology **psicología** *f.* 1.2
Puerto Rican **puertorriqueño/a**
  adj. 1.3
Puerto Rico **Puerto Rico** *m.* 1.1
pull a tooth **sacar una muela**
purchases **compras** *f., pl.* 1.5
purple **morado/a** *adj.* 1.6
purse **bolsa** *f.* 1.6
put **poner** *v.* 1.4
  put on *(clothing)* **ponerse** *v.* 1.7
  put on makeup **maquillarse** *v.*
  1.7

Q

quality **calidad** *f.* 1.6
quarter **trimestre** *m.* 1.2
  quarter after *(time)* **y**
  cuarto 1.1; **y quince** 1.1
  quarter to *(time)*
  menos cuarto 1.1;
  menos quince 1.1
question **pregunta** *f.* 1.2
quiz **prueba** *f.* 1.2

R

radio *(medium)* **radio** *f.* 1.2
rain **llover (o:ue)** *v.* 1.5
  It's raining. **Llueve.** 1.5; **Está**
  lloviendo. 1.5
raincoat **impermeable** *m.* 1.6
read **leer** *v.* 1.3.
  read e-mail **leer correo**
  electrónico 1.4
  read a magazine **leer una**
  revista 1.4
  read a newspaper **leer un**
  periódico 1.4
ready **listo/a** *adj.* 1.5
receive **recibir** *v.* 1.3
recommend **recomendar (e:ie)**
  v. 1.8
recreation **diversión** *f.* 1.4
red **rojo/a** *adj.* 1.6
red-haired **pelirrojo/a** *adj.* 1.3
relatives **parientes** *m., pl.* 1.3
relax **relajarse** *v.* 1.9
remain **quedarse** *v.* 1.7
remember **acordarse (o:ue)** *v.*
  (de) 1.7; **recordar (o:ue)**
  v. 1.4
repeat **repetir (e:i)** *v.* 1.4
request **pedir (e:i)** *v.* 1.4
reservation **reservación** *f.* 1.5
rest **descansar** *v.* 1.2
restaurant **restaurante** *m.* 1.4
retire *(from work)* **jubilarse** *v.* 1.9

return **regresar** *v.* 1.2; **volver (o:ue)** *v.* 1.4
  return trip **vuelta** *f.*
rice **arroz** *m.* 1.8
rich **rico/a** *adj.* 1.6
ride: ride a bicycle **pasear** *v.* **en bicicleta** 1.4
  ride a horse **montar** *v.* **a caballo** 1.5
right **derecha** *f.* 1.2
  be right **tener razón** 1.3
  right away **enseguida** *adv.* 1.9
  right now **ahora mismo** 1.5
  to the right of **a la derecha de** 1.2
  right? (*question tag*) **¿no?** 1.1; **¿verdad?** 1.1
road **camino** *m.*
roast **asado/a** *adj.* 1.8
roast chicken **pollo** *m.* **asado** 1.8
rollerblade **patinar en línea** *v.*
room **habitación** *f.* 1.5; **cuarto** *m.* 1.2; 1.7
roommate **compañero/a** *m., f.* **de cuarto** 1.2
roundtrip **de ida y vuelta** 1.5
  roundtrip ticket **pasaje** *m.* **de ida y vuelta** 1.5
routine **rutina** *f.* 1.7
run **correr** *v.* 1.3
Russian **ruso/a** *adj.* 1.3

S

sad **triste** *adj.* 1.5
safe **seguro/a** *adj.* 1.5
salad **ensalada** *f.* 1.8
sale **rebaja** *f.* 1.6
salesperson **vendedor(a)** *m., f.* 1.6
salmon **salmón** *m.* 1.8
salt **sal** *f.* 1.8
same **mismo/a** *adj.* 1.3
sandal **sandalia** *f.* 1.6
sandwich **sándwich** *m.* 1.8
Saturday **sábado** *m.* 1.2
sausage **salchicha** *f.* 1.8
say **decir** *v.* 1.4
  say (that) **decir (que)** *v.* 1.4, 1.9
  say the answer **decir la respuesta** 1.4
scared: be (very) scared (of) **tener (mucho) miedo (de)** 1.3
schedule **horario** *m.* 1.2
school **escuela** *f.* 1.1
science *f.* **ciencia** 1.2
scuba dive **bucear** *v.* 1.4
sea **mar** *m.* 1.5
season **estación** *f.* 1.5
seat **silla** *f.* 1.2
second **segundo/a** *n., adj.* 1.5

see **ver** *v.* 1.4
  see movies **ver películas** 1.4
  See you. **Nos vemos.** 1.1
  See you later. **Hasta la vista.** 1.1; **Hasta luego.** 1.1
  See you soon. **Hasta pronto.** 1.1
  See you tomorrow. **Hasta mañana.** 1.1
seem **parecer** *v.* 1.6
sell **vender** *v.* 1.6
semester **semestre** *m.* 1.2
separate (from) **separarse** *v.* **(de)** 1.9
separated **separado/a** *adj.* 1.9
September **septiembre** *m.* 1.5
sequence **secuencia** *f.*
serve **servir (e:i)** *v.* 1.8
set (*fixed*) **fijo/a** *adj.* 1.6
seven **siete** *n., adj.* 1.1
seven hundred **setecientos/as** *n., adj.* 1.2
seventeen **diecisiete** *n., adj.* 1.1
seventh **séptimo/a** *n., adj.* 1.5
seventy **setenta** *n., adj.* 1.2
several **varios/as** *adj. pl.* 1.8
shampoo **champú** *m.* 1.7
share **compartir** *v.* 1.3
sharp (*time*) **en punto** 1.1
shave **afeitarse** *v.* 1.7
shaving cream **crema** *f.* **de afeitar** 1.7
she **ella** *sub. pron.* 1.1
shellfish **mariscos** *m., pl.* 1.8
ship **barco** *m.*
shirt **camisa** *f.* 1.6
shoe **zapato** *m.* 1.6
  shoe size **número** *m.* 1.6
  tennis shoes **zapatos** *m., pl.* **de tenis** 1.6
shop **tienda** *f.* 1.6
shopping: to go shopping **ir de compras** 1.5
shopping mall **centro comercial** *m.* 1.6
short (*in height*) **bajo/a** *adj.* 1.3; (*in length*) **corto/a** *adj.* 1.6
shorts **pantalones cortos** *m., pl.* 1.6
should (*do something*) **deber** *v.* **(+ *inf.*)** 1.3
show **mostrar (o:ue)** *v.* 1.4
shower **ducha** *f.* 1.7; **ducharse** *v.* 1.7
shrimp **camarón** *m.* 1.8
siblings **hermanos/as** *m., f. pl.* 1.3
silk **seda** *f.* 1.6
  (made of) silk **de seda** 1.6
silly **tonto/a** *adj.* 1.3
since **desde** *prep.*
sing **cantar** *v.* 1.2
single **soltero/a** *adj.* 1.9
  single room **habitación** *f.* **individual** 1.5

sink **lavabo** *m.* 1.7
sir **señor (Sr.)** *m.* 1.1
sister **hermana** *f.* 1.3
sister-in-law **cuñada** *f.* 1.3
sit down **sentarse (e:ie)** *v.* 1.7
six **seis** *n., adj.* 1.1
six hundred **seiscientos/as** *n., adj.* 1.2
sixteen **dieciséis** *n., adj.* 1.1
sixth **sexto/a** *n., adj.* 1.5
sixty **sesenta** *n., adj.* 1.2
size **talla** *f.* 1.6
  shoe size **número** *m.* 1.6
skate (in-line) **patinar** *v.* **(en línea)** 1.4
skateboard **andar en patineta** *v.* 1.4
ski **esquiar** *v.* 1.4
skiing **esquí** *m.* 1.4
  waterskiing **esquí** *m.* **acuático** 1.4
skirt **falda** *f.* 1.6
sleep **dormir (o:ue)** *v.* 1.4; **sueño** *m.* 1.3
  go to sleep **dormirse (o:ue)** *v.* 1.7
sleepy: be (very) sleepy **tener (mucho) sueño** 1.3
slender **delgado/a** *adj.* 1.3
slippers **pantuflas** *f.* 1.7
small **pequeño/a** *adj.* 1.3
smart **listo/a** *adj.* 1.5
smile **sonreír (e:i)** *v.* 1.9
smoggy: It's (very) smoggy. **Hay (mucha) contaminación.** 1.4
smoke **fumar** *v.* 1.8
smoking section **sección** *f.* **de fumar** 1.8
  nonsmoking section *f.* **sección de no fumar** 1.8
snack **merendar** *v.* 1.8
sneakers **los zapatos de tenis** 1.6
snow **nevar (e:ie)** *v.* 1.5; **nieve** *f.*
snowing: It's snowing. **Nieva.** 1.5; **Está nevando.** 1.5
so **tan** *adv.* 1.5
  so much **tanto** *adv.*
  so-so **regular** 1.1
soap **jabón** *m.* 1.7
soccer **fútbol** *m.* 1.4
sociology **sociología** *f.* 1.2
sock(s) **calcetín (calcetines)** *m.* 1.6
soft drink **refresco** *m.* 1.8
some **algún, alguno/a(s)** *adj.* 1.7; **unos/as** *pron. m., f. pl.; indef. art.* 1.1
somebody **alguien** *pron.* 1.7
someone **alguien** *pron.* 1.7
something **algo** *pron.* 1.7
son **hijo** *m.* 1.3
son-in-law **yerno** *m.* 1.3
soon **pronto** *adv.*

See you soon. **Hasta pronto.**
1.1
sorry
I'm sorry. **Lo siento.** 1.4
I'm so sorry. **Mil perdones.**
1.4; **Lo siento
muchísimo.** 1.4
soup **caldo** *m.* 1.8; **sopa** *f.* 1.8
Spain **España** *f.* 1.1
Spanish (*language*) **español** *m.*
1.2; **español(a)** *adj.* 1.3
spare time **ratos libres** 1.4
speak **hablar** *v.* 1.2
spelling **ortografía** *f.*;
ortográfico/a *adj.*
spend (*money*) **gastar** *v.* 1.6
sport **deporte** *m.* 1.4
sports-related **deportivo/a**
adj. 1.4
spouse **esposo/a** *m., f.* 1.3
spring **primavera** *f.* 1.5
square (*city or town*) **plaza** *f.* 1.4
stadium **estadio** *m.* 1.2
stage **etapa** *f.* 1.9
station **estación** *f.* 1.5
status: marital status **estado** *m.*
civil 1.9
stay **quedarse** *v.* 1.7
steak **bistec** *m.* 1.8
step **etapa** *f.*
stepbrother **hermanastro**
m. 1.3
stepdaughter **hijastra** *f.* 1.3
stepfather **padrastro** *m.* 1.3
stepmother **madrastra** *f.* 1.3
stepsister **hermanastra** *f.* 1.3
stepson **hijastro** *m.* 1.3
still **todavía** *adv.* 1.5
stockings **medias** *f., pl.* 1.6
store **tienda** *f.* 1.6
strawberry **frutilla** *f.* 1.8, **fresa**
stripe **raya** *f.* 1.6
striped **de rayas** 1.6
stroll **pasear** *v.* 1.4
student **estudiante** *m., f.*
1.1, 1.2; **estudiantil** *adj.* 1.2
study **estudiar** *v.* 1.2
stupendous **estupendo/a**
adj. 1.5
style **estilo** *m.*
subway **metro** *m.* 1.5
subway station **estación** *f.*
del metro 1.5
such as **tales como**
suddenly **de repente** *adv.* 1.6
sugar **azúcar** *m.* 1.8
suit **traje** *m.* 1.6
suitcase **maleta** *f.* 1.1
summer **verano** *m.* 1.5
sun **sol** *m.* 1.5
sunbathe **tomar** *v.* **el sol** 1.4
Sunday **domingo** *m.* 1.2
sunglasses **gafas** *f., pl.*
oscuras/de sol 1.6; **lentes**
m. pl. **de sol** 1.6

sunny: It's (very) sunny. **Hace
(mucho) sol.** 1.5
suppose **suponer** *v.* 1.4
sure **seguro/a** *adj.* 1.5
be sure **estar seguro/a** 1.5
surprise **sorprender** *v.* 1.9;
sorpresa *f.* 1.9
sweater **suéter** *m.* 1.6
sweets **dulces** *m., pl.* 1.9
swim **nadar** *v.* 1.4
swimming **natación** *f.* 1.4
swimming pool **piscina** *f.* 1.4

T

table **mesa** *f.* 1.2
take **tomar** *v.* 1.2; **llevar** *v.* 1.6
take a bath **bañarse** *v.* 1.7
take (*wear*) a shoe size *v.*
calzar 1.6
take a shower **ducharse** *v.* 1.7
take off **quitarse** *v.* 1.7
take photos **tomar fotos** 1.5;
sacar fotos 1.5
talk *v.* **hablar** 1.2
tall **alto/a** *adj.* 1.3
tape (*audio*) **cinta** *f.*
tape recorder **grabadora** *f.* 1.1
taste **probar (o:ue)** *v.* 1.8;
saber *v.* 1.8
taste like **saber a** 1.8
tasty **rico/a** *adj.* 1.8; **sabroso/a**
adj. 1.8
taxi **taxi** *m.* 1.5
tea **té** *m.* 1.8
teach **enseñar** *v.* 1.2
teacher **profesor(a)** *m., f.*
1.1, 1.2
team **equipo** *m.* 1.4
television **televisión** *f.* 1.2
tell **contar (o:ue)** *v.* 1.4; **decir**
v. 1.4
tell (*that*) **decir** *v.* **(que)** 1.4, 1.9
tell lies **decir mentiras** 1.4
tell the truth **decir la verdad**
1.4
ten **diez** *n., adj.* 1.1
tennis **tenis** *m.* 1.4
tennis shoes **zapatos** *m., pl.* **de
tenis** 1.6
tent **tienda** *f.* **de campaña**
tenth **décimo/a** *n., adj.* 1.5
terrific **chévere** *adj.*
test **prueba** *f.* 1.2; **examen**
m. 1.2
Thank you. **Gracias.** 1.1
Thank you (very much).
(Muchas) gracias. 1.1
Thank you very, very much.
Muchísimas gracias. 1.9
Thanks (a lot). **(Muchas)
gracias.** 1.1
Thanks again. (*lit. Thanks one
more time.*) **Gracias una vez
más.** 1.9

Thanks for everything. **Gracias
por todo.** 1.9
that (one) **ése, ésa, eso** *pron.*
1.6; **ese, esa** *adj.* 1.6
that (*over there*) **aquél,
aquélla, aquello** *pron.* 1.6;
aquel, aquella *adj.* 1.6
that's me **soy yo** 1.1
the **el** *m., sing.* **la** *f. sing.*, **los** *m.,
pl.* **las** *f., pl.*
their **su(s)** *poss. adj.* 1.3
them **los/las** *pl., d.o. pron.* 1.5;
ellos/as *pron., obj. of prep.* 1.9
to/for them **les** *pl., i.o. pron.*
1.6
then **después** (*afterward*)
adv. 1.7; **entonces** (*as a
result*) *adv.* 1.7; **luego** (*next*)
adv. 1.7
there **allí** *adv.* 1.5
There is/are... **Hay...** 1.1
There is/are not... **No hay...**
1.1
these **éstos, éstas** *pron.* 1.6;
estos, estas *adj.* 1.6
they **ellos** *m., pron.* **ellas** *f., pron.*
thin **delgado/a** *adj.* 1.3
thing **cosa** *f.* 1.1
think **pensar (e:ie)** *v.* 1.4;
(*believe*) **creer** *v.*
think about **pensar en** *v.* 1.4
third **tercero/a** *n., adj.* 1.5
thirst **sed** *f.* 1.3
thirsty: be (very) thirsty **tener
(mucha) sed** 1.3
thirteen **trece** *n., adj.* 1.1
thirty **treinta** *n., adj.* 1.1; 1.2
thirty minutes past the hour **y
treinta; y media** 1.1
this **este, esta** *adj.*; **éste, ésta,
esto** *pron.* 1.6
This is... (*introduction*) **Éste/a
es...** 1.1
those **ésos, ésas** *pron.* 1.6;
esos, esas *adj.* 1.6
those (*over there*) **aquéllos,
aquéllas** *pron.* 1.6; **aquellos,
aquellas** *adj.* 1.6
thousand **mil** *n., adj.* 1.6
three **tres** *n., adj.* 1.1
three hundred
trescientos/as *n., adj.* 1.2
Thursday **jueves** *m., sing.* 1.2
thus (*in such a way*) **así** *adj.*
ticket **pasaje** *m.* 1.5
tie **corbata** *f.* 1.6
time **vez** *f.* 1.6; **tiempo** *m.* 1.4
have a good/bad time **pasarlo
bien/mal** 1.9
What time is it? **¿Qué hora
es?** 1.1
(At) What time...? **¿A qué
hora...?** 1.1
times **veces** *f., pl.* 1.6
two times **dos veces** 1.6

tip **propina** *f.* 1.9
tired **cansado/a** *adj.* 1.5
  be tired **estar cansado/a** 1.5
to **a** *prep.* 1.1
toast (*drink*) **brindar** *v.* 1.9
toasted **tostado/a** *adj.* 1.8
  toasted bread **pan tostado** *m.* 1.8
today **hoy** *adv.* 1.2
  Today is... **Hoy es...** 1.2
together **juntos/as** *adj.* 1.9
toilet **inodoro** *m.* 1.7
tomato **tomate** *m.* 1.8
tomorrow **mañana** *f.* 1.1
  See you tomorrow. **Hasta mañana.** 1.1
tonight **esta noche** *adv.* 1.4
too **también** *adv.* 1.2; 1.7
  too much **demasiado** *adv.* 1.6
tooth **diente** *m.* 1.7
toothpaste **pasta** *f.* **de dientes** 1.7
tortilla **tortilla** *f.* 1.8
tour **excursión** *f.* 1.4
  tour an area **recorrer** *v.*
tourism **turismo** *m.* 1.5
tourist **turista** *m., f.* 1.1; **turístico/a** *adj.*
towel **toalla** *f.* 1.7
town **pueblo** *m.* 1.4
train **tren** *m.* 1.5
  train station **estación** *f.* **(de) tren** *m.* 1.5
translate **traducir** *v.* 1.6
travel **viajar** *v.* 1.2
travel agent **agente** *m., f.* **de viajes** 1.5
traveler **viajero/a** *m., f.* 1.5
trillion **billón** *m.*
trimester **trimestre** *m.* 1.2
trip **viaje** *m.* 1.5
  take a trip **hacer un viaje** 1.5
truth **verdad** *f.*
try **intentar** *v.;* **probar (o:ue)** *v.* 1.8
  try on **probarse (o:ue)** *v.* 1.7
t-shirt **camiseta** *f.* 1.6
Tuesday **martes** *m., sing.* 1.2
tuna **atún** *m.* 1.8
turkey **pavo** *m.* 1.8
twelve **doce** *n., adj.* 1.1
twenty **veinte** *n., adj.* 1.1
twenty-eight **veintiocho** *n., adj.* 1.1
twenty-five **veinticinco** *n., adj.* 1.1
twenty-four **veinticuatro** *n., adj.* 1.1
twenty-nine **veintinueve** *n., adj.* 1.1
twenty-one **veintiún, veintiuno/a** *n., adj.* 1.1

twenty-seven **veintisiete** *n., adj.* 1.1
twenty-six **veintiséis** *n., adj.* 1.1
twenty-three **veintitrés** *n., adj.* 1.1
twenty-two **veintidós** *n., adj.* 1.1
twice **dos veces** *adv.* 1.6
twin **gemelo/a** *m., f.* 1.3
two **dos** *n., adj.* 1.1
  two hundred **doscientos/as** *n., adj.* 1.2
  two times **dos veces** *adv.* 1.6

U

ugly **feo/a** *adj.* 1.3
uncle **tío** *m.* 1.3
under **bajo** *adv.* 1.7; **debajo de** *prep.* 1.2
understand **comprender** *v.* 1.3; **entender (e:ie)** *v.* 1.4
underwear **ropa interior** *f.* 1.6
United States **Estados Unidos (EE.UU.)** *m. pl.* 1.1
university **universidad** *f.* 1.2
unmarried **soltero/a** *adj.*
unpleasant **antipático/a** *adj.* 1.3
until **hasta** *prep.* 1.6
us **nos** *pl., d.o. pron.* 1.5
  to/for us **nos** *pl., i.o. pron.* 1.6
use **usar** *v.* 1.6
useful **útil** *adj.*

V

vacation **vacaciones** *f. pl.* 1.5
  be on vacation **estar de vacaciones** 1.5
  go on vacation **ir de vacaciones** 1.5
various **varios/as** *adj., pl.* 1.8
vegetables **verduras** *pl., f.* 1.8
verb **verbo** *m.*
very **muy** *adv.* 1.1
  very much **muchísimo** *adv.* 1.2
  (Very) well, thank you. **(Muy) bien gracias.** 1.1
video **video** *m.* 1.1
video game **videojuego** *m.* 1.4
vinegar **vinagre** *m.* 1.8
visit **visitar** *v.* 1.4
  visit monuments **visitar monumentos** 1.4
volleyball **vóleibol** *m.* 1.4

W

wait (for) **esperar** *v.* (+ *inf.*) 1.2
waiter/waitress **camarero/a** *m., f.* 1.8

wake up **despertarse (e:ie)** *v.* 1.7
walk **caminar** *v.* 1.2
  take a walk **pasear** *v.* 1.4
  walk around **pasear por** 1.4
walkman **walkman** *m.*
wallet **cartera** *f.* 1.6
want **querer (e:ie)** *v.* 1.4
wash **lavar** *v.*
  wash one's face/hands **lavarse la cara/las manos** 1.7
  wash oneself **lavarse** *v.* 1.7
wastebasket **papelera** *f.* 1.2
watch **mirar** *v.* 1.2; **reloj** *m.* 1.2
  watch television **mirar (la) televisión** 1.2
water **agua** *f.* 1.8
waterskiing *m.* **esquí acuático** 1.4
we **nosotros(as)** *m., f. sub. pron.* 1.1
wear **llevar** *v.* 1.6; **usar** *v.* 1.6
weather **tiempo** *m.*
  The weather is bad. **Hace mal tiempo.** 1.5
  The weather is good. **Hace buen tiempo.** 1.5
wedding **boda** *f.* 1.9
Wednesday **miércoles** *m., sing.* 1.2
week **semana** *f.* 1.2
weekend **fin** *m.* **de semana** 1.4
well **pues** *adv.* 1.2; **bueno** *adv.* 1.2
  (Very) well, thanks. **(Muy) bien, gracias.** 1.1
  well organized **ordenado/a** *adj.*
what? **¿qué?** *pron.* 1.1
  At what time...? **¿A qué hora...?** 1.1
  What day is it? **¿Qué día es hoy?** 1.2
  What do you guys think? **¿Qué les parece?** 1.9
  What is today's date? **¿Cuál es la fecha de hoy?** 1.5
  What nice clothes! **¡Qué ropa más bonita!** 1.6
  What size do you take? **¿Qué talla lleva (usa)?** 1.6
  What time is it? **¿Qué hora es?** 1.1
  What's going on? **¿Qué pasa?** 1.1
  What's happening? **¿Qué pasa?** 1.1
  What's... like? **¿Cómo es...?** 1.3
  What's new? **¿Qué hay de nuevo?** 1.1
  What's the weather like? **¿Qué tiempo hace?** 1.5
  What's your name? **¿Cómo se llama usted?** *form.* 1.1

What's your name? **¿Cómo te llamas (tú)?** *fam.* 1.1
when **cuando** *conj.* 1.7
   When? **¿Cuándo?** *adv.* 1.2
where **donde** *prep.*
   where (to)? (*destination*) **¿adónde?** *adv.* 1.2; (*location*) **¿dónde?** *adv.* 1.1
   Where are you from? **¿De dónde eres (tú)?** *fam.* 1.1; **¿De dónde es (usted)?** *form.* 1.1
   Where is...? **¿Dónde está...?** 1.2
which? **¿cuál?** *pron.* 1.2; **¿qué?** *adj.* 1.2
   In which...? **¿En qué...?** 1.2
   which one(s)? **¿cuál(es)?** *pron.* 1.2
white **blanco/a** *adj.* 1.6
   white wine **vino blanco** 1.8
who? **¿quién(es)?** *pron.* 1.1
   Who is...? **¿Quién es...?** 1.1
whole **todo/a** *adj.*
whose **¿de quién(es)?** *pron., adj.* 1.1
why? **¿por qué?** *adv.* 1.2
widower/widow **viudo/a** *adj.* 1.9
wife **esposa** *f.* 1.3
win **ganar** *v.* 1.4
wind **viento** *m.* 1.5
window **ventana** *f.* 1.2
windy: It's (very) windy. **Hace (mucho) viento.** 1.5
wine **vino** *m.* 1.8
   red wine **vino tinto** 1.8
   white wine **vino blanco** 1.8
winter **invierno** *m.* 1.5
wish **desear** *v.* 1.2

with **con** *prep.* 1.2
   with me **conmigo** 1.4; 1.9
   with you **contigo** *fam.* 1.9
without **sin** *prep.* 1.2
woman **mujer** *f.* 1.1
wool **lana** *f.* 1.6
   (made of) wool **de lana** 1.6
word **palabra** *f.* 1.1
work **trabajar** *v.* 1.2
worldwide **mundial** *adj.*
worried (about) **preocupado/a (por)** *adj.* 1.5
worry (about) **preocuparse** *v.* **(por)** 1.7
   Don't worry. **No se preocupe.** *form.* 1.7; **No te preocupes.** *fam.* 1.7; **Tranquilo.** *adj.*
worse **peor** *adj.* 1.8
worst **el/la peor** *adj.* **lo peor** *n.* 1.8
Would you like to...? **¿Te gustaría...?** *fam.* 1.4
write **escribir** *v.* 1.3
   write a letter/postcard/e-mail message **escribir una carta/una postal/un mensaje electrónico** 1.4
wrong **equivocado/a** *adj.* 1.5
   be wrong **no tener razón** 1.3

X

X-ray **radiografía** *f.*

Y

year **año** *m.* 1.5
   be... years old **tener... años** 1.3

yellow **amarillo/a** *adj.* 1.6
yes **sí** *interj.* 1.1
yesterday **ayer** *adv.* 1.6
yet **todavía** *adv.* 1.5
yogurt **yogur** *m.* 1.8
you *sub pron.* **tú** *fam. sing.*, **usted (Ud.)** *form. sing.*, **vosotros/as** *fam. pl.*, **ustedes (Uds.)** *form. pl.* 1.1; *d. o. pron.* **te** *fam. sing.*, **lo/la** *form. sing.*, **os** *fam. pl.*, **los/las** *form. pl.* 1.5; *obj. of prep.* **ti** *fam. sing.*, **usted (Ud.)** *form. sing.*, **vosotros/as** *fam. pl.*, **ustedes (Uds.)** *form. pl.* 1.9
   (to, for) you *i.o. pron.* **te** *fam. sing.*, **le** *form. sing.*, **os** *fam. pl.*, **les** *form. pl.* 1.6
   You are... **Tú eres...** 1.1
   You're welcome. **De nada.** 1.1; **No hay de qué.** 1.1
young **joven** *adj.* 1.3
   young person **joven** *m., f.* 1.1
   young woman **señorita (Srta.)** *f.*
younger **menor** *adj.* 1.3
   younger brother/sister *m., f.* **hermano/a menor** 1.3
youngest **el/la menor** *m., f.* 1.8
your **su(s)** *poss. adj. form.* 1.3; **tu(s)** *poss. adj. fam. sing.* 1.3; **vuestro/a(s)** *poss. adj. form. pl.* 1.3
youth *f.* **juventud** 1.9

Z

zero **cero** *m.* 1.1

MATERIAS / ACADEMIC SUBJECTS

MATERIAS	ACADEMIC SUBJECTS
la administración de empresas	business administration
la agronomía	agriculture
el alemán	German
el álgebra	algebra
la antropología	anthropology
la arqueología	archaeology
la arquitectura	architecture
el arte	art
la astronomía	astronomy
la biología	biology
la bioquímica	biochemistry
la botánica	botany
el cálculo	calculus
el chino	Chinese
las ciencias políticas	political science
la computación	computer science
las comunicaciones	communications
la contabilidad	accounting
la danza	dance
el derecho	law
la economía	economics
la educación	education
la educación física	physical education
la enfermería	nursing
el español	Spanish
la filosofía	philosophy
la física	physics
el francés	French
la geografía	geography
la geología	geology
el griego	Greek
el hebreo	Hebrew
la historia	history
la informática	computer science
la ingeniería	engineering
el inglés	English
el italiano	Italian
el japonés	Japanese
el latín	Latin
las lenguas clásicas	classical languages
las lenguas romances	Romance languages
la lingüística	linguistics
la literatura	literature
las matemáticas	mathematics
la medicina	medicine
el mercadeo/ la mercadotecnia	marketing
la música	music
los negocios	business
el periodismo	journalism
el portugués	Portuguese
la psicología	psychology
la química	chemistry
el ruso	Russian
los servicios sociales	social services
la sociología	sociology
el teatro	theater
la trigonometría	trigonometry

LOS ANIMALES / ANIMALS

LOS ANIMALES	ANIMALS
la abeja	bee
la araña	spider
la ardilla	squirrel
el ave (f.), el pájaro	bird
la ballena	whale
el burro	donkey
la cabra	goat
el caimán	alligator
el camello	camel
la cebra	zebra
el ciervo, el venado	deer
el cochino, el cerdo, el puerco	pig
el cocodrilo	crocodile
el conejo	rabbit
el coyote	coyote
la culebra, la serpiente, la víbora	snake
el elefante	elephant
la foca	seal
la gallina	hen
el gallo	rooster
el gato	cat
el gorila	gorilla
el hipopótamo	hippopotamus
la hormiga	ant
el insecto	insect
la jirafa	giraffe
el lagarto	lizard
el león	lion
el lobo	wolf
el loro, la cotorra, el papagayo, el perico	parrot
la mariposa	butterfly
el mono	monkey
la mosca	fly
el mosquito	mosquito
el oso	bear
la oveja	sheep
el pato	duck
el perro	dog
el pez	fish
la rana	frog
el ratón	mouse
el rinoceronte	rhinoceros
el saltamontes, el chapulín	grasshopper
el tiburón	shark
el tigre	tiger
el toro	bull
la tortuga	turtle
la vaca	cow
el zorro	fox

EL CUERPO EL CUERPO HUMANO Y LA SALUD

THE HUMAN BODY AND HEALTH

El cuerpo humano

The human body

la barba	beard
el bigote	mustache
la boca	mouth
el brazo	arm
la cabeza	head
la cadera	hip
la ceja	eyebrow
el cerebro	brain
la cintura	waist
el codo	elbow
el corazón	heart
la costilla	rib
el cráneo	skull
el cuello	neck
el dedo	finger
el dedo del pie	toe
la espalda	back
el estómago	stomach
la frente	forehead
la garganta	throat
el hombro	shoulder
el hueso	bone
el labio	lip
la lengua	tongue
la mandíbula	jaw
la mejilla	cheek
el mentón, la barba, la barbilla	chin
la muñeca	wrist
el músculo	muscle
el muslo	thigh
las nalgas, el trasero, las asentaderas	buttocks
la nariz	nose
el nervio	nerve
el oído	(inner) ear
el ojo	eye
el ombligo	navel, belly button
la oreja	(outer) ear
la pantorrilla	calf
el párpado	eyelid
el pecho	chest
la pestaña	eyelash
el pie	foot
la piel	skin
la pierna	leg
el pulgar	thumb
el pulmón	lung
la rodilla	knee
la sangre	blood
el talón	heel
el tobillo	ankle
el tronco	torso, trunk
la uña	fingernail
la uña del dedo del pie	toenail
la vena	vein

Los cinco sentidos

The five senses

el gusto	taste
el oído	hearing
el olfato	smell
el tacto	touch
la vista	sight

La salud

Health

el accidente	accident
alérgico/a	allergic
el antibiótico	antibiotic
la aspirina	aspirin
el ataque cardiaco, el ataque al corazón	heart attack
el cáncer	cancer
la cápsula	capsule
la clínica	clinic
congestionado/a	congested
el consultorio	doctor's office
la curita	adhesive bandage
el/la dentista	dentist
el/la doctor(a), el/la médico/a	doctor
el dolor (de cabeza)	(head)ache, pain
embarazada	pregnant
la enfermedad	illness, disease
el/la enfermero/a	nurse
enfermo/a	ill, sick
la erupción	rash
el examen médico	physical exam
la farmacia	pharmacy
la fiebre	fever
la fractura	fracture
la gripe	flu
la herida	wound
el hospital	hospital
la infección	infection
la inyección	injection
el insomnio	insomnia
el jarabe	(cough) syrup
mareado/a	dizzy, nauseated
el medicamento	medication
la medicina	medicine
las muletas	crutches
la operación	operation
el/la paciente	patient
el/la paramédico/a	paramedic
la pastilla, la píldora	pill, tablet
los primeros auxilios	first aid
la pulmonía	pneumonia
los puntos	stitches
la quemadura	burn
el quirófano	operating room
la radiografía	X-ray
la receta	prescription
el resfriado	cold (illness)
la sala de emergencia(s)	emergency room
saludable	healthy, healthful
sano/a	healthy
el seguro médico	medical insurance
la silla de ruedas	wheelchair
el síntoma	symptom
el termómetro	thermometer
la tos	cough
la transfusión	transfusion

la vacuna	vaccination
la venda	bandage
el virus	virus
cortar(se)	to cut (oneself)
curar	to cure, to treat
desmayar(se)	to faint
enfermarse	to get sick
enyesar	to put in a cast
estornudar	to sneeze
guardar cama	to stay in bed
hinchar(se)	to swell
internar(se) en el hospital	to check into the hospital
lastimarse (el pie)	to hurt (one's foot)
mejorar(se)	to get better; to improve
operar	to operate
quemar(se)	to burn
respirar (hondo)	to breathe (deeply)
romperse (la pierna)	to break (one's leg)
sangrar	to bleed
sufrir	to suffer
tomarle la presión a alguien	to take someone's blood pressure
tomarle el pulso a alguien	to take someone's pulse
torcerse (el tobillo)	to sprain (one's ankle)
vendar	to bandage

EXPRESIONES ÚTILES PARA LA CLASE

USEFUL CLASSROOM EXPRESSIONS

Palabras útiles

Useful words

ausente	absent
el departamento	department
el dictado	dictation
la conversación, las conversaciones	conversation(s)
la expresión, las expresiones	expression(s)
el examen, los exámenes	test(s), exam(s)
la frase	sentence
la hoja de actividades	activity sheet

el horario de clases	class schedule
la oración, las oraciones	sentence(s)
el párrafo	paragraph
la persona	person
presente	present
la prueba	test, quiz
siguiente	following
la tarea	homework

Expresiones útiles

Useful expressions

Abra(n) su(s) libro(s).	Open your book(s).
Cambien de papel.	Change roles.
Cierre(n) su(s) libro(s).	Close your book(s).
¿Cómo se dice ___ en español?	How do you say ___ in Spanish?
¿Cómo se escribe ___ en español?	How do you write ___ in Spanish?
¿Comprende(n)?	Do you understand?
(No) comprendo.	I (don't) understand.
Conteste(n) las preguntas.	Answer the questions.
Continúe(n), por favor.	Continue, please.
Escriba(n) su nombre.	Write your name.
Escuche(n) la cinta (el disco compacto).	Listen to the tape (compact disc).
Estudie(n) la Lección tres.	Study Lesson three.
Haga(n) la actividad (el ejercicio) número cuatro.	Do activity (exercise) number four.
Lea(n) la oración en voz alta.	Read the sentence aloud.
Levante(n) la mano.	Raise your hand(s).
Más despacio, por favor.	Slower, please.
No sé.	I don't know.
Páse(n)me los exámenes.	Pass me the tests.
¿Qué significa ___?	What does ___ mean?
Repita(n), por favor.	Repeat, please.
Siénte(n)se, por favor.	Sit down, please.
Siga(n) las instrucciones.	Follow the instructions.
¿Tiene(n) alguna pregunta?	Do you have any questions?
Vaya(n) a la página dos.	Go to page two.

COUNTRIES & NATIONALITIES

PAÍSES Y NACIONALIDADES

North America

Norteamérica

Canada	Canadá	canadiense
Mexico	México	mexicano/a
United States	Estados Unidos	estadounidense

Central America

Centroamérica

Belize	Belice	beliceño/a
Costa Rica	Costa Rica	costarricense
El Salvador	El Salvador	salvadoreño/a
Guatemala	Guatemala	guatemalteco/a
Honduras	Honduras	hondureño/a
Nicaragua	Nicaragua	nicaragüense
Panama	Panamá	panameño/a

The Caribbean	El Caribe	
Cuba	**Cuba**	*cubano/a*
Dominican Republic	**República Dominicana**	*dominicano/a*
Haiti	**Haití**	*haitiano/a*
Puerto Rico	**Puerto Rico**	*puertorriqueño/a*

South America	Suramérica	
Argentina	**Argentina**	*argentino/a*
Bolivia	**Bolivia**	*boliviano/a*
Brazil	**Brasil**	*brasileño/a*
Chile	**Chile**	*chileno/a*
Colombia	**Colombia**	*colombiano/a*
Ecuador	**Ecuador**	*ecuatoriano/a*
Paraguay	**Paraguay**	*paraguayo/a*
Peru	**Perú**	*peruano/a*
Uruguay	**Uruguay**	*uruguayo/a*
Venezuela	**Venezuela**	*venezolano/a*

Europe	Europa	
Armenia	**Armenia**	*armenio/a*
Austria	**Austria**	*austríaco/a*
Belgium	**Bélgica**	*belga*
Bosnia	**Bosnia**	*bosnio/a*
Bulgaria	**Bulgaria**	*búlgaro/a*
Croatia	**Croacia**	*croata*
Czech Republic	**República Checa**	*checo/a*
Denmark	**Dinamarca**	*danés, danesa*
England	**Inglaterra**	*inglés, inglesa*
Estonia	**Estonia**	*estonio/a*
Finland	**Finlandia**	*finlandés, finlandesa*
France	**Francia**	*francés, francesa*
Germany	**Alemania**	*alemán, alemana*
Great Britain (United Kingdom)	**Gran Bretaña (Reino Unido)**	*británico/a*
Greece	**Grecia**	*griego/a*
Hungary	**Hungría**	*húngaro/a*
Iceland	**Islandia**	*islandés, islandesa*
Ireland	**Irlanda**	*irlandés, irlandesa*
Italy	**Italia**	*italiano/a*
Latvia	**Letonia**	*letón, letona*
Lithuania	**Lituania**	*lituano/a*
Netherlands (Holland)	**Países Bajos (Holanda)**	*holandés, holandesa*
Norway	**Noruega**	*noruego/a*
Poland	**Polonia**	*polaco/a*
Portugal	**Portugal**	*portugués, portuguesa*
Romania	**Rumania**	*rumano/a*
Russia	**Rusia**	*ruso/a*
Scotland	**Escocia**	*escocés, escocesa*
Serbia	**Serbia**	*serbio/a*
Slovakia	**Eslovaquia**	*eslovaco/a*
Slovenia	**Eslovenia**	*esloveno/a*
Spain	**España**	*español(a)*
Sweden	**Suecia**	*sueco/a*
Switzerland	**Suiza**	*suizo/a*
Ukraine	**Ucrania**	*ucraniano/a*
Wales	**Gales**	*galés, galesa*
Yugoslavia	**Yugoslavia**	*yugoslavo/a*

Asia	Asia	
Bangladesh	**Bangladés**	*bangladesí*
Cambodia	**Camboya**	*camboyano/a*
China	**China**	*chino/a*
India	**India**	*indio/a*
Indonesia	**Indonesia**	*indonesio/a*
Iran	**Irán**	*iraní*
Iraq	**Iraq, Irak**	*iraquí*

Israel	**Israel**	*israelí*
Japan	**Japón**	*japonés, japonesa*
Jordan	**Jordania**	*jordano/a*
Korea	**Corea**	*coreano/a*
Kuwait	**Kuwait**	*kuwaití*
Lebanon	**Líbano**	*libanés, libanesa*
Malaysia	**Malasia**	*malasio/a*
Pakistan	**Pakistán**	*pakistaní*
Russia	**Rusia**	*ruso/a*
Saudi Arabia	**Arabia Saudí**	*saudí*
Singapore	**Singapur**	*singapurés, singapuresa*
Syria	**Siria**	*sirio/a*
Taiwan	**Taiwán**	*taiwanés, taiwanesa*
Thailand	**Tailandia**	*tailandés, tailandesa*
Turkey	**Turquía**	*turco/a*
Vietnam	**Vietnam**	*vietnamita*

Africa	**África**	
Algeria	**Argelia**	*argelino/a*
Angola	**Angola**	*angoleño/a*
Cameroon	**Camerún**	*camerunés, camerunesa*
Congo	**Congo**	*congolés, congolesa*
Egypt	**Egipto**	*egipcio/a*
Equatorial Guinea	**Guinea Ecuatorial**	*ecuatoguineano/a*
Ethiopia	**Etiopía**	*etíope*
Ivory Coast	**Costa de Marfil**	*marfileño/a*
Kenya	**Kenia, Kenya**	*keniano/a*
Libya	**Libia**	*libio/a*
Mali	**Malí**	*maliense*
Morocco	**Marruecos**	*marroquí*
Mozambique	**Mozambique**	*mozambiqueño/a*
Nigeria	**Nigeria**	*nigeriano/a*
Rwanda	**Ruanda**	*ruandés, ruandesa*
Somalia	**Somalia**	*somalí*
South Africa	**Sudáfrica**	*sudafricano/a*
Sudan	**Sudán**	*sudanés, sudanesa*
Tunisia	**Tunicia, Túnez**	*tunecino/a*
Uganda	**Uganda**	*ugandés, ugandesa*
Zambia	**Zambia**	*zambiano/a*
Zimbabwe	**Zimbabue**	*zimbabuense*

Australia and the Pacific	**Australia y el Pacífico**	
Australia	**Australia**	*australiano/a*
New Zealand	**Nueva Zelanda**	*neozelandés, neozelandesa*
Philippines	**Filipinas**	*filipino/a*

MONEDAS DE LOS PAÍSES HISPANOS
CURRENCIES OF HISPANIC COUNTRIES

País / COUNTRY	Moneda / CURRENCY
Argentina	el peso
Bolivia	el boliviano
Chile	el peso
Colombia	el peso
Costa Rica	el colón
Cuba	el peso
Ecuador	el sucre, el dólar estadounidense
El Salvador	el colón, el dólar estadounidense
España	el euro
Guatemala	el quetzal, el dólar estadounidense
Guinea Ecuatorial	el franco
Honduras	el lempira
México	el peso
Nicaragua	el córdoba
Panamá	el balboa, el dólar estadounidense
Paraguay	el guaraní
Perú	el sol
Puerto Rico	el dólar estadounidense
República Dominicana	el peso
Uruguay	el peso
Venezuela	el bolívar

EXPRESIONES Y REFRANES

EXPRESSIONS AND SAYINGS

Expresiones y refranes con partes del cuerpo

Expressions and sayings with parts of the body

A cara o cruz	Heads or tails
A corazón abierto	Open heart
A ojos vistas	Clearly, visibly
Al dedillo	Like the back of one's hand
¡Choca/Vengan esos cinco!	Put it there!/Give me five!
Codo con codo	Side by side
Con las manos en la masa	Red-handed
Costar un ojo de la cara	To cost an arm and a leg
Darle a la lengua	To chatter/To gab
De rodillas	On one's knees
Duro de oído	Hard of hearing
En cuerpo y alma	In body and soul
En la punta de la lengua	On the tip of one's tongue
En un abrir y cerrar de ojos	In a blink of the eye
Entrar por un oído y salir por otro	In one ear and out the other
Estar con el agua al cuello	To be up to one's neck with/in
Estar para chuparse los dedos	To be delicious/To be finger-licking good
Hablar entre dientes	To mutter/To speak under one's breath
Hablar por los codos	To talk a lot/To be a chatterbox
Hacer la vista gorda	To turn a blind eye on something
Hombro con hombro	Shoulder to shoulder
Llorar a lágrima viva	To sob/To cry one's eyes out
Metérsele (a alguien) algo entre ceja y ceja	To get an idea in your head
No pegar ojo	Not to sleep a wink
No tener corazón	Not to have a heart
No tener dos dedos de frente	Not to have an ounce of common sense
Ojos que no ven, corazón que no siente	Out of sight, out of mind
Perder la cabeza	To lose one's head
Quedarse con la boca abierta	To be thunderstruck
Romper el corazón	To break someone's heart
Tener buen/mal corazón	Have a good/bad heart
Tener un nudo en la garganta	Have a knot in your throat
Tomarse algo a pecho	To take something too seriously
Venir como anillo al dedo	To fit like a charm/To suit perfectly

Expresiones y refranes con animales

Expressions and sayings with animals

A caballo regalado no le mires el diente.	Don't look a gift horse in the mouth.
Comer como un cerdo	To eat like a pig
Cuando menos se piensa, salta la liebre.	Things happen when you least expect it.
Llevarse como el perro y el gato	To fight like cats and dogs
Perro ladrador, poco mordedor./Perro que ladra no muerde.	His/her bark is worse than his/her bite.
Por la boca muere el pez.	Talking too much can be dangerous.
Poner el cascabel al gato	To stick one's neck out
Ser una tortuga	To be a slowpoke

Expresiones y refranes con alimentos

Expressions and sayings with food

Agua que no has de beber, déjala correr.	If you're not interested, don't ruin it for everybody else.
Con pan y vino se anda el camino.	Things never seem as bad after a good meal.
Contigo pan y cebolla.	You are all I need.
Dame pan y dime tonto.	I don't care what you say, as long as I get what I want.
Descubrir el pastel	To let the cat out of the bag
Dulce como la miel	Sweet as honey
Estar como agua para chocolate	To furious/To be at the boiling point
Estar en el ajo	To be in the know
Estar en la higuera	To have one's head in the clouds
Estar más claro que el agua	To be clear as a bell
Ganarse el pan	To earn a living/To earn one's daily bread
Llamar al pan, pan y al vino, vino.	Not to mince words.
No hay miel sin hiel.	Every rose has its thorn./There's always a catch.
No sólo de pan vive el hombre.	Man doesn't live by bread alone.
Pan con pan, comida de tontos.	Variety is the spice of life.
Ser agua pasada	To be water under the bridge
Ser más bueno que el pan	To be kindness itself
Temblar como un flan	To shake/tremble like a leaf

Expresiones y refranes con colores

Expressions and sayings with colors

Estar verde	To be inexperienced/wet behind the ears
Poner los ojos en blanco	To roll one's eyes
Ponerle a alguien un ojo morado	To give someone a black eye
Ponerse rojo	To turn red/To blush
Ponerse rojo de ira	To turn red with anger
Ponerse verde de envidia	To be green with envy
Quedarse en blanco	To go blank
Verlo todo de color de rosa	To see the world through rose-colored glasses

Refranes	Sayings		
A buen entendedor, pocas palabras bastan.	A word to the wise is enough.	Lo que es moda no incomoda.	You have to suffer in the name of fashion.
Ande o no ande, caballo grande.	Bigger is always better.	Más vale maña que fuerza.	Brains are better than brawn.
A quien madruga, Dios le ayuda.	The early bird catches the worm.	Más vale prevenir que curar.	Prevention is better than cure.
Cuídate, que te cuidaré.	Take care of yourself, and then I'll take care of you.	Más vale solo que mal acompañado.	Better alone than with people you don't like.
De tal palo tal astilla.	A chip off the old block.	Más vale tarde que nunca.	Better late than never.
Del dicho al hecho hay mucho trecho.	Easier said than done.	No es oro todo lo que reluce.	All that glitters is not gold.
Dime con quién andas y te diré quién eres.	A man is known by the company he keeps.	Poderoso caballero es don Dinero.	Money talks.
El saber no ocupa lugar.	One never knows too much.		

COMMON FALSE FRIENDS

False friends are Spanish words that look similar to English words but have very different meanings. While recognizing the English relatives of unfamiliar Spanish words you encounter is an important way of constructing meaning, there are some Spanish words whose similarity to English words is deceptive. Here is a list of some of the most common Spanish false friends.

actualmente ≠ actually
actualmente = nowadays, currently
actually = **de hecho, en realidad, en efecto**

argumento ≠ argument
argumento = plot
argument = **discusión, pelea**

armada ≠ army
armada = navy
army = **ejército**

balde ≠ bald
balde = pail, bucket
bald = **calvo/a**

batería ≠ battery
batería = drum set
battery = **pila**

bravo ≠ brave
bravo = wild; fierce
brave = **valiente**

cándido/a ≠ candid
cándido/a = innocent
candid = **sincero/a**

carbón ≠ carbon
carbón = coal
carbon = **carbono**

casual ≠ casual
casual = accidental, chance
casual = **informal, despreocupado/a**

casualidad ≠ casualty
casualidad = chance, coincidence
casualty = **víctima**

colegio ≠ college
colegio = school
college = **universidad**

collar ≠ collar (of a shirt)
collar = necklace
collar = **cuello (de camisa)**

comprensivo/a ≠ comprehensive
comprensivo/a = understanding
comprehensive = **completo, extensivo**

constipado ≠ constipated
estar constipado/a = to have a cold
to be constipated = **estar estreñido/a**

crudo/a ≠ crude
crudo/a = raw, undercooked
crude = **burdo/a, grosero/a**

divertir ≠ to divert
divertirse = to enjoy oneself
to divert = **desviar**

educado/a ≠ educated
educado/a = well-mannered
educated = **culto/a, instruido/a**

embarazada ≠ embarrassed
estar embarazada = to be pregnant
to be embarrassed = **estar avergonzado/a; dar/tener vergüenza**

eventualmente ≠ eventually
eventualmente = possibly
eventually = **finalmente, al final**

éxito ≠ exit
éxito = success
exit = **salida**

físico/a ≠ physician
físico/a = physicist
physician = **médico/a**

fútbol ≠ football
fútbol = soccer
football = **fútbol americano**

lectura ≠ lecture
lectura = reading
lecture = **conferencia**

librería ≠ library
librería = bookstore
library = **biblioteca**

máscara ≠ mascara
máscara = mask
mascara = **rímel**

molestar ≠ to molest
molestar = to bother, to annoy
to molest = **abusar**

oficio ≠ office
oficio = trade, occupation
office = **oficina**

rato ≠ rat
rato = while, time
rat = **rata**

realizar ≠ to realize
realizar = to carry out; to fulfill
to realize = **darse cuenta de**

red ≠ red
red = net
red = **rojo/a**

revolver ≠ revolver
revolver = to stir, to rummage through
revolver = **revólver**

sensible ≠ sensible
sensible = sensitive
sensible = **sensato/a, razonable**

suceso ≠ success
suceso = event
success = **éxito**

sujeto ≠ subject (topic)
sujeto = fellow; individual
subject = **tema, asunto**

LOS ALIMENTOS / FOODS

Frutas / Fruits

la aceituna	olive
el aguacate	avocado
el albaricoque, el damasco	apricot
la banana, el plátano	banana
la cereza	cherry
la ciruela	plum
el dátil	date
la frambuesa	raspberry
la fresa, la frutilla	strawberry
el higo	fig
el limón	lemon; lime
el melocotón, el durazno	peach
la mandarina	tangerine
el mango	mango
la manzana	apple
la naranja	orange
la papaya	papaya
la pera	pear
la piña	pineapple
el pomelo, la toronja	grapefruit
la sandía	watermelon
las uvas	grapes

Vegetales / Vegetables

la alcachofa	artichoke
el apio	celery
la arveja, el guisante	pea
la berenjena	eggplant
el brócoli	broccoli
la calabaza	squash; pumpkin
la cebolla	onion
el champiñón, la seta	mushroom
la col, el repollo	cabbage
la coliflor	cauliflower
los espárragos	asparagus
las espinacas	spinach
los frijoles, las habichuelas	beans
las habas	fava beans
las judías verdes, los ejotes	string beans, green beans
la lechuga	lettuce
el maíz, el choclo, el elote	corn
la papa, la patata	potato
el pepino	cucumber
el pimentón	bell pepper
el rábano	radish
la remolacha	beet
el tomate, el jitomate	tomato
la zanahoria	carrot

El pescado y los mariscos / Fish and shellfish

la almeja	clam
el atún	tuna
el bacalao	cod
el calamar	squid
el cangrejo	crab
el camarón, la gamba	shrimp
la langosta	lobster
el langostino	prawn
el lenguado	sole; flounder
el mejillón	mussel
la ostra	oyster
el pulpo	octopus
el salmón	salmon
la sardina	sardine
la vieira	scallop

La carne / Meat

la albóndiga	meatball
el bistec	steak
la carne de res	beef
el chorizo	hard pork sausage
la chuleta de cerdo	pork chop
el cordero	lamb
los fiambres	cold cuts, food served cold
el filete	fillet
la hamburguesa	hamburger
el hígado	liver
el jamón	ham
el lechón	suckling pig, roasted pig
el pavo	turkey
el pollo	chicken
el cerdo	pork
la salchicha	sausage
la ternera	veal
el tocino	bacon

Otras comidas / Other foods

el ajo	garlic
el arroz	rice
el azúcar	sugar
el batido	milkshake
el budín	pudding
el cacahuete, el maní	peanut
el café	coffee
los fideos	noodles, pasta
la harina	flour
el huevo	egg
el jugo, el zumo	juice
la leche	milk
la mermelada	marmalade, jam
la miel	honey
el pan	bread
el queso	cheese
la sal	salt
la sopa	soup
el té	tea
la tortilla	omelet (Spain), tortilla (Mexico)
el yogur	yogurt

Cómo describir la comida / Ways to describe food

a la plancha, a la parrilla	grilled
ácido/a	sour
al horno	baked
amargo/a	bitter
caliente	hot
dulce	sweet
duro/a	tough
frío/a	cold
frito/a	fried
fuerte	strong, heavy
ligero/a	light
picante	spicy
sabroso/a	tasty
salado/a	salty

DÍAS FESTIVOS / HOLIDAYS

enero / January

Año Nuevo (1) — New Year's Day
Día de los Reyes Magos (6) — Three Kings Day (Epiphany)
Día de Martin Luther King, Jr. — Martin Luther King, Jr. Day

febrero / February

Día de San Blas (Paraguay) (3) — St. Blas Day (Paraguay)
Día de San Valentín, Día de los Enamorados (14) — Valentine's Day
Día de los Presidentes — Presidents' Day
Carnaval — Carnival (Mardi Gras)

marzo / March

Día de San Patricio (17) — St. Patrick's Day
Nacimiento de Benito Juárez (México) (21) — Benito Juárez's Birthday (Mexico)

abril / April

Semana Santa — Holy Week
Pésaj — Passover
Pascua — Easter
Declaración de la Independencia de Venezuela (19) — Declaration of Independence of Venezuela
Día de la Tierra (22) — Earth Day

mayo / May

Día del Trabajo (1) — Labor Day
Cinco de Mayo (5) (México) — Cinco de Mayo (May 5th) (Mexico)
Día de las Madres — Mother's Day
Independencia Patria (Paraguay) (15) — Independence Day (Paraguay)
Día Conmemorativo — Memorial Day

junio / June

Día de los Padres — Father's Day
Día de la Bandera (14) — Flag Day
Día del Indio (Perú) (24) — Native People's Day (Peru)

julio / July

Día de la Independencia de los Estados Unidos (4) — Independence Day (United States)
Día de la Independencia de Venezuela (5) — Independence Day (Venezuela)
Día de la Independencia de la Argentina (9) — Independence Day (Argentina)
Día de la Independencia de Colombia (20) — Independence Day (Colombia)

Nacimiento de Simón Bolívar (24) — Simón Bolívar's Birthday
Día de la Revolución (Cuba) (26) — Revolution Day (Cuba)
Día de la Independencia del Perú (28) — Independence Day (Peru)

agosto / August

Día de la Independencia de Bolivia (6) — Independence Day (Bolivia)
Día de la Independencia del Ecuador (10) — Independence Day (Ecuador)
Día de San Martín (Argentina) (17) — San Martín Day (anniversary of his death) (Argentina)
Día de la Independencia del Uruguay (25) — Independence Day (Uruguay)

septiembre / September

Día del Trabajo (EE. UU.) — Labor Day (U.S.)
Día de la Independencia de Costa Rica, El Salvador, Guatemala, Honduras y Nicaragua (15) — Independence Day (Costa Rica, El Salvador, Guatemala, Honduras, Nicaragua)
Día de la Independencia de México (16) — Independence Day (Mexico)
Día de la Independencia de Chile (18) — Independence Day (Chile)
Año Nuevo Judío — Jewish New Year
Día de la Virgen de las Mercedes (Perú) (24) — Day of the Virgin of Mercedes (Peru)

octubre / October

Día de la Raza (12) — Columbus Day
Noche de Brujas (31) — Halloween

noviembre / November

Día de los Muertos (2) — All Souls Day
Día de los Veteranos (11) — Veterans' Day
Día de la Revolución Mexicana (20) — Mexican Revolution Day
Día de Acción de Gracias — Thanksgiving
Día de la Independencia de Panamá (28) — Independence Day (Panama)

diciembre / December

Día de la Virgen (8) — Day of the Virgin
Día de la Virgen de Guadalupe (México) (12) — Day of the Virgin of Guadalupe (Mexico)
Januká — Chanukah
Nochebuena (24) — Christmas Eve
Navidad (25) — Christmas
Año Viejo (31) — New Year's Eve

NOTE: In Spanish, dates are written with the day first, then the month. Christmas Day is **el 25 de diciembre**. In Latin America and in Europe, abbreviated dates also follow this pattern. Halloween, for example, falls on 31/10. You may also see the numbers in dates separated by periods: 14.2.07. When referring to centuries, roman numerals are always used. The 16th century, therefore, is **el siglo XVI**.

PESOS Y MEDIDAS

WEIGHTS AND MEASURES

Longitud

El sistema métrico
Metric system

Length

El equivalente estadounidense
U.S. equivalent

milímetro = 0,001 metro
millimeter = 0.001 meter — = 0.039 inch
centímetro = 0,01 metro
centimeter = 0.01 meter — = 0.39 inch
decímetro = 0,1 metro
decimeter = 0.1 meter — = 3.94 inches
metro
meter — = 39.4 inches
decámetro = 10 metros
dekameter = 10 meters — = 32.8 feet
hectómetro = 100 metros
hectometer = 100 meters — = 328 feet
kilómetro = 1.000 metros
kilometer = 1,000 meters — = .62 mile
U.S. system — Metric equivalent
El sistema estadounidense

El equivalente métrico

inch — = 2.54 centimeters
pulgada — **= 2,54 centímetros**
foot = 12 inches — = 30.48 centimeters
pie = 12 pulgadas — **= 30,48 centímetros**
yard = 3 feet — = 0.914 meter
yarda = 3 pies — **= 0,914 metro**
mile = 5,280 feet — = 1.609 kilometers
milla = 5.280 pies — **= 1,609 kilómetros**

Superficie

El sistema métrico
Metric system

Surface Area

El equivalente estadounidense
U.S. equivalent

metro cuadrado — = 10.764 square feet
square meter
área = 100 metros cuadrados — = 0.025 acre
are = 100 square meters
hectárea = 100 áreas — = 2.471 acres
hectare = 100 ares
U.S. system — Metric equivalent
El sistema estadounidense — **El equivalente métrico**

> **yarda cuadrada = 9 pies cuadrados = 0,836 metros cuadrados**
> square yard = 9 square feet = 0.836 square meters
> **acre = 4.840 yardas cuadradas = 0,405 hectáreas**
> acre = 4,840 square yards = 0.405 hectares

Capacidad

El sistema métrico
Metric system

Capacity

El equivalente estadounidense
U.S. equivalent

mililitro = 0,001 litro
milliliter = 0.001 liter — = 0.034 ounces
centilitro = 0,01 litro
centiliter = 0.01 liter — = 0.34 ounces
decilitro = 0,1 litro
deciliter = 0.1 liter — = 3.4 ounces
litro
liter — = 1.06 quarts
decalitro = 10 litros
dekaliter = 10 liters — = 2.64 gallons
hectolitro = 100 litros
hectoliter = 100 liters — = 26.4 gallons
kilolitro = 1.000 litros
kiloliter = 1,000 liters — = 264 gallons
U.S. system — Metric equivalent
El sistema estadounidense — **El equivalente métrico**

ounce — = 29.6 milliliters
onza — **= 29,6 mililitros**
cup = 8 ounces — = 236 milliliters
taza = 8 onzas — **= 236 mililitros**
pint = 2 cups — = 0.47 liters
pinta = 2 tazas — **= 0,47 litros**
quart = 2 pints — = 0.95 liters
cuarto = 2 pintas — **= 0,95 litros**
gallon = 4 quarts — = 3.79 liters
galón = 4 cuartos — **= 3,79 litros**

Peso

El sistema métrico
Metric system

Weight

El equivalente estadounidense
U.S. equivalent

miligramo = 0,001 gramo
milligram = 0.001 gram
gramo
gram — = 0.035 ounce
decagramo = 10 gramos
dekagram = 10 grams — = 0.35 ounces
hectogramo = 100 gramos
hectogram = 100 grams — = 3.5 ounces
kilogramo = 1.000 gramos
kilogram = 1,000 grams — = 2.2 pounds
tonelada (métrica) = 1.000 kilogramos
metric ton = 1,000 kilograms — = 1.1 tons
U.S. system — Metric equivalent
El sistema estadounidense — **El equivalente métrico**

ounce — = 28.35 grams
onza — **= 28,35 gramos**
pound = 16 ounces — = 0.45 kilograms
libra = 16 onzas — **= 0,45 kilogramos**
ton = 2,000 pounds — = 0.9 metric tons
tonelada = 2.000 libras — **= 0,9 toneladas métricas**

Temperatura

Grados centígrados
Degrees Celsius
To convert from Celsius to Fahrenheit, multiply by $\frac{9}{5}$ and add 32.

Temperature

Grados Fahrenheit
Degrees Fahrenheit
To convert from Fahrenheit to Celsius, subtract 32 and multiply by $\frac{5}{9}$

NÚMEROS

Números ordinales

primer, primero/a	1º/1ª
segundo/a	2º/2ª
tercer, tercero/a	3º/3ª
cuarto/a	4º/4ª
quinto/a	5º/5ª
sexto/a	6º/6ª
séptimo/a	7º/7ª
octavo/a	8º/8ª
noveno/a	9º/9ª
décimo/a	10º/10ª

Fracciones

$\frac{1}{2}$	un medio, la mitad
$\frac{1}{3}$	un tercio
$\frac{1}{4}$	un cuarto
$\frac{1}{5}$	un quinto
$\frac{1}{6}$	un sexto
$\frac{1}{7}$	un séptimo
$\frac{1}{8}$	un octavo
$\frac{1}{9}$	un noveno
$\frac{1}{10}$	un décimo
$\frac{2}{3}$	dos tercios
$\frac{3}{4}$	tres cuartos
$\frac{5}{8}$	cinco octavos

Decimales

un décimo	0,1
un centésimo	0,01
un milésimo	0,001

NUMBERS

Ordinal numbers

first	1st
second	2nd
third	3rd
fourth	4th
fifth	5th
sixth	6th
seventh	7th
eighth	8th
ninth	9th
tenth	10th

Fractions

one half	
one third	
one fourth (quarter)	
one fifth	
one sixth	
one seventh	
one eighth	
one ninth	
one tenth	
two thirds	
three fourths (quarters)	
five eighths	

Decimals

one tenth	0.1
one hundredth	0.01
one thousandth	0.001

OCUPACIONES

OCCUPATIONS

el/la abogado/a	lawyer
el actor, la actriz	actor
el/la administrador(a) de empresas	business administrator
el/la agente de bienes raíces	real estate agent
el/la agente de seguros	insurance agent
el/la agricultor(a)	farmer
el/la arqueólogo/a	archaeologist
el/la arquitecto/a	architect
el/la artesano/a	artisan
el/la auxiliar de vuelo	flight attendant
el/la basurero/a	garbage collector
el/la bibliotecario/a	librarian
el/la bombero/a	firefighter
el/la cajero/a	bank teller, cashier
el/la camionero/a	truck driver
el/la cantinero/a	bartender
el/la carnicero/a	butcher
el/la carpintero/a	carpenter
el/la científico/a	scientist
el/la cirujano/a	surgeon
el/la cobrador(a)	bill collector
el/la cocinero/a	cook, chef
el/la comprador(a)	buyer
el/la consejero/a	counselor, advisor
el/la contador(a)	accountant
el/la corredor(a) de bolsa	stockbroker
el/la diplomático/a	diplomat
el/la diseñador(a) (gráfico/a)	(graphic) designer
el/la electricista	electrician
el/la empresario/a de pompas fúnebres	funeral director
el/la especialista en dietética	dietician
el/la fisioterapeuta	physical therapist
el/la fotógrafo/a	photographer
el/la higienista dental	dental hygienist
el hombre/la mujer de negocios	businessperson
el/la ingeniero/a en computación	computer engineer
el/la intérprete	interpreter
el/la juez(a)	judge
el/la maestro/a	elementary school teacher
el/la marinero/a	sailor
el/la obrero/a	manual laborer
el/la oficial de prisión	prision guard
el/la obrero/a de la construcción	construction worker
el/la optometrista	optometrist
el/la panadero/a	baker
el/la paramédico/a	paramedic
el/la peluquero/a	hairdresser
el/la piloto	pilot
el/la pintor(a)	painter
el/la plomero/a	plumber
el/la político/a	politician
el/la programador(a)	computer programer
el/la psicólogo/a	psychologist
el/la quiropráctico/a	chiropractor
el/la redactor(a)	editor
el/la reportero/a	reporter
el/la sastre	tailor
el/la secretario/a	secretary
el/la supervisor(a)	supervisor
el/la técnico/a (en computación)	(computer) technician
el/la vendedor(a)	sales representative
el/la veterinario/a	veterinarian

Fine Art Credits

xviii Pablo Picasso. *Woman with hat.* 1935. Colección: Musée National d'Art Moderne, Centre Georges Pompidou, Paris, France. CNAC/MNAM/Dist. Réunion des Musées Nationaux/Art Resources, NY.
75 (ml) Diego Velázquez. *Las meninas.* 1656. Derechos reservados © Museo Nacional del Prado, Madrid.
113 Oswaldo Guayasamín. *Madre y niño en azul.* 1986. Cortesía Fundación Guayasamín. Quito, Ecuador.
148 Frida Kahlo. *Autorretrato con mono.* 1938. Oil on masonite, overall 16 X12" (40.64 x 30.48 cms). Albright-Knox Art Gallery, Buffalo, New York. Bequest of A. Conger Goodyear, 1966.

Illustration Credits

Hermann Mejía: 5, 14, 15, 17, 18, 22, 23, 29, 54, 56, 67 (b), 81, 91 (b), 94, 102, 103, 105, 127, 131, 138, 155, 162 (l), 165, 168, 173, 177, 179 (b), 193, 213, 215, 228, 229, 234, 238, 248, 251, 275, 285, 289, 302, 312.
Pere Virgili: 2–3, 40–41, 62, 78–79, 91 (t), 116–117, 118, 152–153, 154, 169, 172, 179 (t), 183, 190–191, 214, 226-227, 262-263, 264, 300–301.
Yayo: 9, 47, 85, 123, 161, 197, 223, 271, 307.

Photography Credits

Martín Bernetti: 1, 3, 4, 16 (c, m), 19, 32, 33, 42, 57, 68, 69, 70, 71, 79, 80 (tl, tm, r, bml, bmr, br), 90, 95, 97 (r), 98, 106, 107 (b), 109, 112, 113 (t, ml, b), 117 (b), 139, 142, 144, 182, 205, 209 (tl, tr, ml, mr), 210, 211, 218, 219, 237, 239, 242, 243, 255, 258 (tl, tr, tm), 259 (tl, br), 267, 292, 293, 303, 322 (t).
Carlos Gaudier: 180, 181, 186 (tl, tr, ml, mr), 187 (tl, bl).
Corbis: xvi © Corbis. xvii © Royalty Free. xix © Fabio Cardoso. xxi (l) © Royalty Free. xxvi (t) © Gabe Palmer. xxvi (b) © Creasource. 2 (tl) © John Henley. 11 (tr) © Hans Georg Roth. 19 (r) © 1999 Charles Gupton. 33 © Owen Franken, (tr) © Tony Arruza, © Robert Holmes. 35 (t) © Mart Peterson. 36 (tr) © Robert Holmes. 48 (l) © Gabe Palmer, (r) © Royalty Free. 58 © Charles Gupton. 73 (t) © John Springer. 74 (tr, tl) © Patrick Ward, (m) © Elke Stolzenberg, (b) © Reuters. 75 (br) © Owen Franken, (tl) © Patrick Almasy, (tr) © Jean-Pierre Lescourret. 77 © Ronnie Kaufman. 80 (tr) © LWA-Dann Tardif, (bl) © Ariel Skelley. 86 (tr) © Rafael Pérez/Reuters, (b) © Martial Trezzini/epa. 87 (t) © Reuters. 97 (l) © Warren Morgan. 105 © George Shelley. 107 (m) © Chuck Savage, (t) © José Luis Pelaez, Inc. 108 © Tom & Dee Ann McCarthy. 109 © Royalty Free. 115 © Jon Feingersh. 117 (t) © George Shelley. 119 © Ronnie Kaufman. 124 (b) © Reuters. 125 (t) © Reuters. 134 © José Luis Pelaez, Inc. 141 © Images.com. 143 © AFP Photo/Juan Barreto. 145 © Rick Gómez. 147 (b) © Janet Jarman. 148 (tl) © George D. Lepp, (mr) Peter Guttman, (b) Reuters. 149 (tr) © Bettman, (br) Greg Vaughn. 162 (r) © Jeremy Horner. 163 (b) © Mark A. Johnson. 167 © Ronnie Kaufman. 187 (br) © Steve Chenn. 209 (b) ©Lawrence Manning. 221 (t) © Manuel Zambrana. 225 © Michael Prince. 254 © Michael Pole. 257 (b) © Andrzei Grygiel. 258 (bm) © Charles & Josette Lenars, (lm) © Richard Smith. 259 (bl) © Jeremy Horner. 273 (tr) © Carlos Cazalis, (br) © Carlos Cazalis. 277 © José Luis Pelaez, Inc. 295 (t) © Reuters. 296 (t) © Bob Winsett, (ml, mr, b) © Dave G. Houser. 297 (tl) © Reuters Newmedia, Inc./Jorge Silva, (tr) © Michael & Patricia Fogden, (bl) © Jon Butchofsky-Houser, (br) © Paul W. Liebhardt. 303 © Charles Gupton. 308 ® © PictureNet. 322 (b) © Pablo Corral V. 323 © Patrick Ward. 328 (ml) © Dave G. Houser, (tr, mtr) © Mcduff Everton, (tl) © Pablo Corral V., (mbr) © AFP/Macarena Minguell, (bl, br) © Bettman. 329 (tl) © Wolfgang Kaehler, (bl) © Roger Ressmeyer, (br) © Charles O'rear.
AP Wide World Photos: xviii © Jennifer Grimes. 86 (tl) © David Cantor. 87 (b) © Juanjo Martin. 308 (l) © José Luis Magaña. 309 (t) © Simon Cruz, (b) © Karel Navarro.
Alamy: cover © ImageState. xvii © Kelly Redinger. xxi (r) © Ian Shaw. xxvii (t) © Comstock Images. 49 (b) © Michele Molinari. 149 © Greg Vaughn. 163 (t) © Christopher Pillitz. 235 (t) © PCL.
Getty Images: xix © Digital Vision. xxiii © Frank Micelotta. xxvii (b) © Purestock. 11 (l) © Mark Mainz. 35 (b) © Kevin Winter. 48 (b) © John Glustina. 73 (b) © American Stock. 124 (t) © Javier Soriano/AFP. 125 (b) © Daniel García/AFP. 147 (t) © AFP/AFP. 151 © Robert Harding World Imagery. 187 (tr) PhotoDisk. 199 (l) © Guiseppe Carace, (br) © Mark Mainz, (tr) © Carlos Álvarez. 221 (m) © Lucy Nicholson/AFP. 222 (t,b) © PhotoDisk. 223 (tl) © Don Emmert/AFP. 272 (t) © Thomas del Brase. 308 © Tim Graham. 327 © Alberto Tamargo. 329 (tr) © PhotoDisk.
Lonely Planet Images: xvi (r) © Ann Cecil. 11 (br) © 2000 Wes Walker. 272 (b) © Greg Elms.
Masterfile: 147 © WireImageStock. 256 (bl) © Kevin Dodge. 261 © Mark Leibowitz.
The Picture-desk: 185 (b) © Lions Gate/The Kobal Collection/Bob Greene. 223 (br) © Road Movie Prods/The Kobal Collection.
Misc.: 37 (br) © DominiCanada. 39 © Jimmy Dorantes/Latin Focus. 49 (b) © Russell Gordon/Danita Delimont., Wikapedia. 67 (tr) © Hola Images/Workbook.com. 111 (t,m) images are in the public domain, (bl) © Yoyo (br) © Brentwood. 118 (b) Reprinted by permission of Juana Macíos Alba. 185 (t) © Rodrigo Varela/WireImage.com. 198 (t) © Robert Frerck/Odyssey Productions. 221 (b) © The Celia Cruz Foundation. 222 (tl, bmr) © Robert Frerck/Odyssey Productions. 230 (b) © Yann-Arthus Bertrund. 257 (t) © Maritza López. 269 © Network Productions/IndexStock Imagery. 273 (l) © Studio Bonisolli/StockFood Munich. 295 (b) © Rick Diamond/WireImage.com, (t) © Rick Diamond/WireImage.com.